W9-DGK-208

Western Literature

III

The Modern World

Edited by
Peter Brooks
YALE UNIVERSITY

Under the General Editorship of
A. Bartlett Giamatti
YALE UNIVERSITY

HARCOURT BRACE JOVANOVICH, INC.
NEW YORK CHICAGO SAN FRANCISCO ATLANTA

LIBRARY
College of St. Francis
JOLIET, ILL.

© 1971 by Harcourt Brace Jovanovich, Inc.

All rights reserved. No part of this publication may be reproduced or transmitted in any form or by any means, electronic or mechanical, including photocopy, recording, or any information storage and retrieval system, without permission in writing from the publisher.

ISBN: 0-15-595278-1

Library of Congress Catalog Card Number: 75-152578

Printed in the United States of America

ACKNOWLEDGMENTS

BANTAM BOOKS, INC. for "The Return of the Prodigal Son" by André Gide, translated by Wallace Fowlie. From *French Stories,* edited and translated by Wallace Fowlie. Copyright © 1960 by Bantam Books, Inc.

E. P. DUTTON & CO., INC. for *Six Characters in Search of an Author* by Luigi Pirandello, from *Naked Masks: Five Plays* by Luigi Pirandello. Edited by Eric Bentley. Copyright 1922, 1953, by E. P. Dutton & Co., Inc. Renewal copyright 1950 in the names of Stefano, Fausto and Lietta Pirandello. Dutton Paperback Edition. Reprinted by permission of E. P. Dutton & Co., Inc.

EDITIONS GALLIMARD for "Le Retour de l'Enfant Prodigue" ("The Return of the Prodigal Son") by André Gide. © 1948, Editions Gallimard.

FABER AND FABER LIMITED for "The Love Song of J. Alfred Prufrock" from *Collected Poems 1909–1962* by T. S. Eliot.

FARRAR, STRAUS & GIROUX, INC. for *Benito Cereno* from *The Old Glory* by Robert Lowell, copyright © 1964, 1965, 1968 by Robert Lowell. Translation of "Self-Portrait" from *Imitations,* by Robert Lowell, copyright © 1961 by Robert Lowell. "Le Cygne," from *Notebook, 1967–68,* by Robert Lowell. Reprinted with the permission of Farrar, Straus & Giroux, Inc.

GROVE PRESS, INC. for "The Babylon Lottery" from *Ficciones,* by Jorge Luis Borges, translated from the Spanish by Anthony Kerrigan. Reprinted by permission of Grove Press, Inc. Copyright © 1962 by Grove Press, Inc.

HARCOURT BRACE JOVANOVICH, INC. for "The Love Song of J. Alfred Prufrock," from *Collected Poems 1909–1962* by T. S. Eliot, copyright 1936, by Harcourt Brace Jovanovich, Inc.; copyright © 1963, 1964, by T. S. Eliot. Reprinted by permission of publisher.

WILLIAM HEINEMANN LTD., PUBLISHERS for "The Dream of a Ridiculous Man" from *An Honest Thief and Other Stories* by Fyodor Dostoevsky, translated by Constance Garnett.

808.8
V948
3

ALFRED A. KNOPF, INC. for "Tristan" from *Stories of Three Decades,* by Thomas Mann, translated by H. T. Lowe-Porter. Copyright 1936 and renewed 1964 by Alfred A. Knopf, Inc. Reprinted by permission of the publisher. For "The Guest" from *Exile and the Kingdom,* by Albert Camus, translated by Justin O'Brien. Copyright © 1957, 1958 by Alfred A. Knopf, Inc. Reprinted by permission of the publisher. For "Final Soliloquy of the Interior Paramour." Copyright 1951 by Wallace Stevens. Reprinted from *The Collected Poems of Wallace Stevens* by permission of Alfred A. Knopf, Inc.

THE MACMILLAN COMPANY for *Faust,* Part I, by Johann Wolfgang von Goethe, translated by Bayard Taylor, revised and edited by Stuart Atkins. Reprinted with permission of the Macmillan Company. Copyright © 1962, 1963 by the Crowell-Collier Publishing Company. For "The Dream of a Ridiculous Man," from *An Honest Thief and Other Stories* by Fyodor Dostoevsky, translated from the Russian by Constance Garnett. Reprinted with permission of the Macmillan Company. Printed in Great Britain. For "Leda and the Swan," "Sailing to Byzantium," and "Among School Children" by William Butler Yeats, from *Collected Poems.* Reprinted with permission of The Macmillan Company. Copyright 1928 by The Macmillan Company, renewed 1956 by Georgie Yeats. For "Crazy Jane Talks with the Bishop" by William Butler Yeats, from *Collected Poems.* Reprinted with permission of The Macmillan Company. Copyright 1933 by The Macmillan Company, renewed 1961 by Bertha Georgie Yeats. For "An Acre of Grass" by William Butler Yeats, from *Collected Poems.* Reprinted with permission of The Macmillan Company. Copyright 1940 by Georgie Yeats, renewed 1968 by Bertha Georgie Yeats, Michael Butler Yeats, and Anne Yeats. For "No Second Troy" by William Butler Yeats, from *Collected Poems.* Reprinted with permission of The Macmillan Company. Copyright 1912 by The Macmillan Company, renewed 1940 by Bertha Georgie Yeats.

MARTIN SECKER & WARBURG LIMITED for "The Return of the Prodigal Son" by André Gide, translated by Wallace Fowlie. From *French Stories,* edited and translated by Wallace Fowlie.

THE NEW AMERICAN LIBRARY, INC. for "A Simple Heart" from *Three Tales by Flaubert* translated by Walter J. Cobb. Copyright © 1964 by Walter J. Cobb. Reprinted by permission of The New American Library, Inc., New York. For "Diary of a Madman" from *Diary of a Madman and Other Stories* by Nikolai Gogol, translated by Andrew R. MacAndrew. Copyright © 1960 by Andrew R. MacAndrew. Reprinted by permission of The New American Library, Inc., New York.

NEW DIRECTIONS PUBLISHING CORPORATION for "The Sunflower" translated by Maurice English, from *Selected Poems* by Eugenio Montale. Copyright © 1965 by New Directions Publishing Corporation. Reprinted by permission of New Directions Publishing Corporation. For "Portrait d'une Femme" from *Personae,* by Ezra Pound. Copyright 1926 by Ezra Pound. Reprinted by permission of New Directions Publishing Corporation. For "Casida of the Flight," translated by Stephen Spender and J. L. Gill, from *Selected Poems*

69713

by Federico García Lorca. Copyright 1955 by New Directions Publishing Corporation. Reprinted by permission of New Directions Publishing Corporation.

ROUTLEDGE & KEGAN PAUL LTD. for "Reveries of a Solitary" by Jean-Jacques Rousseau, translated by John Gould Fletcher (George Routledge & Sons, 1927—Broadway Library of XVIII Century French Literature).

SCHOCKEN BOOKS INC. for "A Hunger Artist" by Franz Kafka. Reprinted by permission of Schocken Books Inc. for *The Penal Colony* by Franz Kafka. Copyright © 1948 by Schocken Books Inc.

CHARLES SCRIBNER'S SONS for "The Master Builder" by Henrik Ibsen, translated by Edmund Gosse and William Archer. (Charles Scribner's Sons 1907). "A Clean, Well-Lighted Place" (Copyright 1933 Charles Scribner's Sons; renewal copyright © 1961 by Ernest Hemingway) is reprinted with the permission of Charles Scribner's Sons from *Winner Take Nothing* by Ernest Hemingway.

THE VIKING PRESS, INC. for "Araby" from *Dubliners* by James Joyce. Originally published by B. W. Huebsch, Inc., in 1916. Copyright © 1967 by The Estate of James Joyce. All rights reserved. Reprinted by permission of The Viking Press, Inc. For "Tickets, Please" from *The Complete Short Stories of D. H. Lawrence,* Volume II. Copyright 1922 by Thomas B. Seltzer, Inc., renewed 1950 by Frieda Lawrence. Reprinted by permission of The Viking Press, Inc. For "Malaria" from *Little Novels of Sicily* by D. H. Lawrence. Copyright 1925 by Thomas Seltzer, Inc., renewed 1953 by Frieda Lawrence Ravagli. Reprinted by permission of The Viking Press, Inc.

A. P. WATT & SON for "No Second Troy," "Leda and the Swan," "Crazy Jane Talks with the Bishop," "Sailing to Byzantium," "An Acre of Grass," and "Among School Children," from *Collected Poems* by W. B. Yeats. Reprinted with permission of Mr. Michael B. Yeats and The Macmillan Company of Canada Ltd.

Contents

General Introduction

The three volumes of *Western Literature* are intended to provide the student with a broad view of the literature of the Western world. The volume on the Ancient World contains some of the best representative examples of the Hebraic and Greco-Roman traditions and of the origins of Christian writing. The second volume, covering the Middle Ages, Renaissance, and Enlightenment, opens with a troubadour's lyric to a faraway love and ends with Voltaire's satire on complacent optimism. The third volume, devoted to the Modern World, traces the contemporary spirit from Rousseau to two current masters of the Americas.

Certain principles have guided the editors, both individually and collectively, in their selections. An effort has been made to include, wherever possible, complete works or at least substantial excerpts of large works. This has not always been possible, and in a very few cases it has meant not including an author when no representative work of manageable length could be found. The underlying assumption here is that the artistic integrity of a literary work has primary importance.

The editors have tried to include translations of continental poetry by other notable poets—for example, John Milton's translation of Horace or Ezra Pound's of Cavalcanti—in order to provide the reader not only with distinguished renderings but with instances of the critical operation of one poetic sensibility on another. The editors have also been guided by their sense of the wholeness of literature, by their conviction that literature is the expression of a fundamental human activity, the urge to order memory and desire by making a new world with the imagination. Finally, if there is one overriding principle that informs the selections in these three volumes, it is that what man has written about himself over the centuries is our best indication of where we are, and who we are.

A. B. GIAMATTI
GENERAL EDITOR

Jean-Jacques Rousseau

FROM *Reveries of a Solitary*

TRANSLATED BY JOHN GOULD FLETCHER

Jean-Jacques Rousseau (1712–1778)

JEAN-JACQUES ROUSSEAU WAS BORN IN PROTESTANT GENEVA. THE son of a watchmaker, he was apprenticed to an engraver who was a harsh master, and ran away from Geneva when he was sixteen. Rousseau then began a life of wandering which eventually led him to Paris in 1741, where a treatise on music, an opera, and his sociopolitical writings were to make him a celebrity, and an important figure of Enlightenment liberalism.

As time went on, however, Rousseau became convinced that human happiness, the ideal community, and a life of true freedom were not to be found within the cultivated manners and hypocrisies of society. He remade his life on a pattern of extreme simplicity, quarreled with the worldly philosophers of the Enlightenment, and in 1756 left Paris to live in a country retreat. In 1762, his treatise on education, *Émile,* was confiscated and burned as subversive by Parisian authorities; he fled to Switzerland, then to England, and began to write the story of his life in the *Confessions*. Eight years after his flight, he was allowed to return to Paris on the condition that he write nothing on politics or religion. He pursued the work of self-discovery, begun in the *Confessions,* with the *Dialogues* and the *Reveries of a Solitary*.

Rousseau is the prime source of European Romanticism and perhaps the most important single source of the ideas that have shaped the modern world. His writings touch on a very broad range of subjects and each of them was of almost revolutionary significance for its time. The *Discourse on the Origins of Inequality Among Men* and *The Social Contract* became major texts for the French Revolution of 1789 and for the continuing aspirations of men toward freedom, equality, and dignity. He wrote the first great French novel of Romantic passion in *Julie, or the New Heloise*. In the *Confessions,* he inaugurated the distinctively modern quest for complete sincerity in self-understanding, the modern insistence that the individual personality is of supreme value. The *Reveries of a Solitary* is his last work. It is the best example of his search to define the self, isolated from society, in its relations to the natural world, and to achieve perfect happiness in an existence stripped bare of all the appurtenances of civilization.

The *Reveries* frequently reflects Rousseau's "persecution mania": truly persecuted by civil and religious authorities, and by hostile thinkers like Voltaire, he became more and more obsessed by the idea that his enemies wished to harm him and to destroy his writings. Yet if the *Reveries* often sounds this note, it also shows the uses of solitude, the great serenity which Rousseau was capable of achieving in remembrance of past happiness and under the "gentle law" of nature.

Reveries of a Solitary

FROM THE *First Promenade*

Here am I, then, alone upon the earth, having no brother, or neighbor, or friend, or society but myself. The most sociable and loving of human beings has been proscribed by unanimous agreement. They have sought in the refinements of their hatred whatever torment could be most cruel to my sensitive soul, and they have violently broken all the links which attached me to them. I would fain have loved men in despite of themselves; they have not been able to conceal themselves from my affection, except by ceasing to be men. They are, then, strangers, unknown, nothing finally for me, because they have wished it. But I, detached from them and from all, what am I in myself? That is what remains to be discovered. Unhappily this search must be preceded by a backward glance over my position; that is a mental stage through which I must necessarily pass in order to arrive at myself. . . .

All is ended for me upon the earth; none can now do me good or evil. There remains for me neither anything to hope for nor to fear in this world, and now I am tranquil at the bottom of the gulf, a poor unfortunate mortal, but as undisturbed as God Himself.

All that is external to me, is now strange henceforward. I have, in this world, neither neighbor, nor kinsmen, nor brothers. I am upon this earth as upon a strange planet, whence I have fallen from that which I inhabited. If I recognize anything about me, it is only some object which is afflicting and torturing to my heart; and I cannot cast my eyes upon that which touches and surrounds me without finding always some subject of disdain which rouses my indignation, or of sorrow which afflicts me. Let me remove, then, from my spirit all the painful objects with which I have occupied myself as sorrowfully as uselessly. Alone for the rest of my life, because I cannot find except in myself consolation, hope and peace, I ought not, and do not wish to occupy myself any longer save with myself. It is in this state that I am taking up the sequel of that sincere and severe examination that I once called my *Confessions*. I shall consecrate my last days to the study of myself, and to preparing in advance the account which I shall not be slow to give of myself. Let me devote myself entirely to the sweetness of speaking with my own soul, because that is the only thing of which men cannot rob me. If, by force of reflecting upon my inward propensities, I succeed in putting these in order and correcting the evil that may remain there, my meditations will not be entirely useless, and although I shall not be good for anything upon this earth, I shall not have lost entirely my last days. The leisures of my daily walks have often been filled with delightful contemplations of which I regret having lost the memory. I shall set down in writing those which may still come to me; each time that I reread them will give me new pleasure. I shall forget my sufferings, my persecutors, my opprobrium, in dreaming of the reward which my heart has merited.

These leaves will not be, properly speaking, anything but a formless journal of my reveries. There will be much concerning myself, because a solitary who reflects occupies himself necessarily much with himself. For the rest, all the strange ideas which pass through my head in walking about will equally find a place. I shall say that which I have thought exactly as it has come to me, and also with as little linking together as the ideas of yesterday ordinarily have with those of the day following. But there will always result a new understanding of my nature and my humor, through the knowledge of the sentiments and the thoughts on which my spirit feeds daily, in this strange state in which I am. These leaves can then be regarded as an appendix to my *Confessions,* but I do not give them this title, as I have nothing more to say which can merit being said. My heart has been purified in the crucible of adversity, and I scarcely find, in sounding it carefully, anything that remains of a reprehensible tendency. What could I have still to confess, when all my earthly affections are torn away? I have nothing to praise or blame myself for; I am nothing henceforward among men, and that is all that I can be, having no more a real relation or a veritable companionship with them. Not being able to do any good that does not turn into evil, not being able to act without injury to another or to myself, to abstain has become my unique duty, and I shall fulfil it as much as is in me. But, in this idleness of body, my soul is still active; it still produces sentiments and thoughts, and its inner and moral life seems to be increased by the death of every earthly and temporal interest. My body is nothing to me but an embarrassment, but an obstacle, and I shall in advance disengage myself from it as much as I can.

A situation so singular as this deserves assuredly to be examined and described, and it is to this examination that I have devoted my last leisure. To do it with success, it is necessary to proceed with order and method; but I am incapable of this labor, and it would even remove me from my goal, which is to render an account to myself of the modifications of my soul and of their successions. I shall carry out upon myself to a certain extent the operations which the physicists make upon the air, to understand its daily state. I shall apply the barometer to my soul, and these operations well directed and for long repeated will furnish me with results as sure as those of science. But I shall not extend my enterprise so far. I shall content myself with keeping a register of my operations, without seeking to reduce them into system. I shall carry out the same enterprise as Montaigne,[1] but with a goal entirely contrary to his, because he did not write his *Essays* except for others, and I do not write my reveries except for myself. If, in my extreme age, at the approach of death, I remain, as I hope, in the same mood as I am now, the reading of my reveries will recall to me the pleasure that I tasted in writing them, and thus making reborn for me times gone by, will, so to say, redouble my existence. In spite of men I shall still enjoy the charm of society, and I shall live decrepit with myself in another age, as if I were living with a younger friend.

I wrote my *Confessions* and my *Dialogues* in a continual anxiety about the means of snatching them from the rapacious hands of my persecutors, in order to transmit them, if it were possible, to other generations.[2] The same disquiet does not torment me any more as regards this work; I know it will be useless; and the desire of being better known among men having been extinguished in my heart leaves nothing but a profound indifference to the lot both of my true writings and of the testimonies to my innocence, which already perhaps have been all destroyed forever. Let them spy upon what I am doing, let them worry themselves about these leaves, let them seize upon them, suppress them, falsify them, everything is the same to me henceforward. I do not hide or display them. If they are taken away from me in my lifetime, I cannot be robbed of the pleasure of having written them, nor of the memory of their contents, nor of the solitary meditations of which they are the fruit and of which the source cannot be extinguished except with my soul. If, upon my first calamities, I had not turned against my destiny, and had taken up the position which I take today, all the efforts of men, all their frightful intrigues, would have been without effect upon me, and they would not have troubled my repose by all their plots, any more than they can trouble it henceforward by all their successes. Let them rejoice to their hearts' content at my disgrace, they will not prevent me from rejoicing in my innocence, and from ending my days in peace despite them all.

[1] Michel de Montaigne (1533–1592) made himself the chief subject of study in his *Essays*. [2] Rousseau was convinced that his enemies wished to suppress his autobiographical writings, which had harsh things to say about many of them. In 1776, he attempted to place the manuscript of the *Dialogues* on the altar of Notre-Dame Cathedral to put them under the protection of God.

FROM THE *Second Promenade*

Having, then, formed the project of describing the habitual state of my soul in the most strange position in which a mortal can ever find himself, I saw no way more simple and more sure of executing this enterprise than to make a faithful record of my solitary walks and of the reveries that fill them, when I leave my head entirely free and let my ideas follow their bent without resistance and without trouble. These hours of solitude and meditation are the only ones of the day in which I am fully myself and for myself, without diversion, without obstacle, and where I can truly say I am that which nature has designed.

I soon felt that I had delayed too long in executing this project. My imagination, already less alive, does not enkindle as before at the contemplation of the object which animates it; I am less drunken with the delirium of reverie; there is more of reminiscence than of creation in that which it now produces; the spirit of life is extinguished in me by degrees, my soul does not leap out any more except with a struggle from its narrow envelope, and, lacking the hope of the state to which I aspire because I feel I have right to it, I do not exist now except in memories; so in order to contemplate myself before my decline, it is necessary that I should go back at least some years to the time when, losing all hope here below and not finding more food for my heart upon earth, I accustomed myself little by little to nourish it with its own substance and to seek all its pasturage within myself.

This resource, of which I learned too late, became so fecund that it soon sufficed to compensate me for everything. The habit of entering into myself made me lose finally the feeling and even the remembrance of my evils. I learned thus by my own experience that the source of true happiness is in ourselves, and that it did not depend upon men to make miserable him who knows how to will to be happy. For four or five years, I tasted habitually these internal delights which loving and tender souls find in contemplation. These ravishments, these ecstasies, that I found sometimes in walking thus alone, were enjoyments which I owed to my persecutors: without them, I could not have ever found nor known the treasures which I carried within myself. In the midst of so much richness, how keep a faithful register? In trying to recall to myself so many sweet reveries, instead of describing them I fell back into them again. It is a state which the memory brings back and which one would soon cease to understand by ceasing entirely to feel.

I experienced this effect in the promenades which followed the project of writing the sequel to my *Confessions*, above all in one which I am about to speak of, and in which an unforeseen accident came to break the thread of my ideas and to give them for some time another direction.

On Thursday, October 24, 1776, after dinner I followed the boulevards up to the Rue du Chemin-Vert, by which I gained the heights of Ménilmontant;[3] and from there, taking the paths across the vineyards and meadows, I followed as far as Charonne the smiling landscape which unites the two villages: then I made a detour to return to the same meadows, by taking another road. I amused myself by going over them with that pleasure and interest which agreeable sites have always given me, stopping sometimes to identify plants in the grass. I perceived two which I see very rarely around Paris, and which I found very abundant in this district. One is the *Picris hieracoides* of the composite group, and the other the *Bupleurum falcatum* of the umbelliferous family. This discovery delighted and amused me for a long time, and finished by that of a plant still more rare, especially in a high country, that is to say, the *Cerastium aquaticum,* which, despite the accident which befell me the same day, I found again in a book which I had in my pocket, and put into my herbarium.

Finally, after having gone over in detail many other plants which I saw still in flower, and whose aspect and classification which were familiar to me nevertheless still gave me pleasure, I quitted little by little these slight observations in order to yield myself to the impression, not less agreeable, but more touching, which the whole of the landscape made upon me. For some days the vintage had been harvested; the walkers from the city had already gone home, the peasants also were quitting the fields for the labor of the winter. The country, still green and smiling, but unleafed in part, and already almost desert, offered everywhere the image of solitude and of the approach of winter. There resulted from its aspect a mixed impression, sweet and sad, too analogous to my age and lot that I should fail to make the application to myself. I saw myself at the decline of an innocent and unfortunate life; the soul still full of lively sentiments, and the spirit still ornamented with some flowers, but already withered by sadness and dried up in *ennui.* Alone and abandoned, I felt the chill of the first frosts, and my failing imagination did not people my solitude any more with beings formed according to my own heart. I said to myself with a sigh: What have I done here on earth? I was made for living, and I am dying, without having lived. At least this has not been my fault, and I shall carry back to the Author of my being, if not the offering of good works which men have not allowed to me, at least a host of good but frustrated intentions, of sentiments healthy but made of no effect, and of a patience above the contempt of men. I grew tender at these reflections; I went over again the movements of my soul since youth, and during my mature age, since I have been sequestered from the society of men, and during the long retreat in which I must finish my days. I went back with pleasure over all the affections of my heart, over all its attachments, so tender, but so blind, over the ideas less sad than consoling, with which my spirit has been nourished for some

[3] At that time a village outside Paris, now part of Paris.

years, and I prepared to recall these sufficiently to describe them with a pleasure almost equal to that which I had taken in yielding myself to them. My afternoon passed in these peaceful meditations, and I was returning very content with my day, when, in the midst of my reverie, I was drawn out of it by the event which it remains for me to describe.

I was, about six o'clock, on the descent from Ménilmontant, almost face to face with the Galant Jardinier,[4] when certain persons who were walking in front of me having been suddenly swept aside, I saw rushing towards me a great Danish dog, which flying at full speed in front of a carriage, had no time to check its speed or to turn aside when it perceived me. I judged that the sole means that I had to avoid being thrown down to earth was to make a great leap, so that the dog should pass under me while I was in the air. This idea, more swift than the lightning, and which I had not even the time to reason out or to execute, was the last before my accident. I did not feel the blow, nor the fall, nor anything of what followed, up to the moment when I came to myself.

It was almost night when I came back to consciousness. I found myself between the arms of three or four young people who told me what had happened. The Danish dog, not having been able to check its onrush, was precipitated upon my two legs, and striking me with its body and its speed, made me fall head foremost; the upper jaw, bearing the whole weight of my body, struck upon a very hard pavement, and the fall was the more violent because, the road being downhill, my head was thrown down lower than my feet. The carriage to which the dog belonged followed immediately, and would have passed over my body if the coachman had not reined in his horses upon the instant.

That is what I learned from the recital of those who had picked me up and who held me still when I came to myself. The state in which I found myself in that instant was too singular not to make a description of it here.

The night was coming on. I perceived the sky, some stars, and a little grass. This first sensation was a delicious moment. I did not feel anything except through them. I was born in that instant to life, and it seemed to me that I filled with my light existence all the objects which I perceived. Entirely given up to the present moment, I did not remember anything; I had no distinct notion of my individuality, not the least idea of what had happened to me; I did not know who I was nor where I was; I felt neither evil nor fear, nor trouble. I saw my blood flowing as I might have looked at a brooklet, without dreaming even that this blood in any way belonged to me. I felt in the whole of my being a ravishing charm, to which, each time that I think of it, I find nothing comparable in the whole action of known pleasures.

They asked me where I lived: it was impossible for me to say. I asked where I was; they said on the High Cliff; it was as if they said to me: on

[4] Probably a tavern.

Mount Atlas. It was necessary for me to ask successively the country, the city, and the quarter where I was: still this did not suffice for me to recollect myself; it was necessary for me to walk the whole distance from there to the highroad in order to recall my home and my name. A gentleman whom I do not know, and who had the charity to accompany me for a time, learning that I lived so far away, advised me to take a cab at the Temple to carry me back home. I walked quite well, very softly, without feeling either pain or wound, although I kept spitting blood. But I had an icy shiver which made my loose teeth rattle in a very uncomfortable way. Arrived at the Temple, I thought that, because I walked without trouble, it was better worth while to continue my route, on foot, than to expose myself to perishing of cold in a cab. I thus covered the half-a-league which lay between the Temple to the Rue Platière, walking without trouble, avoiding the obstructions, the carriages, choosing and following my road as well as I could have done in full health. I arrived; I opened the lock which had been put upon the street door, I went up the stairway in darkness, and I finally entered my house without other accident than my fall and its sequels, of which I did not feel anything even then.

The cries of my wife upon seeing me made me understand that I had been more injured than I supposed. I passed the night without understanding or feeling my accident. This is what I felt and found in the morning. I had the upper lip split inside up to the nose; on the outside the skin had preserved it better, and prevented the total separation; four teeth were bent back in the upper jaw, the whole of that part of the face which covered it extremely swollen and bruised, the right thumb sprained and very swollen, the left thumb severely cut, the right arm sprained, the left knee also very swollen, while a strong and painful contusion forbade me totally to bend it. But, with all this fracas, nothing broken, not even a tooth; a good fortune which seemed almost a miracle in a fall like that.[5] . . .

Fifth Promenade

Of all the homes where I have lived (and I have had charming ones) none has made me so truly happy and has left me such tender regrets as the island of St. Peter, in the midst of the Lake of Bienne.[6] This little island, which is called at Neufchâtel the island of La Motte, is scarcely

[5] Rousseau goes on to describe how his accident became the basis for a false report that he was dead, which he ascribes to his enemies' desire to "bury him alive."

[6] In Switzerland, in the Canton of Bern. It was here that Rousseau lived for two months in 1765, after having been forced to flee from France, and then from Motiers-Travers in the Swiss Canton of Neufchâtel, where the townspeople regarded him as an anti-Christ and stoned his house.

known, even in Switzerland. No traveler, so far as I am aware, has made mention of it. However, it is very agreeable, and singularly situated for the happiness of a man who loves to limit himself; for, although I am perhaps the only man to whom his destiny has made this a law, I cannot believe that I am the only one who has a taste so natural, although I have not found it up to now in anyone else.

The shores of the Lake of Bienne are wilder and more romantic than those of the Lake of Geneva, because the rocks and the woods surround the water more closely; but they are not less smiling. If there is less cultivation of fields and vines, fewer houses and woods, there are also more natural greenery, more meadows, more haunts shaded with coppices, more frequent contrasts and undulations of ground close together. As there are not, upon these happy shores, comfortable main roads for carriages, the country is little frequented by travelers; but it is interesting for those solitary contemplatives who love to intoxicate themselves at leisure with the charms of nature, and to meditate in a silence disturbed by no sound except the cry of the eagles, the occasional twittering of birds, and the rolling down of torrents which fall from the mountain. This beautiful basin, with a form almost round, contains two little islands in its midst, the one inhabited and cultivated, of about a half-league in circuit; the other, more small, desert and fallow, which will be destroyed in the end by the transportations of earth which are being carried on incessantly in order to repair the damages which the waves and the storms make to the greater. It is thus that the substance of the weak is always employed to the profit of the powerful.

There is only a single house on the island, but large, agreeable and comfortable, which belongs to the hospital at Berne, as does the island; there a comptroller lives with his family and domestics. It contains a large farmyard, a pigeon-house, and reservoirs for fish. The island, in its small compass, is so varied in its fields and aspects, that it offers all sorts of sites and allows all sorts of cultivation. One finds there fields, vines, woods, fat pastures shaded with woods, and bordered with small trees of every species, which are kept fresh by the proximity of the water; a high terrace, planted with two rows of trees, borders the island in its length, and in the midst of this terrace has been built a fine hall, where the inhabitants of the neighboring banks gather together and dance on Sundays during the vintage season.

It is in this island that I took refuge after the stoning of Motiers. I found the sojourn so charming, I carried on a life so suitable to my humor, that resolved to finish my days there, I had no other disquiet except that I might not be allowed to carry out this plan, which did not accord with that of dragging me to England, of which I already felt the first effects.[7] In the pre-

[7] Rousseau was invited to England by the philosopher David Hume, with whom he soon quarreled. He came to see the English expedition as part of his enemies' "plot."

sentiments which disquieted me, I could have wished that this asylum had been made a perpetual prison, that I had been confined there for the whole of my life, and that by taking from me all power and every hope to leave, I had been forbidden every sort of communication with the mainland, in such a way that ignorant of all that was being done in the world I could have forgotten its existence, and that the world could have forgotten mine also.

I was allowed to pass only two months in this island, but I could have passed there two years, two centuries, and the whole of eternity, without being weary one moment, although I had not, with my wife, other society than that of the receiver,[8] of his wife, and of his servants, who all were in truth very good people, and nothing more; but that was precisely what I needed. I count these two months as the happiest time of my life, and so happy, that it would have sufficed me throughout life, without for a single moment allowing in my soul the desire for a different state.

What then was this happiness, and in what did its enjoyment consist? I shall let it be guessed at by all the men of this century, from the description of the life which I led there. A delicious idleness was the first and the principal enjoyment that I wished to taste in all its sweetness; and all that I did during my stay was nothing but the charming and necessary occupation of a man who is vowed to idleness.

The hope that the Government would not ask more than to leave me in this isolated place where I was entwined by myself, which it was impossible for me to leave without assistance and without being seen, and where I could have neither communication nor correspondence except by the help of the people who surrounded me; that hope, I say, gave me the further hope of finishing my days more quietly than I had passed them; and the idea that I should have the time to arrange my life at leisure made me commence by having no arrangement at all. Transported there suddenly, alone and unprovided for, I sent successively for my wife, my books, and my little luggage, which I had the pleasure of not unlocking, leaving my chests and my trunks as they had arrived and living in the home where I counted upon finishing my days, as in an inn whence I should depart on the morrow. All things, as they were, went so well that to wish to arrange things better was to spoil them. One of my greatest delights was above all to leave my books well boxed up, and not to have a writing-desk. When unlucky letters made me take up the pen to answer, I borrowed with murmurs the writing-pad of the comptroller, and I hastened to return it, in the vain hope of having no need to reborrow it. In place of sad paper-heaps and all that book trade, I filled my room with flowers and seeds; because I was then in the first fervor of my botanizing, for which the doctor of Invernois had inspired in me a taste which soon became a passion. Since I did not wish to

[8] The official in charge of the island.

work any more at writing, there was necessary for me an amusement which pleased me, and which gave me no more trouble than that which a lazy man cares to give. I undertook to make the *Flora* of St. Peter's Island, and to describe all the plants there, without omitting one, in sufficient detail to occupy me for the rest of my days. They say that a German has written a book on lemon-peel; I would have done one on each grain of the fields, on every moss of the wood, on each lichen which carpets the rocks; finally I did not want to leave a blade of grass, a vegetable atom which was not fully described. In consequence of this fine project, every morning after breakfast, which we took together, I went, a magnifying glass in hand, and my *System of Nature*[9] under my arm, to visit a portion of the island, which I had for this purpose divided into small squares, with the intention of going over them one after the other, in each season. Nothing is more singular than the ravishments, the ecstasies which I felt at each observation I had made upon the structure and the vegetable organization, and upon the play of the sexual parts in the fructification, of which the system was then altogether new to me. The distinction of generic characters, of which I had not beforehand the least notion, enchanted me as I verified them in common species, while waiting till rarer varieties were offered to me. The forking of the two long stamens of the self-heal, the springing of those of the nettle and the wall-flower, the bursting of the fruit of the garden-balsam, and of the capsule of the box-bush, a thousand small tricks of fructification, which I observed for the first time, filled me with joy, and I went about asking people if they had seen the horns of the self-heal, as La Fontaine asked if people had read Habakkuk.[10] At the end of two or three hours, I returned laden with an ample harvest, a provision of amusement for the afternoon at home, in case of rain. I spent the rest of the morning in going about with the comptroller, his wife and Thérèse, visiting their workmen and their harvest, often setting hand to the work with them; and often the Bernese who came to see me have found me in a tree, bound about with a sack which I filled with fruits, and which I let down afterwards to earth with a cord. The exercise which I had taken in the morning, and the good humor which is inseparable from it, made the repose of dining very agreeable; but when it was too long prolonged, and the fine weather invited me, I could not wait so long; and while the others were still at the table I escaped, and threw myself alone into a boat which I rowed into the midst of the lake, when the water was calm: and there, stretching myself out at full length in the boat, my eyes turned towards heaven, I let myself go and wander about slowly at the will of the water, sometimes during many hours, plunged into a thousand con-

[9] By the great Swedish botanist, Linnaeus (1707–1778). [10] The French poet Jean de La Fontaine (1621–1695) was impressed by the beauty of a psalm by Baruch (not Habakkuk; this is Rousseau's error), a disciple of the prophet Jeremiah.

fused but delicious reveries, which, without having any well-determined object, nor constancy, did not fail to be in my opinion a hundred times preferable to all that I have found sweetest in what are called the pleasures of life. Often warned by the going down of the sun at the hour of sunset, I found myself so far away from the island, that I was forced to labor with all my strength to arrive before the night closed down. Other times, in place of letting myself drift about in the water, I pleased myself by skirting the green banks of the island, of which the limpid waters and the fresh umbrages have often tempted me to bathe in them. But one of my most frequent navigations was to go from the large to the small island, to disembark and to pass the afternoon, sometimes in very circumscribed promenades in the midst of the thickets of shrubs of every species, and sometimes to establish myself on the top of a sandy hillock, covered with fine grass, with wild thyme, with the flowers of the sanfoin, and with trefoil which apparently had been sown previously, and was very good to lodge rabbits, who could there multiply in peace, without fearing anything, and without harming anything.

I gave this idea to the comptroller, who brought from Neufchâtel male and female specimens, and we went in great state, his wife, one of her sisters, Thérèse and myself, to establish them in the small island, which they commenced to populate before my departure, and where they have prospered without a doubt, if they have been able to sustain the rigor of the winter. The founding of this small colony was a fête. The pilot of the Argonauts was not more proud than I, leading in triumph the company and the rabbits from the large to the small island; and I noted with pride that the wife of the comptroller, who feared the water excessively, and always felt ill upon it, embarked under my conduct with confidence, and did not display any fear during the crossing.

When the agitated lake did not permit me to navigate on it, I passed my afternoon in going over the island, botanizing to right and left, seating myself now in the most pleasant and most solitary nooks, to dream at my ease, sometimes on terraces or mounds, to sweep with my eyes the superb and ravishing surroundings of the lake and its banks, crowned on one side by neighboring mountains, and on the other, enlarged by rich and fertile plains, of which the view was extended to the blue mountains, more distant, which bounded the horizon.

When the evening approached, I descended from the summits of the island, and I went gladly to sit down on the border of the lake, on the shore, in some hidden nook: there, the sound of the waves and the agitation of the water, fixing my senses and driving every other agitation from my soul, plunged it into a delicious reverie, where the night often surprised me without my having perceived it. The flux and reflux of this water, its continuous sound, swelling at intervals, struck ceaselessly my ears and my eyes, substituting itself for the internal movements which reverie extinguished in me, and sufficed to make me feel my existence with pleasure, without taking the trouble to think. From time to time was born some weak and brief reflection on the instability of earthly things, of which the surface of the water offered me the image; but soon these light impressions effaced themselves in the uniformity of continuous movement which rocked me, and which, without any active help from my soul, did not fail to attach me to such an extent that when summoned by the hour and the signal agreed upon, I could not tear away without an effort.

After supper, when the evening was beautiful, we all went together to make a tour of the walk on the terrace, to breathe the air of the lake and its freshness. We rested in the pavilion, we laughed, talked, sung some old song which was far better than modern discord, and finally went to rest content with the day, and not desiring anything but its like for the morning.

Such is, leaving to one side unforeseen and importunate visits, the manner in which I passed my time in this island, during the stay that I made there. Let someone tell me now what there was so attractive to excite in my heart regrets so lively, so tender, and so durable, that at the end of fifteen years it is still impossible for me to think of this beloved habitation, without feeling myself every time still carried away by agitations of desire.

I have remarked in the vicissitudes of a long life that the epochs of the sweetest enjoyments and of the most lively pleasures are not in every case those of which the remembrance draws me and touches me most nearly. These short moments of delirium and of passion, however strong they may be, are nevertheless, by their vivacity itself, only scattered points in the line of life. They are too rare and too rapid to constitute a state; and the happiness which my heart regrets is not composed of fugitive instincts, but a simple and permanent state, which has nothing keen in itself, but the duration of which increases the charm, to the point of finding there the supreme felicity.

All is in a continuous flux upon earth. Nothing keeps a constant and fixed form, and our affections which attach themselves to exterior things pass away and change necessarily like them. Always in advance or behind us, they recall the past, which is no more, or presage the future, which often is not to be; there is nothing solid there to which the heart can attach itself. Therefore one has scarcely here below anything but passing pleasures; for the happiness which lasts, I doubt if it is known. Scarcely is there, in our most living delights, a moment where the heart can truly say to us: I wish that this moment should last forever. And how can one call that happiness which is a fugitive state which leaves our heart unquiet and empty, which makes us regret something beforehand or desire something after?

But if there is a state where the soul finds a position sufficiently solid to repose thereon, and to gather together all its being, without having need for recalling the past, nor to climb on into the future; where time counts for nothing, where the present lasts forever, without marking its duration in any way, and without any trace of succession, without any other sentiment of privation, neither of enjoyment, of pleasure nor pain, of desire nor of fear, than this alone of our existence, and which this feeling alone can fill entirely: so long as this state lasts, he who finds it may be called happy, not with an imperfect happiness, poor and relative, such as that which one finds in the pleasures of life, but with a sufficing happiness, perfect and full, which does not leave in the soul any void which it feels the need of filling. Such is the state in which I found myself often at the island of St. Peter, in my solitary reveries, either resting in my boat which I let drift at the will of the water, or seated on the banks of the agitated lake, or elsewhere at the border of a beautiful river, or of a brooklet murmuring on the sand.

What is the nature of one's enjoyment in such a situation? Nothing external to oneself, nothing except oneself and one's own existence; so long as this state lasts, one suffices to oneself, like God. The sentiment of existence, deprived of all other affection, is in itself a precious sentiment of contentment and of peace, which alone suffices to render this existence dear and sweet to whoever knows how to remove from himself all the sensual and terrestrial impressions which come unceasingly to distract us, and to trouble the sweetness here below. But the greater part of men agitated by continual passions know little of this state, and having tasted it but imperfectly for a few instants, do not retain anything but an obscure and confused idea, which does not permit them to feel the charm. It would not even be good in the present state of affairs, that avid of these sweet ecstasies, they should be disgusted with the active life, of which their needs always being reborn, prescribe to them the duty. But an unfortunate who has been withdrawn from human society, and who can do nothing here below that is useful or good for himself or for others, can find in this state consolations for all human enjoyments which fortune and men cannot remove from him.

It is true that these consolations cannot be felt by all souls, nor in all situations. It is necessary that the heart should be at peace and that no passion should come to trouble the charm. Certain dispositions on the part of the man who experiences them are necessary; it is also necessary in the gathering together of environing objects. There is needed neither an absolute repose nor too much agitation, but a uniform and moderate movement which should have neither shocks nor intervals. Without movement, life is only a lethargy. If the movement is unequal or too strong it awakens; in recalling us to environing objects, it destroys the charm of the reverie and draws us out of ourselves, to put us in an instant under the yoke of fortune and man and to bring us back to the feeling of our unhappiness. An absolute silence leads to sadness; it offers us an image of death; thus the help of a light-hearted imagination is necessary and presents itself naturally to those whom the heavens have gratified with it. The movement which does not come from without, then, is made within us. The repose is less, it is true; but it is also more agreeable when light and sweet ideas, without agitating the depths of the soul, do nothing but brush the surface. There is needed only enough of them to remember oneself while forgetting all one's evils. This species of reverie can be tasted everywhere where one can be tranquil; and I have often thought that at the Bastille, and even in a cell where no object would strike my sight, I could still have dreamed agreeably.

But it is necessary to admit that this was done better and more favorably in a fertile and solitary island, naturally circumscribed and separated from the rest of the world, where nothing offered itself to me but smiling images, where nothing recalled sad remembrances, where the society of the small number of inhabitants was binding and sweet, without being interesting up to the point of occupying me incessantly, where I could finally yield myself the whole day, without obstacles and without cares, to the occupations of my taste or to the softest idleness. The opportunity without a doubt was excellent for a dreamer, who knowing how to nourish himself with agreeable illusions, in the midst of the most displeasing objects, could recall them at ease while adding to them everything which actually struck his senses. On emerging from a long and sweet reverie, seeing myself surrounded with verdure, flowers, birds, and letting my eyes wander afar over romantic banks which bordered a vast extent of clear and crystalline water, I assimilated to my fictions all these amiable objects; and finding myself brought back by degrees to myself and to what surrounded me, I could not distinguish the point of separation between fiction and reality, so much did all concur equally to render dear the solitary and absorbed life that I lived in this fair dwelling. If it could only come again! and if I could only go and end my days in this dear island, without ever leaving it, or ever seeing any inhabitant of the continent who would recall to me the memory of the calamities of every sort which they have been pleased to heap upon me for so many years! They would be soon forgotten forever; without a doubt they would not forget me in the same way; but what would this matter to me, provided that they had no access to me to trouble my repose? Delivered from all the terrestrial passions which the tumult of social life engenders, my soul would frequently leap above this atmosphere and have converse beforehand with the celestial intelligences, of which it hopes to augment the number in a short time. Mankind will take care, I know, not to give me back so sweet an asylum where they would not leave me. But they will not prevent me at least from transporting myself there everyday upon the wings of the imagination, and from tasting during some hours the same pleasure as if I were still inhabiting it. That which I did there was to dream at my ease. In dreaming that I am there, do I not do the same thing? I do even more; to the attraction of an abstract and monotonous reverie, I join the charming images which vivify it. These objects often escape from my senses in my ecstasies;

but now, the more my reverie is profound, the more strongly it paints them. I am often still in the midst of them, and more agreeably even than if I were actually so. The misfortune is, that to the degree in which my imagination becomes tepid, all this comes with more difficulty, and does not endure so long. Alas! it is when one commences to quit one's own carcase that one is the most offended by it!

FROM THE *Seventh Promenade*

. . . I have sometimes thought profoundly, but scarcely with pleasure, almost always against my will, and, as it were, by force. Reverie relaxes and amuses me, reflection wearies and saddens me. To think has always been a painful occupation for me and one without charm. Sometimes my reveries end up in meditation, but more often my meditations end up in reverie; and during these wanderings, my soul strays and soars in the universe, upon the wings of the imagination, in ecstasies which surpass every other enjoyment.

As long as I tasted this in all its purity, every other occupation was always insipid to me; but when once I was thrown into the literary career by outside impulses and felt the fatigue of mental labor and the annoyance of an unfortunate celebrity, I felt at the same time my sweet reveries weaken and become tepid; and soon forced despite myself to occupy myself with my sad situation, I could rarely find these dear ecstasies which for fifty years have held the place of fortune and of glory for me, with no other expenditure than that of time, and have made me, in idleness, the happiest of mortals.

I had even to fear, in my reveries, that my imagination, disturbed by my misfortunes, would turn its activity in that direction only, and that the continual feeling of my woes, oppressing my heart by degrees, would finally cast me down with their weight. In this state, an instinct which is natural to me, making me fly every saddening idea, imposed silence upon my imagination, and, fixing my attention upon those objects which surrounded me, made me, for the first time, absorb in detail the spectacle of Nature, which I had scarcely contemplated except in mass and in its whole.

The trees, the shrubs, the plants, are the ornamentation and the vestment of the earth. Nothing is so sad as the aspect of a naked and treeless country, which displays to the eye nothing but stones, soil, and sands; but, vivified by Nature, and reclad in its wedding robe, in the midst of watercourses and the song of the birds, the earth offers to man, in the harmony of its three kingdoms, a spectacle full of life, of interest and of charm, the one spectacle in the world of which his eyes and his heart are never weary.

The more a contemplator has a sensitive soul, the more he yields himself to ecstasies which excite in him this harmony. A profound and pleasing reverie then fills his senses, and he loses himself with a delicious intoxication in the immensity of the beautiful system with which he feels himself identified. Then all particular objects escape him; he does not see and does not feel anything but everything. It is necessary that some particular circumstance should gather together his ideas and circumscribe his imagination, in order for him to observe in part this universe which he struggles to embrace.

This naturally happened to me when my heart, oppressed by distress, recalled and concentrated all its movements on itself in order to preserve the remains of fervor which were ready to evaporate and to disappear, in the prostration I gradually experienced. I wandered carelessly through the woods and the mountains, not daring to think, for fear of increasing my griefs. My imagination which refuses itself to painful objects, let my senses yield themselves to the light but sweet impressions of surrounding objects. My eyes wandered ceaselessly from one to the other, and it was not possible that in so great a variety it should not find something to hold them despite themselves, and keep them fixed for a long period. . . .

Johann Wolfgang von Goethe

FROM *Faust*

PART ONE

TRANSLATED BY BAYARD TAYLOR
ADAPTED BY STUART ATKINS

Johann Wolfgang von Goethe (1749–1832)

GOETHE'S LIFE HAD AN EPIC SWEEP AND SCOPE, AND HIS LITerary career is a kind of history of literature in itself. He was born in Frankfurt-am-Main, Germany, and attended Leipzig University, the German center of cosmopolitan French Enlightenment culture. He went on to the University of Strasbourg, where he met Gottfried Herder, leader of the literary movement that became known as *Sturm und Drang* ("Storm and Stress"), a first stage in German Romanticism that rejected French neo-Classicism and sought its models in Shakespeare, in folklore, in popular ballads, and in national history.

In 1775 he moved to Weimar, where he became the friend of Grand Duke Karl August, who guaranteed Goethe's financial independence through a series of government appointments. Goethe's presence was to make Weimar an important cultural capital, one of the centers of the new European literature. A major event was Goethe's trip to Italy (1786–1788), which led to a rediscovery of Classical literature and a new style of writing. By the last period of his life, Goethe was a figure of international renown.

From early work in the eighteenth-century French tradition, Goethe moved, under Herder's influence, to the "pre-Romanticism" of his historical play *Götz von Berlichingen* and the novel *The Sorrows of Young Werther,* a story of romantic emotion and suffering which had immense influence on the lives and writings of young Europeans. Goethe's renewed interest in classical literature was expressed in the plays *Iphigenia, Torquato Tasso,* and in the verse narrative, *Hermann and Dorothea.* Goethe also wrote volumes of scientific observations and throughout his life continued to publish poetry, from the first *Poems* of 1771 to the final *Marienbad Elegies* of 1823.

Faust, Goethe's major work, was composed over a long period of time. The first sketches date from the 1770s, and the completed *Faust,* Part I was published in 1808. Part II, a lengthy and complex drama never intended for the stage, was published after Goethe's death, in 1833. The material underlying Goethe's drama is both real and mythic. There was a real Faustus who lived during the Renaissance, and was supposed to have sought universal knowledge through science and black magic. A popular account of his life had been written, and he had become the subject of folklore and folk drama. Goethe knew the legend from his childhood, and it never ceased to preoccupy him. To Goethe, Faust is the eternal seeker who incarnates aspiring mankind at his highest. Mephistopheles offers him an end to quest, a variety of instant pleasures which, if fully accepted as ultimate fulfillment by Faust, would mean an end to his moral being.

Faust

*Prologue in Heaven**

[THE LORD. HEAVENLY HOSTS. *Afterwards,* MEPHISTOPHELES.]
[THE THREE ARCHANGELS *come forward.*]

RAPHAEL. The sun-orb sings, in emulation,
mid brother-spheres, his ancient round;
his path predestined through Creation
he ends with step of thunder-sound.
The angels from the vision splendid
draw power, whose measure none can say;
the lofty works, uncomprehended,
are bright as on the earliest Day.

GABRIEL. And swift, and swift beyond conceiving,
the splendor of the Earth goes round,
Day's Eden-brightness still relieving
the awful Night's intense profound;
the ocean-tides in foam are breaking,
against the rocks' deep bases hurled,
and both, the spheric race partaking,
eternal, swift, are onward whirled.

MICHAEL. And rival storms abroad are surging
from sea to land, from land to sea,
a chain of deepest action forging
round all, in wrathful energy.
There flames a desolation, blazing
before the thunder's crashing way.
Yet, Lord, Thy messengers keep praising
the gentle movement of Thy day.

THE THREE. Since Thou remain'st uncomprehended,

* The "Prologue in the Theater" is omitted here.

this vision gives the angels power,
and all Thy works, sublime and splendid,
are bright as in Creation's hour.

[*Heaven opens.*]

MEPHISTOPHELES. Since Thou, O Lord, deign'st to approach again
and ask us how we do, in manner kindest,
and heretofore to meet myself wert fain,
me, too, among Thy retinue Thou findest.
Forgive, that these I cannot follow after
with lofty speech, though by them scorned and spurned;
my pathos certainly would move Thy laughter,
if Thou hadst not all merriment unlearned.
On sun and planets I'm not to be quoted;
how men torment themselves, is all I've noted.
The little god o' the world sticks to the same old way
and is as whimsical as on Creation's day.
Life somewhat better might content him,
but for the gleam of Light which Thou, from Heaven, hast sent him:
he calls it Reason—thence his power's increased,
to be far beastlier than any beast.
Saving Thy Grace's Presence, he to me
a long-legged grasshopper appears to be,
that springing flies, and flying springs,
and in the grass the same old ditty sings.
Would he just lay amid the grass he grows in!—
each bit of dung he seeks, to stick his nose in!

LORD. Hast thou, then, nothing more to mention?
Com'st ever, thus, with ill intention?
Find'st nothing right on earth, eternally?

MEPHISTOPHELES. No, Lord! I find things there still bad as they can be.
I pity a mankind that passes days so doleful
and have no heart to make them still more woeful.

LORD. Know'st Faust?

MEPHISTOPHELES. The Doctor? °

LORD. Ay; my servant, he!

MEPHISTOPHELES. Forsooth! he serves you after strange devices.
No earthly meat or drink the fool suffices.
His spirit's ferment far aspireth,
half conscious of his frenzied, crazed unrest;

57. *Doctor:* doctor of philosophy.

the fairest stars from Heaven he requireth,
from Earth, the highest raptures and the best,
and all the Near and Far that he desireth
fails to subdue the tumult of his breast.
LORD. Though still confused his service unto Me,
I soon shall lead him to a clearer morning:
sees not the gardener, e'en while buds his tree,
both flower and fruit its future years adorning?
MEPHISTOPHELES. What will you bet? I've still a chance to gain him,
if unto me full leave you give
gently along my road to train him.
LORD. As long as he's on earth, alive,
so long I make no prohibition.
Men err as long as they do strive.
MEPHISTOPHELES. My thanks! I find the dead no acquisition,
and never cared to have them in my keeping.
I much prefer the cheeks through which fresh blood is seeping.
And when a corpse is brought, I close my house:
my fun's that of a cat that's caught a mouse.
LORD. It's up to you as of this hour!
Turn off this spirit from his fountain-head
and lead him, if it's in your power,
along the path that you have planted,
then stand abashed when thou art forced to say:
A good man, in obscurest aspiration,
is well aware of what's the proper way.
MEPHISTOPHELES. Agreed! 'Tis but a short probation.
About my bet I feel no trepidation.
If I fulfill my expectation,
you'll let me triumph with a swelling breast.
Dust shall he eat, and with a zest,
as did a certain snake,° my near relation.
LORD. On that day, too, come uninvited;
the like of thee have never moved My hate.
Of all the spirits of Denial,
the waggish knave least trouble doth create.
Man's active nature, flagging, seeks too soon the level,
unqualified repose he learns to crave;
therefore, quite gladly, the comrade him I gave
who works, excites, and so creates, though devil.
But ye, God's sons in truth and duty,

93. *snake:* that of Genesis, who tempted Eve.

enjoy the rich, the ever-living Beauty!
Creative Power, that works eternal schemes,
clasp you in bonds of Love, propitious ever;
and what in wavering apparition gleams,
fix in its place with thoughts that last forever!

[*Heaven closes; exeunt* ARCHANGELS, *severally*.]

MEPHISTOPHELES [*solus*].
I like to see the Old Man when I'm bored
and have a care to be most civil.
It's really kind of such a noble Lord
to be so human, talking with the Devil.

NIGHT

[*A high-vaulted, narrow, Gothic room.* FAUST *sitting restlessly at a desk.*]

FAUST. I've studied now Philosophy
and Jurisprudence, Medicine,
and e'en, alas! Theology,
from end to end, with labor keen.
Yet here, poor fool! with all my lore
I stand, no wiser than before;
I'm Magister—yea, Doctor,—hight,
and straight or crosswise, wrong or right,
nigh ten years now, with many woes,
I've led my pupils by the nose . . .
and see that nothing can be known!
This knowledge cuts me to the bone.
I'm cleverer, true, than those fops of teachers,
Doctors, Magisters, Clerks, and Preachers;
no scruple or doubt comes now to smite me,
nor Hell nor Devil can longer affright me—
instead, I must all joys forego,
I cannot pretend aught truly to know,
I cannot pretend that I as a teacher
might help or convert a fellow creature.
Besides, I've neither lands nor gold,
nor earth's least pomp or honor hold.
No dog would bear such an existence!
Therefore, from Magic I seek assistance;
my hope is many a secret to reach
through spirit-power and spirit-speech,

and so the bitter task forego
of saying the things I do not know;
'tis to detect the inmost force
which binds the world and guides its course,
all germs and forces to explore—
and bandy empty words no more!
O full and splendid Moon, whom I
have, from this desk, seen climb the sky
so many a midnight, would thy glow
for the last time beheld my woe!
Ever thine eye, most mournful friend,
o'er books and papers saw me bend.
But would that I, on mountains grand,
amid thy blessèd light might stand,
with spirits through mountain caverns hover,
float in thy twilight the meadows over,
and, freed from the fumes of lore that swathe me,
to health in thy dewy fountains bathe me.
Alas! my prison still I see!
This drear, accursed masonry's
a dungeon that the sun attains
but duskly through the painted panes.
Hemmed in by many a toppling heap
of books worm-eaten, gray with dust,
which to the vaulted ceiling creep,
amidst them smoky papers thrust;
with glasses, boxes, round one stacked,
with instruments together hurled,
ancestral lumber jammed in, packed:
that is my world—if such's to call a world!
And do I ask, wherefore my heart
falters, oppressed with unknown needs;
why some inexplicable smart
all movement of my life impedes?
Because—in living Nature's stead,
where God His human creatures set—
in smoke and mould the fleshless dead
and bones of beasts surround me yet.
Away to wider, freer spheres!
And is this Book of Mystery,
where Nostradamus' ° hand appears,

178. *Nostradamus:* the French astrologer and alchemist (1503–1566).

69713

LIBRARY
College of St. Francis
JOLIET, ILL.

not full sufficient company?
When I the starry courses know
and Nature's wise instruction gain,
with light of power my soul shall glow,
as when the spirits spirits entertain.
In vain, this empty brooding here,
though guessed the holy symbols be:
ye Spirits, come—ye hover near—
oh, if you hear me, answer me!

[*He opens the book and sees the sign of the Macrocosm.*°]

Ha! what a sudden rapture leaps from this
I view, through all my senses swiftly flowing!
I feel a youthful, holy, vital bliss
in every vein and fibre newly glowing.
Did once a god these signs and figures write
that calm my inner violent feeling,
my troubled heart to joy unsealing;
that work their will with secret might,
the forces of great Nature, round about, revealing?
Am I a god?—so clear mine eyes!
In these clear symbols I behold
creative Nature to my soul unfold.
What says the sage, now first I recognize:
"The spirit-world no closures fasten—
thy mind is shut, thy heart is dead!
Disciple, up! Undaunted, hasten!
Bathe mortal breast in Dawn's first red!" °

[*He contemplates the sign.*]

How each the Whole its substance gives,
each in the other works and lives!
See heavenly forces rising and descending,
their golden urns reciprocally lending:
on wings that winnow sweet blessing
from heaven through the earth they're pressing,
to fill the All with harmonies caressing.
How grand a show! but, ah! a show alone.
Where, boundless Nature, seize thee for my own?
Where you, O breasts! ye fountains of all Being,
which earth and heaven do sustain,
toward which the withered breast doth strain:

S.D. *Macrocosm:* literally, "the great world"; the universe as a whole. 204. *Dawn's first red:* a favorable hour for successful mystic intuition or experience (here apparently figurative: Faust has momentarily gained a mystic insight).

ye flow, ye feed—and I must pine in vain?
[*He turns the pages angrily, then sees the sign of the* EARTH SPIRIT.°]
How otherwise upon me works this sign!
Thou, Spirit of Earth, to me art nearer:
I feel my powers loftier, clearer,
I glow, as drunk with new-made wine,
my heart has strength to face the world again,
to bear all earthly joy, all earthly pain,
to battle with the hurricane
and not to flinch, though foundering on the main.
Clouds gather over me—
the moon conceals her light—
the lamp's extinguished!
Mists rise!—Red angry rays are darting
around my head—there falls
a horror from the vaulted roof
and seizes me!
I feel thy presence, Spirit I invoke:
reveal thyself!
Ha! in my heart what rendering stroke!
New impulse feeling,
all my senses now are reeling!
I feel thee draw my heart, absorb, exhaust me!
Thou must! thou must! and though my life it cost me!
[*He takes the book and mysteriously utters the sign of the spirit. There is a reddish flame, in which the* EARTH SPIRIT *appears.*]

SPIRIT. Who calls me?
FAUST [*turning away*]. Terrible to see!
SPIRIT. Me hast thou long with might attracted,
long from my sphere the breath exacted,
and now—
FAUST. Woe! I endure not thee!
SPIRIT. To view me is thine aspiration,
my voice to hear, my countenance to see;
thy mighty yearning moveth me,
and here I am!—Does timid perturbation
one more than mortal shake? No cry exalted here!
And where's the breast that from itself a world did bear,

S.D. *Earth Spirit:* as the term is used in *Faust,* the Earth Spirit (*der Erdgeist*) is not, like the Macrocosm, a traditional alchemical-mystic concept (*anima terrae,* etc.), but rather a symbol of the divine spirit manifested in terrestrial activity.

and shaped and cherished, which with joy expanded
to be our peer, with us, the Spirits, banded?
Where art thou, Faust, whose voice has pierced to me,
who towards me pressed with all thine energy?
Art *thou* he, who, my presence breathing, seeing,
trembles through all the depths of being,
a writhing worm, a terror-stricken form?

FAUST. Shall I, O shape of flame, then yield in fear?
'Tis I, 'tis Faust! I am thy peer!

SPIRIT. In the tides of life, in action's storm,
a fluctuant wave,
a shuttle free,
birth and the grave,
an eternal sea,
a weaving, flowing,
life, all-glowing,
at Time's humming loom 'tis my hand that prepares
the garment of life which the Deity wears!

FAUST. Thou, who around the wide world wendest,
thou busy Spirit, how near I feel to thee!

SPIRIT. Thou'rt like the spirit thou comprehendest,
not me! [*Disappears.*]

FAUST [*collapsing*]. Not thee!
Whom then?
I, image of the Godhead,
not even like thee! [*A knock.*]
Damnation! 'Tis, I know, my famulus—
my happiness finds no fruition!
That on the fullness of my vision
the plodding pedant breaks in thus!

[*Enter* WAGNER, *in dressing-gown and nightcap, a lamp in his hand.* FAUST *turns, irritated.*]

WAGNER. Pardon! I heard your declamation—
'twas sure a Grecian tragedy you read?
In that high art I crave indoctrination,
since now it stands one in good stead.
I've often heard it said that preachers
could learn much, with actors as their teachers.

FAUST. Yes, if the priest an actor is by nature,
as haply now and then the case may be.

WAGNER. When, in one's study thus, one's an imprisoned creature
and scarce the world on holidays can see,
save from afar, with glasses, on occasion,

how shall one lead it by persuasion?
FAUST. You'll ne'er attain that, save you know deep feeling
that from the soul arises clear,
serene in primal strength, compelling
the hearts and minds of all who hear.
You sit forever gluing, patching;
stew up the scraps from others' fare;
and, from your heap of ashes hatching
a starveling flame, give it your care.
Let children and apes be admiring,
if to such things your taste impel—
but ne'er from heart to heart you'll speak inspiring,
save from your heart your speech doth well.
WAGNER. Yet how they speak, lets orators succeed.
I feel that I am far behind indeed.
FAUST. Seek thou an honest recompense!
Beware, a tinkling fool to be!
With little art, clear wit and sense
suggest their own delivery.
And if thou'rt moved to speak in earnest,
what need that after words thou yearnest?
Yes, your discourses, with their glittering show,
where ye for men twist thought like shredded paper,
are unrefreshing as the winds that blow
the rustling leaves through chill autumnal vapor.
WAGNER. The rhetor's art is long,
and life, alas! is fleeting.
Yet often, when my critic-duties meeting,
in head and heart I know that something's wrong.
How hard it is to compass the assistance
whereby one rises to the source!
And yet, before they've traveled half the course,
must most poor fellows quit existence.
FAUST. Is parchment, then, the holy fount before thee,
a draught wherefrom thy thirst forever slakes?
No true refreshment can restore thee,
save what from thine own soul spontaneous breaks.
WAGNER. Forgive me! great delight is granted
when, in the spirit of past ages planted,
we mark how, ere our time, a sage has thought,
then see how far and grandly all things we now have brought.
FAUST. O yes, the nearest stars we've passed!
Listen, my friend: the ages that are past

are now a book with seven seals° protected.
What you the Spirit of the Ages call
is nothing but a human mind withal
in which past ages are reflected.
That's why it often seems so sterile!
at the first glance who sees it runs away:
a lumber-garret and an offal-barrel—
at best, a grand-theatrical display
with maxims most pragmatical and hitting,
quite well the mouths of puppet-actors fitting!

WAGNER. But then, the world—the human heart and brain—
of these, all covet some slight apprehension!

FAUST. Yes, of the kind which most attain!
Who dares the child's true name in public mention?
The few, who thereof something really learned,
unwisely frank, with hearts that spurned concealing,
who to the mob laid bare each thought and feeling—
they evermore were crucified and burned.
I pray you, friend, 'tis now the dead of night,
our converse here must be suspended.

WAGNER. I would have shared your watches with delight,
that so our learned talk might be extended.
Tomorrow, though, I'll ask, in Easter leisure,
this and the other question, at your pleasure.
I've sought most zealously to gain in erudition—
though much I know, all knowledge's my ambition. [*Exit.*]

FAUST [*solus*].
That brain alone not loses hope, whose choice is
to stick in shallow trash forevermore,
which digs with hand for buried ore,
and, when it finds an angleworm, rejoices.
How could the voice of such a man intrude
where spirit-fullness compassed me about?
And yet, this once I owe him gratitude,
of mortal men the dullest, without doubt.
For he has torn me from a desperate state
that was about to overwhelm my senses:
the apparition was so giant-great,
it dwarfed and withered all my soul's pretenses.
I, image of the Godhead, who began—

334. *book with seven seals:* see Revelation 5:1.

deeming Eternal Truth secure in nearness—
to sun myself in heavenly light and clearness
and laid aside the earthly man;
I, more than Cherub, whose free force had planned
to flow through Nature's veins in bold pulsation,
to reach beyond, enjoying in creation
the life of gods—behold my expiation!
A thunder-word hath swept me from my stand.
With thee I dare not venture to compare me.
Though I possessed the power to draw thee near me,
the power to keep thee was denied my hand.
When that ecstatic moment held me,
I felt myself so small, so great;
and thou hast ruthlessly repelled me
back upon Man's uncertain fate.
Who is to teach me? What am I to shun?
Am I to heed this impulse or another?
Alas, the things we do, no less than those we suffer,
restrict the ways our life can run.
Some alien substance more and more is cleaving
to all the mind conceives as grand and fair;
when this world's Good is won by our achieving,
the Better, then, is named a cheat and snare.
The fine emotions, whence our lives we mould,
turn, midst the mundane tumult, dumb and cold.
If hopeful Fancy once, in daring flight,
her longings to the Infinite expanded,
still now a narrow space contents her quite,
since Time's wild wave so many a fortune stranded.
Deep in our hearts Dame Care is quickly lurking;
there secret pangs in silence working,
she, restless, rocks herself, disturbing joy and rest;
in newer masks her face is ever dressed,
by turns as house and land, as wife and child, presented,
as fire, water, poison, steel;
we dread the blows we never feel,
and what we never lose is yet by us lamented.
I am not like the gods—that truth is felt too deep!
The worm am I, that in the dust doth creep,
that, while in dust it lives and seeks its bread,
is crushed and buried by the wanderer's tread.
Is not all dust these walls within them hold,
the hundred shelves, which cramp and chain me,

the frippery, the trinkets thousandfold,
that in this mothy den restrain me?
Here shall I find the help I need?
Shall here a thousand volumes teach me only
that men, self-tortured, everywhere must bleed,
that somewhere, once, a happy man sat lonely?—
What mean'st thou by that grin, thou hollow skull,
save that thy brain, like mine a cloudy mirror,
sought reassuring light and then, in twilight dull,
thirsting for truth, went wretchedly to error?
Ye instruments, forsooth, but jeer at me,
your wheels and cogs mere things of wonder;
when at the door, you were my keys to be,
yet, deftly wrought, your bits can move no wards asunder.
Mysterious by Day's broad light,
Nature retains her veil, despite our clamors,
and what she won't reveal to human mind or sight
cannot be wrenched from her with levers, screws or
hammers.
Ye ancient tools—my use ye never knew—,
here, since my father° used you, still ye moulder.
Thou, ancient scroll, hast worn thy smoky hue
since dimly at this desk the lamp was wont to smoulder.
'Twere better far, had I my little idly spent,
than now to sweat beneath its burden, I confess it!
What from ancestral heritage is lent,
ye must make yours, if ye'd possess it:
what serves no use is mere impediment,
the Moment can use naught, save what will serve and bless it.
Yet why is fixed my gaze on yonder point so tightly,
the flask I yonder see a magnet to my eyes?
Why, all around me, glows the air so brightly,
as when in woods at night the mellow moonbeam lies?
I hail thee, wondrous, rarest vial!
and take thee down devoutly for the while,
man's art and wit to venerate in thee.
Thou summary of gentle slumber-potions,
thou essence of death's subtile countermotions,
unto thy master show thy favor free!
I see thee, and the stings of pain diminish,
I grasp thee, and my struggles slowly finish,
the spirit's flood tide ebbing more and more.

435. *ancient tools . . . father:* Faust's father was a doctor of medicine.

Far out to sea my course is now directed,
the gleaming flood's beneath my feet reflected—
a new Day beckons to a newer shore.
  A fiery chariot, borne on buoyant pinions,
sweeps near me now! The time has come for me
to pierce the ether's high, unknown dominions,
to reach new spheres of pure activity!
This godlike rapture, this supreme existence,
can I, but now a worm, deserve and earn?
Yes, resolute to reach some brighter distance,
on earth's fair sun my back I turn!
So let me dare those gates to fling asunder
which every man would fain go slinking by!
'Tis time, through deeds the word of truth to thunder,
that in their courage men with the high gods may vie;
and from that dark pit not to shrink affrighted
where Fancy doth herself to self-born pangs compel;
to struggle toward that pass benighted,
around whose narrow mouth flame all the fires of hell;
to take this step with cheerful resolution,
though nothingness should be the certain, swift conclusion.
  And now come down, thou cup of crystal clearest!
Fresh from thine ancient cover thou appearest,
so many years forgotten to my thought.
Refulgent once at banquets legendary,
the solemn guests thou madest merry
when one thy wassail to the other brought;
the rich and skillful figures o'er thee wrought,
the drinker's duty, rhyme-wise to explain them,
or in one breath below the mark to drain them,
are things for me with youthful memories fraught.
Now to a neighbor shall I pass thee never,
nor on thy curious art to test my wit endeavor,
for here's a juice whence sleep is swiftly got,
It fills with brownish flood thy crystal hollow.
I chose, prepared this—so let it follow
that solemnly, as final drink I swallow,
my festal toast and greeting be to the Morrow brought.

[*He raises the cup to his lips.*]

[CHIMES AND CHORALE.]

ANGELS' CHORUS. Christ is arisen!°

495. *Christ is arisen:* first line of a medieval Easter hymn, which Goethe freely adapts here.

Joy to that Mortal who
man's imperfection knew,
care and annoyance too—
all that's man's prison.

FAUST. What bright clear tones, what hollow droning knell,
drives from my lips the goblet of libation?
Ye booming bells, do ye already tell
of the first hour of Easter's celebration?
Ye choirs, have ye begun the sweet, consoling chant,
sung once, through night of death, by angels ministrant,
new Covenant's affirmation?

WOMEN'S CHORUS. With spices, balm precious,
therewith we arrayed Him,
faithful and gracious,
we tenderly laid Him;
linen to bind Him
cleanlily wound we;
yet when we'd find Him,
no Christ do we see.

ANGELS' CHORUS. Christ is arisen!
Bliss hath invested Him!
Woes that molested Him,
trials that tested Him,
now're a past vision.

FAUST. Why sound for me, earth-bound, your spell,
ye gentle, powerful sounds of heaven?
Peal rather there, where tender mortals dwell!
Your messages I hear, but faith has not been given—
and dearest child of Faith is Miracle.
I venture not to soar to those high regions
whence the glad tidings to us float—
and yet, from childhood up familiar with the note,
to life they now renew my old allegiance.
Once, Heavenly Love sent down a burning kiss
upon my brow, in sabbath silence holy;
then, filled with mystic presage, many bells chimed slowly,
and prayer dissolved me in a fervent bliss.
A sweet, uncomprehended yearning
drove forth my feet through woods and meadows free,
and, while a thousand tears were burning,
I felt a world arise for me.
This song, to youth and all its sports appealing,
proclaimed the Spring's rejoicing holiday.

So Memory holds me now, in childlike feeling,
back from the last, the solemn way.
Sound on, ye songs of heaven, so sweet and mild!
My tears gush forth, and Earth takes back her child!

DISCIPLES' CHORUS. If He, victoriously,
burst from the vaulted
grave and, all-gloriously,
now sits exalted;
if He's, in glow of birth,
rapture creative near:—
ah! to the woe of earth
still are we native here.
If His aspiring
followers Him here miss,
they're tearful, desiring,
Master, Thy bliss!

ANGELS' CHORUS. Christ is arisen,
out of Corruption's womb.
Burst ye your prison,
break from your gloom!
When your deeds adulate,
when love you demonstrate
feeding your fellow men,
teaching them lessons great,
giving them Joy's omen,
then is your Master near,
then is He here!

OUTSIDE THE CITY GATE

[PEOPLE OF EVERY CLASS, *moving away from the city.*]

SOME APPRENTICES. Why do you go that way?
OTHERS. We're off to Hunter's Lodge today.
THE FIRST. We plan to go to the Old Mill and dance.
ONE. Go to the River Tavern's my advice.
A SECOND. The road that way is not so nice.
THE OTHERS. And you then?
A THIRD. With the crowd I'll take my chance.
A FOURTH. Come on along to Burgdorf! There you find, I hear,
the prettiest girls, the very best of beer,
and fighting good enough for any.
A FIFTH. I know that's your idea of fun,

but do you want *another* beating?
Not me! I just detest the place, for one.

SERVANT GIRL. No, no! I'm going back to town again.

A SECOND. We'll surely find him standing by those poplars there.

THE FIRST. So what? Why should I cheer? So then
he'll be beside you everywhere,
and only dance with you. You'll see!
So what is all your fun to me?

THE SECOND. I'm sure he's not alone today—
he'd be with Curly's what I heard him say.

A STUDENT. And how they walk! Say, do you see . . . ?
Those wenches really need our company.
A good strong beer, tobacco when I rest,
and servant-girls diked out—that's what I now like best.

BURGHER'S DAUGHTER. D'you see those handsome fellows, sister?
I really think that's just too bad.
It's servant-girls they're running after,
although the nicest girls as company they've had.

SECOND STUDENT [*to the* FIRST]. Not quite so fast! There come two more behind;
they're dressed quite well and neatly,
and one lives right next door, I find—
a girl that takes my heart completely.
They're walking properly, alone,
but in the end they'll let us come along.

THE FIRST. They're not for me—I don't like formal ways.
Quick! lest our game escape us in the press.
The hand that wields the broom on Saturdays
can best, on Sundays, fondle and caress.

BURGHER. He suits me not at all, our new-made Burgomaster!
Since he's installed, his arrogance grows faster.
How has he helped the town? Just say!
Things worsen here from day to day;
each petty law we must obey
and taxes more than ever pay.

BEGGAR [*sings*]. Good gentlemen and lovely ladies,
so red of cheek and fine of dress,
behold how needful here your aid is,
and see and lighten my distress!
Let me not sing my song too late,—
he's only glad who gives away!
A day that all men celebrate
should be for me a harvest day.

SECOND BURGHER. On Sundays, holidays, there's naught I take delight in
like gossiping of war and war's array,
when off in Turkey, far away,
those foreign armies are a-fighting.
One at the window sits, with glass and friends,
and sees all sorts of ships go down the river gliding;
and blesses then, as home he wends
at eve, our times of peace abiding.

A THIRD. Yes, Neighbor, that's my notion too:
they break their heads, let loose their passions,
and mix things madly through and through,
but we must keep our good old fashions.

OLD WOMAN [*to the* BURGHER'S DAUGHTERS]. Oho! how fine! so handsome and so young!
Who wouldn't look again, that met you?—
Don't act so proud—I'll hold my tongue.
But what you'd like I'll undertake to get you.

BURGHER'S DAUGHTER. Come, Agatha! I shun the witch's sight
in public, lest there be misgiving.
And yet she showed me, on Saint Andrew's Night,°
my future sweetheart, just as he were living.

AGATHA. She showed me mine, in crystal clear,
with several wild young blades, a soldier-lover;
I seek him everywhere, I pry and peer,
and yet his face I don't discover.

SOLDIERS. Castles with lofty
ramparts and towers,
maidens disdainful
in Beauty's array,
both shall be ours!
Bold is the venture,
splendid the pay!
Lads, let the trumpets
for us be suing,
calling to pleasure,
calling to ruin.
Stormy our life is,
such is its boon.
Maidens and castles
capitulate soon.

636. *Saint Andrew's night:* Saint Andrew's eve, November 29, was traditionally the time girls consulted fortune tellers about their future sweethearts.

Bold is the venture,
splendid the pay!
Then go the soldiers
marching away!

[*Enter* FAUST *and* WAGNER.]

FAUST. Released from ice are brook and river,
by the quickening glance of gracious Spring,
as colors of hope to the valley cling.
Now weak old Winter himself must shiver,
withdrawn to the hills, a crownless king,
whence, ever retreating, he sends again
impotent showers of sleet that darkle
in belts across the green of the plain;
but the sun will permit no white to sparkle,
everywhere forms inchoate are stirring,
he brightens the world with palette unerring
and, lacking blossoms, blue, yellow, red,
he takes these gaudy people instead.
Turn thee about, and from this height
back on the town direct thy sight.
Out of the hollow, gloomy gate
the motley throngs come forth elate.
They all enjoy the sunshine's hoard.
They honor the day of the Risen Lord,
for they themselves know resurrection:
from the low, dark rooms, scarce habitable,
from the bonds of work, from trade's restriction,
from the pressing weight of roof and gable,
from the narrow, crushing streets and alleys,
from the churches' solemn and reverend night,
forth they come to cheerful light.
How lively, see! the multitude sallies,
scattering through gardens and fields remote,
how over the river, that broadly dallies,
dances so many a festive boat,
as, overladen, night to sinking,
the last full wherry takes the stream.
Even afar, from hill paths blinking,
men's clothes are colors that softly gleam.
The village bustle, you hear it, then?—
true heaven is here for most of men,
hence great and small cry with delight,
"Here I'm a Man, and that is right."

WAGNER. To stroll with you, Professor, flatters,
'tis honor, profit, unto me;
yet if alone, I'd shun these shallow matters,
since all that's coarse provokes my enmity.
This fiddling, shouting, ten-pin rolling—
I hate the noises of the throng;
they rave, as Satan were their sports controlling,
and call it mirth, and call it song.

PEASANTS [*under the lime-tree*].

DANCE AND SONG

As for the dance the shepherd dressed,
in ribbons, wreath and gayest vest
himself with care arraying,
around the linden lass and lad
already footed it like mad.
Hey-day! hey-day!
and a hey-nonny hey!
the fiddle-bow was playing.
He broke the ranks, no whit afraid,
and with his elbow nudged a maid
who stood, the dance surveying;
the buxom girl then turned and said,
"Now you I call a stupid-head."
Hey-day! hey-day!
and a hey-nonny hey!
"Be decent while you're playing."
Then round the circle went their flight,
they danced to left, they danced to right,
and every skirt went sailing.
They soon grew red, they soon got warm,
then rested, panting, arm in arm,
—hey-day! hey-day!
and a hey-nonny hey!—
to hips their elbows straying.
"And don't be so familiar here!
How many a one has fooled his dear,
waylaying and betraying!"
But still, he coaxed her soon aside,
and round the linden sounded wide
hey-day! hey-day!
and a hey-nonny hey!
loud shouts and fiddle-playing.

OLD PEASANT. Professor, it is good of you

to lend your presence here today,
among our crowd of common folk,
a highly-learned man, to stray.
Our finest tankard here you have,
'tis newly filled for you to take;
in offering it, I boldly wish
that not alone your thirst it slake,—
that every drop it doth embrace
be added to your store of days.

FAUST. I take the cup you kindly reach,
with thanks and health to all and each.

[*The* VILLAGERS *gather around him.*]

THE PEASANT. In truth, 'tis well and fitly timed
that now our day of joy you share,
since heretofore, in evil days,
you gave us so much helping care.
Still many a man is now alive,
saved by your father's skillful hand,
that snatched him from the fever's rage
and stayed the plague in all the land.
'Twas then that you, though but a youth,
went into every house of pain;
many a corpse was carried forth,
but you in health came out again;
no test or trial you then evaded—
a Helping God our helper aided.

ALL. Health to the man, so skilled and tried,
that he as helper long abide!

FAUST. To Him above bow down, my friends,
Who, teaching us to help, help sends.

[*He walks on with* WAGNER.]

WAGNER. With what a feeling, thou great man, must thou
receive the people's honest veneration!
How lucky he, whose gifts outstanding
with such advantages endow!
The father shows thee to his offspring;
all ask, and press in haste to gaze;
the fiddle halts, the dance delays.
Thou goest, they stand in rows to see,
and all the caps are lifted high—
a little more and they would bend the knee
as if the Holy Host came by.

FAUST. A few more steps ascend, as far as that near stone,
a place to break our walk and rest, contented.
Here, lost in thought, I've lingered oft alone
when foolish fasts and prayers my life tormented.
Here, rich in hope and firm in faith,
with tears, wrung hands and sighs I've striven,
the end of that far-spreading death
by force to gain from God in heaven.
Now like contempt the masses' praise doth seem.
Couldst thou but read, within mine inmost spirit,
how little now I deem
that sire or son such praises merit!
My father was an alchemist obscure,
who through the holy spheres of Nature groped and
  wandered
and on them in capricious fashion pondered,
and yet a man of motives pure;
who, in his blackened kitchen bending,
with proved adepts in company,
made, with his recipes unending,
opposing substances agree.
There was the Lion red, a wooer daring,
within the Lily's tepid bath espoused,
and both, tormented then by flame unsparing,
at last in a new bridal chamber housed;
and when appeared, with colors splendid,
the young Queen in her crystal shell,
that was the drug specific.° The patients' woes soon ended—
and none inquired who got well.
Thus we, our hellish medicines compounding,
among these vales and hills surrounding,
worse than the pestilence, have raged.
Thousands were done to death from poison of my giving,
but I must hear from those yet living
the shameless murderers still praised.
WAGNER. Why therefore yield to deep depression?
Does not a good man do his share
by exercising with strict care
the skills passed on to him for his profession?
If one his father honors, as a youth,

800–06. Lion red . . . specific: a description of the production of the philosopher's stone (panacea).

he learns from him without recalcitrance;
if he, as man, augments the stores of truth,
then may his son to higher goals advance.

FAUST. O happy he, who still renews
the hope from Error's deeps to rise for ever!
That which one does not know, one needs to use,
and what one knows, one uses never.
But let us not, by such despondence, so
the fortune of this hour embitter!
Mark how, in evening sunlight's glow,
the cottages against the greenery glitter.
The glow retreats, done is the day of toil;
it onward hastes, old life with new restoring;
ah, that no wing can lift me from the soil,
upon its track to follow, follow soaring!
Then would I see eternal Evening gild
the silent world beneath me glowing,
on fire each mountain peak, with peace each valley filled,
the silver brook to golden rivers flowing.
The mountain chain, with all its gorges deep,
would then no more impede my godlike motion—
before astounded eyes expands the ocean,
with all its inlets warm in sleep.
As, finally, the sun afar is sinking,
a reborn impulse fires my mind
to hasten on, his beams eternal drinking,
the day before me, and the night behind,
above me skies unfurled, the floor of waves beneath me.
A glorious dream! though now its glories fade.
Alas! the wings that lift the mind, no aid
of wings to lift the body can bequeath me.
Yet in each soul is born the pleasure
of yearning onward, upward and away
when o'er our heads, lost in the vaulted azure,
the lark sends down his warbling lay,
when over crags and piny highlands
the poising eagle slowly soars,
when over plains and lakes and islands
the homing crane seeks far-off shores.

WAGNER. I've had, myself, at times some odd caprices,
but never yet such impulse felt as this is.
One soon fatigues, on woods and fields to look,
nor would I beg the bird his wing to spare us.

How otherwise the mental raptures bear us
from page to page, from book to book!
Then winter nights take loveliness untold,
and warmth of happiness fills your whole being;
if then your hands unroll some parchment rare and old,
all heaven descends, and you this earth are fleeing.

FAUST. One impulse art thou conscious of, at best;
O, never seek to know the other!
Two souls, alas! reside within my breast,
and each withdraws from, and repels, its brother:
one to the world is bound in clinging lust,
the other soars, all earthly ties unheeded,
to join ancestral gods, far from this dust,
in fields where naught mundane is needed.
If there be airy spirits near,
'twixt heaven and earth their potent errands plying,
let them from out the golden haze appear
and bear me forth, to bright, new regions flying!
Yes, if a magic mantle once were mine,
to waft me o'er the world at pleasure,
I would not for the costliest stores of treasure,
not for a monarch's robe, the gift resign.

WAGNER. Invoke not thus that well-known throng
which through the evening haze diffused is faring
and danger thousandfold, our race to wrong,
in every quarter is preparing.
Swift from the north their spirit fangs so sharp
sweep down and with their barbèd points assail you;
or from the east they come, to dry and warp
your lungs, till breath and being fail you;
if from the desert sendeth them the South,
with fire on fire your throbbing forehead crowning,
the West soon leads a host to cure the drouth
so that the meadow, field, and you, are drowning.
They gladly hearken, prompt for injury,
gladly obey, because they gladly cheat us;
from Heaven they represent themselves to be,
and lisp like angels when with lies they greet us.
But let us go! 'Tis gray and dusky all,
the air is cold, the vapors fall:
at night, one learns his house to prize.—
Why stand thou thus, with such astonished eyes?
What, in the twilight, can your mind so trouble?

FAUST. Seest thou the black dog coursing there, through grain
and stubble?
WAGNER. Long since—yet deemed it not important in the least.
FAUST. Inspect him close: for what tak'st thou the beast?
WAGNER. Why, for a poodle who has lost its master
and scents about, his track to find.
FAUST. Seest thou the spiral circles, narrowing faster,
which he, approaching, round us seems to wind?
A streaming trail of fire, if I see rightly,
behind his course doth twist and turn.
WAGNER. It may be that your eyes deceive you slightly—
a mere black poodle's all that I discern.
FAUST. It seems to me that with enchanter's cunning
he snares our feet, some future chain to bind.
WAGNER. I see him timidly, in doubt, around us running,
since, in his master's stead, two strangers doth he find.
FAUST. The circle narrows, now he's near!
WAGNER. A dog thou seest, and not a phantom, here.
Behold him stop, upon his belly crawl,
his tail go wagging—canine habits, all.
FAUST. Come, follow us! Come here, at least!
WAGNER. 'Tis the absurdest, drollest beast.
Stand still, and you will see him wait;
address him, and he's with you straight;
if something's lost, he'll quickly bring it,
your cane, if in the stream you fling it.
FAUST. No doubt you're right: no trace of mind, I own,
is in the beast—I see but drill alone.
WAGNER. A dog, when he's well educated,
is by the wisest tolerated.
Your favor, then, he curries not in vain—
some student's clever pupil, I maintain.
[*They enter the city gate.*]

FAUST'S STUDY

FAUST [*enters, with the* DOG].
Behind me field and meadow sleeping
I leave in deep and quiet night,
within whose dread and holy keeping
our better soul awakes to light.

Now wild desires no longer win us,
the deeds of passion cease to chain;
the love of Man revives within us,
the love of God revives again.
Stop running, poodle, nor make such racket and riot!
Why at the threshold wilt snuffing be?
Lie down behind the stove in quiet:
my softest cushion I give to thee.
As thou, outside there, with running and leaping
amused us hast, on the mountain's crest,
so now I take thee into my keeping,
a welcome, if but silent, guest.
Ah, when, within our narrow chamber,
the lamp with friendly luster glows,
there flames within the breast each ember
and in the heart, itself that knows.
Then Hope again lends sweet assistance,
and Reason then resumes her speech;
one yearns, the rivers of existence,
the very founts of life, to reach.
Snarl not, poodle! 'Mid the sounds that rise,
the sacred tones that my soul embrace,
animal noises are out of place.
Of course we know that men despise
what they don't comprehend;
the Good and Beautiful they vilipend,
finding it oft a burdensome measure.
Is the dog, like men, snarling displeasure?
But ah! I feel, though will thereto be stronger,
contentment flows from out my breast no longer.
Why must the stream so soon run dry and fail us,
and thirst once again assail us—
so often my own situation?
And yet, this want may be supplied us:
we call the supernatural to guide us,
we pine and thirst for revelation—
nowhere a purer or brighter flame
than in what men the Gospel name.
I feel impelled its meaning to determine
and in sincerity, withal,
the sacred Text's original
to turn into my own belovèd German.

[*He opens a great tome and makes preparations for writing.*]

'Tis written, "In the beginning was the *Word*." °
Here I am balked! Who, now, can help afford?
The *Word*—impossible so high to rate it;
quite otherwise must I translate it,
if by the Spirit's light I'm truly taught.
I've writ, "In the beginning was the *Thought*."
This first line let me weigh completely,
lest my impatient pen proceed too fleetly.
Is it the *Mind* which works, creates, indeed?
"In the beginning was the *Power*," now I read.
Yet, as I write, a warning is suggested,
that I the sense may not have fairly tested.
The Spirit aids me, now I see the light!
"In the beginning was the *Act*," I write.
  If I'm to share my room with thee,
poodle, no howling, prithee!
no barking, also!
Such a noisy, disturbing fellow
no longer can I suffer near me.
One of us, dost hear me?
must leave, I fear me.
No longer guest-rights I bestow—
the door is open, art free to go.
But what do I see in the creature!
Is that a natural feature?
is't actual fact? or Fancy's shows?
How long and broad my poodle grows!
He rises mightily—
a canine form that cannot be!
What a spectre I've harbored thus!
He resembles a hippopotamus,
with fiery eyes, teeth terrible to see.
O, now am I sure of thee:
to exorcise things half from Hell,
the Key of Solomon° works well.

SPIRITS [*in the corridor*]. Someone within is caught!
Stay without, follow him not!
Like the fox in a snare
quakes the old hell-lynx there.
Take heed—look about!
Back and forth hover,

982. the Word: see John 1:1. *1016. Key of Solomon:* a collection of spells, incantations, etc.

under and over,
and he'll work himself out.
If your aid can avail him,
let it not fail him,
for he, without measure,
has wrought for our pleasure.

FAUST. First, for confronting the creature,
the Spell for the Four's° the right feature:
Salamander, burn glorious!
Writhe, Undine, as bidden!
Sylph, become hidden!
Gnome, be laborious!
Who for the Elements
has no true sense,
unaware
of the powers there—
no Spirit whatever
him dreadeth ever.
O disappear burning,
Salamander!
Flow purling and churning,
o Undine!
Shine in meteor-sheen,
o Sylph!
Come serve us thyself,
Incubus! Incubus!
Spirit, come forth! appear to us!
Of the Four, no feature
lurks in the creature.
Quiet he lies and grins disdain—
not yet, it seems, have I given him pain.
Now shalt thou hear me
more strongly conjure thee!
Art thou, my gay one,
Hell's fugitive stray-one?
The sign witness, now,
before which they bow,
the cohorts of Hell!
With hair all bristling, it begins to swell.
Base Being, hearest thou?!
Knowest and fearest thou

1030. *Spell for the Four:* for the four Elements: salamanders were spirits of fire, undines of water, sylphs of air, gnomes of earth.

the One not created,
named inexpressibly,
who all zones permeated,
pierced irredressibly?
Behind the stove still banned,
see it, an elephant, expand!
It fills the space entire,
mist-like melting, ever faster.
That's enough! Ascend no higher!
Lay thyself at the feet of the Master!
Thou seest, not vain the threats I bring thee:
with holy fire I'll scorch and sting thee!
Wait not to know
the threefold dazzling glow,
wait not to know
the strongest art we reserve us!

MEPHISTOPHELES [*steps forth from behind the stove as the mist is dissipating; he is dressed as a Traveling Scholar*].
Why such a noise? Sir, may I be of service?

FAUST. Was this alone the poodle's core?
A scholar, poor and migrant! The *casus* is diverting.

MEPHISTOPHELES. The learned gentleman I bow before:
you've made me roundly sweat, that's certain!

FAUST. Thy name?

MEPHISTOPHELES. A question hardly worthy of
a man whose mind the Word so much despises;
who has for outward forms no love
and depths of being only prizes.

FAUST. With most of you, the name's a test
whereby your essence is expressed:
Beelzebub's the Lord of Flies,
Apollyon the Destroyer, and Satan Prince of Lies.
Well, who are thou?

MEPHISTOPHELES. Part of that power, little understood,
which always wills the Bad, and always works the Good.

FAUST. What hidden sense in this enigma lies?

MEPHISTOPHELES. I am the Spirit that denies,
and rightly so, for all things, from the Void
called forth, deserve to be destroyed—
'twere better, then, were naught created.
Thus, all which you as sin have rated,
destruction, aught with Evil blent,
all that's my proper element.

FAUST. Thou nam'st thyself a part, yet show'st complete to me?
MEPHISTOPHELES. The modest truth I speak to thee.
Though Man, that microcosmic fool, can see
himself a whole so frequently,
part of the part am I, once All in primal night,
part of the Darkness which brought forth the Light,
the haughty Light, which now demands all space
and claims of Mother Night her ancient place.
And yet the struggle fails, since light, howe'er it weaves,
still, fettered, unto bodies cleaves;
it flows from bodies, bodies beautifies,
by bodies is its course impeded;
and so, but little time is needed,
I hope, ere, as the bodies die, it dies.
FAUST. A noble plan thou art pursuing!
Thou canst not compass general ruin,
and hast on smaller scale begun.
MEPHISTOPHELES. And truly 'tis not much, when all is done.
That which to Naught is in resistance set,
the Something of this clumsy world, has yet,
with all that I have undertaken,
not been by me disturbed or shaken:
from earthquake, tempest, wave, volcano's brand
back into quiet settle sea and land!
And that damned stuff, the brood of beasts and men—
what use, in having that to play with?
how much of it I've made away with,
yet ever circulates more new, fresh blood again!
It makes me furious, such things beholding:
from water, earth and air unfolding,
a thousand germs break forth and grow
in dry, and wet, and warm, and chilly!
And had I not the flame reserved, why, really,
I'd nothing all my own to show.
FAUST. So, to the actively eternal
creative force, in cold disdain
you now oppose the fist infernal,
whose wicked clench is all in vain!
Some other labor should you rather,
strange Son of Chaos, undertake!
MEPHISTOPHELES. Well, we'll consider: thou canst gather
my views when later calls I make.
But could I now myself absent?

FAUST. Why thou shouldst ask, I don't perceive.
We are acquainted now to some extent:
for further visits thou hast leave.
The window's here, the door is yonder;
a chimney, too, would meet your needs.
MEPHISTOPHELES. I must confess that forth I may not wander:
one little obstacle impedes.
The wizard's-foot, that on your threshold made is—
FAUST. The pentagram° prohibits thee?
Why, tell me now, thou son of Hades,
if that prevents, how cam'st thou in to me?
Could such a Spirit be so cheated?
MEPHISTOPHELES. Inspect the thing! The drawing's not completed:
the outer angle, you may see,
is open left—the lines don't fit it.
FAUST. Well, Chance this time has fairly hit it!
And so, thou'rt prisoner to me?
This is a triumph not intended!
MEPHISTOPHELES. The poodle naught remarked as here his way he wended,
but other aspects now obtain:
the devil can't get out again.
FAUST. Try, then, the open window-pane!
MEPHISTOPHELES. For devils and for spectres 'tis a law
that where they've entered in, they also must withdraw.
The former's free to us, we're governed by the second.
FAUST. In Hell itself, then, laws are reckoned?
That's well! So might a compact be
made with you gentlemen—one binding surely?
MEPHISTOPHELES. Whatever's promised shall delight thee purely,
nor skinflint bargain shalt thou see.
But such is not for swift conclusion;
we'll talk about the matter soon.
So now, I do entreat this boon:
leave to withdraw from my intrusion.
FAUST. One moment more I ask thee to remain,
some pleasant tale, before, to tell me.
MEPHISTOPHELES. Release me now, and I'll soon come again;
then thou, at will, mayst question and compel me.
FAUST. Not I did snares around thee cast,
'twas thou who led thyself into the meshes.

1154. *pentagram:* a magical five-pointed star designed to keep away witches and other evil spirits.

Who traps a devil, hold him fast!
not soon a second time he'll catch a prey so precious.
MEPHISTOPHELES. If 'tis your wish, I'm also glad to stay
and serve thee in a social station,
though stipulating that I may
with arts of mine afford thee recreation.
FAUST. To that I willingly agree,
if the diversion pleasant be.
MEPHISTOPHELES. My friend, thou'lt gain, past all pretenses,
more in this hour to soothe thy senses,
than in a year's monotony.
That which the dainty spirits sing thee,
the lovely pictures they shall bring thee,
are more than magic's empty show.
Thy scent will be to bliss invited,
thy palate then with taste delighted,
thy nerves of touch ecstatic glow.
All unprepared, the charm we spin:
we're here together, so begin!
SPIRITS. Vanish, ye darkling
arches above him!
Loveliest weather,
born of blue ether,
break from the sky!
O that the darkling
clouds had departed!
Starlight is sparkling,
tranquiller-hearted
suns are on high.
Heaven's own children
in beauty bewildering
gracefully bending
pass as they hover.
Longing unending
follows them over;
they, with their glowing
garments out-flowing,
cover, in going,
landscape and bower,
where, in seclusion,
lovers are plighted,
lost in illusion.
Bower on bower!

Tendrils unblighted!
Lo! in a shower
grapes that o'ercluster
gush into must or
flow into rivers
of foaming and dashing
wine, that 'mid flashing
gems downward boundeth
from the high places
and, spreading, surroundeth
as crystalline spaces
blossoming forelands,
emerald shore-lands.
And the winged races
taste what delight is,
fly where no night is,
to islands enticing
in luminous motion,
dipping and rising
on waves of the ocean.
Hear men there voicing
songs of rejoicing!
see how they're dancing
o'er leas entrancing—
men whom no towns mure
seek and find pleasure.
Some you see skimming
boldly the highlands,
others are swimming
lakes of the islands,
others are flying—
lifeward all hieing,
off to the distant
stars of existent
rapture and love!

MEPHISTOPHELES. He sleeps. Enough, ye sprites! your airy number
have sung him truly into slumber:
for this performance I your debtor prove.—
Not yet are *thou* the man, to catch the Fiend and hold him!—
With fairest dreams and images infold him,
plunge him in seas of sweet untruth!
Yet, for the threshold's magic which controlled him,
the devil needs a rat's quick tooth.

I'll need no lengthened invocation:
here rustles one that soon will work my liberation.
The Lord of Rats, and eke of mice,
of flies and bedbugs, frogs and lice,
summons thee hither to the doorsill
to gnaw it where, with just a morsel
of oil, he paints the spot for thee—
There com'st thou running out toward me!
To work, at once! The point which made me craven
is forward, near the edge, engraven.
Another bite makes free the door.—
So, dream thy dreams, o Faust, until we meet once more! [*Exit.*]

FAUST [*awakening*]. Am I a second time defeated?
Remains there naught of lofty spirit-sway,
save that I've been, by dream of devil, cheated
and that a poodle ran away?

FAUST'S STUDY

[FAUST, MEPHISTOPHELES.]

FAUST. A knock? Come in! Again my quiet broken?

MEPHISTOPHELES. 'Tis I.

FAUST. Come in!

MEPHISTOPHELES. Thrice must the words be spoken.

FAUST. Come in, then!

MEPHISTOPHELES. Thus thou pleasest me.
I hope we'll suit each other well;
for, thy depression to dispel,
I come, a squire of high degree,
in scarlet suit with golden trimming,
a cloak in silken lustre swimming,
a tall cock's-feather in my hat,
a long, sharp sword for show or quarrel.
And I advise thee, brief and flat,
to don the selfsame gay apparel,
that, from thy cares released, and free,
Life be at last revealed to thee.

FAUST. This life of earth, whatever my attire,
I'd find confining, painful, lonely.
Too old am I for pleasure only,
too young, to be without desire.
What from the world have I to gain?

Thou shalt abstain, renounce, refrain—
such is the everlasting song
that in the ears of all men rings,
that unrelieved, our whole life long,
each hour, in passing, hoarsely sings.
In very terror, I at morn awake,
upon the verge of bitter weeping
to see the day of disappointment break,
to no one hope of mine, not one, its promise keeping,
that e'en the slightest hope of joy
with wilful cavil would diminish,
with life's vexations would destroy
my ardent zeal great works to finish.
Then, too, when night descends, uneasily
upon my couch of sleep I lay me;
there, also, comes no rest to me,
and only some wild dream, to fray me.
The god that in my breast doth dwell
can deeply stir the inner sources;
yet, though it all my faculties impel,
it can't affect external forces.
So, by the burden of my days oppressed,
death I desire, find life a thing unblessed.

MEPHISTOPHELES. And yet is never Death a wholly welcome guest.

FAUST. O fortunate, for whom, when victory glances,
the bloody laurels on the brow he bindeth!
whom, after rapid, maddening dances,
in clasping maiden-arms he findeth!——
O would that I, before that Spirit's might,
ecstatic, reft of life, had sunken.

MEPHISTOPHELES. And yet, by someone, in that Easter night,
a certain liquid was not drunken.

FAUST. Eavesdropping, ha! thy pleasure seems to be.

MEPHISTOPHELES. Omniscient am I not; yet much is known to me.

FAUST. Though some familiar tone, retrieving
my thoughts from torment, led me on,
and sweet, clear echoes came, deceiving
a faith bequeathed from childhood's dawn,
yet now I curse whate'er entices
and snares the soul with visions vain,
with dazzling cheats and dear devices
detains it in the body's cave of pain!
Cursed be, at once, all proud ambitions

wherewith the mind itself deludes!
Cursed be the glare of apparitions
that on the finer sense intrudes!
Cursed be the lying dream's impression
of name, and fame, and laureled brow!
Cursed, all that flatters as possession,
as wife and child, as land and plow!
Cursed Mammon be, when he with treasures
to restless actions spurs our fate,
and cursed when, for indulgent leisures,
he lays for us the pillows straight!
Cursed be the vine's transcendent nectar,
and highest favors Love lets fall!
cursed, also, Hope! cursed Faith, the spectre!
And cursed be Patience most of all!

CHORUS OF SPIRITS° [*invisible*].
Woe! woe!
Thou hast it destroyed,
the beautiful world
with powerful hand;
in ruin 'tis hurled,
by the fist of a demigod shattered!
The scattered
fragments into the Void we carry,
deploring
beauty lost beyond restoring.
Mightiest
of mortal men,
raise it
more splendid again,
in thine own bosom build it anew!
Bid a new career
commence—
show thus good sense—
as fresher songs thou'lt hear,
suited thereto!

MEPHISTOPHELES. These younger dependents
of my attendance
urge thee, in precocious fashion,

1366–85. *Chorus of Spirits:* perhaps neutral nature-spirits, but more probably Mephistophelean in view of the flattering epithets they bestow on Faust. (Ultimately, of course, like all spirit creatures in *Faust,* projections of a dramatic character's—here Faust's—feelings and intuitions.)

to deeds and passion!
Into the world of strife,
out of this lonely life
that of senses and sap has betrayed thee,
they would persuade thee.
This nursing of the pain forgo thee
that, vulture-like, doth feed upon thy breast!
The plainest company there is will show thee
thou art a man among the rest.
I do not mean to thrust
thee into the mob of rabble:
in highest circles I don't travel,
yet, wilt thou to me entrust
thy steps through life, I'll guide thee,
and willing walk beside thee,
will serve thee at once and for ever
with best endeavor
and, if thou'rt satisfied,
as servant, slave, with thee abide.
FAUST. And what shall be my counterservice therefor?
MEPHISTOPHELES. The time is long; thou need'st not now insist.
FAUST. No, no! A devil is an egotist
and is not apt, without some wherefore,
for love of God another to assist.
Speak thy conditions plain and clear:
with such a servant danger comes, I fear.
MEPHISTOPHELES. *Here,* an unwearied slave, I'll wear thy tether
and to thine every nod obedient be;
if we *beyond* meet up together,
then shalt thou do the same for me.
FAUST. That world my scruples naught increases:
when thou hast dashed this world to pieces,
the other, then, its place may fill.
Here, on this earth, my pleasures have their sources,
yon sun beholds my sorrows in his courses;
but if from them my life itself divorces,
let happen all that can or will!—
No more I'll hear my colleagues ponder
if future loves or hates we'll know,
if, in the spheres we dream of yonder,
there's an Above or a Below.
MEPHISTOPHELES. If that's thy mind, 'tis no great venture.

Come, bind thyself by prompt indenture,
and thou mine arts with joy shalt see:
what no man ever saw, I'll give to thee.

FAUST. Canst thou, poor devil, give me whatsoever?
When was a human soul, in its supreme endeavor,
e'er understood by such as thou?
What foods thou hast do never satiate;
thy gold flows red, or soon or late,
quicksilver-like, one's fingers through;
thy games—their winning no man ever knew;
thy girls, too, even from our breast,
beckon our neighbors with their wanton glances;
nor is *thy* honor's godlike zest
more than a meteor that briefly dances.
You'll show me fruits that, e'er they're gathered, rot
and trees that daily with new leafage clothe them!

MEPHISTOPHELES. This latter task alarms me not;
such treasures have I, and can show them.
But still a time must reach us, good my friend,
when peace we crave and more luxurious diet.

FAUST. When on an idler's bed I stretch myself in quiet,
then let, at once, my record end!
Canst thou with lying flattery rule me,
until self-pleased myself I see,
canst thou with rich enjoyment fool me:
let that day be the last for me!
The bet I offer!

MEPHISTOPHELES. Done!

FAUST. And heartily!
When thus I hail the Moment flying:
"Ah, linger still! thou art so fair!"
—then bind me in thy bonds undying,
my final ruin then declare!
Then let the death-bell chime the token,
then art thou from thy service free;
the clock may stop, its hand be broken,
and Time be finished unto me!

MEPHISTOPHELES. Consider well! my memory as good is rated.

FAUST. Thy rights are sure, they need no prop:
my oaths I've never cheaply estimated.
A slave am I, if e'er I stop—
if thine, or whose? 'tis needless to debate it.

MEPHISTOPHELES. At the doctoral banquet° I'll, this day,
as servant, put in my appearance.
One thing!—as accident insurance
give me a line or two, I pray.

FAUST. Demand'st thou, pedant, too, a document?
Hast never known a man, nor proved his word's intent?
Is't not enough, that what I speak today
shall stand, with all my mortal days agreeing?
In all its tides sweeps not the world away?
and shall a promise bind my being?
Yet this delusion in our hearts still sleeps,
and who'd himself therefrom deliver?
Blessed the heart that aye its promise keeps:
no sacrifice will it repent of ever!
But still, a parchment, writ and stamped with care,
a spectre is, which all to shun endeavor.
The word, alas! dies even in the pen,
and wax and goatskin keep the lordship then.
What wilt from me? Base spirit, say!
Brass, marble, parchment, paper, clay?
The terms with graver, quill, or chisel, stated?
I freely leave the choice to thee.

MEPHISTOPHELES. Why heat thyself, thus instantly,
with rhetoric exaggerated?
Each scrap for such a pact is good,
and to subscribe thy name thou'lt need a drop of blood.

FAUST. If thou therewith art fully satisfied,
so let us by the farce abide.

MEPHISTOPHELES. Blood is a juice of rarest quality.

FAUST. Fear not that I this pact shall seek to sever!
The promise that I make—thou'lt see—
is the full sum of mine endeavor.
I have myself inflated all too high:
my proper place is thy estate.
The mighty Spirit deigned me no reply,
and Nature shuts on me her gate.
The thread of Thought for me is broken,
and Knowledge brings disgust unspoken.
Let us the sensual deeps explore,

1471. *doctoral banquet:* Goethe originally planned a satirical Disputation Scene (comic disputations and disquisitions being traditional at academic celebrations), but the reference now serves only to indicate that the long Easter vacation is over—that considerable time has passed since Mephistopheles' first interview with Faust.

to quench the fervors of glowing passion!
Thy marvels wrought in magic fashion
bring forth from out thy endless store!
Plunge we in time's tumultuous dance,
in the rush and roll of circumstance!
Then may delight and distress,
and worry and success,
alternately follow, as best they can:
restless activity proves the man.

MEPHISTOPHELES. No bound or term for you is set.
If everywhere you would be trying
to snatch a rapid bliss in flying,
may what you like agree with you!
Fall to, and fear no indigestion!

FAUST. But thou hast heard, 'tis not of joy a question.
I take the wildering whirl, enjoyment's keenest pain,
enamored hate, exhilarant disdain.
My bosom, of its thirst for knowledge sated,
shall not, henceforth, from any pang be wrested,
and all of life for all mankind created
shall be within my inmost being tested;
the highest, lowest forms my soul shall borrow,
shall heap upon itself their bliss and sorrow,
and thus, my own sole self to all their selves expanded,
I too, at last, shall with them all be stranded.

MEPHISTOPHELES. Believe me, who for many a thousand year
the same tough meat have chewed and tested,
that from the cradle to the bier
no man the ancient leaven has digested!
Trust one of us, this Whole supernal
is made but for a god's delight!
He dwells in splendor, single and eternal,
and *us* he thrusts in darkness, out of sight,
but *you* he dowers with both day and night.

FAUST. Nay, but I will!

MEPHISTOPHELES. A good reply!
One only fear still needs repeating:
the art is long, but time is fleeting.
So let thyself be taught, say I!
Go, place thyself in contact with a poet,
give the rein to his imagination,
then wear the crown, and show it,
with attributes of his creation:

the courage of the lion's breed,
the wild stag's speed,
th' Italian's fiery blood,
the Norseman's fortitude.
Let him find for thee the secret tether
that binds the Noble and Mean together,
and teach thee, feeling youth and pleasure,
to love by rule and hate by measure.
I'd like, myself, such a one to see—
Sir Microcosm his name should be.

FAUST. What am I, then, if 'tis denied my part
the crown of all humanity to win me,
whereto yearns every sense within me?

MEPHISTOPHELES. Why, on the whole, thou'rt . . . what thou art.
Set wigs of million curls upon thy head, to raise thee,
wear shoes an ell in height: the truth betrays thee,
and thou remainest what thou art.

FAUST. I feel, indeed, that I have made the treasure
of human thought and knowledge mine, in vain;
and if I now sit down in restful leisure,
no fount of newer strength is in my brain,
I am no hair's-breadth more in height,
nor nearer to the Infinite.

MEPHISTOPHELES. Good Sir, you see the facts precisely
as they are seen by each and all;
we must arrange them now, more wisely,
before the joys of life shall pall.
Why, hang it all! thy hands and feet
and head—and other parts—are thine.
But things we use, for pleasure meet,
are they less wholly yours or mine?
If I've six stallions in my stall,
are not their forces also lent me?
I speed along, completest man of all,
as though my legs were four and twenty.
Take hold, then! let reflection rest,
and plunge into the world with zest!
I say to thee, a speculative wight
is like a beast on moorlands lean,
that round and round some fiend misleads to evil plight
while all about lie pastures fresh and green.

FAUST. Then how shall we begin?

MEPHISTOPHELES. We'll try a wider sphere.

What place of martyrdom is here!
Is't life, I ask, is't even prudence,
to bore thyself and bore the students?
Let Neighbor Paunch to that attend!
Why plague thyself with threshing straw for ever?
The best thou learnest, in the end
thou dar'st not tell the youngsters ever.
I hear one now—he's hither steering.

FAUST. To see him now, I have no heart.

MEPHISTOPHELES. The poor lad long has been a-waiting,
he should not unconsoled depart.
Thy cap and gown now straightway lend me:
I'll surely play your role with art! [*He invests himself.*]
My wits, be certain, will befriend me.
But fifteen minutes' time is all I need;
for our fine trip, meanwhile, prepare thyself with speed!
[*Exit* FAUST.]

MEPHISTOPHELES [*in* FAUST'*s long robes*].
Reason and knowledge mayst thou well despise,
the highest strength in man that lies:
just let Deception's spirit bind thee
with magic works and shows that blind thee,
and I shall have thee fast and sure.—
Fate such a bold, untrammeled spirit gave him,
as forwards, onwards, ever must endure,
whose overhasty impulse drave him
past earthly joys he might secure.
I'll drag him through a life of riot fast,
through stale inanities at first,
then soon he'll writhe and weaken, stuck at last,
while him, in hot, insatiate thirst,
the dream of drink shall mock, and none shall lave him;
refreshment shall his lips in vain implore,
and even if my charge he weren't, there's naught could save him—
he'll be destroyed for evermore! . . .

There follows a satirical scene with the student, omitted here.

[FAUST *enters.*]

FAUST. Now, whither shall we go?
MEPHISTOPHELES. As best it pleases thee.
The common life, and then the high, we'll see.
With what delight, what profit winning,
thou'lt take, sans fees, the program now beginning!
FAUST. Yet, with the flowing beard I wear,
both ease and grace will fail me there.
Th' attempt will be a futile striving—
I ne'er could learn the easy way of living;
I feel so small with others 'round, and hence
will always feel embarrassments.
MEPHISTOPHELES. My friend, thou soon shalt lose this timid fever:
be self-possessed—for that is *savoir vivre!*
FAUST. How shall we leave the house, and start?
Where hast thou servant, coach and horses?
MEPHISTOPHELES. We'll simply spread this cloak apart,
then through the air direct our courses.
But only, on so bold a flight,
be sure to have thy luggage light!
A little fire-air, which I shall soon prepare us,
above the earth will nimbly bear us:
with little weight, we'll travel swift and clear—
congratulations on thy new career!

In three scenes omitted here, Faust and Mephistopheles join a merry drinking party in Auerbach's Cellar, then go to the Witch's Kitchen, where Faust has a vision of a beautiful woman in the magic mirror and is rejuvenated by the Witch's potion. Then Faust sees Margarete passing in the street and begs Mephistopheles to bring him to her.

EVENING

[*A small, neatly kept room.*]

MARGARETE [*plaiting and binding up the braids of her hair*].
I'd something give, could I but say
who was that gentleman today!
Surely a gallant man was he,
and of a noble family:
so much could I in his face behold—
nor would he, else, have been so bold. [*Exit.*]

[*Enter* MEPHISTOPHELES *and* FAUST.]

MEPHISTOPHELES. Come in, but softly! follow me!

FAUST [*after some moments of silence*]. Leave me alone, I beg of thee.

MEPHISTOPHELES [*prying about*]. Not every girl keeps thing so neat.

[*Exit.*]

FAUST [*looking around*]. O welcome, twilight soft and sweet
that breathes throughout this hallowed shrine!
Sweet pain of love, bind thou with fetters fleet
the heart that on the dew of hope must pine!
How all about a sense impresses
of quiet, order, and content!
This poverty what bounty blesses!
What bliss within this prison here is pent!

[*He throws himself into a leather armchair near the bed.*]

Receive me, thou, that in thine open arms
departed joy and pain were wont to gather!
How oft have children, with their simple charms,
hung here, around this throne where sat the father!
My love, while still a child, perchance,
grateful for gifts that Christmas Day had brought her,
here meekly kissed the grandsire's withered hands.
I feel, O maid! thy very soul
of order and content about me whisper,
that guides thee with a motherly control;
the runner, on thy board, it bids thee neatly spread,
the sand beneath thy feet strew whiter, crisper.
O sweet and godlike hand, to thee 'tis given
to change this cottage to a lower heaven!
And here! [*He lifts one of the bed curtains.*]
What ecstasy is in my blood!
Here could I spend whole hours, delaying.
Here Nature shaped, as if in sportive playing,
the angel blossom from the bud;
here lay the child, with life's warm essence
her tender bosom filled, and fair;
and here was wrought, in thy pure, holy presence,
the form diviner beings wear!
And I? What drew me here with power?
How deeply am I moved, this hour!
What seek I? Why so full my heart, and sore?
Mis'rable Faust! I know thee now no more!
Is there a magic vapor here?
I came, with lust of instant pleasure,

and lie dissolved in dreams of love's sweet leisure!
Are we the sport of every change of air?
 And if, this moment, came she in to me,
how would I for my crime atonement render!
How small the braggart then would be,
prone at her feet, uncertain, tender!

MEPHISTOPHELES [*entering*]. Be quick! I see her down there, coming.

FAUST. Let's go! I never will return!

MEPHISTOPHELES. This box, whose weight is almost numbing,
is now (I'll not say how) our personal concern,
so set it in the press, with haste!
I swear, 'twill turn her head, to spy it:
baubles enough I therein placed
for you to win a second by it.
True, child is child, and play is play.

FAUST. I know not—should I do it?

MEPHISTOPHELES. Ask you, pray?
Yourself, perhaps, would keep the bubble?
Then, I suggest, 'twere fair and just
to spare the lovely day your lust,
and spare to me all further trouble.
You are not miserly, I trust?!
My hands I dirty, I scratch my head,
[*He puts the casket in the press, which he relocks.*]
(But quick, away!)
so that the sweet young maiden may
more easily by you be led;
yet you look as though
to the lecture hall you were forced to go,
as if stood before you, gray and loath,
Physics and Metaphysics both!
But away! [*Exeunt.*]

MARGARETE [*enters, carrying a lamp*].
It is so sultry here, so close, [*she opens a window*]
and yet it's not so warm outside.
I have a feeling strange, like fear almost . . .
Would mother came! where can she bide?
My body's chill, I'm shuddering—
I'm but a silly, fearsome thing!
[*She begins to sing, at the same time undressing.*]

A king in Thule,° long living,
was faithful till the grave;
to him his mistress, dying,
a golden goblet gave.
Naught was to him more precious,
he drained it at every bout;
his eyes with tears ran over,
whene'er he drank thereout.
When came his time of dying,
the towns in his land he told,
naught else to his heir denying
except the goblet of gold.
He sat at the royal banquet
with his knights of high degree,
in the lofty hall of his fathers
in that castle by the sea.
There stood the old carouser,
and drank his life's last glow,
then hurled the hallowed goblet
into the tide below.
He saw it plunging, and filling,
and sinking deep in the sea,
then fell his eyelids for ever,
and never more drank he.

[*She opens the press in order to put away her clothes, and sees the jewel box.*]

How comes that lovely casket here to me?
I locked the press, most certainly.
'Tis passing strange! I wonder what's within it!
Perhaps 'twas brought by someone as a pawn,
and mother gave a loan thereon?
That ribbon seems to hold a key to fit;
I have a mind to open it!—
What is all this? Good Lord! Whence came
such things? Their like I never yet did see!
Rich ornaments, such as a noble dame
on highest holidays might wear!
How would the string of pearls become me?
Ah, who can all this splendor own?

1730. *Thule:* the Latin *ultima Thule,* a fabled land beyond the reach of every traveler.

[She adorns herself with the jewelry, and steps before the mirror.]

Were but the earrings mine alone—
one has at once another air!
What help is beauty, e'en to youth?
One may possess it, but the truth
is this: not more do others care,
their praise is pitying, unsure.
To gold still tends,
on gold depends,
all, all! Alas, we poor!

In three scenes omitted here, Mephistopheles creates an approach to Margarete through her neighbor, Martha. But success depends on Faust's lying and claiming to have seen Martha's husband's grave in Padua, thus proving he is really dead. Faust at first refuses, then agrees to lie.

GARDEN

[MARGARETE *on* FAUST'S *arm.* MARTHA *and* MEPHISTOPHELES *walking up and down.*]

MARGARETE. I feel, the gentleman allows for me,
demeans himself, and shames me by it:
a traveler is so used to be
kindly content with any diet.
I know too well that my poor talking can
ne'er entertain such an experienced man.
FAUST. Thy single word or look more entertains
than all the lore of wisest brains. *[He kisses her hand.]*
MARGARETE. Don't incommode yourself! How could you ever kiss it?
It is so ugly, rough to see!
The work I do—how hard and steady is it!
With money mother's never free. *[They pass out of view.]*
MARTHA. And you, Sir, travel always, do you not?
MEPHISTOPHELES. Alas, that trade and duty us so harry!
With what a pang one leaves so many a spot,
and dares not even now and then to tarry!
MARTHA. In young, wild years it suits men's ways,
this round and round the world in freedom sweeping;
but then come on the evil days,

and as a bachelor, into his grave a-creeping,
none ever found a thing to praise.
MEPHISTOPHELES. I dread to see the way that fate advances.
MARTHA. Then, worthy Sir, improve betimes your chances!
[*They pass.*]
MARGARETE. Yes, out of sight is out of mind!
Your courtesy's an easy grace,
but you have friends in many a place
more sensible than I, and more refined.
FAUST. Be not deceived: what men call sensible
is often vanity and narrowness.
MARGARETE. How so?
FAUST. Ah, that simplicity and innocence ne'er know
themselves, their holy value, and their spell!
that meekness, lowliness, the highest graces
which Nature portions out so lovingly . . .
MARGARETE. Think but one short, brief moment's space on me!
To think on you I have all time and places.
FAUST. No doubt you're much alone?
MARGARETE. Yes, for our household small has grown,
yet must be cared for as our own.
We have no maid. I do the knitting, sewing, sweeping,
the cooking—errands at all hours, in fact.
And mother, in her notions of housekeeping,
is so exact!
Not that she needs so much to keep expenses down—
we, more than others, might have comforts, rather.
A nice estate was left us by my father,
a house, a little garden near the town.
But now my days have less of noise and hurry:
my brother is a soldier,
my little sister's dead.
True, with the child I had my cares—no bed
of ease, yet gladly I would take again the worry,
so very dear was she.
FAUST. An angel, if like thee!
MARGARETE. I brought her up, and she was fond of me.
Father had died before she saw the light,
and mother's case seemed hopeless quite,
so weak and miserable she lay,
recovering then but slowly, day by day.
She could not think, herself, of giving
the poor wee thing its natural living,

and so I nursed it all alone
with milk and water: 'twas my own.
Lulled in my lap with many a song,
it smiled, and squirmed, and got along.
FAUST. The purest bliss was surely then thy dower.
MARGARETE. But surely, also, many a weary hour.
I kept the baby's cradle near
my bed at night; if she but stirred, I'd guess it
and, waking, hear;
and I would nurse it, warm beside me press it,
and oft, to quiet it, my bed forsake,
and dandling back and forth the restless creature take;
then at the washtub stand, at morning's break,
then came the marketing and kitchen-tending—
day after day, the same thing, never ending.
One's spirits, Sir, are thus not always good,
but then one learns to relish rest and food. [*They pass.*]
MARTHA. Yet woman's lot is sad, for it is true:
a stubborn bachelor there's no converting.
MEPHISTOPHELES. It but depends upon the like of you,
and I should turn to better ways than flirting.
MARTHA. Speak plainly, Sir, have you no one detected?
Has not your heart been anywhere subjected?
MEPHISTOPHELES. The proverb says, one's own warm hearth
and a good wife are gold and jewels worth.
MARTHA. I mean, have you not felt the wish, although ne'er so slightly?
MEPHISTOPHELES. I've everywhere, in fact, been entertained politely.
MARTHA. I meant to say, were you not touched in earnest, ever?
MEPHISTOPHELES. One should allow one's self to jest with ladies never.
MARTHA. Ah, you don't understand!
MEPHISTOPHELES. I'm sorry I'm so blind,
but I am sure . . . that you are very kind. [*They pass.*]
FAUST. And me, thou angel! didst thou recognize,
as through the garden gate I came?
MARGARETE. Did you not see it? I cast down my eyes.
FAUST. And thou forgiv'st my freedom, and the blame
to my impertinence befitting,
as the cathedral thou wert quitting?
MARGARETE. I was confused, the like ne'er happened me;
no one could ever speak to my discredit.
Ah, thought I, in my conduct has he read it—

something immodest or unseemly free?
He seemed to have the sudden feeling
that with this wench 'twere very easy dealing.
I will confess, I knew not what appeal
on your behalf, here, in my bosom grew;
but I was angry, with myself, to feel
that I could not be angrier with you.

FAUST. Sweet darling!

MARGARETE. Wait a while! [*She plucks a flower and pulls off its petals one by one.*]

FAUST. Shall that a nosegay be?

MARGARETE. No, it is just in play.

FAUST. How?

MARGARETE. Go! you'll laugh at me.
[*She pulls off petals, murmuring.*]

FAUST. What murmurest thou?

MARGARETE [*half aloud*]. He loves me—loves me not.

FAUST. Thou sweet, angelic soul!

MARGARETE [*continues*]. Loves me—not—loves me—not—
[*She plucks the last petal, and cries out in a charming show of delight.*]
He loves me!

FAUST. Yes, dear child! And let this flower's word
be unto thee an oracle: He loves thee!
Ah, know'st thou what it means? He loves thee!
[*He grasps both her hands.*]

MARGARETE. I shudder, tremble!

FAUST. Be not afraid! And let this look,
let this warm clasp of hands, to thee declare
what never tongue can tell:
to yield one wholly, and to feel a rapture,
in yielding, that must be eternal!
Eternal! for the end would be despair.
No, no,—no ending! no ending!
[MARGARETE *presses his hands, frees herself, and runs off.* FAUST *stands a moment in thought, then follows her.*]

MARTHA [*coming forward*]. The night is falling.

MEPHISTOPHELES. Ay! we must away.

MARTHA. I'd ask you, longer here to tarry,
but evil tongues in this town have full play—
as if no one had anything to fetch and carry,
nor other labor,
but spying all the doings of one's neighbor—
and do whate'er one may, one's talked about perforce.

But where's our couple now?
MEPHISTOPHELES. Flown up the garden path,
the wanton butterflies!
MARTHA. He seems to like the lass.
MEPHISTOPHELES. And she him, too. So runs the world its course.

A SUMMERHOUSE

[MARGARETE *comes in, conceals herself behind the door, puts her finger to her lips, and peeps through the crack.*]

MARGARETE. He comes!
FAUST [*entering*]. Ah, rogue! a tease thou art!
I've got thee! [*He kisses her.*]
MARGARETE [*embracing him, and returning the kiss*].
Dear man! I love thee from my heart.
[MEPHISTOPHELES *knocks.*]
FAUST [*stamping his foot*]. Who's there?
MEPHISTOPHELES. A friend!
FAUST. A beast!
MEPHISTOPHELES. The time to
leave has come.
MARTHA [*coming*]. Yes, Sir, 'tis late.
FAUST. Might I, perhaps, escort you home?
MARGARETE. My mother would . . . Farewell!
FAUST. Ah, can I not remain?
Farewell!
MARTHA. Adieu!
MARGARETE. And soon to meet again!
[*Exeunt* FAUST *and* MEPHISTOPHELES.]
MARGARETE. Dear God! However is it, such
a man can think and know so much?
I stand ashamed and in amaze,
and must assent to all he says.
A poor, unknowing child! and he—
I can't think what he finds in me!

FOREST AND CAVE

FAUST [*solus*]. Spirit sublime, thou gav'st me, gav'st me all
for which I prayed. Not unto me in vain
hast thou thy countenance revealed in fire.
Thou gav'st me Nature as a kingdom grand,
with power to feel and to enjoy it. Thou

not only cold, amazed acquaintance yield'st,
but grantest, that in her profoundest breast
I gaze, as in the bosom of a friend.
The ranks of living creatures thou dost lead
before me, teaching me to know my brothers
in air and water and the silent wood.
And when the storm in forests roars and grinds,
the giant firs, in falling, neighbor boughs
and neighbor trunks with crushing weight bear down,
and falling, fill the hills with hollow thunder,
then to the cave secure thou leadest me,
thou show'st me mine own self, and in my breast
profound and secret miracles unfold.
And when the perfect moon before my gaze
comes up with soothing light, around me float
from every precipice and thicket damp
the silvery phantoms of the ages past,
and temper the austere delight of thought.
    That nothing can be perfect unto man
I now am conscious. With this ecstasy,
which brings me near and nearer to the gods,
thou gav'st the comrade whom I now no more
can do without, though, cold and scornful, he
demeans me to myself, and with a breath,
a word, transforms thy gifts to nothingness.
Within my breast he fans a lawless fire,
unwearied, for that fair and lovely creature.
Thus in desire I hasten to enjoyment,
and in enjoyment pine to feel desire.

MEPHISTOPHELES [*entering*]. Have you not led this life quite long enough?
How can a further test delight you?
'Tis very well, that once one tries the stuff,
but something new must then requite you.

FAUST. Would there were other work for thee!
To plague a day auspicious, thou returnest.

MEPHISTOPHELES. Come, now! I like to let thee be:
thou surely darest not complain in earnest.
The loss of thee were truly very slight,
a comrade crazy, rude, repelling.
One has one's hands full all the day and night!
If what one does, or leaves undone, is right,
from such a face as thine there is no telling.

FAUST. A fine way, that, for thee to talk!
That thou hast bored me, I must thankful be.
MEPHISTOPHELES. Poor man, wouldst thou on earth still walk,
still be, had I not aided thee?
I, for a time at least, have worked thy cure,
of Fancy's maggots purged thee clear;
had I not been, so hadst thou, sure,
sauntered away from this terrestrial sphere.
Why here to caverns, rocky hollows slinking,
sit'st thou, as 'twere an owl a-blinking?
Why suck'st, from sodden moss and dripping stone,
toad-like, thy nourishment alone?
This is no way thy time to pass!
The scholar's in thee still, alas!
FAUST. What fresh and vital forces, canst thou guess,
spring from my commerce with the wilderness?
Yet, if thou hadst the power of guessing,
thou wouldst be devil enough to grudge my soul the blessing.
MEPHISTOPHELES. A blessing drawn from supernatural fountains,
in night and dew to lie upon the mountains,
all heaven and earth in rapture penetrating,
thyself to godhood pridefully inflating,
to grub with yearning force through Earth's dark marrow,
compress the six days' work within thy bosom narrow,
to taste I know not what in haughty power,
thine own ecstatic life on all things shower,
thine earthly self behind thee cast,
and then in lofty instinct, thus—[*with an obscene gesture*]
I daren't say how—to pluck the final flower!
FAUST. For shame!
MEPHISTOPHELES. Thou findest that unpleasant,
and thou art right to cry "For shame!" at present:
one may not name before ears chaste, devout,
what chaste hearts cannot do without.
But, once for all, I grudge thee not the pleasure
of lying to thyself in moderate measure.
Yet such a course thou wilt not long endure:
again thou art already jaded,
and, if it last, thou'lt be o'ercome
by madness, or to horror full succumb.—
Enough of that! Thy love sits lonely yonder,
by all things saddened and oppressed.
Her thoughts and yearnings seek thee, tenderer, fonder;

a mighty love is in her breast.
First came thy passion's flood, all wild,
as when from melted snow a freshet overflows;
with that thou hast her heart imbued,
and now thy stream but shallows shows.
Methinks, instead of in the forests lording,
the noble Sir should find it good,
the love of this young silly child
at once to set about rewarding.
Her time is miserably long;
she haunts her window, watching clouds that stray
o'er the old city-wall and far away.
"Were I a little bird!" ° so runs her song,
day long, and half night long.
Now she is lively, mostly sad,
now, wept beyond her tears;
then again quiet she appears,
but aye love-mad.

FAUST. Serpent! serpent!

MEPHISTOPHELES [*aside*]. Ha! do I trap thee?

FAUST. Get thee away with thine offenses,
reprobate! Name not that woman fair,
nor the desire for her sweet body dare
to bring again before my half-crazed senses!

MEPHISTOPHELES. What wouldst thou, then? She thinks that thou art flown—
and half and half thou art, I own.

FAUST. She's always near, however far I flee;
forget her can I never, nor ever live without her.
if it her lips but touch, I envy, verily,
the body of the Lord.

MEPHISTOPHELES. No doubter
of that am I, my friend! Mine envy oft reposes
on your twin pair that feed among the roses.

FAUST. Away, thou pimp!

MEPHISTOPHELES. Yet I must laugh, although you rail.
The God who fashioned youth and maid
at once acknowledged it the noblest trade
to do procuring to one's own avail.
Be off! It is a woe profound
that for your sweetheart's room you're bound,

2021. *"Were I a little bird,* I'd fly to thee!"

and not to death are driven!
FAUST. Although within her arms be joys of heaven,
although her bosom's warmth I share,
of her distress I'm still aware!
I am a man inconstant, homeless roaming,
a monster without aim or rest,
that like a cataract, down rocks and gorges foaming,
has, maddened, leapt into th' abyss's breast!
And sidewards she, with young unwakened senses,
within her cottage on the alpine field
her simple, homely life commences,
her little world therein concealed.
And I, God's hate flung o'er me,
had not enough, to thrust
the stubborn rocks before me
and strike them into dust!
Her too, her peace, I had to undermine,
thou, Hell, hast claimed this sacrifice as thine!
Help, Devil! through the coming pangs to push me;
what must be, let it quickly be!
Let fall on me her fate, to crush me;
one ruin whelm both her and me!
MEPHISTOPHELES. Again it seethes, again it glows!
Thou fool, go in and comfort her!
When such a head as thine no outlet knows,
it thinks the end must soon occur.
Hail him, who keeps a steadfast mind!
Thou, else, dost well the devil-nature wear:
naught so insipid in the world I find
as is a devil in despair.

MARGARETE'S ROOM

GRETCHEN [*alone at the spinning wheel*].
My heart is sad,
my peace is o'er,
I'll find it never
and nevermore.
When gone is he,
the grave I see,
the world is gall
and bitterness all.

Alas, my head
is racked and crazed,
my thought is lost,
my senses mazed.
My heart is sad,
my peace is o'er,
I'll find it never
and nevermore.
To see him, only,
at the pane I sit,
to meet him, only,
the house I quit.
His lofty gait,
his noble form,
the smile of his mouth,
his glances warm,
and the magic flow
of his talk, the bliss
in the clasp of his hand,
and, ah! his kiss!
My heart is sad,
my peace is o'er,
I'll find it never
and nevermore.
My bosom yearns
for him alone;
ah! might I clasp him,
and hold, and own!
and kiss his mouth,
to heart's desire,
and on his kisses
at last expire!

MARTHA'S GARDEN

[MARGARETE, FAUST.]

MARGARETE. Promise me, Henry!—
FAUST. What I can!
MARGARETE. How is't with thy religion? Say!
Thou art a dear, good-hearted man,
and yet, I think, does not incline that way.
FAUST. Leave that, my child! Thou know'st my love is tender:

for those I love, my life I would surrender,
and, as for faith and church, I grant to each his own.
MARGARETE. That's not enough: we must believe thereon.
FAUST. Must we?
MARGARETE. Would that I had some influence!—
Nor honor'st thou the Holy Sacraments.
FAUST. I honor them.
MARGARETE. Desiring no possession.
'Tis long since thou hast gone to mass or to confession.
Believest thou in God?
FAUST. My darling, who may say
"I believe in God"?
Ask priest or sage an answer to essay,
and it will seem (nor deem it odd)
to mock the asker.
MARGARETE. Art thou then an atheist?!
FAUST. Thou dearest girl, take not my words amiss.
Who dare express Him,
and who profess Him,
saying, "I believe in Him"?
Who, feeling, seeing,
deny His being,
or say that he believe Him not?
The All-enfolding,
the All-upholding,
holds and sustains He not
thee, me, Himself?
Arches not there the sky above us?
Lies not beneath us, firm, the earth?
And rise not, on us shining,
friendly, the everlasting stars?
Look I not, eye to eye, at thee,
and feel'st not, touching
thy mind and heart, the Force
that moveth in eternal mystery,
invisible, visible, round thy life?
With all these things but wholly fill thy heart:
then, when thou in the feeling fully blessèd art,
call it whate'er thou wilt,
call it Bliss! Heart! Love! God!
I have no name to give it!
Feeling is all in all,

name is but sound and smoke,
obscuring Heaven's clear light.
MARGARETE. That is fine, and sounds quite right—
much the same way the pastor spoke,
although in slightly different phrases.
FAUST. The same thing, in all places,
all hearts that beat beneath the heavens' day—
each in its language—say:
why not I, in mine, as well?
MARGARETE. To hear it thus, it may seem passable,
yet some hitch in it there must be,
for thou hast no Christianity.
FAUST. Dear child!
MARGARETE. It long has grieved me deep
that thou that company dost keep.
FAUST. How so?
MARGARETE. The man who's with thee soon and late,
within my very inmost soul I hate;
in all my life there's no thing
has caused my heart such pain and loathing
as his repulsive face has done.
FAUST. Fear him not, my sweetest one!
MARGARETE. I feel his presence like something ill.
I've else, for all, a kindly will,
but, much as my heart to see thee yearneth,
the secret horror of him returneth.
Nor is he honest, do I believe—
if I do him wrong, may God forgive!
FAUST. The world must have all sorts, however.
MARGARETE. Live with the like of him, may I never!
When once inside the door comes he,
he looks around so sneeringly,
and half in wrath:
one sees that in nothing no interest he hath,
'tis written on his very forehead
that love, to him, is a thing abhorrèd.
I am so happy in thine arms,
so free, so yielding, and so warm,
and in his presence stifled seems my heart.
FAUST. Foreboding angel that thou art!
MARGARETE. It overcomes me in such degree
that, if he join us anywhere,

I feel as though I'd lost my love for thee.
When he is by, I could not say a prayer;
this burns within me like a flame.
And surely, Henry, 'tis with thee the same.
FAUST. There now! 'tis just antipathy.
MARGARETE. I now must go.
FAUST. Shall there ne'er be
a chance to rest upon thy breast in quiet,
as heart to heart and soul to soul unite?
MARGARETE. Ah, if I only slept alone,
I'd draw the bolts tonight, for thy desire;
but mother's sleep so light has grown,
and if we were discovered by her,
'twould be my death upon the spot!
FAUST. My angel, have no fear of that!
Here is a phial: in her drink
but three drops of it measure,
and into deepest sleep she'll gently sink.
MARGARETE. What would I not, to give thee pleasure!
It will not harm her, when one tries it?
FAUST. If 'twould, my love, would I advise it?
MARGARETE. O dearest man, if but thy face I see,
I know not what compels me to thy will;
so much have I already done for thee,
that scarcely more is left me to fulfill. [*Exit.*]
[*Enter* MEPHISTOPHELES.]
MEPHISTOPHELES. Thy pert young thing has gone?
FAUST. Hast played the spy
again?
MEPHISTOPHELES. I've heard, most fully, how she drew thee.
The Doctor has been catechized, 'tis plain—
great good, I hope, the thing will do thee!
The girls much like to ascertain
if one is prim and good, as ancient ways demand—
they think that they can then, with ease, take him in hand.
FAUST. Thou monster, wilt nor see nor own
that this true and loving creature,
filled with the faith that must,
she holds, alone
bring bliss, in earnest dread herself doth torture
that she should think the man she so much loves be lost.
MEPHISTOPHELES. Thy sensual, suprasensual desire
lets a mere girl now lead thee by the hook.

FAUST. Abortion, thou, of filth and fire!
MEPHISTOPHELES. And when it comes to faces, she reads them like a book!
When I am nigh, she's not at ease at all,
and sees some hidden sense behind the mask;
she feels that I'm a radical,
or even that to be the Devil's my task.
Well, well—tonight—?
FAUST. What's that to thee?!
MEPHISTOPHELES. Yet my delight 'twill also be!

Two scenes are omitted. In them, Gretchen meets the gossip Lieschen at the well and hears her scorn another seduced girl. She then goes to the ramparts to place flowers before the image of the Virgin and sings a lament.

NIGHT

[*Street, before the door of* MARGARETE*'s house.*]

VALENTINE [*a soldier,* MARGARETE*'s brother*].
When I have sat at some carouse
where each to each his brag allows,
and many a comrade praised to me
his pink of girls right lustily,
with brimming glass would drink her praise:
on elbows propped I then would gaze
and sit in unconcerned repose,
hearing the swagger as it rose.
And stroking then my beard, I'd say,
smiling, the bumper in my hand,
"Each well enough in her own way!
But is there one in all the land
like sister Gretchen, good as gold—
one that to her can a candle hold?"
Cling! clang! "Here's to her!" went around
the board. "He speaks the truth!" cried some,
"In her the flower o' the sex is found!"
And all the swaggerers were dumb.
But now—I could tear my hair, damnation!
and smash the wall in desperation!—
with turned up nose each scamp may face me,
with sneers and stinging taunts disgrace me,

and, like a bankrupt debtor sitting,
a chance-dropped word may set me sweating!
Although I'd thresh them all together,
I cannot call them liars either.
But what comes sneaking there to view?
If I mistake not, there are two.
If *he* is one, I'll get his hide!
He shall not leave the spot alive!

[*Enter* FAUST *and* MEPHISTOPHELES.]

FAUST. As from the window of the sacristy
Upward th' eternal lamp sends forth its glimmer
that, lessening sidewards, fainter grows and dimmer,
till darkness closes from the sky:
so shadows in my bosom gather!

MEPHISTOPHELES. I'm like a sentimental tomcat, rather,
that steals along the fire escapes
and softly past the copings creeps.
And yet I feel quite virtuous—
not over-thievish, nor too lecherous.
I feel in every limb the presage
of glorious Walpurgis' Night:
night after next will see its passage,
when staying awake's a real delight.

FAUST. May not then, too, the treasure risen be,
whose ghostly aura I there glimmering see?

MEPHISTOPHELES. Shalt soon experience the pleasure,
to lift the caldron with its treasure.
I lately gave therein a squint,
saw fine old Brabant-dollars in't.

FAUST. But not a bracelet, not some ring,
for ornament of my darling girl's?

MEPHISTOPHELES. I saw, among the rest, a thing
that seemed to be a string of pearls.

FAUST. That suits me well, for painful is it
to bring no gift when her I visit.

MEPHISTOPHELES. Thou shouldst not find it so annoying,
without any payment to be enjoying.—
Now, while the sky leads forth its starry throng,
thou'lt hear a masterpiece, no work completer:
I'll sing her, first, a moral song,
the surer, afterwards, to cheat her.

[*Sings to the zither.*]

What dost thou here,

with daybreak near,
Kathrina dear,
before thy lover's door:
Beware! The blade
lets in a maid
that out a maid
departeth nevermore.
The coaxing shun
of such a one!
When once 'tis done,
good night to thee, poor thing!
Love's time is brief,
but to no thief
be warm and lief,
but with the wedding ring.

VALENTINE [*advancing*]. Whom wilt thou lure? God's-element!
Rat-catching piper thou! Perdition!
to the Devil, first, the instrument!
to the Devil, next, the cursed musician!

MEPHISTOPHELES. The zither's smashed, for nothing more 'tis fit!

VALENTINE. There's yet a skull that I must split!

MEPHISTOPHELES [*to* FAUST]. Sir Doctor, don't retreat, I pray!
Stand by! I'll lead, and you be wary!
Out with your rapier—don't delay!
You've but to lunge, and I will parry.

VALENTINE. Then parry that!

MEPHISTOPHELES. Why not? 'tis light.

VALENTINE. That, too!

MEPHISTOPHELES. Of course.

VALENTINE. I think the Devil must fight!
What can this be? My hand's becoming lame.

MEPHISTOPHELES [*to* FAUST]. Thrust home!

VALENTINE [*falling*]. O God!

MEPHISTOPHELES. So now the lubber's tame!
But come, away! 'Tis time to disappear:
the cry of *Murder!* I already hear.
With the police I'd easily compound it,
but this means penal court, and I can't get around it.

[*Exit with* FAUST.]

MARTHA [*at a window*]. Come out! come out!

GRETCHEN [*at a window*]. Quick, bring a light!

MARTHA [*as before*]. They yell and parry, swear and fight.

CROWD. There's one already dead!
MARTHA [*coming out*]. The murderers have fled?!
MARGARETE [*coming out*]. Who lies here?
CROWD. It is thy mother's son.
MARGARETE. Almighty God! how terrible!
VALENTINE. *I'm dying!*—that is quickly said,
and quicker yet 'tis done.
Why howl you women there? Instead,
come here and listen, every one! [*All gather around him.*]
My Gretchen, see! still young thou art,
and not the least bit shrewd or smart,
thy trade so much to slight.
So this advice I give in private:
now that thou art become a harlot,
why, be one then, outright!
MARGARETE. My brother! God! such words to me?!
VALENTINE. In this game let our Lord God be!
What's done's already done, alas!
What follows it, must come to pass.
With one begin'st thou secretly,
but soon will others come to thee,
and when a dozen thee have known,
thou soon art known to all the town.
When Shame is born and first appears,
she is in secret brought to light,
and then they use the veil of night
to hide her head and ears;
her life, in fact, they're loath to spare her.
Yet let her grow and strength display,
she walks abroad unveiled by day,
though she's not grown a whit the fairer.
The uglier she is to sight,
the more she seeks the day's broad light.
In truth, the time I can discern
when all good decent folk will turn
from thee, thou whore! and seek protection
as from a corpse that breeds infection.
Thy guilty heart shall sore despair,
when they but look thee in the face!
No golden chain thou'lt longer wear,
nor near the altar find a place;
shalt not, in lace and ribbons flowing,
make merry when the dance is going,

but in dark corners, woe betide thee!
among the beggars and cripples hide thee,
and so, though God Himself forgive,
on earth already damnèd live!
MARTHA. Commend yourself to God for pardon!
Your soul with blasphemy you burden!
VALENTINE. Thou bawd most infamous, be still:
could I thy withered body kill,
I'd hope to gain, with grace to spare,
forgiveness of all sins it bear!
MARGARETE. My brother! This is Hell's own pain!
VALENTINE. I tell thee, from thy tears refrain!
When thou from honor didst depart,
it stabbed me to the very heart.
Now through the slumber of the grave
I go to God, a soldier brave. [*Dies.*]

CATHEDRAL. *Mass, with Organ and Choir*

[MARGARETE, *surrounded by people; her* EVIL SPIRIT *behind her.*]

SPIRIT. How different, Gretchen, then,
when thou, still innocent,
here to the altar cam'st
and from the worn and fingered book
thy prayers didst prattle,
half sport of childhood,
half God within thee!
Gretchen!
where tends they thought?
within thy bosom
lurks what crime?
Pray'st thou for mercy on thy mother's soul,
that by thy fault hath gone to long, long suffering? °
Upon thy threshold, whose the blood?!
And stirreth not and quickens
beneath thy heart a being
that, uneasy, thee disquiets
with its foreboding presence?

2414. *long, long suffering:* because she died in her sleep, unshriven.

MARGARETE. Woe! woe!
Would I were free from the thoughts
that stir and move about within me
despite my will.

CHOIR. *Dies irae, dies illa*
solvet saeclum in favilla.°
[*The organ plays.*]

SPIRIT. Wrath takes thee,
the trumpet peals,
the graves are stirring,
and thy heart,
from quiet dust
for fiery torments
in body resurrected,
throbs to life!

MARGARETE. Would I could leave!
It is as if the organ here
my breath took from me,
as if the singing
my heart would destroy.

CHOIR. *Judex ergo cum sedebit,*
quidquid latet adparebit,
nil inultum remanebit.

MARGARETE. I cannot breathe.
The columned walls
close in upon me,
the vaulted roof
oppresses!—Air!

SPIRIT. Hide thee—yet sin and shame
stay never hidden.
Air?! Light?!
Woe to thee!

CHOIR. *Quid sum miser tunc dicturus,*
quem patronum rogarturus,
cum vix justus sit securus?

SPIRIT. Transfigured faces
must look away from thee.
The pure, their hands to offer,

2424–25, 2439–41, 2451–53. "The day of wrath shall dissolve this world into ashes. When therefore the Judge shall take his seat, whatever is hidden shall appear, nothing shall remain unpunished. What shall I, wretched man, then say? what protector supplicate? when scarcely the just man may be secure!"

shuddering refuse thee.
Woe!
CHOIR. *Quid sum miser tunc dicturus?*
MARGARETE. Good neighbor, please! thy salts!— [*She swoons.*]

WALPURGISNIGHT °

[*The Harz Mountains: region near Schierke and Elend.*
Enter FAUST *and* MEPHISTOPHELES.]

MEPHISTOPHELES. Dost thou not wish a broomstick-steed's assistance?
A lusty he goat I would gladly ride!
The way we take, our goal is yet some distance.
FAUST. As long as from my legs there's no resistance
I am content with walking-stick to stride
What need to make less long our way?!—
Along this labyrinth of vales to wander,
then climb the rocky rampart yonder
from which descends the brook's eternal spray,
that is the seasoning of the traveler's day!
The springtime stirs within the fragrant birches,
and e'en the fir tree feels it now:
can then our limbs escape its gentle searches?
MEPHISTOPHELES. I notice no such thing, I vow!
'Tis winter still within my body,
and on my path I'd wish for frost and snow.
How sadly rises, incomplete and ruddy,
the moon's lone disk, with its belated glow,
and lights so dimly that, as one advances,
at every step one strikes a rock or tree!
So, let me use a jack-o'-lantern's glances!
I see one yonder, burning merrily.
Ho, there! my friend! May we have thine attendance?
Why waste so vainly thy resplendence!
Be kind enough to light us up the steep!
WILL-O'-THE-WISP.° My reverence, I hope, will me enable
to curb my temperament unstable—
a zigzag course is all we're wont to keep.
MEPHISTOPHELES. Oho! Thou'd like mankind to imitate,
but, in the Devil's name! go straight,

WALPURGISNIGHT: the eve of May Day, or May 1. One episode of no significance to modern readers has been omitted from this scene. 2486. *Will-o'-the-Wisp:* traditionally leads travelers to destruction.

or I'll blow out thy being's flickering spark!
WISP. You are the Master of the House, I mark,
and so I'm glad to serve you nicely.
But don't forget, the mountain's magic-mad today,
and if a will-o'-the-wisp must guide you on the way,
you musn't take things too precisely.
FAUST, MEPHISTOPHELES, WISP [*chanting, in rotation*].
We, it seems, have entered newly
magic spheres of dreams enchanted.
Do thy duty, guide us truly,
that our feet be forwards planted
in the vast, deserted spaces!
See them swiftly changing places,
tree on tree beside us trooping,
and the crags above us stooping,
and the rocky snouts, outgrowing,
that are snoring, that are blowing!
O'er the stones, the grasses, flowing,
stream and streamlet seek the hollow.
Are those murmurs? songs that follow?
are they lovers' lamentation,
voices from my exultation,
sounds of hope and love undying?
And their echo, like tradition
often told, sounds faint and hollow.
Hoo-hoo! Shoo-hoo! Nearer hover
jay and screech-owl, and the plover;
are they all awake and crying?
Is't the salamander pushes,
bloated-bellied, through the bushes?
And the roots, like serpents twisted,
through the sand and boulders toiling,
fright us, weirdest links uncoiling
to entrap us, unresisted,
as live knots and gnarls uncanny
feel with polypus-antennae
for the traveler. Mice are flying,
thousand-colored, herdwise hieing
through the moss and through the heather!
And the fireflies wink and darkle,
crowded swarms that soar and sparkle,
and in wildering escort gather!
Tell me if we still are standing,

or if further we're ascending?
All is turning, whirling, blending,
trees and rocks with grinning faces,
wandering lights that spin their mazes,
still increasing and expanding.
MEPHISTOPHELES. Grasp my coattails all undaunted!
Here a lesser peak we're granted,
whence one seëth, with amaze,
Mammon in the mountain blaze.
FAUST. How strangely glimmers through the hollows
a feeble glow, like that of dawn!
and yet its flashing tracks and follows
the deepest gorges, faint and wan.
Here steam, there rolling smoke is sweeping.
Here shines a flame through film of haze—
now like a tender thread 'tis creeping,
now like a fountain leaps and plays,
then winds away, to form a hundred
veins that traverse the valley's plain,
while here, in corner pressed and sundered,
it becomes a single strand again.
Close by gush sparkles incandescent
like scattered showers of gold sands.
And see! in all its height, at present
the rocky rampart blazing stands.
MEPHISTOPHELES. Has not Sir Mammon grandly lighted
his palace for this festal night?
'Tis lucky thou hast seen the sight,
for boisterous guests approach that are invited.
FAUST. How raves the tempest through the air,
with what fierce blows upon my neck 'tis beating!
MEPHISTOPHELES. Unto the old ribs of the rock retreating,
hold fast, lest thou be hurled down the abysses there!
The night with the mist is black.
Hark! how the forests grind and crack!
Frightened, the owls fly scattered.
Hearken! their pillars are shattered,
the evergreen palaces shaking.
Boughs are moaning and breaking;
resounding, the tree trunks thunder,
and roots are twisted asunder!
In frightful and intricate crashing
each on the other is dashing,

and over the wreck-strewn gorges
the tempest whistles and surges!
Hear'st above the voices ringing?
far away, now nearer singing?
Yes, the mountain's side along
sweeps an infuriate glamoring song.

WITCHES [*in chorus*]. The witches ride to the Brocken's top,
the stubble is yellow, and green the crop.
There gathers the crowd for carnival,
while You-Know-Who presides o'er all.
And as we hasten at full speed,
the witch she farts, and stinks her steed.

SOLO VOICE. Alone, old Baubo's° coming now,
riding upon a farrow-sow.

WITCHES. Then honor to whom the honor's due!
Dame Baubo first, to lead our crew!
A fertile sow and a mother too—
all witches gladly follow now!

A VOICE. Which way cam'st thou here?

A VOICE. By Ilsestein.
I peeped at an owl in her nest down there—
it could stare and glare!

A VOICE. Betake thee to Hell!
Why so fast and so fell!?

A VOICE. And she's badly flayed me:
lo! with sores she's paid me!

WITCHES. The way is wide, the way is long:
see, what a wild and crazy throng!
the besom scratches, the pitchwork ill fits,
the child is choked, the mother splits.

WARLOCKS [*first semichorus*].
Like snail in shell encased we crawl,
ahead there go the women all:
when towards the Devil's home we tread,
woman's a thousand steps ahead.

[*Second semichorus.*] That does not cause us to despair,
that woman leads on the way there,
for howsoe'er she hasten may,
man in one leap goes the whole way.

A VOICE [*above*]. Come on, ye down by that rock-edged lake!

VOICES [*from below*]. Aloft we'd fain ourselves betake:

2588–93. *Baubo:* a lewdly amusing nurse in the Greek mysteries of Demeter.

we've washed, and are as neat as ever you will,
yet we're eternally sterile still.

WITCHES *and* WARLOCKS. The wind is hushed, the stars are shy,
the dreary moon forsakes the sky.
Emitting many a magic spark,
our flock roars past here in the dark.

A VOICE [*from below*]. Halt, there! Ho, there!

A VOICE [*above*]. Who calls from the rocky cleft below there?

VOICE [*below*]. Take me, too! Take me along!
I've climbed a full three hundred years
and yet the summit cannot see:
among my equals I want to be!

WITCHES *and* WARLOCKS. The broom supports, the stick will bear,
the fork can lift, the goat's chair—
who cannot levitate tonight
is evermore a ruined wight.

HALF-WITCH [*below*]. With mincing step I've followed long,
but far ahead are those more strong.
At home I have not rest nor cheer,
and yet I can gain neither here.

WITCHES. To give us courage, salves avail;
a rag will answer for a sail,
and any trough our ship supplies;
he ne'er will fly, who now not flies.

WITCHES *and* WARLOCKS. When round the summit whirls our flight,
drop low, and on the ground alight,
and far and wide the heather press
with witchhood's swarms of wantonness! [*They settle.*]

MEPHISTOPHELES. They crowd and push, they roar and clatter,
they whirl and whistle, pull and chatter!
What flame and stench most pestilent,
a truly witch-like element!
Hold fast to me, or soon away you're rent!
Where art thou?

FAUST [*in the distance*]. Here!

MEPHISTOPHELES. What! whirled so far astray?
I am at home, and so can clear the way.
Make room! Sir Tempter comes! Room, gentle rabble, room!
Here, Doctor, hold to me! and with a leap we'll zoom
to a clear space, and from the press be free.
This is too much, e'en for the like of me!
There something sparkles with peculiar glare,
off in those bushes—I've a mind to see!

Come! let's slip in right over there!
FAUST. Thou art indeed perverse! But go! I'll follow straight.
'Tis planned most wisely, if I judge aright!
We climb the Brocken's top on St. Walpurgis' Night,
that arbitrarily ourselves we isolate.
MEPHISTOPHELES. What motley flames there rise and tremble!
A merry club doth there assemble.
One's not alone, though small the company.
FAUST. Up there's where I'd much rather be!
E'en now I see smoke whirl and blaze.
The crowd swarms to the Sire of Evil,
where must be solved so many a riddle.
MEPHISTOPHELES. Though many more would take their place!
Leave to the madding crowd its riot,
while we here house ourselves in quiet.
It is an old, long-practiced trade,
that in the greater world some little worlds are made.
I see young naked witches congregate,
and old ones who keep covered—shrewdly!
On my account be kind, nor treat them rudely:
the effort's small, the fun is great.
And hark! the sound of instruments salutes me.
Let us advance, though ill such rasping suits me!
Come! I insist! Thou must not hesitate—
I'll forward step and introduce you straight,
thy gratitude still further earning.
What say'st thou, friend? This is no small expanse:
unto the end thou scarce canst send thy glance!
A hundred fires in a row are burning.
They dance, they chat, they cook, they drink, they court:
now where, just tell me! is there better sport?
FAUST. Wilt thou, to introduce us to the revel,
assume the part of wizard or of devil?
MEPHISTOPHELES. I'm mostly used, 'tis true, to go incognito,
but on a gala day one should his orders show.
The Garter° does not deck my suit,
but honored and at home is here the cloven foot.
Perceiv'st thou yonder snail that cometh slow and steady?
So well its seeing feelers pry,
that it hath scented me already:
I cannot here disguise me, though I try.

2690. *Garter:* the Order of the Garter, a decoration of nobility.

But come! from fire to fire let us tour;
I'll make the matches if thou'lt be the wooer.
[*To some figures seated around a dying fire.*]
Old gentlemen, why must apart you gather?
Right near the center's where I'd see you rather,
in midst of youthful revels thrown:
one's quite enough alone when one's at home.

GENERAL. Let no one put his trust in nations,
howe'er for them he may have worked and planned,
for with the people, as with women,
youth always seems to get the upper hand.

MINISTER. The world's too far from what is just and sage,
so I praise *elder* statesmen duly;
when *we* were all-in-all, then, truly,
that was a proper Golden Age.

PARVENU. Nor were we fools—were ever ready
to do what people never did.
But now all things have from their bases slid—
just when we thought to keep them set and steady.

AUTHOR. Who, now, a work of moderate sense will read,
a work in which there's nothing flossy?!
And as regards the younger lot, indeed,
they never yet have been so pert and saucy.

MEPHISTOPHELES [*suddenly acting like a very old man*].
I feel our tribe is ripe for Judgment Day.
Since I've, for the last time, the witches' hill ascended,
since to the lees *my* cask is drained away,
the world's days, too, must soon be ended.

HUCKSTER-WITCH. Sweet masters, do not pass me thus!
Lose not your chance, be not so chary!
Examine closely what I carry!
My stock is rare and various.
And yet, there's nothing I've collected
(a stock like mine you'll nowhere find!)
which has not, once, sore hurt inflicted
upon the world, and on mankind.
No dagger's here, that hath not set blood flowing,
no cup, that hath not once, in healthy frame induced,
poured speedy death as poison glowing,
no jewel, but hath some woman sweet seduced,
no sword, but severed pledge for the unwary
or from behind struck down the adversary.

MEPHISTOPHELES. Thou art, good mistress, fully out of fashion!

What's past, is past! What's done, is done!
Novelties were best to spend thy cash on,
by novelties alone are we now won!

FAUST. I'll soon go mad, if things get gayer!
To end all fairs, this is the fair!

MEPHISTOPHELES. Upward is all the vortex striving:
we are but driven whilst we think we're driving!

FAUST. Say, who is that?

MEPHISTOPHELES. Note her especially:
'tis Lilith.°

FAUST. Who?

MEPHISTOPHELES. Adam's first wife is she.
Beware the lure within her lovely tresses,
the only ornament that she doth wear!
When she succeeds therewith a youth to snare,
not soon again doth he escape her jesses.

FAUST. Two women there, one young, one old, are seated,
who've clearly danced already more than needed!

MEPHISTOPHELES. No rest tonight for young or old!
Another dance begins—come now, let us take hold!

FAUST [*dancing with the pretty* YOUNG WITCH].
A lovely dream came once to me,
in which I saw an apple tree.
In it shone lovely apples two
and tempted me to climb thereto.

YOUNG WITCH. Apples have been your great desire
e'er since in Eden was your sire.
And I am moved with joy to know
that such within my garden grow. . . .

MEPHISTOPHELES [*to* FAUST, *who has left the dance*].
Say, why dost thou forsake the lovely maiden
that in the dance so sweetly sang?

FAUST. Because, the while she sang, there sprang
from out her mouth a mouse as red as scarlet.

MEPHISTOPHELES. Let not such trifles, friend, your fun abate,
for such will happen at a pastoral fête.
Enough that 'twas not gray, the leaping varlet!

FAUST. Then saw I—

MEPHISTOPHELES. What?

2745. *Lilith:* considered to be Adams's first wife, according to a rabbinical legend. After the creation of Eve, Lilith became a ghost, seducing men and harming children.

FAUST. But look! Mephisto, seest thou not
a pallid, lovely girl who stays afar and lonely?
Her feet seem gyved, and 'tis with trouble only
she drags along from spot to spot.
I must confess, to me it doth appear
that she is very like my Gretchen dear.

MEPHISTOPHELES. Let the thing be! it is no canny sight.
A lifeless Vision, 'tis, a kind of magic sleight,
an eidolon that's better left alone:
its blank, set stare benumbs the human blood,
and one is almost turned to stone—
you know full well what the Medusa° could!

FAUST. The eyes, methinks, are those of one who suffered
violent death—they're eyes no loving hand hath closed.
That is the breast, that Gretchen to me proffered,
and in that body hath my every joy reposed.

MEPHISTOPHELES. Thou easy fool! therein the sorcery lies!
His own true love it seems to each man's eyes.

FAUST. What horrid pain, what bliss Elysian!
I cannot tear me from that vision.
And, strange! around her lovely throat
a single scarlet strand is gleaming,
no broader than a knife-edge seeming!

MEPHISTOPHELES. You see aright; that mark I also note.
Beneath her arm as well, her head she's fain to carry—
'twas Perseus lopped it off, her ancient adversary.
But why this craving for illusion still?!— . . .

The Walpurgisnight's Dream, an "Intermezzo" which is always cut from performances of Faust, *is omitted here. It ends with the Choir singing,* pianissimo:

Misty veil, like cloud on high,
becomes illuminated.
The branches stir, the reeds do sigh—
and all is dissipated.

2780. *Medusa:* the Gorgon Medusa whose glance turned people to stone. She was slain by the hero Perseus.

FIELD: OVERCAST SKY

[FAUST *and* MEPHISTOPHELES.]

FAUST. In misery! In despair! Long wretchedly astray, and now imprisoned! That sweet, unfortunate creature shut in a prison as a criminal, and prey to fearful torments! To this has it come? to this?—Treacherous, contemptible spirit! thou didst conceal it from me!—Stay! stay! rolling they diabolic eyes in fury! Stay and despite me with thine intolerable presence! Imprisoned! In misery that can never be undone! Delivered up to her own evil spirits, and to condemned, unfeeling fellow-men! And thou hast lulled me, meanwhile, with inane distractions; hast concealed from me her ever growing wretchedness; has suffered her to come to hopeless grief and ruin!

MEPHISTOPHELES. She is not the first.

FAUST. Dog! abominable monster!—Transform him, thou Spirit Infinite! transform the serpent back into that canine form in which he likes to scamper on before me, to roll before the unsuspecting traveler's feet, then leap upon his shoulders when he fell! Transform him once again into that favorite shape, that he may crawl upon his belly in the dust before me, that I may kick the dog, the profligate!—"Not the first"!—The misery! O the misery of it! what no human soul can grasp, that more than one being should have sunk into these depths of misfortune, that the first of them, in her writhing mortal-shame before the eyes of the Eternal Forgiver, did not expiate the guilt of all the others after. The wretchedness of this single one alone pierces the very marrow of my bone and life, whilst thou, indifferent, dost smirk to think about the fate of thousands!

MEPHISTOPHELES. Now we're at our wits' ends again! at the point where your mortal minds break under the strain. Why didst thou enter into alliance with us, if thou art not able to endure its terms. Wilt fly, and art not secure against dizziness?! Did we thrust ourselves upon thee, or thou thyself upon us?!

FAUST. Display not thus thy fang-like teeth to me! Thy sneer fills me with horrible disgust!—Mighty, glorious Spirit, who didst vouchsafe to me thine apparition, who knowest my heart and my soul, why to this felon-comrade fetter me, who feeds on michief and gluts himself with ruin?

MEPHISTOPHELES. Hast thou done?!

FAUST. Rescue her! or woe to thee, and the most fearful curse be upon thee for time without end!

MEPHISTOPHELES. I cannot loosen bonds laid in the name of the Avenger, cannot undo His bolts.—"Rescue her"! Who was it plunged her into ruin, I or thou? [FAUST *looks around wildly.*] Wilt thou reach for thunderbolts? 'Tis well they were not given to you wretched mortals! To crush and slay the innocent man that faces thee out: that is a tyrant's way of finding relief when one is in bad straits.

FAUST. Take me thither! She shall be free!

MEPHISTOPHELES. And the danger to which thou wilt expose thyself? Know that guilt of blood, caused by thy hand, lies on the town! Avenging spirits hover o'er the place where fell the man thou slewest, and lie in wait for the returning murderer.

FAUST. Thou darest call me that! All death and murder seize thee, monster! Take me there, I say, and set her free!

MEPHISTOPHELES. I will conduct thee thither. And what I can do, hear! (Have I all the power that there be in heaven and on earth?!) I will becloud the jailer's senses. Take thou possession of his keys, and lead her forth with human hand! I will keep watch —the magic steeds are ready, and I can conduct you away. So much is in my power.

FAUST. Up and away!

NIGHT: OPEN FIELD

[FAUST *and* MEPHISTOPHELES, *speeding past on black horses.*]

FAUST. What do those there by the gibbet's hill?

MEPHISTOPHELES. I don't know what they're making and brewing.

FAUST. Soaring up, floating down, bowing and bending!

MEPHISTOPHELES. It is a witches' guild.

FAUST. They strew and consecrate.

MEPHISTOPHELES. On! Hurry on!

PRISON

FAUST [*with a bunch of keys and a lamp, standing before a small iron door*]. A horror, long unfelt, comes o'er me,
and Man's collective woes o'erwhelm me, all.
She dwells within the dark, damp walls before me,
whom better feelings made a criminal!
What! I delay to near her?
I dread, once again to see her?

On! my shrinking only brings her death the nearer.

[*He takes hold of the lock; as he does so, a* VOICE *is heard singing behind the door.*]

My mother, the harlot,
she put me to death!
My father, the varlet,
then eaten me hath!
Little sister, so good,
gathered my bones,
so that cool they lay.
And now I'm become a bird o' the wood,
and fly on and away!

FAUST [*unlocking the door*]. She does not dream her lover listens near,
that he the rattling chain and rustling straw can hear.

[*He enters the cell.*]

MARGARETE [*hiding herself on the pallet*]. They come! O death, O bitterness!

FAUST [*softly*]. Quiet! The hour's come that frees thee.

MARGARETE [*casting herself down before him*].
If thou art human, pity my distress!

FAUST. Thy cries will wake the guards, and they will seize thee!

[*He takes hold of the fetters to unlock them.*]

MARGARETE [*on her knees*]. Who, headsman! unto thee such power
over me could give?
Thou'rt come for me at midnight-hour—
have mercy on me, let me live!—
'tis soon enough when we hear matins sung! [*She rises.*]
And I am still so young, so young!
yet now comes death, and ruin!
Fair was I, too, and that was my undoing.
My love was near, but now he's far;
torn lies the wreath, scattered the blossoms are.
Seize me not thus, so violently!
Spare me! What have I done to thee?
Let me not vainly entreat thee—
I never chanced in all my days to meet thee!

FAUST [*aside*]. Shall I survive the grief I see?

MARGARETE. Now am I wholly in thy might.
But let me nurse, please! first my baby—
I've held it close this whole night through—
they took't away, to vex me, maybe—
and now they say I killed it—'tis not true!
Never shall I be happy again.

They make me their song! they're mean to do it!
There's an old tale has the same refrain—
who bade them tell it of me?

FAUST [*falling at her feet*]. Here lieth one who loves thee,
and from thy woe would set thee free.

MARGARETE [*flinging herself beside him*].
O let us kneel and ask the Saints to aid us!
Lo! beneath this paving,
beneath this sill
there seetheth Hades!
The Prince of Hell
in his angry raving
maketh that noise!

FAUST [*loudly*]. Gretchen! Gretchen!

MARGARETE [*listening attentively*]. That was my lover's voice!

[*She springs to her feet; the fetters drop to the ground.*]

I heard him call me! Where is he?
No one shall stop me—I am free!
To his neck will I fly,
upon his heart to lie!
On the threshold he stood, and *Gretchen!* he called.
Though the sound of Hell's weeping and gnashing appalled,
'spite wrathful, infernal mockings all 'round,
I knew that voice's sweet, loving sound.

FAUST. 'Tis I.

MARGARETE. 'Tis thou! O, say it once again!
[*Clasping him.*] 'Tis he! 'Tis he! Where, now, is all my pain—
the anguish of the prison and the chain?
'Tis thou! Thou comest to save,
and I am saved!—
Again the street I see
where first I looked on thee,
and the garden so gay,
where Martha and I waited that day.

FAUST [*urging her toward the door*].
Come! Come with me!

MARGARETE. Stay, now!
I'd like to stay where'er thou stayest [*caressing him*].

FAUST. Away, now!
If longer here delayest,
We shall be made to rue it dearly.

MARGARETE. Kissing thou hast forgotten, clearly!
Absent so short a time as this,

and thou canst no longer kiss?!
Why is my heart so anxious, on thy breast,
where once a heaven thy glances did create,
a heaven thy loving words expressed,
and in thy kiss I'd almost suffocate?
Kiss me!
or I'll kiss thee! [*She embraces him.*]
Alas! they lips are chill,
and still!
How changed in fashion
thy passion!
Who has done me this ill? [*She turns away from him.*]

FAUST. Come, follow me! My darling, be but bold!
I'll hold thee close, with warmth a thousandfold,
if thou'lt but follow! 'Tis all I ask of thee.

MARGARETE [*turning to him*]. And is it thou? Thou—surely, certainly?

FAUST. It is! But come!

MARGARETE. Thou dost unloose my chain,
and to thy arms dost take me once again.
But how is that thou dost not shrink from me?—
Say, dost thou know, my friend, whom thou dost free?

FAUST. Come! the night already is less deep!

MARGARETE. My mother I have put to sleep,
my babe I've drowned.
But was that not a gift we both had owned,
thine, too!?—'Tis thou, though scarcely true it seem!
Give me thy hand! 'Tis not a dream!
Thy dear, dear hand!—But oh, 'tis wet!
Wipe it off! Methinks there's yet
blood thereon.
Ah, God! what hast thou done?!
Sheathe thy sword at last—
I beg thee, put it away!

FAUST. O, let the past be past!—
thy very words do slay!

MARGARETE. Don't die! Thou must outlive us.
I'll tell thee the graves to give us:
thou must begin tomorrow
the work of sorrow!
The best place give to my mother,
then close at her side my brother,
next me, a little away
(but not too far, I pray!),

then my baby lay on my right breast.
No one else shall sleep beside me!—
When at thy side I closely pressed,
that was my highest happiness!
But that is so no longer:
to force myself to touch thee, I'd need be much stronger,
for I feel that thou repellest my kiss.
And yet 'tis thou, so good, so kind to see!

FAUST. If thou feel'st it is I, then come with me!

MARGARETE. Out there!?

FAUST. To freedom!

MARGARETE. If the grave is there,
and death lying in wait, then come!
From here to eternal rest—no further,
no further step, not one!
Thou leavest now? Would I might go along!

FAUST. Thou canst! But will it! Open stands the door.

MARGARETE. I may not go—I've no hopes any more.
Why flee, since they will still my steps waylay!
It's wretched, to have to beg one's food—
and with a bad conscience to boot!
It's wretched, to be far from home, forsaken—
and I'd still be followed and taken!

FAUST. I'll be with thee.

MARGARETE. Be quick! Be quick,
rescue the poor, poor child!
Go! Follow the ridge
along the brook,
over the bridge,
into the wood,
to the left, where the plank is placed—
in the pool!
Seize it in haste!
'Tis trying to rise,
'tis struggling still!
Save it! save it!

FAUST. Exert thy will!
One step, and thou art free!

MARGARETE. If we were only past the hill!
My mother upon a stone I see
(a cold hand is seizing me!),
there sits my mother upon a stone,
her head wags on and on:

she nods not nor beckons, her head's such a weight;
she slept so long that no more she'll wake.
She slept, that we might caress.
Those were the days of happiness!

FAUST. Since words and prayers here naught avail,
I'll venture, then, to bear thee forth.

MARGARETE. No! let me go! I'll suffer no force!
Grasp me not so murderously!
I've done, else, all things for the love of thee.

FAUST. Day is dawning! Dearest! dearest!

MARGARETE. Day? Yes, the day comes—the last day breaks!
My wedding day it was to be.
Tell no one thou hast been before with me!
Alas, no wreath!—
'tis too late, now!
Once again we shall meet,
but not at the dance!
The crowd is thronging, no word is spoken.
The square below
and the streets overflow.
The death-bell tolls, the wand is broken.
I am seized, and bound, and delivered,
have reached the block—they give the sign!
Now, near each neck, has quivered
the blade-edge that darts toward mine.
Mute lies the world like the grave!

FAUST. O had I ne'er been born!

MEPHISTOPHELES [*appearing outside the cell*].
Off! or you're lost! 'Tis dawn!
Useless talking, delaying and praying!
My horses are neighing,
affrighted that morning is near.

MARGARETE. What rises up before us here?
He! he! Suffer him not!
What does he want in this holy spot?
He seeks me!

FAUST. Thou shalt live!

MARGARETE. Judgment of God! myself to thee I give.

MEPHISTOPHELES [*to* FAUST]. Come! come! or I'll abandon her and thee.

MARGARETE. Thine am I, Father! Rescue me!
Ye angels, holy cohorts, guard me,
compass me about, from evil ward me!
Henry! I shudder at the thought of thee.

MEPHISTOPHELES. She is judged!
VOICE [*from above*]. She is saved!
MEPHISTOPHELES [*to* FAUST]. Away, with me!
[*He disappears with* FAUST.]
MARGARETE'S VOICE [*from within, dying away*]. Henry! Henry!

Selected Poems of William Wordsworth

William Wordsworth (1770–1850)

WILLIAM WORDSWORTH WAS BORN IN THE LAKE DISTRICT of northern England, a region of great natural beauty which was to be his home for most of his life and a source of imaginative power and joy in almost all of his poetry. He was a mediocre student at Cambridge University, where he took his degree in 1791. After graduation, Wordsworth spent a year in France, then in the midst of its great revolution, and underwent his own "radicalization" during the French struggle for liberty, equality, and fraternity. While in France he had an affair with a somewhat older Frenchwoman, Annette Vallon, by whom he had a daughter. Back in England, he initially chafed at his country's reactionary policies, but gradually lost sympathy with the revolutionary cause (which led to the Reign of Terror and then to Napoleonic dictatorship). He ended his life a nationally honored figure, Poet Laureate of England, and a conservative.

Wordsworth's major creative period lies between 1797 and 1807. During this time, he and Samuel Taylor Coleridge forged a new and revolutionary poetics, which they demonstrated first in the *Lyrical Ballads* of 1798. In the famous "Preface" to the second edition of the volume, Wordsworth maintained that poetry must no longer be written in the flowery "poetic" diction inherited from the Renaissance and codified during the eighteenth century but in the ordinary speech of ordinary men. A poet, he said, is "a man speaking to men." It was his effort to use direct, colloquial speech, to make it embody deeply felt human emotion, and to transform the common experiences of men into subjects of poetic meditation that made poems like "Tintern Abbey" a new mode in English poetry. Despite the initial hostility of critics, the Wordsworthian mode ultimately prevailed.

Wordsworth's poetry celebrates nature. In his works, "nature" is not merely natural beauty but the source of creative vitality and moral force. His long autobiographical poem, *The Prelude,* describes how he lost his childhood oneness with nature, became estranged from it, and then later returned to it more consciously, seeking to found his life on its dictates and his poetry on the concrete images that show man's spiritual investment in nature. The "Immortality Ode," as well as "Tintern Abbey," deals with the successive stages of the poet's awareness of the universal laws immanent in nature and the mind's imaginative effort to understand itself in terms of nature.

Selected Poems

Lines

Composed a Few Miles Above Tintern Abbey on Revisiting the Banks of the Wye During a Tour. July 13, 1798

Five years have passed; five summers, with the length
Of five long winters! and again I hear
These waters, rolling from their mountain-springs
With a soft inland murmur.—Once again
Do I behold these steep and lofty cliffs,
That on a wild secluded scene impress
Thoughts of more deep seclusion; and connect
The landscape with the quiet of the sky.
The day is come when I again repose
Here, under this dark sycamore, and view
These plots of cottage-ground, these orchard-tufts,
Which at this season, with their unripe fruits,
Are clad in one green hue, and lose themselves
'Mid groves and copses. Once again I see
These hedgerows, hardly hedgerows, little lines
Of sportive wood run wild: these pastoral farms,
Green to the very door; and wreaths of smoke
Sent up, in silence, from among the trees!
With some uncertain notice, as might seem
Of vagrant dwellers in the houseless woods,
Or of some hermit's cave, where by his fire
The hermit sits alone.

These beauteous forms,
Through a long absence, have not been to me
As is a landscape to a blind man's eye;
But oft, in lonely rooms, and 'mid the din
Of towns and cities, I have owed to them
In hours of weariness, sensations sweet,

Felt in the blood, and felt along the heart;
And passing even into my purer mind,
With tranquil restoration—feelings too
Of unremembered pleasure: such, perhaps,
As have no slight or trivial influence
On that best portion of a good man's life,
His little, nameless, unremembered acts
Of kindness and of love. Nor less, I trust,
To them I may have owed another gift,
Of aspect more sublime; that blessèd mood
In which the burthen of the mystery,
In which the heavy and the weary weight
Of all this unintelligible world,
Is lightened—that serene and blessèd mood,
In which the affections gently lead us on—
Until, the breath of this corporeal frame
And even the motion of our human blood
Almost suspended, we are laid asleep
In body, and become a living soul;
While with an eye made quiet by the power
Of harmony, and the deep power of joy,
We see into the life of things.

If this
Be but a vain belief, yet, oh! how oft—
In darkness and amid the many shapes
Of joyless daylight; when the fretful stir
Unprofitable, and the fever of the world,
Have hung upon the beatings of my heart—
How oft, in spirit, have I turned to thee,
O sylvan Wye! thou wanderer through the woods.
How often has my spirit turned to thee!

And now, with gleams of half-extinguished thought,
With many recognitions dim and faint,
And somewhat of a sad perplexity,
The picture of the mind revives again;
While here I stand, not only with the sense
Of present pleasure, but with pleasing thoughts
That in this moment there is life and food
For future years. And so I dare to hope,
Though changed, no doubt, from what I was when first
I came among these hills; when like a roe

I bounded o'er the mountains, by the sides
Of the deep rivers, and the lonely streams,
Wherever nature led: more like a man
Flying from something that he dreads than one
Who sought the thing he loved. For nature then
(The coarser pleasures of my boyish days,
And their glad animal movements all gone by)
To me was all in all.—I cannot paint
What then I was. The sounding cataract
Haunted me like a passion; the tall rock,
The mountain, and the deep and gloomy wood,
Their colors and their forms, were then to me
An appetite; a feeling and a love,
That had no need of a remoter charm,
By thought supplied, nor any interest
Unborrowed from the eye.—That time is past,
And all its aching joys are now no more,
And all its dizzy raptures. Not for this
Faint I, nor mourn nor murmur; other gifts
Have followed; for such loss, I would believe,
Abundant recompense. For I have learned
To look on nature, not as in the hour
Of thoughtless youth; but hearing oftentimes
The still, sad music of humanity,
Nor harsh nor grating, though of ample power
To chasten and subdue. And I have felt
A presence that disturbs me with the joy
Of elevated thoughts; a sense sublime
Of something far more deeply interfused,
Whose dwelling is the light of setting suns,
And the round ocean and the living air,
And the blue sky, and in the mind of man:
A motion and a spirit, that impels
All thinking things, all objects of all thought,
And rolls through all things. Therefore am I still
A lover of the meadows and the woods
And mountains; and of all that we behold
From this green earth; of all the mighty world
Of eye, and ear—both what they half create,
And what perceive; well pleased to recognize
In nature and the language of the sense
The anchor of my purest thoughts, the nurse,

The guide, the guardian of my heart, and soul
Of all my moral being.

Nor perchance,
If I were not thus taught, should I the more
Suffer my genial spirits to decay:
For thou art with me here upon the banks
Of this fair river; thou my dearest friend,
My dear, dear friend; and in thy voice I catch
The language of my former heart, and read
My former pleasures in the shooting lights
Of thy wild eyes. Oh! yet a little while
May I behold in thee what I was once,
My dear, dear sister! and this prayer I make,
Knowing that Nature never did betray
The heart that loved her; 'tis her privilege,
Through all the years of this our life, to lead
From joy to joy: for she can so inform
The mind that is within us, so impress
With quietness and beauty, and so feed
With lofty thoughts, that neither evil tongues,
Rash judgments, nor the sneers of selfish men,
Nor greetings where no kindness is, nor all
The dreary intercourse of daily life,
Shall e'er prevail against us, or disturb
Our cheerful faith, that all which we behold
Is full of blessings. Therefore let the moon
Shine on thee in thy solitary walk;
And let the misty mountain winds be free
To blow against thee: and, in after years,
When these wild ecstasies shall be matured
Into a sober pleasure; when thy mind
Shall be a mansion for all lovely forms,
Thy memory be as a dwelling place
For all sweet sounds and harmonies; oh! then,
If solitude, or fear, or pain, or grief
Should be thy portion, with what healing thoughts
Of tender joy wilt thou remember me,
And these my exhortations! Nor, perchance—
If I should be where I no more can hear
Thy voice, nor catch from thy wild eyes these gleams
Of past existence—wilt thou then forget
That on the banks of this delightful stream

We stood together; and that I, so long
A worshiper of Nature, hither came
Unwearied in that service; rather say
With warmer love—oh! with far deeper zeal
Of holier love. Nor wilt thou then forget,
That after many wanderings, many years
Of absence, these steep woods and lofty cliffs,
And this green pastoral landscape, were to me
More dear, both for themselves and for thy sake!

*The Simplon Pass**

—Brook and road
Were fellow travellers in this gloomy Pass,
And with them did we journey several hours
At a slow step. The immeasurable height
Of woods decaying, never to be decayed,
The stationary blasts of waterfalls,
And in the narrow rent, at every turn,
Winds thwarting winds bewildered and forlorn,
The torrents shooting from the clear blue sky,
The rocks that muttered close upon our ears,
Black drizzling crags that spake by the wayside
As if a voice were in them, the sick sight
And giddy prospect of the raving stream,
The unfettered clouds and region of the heavens,
Tumult and peace, the darkness and the light—
Were all like workings of one mind, the features
Of the same face, blossoms upon one tree,
Characters of the great Apocalypse,
The types and symbols of Eternity,
Of first, and last, and midst, and without end.

A Slumber Did My Spirit Seal

A slumber did my spirit seal;
I had no human fears;
She seemed a thing that could not feel
The touch of earthly years.

* *The Simplon Pass:* a pass through the Alps between Italy and Switzerland.

No motion has she now, no force;
She neither hears nor sees;
Rolled round in earth's diurnal course,
With rocks, and stones, and trees.

Composed upon Westminster Bridge, September 3, 1802

Earth has not anything to show more fair:
Dull would he be of soul who could pass by
A sight so touching in its majesty:
This city now doth, like a garment, wear
The beauty of the morning; silent, bare,
Ships, towers, domes, theaters, and temples lie
Open unto the fields, and to the sky;
All bright and glittering in the smokeless air.
Never did sun more beautifully steep
In his first splendor, valley, rock, or hill;
Ne'er saw I, never felt, a calm so deep!
The river glideth at his own sweet will:
Dear God! the very houses seem asleep;
And all that mighty heart is lying still!

The Solitary Reaper

Behold her, single in the field,
Yon solitary Highland lass!
Reaping and singing by herself;
Stop here, or gently pass!
Alone she cuts and binds the grain,
And sings a melancholy strain;
O listen! for the vale profound
Is overflowing with the sound.

No nightingale did ever chaunt
More welcome notes to weary bands
Of travelers in some shady haunt,
Among Arabian sands:
A voice so thrilling ne'er was heard
In springtime from the cuckoo-bird,

Breaking the silence of the seas
Among the farthest Hebrides.

Will no one tell me what she sings?—
Perhaps the plaintive numbers flow
For old, unhappy, far-off things,
And battles long ago:
Or is it some more humble lay,
Familiar matter of today?
Some natural sorrow, loss, or pain,
That has been, and may be again?

Whate'er the theme, the maiden sang
As if her song could have no ending;
I saw her singing at her work,
And o'er the sickle bending:—
I listened, motionless and still;
And, as I mounted up the hill,
The music in my heart I bore,
Long after it was heard no more.

Ode

Intimations of Immortality from Recollections of Early Childhood

I

There was a time when meadow, grove, and stream,
The earth, and every common sight,
        To me did seem
    Apparelled in celestial light,
The glory and the freshness of a dream.
It is not now as it hath been of yore;—
    Turn wheresoe'er I may,
        By night or day,
The things which I have seen I now can see no more.

II

        The Rainbow comes and goes,
        And lovely is the Rose;
        The Moon doth with delight
  Look round her when the heavens are bare;
    Waters on a starry night

Are beautiful and fair;
The sunshine is a glorious birth;
But yet I know, where'er I go,
That there hath past away a glory from the earth.

III

Now, while the birds thus sing a joyous song,
And while the young lambs bound
As to the tabor's sound,
To me alone there came a thought of grief:
A timely utterance gave that thought relief,
And I again am strong:
The cataracts blow their trumpets from the steep;
No more shall grief of mine the season wrong;
I hear the Echoes through the mountains throng,
The Winds come to me from the fields of sleep,
And all the earth is gay;
Land and sea
Give themselves up to jollity,
And with the heart of May
Doth every Beast keep holiday;—
Thou Child of Joy,
Shout round me, let me hear thy shouts, thou happy Shepherd-boy!

IV

Ye blessed Creatures, I have heard the call
Ye to each other make; I see
The heavens laugh with you in your jubilee;
My heart is at your festival,
My head hath its coronal,
The fulness of your bliss, I feel—I feel it all.
Oh evil day! if I were sullen
While Earth herself is adorning,
This sweet May-morning,
And the Children are culling
On every side,
In a thousand valleys far and wide,
Fresh flowers; while the sun shines warm,
And the Babe leaps up on his Mother's arm:—
I hear, I hear, with joy I hear!
—But there's a Tree, of many, one,

A single Field which I have looked upon,
Both of them speak of something that is gone;
The Pansy at my feet
Doth the same tale repeat:
Whither is fled the visionary gleam?
Where is it now, the glory and the dream?

V

Our birth is but a sleep and a forgetting:
The Soul that rises with us, our life's Star,
Hath had elsewhere its setting,
And cometh from afar:
Not in entire forgetfulness,
And not in utter nakedness,
But trailing clouds of glory do we come
From God, who is our home:
Heaven lies about us in our infancy!
Shades of the prison-house begin to close
Upon the growing Boy,
But He beholds the light, and whence it flows,
He sees it in his joy;
The Youth, who daily farther from the east
Must travel, still is Nature's Priest,
And by the vision splendid
Is on his way attended;
At length the Man perceives it die away,
And fade into the light of common day.

VI

Earth fills her lap with pleasures of her own;
Yearnings she hath in her own natural kind,
And, even with something of a Mother's mind,
And no unworthy aim,
The homely Nurse doth all she can
To make her Foster-child, her Inmate Man,
Forget the glories he hath known,
And that imperial palace whence he came.

VII

Behold the Child among his new-born blisses,
A six years' Darling of a pigmy size!
See, where 'mid work of his own hand he lies,
Fretted by sallies of his mother's kisses,
With light upon him from his father's eyes!
See, at his feet, some little plan or chart,
Some fragment from his dream of human life,
Shaped by himself with newly-learnèd art;
A wedding or a festival,
A mourning or a funeral;
And this hath now his heart,
And unto this he frames his song:
Then will he fit his tongue
To dialogues of business, love, or strife;
But it will not be long
Ere this be thrown aside,
And with new joy and pride
The little Actor cons another part;
Filling from time to time his "humorous stage"
With all the Persons, down to palsied Age,
That Life brings with her in her equipage;
As if his whole vocation
Were endless imitation.

VIII

Thou, whose exterior semblance doth belie
Thy Soul's immensity;
Thou best Philosopher, who yet dost keep
Thy heritage, thou Eye among the blind,
That, deaf and silent, read'st the eternal deep,
Haunted for ever by the eternal mind,—
Mighty Prophet! Seer blest!
On whom those truths do rest,
Which we are toiling all our lives to find,
In darkness lost, the darkness of the grave;
Thou, over whom thy Immortality
Broods like the Day, a Master o'er a Slave,
A Presence which is not to be put by;
To whom the grave
Is but a lonely bed without the sense or sight

Of day or the warm light,
A place of thought where we in waiting lie;
Thou little Child, yet glorious in the might
Of heaven-born freedom on thy being's height,
Why with such earnest pains dost thou provoke
The years to bring the inevitable yoke,
Thus blindly with thy blessedness at strife?
Full soon thy Soul shall have her earthly freight,
And custom lie upon thee with a weight,
Heavy as frost, and deep almost as life!

IX

O joy! that in our embers
Is something that doth live,
That nature yet remembers
What was so fugitive!
The thought of our past years in me doth breed
Perpetual benediction: not indeed
For that which is most worthy to be blest—
Delight and liberty, the simple creed
Of Childhood, whether busy or at rest,
With new-fledged hope still fluttering in his breast:—
Not for these I raise
The song of thanks and praise;
But for those obstinate questionings
Of sense and outward things,
Fallings from us, vanishings;
Blank misgivings of a Creature
Moving about in worlds not realised,
High instincts before which our mortal Nature
Did tremble like a guilty Thing surprised:
But for those first affections,
Those shadowy recollections,
Which, be they what they may,
Are yet the fountain-light of all our day,
Are yet a master-light of all our seeing;
Uphold us, cherish, and have power to make
Our noisy years seem moments in the being
Of the eternal Silence: truths that wake,
To perish never:
Which neither listlessness, nor mad endeavour,
Nor Man nor Boy,

Nor all that is at enmity with joy,
Can utterly abolish or destroy!
Hence in a season of calm weather
Though inland far we be,
Our Souls have sight of that immortal sea
Which brought us hither,
Can in a moment travel thither,
And see the Children sport upon the shore,
And hear the mighty waters rolling evermore.

X

Then sing, ye Birds, sing, sing a joyous song!
And let the young Lambs bound
As to the tabor's sound!
We in thought will join your throng,
Ye that pipe and ye that play,
Ye that through your hearts to-day
Feel the gladness of the May!
What though the radiance which was once so bright
Be now for ever taken from my sight,
Though nothing can bring back the hour
Of splendour in the grass, of glory in the flower;
We will grieve not, rather find
Strength in what remains behind;
In the primal sympathy
Which having been must ever be;
In the soothing thoughts that spring
Out of human suffering;
In the faith that looks through death,
In years that bring the philosophic mind.

XI

And O, ye Fountains, Meadows, Hills, and Groves,
Forebode not any severing of our loves!
Yet in my heart of hearts I feel your might;
I only have relinquished one delight
To live beneath your more habitual sway.
I love the Brooks which down their channels fret,
Even more than when I tripped lightly as they;
The innocent brightness of a new-born Day
Is lovely yet;

The Clouds that gather round the setting sun
Do take a sober colouring from an eye
That hath kept watch o'er man's mortality;
Another race hath been, and other palms are won.
Thanks to the human heart by which we live,
Thanks to its tenderness, its joys, and fears,
To me the meanest flower that blows can give
Thoughts that do often lie too deep for tears.

Romantic Poetry

THIS SELECTION OF ROMANTIC POETRY FROM FIVE COUNTRIES represents styles and themes so diverse that their grouping together may seem arbitrary. Nonetheless, these poets all do belong to a common spirit—and a common revolution—in poetry. In part the revolution is one of literary form and language, an effort to break from earlier conventions of vocabulary and diction and to write in a more direct, spontaneous, and lyrical manner. But more importantly it is a revolution of sensibility and outlook. As with Rousseau, and also Faust, the primary reality for these poets is the self, the individual personality in its confrontation with the world and its subjective interpretation of reality. The Enlightenment's inquisitiveness about the universe and its laws has given way to man's introspective search for the obscure forces that make him act. The individual's feelings, his emotional responses, have gained precedence over reason as the guide to truth and beauty.

"Nature" is of course a prime setting, force, and image in Romantic poetry. If nature can be a source of intense emotional experience for all these poets, and the foundation of right feeling and behavior, it also may put man face to face with his own aloneness in the world. Much Romantic poetry deals with the sense of alienation that arises when man realizes his separation from the natural world: the curse—as well as the privilege—brought by self-consciousness, the burden of the mind that tells us we are different from animals and trees and prevents us from participating in the organic cycles of nature.

Such a realization may lead to an attitude of revolt, which is the stance of the Byronic hero who protests society and, beyond that, the whole ordering of the universe. Or it may lead to the exercise of visionary powers, as the poet tries to recompose a sense of the unity of being. The visionary element is important in much Romantic poetry: in a world where the old principles of civil and religious order had been shaken, even shattered, where society was beginning to feel the effects of industrialization, the division of labor, and class conflict, it became the task of the imagination to create the vital unifying principles by which man could live. And it is to the individual imagination—of the self, of society, of the universe—that most Romantic poets finally attach the highest importance.

Romantic Poetry

William Blake (1757–1827)

Blake, a mystic in search of a new religious mythology, was a fierce antagonist of rationalism and the scientific outlook.

Mock on, Mock on, Voltaire, Rousseau

Mock on, Mock on, Voltaire, Rousseau:°
Mock on, Mock on; 'tis all in vain!
You throw the sand against the wind,
And the wind blows it back again.

And every sand becomes a Gem
Reflected in the beams divine;
Blown back they blind the mocking Eye,
But still in Israel's paths they shine.

The Atoms of Democritus
And Newton's Particles of light°
Are sand upon the Red sea shore,
Where Israel's tents do shine so bright.

George Gordon, Lord Byron (1788–1824)

During the nineteenth century, Byron was considered the Romantic rebel par excellence. Indeed, his very name has come to stand for a certain kind of rebel: the man who pits himself against society and the cosmic order.

1. Voltaire, Rousseau: in Blake's view, two representatives of the skepticism of the Enlightenment. *9–10. Atoms . . . light:* Democritus (Greek philosopher, 460?–362? B.C.) claimed that everything was made up of structures of atoms; Newton developed a corpuscular theory of light.

Prometheus

Titan! to whose immortal eyes
The sufferings of mortality,
Seen in their sad reality,
Were not as things that gods despise;
What was thy pity's recompense?
A silent suffering, and intense;
The rock, the vulture, and the chain,
All that the proud can feel of pain,
The agony they do not show,
The suffocating sense of woe,
Which speaks but in its loneliness,
And then is jealous lest the sky
Should have a listener, nor will sigh
Until its voice is echoless.

Titan! to thee the strife was given
Between the suffering and the will,
Which torture where they cannot kill;
And the inexorable Heaven,
And the deaf tyranny of Fate,
The ruling principle of Hate,
Which for its pleasure doth create
The things it may annihilate,
Refused thee even the boon to die:
The wretched gift eternity
Was thine—and thou hast borne it well.
All that the Thunderer° wrung from thee
Was but the menace which flung back
On him the torments of thy rack;
The fate° thou didst so well foresee,
But would not to appease him tell;
And in thy silence was his sentence,
And in his soul a vain repentance,
And evil dread so ill dissembled,
That in his hand the lightnings trembled.

Thy Godlike crime was to be kind,
To render with thy precepts less
The sum of human wretchedness,

26. *Thunderer:* Jupiter. 29. *The fate:* Prometheus foresaw Jupiter's downfall and would not reveal how it would happen.

And strengthen man with his own mind;
But baffled as thou wert from high,
Still in thy patient energy,
In the endurance, and repulse
  Of thine impenetrable spirit,
Which Earth and Heaven could not convulse,
  A mighty lesson we inherit:
Thou art a symbol and a sign
  To mortals of their fate and force;
Like thee, man is in part divine,
  A troubled stream from a pure source;
And man in portions can foresee
His own funereal destiny;
His wretchedness, and his resistance,
And his sad unallied existence:
To which his spirit may oppose
Itself—and equal to all woes,
  And a firm will, and a deep sense,
Which even in torture can descry
  Its own concenter'd recompense,
Triumphant where it dares defy,
And making death a victory.

John Keats (1795–1821

In his brief career, Keats achieved a poetry of a rich, vibrant sensuousness comparable to Shakespeare's.

When I Have Fears

When I have fears that I may cease to be
Before my pen has gleaned my teeming brain,
Before high-pilèd books, in charact'ry,
Hold like rich garners the full-ripened grain;
When I behold, upon the night's starred face,
Huge cloudy symbols of a high romance,
And think that I may never live to trace
Their shadows, with the magic hand of chance;
And when I feel, fair creature of an hour,

That I shall never look upon thee more,
Never have relish in the faery power
Of unreflecting love!—then on the shore
Of the wide world I stand alone, and think
Till Love and Fame to nothingness do sink.

Ode to a Nightingale

My heart aches, and a drowsy numbness pains
My sense, as though of hemlock I had drunk,
Or emptied some dull opiate to the drains
One minute past, and Lethe°-wards had sunk:
'Tis not through envy of thy happy lot,
But being too happy in thine happiness—
That thou, light-wingéd Dryad° of the trees,
In some melodious plot
Of beechen green, and shadows numberless,
Singest of summer in full-throated ease.

O, for a draught of vintage! that hath been
Cooled a long age in the deep-delvéd earth,
Tasting of Flora° and the country green,
Dance, and Provençal song, and sunburnt mirth!
O for a beaker full of the warm South,
Full of the true, the blushful Hippocrene,°
With beaded bubbles winking at the brim,
And purple-stainéd mouth;
That I might drink, and leave the world unseen,
And with thee fade away into the forest dim:

Fade far away, dissolve, and quite forget
What thou among the leaves hast never known,
The weariness, the fever, and the fret
Here, where men sit and hear each other groan;
Where palsy shakes a few, sad, last gray hairs,
Where youth grows pale, and specter-thin, and dies;
Where but to think is to be full of sorrow
And leaden-eyed despairs,
Where Beauty cannot keep her lustrous eyes,
Or new Love pine at them beyond tomorrow.

4. *Lethe:* river of forgetfulness in Hades. 7. *Dryad:* wood nymph. 13. *Flora:* goddess of flowers. 16. *Hippocrene:* fountain of the Muses on Mt. Helicon.

Away! away! for I will fly to thee,
  Not charioted by Bacchus° and his pards,
But on the viewless wings of Poesy,
  Though the dull brain perplexes and retards:
Already with thee! tender is the night,
  And haply the Queen-Moon is on her throne,
    Clustered around by all her starry Fays;
        But here there is no light,
  Save what from heaven is with the breezes blown
    Through verdurous glooms and winding mossy ways.

I cannot see what flowers are at my feet,
  Nor what soft incense hangs upon the boughs,
But, in embalméd darkness, guess each sweet
  Wherewith the seasonable month endows
The grass, the thicket, and the fruit tree wild;
  White hawthorn, and the pastoral eglantine;
    Fast fading violets covered up in leaves;
        And mid-May's eldest child,
  The coming musk-rose, full of dewy wine,
    The murmurous haunt of flies on summer eves.

Darkling° I listen; and, for many a time
  I have been half in love with easeful Death,
Called him soft names in many a muséd rhyme,
  To take into the air my quiet breath;
Now more than ever seems it rich to die,
  To cease upon the midnight with no pain,
    While thou art pouring forth thy soul abroad
        In such an ecstasy!
  Still wouldst thou sing, and I have ears in vain—
    To thy high requiem become a sod.

Thou was not born for death, immortal Bird!
  No hungry generations tread thee down;
The voice I hear this passing night was heard
  In ancient days by emperor and clown:
Perhaps the selfsame song that found a path
  Through the sad heart of Ruth,° when, sick for home,

32. *Bacchus:* god of wine whose chariot is drawn by leopards (*pards*). 51. *Darkling:* in darkness. 66. *Ruth:* Biblical figure who left her native land to live with Naomi, her mother-in-law. See The Book of Ruth.

She stood in tears amid the alien corn;
The same that ofttimes hath
Charmed magic casements, opening on the foam
Of perilous seas, in faery lands forlorn.

Forlorn! the very word is like a bell
To toll me back from thee to my sole self!
Adieu! the fancy cannot cheat so well
As she is famed to do, deceiving elf.
Adieu! adieu! thy plaintive anthem fades
Past the near meadows, over the still stream,
Up the hill side; and now 'tis buried deep
In the next valley-glades:
Was it a vision, or a waking dream?
Fled is that music:—Do I wake or sleep?

Ode on a Grecian Urn

Thou still unravished bride of quietness,
Thou foster-child of silence and slow time,
Sylvan historian, who canst thus express
A flowery tale more sweetly than our rhyme:
What leaf-fringed legend haunts about thy shape
Of deities or mortals, or of both,
In Tempe or the dales of Arcady? °
What men or gods are these? What maidens loath?
What mad pursuit? What struggle to escape?
What pipes and timbrels? What wild ecstasy?

Heard melodies are sweet, but those unheard
Are sweeter; therefore, ye soft pipes, play on;
Not to the sensual ear, but, more endeared,
Pipe to the spirit ditties of no tone:
Fair youth, beneath the trees, thou canst not leave
Thy song, nor ever can those trees be bare;
Bold lover, never, never canst thou kiss,
Though winning near the goal—yet, do not grieve;
She cannot fade, though thou hast not thy bliss,
Forever wilt thou love, and she be fair!

7. *Tempe, Arcady:* Greek sites traditionally associated with pastoral poetry.

Ah, happy, happy boughs! that cannot shed
  Your leaves, nor ever bid the spring adieu;
And, happy melodist, unwearièd,
  Forever piping songs forever new;
More happy love! more happy, happy love!
  Forever warm and still to be enjoyed,
    Forever panting, and forever young;
All breathing human passion far above,
  That leaves a heart high-sorrowful and cloyed,
    A burning forehead, and a parching tongue.

Who are these coming to the sacrifice?
  To what green altar, O mysterious priest,
Lead'st thou that heifer lowing at the skies,
  And all her silken flanks with garlands dressed?
What little town by river or sea shore,
  Or mountain-built with peaceful citadel,
    Is emptied of this folk, this pious morn?
And, little town, thy streets forevermore
  Will silent be; and not a soul to tell
    Why thou art desolate, can e'er return.

O Attic shape! Fair attitude! with brede
  Of marble men and maidens overwrought,
With forest branches and the trodden weed;
  Thou, silent form, dost tease us out of thought
As doth eternity: Cold Pastoral!
  When old age shall this generation waste,
    Thou shalt remain, in midst of other woe
Than ours, a friend to man, to whom thou say'st,
  "Beauty is truth, truth beauty,"—that is all
    Ye know on earth, and all ye need to know.

Percy Bysshe Shelley (1792–1822)

Shelley was in many ways the most intellectually ambitious of the English Romantic poets—the one who made the most difficult demands on poetry and the highest claims for the poet's guiding role in human society.

Ode to the West Wind

I

O wild West Wind, thou breath of Autumn's being,
Thou, from whose unseen presence the leaves dead
Are driven, like ghosts from an enchanter fleeing,

Yellow, and black, and pale, and hectic red,
Pestilence-stricken multitudes: O thou,
Who chariotest to their dark wintry bed

The wingéd seeds, where they lie cold and low,
Each like a corpse within its grave, until
Thine azure sister of the Spring shall blow

Her clarion o'er the dreaming earth, and fill
(Driving sweet buds like flocks to feed in air)
With living hues and odors plain and hill:

Wild Spirit, which art moving everywhere;
Destroyer and preserver; hear, oh, hear!

II

Thou on whose stream, mid the steep sky's commotion,
Loose clouds like earth's decaying leaves are shed,
Shook from the tangled boughs of Heaven and Ocean,

Angels of rain and lightning: there are spread
On the blue surface of thine aery surge,
Like the bright hair uplifted from the head

Of some fierce Maenad,° even from the dim verge
Of the horizon to the zenith's height,
The locks of the approaching storm. Thou dirge

Of the dying year, to which this closing night
Will be the dome of a vast sepulchre,
Vaulted with all thy congregated might

Of vapors, from whose solid atmosphere
Black rain, and fire, and hail will burst: oh, hear!

21. *Maenad:* one of the women followers of Bacchus, inspired by the god to ecstatic frenzy.

III

Thou who didst waken from his summer dreams
The blue Mediterranean, where he lay,
Lulled by the coil of his crystálline streams,

Beside a pumice isle in Baiae's bay,°
And saw in sleep old palaces and towers
Quivering within the wave's intenser day,

All overgrown with azure moss and flowers
So sweet, the sense faints picturing them! Thou
For whose path the Atlantic's level powers

Cleave themselves into chasms, while far below
The sea-blooms and the oozy woods which wear
The sapless foliage of the ocean, know

Thy voice, and suddenly grow gray with fear,
And tremble and despoil themselves: oh, hear!

IV

If I were a dead leaf thou mightest bear,
If I were a swift cloud to fly with thee;
A wave to pant beneath thy power, and share

The impulse of thy strength, only less free
Than thou, O uncontrollable! If even
I were as in my boyhood, and could be

The comrade of thy wanderings over Heaven,
As then, when to outstrip thy skyey speed
Scarce seemed a vision; I would ne'er have striven

As thus with thee in prayer in my sore need.
Oh, lift me as a wave, a leaf, a cloud!
I fall upon the thorns of life! I bleed!

A heavy weight of hours has chained and bowed
One too like thee; tameless, and swift, and proud.

V

Make me thy lyre, even as the forest is:
What if my leaves are falling like its own!
The tumult of thy mighty harmonies

32. *Baiae's bay:* near Naples, the site of a Roman town.

Will take from both a deep, autumnal tone,
Sweet though in sadness. Be thou, Spirit fierce,
My spirit! Be thou me, impetuous one!

Drive my dead thoughts over the universe
Like withered leaves to quicken a new birth!
And, by the incantation of this verse,

Scatter, as from an unextinguished hearth
Ashes and sparks, my words among mankind!
Be through my lips to unawakened earth

The trumpet of a prophecy! O Wind,
If Winter comes, can Spring be far behind?

Friedrich Hölderlin (1770–1843)

Hölderlin is generally regarded as one of the greatest lyric poets of early German Romanticism. His works reflect his admiration of ancient Greece and his deep pessimism, a combination that was very characteristic of some German art and literature during the early nineteenth century.

*To the Parcae**

Grant me a single summer, oh powerful ones!
    And an autumn for my ripening song,
        That my heart more willingly then,
            Sated with sweet playing, may die.

A soul which in life was denied its
    Divine right finds no rest even down in Orkus;°
        But if I once achieve that holiness
            Which I have at heart, my poem,

Then welcome, oh silence of the shadow-world!
    I am at peace, though my song has not
        Accompanied me below; I lived
            Once like the gods and have no need of more.

—TR. CYRUS HAMLIN

* *Parcae:* the Fates. 6. *Orkus:* the land of the dead.

Heinrich Heine (1797–1856)

Although usually grouped with the Romantics, Heine stands apart from them by his ironic attitude toward excessively idealized passion and what he considered a Romantic tendency to seek escape from reality.

Shipwrecked

Hope and love! All in ruins!
And I myself, like a corpse
Thrown sullenly up by the sea,
Lie on the beach,
On the desolate, bare beach.
Before me heaves the watery waste,
Behind me lies but sorrow and misery,
And above me move the clouds,
The formless grey daughters of the air,
Who draw water
Out of the sea in foggy buckets,
And haul and haul it wearily,
And pour it out into the sea again,
A gloomy, boring business,
And useless, like my own life.

The waves murmur, the gulls shriek,
Old memories blow on the breeze,
Forgotten dreams, vanished images,
Emerge, tormentingly sweet.

There lives a woman in the north,
A beautiful woman, royally beautiful.
A lustful white garment
Embraces the slender cypress figure;
The dark mass of curls,
Like a blissful night
Pouring from her braid-crowned head,
Wreathes, dreamily sweet,
The sweet, pale visage,
And from the sweet, pale visage,
Gleams an eye, great and mighty,
Like a black sun.

Oh, black sun, how often,
Delightfully often, did I drink from thee
The wild flames of rapture,
And stood and reeled, fire-intoxicated—
Then there hovered, gentle as a dove, a smile
Over the short-skirted, proud lips,
And the short-skirted, proud lips
Breathed words, sweet as moonlight,
And tender as the fragrance of a rose—
And my soul arose
And flew, like an eagle, up into the heavens!

Be silent, waves and gulls!
All is gone, happiness and hope,
Hope and love! I lie on the ground.
A desolate, shipwrecked man,
And press my white-hot visage
Into the damp sand.

—TR. JEFFREY L. SAMMONS

Victor Hugo (1802–1885)

Hugo was the leader of the French Romantic movement. Indeed, French Romanticism is traditionally dated from the performance of his play *Hernani*. Hugo was enormously influential and successful during his own lifetime as playwright, novelist, and poet; and today he is recognized as a visionary writer of great imaginative power.

Mors

I saw that reaper. In her field she strode,
Reaping and harvesting all that she mowed,
Black skeleton, letting the twilight pass—
All tremble at its shadow in the grass—
Man kept the glimmering of the scythe in sight
Under triumphant arches, triumphers quite
Tumbled; in desert Babylon alone
Throne she turned scaffold, scaffold into throne;
Gold into dust, and children into birds;

Mothers' eyes, rivers; roses into turds.
"Give me back this little being," women cried,
"Why was it made to live, just to have died?"
Only one sob rang out through all the lands,
Black pallets put forth bony-fingered hands;
A chill wind rustled through unnumbered shrouds;
Under the dismal scythe, bewildered crowds
Resembled shivering herds in shadowed flight:
Under their mournful feet, terror and night.
Behind her, his forehead bathed in gentle flame,
With souls in sheaves, a smiling angel came.

—TR. JOHN HOLLANDER

Giacomo Leopardi (1798–1837)

Leopardi was both a scholar and a poet. His poems, considered to be among the finest written in nineteenth-century Italy, are usually suffused with a gentle melancholy.

The Infinite

Dear to me always was this lonely hill,
and this hedgerow, that cuts the greater part
of the horizon farthest from my view.
But gazing out from my seat here
I shape the endless spaces there beyond,
and the transcendent silences and deepest
quiet, in my thought; until, almost,
the heart is for a moment terrified.
And as I hear the wind stream through these woods,
I then begin to match this voice to that
infinite silence; and I remember the eternal
and the dead seasons, and that living present
giving its own sound. And so amidst
this vast immensity, my thought drowns;
and sinking in this sea is sweet to me.

—TR. A. BARTLETT GIAMATTI

Alfred, Lord Tennyson (1809–1892)

Tennyson, usually classified as a Victorian poet, develops and modifies many Romantic attitudes. His "Ulysses" is one of the chief examples of the dramatic monologue form, which was later exploited by T. S. Eliot in his "Love Song of J. Alfred Prufrock."

Ulysses

It little profits that an idle king,
By this still hearth, among these barren crags,
Matched with an aged wife, I mete and dole
Unequal laws unto a savage race,
That hoard, and sleep, and feed, and know not me.
I cannot rest from travel; I will drink
Life to the lees; all times I have enjoyed
Greatly, have suffered greatly, both with those
That loved me, and alone; on shore, and when
Through scudding drifts the rainy Hyades°
Vexed the dim sea: I am become a name;
For always roaming with a hungry heart
Much have I seen and known; cities of men
And manners, climates, councils, governments,
Myself not least, but honored of them all;
And drunk delight of battle with my peers,
Far on the ringing plains of windy Troy.
I am a part of all that I have met;
Yet all experience is an arch wherethrough
Gleams that untraveled world, whose margin fades
Forever and forever when I move.
How dull it is to pause, to make an end,
To rust unburnished, not to shine in use!
As though to breathe were life. Life piled on life
Were all too little, and of one to me
Little remains; but every hour is saved
From that eternal silence, something more,
A bringer of new things; and vile it were
For some three suns to store and hoard myself,
And this gray spirit yearning in desire

10. *Hyades:* nymphs.

To follow knowledge like a sinking star,
Beyond the utmost bound of human thought.
    This is my son, mine own Telemachus
To whom I leave the scepter and the isle—
Well-loved of me, discerning to fulfill
This labor, by slow prudence to make mild
A rugged people, and through soft degrees
Subdue them to the useful and the good.
Most blameless is he, centered in the sphere
Of common duties, decent not to fail
In offices of tenderness, and pay
Meet adoration to my household gods,
When I am gone. He works his work, I mine.
    There lies the port; the vessel puffs her sail;
There gloom the dark broad seas. My mariners,
Souls that have toiled, and wrought, and thought with me—
That ever with a frolic welcome took
The thunder and the sunshine, and opposed
Free hearts, free foreheads—you and I are old;
Old age hath yet his honor and his toil;
Death closes all; but something ere the end,
Some work of noble note, may yet be done,
Not unbecoming men that strove with gods.
The lights begin to twinkle from the rocks;
The long day wanes; the slow moon climbs; the deep
Moans round with many voices. Come, my friends,
'Tis not too late to seek a newer world.
Push off, and sitting well in order smite
The sounding furrows; for my purpose holds
To sail beyond the sunset, and the baths
Of all the western stars, until I die.
It may be that the gulfs will wash us down;
It may be we shall touch the Happy Isles,
And see the great Achilles, whom we knew.
Though much is taken, much abides; and though
We are not now that strength which in old days
Moved earth and heaven, that which we are, we are;
One equal temper of heroic hearts,
Made weak by time and fate, but strong in will
To strive, to seek, to find, and not to yield.

Walt Whitman (1819–1892)

Walt Whitman was at first a rambunctious journalist and later a master poet. His poems, unconventional in language, form, and subject, dramatize an enormous ego taking hold of the world of sense and making it his own.

From Pent-up Aching Rivers

From pent-up, aching rivers,
From that of myself, without which I were nothing,
From what I am determin'd to make illustrious, even if I stand
 sole among men,
From my own voice resonant, singing the phallus,
Singing the song of procreation,
Singing the need of superb children, and therein superb grown
 people,
Singing the muscular urge and the blending,
Singing the bedfellow's song, (O resistless yearning!
O for any and each, the body correlative attracting!
O for you, whoever you are, your correlative body! O it, more
 than all else, you delighting!)
From the hungry gnaw that eats me night and day,
From native moments, from bashful pains, singing them,
Singing something yet unfound, though I have diligently sought
 it, many a long year,
Singing the true song of the Soul, fitful, at random,
Renascent with grossest Nature, or among animals,
Of that, of them, and what goes with them; my poems informing,
Of the smell of apples and lemons, of the pairing of birds,
Of the wet of woods, of the lapping of waves,
Of the mad pushes of waves upon the land, I them chanting,
The overture lightly sounding, the strain anticipating,
The welcome nearness, the sight of the perfect body,
The swimmer swimming naked in the bath, or motionless on his
 back lying and floating,
The female form approaching—I, pensive, love-flesh tremulous,
 aching,
The divine list, for myself or you, or for any one, making,

The face, the limbs, the index from head to foot, and what it arouses,
The mystic deliria, the madness amorous, the utter abandonment,
(Hark close, and still, what I now whisper to you,
I love you, O you entirely possess me.
O I wish that you and I escape from the rest, and go utterly off, O free and lawless,
Two hawks in the air, two fishes swimming in the sea not more lawless than we;)
The furious storm through me careering, I passionately trembling,
The oath of the inseparableness of two together, of the woman that loves me, and whom I love more than my life, that oath swearing,
(O I willingly stake all, for you!
O let me be lost, if it must be so!
O you and I, what is it to us what the rest do or think?
What is all else to us? only that we enjoy each other, and exhaust each other, if it must be so;)
From the master, the pilot I yield the vessel to,
The general commanding me, commanding all, from him permission taking;
From time the programme hastening, (I have loiter'd too long, as it is,)
From sex, from the warp and from the woof,
From privacy, from frequent repinings alone,
From plenty of persons near, and yet the right person not near,
From the soft sliding of hands over me, and thrusting of fingers through my hair and beard,
From the long sustain'd kiss upon the mouth or bosom,
From the close pressure that makes me or any man drunk, fainting with excess,
From what the divine husband knows, from the work of fatherhood;
From exultation, victory, and relief, from the bedfellow's embrace in the night,
From the act-poems of eyes, hands, hips, and bosoms,
From the cling of the trembling arm,
From the bending curve and the clinch,
From side by side, the pliant coverlid off-throwing,
From the one so unwilling to have me leave, and me just as unwilling to leave,

(Yet a moment, O tender waiter, and I return,)
From the hour of shining stars and dropping dews,
From the night, a moment, I emerging, flitting out,
Celebrate you, act divine, and you, children prepared for,
And you, stalwart loins.

Honoré de Balzac

Facino Cane

TRANSLATED BY
KATHERINE PRESCOTT WORMELEY

Honoré de Balzac (1799–1850)

HONORÉ BALZAC (THE ARISTOCRATIC "DE" WAS HIS OWN ADDItion) was born in the provincial town of Tours and, like so many of the young men in his novels, came to Paris to seek his fortune. His family wanted him to become a lawyer, but instead he moved into a garret and wrote, at first hack novels published under pseudonyms, in order to make a living. In 1829 came *The Last of the Chouans,* the first novel he thought good enough to bear his own name. He also plunged into a succession of business ventures in the search for rapid wealth, but each failed and drove him further into debt. Despite his vast production of novels and short stories, and their great popular success, he remained in debt most of his life. Pursued by creditors, ever behind in his commitments, working sometimes around the clock to fulfill contracts and satisfy editors (and consequently producing some very mediocre work), he aged prematurely, fell ill, and died shortly after marrying an aristocratic foreign admirer, the Countess Hanska, with whom he had been in correspondence for many years.

Balzac's life was spent primarily in the writing of *The Human Comedy,* a kind of super-novel made up of over ninety individual novels and designed to give a total picture of the French society in his time. Balzac's enormous energy and passion for life finally expressed themselves in an imaginary life which has probably never been equaled. "I carry a whole society in my head," said Balzac. *The Human Comedy* is peopled by over 2,000 characters, many of whom reappear from one novel to another. This great edifice is unfinished and asymmetrical, it has gaps and overlaps, but it gives an extraordinarily rich and convincing picture of France, especially Paris, in the first third of the nineteenth century. It is the picture of a society caught in frenetic movement, ruled by ambition and the lust for money and power, and headed toward chaos.

Balzac liked to compare himself to a zoologist, classifying the human species and subspecies. He gives careful attention not only to different human types but also to their environments—the places where they live and the objects they surround themselves with and define themselves by. Yet Balzac's temperament was really less scientific than visionary, even mystical: beyond the real, behind the surface of things, he sought the emotional and intellectual principles that drive men and create the human drama. Like the narrator of *Facino Cane,* he thought of himself as endowed with a "second sight" with which he penetrated into men's souls and life's secrets.

The fame of such novels as *The Fatal Skin, Eugénie Grandet, Père Goriot, Lost Illusions,* and *Cousin Bette* has often obscured the fact that Balzac was also a master of the short story, the succinct presentation of a character in a revealing instant.

Facino Cane

I was then living in a little street which you probably do not know, the rue de Lesdiguières, which begins at the rue Saint-Antoine opposite to the fountain near the place de la Bastille, and opens into the rue de la Cerisaie. Love of science had driven me to a garret, where I worked during the night, passing my days in the library of Monsieur, which was near by. I lived frugally, taking upon me the conditions of monastic life, so essential to workers. I seldom walked for pleasure as far as the boulevard Bourdon, even when the weather was fine. One sole passion drew me away from my studious habits; but even that was a form of study. I walked the streets to observe the manners and ways of the faubourg, to study its inhabitants and learn their characters. Ill-dressed as the workmen themselves, and quite as indifferent to the proprieties, there was nothing about me to put them on their guard. I mingled in their groups, watched their bargains, heard their disputes, at the hour when their day's work ended. The faculty of observation had become intuitive with me; I could enter the souls of others, while still conscious of their bodies—or rather, I grasped external details so thoroughly that my mind instantly passed beyond them; I possessed, in short, the faculty of living the life of the individual on whom I exercised my observation, and of substituting myself for him, like the dervish in the Arabian Nights who assumed the body and soul of those over whom he pronounced certain words.

Often, between eleven o'clock and midnight, when I met some workman and his wife returning home from the Ambigu-Comique,[1] I amused myself by following them from the boulevard du Pont-aux-Choux to the boulevard Beaumarchais. These worthy folks usually talked first of the piece they had just seen; then, from one thing to another, they came to their own affairs; the mother dragged her child along by the hand without paying attention to his complaints or inquiries; husband and wife counted up their gains; told what they expected to make on the morrow, and spent that sum in fancy in a dozen different ways. Then they dropped into household details, groaned over the excessive cost of potatoes, or the coldness of the winter, the increased price of fuel, and the energetic remonstrances they were forced to

[1] A popular theatre.

make to the baker. Their discussions often grew heated, and each side betrayed his and her character in picturesque language. As I listened to these persons, I imbibed their life, I felt their ragged clothing on my back, my feet walked in their broken shoes; their desires, their wants, passed into my soul, or my soul passed into theirs. It was the dream of a waking man. I grew angry, with them, against some foreman who ill-used them; against annoying customers who obliged them to call many times before they could get their money. To quit my own life, to become some other individual through the exaltation of a moral faculty, and to play this game at will, was the relaxation of my studious hours.

To what have I owed this gift? Was it second-sight? Is it one of those qualities the abuse of which leads to insanity? I have never sought to discover the causes of this power. I only know that I possess it, and use it; that is enough for me. You must know that ever since I became aware of this faculty, I have decomposed the elements of those heterogeneous masses called the People, and I have analyzed them in a manner that enables me to appraise both their good and evil qualities. I knew, before the time came to prove it, what use "*the* faubourg" would be put to—that seminary of revolution from which have emerged heroes, inventors, practically learned men, knaves, scoundrels, virtues, vices; all repressed by poverty, stifled by want, drowned in wine, worn-out by the use of strong liquors. You cannot imagine how many lost epics, how many forgotten dramas there are in this city of sorrows! how many horrible things, how many glorious things! Imagination cannot reach to a full conception of what is hidden here, in quest of which no man can go; he would be forced to descend too low to find these startling scenes of tragedy or of comedy, masterpieces to which, often, mere accident gives birth. I hardly know why I have so long refrained from telling you the following story; it is one of the many curious tales put away in a bag from which memory pulls them forth capriciously, like numbers in a lottery. I have others quite as singular buried in my mind, but you may depend upon it, they shall see the light some day.

One morning my charwoman, the wife of a laboring man, asked me to honor the wedding of her sister with my presence. To make you understand the sort of wedding it was likely to be, I must tell you that I paid forty sous a month to this poor creature, who came every morning to make my bed, clean my shoes, brush my clothes, sweep the room, and prepare my breakfast; the rest of her time was spent in turning the crank of an engine—a form of hard labor which brought her in ten sous a day. Her husband, a cabinet-maker, earned four francs; but as these parents had three children, their wages were barely enough for a decent living. I have never seen more solid honesty than that of this man and woman. For five years after I left the neighborhood, mère Vaillant always came to wish me happy returns on my birthday, bringing with her a bunch of flowers and some oranges—poor soul, who never in her life could lay by ten sous. Poverty brought us near together. I was never able to give her more than ten francs, often borrowed for the occasion. This may explain my promise to go to the wedding; I expected to revel in the happiness of these poor creatures.

The feast and the ball took place at the house of a wine-merchant in the rue de Charenton, in a large room, lighted by lamps with tin reflectors and hung with a paper that was greasy behind the wooden seats which ran round the walls. In this room were assembled eighty persons in their Sunday clothes, bedizened with ribbons and nosegays, dancing with flushed faces as if the world were coming to an end. The bride and bridegroom kissed each other to the general satisfaction, with a chorus of "Hey, hey's," and "Ha, ha's," which were significant but really less indecent than the timid glances of well-educated young girls. The whole company gave evidence of a coarse enjoyment which had something contagious in it.

However, neither the characteristics of this assembly, nor the wedding, nor anything concerning it, has to do with my story. Remember only the oddness of the setting; see the shabby room, painted red, smell the fumes of wine, hear the roars of delight, imagine yourself in *the* faubourg, among these workmen, these old men, these poor women, giving themselves up to enjoyment for one night.

The orchestra consisted of three blind men from the Quinze-Vingts;[2] the first a violin, the second a clarionet, the third a flute. The three were paid, in a lump, seven francs for the evening. At that price they were not likely to give Rossini nor Beethoven; they played what they would and as they could; and no one found fault with them, out of delicacy. Their music assaulted my tympanum so violently that after one glance at the assembled company I looked at the blind trio and was instantly moved to forgiveness when I saw their uniform. The musicians were seated in the recess of a window, and it was necessary to stand quite near them to distinguish their faces; I did not go up to them at once, but when I did so the wedding and the music became as nought, my curiosity was excited to the highest pitch, for my soul passed into the body of the player of the clarionet. The violin and the flute both had common faces, the well-known face of the blind, full of a contentious spirit, attentive and serious; but that of the clarionet presented one of those phenomena which instantly arrest the attention of artists and philosophers.

Imagine to yourself a plaster mask of Dante lighted by the ruddy glare of an oil lamp, and surmounted by a forest of silvery-white hair. The bitter and distressful expression of that magnificent head was increased by the man's blindness, for the dead eyes lived anew through thought; burning gleams

[2] The Quinze-Vingts is a hospital in Paris, founded by Louis IX (Saint-Louis) for three hundred knights whose eyes were put out by the Saracens.

were emitted from the sightless balls, produced by one incessant, solitary desire, vigorously stamped on that projecting brow, which was furrowed by wrinkles like the courses of a stone wall. The old man blew his instrument as he pleased, paying no attention to time or tune; his fingers went up or down, pressing the old stops by a mere mechanical habit; he took no pains to avoid *couacs* (to use an orchestral term for the quacking of false notes), but the dancers paid no attention to them, neither did the two acolytes of my Italian—for I felt sure he was an Italian, and so he proved. There was something grand and despotic in this old Homer who bore a forgotten or unknown Odyssey within him; a grandeur so real that it still triumphed even in its overthrow; a despotism so undying that it mastered poverty. None of the violent passions which lead men to good as well as to evil, making one a hero and another a galley-slave, were lacking in that face so nobly modelled, so lividly Italian; shaded by gray eyebrows which threw their shadow over those blind cavities, where the apparition of the light of thought made the spectator shudder, as one who sees a band of brigands armed with daggers issuing from a cavern's mouth. There was a lion in that cage of flesh, a lion who spent his useless rage against the iron bars of his prison. The conflagration of despair had died to ashes, the lava had stiffened and was cold; but furrows, convulsions, a little smoke bore witness to the violence of the eruption and the ravages of the flames. These ideas, suggested by the sight of that man, were as hot in his soul as they were cold and dead upon his face.

Between each quadrille the violin and the flute, solemnly concerned for glass and bottle, hung their instruments to a button of each shabby coat and moved their hands cautiously to a little table on which their refreshments stood; always offering a full glass to the Italian, who was unable to reach it for himself, the table being placed behind his chair. Each time that his companions paid him this attention the clarionet thanked them with a friendly nod. Their movements were all performed with the precision which is so noticeable among the pensioners of the Quinze-Vingts, and leads one almost to imagine that those blind men see. I approached the musicians to hear them talk, but when I was near them they evidently studied me and seemed aware that I was not a working-man; they grew reserved at once.

"What countryman are you, —you who play the clarionet?" I said.

"I come from Venice," answered the blind man with a slight Italian accent.

"Were you born blind or did you become so?"

"I became so," he answered, quickly, "a cursed paralysis of the retina."

"Venice is a beautiful city; I have always longed to go there."

The old man's face lighted up, his wrinkles quivered, and he showed signs of strong emotion.

"If I went with you you would not lose your time," he said, significantly.

"Don't talk to him of Venice," said the violin. "If you do, the doge will be unmanageable; and he has got two bottles already under his waistcoat, the prince!"

"Come, play away, père Canet!" cried the flute.

All three began to play; but all the time they were executing four quadrilles the Venetian seemed to be scenting me, as though he guessed the sudden and extreme interest I felt in him. His countenance lost its chilling aspect of distress; something like hope enlivened his features and slid like a blue flame among their wrinkles; he smiled and wiped his brow, that bold and awful brow, and even assumed the gayety of a man who mounts a hobby.

"How old are you?" I asked him.

"Eighty-two."

"When did you become blind?"

"Nearly fifty years ago," he replied, in a tone that showed me his grief was not caused by the loss of sight only, but by the loss of some great power of which he had been robbed.

"Why do they call you doge?" I asked.

"Oh! that is a joke," he replied. "I am a patrician of Venice, and might have been a doge like any other."

"What is your name?"

"Here," he said, "they call me père Canet. My name is always written thus on the registers; but in Italy I am Marco Facino Cane, Principe di Varese."

"What! you are descended from the famous captain, Facino Cane, whose conquests passed to the Duke of Milan?"

"*È vero,*" he replied. "At that time Cane's son took refuge in Venice to escape being killed by the Visconti, and had himself inscribed on the *Libro d'oro*. But now neither Cane nor Golden Book remain of all that past!" and he made a dreadful gesture of extinct patriotism and of hatred for all things human.

"But if you were senator of Venice you ought to be rich; how is it you have lost your wealth?"

At this question he raised his head, with a tragic movement, as if to gaze fixedly at me, and replied—

"Through misfortune."

He no longer thought of drinking, and refused with his hand a glass which the old flute was offering him at this moment; then he bowed his head.

These details were not of a nature to extinguish my curiosity. During the quadrille which the three machines now played, I gazed at the old Venetian noble with the excited feelings natural to a young man of twenty. I saw Venice and the Adriatic; I beheld the ruined city in that ruined face; I floated amid those palaces so dear to their inhabitants; I passed from the

Rialto to the Salute, from the riva degli Schiavoni to the Lido; then back to the marvellous San Marco, so original and so sublime; I looked at the windows of the Casa d'Oro, each with its different tracery; I contemplated, as I glided past, those old *palazzi* so rich in marbles, and all those many wonders with which the scholar sympathizes, the more because he colors them with knowledge, and is conscious that their present reality is powerless to depoetize his dream. In fancy I reviewed the life of this descendant of the famous *condottiere;* I looked for traces of his misfortunes and for the causes of the physical and moral degradation which rendered his sudden gleam of greatness and revived nobility more striking still. Our thoughts were no doubt in common, his and mine; for I believe that blindness renders mental communication far more rapid by preventing the attention from frittering itself away on outside objects. The proof of our sympathetic thought was not long in coming. Facino Cane ceased playing, rose, came up to me and said, "Let us go!" in a tone and manner which struck me like an electric shock. I gave him my arm, and we went out.

When we reached the street he said: "Take me to Venice! will you take me there? will you have faith in me? If you will, you shall be richer than the ten richest merchants in Amsterdam or London; richer than the Rothschilds; rich with all the riches of the Arabian Nights."

I thought him mad; but there was a power in his voice that compelled my obedience. I allowed him to guide me, and he proceeded toward the fosses of Belleville as if he had eyes to see. He seated himself on a stone in a very solitary spot where the bridge by which the canal Saint-Martin now communicates with the Seine was subsequently built. I sat upon another stone directly facing the old man, whose white hairs glittered like silver threads in the effulgence of the moon. The silence about us, scarcely broken by the rumbling noises of the distant boulevard, the clearness of the night, all contributed to the weird aspect of the scene.

"You talk of millions to a young man," I said, "and you think he would hesitate to face a thousand evils to obtain them! Are you not jesting with me?"

"May I die without confession," he said vehemently, "if what I tell you is not true. I was twenty years old, as you are now; I was rich, I was handsome, I was noble. I began with the first madness, love. I loved as men do not love in these days—enough to hide in a coffer and risk a poignard without receiving anything more than the promise of a kiss. To die for *her* seemed to me to live a lifetime. In 1760 I loved a Vendramini, a girl of eighteen, married to a Sagredo, one of the richest senators, a man of thirty, frantically in love with his wife. My mistress and I were as innocent as two cherubim when the *sposo* surprised us talking of love; I was unarmed, his sword missed me; I sprang at his throat and strangled him with both hands as you wring the neck of a chicken. I wanted to fly with Bianca, but she would not go with me. Such are women! I went alone; I was condemned; my property confiscated to my heirs; but I carried off my diamonds, five Titians rolled up, and all my gold. I went to Milan, where I was not molested; my affair was of no interest to the State.

"Allow me a little remark before continuing my story," he said, after a pause. "Whether a woman's fancies affect the child she conceives and bears I know not, but it is certain that my mother had a passion for gold during her pregnancy. I have a monomania for it, the gratification of which is so essential to my life that all through my vicissitudes I am never without gold in my possession; I handle it, finger it, incessantly; when I was young I wore jewelry, and I always carried two or three hundred ducats about me."

So saying, he drew two ducats from his pocket and showed them to me.

"I *feel* the presence of gold. Though blind, I can always stop before a jeweller's window. That passion was my ruin; I became a gambler for the sake of gold. I was not a swindler, but I was swindled, and was ruined. When I had no longer any money I was seized with a desperate desire to see Bianca. I returned secretly to Venice; I found her. I was happy for six months, hidden in her house and fed by her. I thought with delight that I should end my days in that way. But Bianca was sought in marriage by the Proveditore. He suspected a rival (in Italy they scent rivals); he watched us, and surprised us, the scoundrel! Fancy what a struggle it was! But I did not kill him; I only wounded him severely. That affair destroyed my happiness. From that day forth I never found a second Bianca. I have enjoyed great pleasures; I lived at the court of Louis XV among the most celebrated women; but nowhere have I found the noble qualities, the grace, the love of my dear Venetian lady. The Proveditore had his people within call; the palace was surrounded, invaded. I defended myself, that I might die before Bianca's eyes. Formerly she would not fly with me; now, after six months' happiness, she desired to die my death, and received several wounds. A huge mantle was thrown over me, and I was rolled in it, carried to a gondola, and thrown into a dungeon in the vaults of the ducal palace. I was twenty-two years old, and I held the hilt of my broken sword so firmly that to get it from me they would have had to cut off my wrist. By remarkable luck—or rather, inspired by a sense of precaution, I hid that bit of iron in a corner of the vault, thinking it might some day help me. I was nursed and cared for. My wounds were not mortal. At twenty-two we can live through everything. Doubtless I was to die decapitated. I pretended continued illness to gain time. I felt sure I was in a dungeon adjoining the canal. My plan was to escape by tunnelling the wall and swimming across the canal, at the risk of being drowned. Here is the reasoning on which I rested my hopes: each time the jailer opened the door to bring my food I read the indications written on the walls, such as, 'Palace side,' 'Canal side,' 'Subterranean side,' and I came at last to conceive a plan of escape connected with the existing state of the ducal palace, which has never been finished. With the genius that the hope of freedom inspires, and by feeling with my fingers along the face of a stone, I contrived to decipher an Arabic inscription by which the inscriber informed his successors that he had loosened two stones in the lower course and had tunnelled eleven feet under ground. To continue his work it was necessary to spread the fragments of stone and mortar over the floor of the dungeon itself. Even if the jailers or the inquisitors had not been, as they were, so satisfied with the construction of the massive building that no watch was kept on the interior, it would always have been easy to raise the level of the soil gradually because of the position of the cells, which were at the bottom of a flight of steps. This immense toil had all been wasted, at least for the man who had undertaken it, for its unfinished condition was a proof of his death. His devoted labor would be lost forever unless some succeeding prisoner should have a knowledge of Arabic. Fortunately, I had studied the oriental languages in the Armenian convent. A sentence inscribed on the back of the stone told the fate of the unfortunate man, who died a victim to his enormous wealth, which Venetian greed had coveted and seized.

"It took me a month," continued the old man, who had paused to consider his words, "before I came to any result. While I worked, and during the moments when overcome by fatigue I rested, I could hear the sound of gold, I saw gold glittering before me, I was dazzled by the light of diamonds. Wait, wait! I have more to tell. One night my blunted steel struck wood. I sharpened that fragment of a sword and cut a hole in the wood. To do this work I wriggled like a snake on my belly; I even went naked to work, as the moles do, with my hands in front of me, propelling my body by the stones. The night but one before I was to be taken up for judgment I resolved on a final effort. My broken blade made a hole in the wood and touched nothing beyond it. Imagine my astonishment at what I saw when I applied an eye to the hole. I found myself at the roof of a vault where the feeble glimmer of a light showed me heaps of gold. The doge and one of the Ten were in this vault; I heard their voices, and what they said informed me that here was the secret treasure of the Republic, the offerings of the doges, the reservation of spoils, called the 'perquisite of Venice,' which was levied on the proceeds of the expeditions. I was saved! When the jailer came I proposed to him to assist my escape and to fly with me, carrying all that we could possibly take with us. He agreed; he did not even hesitate. A vessel was just sailing for the Levant; all precautions were taken. Bianca, to whom my accomplice went, approved my plans. Not to excite suspicion, she was to follow and rejoin me in Smyrna. The next night we enlarged the hole and climbed down upon the treasure.

"What a night! what a night!" cried the old man, quivering at the recollection. "I saw four huge tuns overflowing with gold. In the adjoining vault silver was amassed in two great heaps, leaving a path between them to cross the room, which they filled to the height of six feet. I thought the gaoler would have gone mad; he sang, he danced, he laughed, he jumped upon the gold. I threatened to strangle him if he wasted time, or continued to make a noise. In his delirium he did not see a table on which the precious stones were piled. I sprang to them and filled my sailor jacket and the pockets of my trousers. Good God! I could not take a third of the dazzling heap. Under that table were bars of gold. I persuaded my companion to fill as many sacks with gold as we were able to carry; pointing out to him that gold could not lead to our discovery in a foreign land; 'whereas,' I said, 'jewels and precious stones would certainly be recognized.' But however great our longing, we could take only two thousand pounds of gold, and even they necessitated six trips across the prison to the gondola. The sentinel at the water-gate was in our pay, bought by ten pounds of gold. As for the gondoliers, they thought they were employed for the Republic. At break of day we started. When fairly at sea and I could think of what had happened—when I recalled my sensations and saw again in my mind's eye that vast treasury where, according to my valuation, I had been forced to leave behind me thirty millions of silver, twenty millions of gold, and many millions in diamonds, pearls, and rubies—I became, as it were, insane. The fever of gold was upon me.

"Well," he continued, after a moment's silence, "we landed at Smyrna, and immediately reembarked for France. As we boarded the French vessel God was so good as to relieve me of my accomplice. At the moment, I did not reflect on the consequences of this accident, in which I then rejoiced heartily. We were so completely enervated with toil and emotion that we sat partly stupefied, without a word to each other, waiting for perfect safety before we dared to enjoy our good fortune at our ease. It is not surprising that the fellow's head turned giddy— You will see how God punished me. I thought I was safe and happy after selling two-thirds of my diamonds in London and Amsterdam, and putting my gold into commercial property. I lived hidden in Madrid for five years; then, in 1770, I came to Paris under a Spanish name, and led a brilliant life. Bianca was dead. In the midst of my pleasures, in the full enjoyment of millions, I was struck blind. No doubt this affliction was originally caused by living in a dungeon and working through the stone wall—unless indeed my faculty for seeing gold entailed an abuse of visual power which predestined me to lose my sight. At this particular time I was in love with a woman whom I thought of marrying. I had told her the secret of my name; she herself belonged to a powerful family, and I hoped much from the favor shown to me by Louis XV. I placed great confidence in this woman, who was a friend of Madame du Barry; she advised me to consult an oculist in London. After a stay of some months in that city, she one day abandoned me in Hyde Park, robbing me of all my property and leaving me helpless; for, compelled as I was to hide my name in dread of Venetian vengeance, I could ask succor from no one. I feared Venice. My infirmity was worked upon to my ruin by spies whom that woman placed about me. I will spare you a series of adventures worthy of Gil Blas. Your Revolution took place. I was forced to enter the Quinze-Vingts, where the woman placed me after keeping me two years in a madhouse, declaring that I was insane. I have never been able to kill her, for I could not see her, and I was too poor to buy another man's arm. If, before losing Benedetto Carpi, the jailer, I had inquired from him the exact position of my dungeon, I might have gone to Venice when the Republic was abolished by Napoleon and rediscovered the treasure vault— But now, hear me! in spite of my blindness, let us go to Venice! I can find the door of my dungeon; I can see gold through the thickest wall; I can feel it in the water under which it is sunk! The events which have overthrown the power of Venice are such that the secret of this treasure must have died with Vendramino, Bianca's brother, a doge who, I always hoped, would have made my peace with the Ten. I wrote letters to the First Consul, I proposed a bargain to the Emperor of Austria—they both treated me as a lunatic. Come! let us go to Venice! We shall start beggars and come back with millions; I will recover my estates, and you shall be my heir; you shall be Principe di Varese!"

Bewildered by this tale, which had all the magnitude of a poem to my imagination, and by the aspect of that white head against the black waters that surrounded the Bastille—still waters like those of the canals of Venice—I could not answer. Facino Cane thought, no doubt, that I judged him, as others did, with contemptuous pity; he made a gesture eloquent with the whole philosophy of despair. His narrative had recalled to his mind the happy days of Venice; he seized his clarionet and sadly played a Venetian air, a *barcarole* which revived his his early gift, the musical gift of a patrician in love. It was, as it were, the *Super flumina Babylonis*. Tears filled my eyes. If some belated pedestrian had passed along the boulevard Bourdon he would have stopped to listen to this exile's prayer, this last regret for a lost name, with which was mingled the memory of Bianca. But gold recovered its ascendency; the fatal passion stamped out the gleam of youth and love.

"I see that treasure everywhere," he cried, "at all times, waking or asleep; I walk in the midst of it; the diamonds sparkle. I am not so blind as you fancy; gold and diamonds illumine my night — the night of the last Facino Cane, for my title passes to the Memmi. My God! the murderer's punishment began too soon! *Ave Maria*—"

He recited a few prayers which I could not hear.

"We will go to Venice," I said, as he rose.

"I have found my helper at last!" he cried, his face flaming. I led him back on my arm; he pressed my hand at the gates of the Quinze-Vingts as some of the wedding party passed noisily by us.

"Shall we start tomorrow?" he said.

"As soon as we get money enough."

"But we can go on foot; we will beg our way—I am robust, and gold, the sight of gold before me makes me young."

Facino Cane died during that winter after a lingering illness of two months. The poor old man had taken cold.

Nikolai Gogol

The Diary of a Madman

TRANSLATED BY ANDREW R. MAC ANDREW

Nikolai Gogol (1809–1852)

NIKOLAI GOGOL, THE SON OF A SMALL LANDOWNER IN THE Russian Ukraine, was educated in a boarding school in the Ukrainian town of Niezhin. At the age of nineteen he left for the imperial capital of St. Petersburg, where he entered government service and worked in various positions for about fifteen months. He taught school for a while and planned a volume on medieval history, which was never written but which brought him a post at the University of St. Petersburg. During this period he also wrote fiction, and in 1831–32 published two volumes of short stories based on Ukrainian folk tales, *Evenings on a Farm in Dikanka,* which were well received. Other tales, including "The Diary of a Madman," "The Nose," the first version of *Taras Bulba,* and early work on "The Overcoat" date from this most productive period of Gogol's life.

In 1836 his play *The Inspector General* was produced and aroused much controversy, which Gogol tended to regard as general hostility. He left Russia for Germany, Switzerland, Paris, and chiefly Rome, returning permanently to Russia only twelve years later. His major work, the novel *Dead Souls,* was completed during this period of voluntary exile. Published in Russia in 1842, it was an immediate success. During the next ten years, Gogol labored over a sequel to *Dead Souls,* making fresh starts, revising, but never achieving a satisfactory result. He burned the manuscript ten days before his death.

Gogol has often been considered the founder of Russian realism. A political and social liberal, he portrayed compassionately the fate of the wretched. There is some truth in this view, but we may be more impressed by the Romantic temper of his realism, his extraordinary fantasy, his use of the grotesque, the weird, and the unbalanced to create a rich and feverish inner life for his petty, even insignificant, characters. Gogol was a man possessed by a sense of destiny; he felt he had a messianic mission to lead his countrymen to moral regeneration. At the same time, this feeling was undermined by guilt and doubts, a sense of failure and great unhappiness. Some of this grandiose ambition, and the accompanying doubts, can be felt in the sublimely mad visions of the miserable bureaucrat who bares his soul in "The Diary of a Madman."

The Diary of a Madman

October 3

An extraordinary thing happened today. I got up rather late, and when Marva brought my boots, I asked her the time. Hearing that ten had struck quite a while before, I dressed in a hurry. I must say I'd as soon have skipped the office altogether, knowing the sour look the Chief of my Division would give me. For a long time now he has been telling me: "How come, my man, you're always in such a muddle? Sometimes you dart around like a house on fire, and get your work in such a tangle the Devil himself couldn't put it straight; you're likely to start a new heading with a small letter and give no date or reference number." The vicious old crane! He must envy me for sitting in the Director's room and sharpening his quills. So I wouldn't have gone to the office if not in hopes of seeing the cashier and trying to get even a small advance on my salary out of the Jew. What a creature he is! The Last Judgment will come before you'll get a month's pay out of him in advance. Even if there's a dire emergency, you can beg till something bursts inside you; he won't give in, the hoary monster. Yet at home his own cook slaps him around. Everyone knows that. I see no advantage in working in our department. No side benefits whatever. It's not like working, say, for the City Administration or in the Justice Department. There you may see someone nesting in a corner and scribbling away. He may be wearing a shabby coat and have a snout that you'd want to spit at. But then, just take a look at the summer house he rents! And don't even think of offering him a gilt china cup: this, he'd say, may be all right for a doctor. But he—he must have a pair of horses maybe, or a carriage, or a beaver fur—300 rubles' worth or so. And he looks so quiet and sounds so deferential and polite: "Would you," he'll say, "be so kind as to lend me your penknife to sharpen my quill, if you please." But he'll strip a petitioner naked, except perhaps for his shirt. On the other hand, though, to work in our department carries more prestige. The people of the City Administration have never dreamt of such cleanliness. Then we have red mahogany tables and our superiors always address us politely. Yes, if it weren't for the prestige, I confess I'd have left the department long ago.

I put on my old overcoat and, as it was pouring rain, took my umbrella.

The streets were quite deserted except for some peasant women, their skirts thrown over their heads, a few merchants under umbrellas, and a coachman here and there. As for decent people there was only our kind, the civil-service clerk, squelching along. I saw him at a street crossing. And as soon as I saw him I said to myself: "You're not on your way to the office, my man. You're after that one trotting ahead over there and it's her legs you're staring at." What a rogue your civil servant is! When it comes to such matters, he can take on an army officer any day. He'll try to pick up anything under a bonnet. I was passing by a store, thinking about all this, when a carriage stopped in front of it. I recognized it at once: it belonged to the Director of our Department, himself. But, I thought, he cannot possibly need anything here—it must be his daughter. I pressed myself against the wall. The footman opened the carriage door and she fluttered out like a little bird. Ah, how she looked around, first right, then left, how her eyes and eyebrows flashed past me! . . . Oh God, I'm lost, lost forever. And why did she have to drive out in the pouring rain? Try and deny after that, that women have a passion for clothing. She did not recognize me. Besides, I was trying to hide myself; my coat was quite stained and out of fashion too. Nowadays, they are wearing long collars on their coats while I had two very short ones, one on top of the other. Her lap dog was too slow to get into the store while the door was open and had to stay in the street. I know this little dog. She's called Madgie. Then, a minute or so later, I heard a thin little voice: "Hello, Madgie." I'll be damned! Who's that talking? I turned around and saw two ladies walking under their umbrellas: one old, the other young and pretty. But they had already passed when I heard again, just next to me: "You ought to be ashamed, Madgie!" What on earth was going on? I saw Madgie and a dog that had been following the two ladies sniffing at one another. "Maybe I'm drunk," I said to myself, "but it's not likely. It doesn't happen to me very often." "No, Fidele, you're wrong." With my own eyes I saw Madgie forming the words, "I was, bow-wow, I was, bow-ow-ow, very sick." Talk about a lap dog! I must say I was quite surprised to hear her talking. Later, however, when I had properly sized up the situation, I was no longer surprised. As a matter of fact, the world has seen many similar occurrences before. I've heard that, in England, a fish broke surface and uttered a couple of words in such an outlandish language that scholars have been trying to work out their meaning for three years—so far in vain. Then, too, I read in the newspapers about two cows who went into a store and asked for a pound of tea. But I'll confess that I was much more bewildered when Madgie said: "I *did* write you, Fidele. Perhaps Fido didn't give you my letter." Now, I'd be willing to forfeit a month's pay if I've ever heard of a dog that could write. Only a gentleman can write correctly anyway. Of course, one finds some scribbling shopkeepers—even serfs—but that sort of writing is mostly mechanical; no commas, periods, or spelling. So I was surprised. I'll confess that recently I have been seeing and hearing things that no one else has ever seen or heard. "Let's," I said to myself, "follow this little dog and find out who she is and what her thoughts are." I opened my umbrella and followed the ladies. We crossed Pea Street, from there on to Tradesman's Avenue, turned into Carpenter's Lane, and finally stopped before a large building near Cuckoo Bridge. "I know this house," I said to myself, "it's the Zverkov house." What a house! Who isn't to be found there! There are so many cooks, so many Poles! And it teems with my fellow civil servants; they sit there on top of one another, like dogs. I have a friend there who can play the trumpet quite well. The ladies went up to the fifth floor. "Fine," I thought, "I won't go in now. I'll make a note of the place and wait for the first opportunity."

October 4

Today is Wednesday and that's why I was in our Director's study at his home. I purposely came in early, settled down and sharpened all the quills. Our Director must be a very brilliant man. His study is crammed with bookcases. I looked at some of the titles: such erudition all over the place—cuts an ordinary person off completely; they're all in French or German. And just look into his face, good gracious! What a lot of importance shines in his eyes! I've never heard him utter an unnecessary word. Except, perhaps, when one hands him some documents, he may ask: "How's the weather outside?" "It's quite damp, sir," Yes, he's different from our kind. A public figure! Nevertheless, I feel that he has taken a special liking to me. If only his daughter . . . Ah, what a rogue I am! Never mind, never mind . . . Quiet! . . . I was reading the *Bee*. Aren't the French a stupid race? Whatever can they be driving at? I'd like to take them all and give each one of them a good thrashing. In the same journal I also read a very nice description of a ball by a landowner from Kursk. Kursk landowners certainly write well. . . . Whereupon I noticed that it was striking twelve-thirty and our Director still hadn't left his bedroom. But then, around one-thirty, a thing happened that no pen can adequately describe. The door opened; I thought it was the Director and jumped up from my desk holding the documents in my hand; but it was her, in person! Holy Fathers, the way she was dressed! Her dress was white, all fluffy, like a swan, and when she looked at me, I swear it was like the sun! She nodded to me and said: "Hasn't Papa been in here?" What a voice! A canary, an absolute canary. "Ma'am," I was on the point of saying, "don't have me put to death. But if you do decide that I must die, let it be by your own aristocratic little hand." But my tongue would not obey me and I only muttered, "No, ma'am." Her glance slid from me to the books and she dropped her handkerchief. I rushed like mad, slipped on the blasted parquet and almost smashed my nose. But somehow

I recovered my balance and picked it up. Holy Saints, what a hanky! Such fine, delicate linen, and amber, sheer amber. It exuded aristocracy. She said, "Thank you" and smiled, but so faintly that her divine lips hardly moved, and then she left. I remained seated there and after another hour, a footman came in and told me: "You may go home, the master has gone out." The flunky is the one thing I cannot stand. They're always sprawled out in the entrance hall, not even bothering to acknowledge my existence with a little nod. Once, one of those lumps actually offered me snuff, and without even getting up. Don't you know, you stupid flunky, that I am a civil servant and that I come from a respectable family? Still, I picked up my hat and pulled on my overcoat unaided since those gents wouldn't think of helping you, and left. At home, I lay on my bed most of the time. Then I copied an excellent poem:

Without you one hour crept
  Slowly like a year.
"Is my life worth while," I wept,
  "When you are not near?"

Sounds like Pushkin.[1] In the evening, I put on my overcoat and walked over to the Director's house and waited by the gate for quite a while to see whether she wouldn't come out and get into her carriage. But she didn't.

November 6

Something has got into the Chief of my Division. When I arrived at the office he called me and began as follows: "Now then, tell me. What's the matter with you?" "What do you mean? Nothing," I said. "Come, try to understand; aren't you over forty? Time to be a bit wiser. What do you fancy you are? Don't imagine I can't see what you're up to. I know you're trailing after the Director's daughter. Just look at yourself—what are you? Just nothing. You haven't a penny to your name. Look in the mirror. How can you even think of such things?" The hell with him! Just because he's got a face like a druggist's bottle and that quiff of hair on his head all curled and pomaded, and because he holds his head up in the air like that, he thinks he can get away with anything. I see through his indignation. He's envious; perhaps he's noticed the marks of favor bestowed upon me. A lot I care what he says. So he's a Divisional Chief, so what! So he hangs out his gold watch chain and has custom-made boots at thirty rubles. Let him be damned. Perhaps he imagines I had a shopkeeper or a tailor for a father. I'm a gentleman! And I can be promoted too. I'm only forty-two, an age

[1] Alexander Pushkin (1799–1837), famous Russian poet and dramatist.

when one's career is really just beginning. Wait, my friend, I'll go higher than you yet, and, God willing, very, very much higher. Then I'll have a social position beyond your dreams. Do you imagine you're the only one to have dignity? Give me a fashionable new coat, let me wear a tie like yours, and you won't be worthy to shine my shoes. My lack of means—that's the only trouble.

November 8

Went to the theater. The play was about the Russian fool Filatka. Laughed a lot. They had a vaudeville show as well, full of amusing verses lampooning lawyers, so outspoken that I wondered how it got past the censor; as to the merchants, it says plainly that they swindle the people, that their sons wallow in debauchery and elbow their way into society. There was also an amusing couplet which complained about the way newspapermen criticize everything and asked the audience for protection from them. Playwrights write very amusing plays nowadays. I love going to the theater. As soon as I get hold of a few pennies, I can't help myself, I go. But civil servants are such swine . . . you won't catch clods like them going to the theater, not even if they're given free tickets. One actress sang really well. . . . It made me think of . . . What a rogue I am! Never mind, never mind . . . silence!

November 9

Left for the office at eight. The Divisional Chief pretended he hadn't noticed me come in. And I also acted as though nothing had happened between us. I went through the papers and sorted them out. Left at four. On the way home, passed by the Director's house but didn't see anyone. After dinner, mostly lay on my bed.

Today, I sat in the Director's study and sharpened twenty-three quills for him, and four quills for . . . oh-oh . . . her. He likes to have as many quills to hand as possible. My, how brainy he must be! Usually he doesn't say much but I guess he must be weighing everything in that head of his. I'd like to know what he has on his mind most of the time, what's cooking up there. I'd like to have a closer look at these people, how they live, with all their subtle innuendoes and courtly jokes; I wish I knew how they behave and what they do among themselves. I've often tried to engage the Director in conversation but I'm damned if it's ever come off. I've managed to say it's warm or cold outside and that is absolutely as far as I've got. One day I'd like just to step into their drawing room. The door is ajar sometimes and from there I can see another door, leading to another room. That drawing room! You should see how it's decorated. All those mirrors and fine pieces of porcelain. I'd also like to see the part where her rooms are. That's where I'd really like to go! I'd like to peep into her boudoir, and see all those little jars and bottles of hers standing there amidst the sort of flowers one doesn't even dare breathe on; to have a glimpse at the dress she has thrown off, lying there looking more like air than a dress. It would be wonderful to glance into her bedroom. . . . Miracles must happen there. It's a paradise surpassing the heavenly one. What wouldn't I give to see the little stool upon which her delicate foot descends when she gets out of bed and watch how an incredibly fine, immaculate stocking is pulled up her leg. . . . Oh, the roguish thoughts! . . . Never mind . . . never mind . . . silence!

But today something suddenly became clear to me when I recalled the conversation between the two dogs I'd overheard on Nevsky Avenue. Fine, I said to myself, now I'll find out everything. I must get hold of the letters exchanged between those nasty mutts. I'm sure to find out something. Now I'll confess that, at one point, I almost called Madgie and said to her: "Listen, Madgie, we are alone now. If you wish, I'll even lock the door so that no one'll see us. Tell me everything you know about your mistress: what she's like and all that. And don't worry, I swear I'll not repeat a thing to anyone." But the sly little mutt just sort of shrank into herself, put her tail between her legs, and left the room in silence, as though she hadn't heard a thing. For a long time I've suspected that dogs are much more intelligent than men; I was even certain that they could speak and simply chose not to out of a peculiar stubbornness. A dog is an extraordinary politician and notices everything, every step a human takes. Still, whatever happens, tomorrow I'll go to the Zverkov house and question Fidele and, if possible, I'll lay my hand on Madgie's letters to her.

November 12

At 2:00 P.M. I went out determined to find Fidele and question her. I can't stand the smell of cabbage which comes pouring out of all the greengrocers along Tradesman's Avenue. This, and the infernal stench from under the gates of every house, sent me scurrying, holding my nose. And all the soot and smoke that they let pour out of the vile workshops make it a quite unsuitable place for a person of breeding to take a stroll. When I reached the sixth floor and rang the bell, out came a girl with little freckles and not too bad-looking at that. I recognized her at once. She was the one I had seen walking with the old woman. She blushed a little and I immediately saw through her: what you need, my dear, is a husband. "What do you want?" she asked. "I want to have a talk with your doggie."

The girl was stupid. I could see from the start how stupid she was! At that moment the mutt ran in yapping furiously and as I was trying to grab her, the repulsive creature almost caught my nose between her teeth. But then I saw her basket in the corner—which was just what I was looking for! I went over to it and felt under the straw and, to my great joy, I found a small bundle of papers. Seeing what I was doing, the nasty little cur first took a bite out of my calf; then, when upon further sniffing she found that I had taken her letters, she began whining and making up to me, but I told her, "Oh no, my dear. See you later!" And off I went. I believe the girl mistook me for a madman—she seemed very frightened indeed.

Once home, I wanted to get down to work immediately to have those letters sorted before dark, since I can't see too well by candlelight. But for some reason Marva decided to scrub the floor just then. Those stupid Finns always succumb to their obsession for cleanliness at the worst moments. So I went out for a walk to think it all over. Now, finally, I'll find out everything about these intrigues and plots; I'll understand all the little wheels and springs and get to the bottom of the matter. These letters will explain. Dogs are a clever race. They know all about intrigue and so it's all bound to be in their letters: all there is to know about the Director's character and actions. And she, she too is sure to be mentioned . . . but never mind that . . . silence! I came home toward evening. Most of the time, I lay on my bed.

November 13

Let's see now. This letter looks quite legible, though there *is* something canine about the handwriting:

> Dear Fidele, I still find it difficult to get accustomed to the commonness of your name. Couldn't they find a better one for you? Fidele, like Rose, is very ordinary, but all that's beside the point. I'm very glad we have decided to write to each other.

The spelling is very good. It's even punctuated correctly. This is considerably better than our Divisional Chief can do, although he claims to have gone to some university or other. Let's see further on:

> I believe that sharing feelings and impressions with another is one of the main blessings in life. . . .

Hm! The thought is stolen from a work translated from the German. The author's name escapes me now.

> I speak from experience although I've never been much further than the gates of our house. But then, isn't my life full of blessings? My young mistress, whom her papa calls Sophie, is crazy about me.

Ouch! Never mind, never mind. Silence!

> Papa often pets me too. I drink tea and coffee with cream. I must tell you, my dear, that I am not in the least tempted by the half-gnawed bones which our Fido chews on in the kitchen. I only like the bones of game and, even then, only if the marrow hasn't been sucked out by someone else. A mixture of sauces is nice as long as they contain no capers or vegetables. What I hate is people who give dogs the little pellets they knead out of bread. Some person sitting at the table, who has previously touched all sorts of filthy things, begins to knead a piece of bread with those same hands, then calls you and thrusts the pellet into your mouth. It is awkward somehow to refuse and, disgusted, you eat it up. . . .

What's that all about? What rubbish! As though there weren't more interesting things to write about. Let's see the next page. There may be something less stupid.

> Now, I'll tell you with pleasure what goes on in this household. I have mentioned the main character, whom Sophie calls Papa. He's a very strange man. . . .

At last! I knew they had very shrewd judgment, whatever the subject. Let's see what Papa's like.

> . . . a very strange man. He's usually silent. He speaks very little, but a week ago he never stopped saying to himself: Will I get it or not? Once he even asked me: What do you say, Madgie, will I get it or won't I? I could make no sense out of it so I smelled his shoe and left the room. Then, a week later, Papa came home overjoyed. All that morning formally dressed people came and congratulated him. At dinner Papa was gayer than I'd ever seen him before, and after dinner, he picked me up and held me level with his chest, saying: Look, Madgie, what's this? I saw some sort of a ribbon. I sniffed at it but it had no fragrance whatever. Finally, discreetly, I gave it a lick: slightly salty.

Hm. The mutt really goes too far . . . she needs a good whipping . . . So he is that vain is he? I must take it into account.

> Good-bye, my dear, I must run along . . . blah-blah-blah-blah . . . will finish this letter tomorrow. Hello, I am back with you. Today my mistress, Sophie . . .

Aha! Let's see what she says about Sophie. I really *am* a rogue! But never mind, never mind. Let's go on.

> . . . my mistress, Sophie, was in a terrific to-do. She was getting ready for a ball and I intended to take advantage of her absence and write to you. Sophie is always very happy when she's about to leave for a ball but is always very irritable while she's getting dressed for it. You know, my dear, I personally can see no pleasure in going to a ball. Sophie usually returns home from balls at 6 A.M., and I can tell by her pale and emaciated features that the poor thing hasn't been given a bite to eat. I confess I could never lead such a life. If I had to go without game in sauce or chicken wing stews, I don't know what would become of me. A sauce is not at all bad with porridge. But nothing can make carrots, turnips, and artichokes palatable. . . .

The style is very jerky. You can see that it's not written by a man. She starts off all right and then lapses into dogginess. Let's see another letter. Looks rather long . . . hm . . . no date . . . .

> Oh, my dear, how strongly I feel the approach of spring. My heart beats as though it were waiting for something. In my ears, there's a constant buzz. Very often I listen so intently behind doors that I raise my front paw. And, confidentially, I have plenty of suitors. I often sit by the window and watch them. If only you could see some of them, they're so ugly. There is a horrible mongrel with stupidity written all over him, who swaggers along the street and imagines he is a person of breeding and that everyone is bound to admire him. I paid no attention to him, as though I hadn't even noticed him. Then you should have seen the terrifying Great Dane that stopped in front of my window! If that one stood up on his hind legs, which, incidentally, the clod is incapable of doing, he would be a head taller than Sophie's Papa, who's quite tall himself and fat besides. Moreover, the lump seems to be very arrogant. I growled at him but it didn't put him off in the least. He just hung his tongue out, drooped his huge ears, and kept staring at my window, the oaf! But, my dear, you don't really imagine, do you, that my heart is indifferent to all the hopefuls? . . . You should have seen the dashing young lover that came jumping over the fence into our courtyard. His name is Treasure and he has such a nice face. . . .

Ah, damn it all! What rubbish! How much of her letters is she going to fill with such stupid stuff? I'm after *people,* not dogs! I need spiritual food and I am served these inanities. . . . Let's skip a page, perhaps we'll find something more interesting. . . .

> . . . Sophie was sitting at the table sewing something. I was looking out of the window; I like to watch people in the street. Suddenly the manservant came in and announced someone. "Show him in!" Sophie said. She hugged me hard and murmured, "Oh Madgie, darling, if you only knew who that is. He's a Guards officer, his hair is black and his eyes are so dark and so light at the same time . . . like fire." And Sophie rushed out. A minute later a young officer with black side whiskers appeared. He went to the mirror and smoothed his hair; then he looked around the room. I growled a little and settled down by my window. Soon Sophie came back, greeted him gaily, while I pretended to be busy looking out of the window. In fact, however, I turned my head sideways a little, so that I could catch what they said. You cannot imagine, Fidele dear, the silliness of that conversation. They spoke about some lady who, during a dance, kept doing a certain step instead of the one she was expected to do, then about somebody called Bobov, who looked like a stork and almost fell over, then about one Lidina, who thought she had blue eyes when they were really green, and so on and on. Oh no, I said to myself, this officer doesn't compare to Treasure. Heavens, what a difference! To start with, the officer has a wide face, quite bald except for his side whiskers which, in fact, look like a black kerchief tied around it, whereas Treasure's face is narrow and fine and he has a sweet white patch on his brow. Treasure's waist is incomparably slenderer than the officer's, and his eyes, his gestures, and his ways are vastly superior. Really, a tremendous difference! I wonder what she finds in her officer. What on earth can she admire in him? . . .

Yes, here I tend to agree. Something seems wrong. It is quite unbelievable that this officer should have swept her off her feet. Let's see:

> If she likes the officer, I think she'll soon be liking the civil-service clerk who sits in Papa's study. That one, my dear, is a real scarecrow. He looks a bit like a turtle caught in a bag. . . .

Which clerk can that be? . . .

> He has a funny name and he's always sitting sharpening quills. The hair on his head is like straw. Papa sends him on errands like a servant. . . .

The filthy cur seems to be trying to get its own back! Why is my hair like straw?

Sophie can hardly control her laughter when she sees him.

You wretched, lying dog! What a filthy, poisonous tongue! As if I didn't know it's all your jealousy. I know whose tricks these are. I recognize the hand of the Divisional Chief here. For some reason, that man has sworn undying hatred for me and he is trying to harm me, to harm me every minute of the day and night. Still, let's see one more letter. It may make it clear.

> My dear Fidele, forgive me for not writing to you all this time. I've been going around in absolute ecstasy. I agree, without reservation, with the philosopher who said that love is a second life. Moreover, a lot of things are changing in our household. The officer comes every day now. Sophie is madly in love with him. Papa is very gay. I even heard our Gregory, who always talks to himself while sweeping the floors, say that the wedding is close at hand, because Papa always wanted to see Sophie married to a high official or to an army officer with a brilliant career ahead of him. . . .

Hell! . . . I can't go on. . . . High officials, senior officers, they get all the best things in this world. You discover a crumb of happiness, you reach out for it and then along comes a high official or an officer and snatches it away. Goddammit! I would like so much to become a high official myself and not just to obtain her hand in marriage either. No, I'd like to be a high official just so that I could watch them jump around for my benefit; I'd listen for a while to their courtly jokes and innuendoes and then tell them what they could do with themselves. It hurts, though. Oh hell! . . . I tore the stupid little dog's letter to shreds.

December 3

Impossible! Lies! There can't be a wedding. So what if he has a commission in the Guards? That's nothing but position, you can't touch it with your hand. A Guards officer does not have a third eye in the middle of his forehead, his nose is not made of gold but the same stuff as mine or anyone else's and he uses it to sniff not to eat, for sneezing not for coughing. I've often tried to discover where all these differences lie. Why am I a clerk? Why should I be a clerk? Perhaps I'm really a general or a count and only seem to be a clerk? Maybe I don't really know who I am? There are plenty of instances in history when somebody quite ordinary, not necessarily an aristocrat, some middle-class person or even a peasant, suddenly turns out to be a public figure and perhaps even the ruler of a country. If a peasant can turn into someone so important, where are the limits to the possibilities for a man of breeding? Imagine, for instance, me, entering a room in a general's uniform. There's an epaulet on my right shoulder, an epaulet on my left, a blue ribbon across my chest. How would that be? What tune would my beauty sing then? And Papa himself, our Director, what would he say? Ow, he's so vain! He's a Mason, no mistake about it, although he may pretend to be this or that; I noticed from the start that when he shakes hands, he sticks out two fingers only. But I can't be promoted to general or governor or anything like that overnight. What I'd like to know is, why am I a clerk? Why precisely a clerk?

December 5

I read the newspapers all morning. Strange things are happening in Spain. I can't even make them out properly. They write that the throne has been vacated and that the ranking grandees are having difficulty in selecting an heir. It seems there's discontent. Sounds very strange to me. How can a throne be vacant? They say that some donna may accede. A donna cannot accede to a throne. It's absolutely impossible. A king should sit on a throne. But they say there is no king. It's impossible that there should be no king. There must be a king but he's hidden away somewhere in anonymity. It's even possible that he's around but is being forced to remain in hiding for family reasons or for fear of some neighboring country such as France. Or there may be other reasons.

December 8

I was on the point of going to the office but various considerations held me back. I couldn't get those Spanish affairs out of my head. How can a donna possibly become ruler? They won't allow it. In the first place, England won't stand for it. Then we must keep in mind the political setup of the rest of Europe: the Austrian Emperor, our Tsar. . . . I confess I was so perturbed and hurt by these events that I could do nothing all day. Marva remarked that I was very absent-minded during dinner. . . . In fact, I believe I absent-mindedly threw a couple of plates on the floor, where they broke at once. After dinner, I walked the streets, uphill and downhill. Came across nothing of interest. Then, mostly lay on my bed and thought about the Spanish question.

Year 2000, April 43

This is a day of great jubilation. Spain has a king. They've found him. *I* am the King. I discovered it today. It all came to me in a flash. It's incredible to me now that I could have imagined that I was a civil-service clerk. How could such a crazy idea ever have entered my head? Thank God no one thought of slapping me into a lunatic asylum. Now I see everything clearly, as clearly as if it lay in the palm of my hand. But what was happening to me before? Then things loomed at me out of a fog. Now, I believe that all troubles stem from the misconception that human brains are located in the head. They are not: human brains are blown in by the winds from somewhere around the Caspian Sea.

Marva was the first to whom I revealed my identity. When she heard that she was facing the King of Spain, she flung up her hands in awe. She almost died of terror. The silly woman had never seen a King of Spain before. However, I tried to calm her and, speaking graciously, did my best to assure her of my royal favor. I was not going to hold against her all the times she had failed to shine my boots properly. The masses are so ignorant. One can't talk to them on lofty subjects. Probably she was so frightened because she thought that all kings of Spain are like Philip II. But I carefully pointed out that I wasn't like Philip II at all. I didn't go to the office. The hell with it. No, my friends, you won't entice me there now; never again shall I copy your dreadful documents.

Martober 86. Between day and night

Today, our Divisional Chief sent someone to make me go to the office. I hadn't been there for over three weeks. I went, just for a lark. The Divisional Chief expected me to come apologizing to him but I just looked at him indifferently, with not too much ire, nor too much benevolence either; then I sat down in my usual place as though unaware of the people around me. I looked around at all that scribbling rabble and thought: If only you had an inkling of who's sitting here among you, oh Lord, what a fuss you'd make. There'd be a terrific to-do and the Divisional Chief himself would bow deeply to me, as he does to the Director. They put some papers in front of me which I was supposed to abstract or something. I didn't even stir. A few minutes later, there was a general commotion. They said the Director was on his way. Several clerks jumped up, hoping he'd notice them. But I didn't budge. When word came that the Director was about to pass through our Division, they all buttoned up their coats. I did nothing of the sort. What kind of a Director does he think he is? Who says I should get up for him? Never! He's an old cork, not a Director. Yes, but an ordinary cork, the kind used for stoppering a bottle. That's all he is. But the funniest thing of all was when they gave me a paper to sign. They expected I'd sign it in the corner: head clerk such and such. Well, let them think again. I wrote in the main space, the one reserved for the Director's signature: Ferdinand VIII. You should have witnessed the awed silence that followed; but I merely waved my hand graciously and said: "Dispense with the manifestation of allegiance!" and walked out of the room. From there, I went straight to the Director's house. He was not at home. The footman tried to stop me from going in but what I said made his arms drop limp at his sides. I went straight to her boudoir. She was sitting in front of her mirror. She jumped up and stepped back, away from me. Still I did not tell her that I was the King of Spain. I simply told her that she couldn't even imagine the happiness awaiting her and that despite all our enemies' intrigues, we would be together. I did not want to say more and left. Oh, women are such perfidious things! Only now did I understand what a woman is like. So far, no one has found out whom Woman is in love with. I was the first to discover it: Woman is in love with the Devil. And I'm not joking either. Physicists write a lot of drivel about her being this, that and the other. She loves only the Devil. Look, do you see over there, in the front tier of the boxes? She raises her lorgnette. You think she's looking at that fat man with the star over there? Nothing of the sort. She's staring at the Devil, the Devil hiding behind the fat man's back. See, now he has hidden himself in the star and he's beckoning to her with his finger! And she'll marry him too. She will for sure. As for all the rest of them, all those who lick boots and proclaim their patriotism, all they really want is annuities and more annuities. Some patriots! They'd sell their mother, their father, and their God for money, the strutting betrayers of Christ! And all this crazy ambition and vanity comes from the little bubble under the tongue which has a tiny worm about the size of a pinhead in it, and it's all the work of a barber on Pea Street. I can't recall his name but the moving force behind it all is the Sultan of Turkey who pays the barber to spread Mohammedanism all over the world. They say that in France, already, the majority of the people have embraced the Mohammedan faith.

No date. A day without date

Went along Nevsky Avenue incognito. Saw the Tsar riding past. Everybody was doffing his hat, and so did I. I gave no sign that I was the King of Spain. I thought it would be undignified to reveal my identity there, in front of all those people, that it would be more proper to be presented at Court first. What has prevented me so far is the fact that I haven't got Spanish royal attire. If only I could get hold of a royal mantle of some sort. I thought of having one made but tailors are so stupid. Besides, they don't seem to be interested in their trade nowadays and go in for speculation, so that most of them end up mending roads. I decided to make a mantle out of my best coat, which I had only worn twice. But I didn't want those good-for-nothings to mess it all up—I preferred to do it myself. I locked my door so as not to be seen. I had to cut my coat to ribbons with the scissors since a mantle has a completely different style.

Can't remember the day.
Nor was there a month. Damned if
I know what's been going on

The mantle is ready. Marva really let out a yell when I put it on. Even so, I still don't feel ready to be presented at Court. My retinue hasn't as yet arrived from Spain. The absence of a retinue would be incompatible with my dignity. I'm expecting them at any time.

1st Date

I'm puzzled by the unaccountable delay in the arrival of my retinue. What can be holding them up? I went to the post office and inquired whether the Spanish delegates had arrived. But the postmaster is an utter fool and knows nothing: No, he says, there are no Spanish delegates around here but if you wish to mail a letter, we'll accept it. What the hell is he talking about? What letter? Letter my foot! Let druggists write letters. . . .

Madrid, Februarius the thirtieth

So I'm in Spain. It all happened so quickly that I hardly had time to realize it. This morning the Spanish delegation finally arrived for me and we all got into a carriage. I was somewhat bewildered by the extraordinary speed at which we traveled. We went so fast that in half an hour we reached the Spanish border. But then, nowadays there are railroads all over Europe and the ships go so fast too. Spain is a strange country. When we entered the first room, I saw a multitude of people with shaven heads. I soon realized, though, that these must be Dominican or Capuchin monks because they always shave their heads. I also thought that the manners of the King's Chancellor, who was leading me by the hand, were rather strange. He pushed me into a small room and said: "You sit quiet and don't you call yourself King Ferdinand again or I'll beat the nonsense out of your head." But I knew that I was just being tested and refused to submit. For this, the Chancellor hit me across the back with a stick, twice, so painfully that I almost let out a cry. But I contained myself, remembering that this is customary procedure among knights on initiation into an exalted order. To this day, they adhere to the chivalric code in Spain.

Left to myself, I decided to devote some time to affairs of state. I have discovered that China and Spain are the same thing and it's only ignorance that makes people take them for two separate countries. I advise anybody who doubts it to take a piece of paper and write the word "Spain" and they'll see for themselves that it comes out "China." I also gave much thought to a sad event that must occur tomorrow at seven o'clock. As foreseen by the famous English chemist Wellington, the Earth will mount the Moon. I confess I was deeply worried when I thought of the Moon's extraordinary sensitivity and fragility. The Moon, of course, is made in Hamburg, and I must say they do a very poor job. I wonder why England doesn't do something about it. It's a lame cooper that makes the Moon, and it's quite obvious that the fool has no conception of what the Moon should be. He uses tarred rope and olive oil and that's why the stench is so awful all over the Earth and we are forced to plug our noses. And that's why the Moon itself is such a delicate ball that men cannot live there—only noses. And that's why we can't see our own noses: they are all on the Moon. And when I thought what a heavy thing the Earth is and that, sitting down on the Moon, it would crush our noses into a powder, I became so worried that I put on my socks and shoes and rushed into the State Council Room to order my police force to stand by to prevent the Earth from mounting the Moon. The Capuchin monks I found in the State Council Room were very clever people and when I said, "Gentlemen, let's save the Moon, the Earth is preparing to mount it," they all rushed at once to execute my royal wish and many tried to climb the wall to reach the Moon. But at that moment, the Grand Chancellor came in. As soon as they saw him, they scattered. Being the King, I remained there alone. But to my surprise, the Chancellor hit me with his stick and chased me into my room. Such is the power of popular tradition in Spain!

January of the same year which happened after Februarius

I still can't make out what sort of a place Spain is. The customs and the etiquette at the Court are quite incredible. I don't see, I don't grasp it, I don't understand at all! Today, they shaved my head, although I shouted with all my might that I did not want to become a monk. But then they began to drip cold water on my head and everything went blank. Never have I been through such hell. I just can't understand the point of this peculiar custom, so stupid, so senseless. And the irresponsibility of the kings who never got around to outlawing this custom is quite beyond me.

Some indications make me wonder whether I haven't fallen into the hands of the Inquisition. Maybe the man I took for the Chancellor is really the Grand Inquisitor himself? But then, I can't see how the King can be subjected to the Inquisition. True, this could be the work of France, especially Polignac. That Polignac is an absolute beast. He has sworn to drive me to my death. And so he maneuvers on and on. But I know, my fine fellow, that you in turn are being led by the English. The English are great politicians. They sow the seeds of dissension everywhere. The whole world knows that when England takes snuff, France sneezes.

25th Date

Today, the Grand Inquisitor entered my room. I heard his steps approaching while he was still far off and hid under a chair. He looked around and, not seeing me, he began to call out. First he shouted my name and civil-service rank. I remained silent. Then, Ferdinand VIII, King of Spain! I was about to stick my head out but thought to myself: No, they won't get me that way! They may want to pour cold water on my head again. But he saw me and chased me out from under the chair with his stick. His damn stick hurts dreadfully. But my very latest discovery made me feel better: I had found that every rooster has his own Spain and he has it under his feathers. The Grand Inquisitor left very angry, threatening me with some punishment or other. Of course, I completely ignored his helpless fury. I knew he was a puppet. A tool of England.

da 34 te Mnth. Yr. yraurbeF 349

No, I have no strength left. I can't stand any more. My God! What they're doing to me! They pour cold water on my head. They don't listen to me, they don't hear me, they don't see me. What have I done to them? Why do they torture me so? What do they want from me? What can I give them? I haven't anything to give. I have no strength, I cannot bear this suffering, my head is on fire, and everything goes around me in circles. Save me! Take me away from here! Give me a carriage with horses swift as wind! Drive on, coachman, let the harness bells ring! Soar upward, my horses, carry me away from this world! Further, further, where I will see nothing, nothing. There is the sky smoking before me. A star twinkles far away, the forest rushes past with its dark trees and the crescent moon. The violet fog is a carpet underfoot. I hear the twanging of a guitar string through the fog; on one side, the sea, and on the other, Italy. Then Russian huts come into sight. Perhaps that's my house over there, looking blue in the distance. And isn't that my mother sitting by the window? Mother, save your wretched son! Let your tears fall on his sick head! See how they torture him! Hold me, a poor waif, in your arms. There's no room for him in this world. They are chasing him. Mother, take pity on your sick child. . . .

And, by the way, have you heard that the Dey of Algiers has a wart right under his nose?

Nathaniel Hawthorne

Young Goodman Brown

Nathaniel Hawthorne (1804–1864)

BORN IN SALEM, MASSACHUSETTS, WHERE ONE OF HIS ANCESTORS had been a judge in the famous seventeenth-century witchcraft trials, Nathaniel Hawthorne came from a long line of New England Puritans. He graduated from Bowdoin College in 1825, then devoted himself to writing. For many years he published tales anonymously and made little money. He joined the experimental socialist community at Brook Farm for a time. His first collection of stories, *Twice-Told Tales,* was published in 1837 and was followed by a second series in 1842. He married and settled down in Concord, where he saw much of two of the leading minds of his time, Ralph Waldo Emerson and Henry David Thoreau. Later Herman Melville was to become his closest literary friend.

Hawthorne's first great novel, *The Scarlet Letter,* was published in 1850. It was followed by *The House of Seven Gables,* which made him famous, and by *The Blithedale Romance,* which satirized the optimistic utopian reformism of many of his contemporaries. He went to England in 1853 as U.S. Consul in Liverpool, then traveled in Italy where he completed his last novel, *The Marble Faun.* He returned to Concord in 1860 and struggled without success to finish several works of fiction.

Hawthorne was harshly critical of the Puritans from whom he was descended—he could not accept their dogmas and he hated their bigotry and narrow-minded arrogance—but Puritanism nonetheless determined much of his outlook. In an age whose intellectual life was characterized in large measure by Romantic optimism, Hawthorne was a dissenter who believed that evil was a real presence in life. The chief mortal sin of the Puritans, pride, is everywhere present in Hawthorne's writings in secularized form: as human isolation, as the failure to love, as the failure to understand the interdependency of men.

It is not easy to label the manner of Hawthorne's fiction; it is situated somewhere between realism on the one hand and allegory on the other. Perhaps we can most properly call it "symbolist," in that reality in Hawthorne's stories constantly tends toward the symbolic and the emblematic, but is never reduced to the fixed content of allegory. Truth is never easily discoverable in Hawthorne's universe; it is surrounded by ambiguities, ironies, and false appearances. In *Young Goodman Brown,* as in many of his tales, elements of the setting and the narrative—for example, the journey into the dark forest, the Satanic communion, the characters' names—form a complex drama whose reality and meaning are problematical.

Young Goodman Brown

Young Goodman Brown came forth at sunset into the street at Salem village; but put his head back, after crossing the threshold, to exchange a parting kiss with his young wife. And Faith, as the wife was aptly named, thrust her own pretty head into the street, letting the wind play with the pink ribbons of her cap while she called to Goodman Brown.

"Dearest heart," whispered she, softly and rather sadly, when her lips were close to his ear, "prithee put off your journey until sunrise and sleep in your own bed tonight. A lone woman is troubled with such dreams and such thoughts that she's afeard of herself sometimes. Pray tarry with me this night, dear husband, of all nights in the year."

"My love and my Faith," replied young Goodman Brown, "of all nights in the year, this one night must I tarry away from thee. My journey, as thou callest it, forth and back again, must needs be done 'twixt now and sunrise. What, my sweet, pretty wife, dost thou doubt me already, and we but three months married?"

"Then God bless you!" said Faith, with the pink ribbons; "and may you find all well when you come back."

"Amen!" cried Goodman Brown. "Say thy prayers, dear Faith, and go to bed at dusk, and no harm will come to thee."

So they parted; and the young man pursued his way until, being about to turn the corner by the meeting-house, he looked back and saw the head of Faith still peeping after him with a melancholy air, in spite of her pink ribbons.

"Poor little Faith!" thought he, for his heart smote him. "What a wretch am I to leave her on such an errand! She talks of dreams, too. Methought as she spoke there was trouble in her face, as if a dream had warned her what work is to be done tonight. But no, no; 'twould kill her to think it. Well, she's a blessed angel on earth; and after this one night I'll cling to her skirts and follow her to heaven."

With this excellent resolve for the future, Goodman Brown felt himself justified in making more haste on his present evil purpose. He had taken a dreary road, darkened by all the gloomiest trees of the forest, which barely stood aside to let the narrow path creep through, and closed immediately behind. It was all as lonely as could be; and there is this peculiarity in such a solitude, that the traveller knows not who may be concealed by the innumerable trunks and the thick boughs overhead; so that with lonely footsteps he may yet be passing through an unseen multitude.

"There may be a devilish Indian behind every tree," said Goodman Brown to himself; and he glanced fearfully behind him as he added, "What if the devil himself should be at my very elbow!"

His head being turned back, he passed a crook of the road, and, looking forward again, beheld the figure of a man, in grave and decent attire, seated at the foot of an old tree. He arose at Goodman Brown's approach and walked onward side by side with him.

"You are late, Goodman Brown," said he. "The clock of the Old South was striking as I came through Boston, and that is full fifteen minutes agone."

"Faith kept me back a while," replied the young man, with a tremor in his voice, caused by the sudden appearance of his companion, though not wholly unexpected.

It was now deep dusk in the forest, and deepest in that part of it where these two were journeying. As nearly as could be discerned, the second traveller was about fifty years old, apparently in the same rank of life as Goodman Brown, and bearing a considerable resemblance to him, though perhaps more in expression than features. Still they might have been taken for father and son. And yet, though the elder person was as simply clad as the younger, and as simple in manner too, he had an indescribable air of one who knew the world, and who would not have felt abashed at the governor's dinner table or in King William's court, were it possible that his affairs should call him thither. But the only thing about him that could be fixed upon as remarkable was his staff, which bore the likeness of a great black snake, so curiously wrought that it might almost be seen to twist and wriggle itself like a living serpent. This, of course, must have been an ocular deception, assisted by the uncertain light.

"Come, Goodman Brown," cried his fellow-traveller, "this is a dull pace for the beginning of a journey. Take my staff, if you are so soon weary."

"Friend," said the other, exchanging his slow pace for a full stop, "having kept covenant by meeting thee here, it is my purpose now to return whence I came. I have scruples touching the matter thou wot'st of."

"Sayest thou so?" replied he of the serpent, smiling apart. "Let us walk on, nevertheless, reasoning as we go; and if I convince thee not thou shalt turn back. We are but a little way in the forest yet."

"Too far! too far!" exclaimed the goodman, unconsciously resuming his walk. "My father never went into the woods on such an errand, nor his father before him. We have been a race of honest men and good Christians since the days of the martyrs; and shall I be the first of the name of Brown that ever took this path and kept"—

"Such company, thou wouldst say," observed the elder person, interpreting his pause. "Well said, Goodman Brown! I have been as well acquainted with your family as with ever a one among the Puritans; and that's no trifle to say. I helped your grandfather, the constable, when he lashed the Quaker woman so smartly through the streets of Salem; and it was I that brought your father a pitchpine knot, kindled at my own hearth, to set fire to an Indian village, in King Philip's war. They were my good friends, both; and many a pleasant walk have we had along this path, and returned merrily after midnight. I would fain be friends with you for their sake."

"If it be as thou sayest," replied Goodman Brown, "I marvel they never spoke of these matters; or, verily, I marvel not, seeing that the least rumor of the sort would have driven them from New England. We are a people of prayer, and good works to boot, and abide no such wickedness."

"Wickedness or not," said the traveller with the twisted staff, "I have a very general acquaintance here in New England. The deacons of many a church have drunk the communion wine with me; the selectmen of divers towns make me their chairman; and a majority of the Great and General Court are firm supporters of my interest. The governor and I, too—But these are state secrets."

"Can this be so?" cried Goodman Brown, with a stare of amazement at his undisturbed companion. "Howbeit, I have nothing to do with the governor and council; they have their own ways, and are no rule for a simple husbandman like me. But, were I to go on with thee, how should I meet the eye of that good old man, our minister, at Salem village? Oh, his voice would make me tremble both Sabbath day and lecture day."

Thus far the elder traveller had listened with due gravity; but now burst into a fit of irrepressible mirth, shaking himself so violently that his snake-like staff actually seemed to wriggle in sympathy.

"Ha! ha! ha!" shouted he again and again; then composing himself, "Well, go on, Goodman Brown, go on; but, prithee, don't kill me with laughing."

"Well, then, to end the matter at once," said Goodman Brown, considerably nettled, "there is my wife, Faith. It would break her dear little heart; and I'd rather break my own."

"Nay, if that be the case," answered the other, "e'en go thy ways, Goodman Brown. I would not for twenty old women like the one hobbling before us that Faith should come to any harm."

As he spoke he pointed his staff at a female figure on the path, in whom Goodman Brown recognized a very pious and exemplary dame, who had taught him his catechism in youth, and was still his moral and spiritual adviser, jointly with the minister and Deacon Gookin.

"A marvel, truly, that Goody Cloyse should be so far in the wilderness at nightfall," said he. "But with your leave, friend, I shall take a cut through the woods until we have left this Christian woman behind. Being a stranger to you, she might ask whom I was consorting with and whither I was going."

"Be it so," said his fellow-traveller. "Betake you to the woods, and let me keep the path."

Accordingly the young man turned aside, but took care to watch his companion, who advanced softly along the road until he had come within a staff's length of the old dame. She, meanwhile, was making the best of her way, with singular speed for so aged a woman, and mumbling some indistinct words—a prayer, doubtless—as she went. The traveller put forth his staff and touched her withered neck with what seemed the serpent's tail.

"The devil!" screamed the pious old lady.

"Then Goody Cloyse knows her old friend?" observed the traveller, confronting her and leaning on his writhing stick.

"Ah, forsooth, and is it your worship indeed?" cried the good dame. "Yea, truly is it, and in the very image of my old gossip, Goodman Brown, the grandfather of the silly fellow that now is. But—would your worship believe it?—my broomstick hath strangely disappeared, stolen, as I suspect, by that unhanged witch, Goody Cory, and that, too, when I was all anointed with the juice of smallage, and cinquefoil, and wolf's bane"—

"Mingled with fine wheat and the fat of a new-born babe," said the shape of old Goodman Brown.

"Ah, your worship knows the recipe," cried the old lady, cackling aloud. "So, as I was saying, being all ready for the meeting, and no horse to ride on, I made up my mind to foot it; for they tell me there is a nice young man to be taken into communion tonight. But now your good worship will lend me your arm, and we shall be there in a twinkling."

"That can hardly be," answered her friend. "I may not spare you my arm, Goody Cloyse; but here is my staff, if you will."

So saying, he threw it down at her feet, where, perhaps, it assumed life, being one of the rods which its owner had formerly lent to the Egyptian magi. Of this fact, however, Goodman Brown could not take cognizance. He had cast up his eyes in astonishment, and, looking down again, beheld neither Goody Cloyse nor the serpentine staff, but his fellow-traveller alone, who waited for him as calmly as if nothing had happened.

"That old woman taught me my catechism," said the young man; and there was a world of meaning in this simple comment.

They continued to walk onward, while the elder traveller exhorted his companion to make good speed and persevere in the path, discoursing so aptly that his arguments seemed rather to spring up in the bosom of his auditor than to be suggested by himself. As they went, he plucked a branch of maple to serve for a walking stick, and began to strip it of the twigs and little boughs, which were wet with evening dew. The moment his fingers touched them they became strangely withered and dried up as with a week's sunshine. Thus the pair proceeded, at a good free pace, until suddenly, in a gloomy hollow of the road, Goodman Brown sat himself down on the stump of a tree and refused to go any farther.

"Friend," said he, stubbornly, "my mind is made up. Not another step will I budge on this errand. What if a wretched old woman do choose to go to the devil when I thought she was going to heaven: is that any reason why I should quit my dear Faith and go after her?"

"You will think better of this by and by," said his acquaintance, composedly. "Sit here and rest yourself a while; and when you feel like moving again, there is my staff to help you along."

Without more words, he threw his companion the maple stick, and was as speedily out of sight as if he had vanished into the deepening gloom. The young man sat a few moments by the roadside, applauding himself greatly, and thinking with how clear a conscience he should meet the minister in his morning walk, nor shrink from the eye of good old Deacon Gookin. And what calm sleep would be his that very night, which was to have been spent so wickedly, but so purely and sweetly now, in the arms of Faith! Amidst these pleasant and praiseworthy meditations, Goodman Brown heard the tramp of horses along the road, and deemed it advisable to conceal himself within the verge of the forest, conscious of the guilty purpose that had brought him thither, though now so happily turned from it.

On came the hoof tramps and the voices of the riders, two grave old voices, conversing soberly as they drew near. These mingled sounds appeared to pass along the road, within a few yards of the young man's hiding-place; but, owing doubtless to the depth of the gloom at that particular spot, neither the travellers nor their steeds were visible. Though their figures brushed the small boughs by the wayside, it could not be seen that they intercepted, even for a moment, the faint gleam from the strip of bright sky athwart which they must have passed. Goodman Brown alternately crouched and stood on tiptoe, pulling aside the branches and thrusting forth his head as far as he durst without discerning so much as a shadow. It vexed him the more, because he could have sworn, were such a thing possible, that he recognized the voices of the minister and Deacon Gookin, jogging along quietly, as they were wont to do, when bound to some ordination or ecclesiastical council. While yet within hearing, one of the riders stopped to pluck a switch.

"Of the two, reverend sir," said the voice like the deacon's, "I had rather miss an ordination dinner than tonight's meeting. They tell me that some of our community are to be here from Falmouth and beyond, and others from Connecticut and Rhode Island, besides several of Indian powwows, who, after their fashion, know almost as much deviltry as the best of us. Moreover, there is a goodly young woman to be taken into communion."

"Mighty well, Deacon Gookin!" replied the solemn old tones of the minister. "Spur up, or we shall be late. Nothing can be done you know until I get on the ground."

The hoofs clattered again; and the voices, talking so strangely in the empty air, passed on through the forest, where no church had ever been gathered or solitary Christian prayed. Whither, then, could these holy men be journeying so deep into the heathen wilderness? Young Goodman Brown caught hold of a tree for support, being ready to sink down on the ground, faint and overburdened with the heavy sickness of his heart. He looked up to the sky, doubting whether there really was a heaven above him. Yet there was the blue arch, and the stars brightening in it.

"With heaven above and Faith below, I will yet stand firm against the devil!" cried Goodman Brown.

While he still gazed upward into the deep arch of the firmament and had lifted his hands to pray, a cloud, though no wind was stirring, hurried across the zenith and hid the brightening stars. The blue sky was still visible, except directly overhead, where this black mass of cloud was sweeping swiftly northward. Aloft in the air, as if from the depths of the cloud, came a confused and doubtful sound of voices. Once the listener fancied that he could distinguish the accents of townspeople of his own, men, and women, both pious and ungodly, many of whom he had met at the communion table, and had seen others rioting at the tavern. The next moment, so indistinct were the sounds, he doubted whether he had heard aught but the murmur of the old forest, whispering without a wind. Then came a stronger swell of those familiar tones, heard daily in the sunshine at Salem village, but never until now from a cloud of night. There was one voice of a young woman, uttering lamentations, yet with an uncertain sorrow, and entreating for some favor, which, perhaps, it would grieve her to obtain; and all the unseen multitude, both saints and sinners, seemed to encourage her onward.

"Faith!" shouted Goodman Brown, in a voice of agony and desperation; and the echoes of the forest mocked him, crying, "Faith! Faith!" as if bewildered wretches were seeking her all through the wilderness.

The cry of grief, rage, and terror was yet piercing the night, when the unhappy husband held his breath for a response. There was a scream, drowned immediately in a louder murmur of voices, fading into far-off laughter, as the dark cloud swept away, leaving the clear and silent sky above Goodman Brown. But something fluttered lightly down through the air and caught on the branch of a tree. The young man seized it, and beheld a pink ribbon.

"My Faith is gone!" cried he, after one stupefied moment. "There is no good on earth; and sin is but a name. Come, devil; for to thee is this world given."

And, maddened with despair, so that he laughed loud and long, did Goodman Brown grasp his staff and set forth again, at such a rate that he seemed to fly along the forest path rather than to walk or run. The road grew wilder and drearier and more faintly traced, and vanished at length, leaving him in the heart of the dark wilderness, still rushing onward with the instinct that guides mortal man to evil. The whole forest was peopled with frightful sounds—the creaking of the trees, the howling of wild beasts, and the yell of Indians; while sometimes the wind tolled like a distant church bell, and sometimes gave a broad roar around the traveller, as if all Nature were laughing him to scorn. But he was himself the chief horror of the scene, and shrank not from its other horrors.

"Ha! ha! ha!" roared Goodman Brown when the wind laughed at him. "Let us hear which will laugh loudest. Think not to frighten me with your deviltry. Come witch, come wizard, come Indian powwow, come devil himself, and here comes Goodman Brown. You may as well fear him as he fear you."

In truth, all through the haunted forest there could be nothing more frightful than the figure of Goodman Brown. On he flew among the black pines, brandishing his staff with frenzied gestures, now giving vent to an inspiration of horrid blasphemy, and now shouting forth such laughter as set all the echoes of the forest laughing like demons around him. The fiend in his own shape is less hideous than when he rages in the breast of man. Thus sped the demoniac on his course, until, quivering among the trees, he saw a red light before him, as when the felled trunks and branches of a clearing have been set on fire, and throw up their lurid blaze against the sky, at the hour of midnight. He paused, in a lull of the tempest that had driven him onward, and heard the swell of what seemed a hymn, rolling solemnly from a distance with the weight of many voices. He knew the tune; it was a familiar one in the choir of the village meeting-house. The verse died heavily away, and was lengthened by a chorus, not of human voices, but of all the sounds of the benighted wilderness pealing in awful harmony together. Goodman Brown cried out, and his cry was lost to his own ear by its unison with the cry of the desert.

In the interval of silence he stole forward until the light glared full upon his eyes. At one extremity of an open space, hemmed in by the dark wall of the forest, arose a rock, bearing some rude, natural resemblance either to an altar or a pulpit, and surrounded by four blazing pines, their tops aflame, their stems untouched, like candles at an evening meeting. The mass of foliage that had overgrown the summit of the rock was all on fire, blazing high into the night and fitfully illuminating the whole field. Each pendent twig and leafy festoon was in a blaze. As the red light arose and fell, a numerous congregation alternately shone forth, then disappeared in shadow, and again grew, as it were, out of the darkness, peopling the heart of the solitary woods at once.

"A grave and dark-clad company," quoth Goodman Brown.

In truth they were such. Among them, quivering to and fro between gloom and splendor, appeared faces that would be seen next day at the council board of the province, and others which, Sabbath after Sabbath, looked devoutly heavenward, and benignantly over the crowded pews, from the holiest pulpits in the land. Some affirm that the lady of the governor was there. At least there were high dames well known to her, and wives of honored husbands, and widows, a great multitude, and ancient maidens, all of excellent repute, and fair young girls, who trembled lest their mothers should espy them. Either the sudden gleams of light flashing over the obscure field bedazzled Goodman Brown, or he recognized a score of the church members of Salem village famous for their especial sanctity. Good old Deacon Gookin had arrived, and waited at the skirts of that venerable saint, his revered pastor. But, irreverently consorting with these grave, reputable, and pious people, these elders of the church, these chaste dames and dewy virgins, there were men of dissolute lives and women of spotted fame, wretches given over to all mean and filthy vice, and suspected even of horrid crimes. It was strange to see that the good shrank not from the wicked, nor were the sinners abashed by the saints. Scattered also among their pale-faced enemies were the Indian priests, or powwows, who had often scared their native forest with more hideous incantations than any known to English witchcraft.

"But where is Faith?" thought Goodman Brown; and, as hope came into his heart, he trembled.

Another verse of the hymn arose, a slow and mournful strain, such as the pious love, but joined to words which expressed all that our nature can conceive of sin, and darkly hinted at far more. Unfathomable to mere mortals is the lore of fiends. Verse after verse was sung; and still the chorus of the desert swelled between like the deepest tone of a mighty organ; and with the final peal of that dreadful anthem there came a sound, as if the roaring wind, the rushing streams, the howling beasts, and every other voice of the unconcerted wilderness were mingling and according with the voice of guilty man in homage to the prince of all. The four blazing pines threw up a loftier flame, and obscurely discovered shapes and visages of horror on the smoke wreaths above the impious assembly. At the same moment the fire on the rock shot redly forth and formed a glowing arch above its base, where now appeared a figure. With reverence be it spoken, the figure bore no slight similitude, both in garb and manner, to some grave divine of the New England churches.

"Bring forth the converts!" cried a voice that echoed through the field and rolled into the forest.

At the word, Goodman Brown stepped forth from the shadow of the trees and approached the congregation, with whom he felt a loathful brotherhood by the sympathy of all that was wicked in his heart. He could have well-nigh sworn that the shape of his own dead father beckoned him to advance, looking downward from a smoke wreath, while a woman, with dim features of despair, threw out her hand to warn him back. Was it his mother? But he had no power to retreat one step, nor to resist, even in thought, when the minister and good old Deacon Gookin seized his arms and led him to the blazing rock. Thither came also the slender form of a veiled female, led between Goody Cloyse, that pious teacher of the catechism, and Martha Carrier, who had received the devil's promise to be queen of hell. A rampant hag was she. And there stood the proselytes beneath the canopy of fire.

"Welcome, my children," said the dark figure, "to the communion of your race. Ye have found thus young your nature and your destiny. My children, look behind you!"

They turned; and flashing forth, as it were, in a sheet of flame, the fiend worshippers were seen; the smile of welcome gleamed darkly on every visage.

"There," resumed the sable form, "are all whom ye have reverenced from youth. Ye deemed them holier than yourselves, and shrank from your own sin, contrasting it with their lives of righteousness and prayerful aspirations heavenward. Yet here are they all in my worshipping assembly. This night it shall be granted you to know their secret deeds: how hoary-bearded elders of the church have whispered wanton words to the young maids of their households; how many a woman, eager for widows' weeds, has given her husband a drink at bedtime and let him sleep his last sleep in her bosom; how beardless youths have made haste to inherit their fathers' wealth; and how fair damsels—blush not, sweet ones—have dug little graves in the garden, and bidden me, the sole guest to an infant's funeral. By the sympathy of your human hearts for sin ye shall scent out all the places—whether in church, bed-chamber, street, field, or forest—where crime has been committed, and shall exult to behold the whole earth one stain of guilt, one mighty blood spot. Far more than this. It shall be yours to penetrate, in every bosom, the deep mystery of sin, the fountain of all wicked arts, and which inexhaustibly supplies more evil impulses than human power —than my power at its utmost—can make manifest in deeds. And now, my children, look upon each other."

They did so; and, by the blaze of the hell-kindled torches, the wretched man beheld his Faith, and the wife her husband, trembling before that unhallowed altar.

"Lo, there ye stand, my children," said the figure, in a deep and solemn tone, almost sad with its despairing awfulness, as if his once angelic nature could yet mourn for our miserable race. "Depending upon one another's hearts, ye had still hoped that virtue were not all a dream. Now are ye undeceived. Evil is the nature of mankind. Evil must be your only happiness. Welcome again, my children, to the communion of your race."

"Welcome," repeated the fiend worshippers, in one cry of despair and triumph.

And there they stood, the only pair, as it seemed, who were yet hesitating on the verge of wickedness in this dark world. A basin was hollowed, naturally, in the rock. Did it contain water, reddened by the lurid light? or was it blood? or, perchance, a liquid flame? Herein did the shape of evil dip his hand and prepare to lay the mark of baptism upon their foreheads, that they might be partakers of the mystery of sin, more conscious of the secret guilt of others, both in deed and thought, than they could now be of their own. The husband cast one look at his pale wife, and Faith at him. What polluted wretches would the next glance show them to each other, shuddering alike at what they disclosed and what they saw!

"Faith! Faith!" cried the husband, "look up to heaven, and resist the wicked one."

Whether Faith obeyed he knew not. Hardly had he spoken when he found himself amid calm night and solitude, listening to a roar of the wind which died heavily away through the forest. He staggered against the rock, and felt it chill and damp; while a hanging twig, that had been all on fire, besprinkled his check with the coldest dew.

The next morning young Goodman Brown came slowly into the street of Salem village, staring around him like a bewildered man. The good old minister was taking a walk along the graveyard to get an appetite for breakfast and meditate his sermon, and bestowed a blessing, as he passed, on Goodman Brown. He shrank from the venerable saint as if to avoid an anathema. Old Deacon Gookin was at domestic worship, and the holy words of his prayer were heard through the open window. "What God doth the wizard pray to?" quoth Goodman Brown. Goody Cloyse, that excellent old Christian, stood in the early sunshine at her own lattice, catechizing a little girl who had brought her a pint of morning's milk. Goodman Brown snatched away the child as from the grasp of the fiend himself. Turning the corner by the meeting-house, he spied the head of Faith, with the pink ribbons, gazing anxiously forth, and bursting into such joy at sight of him that she skipped along the street and almost kissed her husband before the whole village. But Goodman Brown looked sternly and sadly into her face, and passed on without a greeting.

Had Goodman Brown fallen asleep in the forest and only dreamed a wild dream of a witch-meeting?

Be it so if you will; but, alas! it was a dream of evil omen for young Goodman Brown. A stern, a sad, a darkly meditative, a distrustful, if not a desperate man did he become from the night of that fearful dream. On the Sabbath day, when the congregation were singing a holy psalm, he could not listen because an anthem of sin rushed loudly upon his ear and drowned all the blessed strain. When the minister spoke from the pulpit with power and fervid eloquence, and, with his hand on the open Bible, of the sacred truths of our religion, and of saint-like lives and triumphant deaths, and of future bliss or misery unutterable, then did Goodman Brown turn pale, dreading lest the roof should thunder down upon the gray blasphemer and his hearers. Often, waking suddenly at midnight, he shrank from the bosom of Faith; and at morning or eventide, when the family knelt down at prayer, he scowled and muttered to himself, and gazed sternly at his wife, and turned away. And when he had lived long, and was borne to his grave a hoary corpse, followed by Faith, an aged woman, and children and grandchildren, a goodly procession, besides neighbors not a few, they carved no hopeful verse upon his tombstone, for his dying hour was gloom.

Gustave Flaubert

A Simple Heart

TRANSLATED BY WALTER J. COBB

Gustave Flaubert (1821–1880)

ROUEN, IN NORMANDY, THE NORTHERLY PART OF FRANCE THAT serves as the setting for both the famous novel *Madame Bovary* and "A Simple Heart," was the birthplace of Gustave Flaubert. The son of a famous surgeon, Flaubert was sent to Paris in 1840 to study law, but failed his final examinations and eventually came back to Normandy to write. Apart from a two-year trip to the Near East, he led a cloistered life largely dedicated to his art, which he pursued with a passion, even a mania, for precision and beauty which has perhaps never been equaled by any other novelist and which was to make him the patron saint of later craftsmen of fiction.

Flaubert's youthful writings are Romantic in manner, and a yearning for the exotic remained a constant element of his art; it can be felt most strongly in works like *Salammbô* and *The Temptation of Saint Anthony*. But Flaubert strove to suppress the romantic element in himself and to base his fiction on an accurate rendering of the real and the ordinary, which, paradoxically, he detested. In *Madame Bovary,* a novel which Flaubert spent five years writing, the romantic element is treated both with sympathetic understanding and with harsh irony. Emma Bovary's sentimental longings are constantly undercut by the banal realities of her existence and eventually lead her to a sordid death. In *Sentimental Education,* Flaubert attempted to recount the "moral history" of his own generation: all the frustrations and deceptions of aspiring youth in the modern wasteland of failed ideals and betrayed revolutions. And in the unfinished *Bouvard and Pécuchet* (published in 1881), he summed up his lifelong hatred of the stultifying middle class, its moral and mental commonplaces, and the joyless, hypocritical world it had created.

"A Simple Heart" (one of the *Three Tales* published in 1877) shows clearly Flaubert's careful attention to the ordinary and the humble and his search for a style that would transform the ordinary and humble into a thing of beauty.

A Simple Heart

I

For half a century the womenfolk of Pont-l'Évêque begrudged Mme. Aubain her servant, Félicité.

For one hundred francs a year she cooked and did the housework, sewed, washed, ironed, and knew how to bridle a horse, how to "fatten" the chickens, how to make butter, and she remained loyal to her mistress who, it must be noted, was not a very easy person to get along with.

Mme. Aubain had married a handsome fellow, without means, who had died at the beginning of the year 1809, leaving her with two very young children and many debts. At that time she sold what landed property she possessed, except two farms, one at Toucques and another at Geffosses, the income of which brought her, at most, five thousand francs a year; and she gave up her house at Saint Melaine to move into another less costly to maintain a house that had belonged to her ancestors and that was situated behind the market square.

This house, with its slate roof, stood between an alley and a little street that led to the river. Inside it had different levels which caused one to stumble. A narrow vestibule separated the kitchen from the parlor where Mme. Aubain, seated near the casement window in her wicker chair, spent the entire day. Against the wainscoting, painted white, were aligned eight mahogany chairs. A pyramid of wooden boxes and pasteboard cartons were piled up on an old piano, underneath a barometer. Two small stuffed armchairs flanked the yellow marble fireplace, in the style of Louis XV. The clock in the center depicted a temple of Vesta—the whole room smelled slightly musty, because the floor was on a level lower than the garden.

On the first floor, there was first Madame's bedroom, very large, papered in a pale flower design, with a portrait of "Monsieur" in a foppish costume on the wall. A smaller room in which were to be seen two children's beds, without mattresses, adjoined hers. Next came the salon, always kept locked, and cluttered with furniture covered over with sheets. Then a corridor led to the study; books and miscellaneous papers filled the shelves of a bookcase, the three sections of which surrounded a large desk made of black wood. The two panels in the corner were almost completely covered with pen sketches, water colors, and engravings by Audran[1]—souvenirs of better times and vanished luxury. A dormer window on the second floor lighted Félicité's room, which overlooked the fields.

Félicité rose at daybreak so as not to miss mass, and she worked till evening without interruption; then, when dinner was over, the dishes done, the door bolted, she would smother the burning log in the ashes and fall asleep before the hearth, her rosary beads still in her hand. No one was better at stubborn bargaining in the marketplace than she. As for cleanliness, the shine on her pots and pans was the despair of the other servants. Very thrifty, she ate slowly and gathered together with her finger the bread crumbs on the table—her bread, which weighed twelve pounds, was especially baked for her, and lasted twenty days.

During all seasons she wore a calico neckerchief over her shoulders, pinned at the back, a bonnet hiding her hair, gray stockings, a red petticoat, and over her bodice an apron like those worn by hospital nurses.

Her face was thin and her voice sharp. At twenty-five, people took her to be forty. After she reached fifty, she showed no age at all; and always taciturn, with her erect posture and measured movements, she seemed like a woman made of wood, performing like an automaton.

II

Like any other, Félicité had had her love story.

Her father, a stonemason, had been killed by a fall from a scaffold. Then her mother died, her sisters wandered away, a farmer took her in and employed her, while still very young, to watch over his cows in the pasture. She shivered in her thin rags; drank water, lying on her stomach, from ponds; for no reason received whippings, and finally was sent away because of a theft of thirty sous—a crime she had not committed. She went to another farm, tended the poultry yard, and because she pleased her employers the other servants became jealous of her.

One evening in August (she was then eighteen) she was taken to a party at Colleville. Immediately she was bewildered, dazzled by the noise of the fiddlers, the lights hanging from the trees, the medley of costumes, the laces, the gold crosses, the immense crowd of people all bustling about. She was standing modestly aside, when a young, well-dressed man, smoking a pipe while resting his elbows on the shaft of a cart, came over and asked her to dance. He bought her cider, coffee and cakes, and a silk scarf, and, imagining that she guessed what he was thinking about, offered to take her home. On their way past a field of oats, he threw her backward very roughly. She was frightened and began to scream. He ran off.

[1] Gérard Audran (1640–1703), who made engravings from the works of famous painters of his time.

Another evening, on the road to Beaumont, she wanted to pass a large wagon of hay that was going along slowly, and brushing against the wheels, she recognized Théodore.

He addressed her calmly, saying that she must forgive him everything, since it was "the fault of the drink."

She did not know what to say; and she wanted to run away.

Immediately he began to speak about the harvesting and the important people of the commune, for his father had left Colleville and had taken over the farm at Écots, so that now they were neighbors. "Oh!" she said. He went on to say that they wanted him to settle down. However, he was in no hurry, and was going to wait till he found a wife to his taste. She lowered her head. Then he asked her had she thought of marriage. She replied, smiling, that it wasn't nice to make fun of her.

"But I'm not making fun of you, I swear!" said he, putting his left arm around her waist. She walked along leaning on him. They slowed their pace. The wind was gentle, stars were shining; in front of them the huge hay wagon swayed from side to side; the four horses, dragging their hoofs, were stirring up dust. Then suddenly the horses veered to the right. He kissed her once more. She disappeared into the darkness.

The following week, Théodore had several meetings with her.

They met in remote farmyards, behind walls, or under some isolated tree. She was not innocent like well-bred young ladies—she had learned from being around animals; but reason and her self-esteem kept her from giving in. Her resistance exasperated Théodore's passion, so much so that to satisfy it (or perhaps naively) he proposed marriage to her. At first she doubted his sincerity, but he made strong vows of love.

Soon afterward, he confessed to her a troublesome bit of news: his parents, the year before, had bought him a substitute for the army, but any day now he could be drafted again; the idea of military service frightened him. Félicité interpreted this cowardice as proof of his affection, and it redoubled hers. She stole away at night to meet him, and while they were together Théodore tortured her with his problems and entreaties.

At last, he declared that would go himself to the prefecture for information, and that he would inform her of what he found out on the following Sunday, between eleven o'clock and midnight.

When the moment arrived she hastened to her lover.

In his stead, she found one of his friends.

He told her that she was never to see Théodore again. To prevent himself from being drafted, Théodore had married a very rich *old* lady, Mme. Lehoussais of Toucques.

Félicité, beside herself with grief, threw herself to the ground, uttering cries, and calling upon the merciful God above. All alone she stayed there in the fields, and wept till morning. Then she went back to the farm and announced that she was leaving; and, at the end of the month, when she had received her wages, she bundled up her few little belongings in a handkerchief and went to Pont-l'Évêque.

In front of the inn, she made some inquiries of a woman wearing a widow's cap, and who, it just so happened, was looking for a cook. This young girl did not know much, but she seemed so willing and was asking for so little that Mme. Aubain ended by saying: "All right, I'll take you!"

Fifteen minutes later, Félicité was settled in her new house.

At first, she lived there in a sort of fear and trembling caused by "the tone of the house" and by the vivid memory of "Monsieur" which hovered over everything! Madame's children, Paul and Virginie, one seven and the other four, respectively, seemed to her to be made of some rare substance; she liked to carry them piggyback. But Mme. Aubain forbade her to kiss them too often, which mortified Félicité. However, she was happy. The gentleness of her surroundings had softened her grief.

Every Thursday, the close friends of Mme. Aubain used to come for a game of "Boston." Félicité had to get the cards and foot warmers ready in advance. They always arrived precisely at eight and left before the clock struck eleven.

Every Monday morning, the junk dealer who lived on the same street used to spread out his wares on the ground. Then the whole town was filled with the hum of many voices—together with the neighing of horses, the bleating of sheep, the grunting of pigs, and the rattle of carts down the street. About noon, when market time reached its peak, a tall, old peasant with a hooked nose, wearing his cap on the back of his head, would appear and stand in the doorway—this was Robelin, a farmer of Geffosses. A little while later, Liébard, a farmer from Toucques, short, ruddy, corpulent, wearing a gray coat and spurs, appeared in the same place.

Both brought chickens and cheeses to their landlady, Mme. Aubain. Invariably Félicité would cunningly outwit them, and they would go away with more respect for her shrewdness.

At various times, the Marquis of Gremanville, one of Mme. Aubain's uncles, used to visit her. He had ruined himself by debauchery and was now living in Falaise on his last bit of farmland. He invariably came at lunch time, accompanied by a dreadful poodle that always dirtied the furniture with its paws. Despite his efforts to play the role of the gentleman (he would raise his hat every time he said, "my late father"), force of habit compelled him to drink one glass after another and to blurt out risqué stories. Félicité would politely usher him out the door, saying "You have had enough, Monsieur de Gremanville! Some other time!" And she would shut the door on him.

To M. Bourais, a retired lawyer, the door was invitingly opened. His white cravat, his bald head, his frilled shirt, his full-fitting brown frock coat, his way of flourishing his arm when he took snuff—his whole person produced in her a certain excitement such as we all experience at the sight of extraordinary men.

As he was the manager of Madame's properties, he spent hours with her in "Monsieur's" study, all the time fearful of compromising his position. He had great respect for the bench. Moreover, he had some pretensions to being a Latin scholar.

To make learning pleasant for the children, he gave them a geography book consisting of prints. There were representative scenes from all over the world: cannibals with feathered headdresses; a monkey carrying away a damsel; Bedouins in the desert; a whale being harpooned, and so on.

Paul explained these pictures to Félicité. And this was the extent of her literary education.

The children's education was in the hands of Guyot, a wretched individual working at the Town Hall, who was famous for his beautiful handwriting and for the way he sharpened his penknife on his boot.

When the weather was clear, they all used to start early for the Geffosses farm.

The farmyard is on the side of a slope, with the house in the middle; and the sea, from a distance, looks like a gray blot.

Félicité would take out slices of cold meat from her basket, and they all would eat in a room that adjoined the milk house. It was all that remained of a once elegant country house. Now the wallpaper hung like tattered ribbons, and rustled with the drafts from the window. Mme. Aubain would bow her head, weighed down by memories of the past; the children would no longer dare to speak. "Go out and play!" she would say to them; and off they would go.

Paul climbed up in the barn, caught birds, played ducks and drakes, or tapped with a stick the huge barrels that rumbled like drums.

Virginie fed the rabbits and scampered away to pick cornflowers, her legs moving so quickly that you could see her little lace-trimmed drawers.

One autumn evening they were returning through the fields.

The moon in its first quarter lit a segment of the sky, and a haze floated like a scarf over the winding Toucques river. Cattle, lying in the middle of the meadow, gazed contentedly at these four people. In the third pasture, some of the cows got up and circled them. "Don't be afraid!" said Félicité, and stroking the back of the one nearest to her, she murmured a sort of lament. It turned around and the others did the same. But, when they crossed the next field, they heard a loud bellow. It was a bull, hidden in the haze. He came toward the two women. Mme. Aubain was about to run. "No, no, not so fast!" Nevertheless, though they quickened their steps, they heard back of them the sound of snorting, coming closer and closer. His hoofs beat like hammer blows on the meadow grass. Now he was galloping toward them!

Félicité turned around and, with both hands, snatched up clods of turf to throw into the bull's eyes. He lowered his head, shook his horns, and, trembling with fury, bellowed terrribly. Mme. Aubain, at the end of the pasture with the two little ones, looked frantically for a way to get over the high bank. Félicité backed steadily away from the bull, throwing grass and dirt at him all the time, to blind him, while at the same time she shouted, "Hurry! Hurry!"

Mme. Aubain jumped into the ditch, pushing Virginie, then Paul, in front of her. She stumbled several times, struggling to climb the bank, and by sheer courage finally succeeded.

The bull had backed Félicité against a fence; his slaver spattered her face; a second more and he would have gored her. She just had time to crawl between two fence rails. The huge animal stopped, amazed.

At Pont-l'Évêque, they talked of this adventure for many years. However, Félicité was not proud of it, nor did she think that she had done anything heroic.

Virginie took up all her time—for, as a result of her fright, she had developed a nervous disorder, and M. Poupart, the physician, advised seabaths for her at Trouville.

At that time not many people frequented Trouville. Mme. Aubain sought information about the place, consulted with Bourais, and made preparations as if embarking on a long voyage.

They sent off her baggage the day before, in Liébard's cart. The next day, he brought to the house two horses, one of which had a lady's saddle, with a velvet back; the other had a cloak rolled up like a seat on the crupper.

Mme. Aubain mounted her horse, behind Liébard. Félicité took charge of Virginie, and Paul rode M. Lechaptois' donkey, lent to him on condition that he take good care of it.

The road was so bad that it took two hours to go five miles. The horses sank into mud up to their pasterns, and had to make strenuous movements with their haunches to extricate themselves; they would sometimes stumble in ruts; other times they had to leap over them. In some places Liébard's mare would stop all of a sudden. Patiently he would wait for her to go on again; meantime he talked about the people whose property bordered the road, interpolating moral reflections on the story told. Thus, while they were in the middle of Toucques, as they were passing under a window full of nasturtiums, he remarked, shrugging his shoulders: "There's that Mme. Lehoussais, who instead of taking in a young man . . ." Félicité did not hear the rest; the horses were trotting; the donkey was galloping. They all filed down the path, a gate swung open, two boys appeared, and they dismounted in front of a dung heap on the very threshold.

When Mme. Liébard spotted her mistress, she was profuse in her expressions of delight. She served her a luncheon of sirloin of beef, tripe, black pudding, a fricassee of chicken, frothy cider, a fruit tart, and plums in brandy—all the time paying the Madame polite compliments, saying how wonderful she looked, how Mademoiselle was becoming "magnificent," and how Paul was growing so strong. Nor did she forget their deceased grandparents, whom the Liébards had known, as they had been in the service of the family for generations. The farm, like them, had the quality of oldness. The ceiling beams were worm-eaten, the walls black with smoke, the window panes gray with dust. On an oak sideboard were set all sorts of utensils, jugs, dishes, pewter bowls, wolf-traps, and sheep shears; and a big syringe made the children laugh. There was not a tree in the three courtyards that did not have mushrooms growing at its base or a tuft of mistletoe on its branches. The wind had blown some of the trees down. They had begun to grow again in the middle; and all of them were bent under the weight of the apples. The thatched roofs, like brown velvet and varying in thickness, had withstood the most violent gales. However, the wagon shed was falling into ruin. Mme. Aubain said she would tend to it later, and ordered the animals to be resaddled.

It was another half hour before they arrived in Trouville. The little caravan dismounted to pass Écores—a cliff jutting out over some boats—and three minutes later, at the end of the quay, they entered the courtyard of the "Golden Lamb" kept by Mme. David.

Virginie, from the very first days there, began to feel less weak—the result of the change of air and the effect of the baths, which she took in her chemise, for want of a bathing costume. Her nurse dressed her in a customhouse shed, which was used by the bathers.

In the afternoon, with the donkey, they rode off beyond the Roches-Noires, in the direction of Hennequeville. The path rose, at first, over hilly terrain like the lawn of a park; then it reached a plateau where meadows alternated with plowed fields. By the edge of the road, in briar thickets, stood holly bushes; here and there, a great lifeless tree made zigzags in the blue sky with its naked branches.

Nearly always they would rest awhile in a meadow, with Deauville to their left, Le Havre to the right, and before them the open sea. It sparkled in the sun, smooth like a mirror, so calm that you could hardly hear its murmuring. Unseen sparrows chirped, and the immense vault of heaven hung over everything. Mme. Aubain sat on the ground, doing her sewing; Virginie, next to her, plaited rushes; Félicité was weeding some lavender flowers; Paul was bored and wanted to go back.

On other occasions, they would go by boat across the Toucques, looking for shells. At low tide, they found sea urchins, starfish, and jellyfish; and the children would chase the flakes of foam carried by the wind. The waves, breaking on the sand, unrolled sleepily along the beach. The latter stretched as far as you could see, but on the landward side, it ended in the dunes that separated it from the Marais, a wide meadow shaped like an arena. When they returned that way, Trouville, on the hill slope in the background, loomed larger with every step, and its houses, with their uneven rooftops, seemed to be spread in colorful disorder.

On days when it was too hot, they did not leave their room. The dazzling brightness from outside made golden streaks through the venetian blinds. The village was silent. No one was to be seen on the sidewalks below. The all-pervading silence intensified the peacefulness. In the distance the hammers of the caulkers tapped on the hulls of the boats and a warm breeze wafted up the odor of tar.

The chief amusement was watching the ships return. As soon as they had passed the buoys, they began to maneuver. They lowered the sails on two of the three masts, and, with the foresail swelling like a balloon, they moved in gliding fashion over the chopping waves, until they reached the middle of the harbor where they suddenly dropped anchor. Then the boat docked against the pier. The sailors threw squirming fish over the side; a line of carts was awaiting them, and women in cotton bonnets rushed forward to take the baskets and to kiss their men.

One day one of them came up to Félicité, who, a little later, went to her room overjoyed. She had found a sister, Nastasie Barette, whose married name was Leroux, nursing an infant; and on her right-hand side was another child, and at her left was a little cabin boy with his hands on his hips and a beret cocked over his ear.

After fifteen minutes, Mme. Aubain sent them away.

But they were always to be seen outside her kitchen or on their walks. The husband never appeared.

Félicité took a liking to them. She bought them a blanket, some shirts, and a stove; it was obvious they were taking advantage of her. And this weakness of hers annoyed Mme. Aubain, who, moreover, did not like the familiar ways of Félicité's nephew with her son. And, as Virginie was coughing and the weather was no longer good, she decided to go back to Pont-l'Évêque.

M. Bourais advised her on the choice of a school for Paul. The one at Caen was considered to be the best, so he was sent there. He said his good-byes bravely and was content to be going to live in a house where he would have companions his age.

Mme. Aubain resigned herself to her son's departure, because it was necessary. Virginie thought about it less and less. Félicité missed his noise. But a new interest diverted her: from Christmas time onward, she took the little girl to her catechism lesson every day.

III

When she had made her genuflection at the door of the church, Félicité walked under the lofty nave between the double row of chairs, opened Mme. Aubain's pew, sat down, and gazed around.

The choir stalls were filled with boys on the right and girls on the left; the curé was standing next to the lectern. One stained-glass window in the apse depicted the Holy Ghost hovering over the Virgin; another showed her on her knees before the Christ Child, and behind the tabernacle a group carved in wood depicted St. Michael overcoming the dragon.

The priest began with an outline of Sacred History. Félicité formed vivid pictures in her mind of Paradise, the Flood, the Tower of Babel, cities in flames, people dying, idols being overturned. She learned from these bewildering scenes a reverence for the Most High and a fear of His wrath. Then, she wept when the Passion was narrated. Why had they crucified Him—He who loved the little children, He who fed the multitudes, He who cured the blind, and He who had consented, out of meekness, to be born among the poor in a stable? The sowings, the harvests, the wine presses, all these familiar things the Gospel speaks of, were a part of her life; they had been sanctified by God's sojourn on earth. She loved lambs more tenderly out of love for the Lamb, and doves because of the Holy Ghost.

She found it difficult to imagine His person, for He was not only a bird, but a flame as well, and at still other times, a breath. She thought perhaps it is His light that hovers at night on the edge of the marshes, His breath that moves the clouds, His voice that gives the bells their harmony! Thus she sat in adoration, delighting in the cool walls and the peacefulness of the church.

As for Church dogmas, she did not understand or even try to understand them. The priest gave his sermon, the children recited, and she finally fell asleep. She woke up again with a start, when the people, leaving the church, clattered with their wooden shoes on the flagstones.

This is how Félicité, whose religious education had been neglected in her youth, learned her catechism—by hearing it repeated; and from that time on she imitated all of Virginie's practices, fasting when she did and going to confession with her. On Corpus Christi they made a small altar together.

She had looked forward with consternation to Virginie's first communion. Félicité made much ado about the little girl's rosary beads, her shoes, her prayerbook, her gloves. How she trembled as she helped Virginie's mother dress the child!

All through the mass, Félicité felt a terrible anxiety. She could not see one side of the choir—M. Bourais was in the way; but just in front of her, the band of young virgins, wearing white crowns over their lowered veils, looked to her like a field of snow. From afar she could recognize her precious little Virginie by her slender neck and by her enraptured bearing.

The altar bell tinkled. Heads bowed. There was silence. When the organ began to play again, the choir members and the whole congregation chanted the *Agnus Dei*. Then the boys began to move from their pews. After them the girls rose. Reverently, with their hands joined, they made their way to the brilliantly lit altar, and knelt on the first step, to receive the Divine Host in turn. Afterward they came back to their *prie-dieus* in the same order.

When it was Virginie's turn, Félicité leaned forward to see her; and in imagination, stimulated by genuine affection, she felt that she herself was this child. Virginie's face became her own; Virginie's dress clothed her; Virginie's heart throbbed in her own breast; when Virginie opened her mouth and closed her eyes, Félicité almost fainted.

Early the next morning, she went to the sacristy and asked M. le Curé to give her communion. She received it with devotion, but she did not feel the same ecstatic rapture.

Mme. Aubain wanted to make an accomplished person of her daughter; and, as Guyot could not teach her either English or music, she decided to board Virginie in the Ursuline Convent at Honfleur.

Virginie did not object. Félicité sighed and thought Madame was unfeeling. Then she decided that her mistress was, perhaps, right. These things were too much for Félicité to grasp.

So, one day, an old coach stopped in front of the door, and out stepped a nun who had come to fetch Virginie. Félicité lifted Virginie's baggage to the top of the vehicle, gave some instructions to the driver, and put on the seat six jars of jam, a dozen pears, and a bouquet of violets.

Virginie, at the last moment, began to sob; she hugged her mother who kissed her on the forehead and kept saying, "Come on, now! Be brave. Don't cry!" The side step was raised and the coach drove off.

Then Mme. Aubain broke down. That evening all her friends—the Lormeau family, Mme. Lechaptois, the Rochefeville ladies, M. de Houppeville, and Bourais—came to comfort her.

At first, her daughter's absence caused Mme. Aubain much grief. But three times a week she received a letter from Virginie. She wrote to her daughter on the other days, took strolls in the garden, or read a little, and in this way managed to fill the lonely hours.

Every morning, regularly, Félicité would go into Virginie's room and look around. It distressed her not to have to comb the girl's hair any more, not to lace her shoes, not to tuck her into bed—not to see her perpetually radiant face, not to hold her hand anymore when they went out together. For want of something to do, Félicité tried making lace, but her clumsy fingers broke the threads; she could not do anything, she could not sleep, and was, to use her own expression, "done in." To "distract herself," she asked permission to have her nephew Victor visit her.

He came on Sundays after mass—rosy-cheeked, bare-chested, and smelling of the fields he had crossed. Immediately Félicité set the table and they sat down to lunch facing each other. Félicité, eating as little as possible to save expense, stuffed him so much that finally he fell asleep. When vespers sounded, she woke him, brushed his trousers, knotted his tie, and went to the church with him, leaning on his arm with a kind of maternal pride.

His parents always instructed him to get something out of her—either a box of brown sugar, some soap, some brandy, or sometimes even money. He always brought his old clothes to Félicité to be mended. She was happy to do this task because it meant he had to come back.

In August his father took him off on a cruise along the coast.

It was vacation time, and the arrival of the children consoled her in the absence of her nephew. But Paul was getting contrary and Virginie was now too old to be addressed familiarly. Now there was a barrier—a feeling of uneasiness—between Virginie and Félicité.

Victor went to Morlaix, Dunkirk, and then to Brighton; and on his return from each trip he brought Félicité a present. The first time it was a box made of sea shells; then it was a coffee cup; from his third trip it was a large gingerbread man. Victor was becoming good-looking: he was well-built, he wore a small mustache, his eyes were attractively frank, and he cocked his small leather cap back like a pilot's. He amused her by telling stories mixed with sailors' lingo.

One Monday, July 14, 1819 (she never forgot the date), Victor told her that he had signed up for a long voyage, and that during the night of the following day, he would take the Honfleur boat to join his schooner which was to weigh anchor from Le Havre soon afterward. He would, perhaps, be gone for two years.

The thought of such a long absence dismayed Félicité, and, to say good-bye to him again, on Wednesday evening, after Madame's dinner, she put on her clogs and traveled the long twelve miles between Pont-l'Évêque and Honfleur.

When she arrived at the Calvary instead of turning left, she went right, got lost in the shipyards, and had to retrace her steps. Some people whom she approached advised her to hurry along. She went all around the ship-filled harbor, stumbling over the moorings. Where the ground sloped, lights criss-crossed. Félicité thought she was losing her mind, for she saw horses in the heavens.

On the wharf's edge, horses, frightened by the sea, were neighing. A crane was lifting them and lowering them into a boat where passengers were jostling one another amid cider casks, baskets of cheese, and grain sacks.

Over the cackling of the chickens, one could hear the captain cursing. A cabin boy, undisturbed by all the confusion, leaned over the bow.

Félicité, who had not recognized him, suddenly called, "Victor!" He raised his head; she darted toward him, but at that moment the gangplank was raised.

The boat, towed by singing women, eased away from the wharf. Her hull creaked, and heavy water lashed against the prow. The sail had been turned around, hence no one could be seen any longer on her decks. On the silvery, moonlit sea, she became a black spot that gradually faded out of sight, then sank below the horizon.

As Félicité passed Calvary she wanted to commend to God this boy whom she loved most. She stood there a long time praying, her face bathed in tears, her eyes raised to heaven.

The town slept; only custom officials walked about. There was the sound of water, like that of a torrent, pouring through the holes of a sluice. The town clock struck two.

The convent reception room would not be open before morning. If she was late, Madame would surely be annoyed; so, in spite of a great desire to see Virginie, she returned home. The serving girls of the inn were just getting up when she reached Pont-l'Évêque.

"For months and months that poor boy is going to be tossing about on the waves!" thought Félicité. She had not been frightened by his previous voyages. One always returned safely from England or Brittany; but America, the colonies, the islands—all these were lost in a hazy region at the other end of the world.

From this moment on, Félicité thought of nothing but her nephew. On sunny days, she imagined he was thirsty; when it was stormy, she feared for him the lightning. As she listened to the wind howling down the chimney or heard it carrying off the slates, she saw him battered by this same storm, as he clung to the top of a broken masthead, his body bent back under the wash of the waves. At other times—remembering the geography prints—she imagined him being eaten by cannibals, captured by apes in the jungle, or lying dead on some deserted beach. But never did she speak of these secret apprehensions.

Mme. Aubain had her own apprehensions about her daughter.

The good nuns thought Virginie an affectionate but delicate child. The least bit of excitement upset her. She had to give up her piano lessons.

Her mother demanded from the convent authorities a regular flow of letters. One morning when there was no mail, she became very impatient; she walked up and down her room from the chair to the window. It was very strange indeed! No mail in four days!

To console her, Félicité said, "Look at me, Madame, it has been six months since I received any . . . !"

"From whom? . . ."

"Why . . . from my nephew!" meekly replied the servant.

"Oh! your nephew!" Mme. Aubain began to pace again, shrugging her shoulders as if to say: "I wasn't thinking of him! . . . Besides, he is nothing to me! A cabin boy, a little scamp! . . . While my daughter . . . just think!"

Félicité, though accustomed to rudeness, felt indignant at Madame, but overlooked it as usual.

It seemed very natural to her that one could lose one's head over a little girl.

The two children, Virginie and her nephew, were equally dear to her—they both shared her heart! And their destinies were to be the same.

The druggist told her that Victor's boat had docked in Havana. He had read this bit of news in a newspaper.

On account of cigars, she imagined Havana to be a country where everyone did nothing but smoke. She could visualize Victor moving among the Negroes in a cloud of tobacco fumes. Could one "in case of necessity" return from Havana by land, she wondered. How far was it from Pont-l'Évêque? For answers to these questions, she turned to M. Bourais.

He took out his atlas and began explaining longitudes; and smiled in a pedantic manner at Félicité's amazement. Then with his pencil he pointed to an almost imperceptible black dot on an oval spot, and said, "Here it is." She leaned over the map. This network of colored lines blurred her vision and meant nothing to her; and when Bourais asked her to say what was puzzling her, she begged him to point to the house where Victor was staying. Bourais threw up his arms, sneezed, and roared with laughter; such simplicity was sheer joy to him. But Félicité did not understand why he was so amused—how could she when she perhaps expected to see her nephew's portrait on the map—so limited was her understanding!

It was two weeks afterward that Liébard came into the kitchen at market time as usual, and handed her a letter from her brother-in-law. Since neither of them could read, she took it to her mistress.

Mme. Aubain, who was counting stitches in her knitting, put her work aside, opened the letter, trembled, and with a look full of meaning, said in a low voice, "It is bad news . . . that they have to tell you. Your nephew . . . ."

He was dead. The letter said no more.

Félicité slumped into a chair, and leaned her head back. She closed her eyelids which had suddenly become pink. Then, with her head down, her hands hanging idly, her eyes fixed, she kept saying over and over, "Poor boy! Poor little boy!"

Liébard, murmuring sighs of consolation, watched her. Mme. Aubain was still shaking a little. She suggested to Félicité that she go visit with her sister at Trouville.

Félicité made a gesture to indicate there was no need to do so.

There was silence. Liébard thought it wise that they leave Félicité alone.

Then Félicité said, "They don't care! It means nothing to them!"

She dropped her head again, but, from time to time, she mechanically picked up the long knitting needles from the worktable.

Women passed in the courtyard with their barrows of dripping linen.

Seeing them through the window, Félicité remembered her own washing. Having soaked it the day before, she had to rinse it today; and she left the room.

Her plank and wooden bucket were down by the Toucques. She threw a pile of underclothing on the river bank, rolled up her sleeves, and took the paddle in her hand. The heavy beating she gave her laundry could be heard in the nearby gardens. The meadows were empty, the wind made ripples on the surface of the water; while deep down, tall weeds swayed, like the hair of corpses floating in the water. Félicité suppressed her grief and was very brave till evening; but in her room, she broke down completely and lay on her bed with her face buried in the pillow and her hands clenched against her temples.

Much later, she heard from the captain himself the circumstances of Victor's death. He had had yellow fever. Four doctors had held him while they bled him—too much—at the hospital. He died immediately and the head doctor said: "There! Another one!"

Victor's parents had always been brutal to him. Félicité preferred not to see them again; and they in turn made no attempt to see her, either because they had forgotten about her, or because of the callousness of the poor.

Meanwhile, at the convent, Virginie became weaker. Congestion in her lungs, coughing, a continuous fever, and splotches on her cheekbones indicated some deep-seated illness. M. Poupart prescribed a few days in Provence. Mme. Aubain agreed to that, and would have brought her daughter home at once were it not for the climate of Pont-l'Évêque.

She chartered a carriage and was driven to the convent every Tuesday. There is a terrace in the garden from which you can see the Seine. Virginie would walk there on her mother's arm, over the fallen vine leaves. Sometimes the sun piercing through the clouds made her blink, as she gazed at the distant sails and the whole horizon—from the Château of Tancarville to the lighthouse of Le Havre. Then they would rest under an arbor. Her mother had with her a little flask of excellent Malaga wine, and, laughing at the idea of getting a little tipsy, Virginie would drink just a little, no more.

She regained strength. Autumn passed pleasantly. Félicité reassured Mme. Aubain. But, one evening when she had been running errands in the neighborhood, she saw on her return M. Poupart's carriage in front of the door. He was in the vestibule. Mme. Aubain was tying on her hat.

"Give me my foot warmer, my handbag, and gloves! Hurry!"

Virginie had pneumonia. Perhaps her case was already hopeless.

"Not yet!" said the doctor and both got into his carriage, under whirling flakes of snow. Night was falling. It was very cold.

Félicité rushed into church to light a candle. Then she ran after the carriage which she overtook an hour later. She had jumped nimbly on behind, and was holding on to the straps, when she suddenly thought: "The courtyard isn't locked! Suppose thieves break in!" And she jumped off.

At dawn of the following day, she went to the doctor's house. He had returned, but had left again for the country. Then she stayed at the inn, thinking some stranger would bring a letter. Finally, at dusk, she took the Lisieux stagecoach.

The convent was at the bottom of a steep lane. About half way down, Félicité heard strange sounds—a death knell. "It's for someone else," she thought. But she knocked violently on the door.

After several minutes, she heard the shuffling of slippers; the door was opened a crack and a nun appeared.

The good sister, with a compassionate air, said that Virginie "had just passed away." At that moment, the tolling at Saint-Léonard's became louder.

Félicité went up to the second floor of the convent.

From the doorway she could see Virginie lying on her back, her hands folded, her mouth open, and her head tilted back under an overhanging black cross between two motionless curtains, less pale than her face. Mme. Aubain, clutching the foot of the bed, was sobbing uncontrollably. The Mother Superior was standing on the right. Three candles on the dresser made shafts of red light, and mist whitened the windowpanes. Some nuns led Mme. Aubain away.

For two nights Félicité did not leave her death watch. She repeated the same prayers, sprinkled the sheets with holy water, sat down again, and gazed at the dead girl. At the end of the first night, she noticed that the face had yellowed, the lips had turned blue, the nose was sharper and the eyes were deeper. She kissed them several times, and would not have been surprised if they had opened again; for to minds like hers the supernatural is quite simple. She dressed her, wrapped her in a shroud, laid her body in the coffin, arranged her hair and placed a wreath upon her head. The hair was blond and extraordinarily long for her age. Félicité cut a thick lock of it and slipped half of it into Virginie's bosom. She resolved never to part with hers.

The corpse was brought back to Pont-l'Évêque, according to the wishes of Mme. Aubain, who followed the hearse in a closed carriage.

After the mass, it took another three-quarters of an hour to reach the cemetery. Paul, sobbing, walked ahead of the cortege. M. Bourais walked behind, followed by the principal residents of the village, the women wearing black mantles, and Félicité. She was thinking of her nephew, and because she had not been able to pay these respects to him, her sadness was intensified, as if he were being interred with Virginie.

Mme. Aubain's despair knew no limits.

At first she cried out against God, thinking it unjust for Him to have taken her daughter—Virginie who had never hurt anyone, and whose soul was so pure! But no! She should have taken her to the south. Other doctors could have saved her! She railed at herself, she wanted to join Virginie in death, she cried out distressfully in her dreams. One dream especially haunted her. Her husband, dressed like a sailor, came back from a long voyage and told her tearfully that he had received orders to take Virginie away. Then, they both tried to find a hiding place somewhere.

Once Mme. Aubain came in from the garden terribly upset. A little while before (she could point out the spot) the father and daughter, standing side by side, had appeared to her; they did nothing; they just looked at her.

For several months she kept to her room—apathetic. Félicité reproached her gently, saying her mistress must take care of herself for the sake of her son, and in remembrance of "her."

"Her?" replied Mme. Aubain as though she were emerging from sleep. "Ah yes! . . . Yes! You do not forget her!" This was an allusion to the cemetery which Mme. Aubain was strictly forbidden to visit.

Félicité went there every day.

At exactly four o'clock, she would go by the houses, climb the hill, open the gate, and come to Virginie's grave. There was a little column of pink marble with a plaque at its base, to which was fastened a chain that enclosed a miniature garden. The borders disappeared under beds of flowers. Félicité watered the plants, upturned the gravel, and knelt down better to dress the ground. Mme. Aubain, when at last she could visit the grave, felt a relief and a kind of consolation.

The years slipped by uneventfully and without any incidents other than the return of the great feast days: Easter, Assumption, All Saints' Day. Only household events were spoken of as important in the years that followed: for example, in 1825, two workmen whitewashed the vestibule; in 1827, part of the roof, falling into the courtyard, almost killed a man; in the summer of 1827, it became Madame's turn to offer the consecrated bread; Bourais, about this time, was mysteriously not around; and the old acquaintances one by one went away: Guyot, Liébard, Mme. Lechaptois, Robelin, Uncle Gremanville, who had been paralyzed for a long time now.

One night the driver of the mail coach announced in Pont-l'Évêque the

July Revolution.[2] A new subprefect was appointed a few days later: Baron de Larsonnière, an ex-consular official in America, and a man who had brought with him, in addition to his wife, his sister-in-law and her three daughters, almost grown up. They could be seen on their lawn, dressed in loose-fitting blouses; they had a Negro servant and a parrot. They paid a visit to Mme. Aubain, who returned their call promptly. Whenever Félicité saw them coming, she always ran to her mistress to forewarn her. But the only thing really capable of arousing Madame was letters from her son.

He could not follow any profession, since he spent most of his time in taverns. She paid his debts, but he contracted others; and the sighs that Mme. Aubain uttered, as she sat knitting by the window, reached Félicité as she turned her spinning wheel in the kitchen.

They took walks together along the espalier, and talked always about Virginie, wondering whether such and such would have pleased her, or what she would probably have said on this or that occasion.

All her little belongings were in a cupboard in the room with two beds. Mme. Aubain inspected them as seldom as possible. One summer day she resigned herself to doing so, and moths flew out of the cupboard.

Her dresses were arranged under a shelf on which sat three dolls, some hoops, a doll's house, and the basin that she used daily. They took out her petticoats, stockings, and handkerchiefs and spread them on the two beds, before folding them again. The sun, shining on these pitiful objects, brought out the spots and the creases made by the movements of Virginie's body. Outside the sky was blue, the air was warm, a blackbird warbled. Everything seemed vibrant with a heartfelt sweetness. They found a little hat of deeply piled plush, chestnut-colored; but it was all motheaten. Félicité wanted it for herself. They looked at each other and their eyes filled with tears; at last the mistress opened her arms and the servant threw herself into them. They held each other close, assuaging their grief in a kiss that made them equal.

This was the first time in their lives, for Mme. Aubain was not demonstrative by nature. Félicité was as grateful as if she had been presented with a gift; and from then on she cherished Mme. Aubain with a devotion that was almost animal and with an almost religious veneration.

The kindness of her heart grew.

When she heard in the street the drums of a marching regiment, she stood at the front door with a pitcher of cider and asked the soldiers to drink. She took care of cholera patients. She protected the Poles,[3] and there was even one who wanted to marry her. But they quarreled, for one morn-

[2] The revolution of July 1830, by which the Bourbons were driven from the throne and Louis-Philippe became "King of the French." [3] Many Poles came to France after the Polish uprising against Russia in 1831 was crushed.

ing, returning from the Angelus, she found that he had entered her kitchen, prepared a salad, and was nonchalantly eating it.

After the Poles came Papa Colmiche, an old man who was supposed to have been guilty of some atrocities in '93.[4] He lived along the riverbank, in a tumble-down pigsty. The little boys used to spy on him through cracks in the wall and throw stones at him that always landed on the squalid bed where he lay, continually racked by a cough. His hair was long, his eyes inflamed, and on his arm grew a tumor bigger than his head. Félicité supplied him with linen and tried to keep his miserable hut clean. It was her wish to have him installed in the bakehouse without his annoying Madame. When the tumor opened, she dressed it every day. Sometimes she brought him some cake. She used to lay him in the sun on a bed of straw. The poor old fellow, slobbering and shaking, would thank her in his weak voice. He was afraid of losing her, and would stretch out his hand when he saw her going away. He died. She had a mass said for the repose of his soul.

On that day, fortune smiled on her: at the dinner hour, the Negro servant of Mme. de Larsonnière came carrying the parrot in a cage, with perch, chain, and padlock. A note from the baroness informed Mme. Aubain that, because her husband was promoted to a prefecture, they were leaving that evening; and she begged her to accept the bird as a remembrance and a mark of her esteem.

For a long time this bird had occupied Félicité's thoughts, because he came from America and America reminded her of Victor—so much so that she questioned the Negro about that country. Once she had even remarked: "How happy Madame would be to have him!"

The Negro had told this to his mistress, and since she could not take the bird with her, she disposed of him in this fashion.

IV

The parrot was called Loulou. His body was green, the tip of his wings pink, his forehead blue, and his throat golden.

But he had the tiresome habit of biting his perch, plucking his feathers, scattering his mess about, and spattering the water of his bath. Mme. Aubain thought the bird was a nuisance and gave him to Félicité to keep.

She set out to train the parrot; soon he could repeat: "Nice boy," "Your servant, sir," "Hello, Mary!" He was placed next to the door, and people were surprised that he would not answer to Jacquot, for weren't all parrots called Jacquot? They likened him to a turkey, to a log of wood; and each time they did so Félicité was hurt to the quick! But Loulou was curiously stubborn! He stopped talking when one looked at him!

[4] 1793, the year of the Reign of Terror during the French Revolution.

Yet he liked company, for on Sunday, while those Rochefeuille ladies, M. de Houppeville, and some new habitués—Onfray the apothecary, M. Varin, and Captain Mathieu—were playing cards, he would beat the windowpanes with his wings, and would fling himself about so violently that it was impossible to hear oneself speak.

Bourais' face, undoubtedly, struck him as being very funny. As soon as he spotted Bourais, he would begin to laugh—to laugh with all his might. His noises reverberated through the courtyard, echoes repeated them, the neighbors stood at their windows and laughed too. Therefore, so as not to be seen by the parrot, M. Bourais would slither along the wall, hiding his face under his hat, and, getting down to the river, would enter the house by the garden door. The looks he then shot at the bird were far from tender.

Loulou had been slapped by the butcher boy for taking the liberty of putting his head into the meat basket. Since then, the bird always tried to pinch him through his shirt. Fabu threatened to wring Loulou's neck, although he was not cruel, in spite of his tattooed arms and long sideburns. On the contrary! He was rather fond of the parrot and, in a jovial mood, he even wanted to teach him some curse words. Félicité, alarmed by all these tricks, removed the parrot to the kitchen.

Later, his little chain was removed and he roamed about the house. He would come downstairs by hooking his curved beak on the steps, lifting first his right leg, then his left. Félicité was afraid that all these gymnastics would make the bird dizzy. Sure enough, he did become ill and could neither talk nor eat. There was a thickness under his tongue such as chickens sometimes develop. She cured him by scratching out this thickness with her fingernail.

M. Paul, one day, had the effrontery to blow cigar smoke into the parrot's nostrils. Another time, when Mme. Lormeau was teasing him with the end of her parasol, Loulou snapped at the metal ring. Finally, the bird got lost.

Félicité had put him on the grass to give him some fresh air and had gone away for a minute. When she returned, the parrot was gone! First, she searched in the bushes, then by the riverbank, and on the roofs, paying no attention to her mistress who was screaming, "Be careful! You must be out of your mind!"

Then Félicité looked in all the gardens of Pont-l'Évêque, and she stopped everyone passing by—"You haven't seen my parrot, by chance, have you?" To those who did not know the bird, she gave a description. Suddenly, she thought she spotted something green fluttering behind the mill at the bottom of the hill. But when she approached—nothing! A peddler told her he had seen a parrot a little while ago at Saint-Melaine, in Mère Simon's shop. She ran all the way. They didn't know what she was talking about. Finally, she came home, exhausted, her slippers in shreds, her heart broken by disappointment. As she was sitting on a bench close to Mme. Aubain and was telling her everywhere she had been, a light weight fell on her shoulder. It was Loulou! What the devil had he been doing? Probably taking a stroll in the neighborhood!

Félicité had trouble getting over this—or rather, she never did recover from it.

As a result of a cold, Félicité had an attack of quinsy, and a little later an ear infection. Three years later she was deaf; and she spoke very loud, even in church. Though her sins might have been bruited abroad to all corners of the diocese without shame to her or scandal to anyone, the parish priest thought it best henceforth to hear her confession only in the sacristy.

Imaginary buzzings in the head added to her afflictions. Often her mistress would say to her: "My word, how stupid you are!" She would simply answer, "Yes, Madame," and go look for something to do near her.

The small scope of her ideas became smaller still, and the pealing of the church bells and the lowing of the cattle ceased to exist for her. All living creatures moved about silently as ghosts. The only sound that she could hear now was the voice of the parrot.

As if to distract her, Loulou would mimic the tic-tac of the turnspit, the shrill cry of the fish vendor, the noise of the carpenter's saw across the road, and when the bell rang, he would imitate Mme. Aubain—"Félicité! The door, the door!"

They had conversations, Loulou incessantly repeating the three short phrases in his repertory, to which Félicité would reply with phrases just as disconnected, but in which there was deep sincerity. Loulou was almost a son and lover to her in her isolated world. He would climb on her fingers, nibble at her lips, and cling to her kerchief; and, when she leaned forward, shaking her head as nurses do, the long wings of her bonnet and those of the bird moved together.

When the clouds were banked on top of one another and the thunder began to roll, Loulou would utter cries, remembering, perhaps, the downpours in his native forests. Teeming rain made him absolutely mad with joy; he fluttered about wildly, he climbed the ceiling, knocked everything over, and went out through the window to splash in the garden; but he would come back quickly and alight on one of the andirons, and hopping about to dry his feathers, he would show first his tail, then his beak.

One morning in the terrible winter of 1837, when Félicité had put Loulou in front of the fireplace because of the cold, she found him dead, in the center of his cage, his head down, and his claws clutching the wire bars. Undoubtedly, he had died of a congestion. But Félicité thought he had been poisoned with parsley, and despite all lack of evidence, she suspected Fabu.

She wept so bitterly that her mistress said to her: "Well then, have the bird stuffed."

She asked the pharmacist's advice, since he had always been kind to the parrot.

He wrote to Le Havre. A certain man named Fellacher undertook the job. But as parcels sometimes got lost when sent by the stagecoach, she decided to take it herself as far as Honfleur.

Leafless apple trees lined both sides of the road. Ice covered the ditches. Dogs barked on the farms. Félicité, with her hands under her cloak, carrying her basket, and wearing her little black sabots, walked briskly along in the middle of the road.

She went through the forest, passed Haut-Chêne, and reached Saint-Gatien.

Behind her, in a cloud of dust, gathering speed down a steep hill, came a mail coach, with horses at full gallop, like the wind. Seeing this woman who was not paying any attention, the driver stood up, and the postilion shouted, too. All the while the four horses which the driver could not hold back gained speed. The first two horses grazed Félicité. With a pull on the reins, he veered to the side, but, furious, he raised his arm, and in full flight, with his heavy whip he gave her such a lash from her stomach to her neck that she fell on her back.

Her first action, when she regained consciousness, was to open the basket. Fortunately, Loulou was all right. She felt a burning on her right cheek, and when she touched it, her hands were red. The blood was streaming.

She sat down on a pile of stones and dabbed her face with a handkerchief; then she ate a crust of bread which she had put in her basket just in case, and took consolation for her own wound in gazing at the bird.

When she arrived at Ecquemauville, she could see below the lights of Honfleur, which twinkled in the night like a cluster of stars; the sea, beyond, spread out indistinctly. Then weakness forced her to stop; and her wretched childhood, the disillusion of her first love, the departure of her nephew, Virginie's death, all came back to her like the waves of a tide, rising to her throat and choking her.

Later she spoke to the captain of the boat; and without telling him what she was sending, she gave him instructions.

Fellacher kept the parrot a long time. He was always promising it for the following week. At the end of six months he announced it had been dispatched in a box; and then nothing more was heard about it. It seemed that Loulou was never coming back. "They have stolen him from me!" she thought.

Finally he did arrive—and how wonderful he looked sitting upright on a branch that was screwed to a mahogany base. One foot was held in the air. His head was tilted sidewise, and he was biting on a nut that the taxidermist, carried away by a flair for the grandiose, had painted gold!

Félicité put Loulou in her room.

This place, to which she admitted few, had so many religious objects and so many unusual things that it looked like a chapel and a bazaar combined.

A large wardrobe made it difficult to open the door. Opposite the window overlooking the garden, a small circular window looked down upon the courtyard. On a table near the folding bed stood a water pitcher, two combs, and a bar of blue soap on a chipped plate. On the walls hung rosary beads, medallions, several statues of the Virgin, and a holy water font made of a coconut; on the commode, covered with a cloth like that on altars, stood the box made of shells which Victor had given to her, a watering can, a balloon, some writing books, the geography picture book, and a pair of boots. Fastened by its ribbons to a nail on the mirror hung the small plush hat! Félicité carried this kind of respect to such extremes that she even kept one of Monsieur's frock coats. All the old things Mme. Aubain no longer wanted Félicité took to her room. For this reason there were artificial flowers on the edge of the commode, and a portrait of the Comte d'Artois[5] in the recess of the dormer window.

By means of a small shelf, Loulou was set prominently on the chimney piece that projected into the room. Every morning, when Félicité woke up, she could see him in the dawn's light, and she would recall painlessly and peacefully the old days with their insignificant events down to their last detail.

Communicating with no one, she lived in a kind of sleep-walking trance. The Corpus Christi processions rejuvenated her. She would go to her neighbors begging tapers and mats with which to decorate the altar being erected in the street.

In church she always sat gazing at the stained-glass window that portrayed the Holy Ghost, and noticed there was something of the parrot about it. The resemblance seemed to her more pronounced in a picture that depicted the Baptism of Our Lord. With its purple wings and its emerald body, it was really Loulou's portrait.

She bought this picture and hung it in the place formerly occupied by the Comte d'Artois—so that, with one glance, she could see them together. They became associated in her mind, the parrot becoming sanctified by this association with the Holy Ghost, which became more real in her eyes and easier to comprehend. God the Father, to reveal Himself, could not have chosen a dove, since those birds have no voices, but rather one of Loulou's ancestors. And Félicité, although she looked at the picture as she said her prayers, would turn from time to time toward the parrot.

She wanted to join the Ladies of the Blessed Virgin, but Mme. Aubain dissuaded her.

Then a great event occurred: Paul's marriage.

After having been in succession a clerk in a notary's office, in business, in the customs office, in the revenue service, and having even made efforts to

[5] Title of Charles X before he became king in 1824. He was the last Bourbon king and was overthrown in 1830, and died in exile in 1836.

get into the bureau of waters and forests—suddenly, at thirty-six, by an inspiration from heaven, he had discovered his career: that of registrar! He showed such aptitude for this kind of work that an inspector had offered him his daughter in marriage, promising to use his influence on Paul's behalf.

Paul, serious-minded now, brought the girl to see his mother.

She sniffed at the ways of Pont-l'Évêque, gave herself the airs of a princess, and hurt Félicité's feelings. Mme. Aubain felt relieved when the visitor left.

The following week news was brought of Bourais' death in an inn in lower Brittany. Rumors of suicide were later confirmed and doubts of his integrity were raised. Mme. Aubain pored over his accounts, and it didn't take her long to discover a long list of his misdeeds: embezzlements, fictitious sales of wood, forged receipts, etc. Besides that, he had an illegitimate child, and "relations with a certain person from Dozulé."

These scandalous acts distressed Madame very much. In March 1853, she was seized with a pain in her chest; her tongue was coated, and leeches did not give her any relief. On the ninth evening she died, having just reached her seventy-second birthday.

Everyone thought she was younger than she really was, because of her brown hair, braids of which framed her pallid, pockmarked face. Few friends regretted her passing, for with her haughty manner she kept people at a distance.

But Félicité mourned her as masters are seldom mourned. That Madame should have died before her disturbed her thoughts, seemed to her contrary to the nature of things, something inadmissible and monstrous.

Ten days later (the time it took to travel from Besançon) the heirs arrived. The daughter-in-law rummaged through drawers, selected certain pieces of furniture, sold the rest. Then they left, and, Paul returned to his registering.

Madame's armchair, her small round table, her foot warmer, the eight chairs were gone! On the walls were yellow squares that marked where pictures used to hang. They had carried off the two beds, with the mattresses, and Virginie's belongings were no longer to be seen in the cupboard! Félicité, numb with sadness, wandered from floor to floor.

Next day there was a notice on the door. The apothecary shouted in her ear that the house was for sale.

She staggered and had to sit down. What distressed her most of all was that she might have to give up her room—so comfortable for poor little Loulou. Gazing at the bird with a look of anguish, she prayed to the Holy Ghost. She had formed the idolatrous habit of saying her prayers on her knees in front of the parrot. Sometimes the sun breaking through the window caught his glass eye, and a long luminous ray would dart from it, throwing Félicité into ecstasy.

She had an income of three hundred and eighty francs a year, willed to her by Mme. Aubain. The garden provided her with vegetables. As for clothes, she had enough to last till the end of her days, and she saved on lighting by going to bed at dusk.

She rarely went out, in order to avoid the secondhand shop where some pieces of the old furniture were displayed for sale. Ever since her shock, she dragged one leg; and as her strength was failing Mère Simon, whose grocery business had fallen into ruin, used to come every morning to chop her wood and pump her water.

Félicité's eyesight became weak.

The shutters of the house would no longer open. Many years passed, but the place was not rented or sold.

For fear of being turned out, Félicité never asked for repairs. The laths of the roof began to rot, so that for a whole year the bolster of her bed was damp. After Easter she began to spit blood.

This time Mère Simon called a doctor. Félicité wanted to know what was the matter with her. But, too deaf to hear, she caught only one word: "Pneumonia." It was familiar enough to her and she answered, softly, "Ah! like Madame," thinking it natural that she should thus follow her mistress.

The time for preparing the altars was nearing. The first of them was always erected at the bottom of the hill, the second in front of the post office, and the third about halfway down the street. There was some difference of opinion concerning this last-mentioned, and the parishioners at last decided to put it in Mme. Aubain's courtyard.

The pain in Félicité's chest and her fever continued to increase. Félicité was annoyed because she could do nothing for the altar. If only she could have at least put something on it. Then she thought of the parrot. But the neighbors objected: it wasn't proper. However, the curé granted permission and this made her so happy that she begged him to accept Loulou, her sole valuable possession, when she died.

From Tuesday to Saturday, the eve of Corpus Christi, she coughed more and more. By the evening, her face was pinched, her lips clung to her gums, and she began to vomit, and next day at early dawn, feeling very weak, she sent for a priest.

Three kindly old women stood around while she received extreme unction. Then she said she wanted to speak to Fabu.

He came in his Sunday clothes, ill at ease in this sad atmosphere.

"Forgive me," she said, with an effort to extend her arm, "I thought it was you who had killed him!"

What did she mean by this nonsense? Suspecting a man like him of being a murderer! He was indignant, and was about to make a scene.

"As you can see, she makes no sense at all."

Every once in a while Félicité would talk to shadows. The three ladies went away and Mère Simon went to breakfast.

A little later Mère Simon took Loulou and, holding him near Félicité, said: "Come, now, say goodbye to him!"

Though he was not a corpse, the worms had begun to devour the dead bird; one of his wings was broken, and the stuffing was coming out of his body. But Félicité, now blind, kissed Loulou's forehead, and pressed him against her cheek. Mère Simon took him away and placed him on the altar.

V

A scent of summer drifted from the meadow; flies buzzed; the sun made the surface of the river glisten and heated the slate roofs. Mère Simon had come back into the room, and was dozing peacefully.

The tolling of the church bell awakened her; the people were coming from vespers. Félicité's delirium ceased. She thought of the procession, and saw it as if she had been there.

All the children from the schools, the choir singers together with the firemen, walked along on the pavement while in the middle of the road marched first the verger armed with his halberd, the beadle carrying his large cross, the schoolmaster watching his small charges, and the sister anxious for her little girls; three of the cutest of these, with curls like angels, were throwing rose petals in the air; the deacon, with his arms outstretched, was leading the music; and two incense bearers bowed at every step in front of the Blessed Sacrament, carried by M. le Curé wearing a beautiful chasuble, beneath a flaming red canopy, held by four churchwardens. Waves of people surged behind, between the white cloths covering the walls of the houses. They arrived at the foot of the hill.

Beads of cold sweat dampened Félicité's temples. Mère Simon sponged them with a piece of cloth, saying to herself that one day she would have to go too.

The murmur of the crowd mounted; for a moment, it was very loud, then it faded.

A fusillade rattled the windowpanes. It was the postilions saluting the monstrance. Félicité rolled her eyes and said as softly as she could:

"Is he all right?" She was anxiously thinking of her parrot.

Her death agony began. A rattle, more and more violent, shook her sides. Froth appeared at the corners of her mouth and her whole body was trembling.

Soon, above the blaring of the wind instruments, the clear voices of the children and the deep voices of men could be distinguished. At intervals, all was silent, except for the tread of feet shuffling over the strewn flowers, sounding like sheep on the grass.

The priests appeared in the courtyard. Mère Simon climbed on one of the chairs to look through the round window. In this way she could look down upon the altar.

Green wreaths hung from the altar, which was decorated with a flounce of English lace. In the middle there was a small receptacle containing relics; two orange trees stood at the corners, and all along were silver candlesticks and porcelain vases, filled with sunflowers, lilies, peonies, foxgloves, and tufts of hydrangea. This mass of brilliant colors banked from the level of the altar to the rug spread over the pavement. Strange objects caught the eye: a vermilion sugar bowl held a wreath of violets; pendants of Alençon stone glittered on the moss; two Chinese screens depicted landscapes. Loulou, concealed by the roses, showed nothing but his blue forehead, like a piece of lapis lazuli.

The churchwardens, choristers, and children stood in rows on three sides of the courtyard. The priest ascended the steps slowly, and put down his great, shining, golden monstrance on the lacework cloth. All knelt. There was a deep silence; and the censers, swinging to and fro, glided on their little chains.

A blue cloud of smoke rose to Félicité's room. She distended her nostrils, breathing it in with a mystical sensuousness; then she closed her eyes. Her lips were smiling. The beating of her heart became fainter and fainter, softer like an exhausted fountain, like a fading echo; and when she breathed her last breath, she thought she saw in the opening heavens a gigantic parrot, hovering above her head.

Fyodor Dostoevsky

The Dream of a Ridiculous Man

TRANSLATED BY CONSTANCE GARNETT

Fyodor Dostoevsky (1821–1881)

Fyodor Dostoevsky was born in Moscow. His father was a doctor who became a landowner with serfs. Dostoevsky was educated at the Military Engineering Academy in St. Petersburg and entered civil service as a draftsman, but soon resigned because he feared that his writing would displease his superiors. His first novel, *Poor People,* was warmly received; *The Double,* which followed shortly after, was a failure.

Dostoevsky became involved in a socialist secret society. In 1849 he was arrested, and brought before a firing squad. He escaped death only by a last-minute reprieve, which transmuted his sentence to hard labor in Siberia, where he spent four years wearing chains. When released in 1854, he was made a soldier and sent to the Mongolian frontier. Finally he was restored to his rights as a member of the landowning class, and in 1859 was allowed to return to St. Petersburg, where he founded a review which was soon suppressed although Dostoevsky had now become a nationalist and a conservative.

Dostoevsky traveled in Western Europe, gambled compulsively, became involved in complicated emotional relationships, and suffered frequent epileptic fits. He published *Crime and Punishment* in 1866, then married his secretary (his second wife) and left Russia again to escape his creditors. Caught in grinding poverty, the two wandered in Germany, Italy, and Switzerland. It was only in 1871, when the first part of *The Possessed* was published and gained popular success, that Dostoevsky returned to Russia. He started another periodical and gained fame and a measure of financial ease. *The Brothers Karamazov* was published shortly before his death.

Dostoevsky's novels owe something to the sensationalism and melodrama of much Romantic fiction. But in Dostoevsky the "thriller" has become internalized; it has become the instrument for plumbing man's inner darkness, violence, and self-loathing. Perhaps no other novelist has given so compelling a picture of the range of human degradation and of the human need to confess the crimes of the mind. Yet this degradation and universal guilt of man are the foundations of Dostoevsky's mystical Christianity, an insistence on the possibility of salvation for whoever, in saintlike fashion, assumes the burden of guilt and affirms the fraternity of mankind.

A recurrent theme in Dostoevsky's work is the validity of a man-made utopia, something he had believed in during his socialist phase and then finally rejected as only a vehicle to enslave man. True freedom, he came to believe, cannot be found in an engineered happiness but only through human suffering. The anguished, rambling confession of the self-proclaimed "ridiculous man" is centrally concerned with this problem.

The Dream of a Ridiculous Man

I

I am a ridiculous person. Now they call me a madman. That would be a promotion if it were not that I remain as ridiculous in their eyes as before. But now I do not resent it, they are all dear to me now, even when they laugh at me—and, indeed, it is just then that they are particularly dear to me. I could join in their laughter—not exactly at myself, but through affection for them, if I did not feel so sad as I look at them. Sad because they do not know the truth and I do know it. Oh, how hard it is to be the only one who knows the truth! But they won't understand that. No, they won't understand it.

In old days I used to be miserable at seeming ridiculous. Not seeming, but being. I have always been ridiculous, and I have known it, perhaps, from the hour I was born. Perhaps from the time I was seven years old I knew I was ridiculous. Afterwards I went to school, studied at the university, and, do you know, the more I learned, the more thoroughly I understood that I was ridiculous. So that it seemed in the end as though all the sciences I studied at the university existed only to prove and make evident to me as I went more deeply into them that I was ridiculous. It was the same with life as it was with science. With every year the same consciousness of the ridiculous figure I cut in every relation grew and strengthened. Every one always laughed at me. But not one of them knew or guessed that if there were one man on earth who knew better than anybody else that I was absurd, it was myself, and what I resented most of all was that they did not know that. But that was my own fault; I was so proud that nothing would have ever induced me to tell it to any one. This pride grew in me with the years; and if it had happened that I allowed myself to confess to any one that I was ridiculous, I believe that I should have blown out my brains the same evening. Oh, how I suffered in my early youth from the fear that I might give way and confess it to my schoolfellows. But since I grew to manhood, I have for some unknown reason become calmer, though I realised my awful characteristic more fully every year. I say "unknown," for to this day I cannot tell why it was. Perhaps it was owing to the terrible misery that was growing in my soul through something which was of more consequence than anything else about me: that something was the conviction that had come upon me that *nothing in the world mattered.* I had long had an inkling of it, but the full realisation came last year almost suddenly. I suddenly felt that it was all the same to me whether the world existed or whether there had never been anything at all: I began to feel with all my being that there was *nothing existing.* At first I fancied that many things had existed in the past, but afterwards I guessed that there never had been anything in the past either, but that it had only seemed so for some reason. Little by little I guessed that there would be nothing in the future either. Then I left off being angry with people and almost ceased to notice them. Indeed this showed itself even in the pettiest trifles: I used, for instance, to knock against people in the street. And not so much from being lost in thought: what had I to think about? I had almost given up thinking by that time; nothing mattered to me. If at least I had solved my problems! Oh, I had not settled one of them, and how many they were! But I gave up caring about anything, and all the problems disappeared.

And it was after that that I found out the truth. I learnt the truth last November—on the third of November, to be precise—and I remember every instant since. It was a gloomy evening, one of the gloomiest possible evenings. I was going home at about eleven o'clock, and I remember that I thought that the evening could not be gloomier. Even physically. Rain had been falling all day, and it had been a cold, gloomy, almost menacing rain, with, I remember, an unmistakable spite against mankind. Suddenly between ten and eleven it had stopped, and was followed by a horrible dampness, colder and damper than the rain, and a sort of steam was rising from everything, from every stone in the street, and from every by-lane if one looked down it as far as one could. A thought suddenly occurred to me, that if all the street lamps had been put out it would have been less cheerless, that the gas made one's heart sadder because it lighted it all up. I had had scarcely any dinner that day, and had been spending the evening with an engineer, and two other friends had been there also. I sat silent—I fancy I bored them. They talked of something rousing and suddenly they got excited over it. But they did not really care, I could see that, and only made a show of being excited. I suddenly said as much to them. "My friends," I said, "you really do not care one way or the other." They were not offended, but they all laughed at me. That was because I spoke without any note of reproach, simply because it did not matter to me. They saw it did not, and it amused them.

As I was thinking about the gas lamps in the street I looked up at the sky. The sky was horribly dark, but one could distinctly see tattered clouds, and between them fathomless black patches. Suddenly I noticed in one of these patches a star, and began watching it intently. That was because that star gave me an idea: I decided to kill myself that night. I had firmly determined to do so two months before, and poor as I was, I bought a splendid revolver that very day, and loaded it. But two months had passed and it was still lying in my drawer; I was so utterly indifferent that I wanted to seize a moment when I would not be so indifferent—why, I don't know. And so for two months every night that I came home I thought I would shoot myself. I kept waiting for the right moment. And so now this star gave me a thought. I made up my mind that it should certainly be that night. And why the star gave me the thought I don't know.

And just as I was looking at the sky, this little girl took me by the elbow. The street was empty, and there was scarcely any one to be seen. A cabman was sleeping in the distance in his cab. It was a child of eight with a kerchief on her head, wearing nothing but a wretched little dress all soaked with rain, but I noticed particularly her wet broken shoes and I recall them now. They caught my eye particularly. She suddenly pulled me by the elbow and called me. She was not weeping, but was spasmodically crying out some words which she could not utter properly, because she was shivering and shuddering all over. She was in terror about something, and kept crying, "Mammy, mammy!" I turned facing her, I did not say a word and went on; but she ran, pulling at me, and there was that note in her voice which in frightened children means despair. I know that sound. Though she did not articulate the words, I understood that her mother was dying, or that something of the sort was happening to them, and that she had run out to call some one, to find something to help her mother. I did not go with her; on the contrary, I had an impulse to drive her away. I told her first to go to a policeman. But clasping her hands, she ran beside me sobbing and gasping, and would not leave me. Then I stamped my foot, and shouted at her. She called out "Sir! sir! . . ." but suddenly abandoned me and rushed headlong across the road. Some other passer-by appeared there, and she evidently flew from me to him.

I mounted up to my fifth storey. I have a room in a flat where there are other lodgers. My room is small and poor, with a garret window in the shape of a semicircle. I have a sofa covered with American leather, a table with books on it, two chairs and a comfortable arm-chair, as old as old can be, but of the good old-fashioned shape. I sat down, lighted the candle, and began thinking. In the room next to mine, through the partition wall, a perfect Bedlam was going on. It had been going on for the last three days. A retired captain lived there, and he had half a dozen visitors, gentlemen of doubtful reputation, drinking vodka and playing *stoss* with old cards. The night before there had been a fight, and I know that two of them had been for a long time engaged in dragging each other about by the hair. The landlady wanted to complain, but she was in abject terror of the captain. There was only one other lodger in the flat, a thin little regimental lady, on a visit to Petersburg, with three little children who had been taken ill since they came into the lodgings. Both she and her children were in mortal fear of the captain, and lay trembling and crossing themselves all night, and the youngest child had a sort of fit from fright. That captain, I know for a fact, sometimes stops people in the Nevsky Prospect and begs. They won't take him into the service, but strange to say (that's why I am telling this), all this month that the captain has been here his behaviour has caused me no annoyance. I have, of course, tried to avoid his acquaintance from the very beginning, and he, too, was bored with me from the first; but I never care how much they shout the other side of the partition nor how many of them there are in there: I sit up all night and forget them so completely that I do not even hear them. I stay awake till daybreak, and have been going on like that for the last year. I sit up all night in my arm-chair at the table, doing nothing. I only read by day. I sit—don't even think; ideas of a sort wander through my mind and I let them come and go as they will. A whole candle is burnt every night. I sat down quietly at the table, took out the revolver and put it down before me. When I had put it down I asked myself, I remember, "Is that so?" and answered with complete conviction, "It is." That is, I shall shoot myself. I knew that I should shoot myself that night for certain, but how much longer I should go on sitting at the table I did not know. And no doubt I should have shot myself if it had not been for that little girl.

II

You see, though nothing mattered to me, I could feel pain, for instance. If any one had struck me it would have hurt me. It was the same morally: if anything very pathetic happened, I should have felt pity just as I used to do in old days when there were things in life that did matter to me. I had felt pity that evening. I should have certainly helped a child. Why, then, had I not helped the little girl? Because of an idea that occurred to me at the time: when she was calling and pulling at me, a question suddenly arose before me and I could not settle it. The question was an idle one, but I was vexed. I was vexed at the reflection that if I were going to make an end of myself that night, nothing in life ought to have mattered to me. Why was it that all at once I did not feel that nothing mattered and was sorry for the little girl? I remember that I was very sorry for her, so much so that I felt a strange pang, quite incongruous in my position. Really I do not know better how to convey my fleeting sensation at the moment, but the sensation persisted at home when I was sitting at the table, and I was very much irritated as I had not been for a long time past. One reflection followed another. I saw clearly that so long as I was still a human being and not nothingness, I was alive and so could suffer, be angry and feel shame at my actions. So be it. But if I am going to kill myself, in two hours, say, what is the little girl to me and what have I to do with shame or with anything else in the world? I shall turn into nothing, absolutely nothing. And can it really be true that the consciousness that I shall *completely* cease to exist immediately and so everything else will cease to exist, does not in the least affect my feeling of pity for the child nor the feeling of shame after a contemptible action? I stamped and shouted at the unhappy child as though to say—not only I feel no pity, but even if I behave inhumanly and contemptibly, I am free to, for in another two hours everything will be extinguished. Do you believe that that was why I shouted that? I am almost convinced of it now. It seemed clear to me that life and the world somehow depended upon me now. I may almost say that the world now seemed created for me alone: if I shot myself the world would cease to be at least for me. I say nothing of its being likely that nothing will exist for any one when I am gone, and that as soon as my consciousness is extinguished the whole world will vanish too and become void like a phantom, as a mere appurtenance of my consciousness, for possibly all this world and all these people are only me myself. I remember that as I sat and reflected, I turned all these new questions that swarmed one after another quite the other way, and thought of something quite new. For instance, a strange reflection suddenly occurred to me, that if I had lived before on the moon or on Mars and there had committed the most disgraceful and dishonourable action and had there been put to such shame and ignominy as one can only conceive and realise in dreams, in nightmares, and if, finding myself afterwards on earth, I were able to retain the memory of what I had done on the other planet and at the same time knew that I should never, under any circumstances, return there, then looking from the earth to the moon—*should I care or not?* Should I feel shame for that action or not? These were idle and superfluous questions for the revolver was already lying before me, and I knew in every fibre of my being that *it* would happen for certain, but they excited me and I raged. I could not die now without having first settled something. In short, the child had saved me, for I put off my pistol shot for the sake of these questions. Meanwhile the clamour had begun to subside in the captain's room: they had finished their game, were settling down to sleep, and meanwhile were grumbling and languidly winding up their quarrels. At that point I suddenly fell asleep in my chair at the table—a thing which had never happened to me before. I dropped asleep quite unawares.

Dreams, as we all know, are very queer things: some parts are presented with appalling vividness, with details worked up with the elaborate finish of jewelery, while others one gallops through, as it were, without noticing them at all, as, for instance, through space and time. Dreams seem to be spurred on not by reason but by desire, not by the head but by the heart, and yet what complicated tricks my reason has played sometimes in dreams, what utterly incomprehensible things happen to it! My brother died five years ago, for instance. I sometimes dream of him; he takes part in my affairs, we are very much interested, and yet all through my dream I quite know and remember that my brother is dead and buried. How is it that I am not surprised that, though he is dead, he is here beside me and working with me? Why is it that my reason fully accepts it? But enough. I will begin about my dream. Yes, I dreamed a dream, my dream of the third of November. They tease me now, telling me it was only a dream. But does it matter whether it was a dream or reality, if the dream made known to me the truth? If once one has recognised the truth and seen it, you know that it is the truth and that there is no other and there cannot be, whether you are asleep or awake. Let it be a dream, so be it, but that real life of which you make so much I had meant to extinguish by suicide, and my dream, my dream—oh, it revealed to me a different life, renewed, grand and full of power!

Listen.

III

I have mentioned that I dropped asleep unawares and even seemed to be still reflecting on the same subjects. I suddenly dreamt that I picked up the revolver and aimed it straight at my heart—my heart, and not my head; and I had determined beforehand to fire at my head, at my right temple. After aiming at my chest I waited a second or two, and suddenly my candle, my table, and the wall in front of me began moving and heaving. I made haste to pull the trigger.

In dreams you sometimes fall from a height, or are stabbed, or beaten, but you never feel pain unless, perhaps, you really bruise yourself against the bedstead, then you feel pain and almost always wake up from it. It was the same in my dream. I did not feel any pain, but it seemed as though with my shot everything within me was shaken and everything was suddenly dimmed, and it grew horribly black around me. I seemed to be blinded and benumbed, and I was lying on something hard, stretched on my back; I saw nothing, and could not make the slightest movement. People were walking and shouting around me, the captain bawled, the landlady shrieked—and suddenly another break and I was being carried in a closed coffin. And I felt how the coffin was shaking and reflected upon it, and for the first time the idea struck me that I was dead, utterly dead, I knew it and had no doubt of it, I could neither see nor move and yet I was feeling and reflecting. But I was soon reconciled to the position, and as one usually does in a dream, accepted the facts without disputing them.

And now I was buried in the earth. They all went away, I was left alone, utterly alone. I did not move. Whenever before I had imagined being buried the one sensation I associated with the grave was that of damp and cold. So now I felt that I was very cold, especially the tips of my toes, but I felt nothing else.

I lay still, strange to say I expected nothing, accepting without dispute that a dead man had nothing to expect. But it was damp. I don't know how long a time passed—whether an hour, or several days, or many days. But all at once a drop of water fell on my closed left eye, making its way through a coffin lid; it was followed a minute later by a second, then a minute later by a third—and so on, regularly every minute. There was a sudden glow of profound indignation in my heart, and I suddenly felt in it a pang of physical pain. "That's my wound," I thought; "that's the bullet. . . ." And drop after drop every minute kept falling on my closed eyelid. And all at once, not with my voice, but with my whole being, I called upon the power that was responsible for all that was happening to me:

"Whoever you may be, if you exist, and if anything more rational than what is happening here is possible, suffer it to be here now. But if you are revenging yourself upon me for my senseless suicide by the hideousness and absurdity of this subsequent existence, then let me tell you that no torture could ever equal the contempt which I shall go on dumbly feeling, though my martyrdom may last a million years!"

I made this appeal and held my peace. There was a full minute of unbroken silence and again another drop fell, but I knew with infinite unshakable certainty that everything would change immediately. And behold my grave suddenly was rent asunder, that is, I don't know whether it was opened or dug up, but I was caught up by some dark and unknown being and we found ourselves in space. I suddenly regained my sight. It was the dead of night, and never, never had there been such darkness. We were flying through space far away from the earth. I did not question the being who was taking me; I was proud and waited. I assured myself that I was not afraid, and was thrilled with ecstasy at the thought that I was not afraid. I do not know how long we were flying, I cannot imagine; it happened as it always does in dreams when you skip over space and time, and the laws of thought and existence, and only pause upon the points for which the heart yearns. I remember that I suddenly saw in the darkness a star. "Is that Sirius?" I asked impulsively, though I had not meant to ask any questions.

"No, that is the star you saw between the clouds when you were coming home," the being who was carrying me replied.

I knew that it had something like a human face. Strange to say, I did not like that being, in fact I felt an intense aversion for it. I had expected complete non-existence, and that was why I had put a bullet through my heart. And here I was in the hands of a creature not human, of course, but yet living, existing. "And so there is life beyond the grave," I thought with the strange frivolity one has in dreams. But in its inmost depth my heart remained unchanged. "And if I have got to exist again," I thought, "and live once more under the control of some irresistible power, I won't be vanquished and humiliated."

"You know that I am afraid of you and despise me for that," I said suddenly to my companion, unable to refrain from the humiliating question which implied a confession, and feeling my humiliation stab my heart as with a pin. He did not answer my question, but all at once I felt that he was not even despising me, but was laughing at me and had no compassion for me, and that our journey had an unknown and mysterious object that concerned me only. Fear was growing in my heart. Something was mutely and painfully communicated to me from my silent companion, and permeated my whole being. We were flying through dark, unknown space. I had for some time lost sight of the constellations familiar to my eyes. I knew that there were stars in the heavenly spaces the light of which took thousands or millions of years to reach the earth. Perhaps we were already flying through those spaces. I expected something with a terrible anguish that tortured my heart. And suddenly I was thrilled by a familiar feeling that stirred me to the depths: I suddenly caught sight of our sun! I knew that it could not be *our* sun, that gave life to *our* earth, and that we were an infinite distance from our sun, but for some reason I knew in my whole being that it was a sun exactly like ours, a duplicate of it. A sweet, thrilling feeling resounded with ecstasy in my heart: the kindred power of the same light which had given me light stirred an echo in my heart and awakened it, and I had a sensation of life, the old life of the past for the first time since I had been in the grave.

"But if that is the sun, if that is exactly the same as our sun," I cried, "where is the earth?"

And my companion pointed to a star twinkling in the distance with an emerald light. We were flying straight towards it.

"And are such repetitions possible in the universe? Can that be the law of Nature? . . . And if that is an earth there, can it be just the same earth as ours . . . just the same, as poor, as unhappy, but precious and beloved for ever, arousing in the most ungrateful of her children the same poignant love for her that we feel for our earth?" I cried out, shaken by irresistible, ecstatic love for the old familiar earth which I had left. The image of the poor child whom I had repulsed flashed through my mind.

"You shall see it all," answered my companion, and there was a note of sorrow in his voice.

But we were rapidly approaching the planet. It was growing before my eyes; I could already distinguish the ocean, the outline of Europe; and suddenly a feeling of a great and holy jealousy glowed in my heart.

"How can it be repeated and what for? I love and can love only that earth which I have left, stained with my blood, when, in my ingratitude, I quenched my life with a bullet in my heart. But I have never, never ceased to love that earth, and perhaps on the very night I parted from it I loved it more than ever. Is there suffering upon this new earth? On our earth we can only love with suffering and through suffering. We cannot love otherwise, and we know of no other sort of love. I want suffering in order to love. I long, I thirst, this very instant, to kiss with tears the earth that I have left, and I don't want, I won't accept life on any other!"

But my companion had already left me. I suddenly, quite without noticing how, found myself on this other earth, in the bright light of a sunny day, fair as paradise. I believe I was standing on one of the islands that make up on our globe the Greek archipelago, or on the coast of the mainland facing that archipelago. Oh, everything was exactly as it is with us, only everything seemed to have a festive radiance, the splendour of some great, holy triumph attained at last. The caressing sea, green as emerald, splashed softly upon the shore and kissed it with manifest, almost conscious love. The tall, lovely trees stood in all the glory of their blossom, and their innumerable leaves greeted me, I am certain, with their soft, caressing rustle and seemed to articulate words of love. The grass glowed with bright and fragrant flowers. Birds were flying in flocks in the air, and perched fearlessly on my shoulders and arms and joyfully struck me with their darling, fluttering wings. And at last I saw and knew the people of this happy land. They came to me of themselves, they surrounded me, kissed me. The children of the sun, the children of their sun—oh, how beauiful they were! Never had I seen on our own earth such beauty in mankind. Only perhaps in our children, in their earliest years, one might find some remote, faint reflection of this beauty. The eyes of these happy people shone with a clear brightness. Their faces were radiant with the light of reason and fulness of a serenity that comes of perfect understanding, but those faces were gay; in their words and voices there was a note of childlike joy. Oh, from the first moment, from the first glance at them, I understood it all! It was the earth untarnished by the Fall; on it lived people who had not sinned. They lived just in such a paradise as that in which, according to all the legends of mankind, our first parents lived before they sinned; the only difference was that all this earth was the same paradise. These people, laughing joyfully, thronged round me and caressed me; they took me home with them, and each of them tried to reassure me. Oh, they asked me no questions, but they seemed, I fancied, to know everything without asking, and they wanted to make haste and smoothe away the signs of suffering from my face.

IV

And do you know what? Well, granted that it was only a dream, yet the sensation of the love of those innocent and beautiful people has remained with me for ever, and I feel as though their love is still flowing out to me from over there. I have seen them myself, have known them and been convinced; I loved them, I suffered for them afterwards. Oh, I understood at once even at the time that in many things I could not understand them at all; as an up-to-date Russian progressive and contemptible Petersburger, it struck me as inexplicable that, knowing so much, they had, for instance, no science like ours. But I soon realised that their knowledge was gained and fostered by intuitions different from those of us on earth, and that their aspirations, too, were quite different. They desired nothing and were at peace; they did not aspire to knowledge of life as we aspire to understand it, because their lives were full. But their knowledge was higher and deeper than ours; for our science seeks to explain what life is, aspires to understand it in order to teach others how to live, while they without science knew how to live; and that I understood, but I could not understand their knowledge. They showed me their trees, and I could not understand the intense love with which they looked at them; it was as though they were talking with creatures like themselves. And perhaps I shall not be mistaken if I say that they conversed with them. Yes, they had found their language, and I am convinced that the trees understood them. They looked at all Nature like that—at the animals who lived in peace with them and did not attack them, but loved them, conquered by their love. They pointed to the stars and told me something about them which I could not understand, but I am convinced that they were somehow in touch with the stars, not only in thought, but by some living channel. Oh, these people did not persist in trying to make me understand them, they loved me without that, but I knew that they would never understand me, and so I hardly spoke to them about our earth. I only kissed in their presence the earth on which they lived and mutely worshipped them themselves. And they saw that and let me worship them without being abashed at my adoration, for they themselves loved much. They were not unhappy on my account when at times I kissed their feet with tears, joyfully conscious of the love with which they would respond to mine. At times I asked myself with wonder how it was they were able never to offend a creature like me, and never once to arouse a feeling of jealousy or envy in me? Often I wondered how it could be that, boastful and untruthful as I was, I never talked to them of what I knew—of which, of course, they had no notion—that I was never tempted to do so by a desire to astonish or even to benefit them.

They were as gay and sportive as children. They wandered about their lovely woods and copses, they sang their lovely songs; their fare was light—the fruits of their trees, the honey from their woods, and the milk of the animals who loved them. The work they did for food and raiment was brief and not laborious. They loved and begot children, but I never noticed in them the impulse of that *cruel* sensuality which overcomes almost every man on this earth, all and each, and is the source of almost every sin of mankind on earth. They rejoiced at the arrival of children as new beings to share their happiness. There was no quarrelling, no jealousy among them, and they did not even know what the words meant. Their children were the children of all, for they all made up one family. There was scarcely any illness among them, though there was death; but their old people died peacefully, as though falling asleep, giving blessings and smiles to those who surrounded them to take their last farewell with bright and loving smiles. I never saw grief or tears on those occasions, but only love, which reached the point of ecstasy, but a calm ecstasy, made perfect and contemplative. One might think that they were still in contact with the departed after death, and that their earthly union was not cut short by death. They scarcely understood me when I questioned them about immortality, but evidently they were so convinced of it without reasoning that it was not for them a question at all. They had no temples, but they had a real living and uninterrupted sense of oneness with the whole of the universe; they had no creed, but they had a certain knowledge that when their earthly joy had reached the limits of earthly nature, then there would come for them, for the living and for the dead, a still greater fulness of contact with the whole of the universe. They looked forward to that moment with joy, but without haste, not pining for it, but seeming to have a foretaste of it in their hearts, of which they talked to one another.

In the evening before going to sleep they liked singing in musical and harmonious chorus. In those songs they expressed all the sensations that the parting day had given them, sang its glories and took leave of it. They sang the praises of Nature, of the sea, of the woods. They liked making songs about one another, and praised each other like children; they were the simplest songs, but they sprang from their hearts and went to one's heart. And not only in their songs but in all their lives they seemed to do nothing but admire one another. It was like being in love with each other, but an all-embracing, universal feeling.

Some of their songs, solemn and rapturous, I scarcely understood at all. Though I understood the words I could never fathom their full significance. It remained, as it were, beyond the grasp of my mind, yet my heart unconsciously absorbed it more and more. I often told them that I had had a presentiment of it long before, that this joy and glory had come to me on our earth in the form of a yearning melancholy that at times approached insufferable sorrow; that I had had a foreknowledge of them all and of their glory in the dreams of my heart and the visions of my mind; that often on our earth I could not look at the setting sun without tears . . . that in my hatred for the men of our earth there was always a yearning anguish: why could I not hate them without loving them? why could I not help forgiving them? and in my love for them there was a yearning grief: why could I not love them without hating them? They listened to me, and I saw they could not conceive what I was saying, but I did not regret that I had spoken to them of it: I knew that they understood the intensity of my yearning anguish over those whom I had left. But when they looked at me with their sweet eyes full of love, when I felt that in their presence my heart, too, became as innocent and just as theirs, the feeling of the fulness of life took my breath away, and I worshipped them in silence.

Oh, every one laughs in my face now, and assures me that one cannot dream of such details as I am telling now, that I only dreamed or felt one sensation that arose in my heart in delirium and made up the details myself when I woke up. And when I told them that perhaps it really was so, my God, how they shouted with laughter in my face, and what mirth I caused! Oh, yes, of course I was overcome by the mere sensation of my dream, and that was all that was preserved in my cruelly wounded heart; but the actual forms and images of my dream, that is, the very ones I really saw at the very time of my dream, were filled with such harmony, were so lovely and enchanting and were so actual, that on awakening I was, of course, incapable of clothing them in our poor language, so that they were bound to become blurred in my mind; and so perhaps I really was forced afterwards to make up the details, and so of course to distort them in my passionate desire to convey some at least of them as quickly as I could. But on the other hand, how can I help believing that it was all true? It was perhaps a thousand times brighter, happier and more joyful than I describe it. Granted that I dreamed it, yet it must have been real. You know, I will tell you a secret: perhaps it was not a dream at all! For then something happened so awful, something so horribly true, that it could not have been imagined in a dream. My heart may have originated the dream, but would my heart alone have been capable of originating the awful event which happened to me afterwards? How could I alone have invented it or imagined it in my dream? Could my petty heart and my fickle, trivial mind have risen to such a revelation of truth? Oh, judge for yourselves: hitherto I have concealed it, but now I will tell the truth. The fact is that I . . . corrupted them all!

V

Yes, yes, it ended in my corrupting them all! How it could come to pass I do not know, but I remember it clearly. The dream embraced thousands of years and left in me only a sense of the whole. I only know that I was the cause of their sin and downfall. Like a vile trichina, like a germ of the plague infecting whole kingdoms, so I contaminated all this earth, so happy and sinless before my coming. They learnt to lie, grew fond of lying, and discovered the charm of falsehood. Oh, at first perhaps it began innocently, with a jest, coquetry, with amorous play, perhaps indeed with a germ, but that germ of falsity made its way into their hearts and pleased them. Then sensuality was soon begotten, sensuality begot jealousy, jealousy—cruelty. . . . Oh, I don't know, I don't remember; but soon, very soon the first blood was shed. They marvelled and were horrified, and began to be split up and divided. They formed into unions, but it was against one another. Reproaches, upbraidings followed. They came to know shame, and every union began waving its flags. They began torturing animals, and the shame brought them to virtue. The conception of honour sprang up, and animals withdrew from them into the forests and became hostile to them. They began to struggle for separation, for isolation, for individuality, for mine and thine. They began to talk in different languages. They became acquainted with sorrow and loved sorrow; they thirsted for suffering, and said that truth could only be attained through suffering. Then science appeared. As they became wicked they began talking of brotherhood and humanitarianism, and understood those ideas. As they became criminal, they invented justice and drew up whole legal codes in order to observe it, and to ensure their being kept, set up a guillotine. They hardly remembered what they had lost, in fact refused to believe that they had ever been happy and innocent. They even laughed at the possibility of this happiness in the past, and called it a dream. They could not even imagine it in definite form and shape, but, strange and wonderful to relate, though they lost all faith in their past happiness and called it a legend, they so longed to be happy and innocent once more that they succumbed to this desire like children, made an idol of it, set up temples and worshipped their own idea, their own desire; though at the same time they fully believed that it was unattainable and could not be realised, yet they bowed down to it and adored it with tears! Nevertheless, if it could have happened that they had returned to the innocent and happy condition which they had lost, and if some one had shown it to them again and had asked them whether they wanted to go back to it, they would certainly have refused. They answered me:

"We may be deceitful, wicked and unjust, we *know* it and weep over it, we grieve over it; we torment and punish ourselves more perhaps than that merciful Judge Who will judge us and whose Name we know not. But we have science, and by means of it we shall find the truth and we shall arrive at it consciously. Knowledge is higher than feeling, the consciousness of life is higher than life. Science will give us wisdom, wisdom will reveal the laws, and the knowledge of the laws of happiness is higher than happiness."

That is what they said, and after saying such things every one began to love himself better than any one else, and indeed they could not do otherwise. All became so jealous of the rights of their own personality that they did their very utmost to curtail and destroy them in others, and made that the chief thing in their lives. Slavery followed, even voluntary slavery; the weak eagerly submitted to the strong, on condition that the latter aided them to subdue the still weaker. Then there were saints who came to these people, weeping, and talked to them of their pride, of their loss of harmony and due proportion, of their loss of shame. They were laughed at or pelted with stones. Holy blood was shed on the threshold of the temples. Then there arose men who began to think how to bring all people together again, so that everybody, while still loving himself best of all, might not interfere with others, and all might live together in something like a harmonious society. Regular wars sprang up over this idea. All the combatants at the same time firmly believed that science, wisdom and the instinct of self-preservation would force men at last to unite into a harmonious and rational society; and so, meanwhile, to hasten matters, "the wise" endeavoured to exterminate as rapidly as possible all who were "not wise" and did not understand their idea, that the latter might not hinder its triumph. But the instinct of self-preservation grew rapidly weaker; there arose men, haughty and sensual, who demanded all or nothing. In order to obtain everything they resorted to crime, and if they did not succeed—to suicide. There arose religions with a cult of non-existence and self-destruction for the sake of the everlasting peace of annihilation. At last these people grew weary of their meaningless toil, and signs of suffering came into their faces, and then they proclaimed that suffering was a beauty, for in suffering alone was there meaning. They glorified suffering in their songs. I moved about among them, wringing my hands and weeping over them, but I loved them perhaps more than in old days when there was no suffering in their faces and when they were innocent and so lovely. I loved the earth they had polluted even more than when it had been a paradise, if only because sorrow had come to it. Alas! I always loved sorrow and tribulation, but only for myself, for myself; but I wept over them, pitying them. I stretched out my hands to them in despair, blaming, cursing and despising myself. I told them that all this was my doing, mine alone; that it was I had brought them corruption, contamination and falsity. I besought them to crucify me, I taught them how to make a cross. I could not kill myself, I had not the strength, but I wanted to suffer at their hands. I yearned for suffering, I longed that my blood should be drained to the last drop in these agonies. But they only laughed at me, and began at last to look upon me as crazy. They justified me, they declared that they had only got what they wanted themselves, and that all that now was could not have been otherwise. At last they declared to me that I was becoming dangerous and that they should lock me up in a madhouse if I did not hold my tongue. Then such grief took possession of my soul that my heart was wrung, and I felt as though I were dying; and then . . . then I awoke.

It was morning, that is, it was not yet daylight, but about six o'clock. I woke up in the same arm-chair; my candle had burnt out; every one was asleep in the captain's room, and there was a stillness all round, rare in our flat. First of all I leapt up in great amazement: nothing like this had ever happened to me before, not even in the most trivial detail; I had never, for instance, fallen asleep like this in my arm-chair. While I was standing and coming to myself I suddenly caught sight of my revolver lying loaded, ready—but instantly I thrust it away! Oh, now, life, life! I lifted up my hands and called upon eternal truth, not with words but with tears; ecstasy, immeasurable ecstasy flooded my soul. Yes, life and spreading the good tidings! Oh, I at that moment resolved to spread the tidings, and resolved it, of course, for my whole life. I go to spread the tidings, I want to spread the tidings—of what? Of the truth, for I have seen it, have seen it with my own eyes, have seen it in all its glory.

And since then I have been preaching! Moreover I love all those who laugh at me more than any of the rest. Why that is so I do not know and cannot explain, but so be it. I am told that I am vague and confused, and if I am vague and confused now, what shall I be later on? It is true indeed: I am vague and confused, and perhaps as time goes on I shall be more so. And of course I shall make many blunders before I find out how to preach, that is, find out what words to say, what things to do, for it is a very difficult task. I see all that as clear as daylight, but, listen, who does not make mistakes? And yet, you know, all are making for the same goal, all are striving in the same direction anyway, from the sage to the lowest robber, only by different roads. It is an old truth, but this is what is new: I cannot go far wrong. For I have seen the truth; I have seen and I know that people can be beautiful and happy without losing the power of living on earth. I will not and cannot believe that evil is the normal condition of mankind. And it is just this faith of mine that they laugh at. But how can I help believing it? I have seen the truth—it is not as though I had invented it with my mind, I have seen it, seen it, and *the living image* of it has filled my soul for ever. I have seen it in such full perfection that I cannot believe that it is impossible for people to have it. And so how can I go wrong? I shall make some slips no doubt, and shall perhaps talk in second-hand language, but not for long: the living image of what I saw will always be with me and will always correct and guide me. Oh, I am full of courage and freshness, and I will go on and on if it were for a thousand years! Do you know, at first I meant to conceal the fact that I corrupted them, but that was a mistake—that was my first mistake! But truth whispered to me that I was *lying,* and preserved me and corrected me. But how establish paradise—I don't know, because I do not know how to put it into words. After my dream I lost command of words. All the chief words, anyway, the most necessary ones. But never mind, I shall go and I shall keep talking, I won't leave off, for anyway I have seen it with my own eyes, though I cannot describe what I saw. But the scoffers do not understand that. It was a dream, they say, delirium, hallucination. Oh! As though that meant so much! And they are so proud! A dream! What is a dream? And is not our life a dream? I will say more. Suppose that this paradise will never come to pass (that I understand), yet I shall go on preaching it. And yet how simple it is: in one day, *in one hour* everything could be arranged at once! The chief thing is to love others like yourself, that's the great thing, and that's everything; nothing else is wanted—you will find out at once how to arrange it all. And yet it's an old truth which has been told and retold a billion times—but it has not formed part of our lives! The consciousness of life is higher than life, the knowledge of the laws of happiness is higher than happiness—that is what one must contend against. And I shall. If only every one wants it, it can all be arranged at once.

And I tracked out that little girl . . . and I shall go on and on!

Henry James

The Real Thing

Henry James (1843–1916)

HENRY JAMES, BORN INTO A RICH AND TALENTED NEW YORK family, began writing at an early age, under the influence of Balzac. When, after years of indecision, he finally chose literature as his life's career, he left America to settle in Paris, where he hoped to learn his art from such master craftsmen as Flaubert and Guy de Maupassant. But though he admired the artistry of French fiction, he felt himself an outcast in Paris and moved on to London. He remained an expatriate for the rest of his life, with only short visits to America, and died a British citizen.

James's recognition of the "complex fate of being an American" was of central importance to his life and his fiction. He found America—even the cultivated America of New York and Boston upper class—lacking the subtle structures of civilization, the institutions, customs, and manners that should provide the substance of fiction. Life in America seemed too "thin" to allow James to work out the complex social and psychological dramas which appealed to him. Yet his tortured, subtle, deep ethical consciousness is in many ways peculiarly American. Many of James's most famous novels, notably *The American, Portrait of a Lady, The Wings of the Dove, The Ambassadors,* and *The Golden Bowl,* dramatize the experience of naive Americans undergoing initiation—painfully, tragically, but often with a sense of illumination—into the rich and treacherous complexities of European civilization.

Like Flaubert, James was a wholly conscious craftsman who elaborated his fictions with fine attention to form, style, and nuance. His critical writings on the novel are among the finest we possess, and indeed they provide the base for most modern analysis of how fiction is "put together" and how it "works." With such an attention to craft, it should be no surprise that so many of his novels, and especially his tales, deal with working artists and the interrelationships of "art" and "reality." One such story is "The Real Thing."

The Real Thing

I

When the porter's wife (she used to answer the house-bell), announced "A gentleman—with a lady, sir," I had, as I often had in those days, for the wish was father to the thought, an immediate vision of sitters. Sitters my visitors in this case proved to be; but not in the sense I should have preferred. However, there was nothing at first to indicate that they might not have come for a portrait. The gentleman, a man of fifty, very high and very straight, with a moustache slightly grizzled and a dark gray walking coat admirably fitted, both of which I noted professionally—I don't mean as a barber or yet as a tailor—would have struck me as a celebrity if celebrities often were striking. It was a truth of which I had for some time been conscious that a figure with a good deal of frontage was, as one might say, almost never a public institution. A glance at the lady helped to remind me of this paradoxical law: she also looked too distinguished to be a "personality." Moreover one would scarcely come across two variations together.

Neither of the pair spoke immediately—they only prolonged the preliminary gaze which suggested that each wished to give the other a chance. They were visibly shy; they stood there letting me take them in—which, as I afterwards perceived, was the most practical thing they could have done. In this way their embarrassment served their cause. I had seen people painfully reluctant to mention that they desired anything so gross as to be represented on canvas; but the scruples of my new friends appeared almost insurmountable. Yet the gentleman might have said "I should like a portrait of my wife," and the lady might have said "I should like a portrait of my husband." Perhaps they were not husband and wife—this naturally would make the matter more delicate. Perhaps they wished to be done together—in which case they ought to have brought a third person to break the news.

"We come from Mr. Rivet," the lady said at last, with a dim smile which had the effect of a moist sponge passed over a "sunk" piece of painting, as well as of a vague allusion to vanished beauty. She was as tall and straight, in her degree, as her companion, and with ten years less to carry. She looked as sad as a woman could look whose face was not charged with expression; that is her tinted oval mask showed friction as an exposed surface shows it. The hand of time had played over her freely, but only to simplify. She was slim and stiff, and so well dressed, in dark blue cloth, with lappets and pockets and buttons, that it was clear she employed the same tailor as her husband. The couple had an indefinable air of prosperous thrift—they evidently got a good deal of luxury for their money. If I was to be one of their luxuries it would behoove me to consider my terms.

"Ah, Claude Rivet recommended me," I inquired; and I added that it was very kind of him, though I could reflect that, as he only painted landscape, this was not a sacrifice.

The lady looked very hard at the gentleman, and the gentleman looked round the room. Then staring at the floor a moment and stroking his moustache, he rested his pleasant eyes on me with the remark: "He said you were the right one."

"I try to be, when people want to sit."

"Yes, we should like to," said the lady anxiously.

"Do you mean together?"

My visitors exchanged a glance. "If you could do anything with *me,* I suppose it would be double," the gentleman stammered.

"Oh yes, there's naturally a higher charge for two figures than for one."

"We would like to make it pay," the husband confessed.

"That's very good of you," I returned, appreciating so unwonted a sympathy—for I supposed he meant pay the artist.

A sense of strangeness seemed to dawn on the lady. "We mean for the illustrations—Mr. Rivet said you might put one in."

"Put one in—an illustration?" I was equally confused.

"Sketch her off, you know," said the gentleman, coloring.

It was only then that I understood the service Claude Rivet had rendered me; he had told them that I worked in black and white, for magazines, for storybooks, for sketches of contemporary life, and consequently had frequent employment for models. These things were true, but it was not less true (I may confess it now—whether because the aspiration was to lead to everything or to nothing I leave the reader to guess), that I couldn't get the honors, to say nothing of the emoluments, of a great painter of portraits out of my head. My "illustrations" were my potboilers; I looked to a different branch of art (far and away the most interesting it had always seemed to me), to perpetuate my fame. There was no shame in looking to it also to make my fortune; but that fortune was by so much further from being made from the moment my visitors wished to be "done" for nothing. I was disappointed, for in the pictorial sense I had immediately *seen* them. I had seized their type—I had already settled what I would do with it. Something that wouldn't absolutely have pleased them, I afterwards reflected.

"Ah, you're—you're—a—?" I began, as soon as I had mastered my surprise. I couldn't bring out the dingy word "models;" it seemed to fit the case so little.

"We haven't had much practice," said the lady.

"We've got to *do* something, and we've thought that an artist in your line might perhaps make something of us," her husband threw off. He further mentioned that they didn't know many artists and that they had gone first, on the off chance (he painted views of course, but sometimes put in figures—perhaps I remembered), to Mr. Rivet, whom they had met a few years before at a place in Norfolk where he was sketching.

"We used to sketch a little ourselves," the lady hinted.

"It's very awkward, but we absolutely *must* do something," her husband went on.

"Of course, we're not so *very* young," she admitted, with a wan smile.

With the remark that I might as well know something more about them, the husband had handed me a card extracted from a neat new pocketbook (their appurtenances were all of the freshest) and inscribed with the words "Major Monarch." Impressive as these words were they didn't carry my knowledge much further; but my visitor presently added: "I've left the army, and we've had the misfortune to lose our money. In fact our means are dreadfully small."

"It's an awful bore," said Mrs. Monarch.

They evidently wished to be discreet—to take care not to swagger because they were gentlefolks. I perceived they would have been willing to recognize this as something of a drawback, at the same time that I guessed at an underlying sense—their consolation in adversity—that they *had* their points. They certainly had; but these advantages struck me as preponderantly social; such for instance as would help to make a drawing room look well. However, a drawing room was always, or ought to be, a picture.

In consequence of his wife's allusion to their age Major Monarch observed: "Naturally, it's more for the figure that we thought of going in. We can still hold ourselves up." On the instant I saw that the figure was indeed their strong point. His "naturally" didn't sound vain, but it lighted up the question. "*She* has got the best," he continued, nodding at his wife, with a pleasant after-dinner absence of circumlocution. I could only reply, as if we were in fact sitting over our wine, that this didn't prevent his own from being very good; which led him in turn to rejoin: "We thought that if you ever have to do people like us, we might be something like it. *She,* particularly—for a lady in a book, you know."

I was so amused by them that, to get more of it, I did my best to take their point of view; and though it was an embarrassment to find myself appraising physically, as if they were animals on hire or useful blacks, a pair of whom I should have expected to meet only in one of the relations in which criticism is tacit, I looked at Mrs. Monarch judicially enough to be able to exclaim, after a moment, with conviction: "Oh yes, a lady in a book!" She was singularly like a bad illustration.

"We'll stand up, if you like," said the Major; and he raised himself before me with a really grand air.

I could take his measure at a glance—he was six feet two and a perfect gentleman. It would have paid any club in process of formation and in want of a stamp to engage him at a salary to stand in the principal window. What struck me immediately was that in coming to me they had rather missed their vocation; they could surely have been turned to better account for advertising purposes. I couldn't of course see the thing in detail, but I could see them make someone's fortune—I don't mean their own. There was something in them for a waistcoat-maker, an hotel-keeper, or a soap-vendor. I could imagine "We always use it" pinned on their bosoms with the greatest effect; I had a vision of the promptitude with which they would launch a *table d'hôte*.

Mrs. Monarch sat still, not from pride but from shyness, and presently her husband said to her: "Get up my dear and show how smart you are." She obeyed, but she had no need to get up to show it. She walked to the end of the studio, and then she came back blushing, with her fluttered eyes on her husband. I was reminded of an incident I had accidentally had a glimpse of in Paris—being with a friend there, a dramatist about to produce a play—when an actress came to him to ask to be intrusted with a part. She went through the paces before him, walked up and down as Mrs. Monarch was doing. Mrs. Monarch did it quite as well, but I abstained from applauding. It was very odd to see such people apply for such poor pay. She looked as if she had ten thousand a year. Her husband had used the word that described her: she was, in the London current jargon, essentially and typically "smart." Her figure was, in the same order of ideas, conspicuously and irreproachably "good." For a woman of her age her waist was surprisingly small, her elbow moreover had the orthodox crook. She held her head at the conventional angle; but why did she come to *me*? She ought to have tried on jackets at a big shop. I feared my visitors were not only destitute, but "artistic"—which would be a great complication. When she sat down again I thanked her, observing that what a draughtsman most valued in his model was the faculty of keeping quiet.

"Oh, *she* can keep quiet," said Major Monarch. Then he added, jocosely: "I've always kept her quiet."

"I'm not a nasty fidget, am I?" Mrs. Monarch appealed to her husband.

He addressed his answer to me. "Perhaps it isn't out of place to mention—because we ought to be quite businesslike, oughtn't we?—that when I married her she was known as the Beautiful Statue."

"Oh dear!" said Mrs. Monarch, ruefully.

"Of course I should want a certain amount of expression," I rejoined.

"Of *course*!" they both exclaimed.

"And then I suppose you know that you'll get awfully tired."

"Oh, we *never* get tired!" they eagerly cried.

"Have you had any kind of practice?"

They hesitated—they looked at each other. "We've been photographed, *immensely*," said Mrs. Monarch.

"She means the fellows have asked us," added the Major.

"I see—because you're so good-looking."

"I don't know what they thought, but they were always after us."

"We always got our photographs for nothing," smiled Mrs. Monarch.

"We might have brought some, my dear," her husband remarked.

"I'm not sure we have any left. We've given quantities away," she explained to me.

"With our autographs and that sort of thing," said the Major.

"Are they to be got in the shops?" I inquired, as a harmless pleasantry.

"Oh, yes; *hers*—they used to be."

"Not now," said Mrs. Monarch, with her eyes on the floor.

II

I could fancy the "sort of thing" they put on the presentation copies of their photographs, and I was sure they wrote a beautiful hand. It was odd how quickly I was sure of everything that concerned them. If they were now so poor as to have to earn shillings and pence, they never had had much of a margin. Their good looks had been their capital, and they had good-humoredly made the most of the career that this resource marked out for them. It was in their faces, the blankness, the deep intellectual repose of the twenty years of country-house visiting which had given them pleasant intonations. I could see the sunny drawing rooms, sprinkled with periodicals she didn't read, in which Mrs. Monarch had continuously sat; I could see the wet shrubberies in which she had walked, equipped to admiration for either exercise. I could see the rich covers the Major had helped to shoot and the wonderful garments in which, late at night, he repaired to the smoking room to talk about them. I could imagine their leggings and waterproofs, their knowing tweeds and rugs, their rolls of sticks and cases of tackle and neat umbrellas; and I could evoke the exact appearance of their servants and the compact variety of their luggage on the platforms of country stations.

They gave small tips, but they were liked; they didn't do anything themselves, but they were welcome. They looked so well everywhere; they gratified the general relish for stature, complexion, and "form." They knew it without fatuity or vulgarity, and they respected themselves in consequence.

They were not superficial; they were thorough and kept themselves up—it had been their line. People with such a taste for activity had to have some line. I could feel how, even in a dull house, they could have been counted upon for cheerfulness. At present something had happened—it didn't matter what, their little income had grown less, it had grown least—and they had to do something for pocket money. Their friends liked them, but didn't like to support them. There was something about them that represented credit—their clothes, their manners, their type; but if credit is a large empty pocket in which an occasional chink reverberates, the chink at least must be audible. What they wanted of me was to help to make it so. Fortunately they had no children—I soon divined that. They would also perhaps wish our relations to be kept secret: this was why it was "for the figure"—the reproduction of the face would betray them.

I liked them—they were so simple; and I had no objection to them if they would suit. But, somehow, with all their perfections I didn't easily believe in them. After all they were amateurs, and the ruling passion of my life was the detestation of the amateur. Combined with this was another perversity—an innate preference for the represented subject over the real one: the defect of the real one was so apt to be a lack of representation. I liked things that appeared; then one was sure. Whether they *were* or not was a subordinate and almost always a profitless question. There were other considerations, the first of which was that I already had two or three people in use, notably a young person with big feet, in alpaca, from Kilburn, who for a couple of years had come to me regularly for my illustrations and with whom I was still—perhaps ignobly—satisfied. I frankly explained to my visitors how the case stood; but they had taken more precautions than I supposed. They had reasoned out their opportunity, for Claude Rivet had told them of the projected *édition de luxe* of one of the writers of our day—the rarest of the novelists—who, long neglected by the multitudinous vulgar and dearly prized by the attentive (need I mention Philip Vincent?) had had the happy fortune of seeing, late in life, the dawn and then the full light of a higher criticism—an estimate in which, on the part of the public, there was something really of expiation. The edition in question, planned by a publisher of taste, was practically an act of high reparation; the woodcuts with which it was to be enriched were the homage of English art to one of the most independent representatives of English letters. Major and Mrs. Monarch confessed to me that they had hoped I might be able to work *them* into my share of the enterprise. They knew I was to do the first of the books, *Rutland Ramsay,* but I had to make clear to them that my participation in the rest of the affair—this first book was to be a test—was to depend on the satisfaction I should give. If this should be limited my employers would drop me without a scruple. It was therefore a crisis for me, and naturally I was making special preparation, looking about for new people, if they should be necessary, and securing the best types. I admitted however that I should like to settle down to two or three good models who would do for everything.

"Should we have often to—a—put on special clothes?" Mrs. Monarch timidly demanded.

"Dear, yes—that's half the business."

"And should we be expected to supply our own costumes?"

"Oh, no; I've got a lot of things. A painter's models put on—or put off—anything he likes."

"And do you mean—a—the same?"

"The same?"

Mrs. Monarch looked at her husband again.

"Oh, she was just wondering," he explained, "if the costumes are in *general* use." I had to confess that they were, and I mentioned further that some of them (I had a lot of genuine, greasy last-century things) had served their time, a hundred years ago, on living, world-stained men and women. "We'll put on anything that *fits*," said the Major.

"Oh, I arrange that—they fit in the pictures."

"I'm afraid I should do better for the modern books. I would come as you like," said Mrs. Monarch.

"She has got a lot of clothes at home: they might do for contemporary life," her husband continued.

"Oh, I can fancy scenes in which you'd be quite natural." And indeed I could see the slipshod rearrangements of stale properties—the stories I tried to produce pictures for without the exasperation of reading them—whose sandy tracts the good lady might help to people. But I had to return to the fact that for this sort of work—the daily mechanical grind—I was already equipped; the people I was working with were fully adequate.

"We only thought we might be more like *some* characters," said Mrs. Monarch mildly, getting up.

Her husband also rose; he stood looking at me with a dim wistfulness that was touching in so fine a man. "Wouldn't it be rather a pull sometimes to have—a—to have—?" He hung fire; he wanted me to help him by phrasing what he meant. But I couldn't—I didn't know. So he brought it out, awkwardly: "The *real* thing; a gentleman, you know, or a lady." I was quite ready to give a general assent—I admitted that there was a great deal in that. This encouraged Major Monarch to say, following up his appeal with an unacted gulp: "It's awfully hard—we've tried everything." The gulp was communicative; it proved too much for his wife. Before I knew it Mrs. Monarch had dropped again upon a divan and burst into tears. Her husband sat down beside her, holding one of her hands; whereupon she quickly dried her eyes with the other, while I felt embarrassed as she looked up at me. "There isn't a confounded job I haven't applied for—waited for—prayed for. You can fancy we'd be pretty bad at first. Secretaryships and that sort of thing? You might as well ask for a peerage. I'd be *anything*—I'm strong; a messenger or a coalheaver. I'd put on a gold-laced cap and open carriage doors in front of the haberdasher's; I'd hang about a station, to carry portmanteaux; I'd be a postman. But they won't *look* at you; there are thousands, as good as yourself, already on the ground. *Gentlemen,* poor beggars, who have drunk their wine, who have kept their hunters!"

I was as reassuring as I knew how to be, and my visitors were presently on their feet again while, for the experiment, we agreed on an hour. We were discussing it when the door opened and Miss Churm came in with a wet umbrella. Miss Churm had to take the omnibus to Maida Vale and then walk half a mile. She looked a trifle blowsy and slightly splashed. I scarcely ever saw her come in without thinking afresh how odd it was that, being so little in herself, she should yet be so much in others. She was a meager little Miss Churm, but she was an ample heroine of romance. She was only a freckled cockney, but she could represent everything from a fine lady to a shepherdess; she had the faculty, as she might have had a fine voice or long hair. She couldn't spell, and she loved beer, but she had two or three "points," and practice, and a knack, and mother-wit, and a kind of whimsical sensibility, and a love of the theater, and seven sisters, and not an ounce of respect, especially for the "h." The first thing my visitors saw was that her umbrella was wet, and in their spotless perfection they visibly winced at it. The rain had come on since their arrival.

"I'm all in a soak; there *was* a mess of people in the bus. I wish you lived near a station," said Miss Churm. I requested her to get ready as quickly as possible, and she passed into the room in which she always changed her dress. But before going out she asked me what she was to get into this time.

"It's the Russian princess, don't you know?" I answered; "the one with the 'golden eyes,' in black velvet, for the long thing in the *Cheapside*."

"Golden eyes? I *say*!" cried Miss Churm, while my companions watched her with intensity as she withdrew. She always arranged herself, when she was late, before I could turn round; and I kept my visitors a little, on purpose, so that they might get an idea, from seeing her, what would be expected of themselves. I mentioned that she was quite my notion of an excellent model—she was really very clever.

"Do you think she looks like a Russian princess?" Major Monarch asked, with lurking alarm.

"When I make her, yes."

"Oh, if you have to *make* her—!" He reasoned, acutely.

"That's the most you can ask. There are so many that are not makeable."

"Well now, *here's* a lady"—and with a persuasive smile he passed his arm into his wife's—"who's already made!"

"Oh, I'm not a Russian princess," Mrs. Monarch protested, a little coldly. I could see that she had known some and didn't like them. There, immediately, was a complication of a kind that I never had to fear with Miss Churm.

This young lady came back in black velvet—the gown was rather rusty and very low on her lean shoulders—and with a Japanese fan in her red hands. I reminded her that in the scene I was doing she had to look over someone's head. "I forget whose it is; but it doesn't matter. Just look over a head."

"I'd rather look over a stove," said Miss Churm; and she took her station near the fire. She fell into position, settled herself into a tall attitude, gave a certain backward inclination to her head and a certain forward drop to her fan, and looked, at least to my prejudiced sense, distinguished and charming, foreign and dangerous. We left her looking so, while I went downstairs with Major and Mrs. Monarch.

"I think I could come about as near it as that," said Mrs. Monarch.

"Oh, you think she's shabby, but you must allow for the alchemy of art."

However, they went off with an evident increase of comfort, founded on their demonstrable advantage in being the real thing. I could fancy them shuddering over Miss Churm. She was very droll about them when I went back, for I told her what they wanted.

"Well, if *she* can sit I'll tyke to bookkeeping," said my model.

"She's very ladylike," I replied, as an innocent form of aggravation.

"So much the worse for *you*. That means she can't turn round."

"She'll do for the fashionable novels."

"Oh yes, she'll *do* for them!" my model humorously declared. "Ain't they bad enough without her?" I had often sociably denounced them to Miss Churm.

III

It was for the elucidation of a mystery in one of these works that I first tried Mrs. Monarch. Her husband came with her, to be useful if necessary—it was sufficiently clear that as a general thing he would prefer to come with her. At first I wondered if this were for "propriety's" sake—if he were going to be jealous and meddling. The idea was too tiresome, and if it had been confirmed it would speedily have brought our acquaintance to a close. But I soon saw there was nothing in it and that if he accompanied Mrs. Monarch it was (in addition to the chance of being wanted) simply because he had nothing else to do. When she was away from him his occupation was gone—she never *had* been away from him. I judged, rightly, that in their awkward situation their close union was their main comfort and that this union had no weak spot. It was a real marriage, an encouragement for the hesitating, a nut for pessimists to crack. Their address was humble (I remember afterwards thinking it had been the only thing about them that was really professional), and I could fancy the lamentable lodgings in which the Major would have been left alone. He could bear them with his wife—he couldn't bear them without her.

He had too much tact to try and make himself agreeable when he couldn't be useful; so he simply sat and waited, when I was too absorbed in my work to talk. But I liked to make him talk—it made my work, when it didn't interrupt it, less sordid, less special. To listen to him was to combine the excitement of going out with the economy of staying at home. There was only one hindrance: that I seemed not to know any of the people he and his wife had known. I think he wondered extremely, during the term of our intercourse, whom the deuce I *did* know. He hadn't a stray sixpence of an idea to fumble for; so we didn't spin it very fine—we confined ourselves to questions of leather and even of liquor (saddlers and breeches-makers and how to get good claret cheap), and matters like "good trains" and the habits of small game. His lore on these last subjects was astonishing, he managed to interweave the stationmaster with the ornithologist. When he couldn't talk about greater things he could talk cheerfully about smaller, and since I couldn't accompany him into reminiscences of the fashionable world he could lower the conversation without a visible effort to my level.

So earnest a desire to please was touching in a man who could so easily have knocked one down. He looked after the fire and had an opinion on the draft of the stove, without my asking him, and I could see that he thought many of my arrangements not half clever enough. I remember telling him that if I were only rich I would offer him a salary to come and teach me how to live. Sometimes he gave a random sigh, of which the essence was: "Give me even such a bare old barrack as *this,* and I'd do something with it!" When I wanted to use him he came alone; which was an illustration of the superior courage of women. His wife could bear her solitary second floor, and she was in general more discreet; showing by various small reserves that she was alive to the propriety of keeping our relations markedly professional—not letting them slide into sociability. She wished it to remain clear that she and the Major were employed, not cultivated, and if she approved of me as a superior, who could be kept in his place, she never thought me quite good enough for an equal.

She sat with great intensity, giving the whole of her mind to it, and was capable of remaining for an hour almost as motionless as if she were before a photographer's lens. I could see she had been photographed often, but somehow the very habit that made her good for that purpose unfitted her for mine. At first I was extremely pleased with her ladylike air, and it was a satisfaction, on coming to follow her lines, to see how good they were and how far they could lead the pencil. But after a few times I began to find her too insurmountably stiff; do what I would with it my drawing looked like a photograph or a copy of a photograph. Her figure had no variety of expression—she herself had no sense of variety. You may say that this was my business, was only a question of placing her. I placed her in every conceivable position, but she managed to obliterate their differences. She was always a lady certainly, and into the bargain was always the same lady. She was the real thing, but always the same thing. There were moments when I was oppressed by the serenity of her confidence that she *was* the real thing. All her dealings with me and all her husband's were an implication that this was lucky for *me*. Meanwhile I found myself trying to invent types that approached her own, instead of making her own transform itself—in the clever way that was not impossible, for instance, to poor Miss Churm. Arrange as I would and take the precautions I would, she always, in my pictures, came out too tall—landing me in the dilemma of having represented a fascinating woman as seven feet high, which, out of respect perhaps to my own very much scantier inches, was far from my idea of such a personage.

The case was worse with the Major—nothing I could do would keep *him* down, so that he became useful only for the representation of brawny giants. I adored variety and range, I cherished human accidents, the illustrative note; I wanted to characterize closely, and the thing in the world I most hated was the danger of being ridden by a type. I had quarreled with some of my friends about it—I had parted company with them for maintaining that one *had* to be, and that if the type was beautiful (witness Raphael and Leonardo), the servitude was only a gain. I was neither Leonardo nor Raphael; I might only be a presumptuous young modern searcher, but I held that everything was to be sacrificed sooner than character. When they averred that the haunting type in question could easily *be* character, I retorted, perhaps superficially: "Whose?" It couldn't be everybody's—it might end in being nobody's.

After I had drawn Mrs. Monarch a dozen times I perceived more clearly than before that the value of such a model as Miss Churm resided precisely in the fact that she had no positive stamp, combined of course with the other fact that what she did have was a curious and inexplicable talent for imitation. Her usual appearance was like a curtain which she could draw up at a request for a capital performance. This performance was simply suggestive; but it was a word to the wise—it was vivid and pretty. Sometimes, even, I thought it, though she was plain herself, too insipidly pretty; I made it a reproach to her that the figures drawn from her were monotonously (*bêtement,* as we used to say) graceful. Nothing made her more angry: it was so much her pride to feel that she could sit for characters that had nothing in common with each other. She would accuse me at such moments of taking away her "reputytion."

It suffered a certain shrinkage, this queer quality, from the repeated visits of my new friends. Miss Churm was greatly in demand, never in want of employment, so I had no scruple in putting her off occasionally, to try them more at my ease. It was certainly amusing at first to do the real thing—it was amusing to do Major Monarch's trousers. They *were* the real thing, even if he did come out colossal. It was amusing to do his wife's back hair (it was so mathematically neat) and the particular "smart" tension of her tight stays. She lent herself especially to positions in which the face was somewhat averted or blurred; she abounded in ladylike back views and *profils perdus*. When she stood erect she took naturally one of the attitudes in which court painters represent queens and princesses; so that I found myself wondering whether, to draw out this accomplishment, I couldn't get the editor of the *Cheapside* to publish a really royal romance, "A Tale of Buckingham Palace." Sometimes, however, the real thing and the make-believe came into contact; by which I mean that Miss Churm, keeping an appointment or coming to make one on days when I had much work in hand, encountered her invidious rivals. The encounter was not on their part, for they noticed her no more than if she had been the housemaid; not from intentional loftiness, but simply because, as yet, professionally, they didn't know how to fraternize as I could guess that they would have liked—or at least that the Major would. They couldn't talk about the omnibus—they always walked; and they didn't know what else to try—she wasn't interested in good trains or cheap claret. Besides, they must have felt—in the air—that she was amused at them, secretly derisive of their ever knowing how. She was not a person to conceal her skepticism if she had had a chance to show it. On the other hand Mrs. Monarch didn't think her tidy; for why else did she take pains to say to me (it was going out of the way, for Mrs. Monarch) that she didn't like dirty women?

One day when my young lady happened to be present with my other sitters (she even dropped in, when it was convenient, for a chat), I asked her to be as good as to lend a hand in getting tea—a service with which she was familiar and which was one of a class that, living as I did in a small way, with slender domestic resources, I often appeal to my models to render. They liked to lay hands on my property, to break the sitting, and sometimes the china—I made them feel Bohemian. The next time I saw Miss Churm after this incident she surprised me greatly by making a scene about it—she accused me of having wished to humiliate her. She had not resented the outrage at the time, but had seemed obliging and amused, enjoying the comedy of asking Mrs. Monarch, who sat vague and silent, whether she would have cream and sugar, and putting an exaggerated simper into the question. She had tried intonations—as if she too wished to pass for the real thing; till I was afraid my other visitors would take offense.

Oh, *they* were determined not to do this; and their touching patience was the measure of their great need. They would sit by the hour, uncomplaining, till I was ready to use them; they would come back on the chance of being wanted and would walk away cheerfully if they were not. I used to go to the door with them to see in what magnificent order they retreated. I tried to find other employment for them—I introduced them to several artists. But they didn't "take," for reasons I could appreciate, and I became conscious, rather anxiously, that after such disappointments they fell back upon me with a heavier weight. They did me the honor to think that it was I who was most *their* form. They were not picturesque enough for the painters, and in those days there were not so many serious workers in black and white. Besides, they had an eye to the great job I had mentioned to them—they had secretly set their hearts on supplying the right essence for my pictorial vindication of our fine novelist. They knew that for this undertaking I should want no costume effects, none of the frippery of past ages—that it was a case in which everything would be contemporary and satirical and, presumably, genteel. If I could work them into it their future would be assured, for the labor would of course be long and the occupation steady.

One day Mrs. Monarch came without her husband—she explained his absence by his having had to go to the City. While she sat there in her usual anxious stiffness there came, at the door, a knock which I immediately recognized as the subdued appeal of a model out of work. It was followed by the entrance of a young man whom I easily perceived to be a foreigner and who proved in fact an Italian acquainted with no English word but my name, which he uttered in a way that made it seem to include all others. I had not then visited his country, nor was I proficient in his tongue; but as he was not so meanly constituted—what Italian is?—as to depend only on that member for expression he conveyed to me, in familiar but graceful mimicry, that he was in search of exactly the employment in which the lady before me was engaged. I was not struck with him at first, and while I continued to draw I emitted rough sounds of discouragement and dismissal. He stood his ground, however, not importunately, but with a dumb, doglike fidelity in his eyes which amounted to innocent impudence—the manner of a devoted servant (he might have been in the house for years) unjustly suspected. Suddenly I saw that this very attitude and expression made a picture, whereupon I told him to sit down and wait till I should be free. There was another picture in the way he obeyed me, and I observed as I worked that there were others still in the way he looked wonderingly, with his head thrown back, about the high studio. He might have been crossing himself in St. Peter's. Before I finished I said to myself: "The fellow's a bankrupt orange-monger, but he's a treasure."

When Mrs. Monarch withdrew he passed across the room like a flash to open the door for her, standing there with the rapt, pure gaze of the young Dante spellbound by the young Beatrice. As I never insisted, in such situations, on the blankness of the British domestic, I reflected that he had the making of a servant (and I needed one, but couldn't pay him to be only that), as well as of a model; in short I made up my mind to adopt my bright adventurer if he would agree to officiate in the double capacity. He jumped at my offer, and in the event my rashness (for I had known nothing about him) was not brought home to me. He proved a sympathetic though a desultory ministrant, and had in a wonderful degree the *sentiment de la pose.*[1] It was uncultivated, instinctive; a part of the happy instinct which had guided him to my door and helped him to spell out my name on the card nailed to it. He had had no other introduction to me than a guess, from the shape of my high north window, seen outside, that my place was a studio and that as a studio it would contain an artist. He had wandered to England in search of fortune, like other itinerants, and had embarked, with a partner and a small green handcart, on the sale of penny ices. The ices had melted away and the partner had dissolved in their train. My young man wore tight yellow trousers with reddish stripes and his name was Oronte. He was sallow but fair, and when I put him into some old clothes of my own he looked like an Englishman. He was as good as Miss Churm, who could look, when required, like an Italian.

IV

I thought Mrs. Monarch's face slightly convulsed when, on her coming back with her husband, she found Oronte installed. It was strange to have to recognize in a scrap of a *lazzarone*[2] a competitor to her magnificent Major. It was she who scented danger first, for the Major was anecdotically unconscious. But Oronte gave us tea, with a hundred eager confusions (he had never seen such a queer process), and I think she thought better of me for having at last an "establishment." They saw a couple of drawings that I had made of the establishment, and Mrs. Monarch hinted that it never would have struck her that he had sat for them. "Now the drawings you make from *us,* they look exactly like us," she reminded me, smiling in triumph; and I recognized that this was indeed just their defect. When I drew the Monarchs I couldn't, somehow, get away from them—get into the character I wanted to represent; and I had not the least desire my model should be discoverable in my picture. Miss Churm never was, and Mrs. Monarch thought I hid her, very properly because she was vulgar;

[1] "A feeling for how to pose." [2] A Neapolitan word for loafer, beggar.

whereas if she was lost it was only as the dead who go to heaven are lost—in the gain of an angel the more.

By this time I had got a certain start with *Rutland Ramsay*, the first novel in the great projected series; that is I had produced a dozen drawings, several with the help of the Major and his wife, and I had sent them in for approval. My understanding with the publishers, as I have already hinted, had been that I was to be left to do my work, in this particular case, as I liked, with the whole book committed to me; but my connection with the rest of the series was only contingent. There were moments when, frankly, it *was* a comfort to have the real thing under one's hand; for there were characters in *Rutland Ramsay* that were very much like it. There were people presumably as straight as the Major and women of as good a fashion as Mrs. Monarch. There was a great deal of country-house life—treated, it is true, in a fine, fanciful, ironical, generalized way—and there was a considerable implication of knickerbockers and kilts. There were certain things I had to settle at the outset; such things for instance as the exact appearance of the hero, the particular bloom of the heroine. The author of course gave me a lead, but there was a margin for interpretation. I took the Monarchs into my confidence, I told them frankly what I was about, I mentioned my embarrassments and alternatives. "Oh, take *him*." Mrs. Monarch murmured sweetly, looking at her husband; and "What could you want better than my wife?" the Major inquired, with the comfortable candor that now prevailed between us.

I was not obliged to answer these remarks—I was only obliged to place my sitters. I was not easy in mind, and I postponed, a little timidly perhaps, the solution of the question. The book was a large canvas, the other figures were numerous, and I worked off at first some of the episodes in which the hero and the heroine were not concerned. When once I had set *them* up I should have to stick to them—I couldn't make my young man seven feet high in one place and five feet nine in another. I inclined on the whole to the latter measurements, though the Major more than once reminded me that *he* looked about as young as anyone. It was indeed quite impossible to arrange him, for the figure, so that it would have been difficult to detect his age. After the spontaneous Oronte had been with me a month, and after I had given him to understand several different times that his native exuberance would presently constitute an insurmountable barrier to our further intercourse, I waked to a sense of his heroic capacity. He was only five feet seven, but the remaining inches were latent. I tried him almost secretly at first, for I was really rather afraid of the judgment my other models would pass on such a choice. If they regarded Miss Churm as little better than a snare, what would they think of the representation by a person so little the real thing as an Italian street vendor of a protagonist formed by a public school?

If I went a little in fear of them it was not because they bullied me, because they had got an oppressive foothold, but because in their really pathetic decorum and mysteriously permanent newness they counted on me so intensely. I was therefore very glad when Jack Hawley came home: he was always of such good counsel. He painted badly himself, but there was no one like him for putting his finger on the place. He had been absent from England for a year; he had been somewhere—I don't remember where—to get a fresh eye. I was in a good deal of dread of any such organ, but we were old friends; he had been away for months and a sense of emptiness was creeping into my life. I hadn't dodged a missile for a year.

He came back with a fresh eye, but with the same old black velvet blouse, and the first evening he spent in my studio we smoked cigarettes till the small hours. He had done no work himself, he had only got the eye; so the field was clear for the production of my little things. He wanted to see what I had done for the *Cheapside,* but he was disappointed in the exhibition. That at least seemed the meaning of two or three comprehensive groans which, as he lounged on my big divan, on a folded leg, looking at my latest drawings, issued from his lips with the smoke of the cigarette.

"What's the matter with you?" I asked.

"What's the matter with *you*?"

"Nothing save that I'm mystified."

"You are indeed. You're quite off the hinge. What's the meaning of this new fad?" And he tossed me, with visible irreverence, a drawing in which I happened to have depicted both my majestic models. I asked if he didn't think it good, and he replied that it struck him as execrable, given the sort of thing I had always represented myself to him as wishing to arrive at; but I let that pass, I was so anxious to see exactly what he meant. The two figures in the picture looked colossal, but I supposed this was *not* what he meant, inasmuch as, for aught he knew to the contrary, I might have been trying for that. I maintained that I was working exactly in the same way as when he last had done me the honor to commend me. "Well, there's a big hole somewhere," he answered; "wait a bit and I'll discover it." I depended upon him to do so: where else was the fresh eye? But he produced at last nothing more luminous than "I don't know—I don't like your types." This was lame, for a critic who had never consented to discuss with me anything but the question of execution, the direction of strokes, and the mystery of values.

"In the drawings you've been looking at I think my types are very handsome."

"Oh, they won't do!"

"I've had a couple of new models."

"I see you have. *They* won't do."

"Are you very sure of that?"

"Absolutely—they're stupid."

"You mean *I* am—for I ought to get round that."

"You *can't*—with such people. Who are they?"

I told him, as far as was necessary, and he declared, heartlessly: "*Ce sont des gens qu'il faut mettre à la porte.*" [3]

"You've never seen them; they're awfully good," I compassionately objected.

"Not seen them. Why, all this recent work of yours drops to pieces with them. It's all I want to see of them."

"No one else has said anything against it—the *Cheapside* people are pleased."

"Everyone else is an ass, and the *Cheapside* people the biggest asses of all. Come, don't pretend, at this time of day, to have pretty illusions about the public, especially about publishers and editors. It's not for *such* animals you work—it's for those who know, *coloro che sanno;* so keep straight for *me* if you can't keep straight for yourself. There's a certain sort of thing you tried for from the first—and a very good thing it is. But this twaddle isn't *in* it." When I talked with Hawley later about *Rutland Ramsay* and its possible successors he declared that I must get back into my boat again or I would go to the bottom. His voice in short was the voice of warning.

I noted the warning, but I didn't turn my friends out of doors. They bored me a good deal; but the very fact that they bored me admonished me not to sacrifice them—if there was anything to be done with them—simply to irritation. As I look back at this phase they seem to me to have pervaded my life not a little. I have a vision of them as most of the time in my studio, seated, against the wall, on an old velvet bench to be out of the way, and looking like a pair of patient courtiers in a royal antechamber. I am convinced that during the coldest weeks of the winter they held their ground because it saved them fire. Their newness was losing its gloss, and it was impossible not to feel that they were objects of charity. Whenever Miss Churm arrived they went away, and after I was fairly launched in *Rutland Ramsay* Miss Churm arrived pretty often. They managed to express to me tacitly that they supposed I wanted her for the low life of the book, and I let them suppose it, since they had attempted to study the work—it was lying about the studio—without discovering that it dealt only with the highest circles. They had dipped into the most brilliant of our novelists without deciphering many passages. I still took an hour from them, now and again, in spite of Jack Hawley's warning: it would be time enough to dismiss them, if dismissal should be necessary, when the rigor of the season was over. Hawley had made their acquaintance—he had met them at my fireside—and thought them a ridiculous pair. Learning that he was

[3] "These are people you must get rid of."

a painter they tried to approach him, to show him too that they were the real thing; but he looked at them, across the big room, as if they were miles away: they were a compendium of everything that he most objected to in the social system of his country. Such people as that, all convention and patent leather, with ejaculations that stopped conversation, had no business in a studio. A studio was a place to learn to see, and how could you see through a pair of feather beds?

The main inconvenience I suffered at their hands was that, at first, I was shy of letting them discover how my artful little servant had begun to sit for me for *Rutland Ramsay*. They knew that I had been odd enough (they were prepared by this time to allow oddity to artists) to pick a foreign vagabond out of the streets, when I might have had a person with whiskers and credentials; but it was some time before they learned how high I rated his accomplishments. They found him in an attitude more than once, but they never doubted I was doing him as an organ grinder. There were several things they never guessed, and one of them was that for a striking scene in the novel, in which a footman briefly figured, it occurred to me to make use of Major Monarch as the menial. I kept putting this off, I didn't like to ask him to don the livery—besides the difficulty of finding a livery to fit him. At last, one day late in the winter, when I was at work on the despised Oronte (he caught one's idea in an instant), and was in the glow of feeling that I was going very straight, they came in, the Major and his wife, with their society laugh about nothing (there was less and less to laugh at), like country callers—they always reminded me of that—who have walked across the park after church and are presently persuaded to stay to luncheon. Luncheon was over, but they could stay to tea—I knew they wanted it. The fit was on me, however, and I couldn't let my ardor cool and my work wait, with the fading daylight, while my model prepared it. So I asked Mrs. Monarch if she would mind laying it out—a request which, for an instant, brought all the blood to her face. Her eyes were on her husband's for a second, and some mute telegraphy passed between them. Their folly was over the next instant; his cheerful shrewdness put an end to it. So far from pitying their wounded pride, I must add, I was moved to give it as complete a lesson as I could. They bustled about together and got out the cups and saucers and made the kettle boil. I know they felt as if they were waiting on my servant, and when the tea was prepared I said: "He'll have a cup, please—he's tired." Mrs. Monarch brought him one where he stood, and he took it from her as if he had been a gentleman at a party, squeezing a crush-hat with an elbow.

Then it came over me that she had made a great effort for me—made it with a kind of nobleness—and that I owed her a compensation. Each time I saw her after this I wondered what the compensation could be. I couldn't go on doing the wrong thing to oblige them. Oh, it *was* the wrong thing, the stamp of the work for which they sat—Hawley was not the only person to say it now. I sent in a large number of the drawings I had made for *Rutland Ramsay,* and I received a warning that was more to the point than Hawley's. The artistic adviser of the house for which I was working was of opinion that many of my illustrations were not what had been looked for. Most of these illustrations were the subjects in which the Monarchs had figured. Without going into the question of what *had* been looked for, I saw at this rate I shouldn't get the other books to do. I hurled myself in despair upon Miss Churm, I put her through all her paces. I not only adopted Oronte publicly as my hero, but one morning when the Major looked in to see if I didn't require him to finish a figure for the *Cheapside,* for which he had begun to sit the week before, I told him that I had changed my mind—I would do the drawing from my man. At this my visitor turned pale and stood looking at me. "Is *he* your idea of an English gentleman?" he asked.

I was disappointed, I was nervous, I wanted to get on with my work; so I replied with irritation: "Oh, my dear Major—I can't be ruined for *you*!"

He stood another moment; then, without a word, he quitted the studio. I drew a long breath when he was gone, for I said to myself that I shouldn't see him again. I had not told him definitely that I was in danger of having my work rejected, but I was vexed at his not having felt the catastrophe in the air, read with me the moral of our fruitless collaboration, the lesson that, in the deceptive atmosphere of art, even the highest respectability may fail of being plastic.

I didn't owe my friends money, but I did see them again. They reappeared together, three days later, and under the circumstances there was something tragic in the fact. It was a proof to me that they could find nothing else in life to do. They had threshed the matter out in a dismal conference—they had digested the bad news that they were not in for the series. If they were not useful to me even for the *Cheapside* their function seemed difficult to determine, and I could only judge at first that they had come, forgivingly, decorously, to take a last leave. This made me rejoice in secret that I had little leisure for a scene; for I had placed both my other models in position together and I was pegging away at a drawing from which I hoped to derive glory. It had been suggested by the passage in which Rutland Ramsay, drawing up a chair to Artemisia's piano stool, says extraordinary things to her while she ostensibly fingers out a difficult piece of music. I had done Miss Churm at the piano before—it was an attitude in which she knew how to take on an absolutely poetic grace. I wished the two figures to "compose" together, intensely, and my little Italian had entered perfectly into my conception. The pair were vividly before me, the piano had been pulled out; it was a charming picture of blended youth and murmured love, which I had only to catch and keep. My visitors stood and looked at it, and I was friendly to them over my shoulder.

They made no response, but I was used to silent company and went on with my work, only a little disconcerted (even though exhilarated by the sense that *this* was at last the ideal thing) at not having got rid of them after all. Presently I heard Mrs. Monarch's sweet voice beside, or rather above me: "I wish her hair was a little better done." I looked up and she was staring with a strange fixedness at Miss Churm, whose back was turned to her. "Do you mind my just touching it?" she went on—a question which made me spring up for an instant, as with the instinctive fear that she might do the young lady a harm. But she quieted me with a glance I shall never forget—I confess I should like to have been able to paint *that*—and went for a moment to my model. She spoke to her softly, laying a hand upon her shoulder and bending over her; and as the girl, understanding, gratefully assented, she disposed her rough curls, with a few quick passes, in such a way as to make Miss Churm's head twice as charming. It was one of the most heroic personal services I have ever seen rendered. Then Mrs. Monarch turned away with a low sigh and, looking about her as if for something to do, stooped to the floor with a noble humility and picked up a dirty rag that had dropped out of my paintbox.

The Major meanwhile had also been looking for something to do and, wandering to the other end of the studio, saw before him my breakfast things, neglected, unremoved. "I say, can't I be useful *here*?" he called out to me with an irrepressible quaver. I assented with a laugh that I fear was awkward and for the next ten minutes, while I worked, I heard the light clatter of china and the tinkle of spoons and glass. Mrs. Monarch assisted her husband—they washed up my crockery, they put it away. They wandered off into my little scullery, and I afterwards found that they had cleaned my knives and that my slender stock of plate had an unprecedented surface. When it came over me, the latent eloquence of what they were doing, I confess that my drawing was blurred for a moment—the picture swam. They had accepted their failure, but they couldn't accept their fate. They had bowed their heads in bewilderment to the perverse and cruel law in virtue of which the real thing could be so much less precious than the unreal; but they didn't want to starve. If my servants were my models, my models might be my servants. They would reverse the parts—the others would sit for the ladies and gentlemen, and *they* would do the work. They would still be in the studio—it was an intense dumb appeal to me not to turn them out. "Take us on," they wanted to say—"we'll do *anything*."

When all this hung before me the *afflatus* vanished—my pencil dropped from my hand. My sitting was spoiled and I got rid of my sitters, who were also evidently rather mystified and awestruck. Then, alone with the Major and his wife, I had a most uncomfortable moment. He put their prayer into a single sentence: "I say, you know—just let *us* do for you, can't you?" I couldn't—it was dreadful to see them emptying my slops; but I pretended I could to oblige them for about a week. Then I gave them a sum of money to go away; and I never saw them again. I obtained the remaining books, but my friend Hawley repeats that Major and Mrs. Monarch did me a permanent harm, got me into a second-rate trick. If it be true I am content to have paid the price—for the memory.

Henrik Ibsen

The Master Builder

TRANSLATED BY
EDMUND GOSSE AND WILLIAM ARCHER

Henrik Ibsen (1828–1906)

Henrik Ibsen is a rare example of an author from a small country, writing in a little-known language, who gained international fame and influence during his lifetime. He was born in Skien, Norway, into a completely impoverished family. He served as a druggist's apprentice, then in 1850 managed to enroll in the university at Christiana (now Oslo). But the following year he went to Bergen to work as playwright and stage manager for the Norwegian Theater, and then became director of a theater in Christiana. Disappointed by his country's refusal to aid in the movement for Scandinavian unity, he went into voluntary exile in 1864, and began a life of wandering that took him to Rome, Dresden, Munich, and many other places. In 1891, he finally returned to Christiana, where, though by now famous and honored, he lived a secluded life.

Ibsen's first major contribution to the renewal of European drama was the seriousness, the honesty, and the realism with which he treated contemporary social problems. Learning from the techniques of the "well-made play" which the French had brought to perfection—plays in which plot, suspense, the characters' entrances and exits were all worked out with precision and plausibility—he went beyond the traditional, often rather frivolous, sentimental, or melodramatic subjects of such plays to dramatize the enslaved condition of women in society, the corruption of journalism and politics, the effects of social hypocrisy, and the difficulties of personal honesty and liberation in bourgeois society. His first major play in this serious social vein was *Pillars of Society,* followed by *A Doll's House, Ghosts, An Enemy of the People, The Wild Duck,* and *Hedda Gabler.*

Yet Ibsen cannot be defined by his social and psychological realism alone. Especially in such late plays as *Rosmersholm, The Master Builder,* and *John Gabriel Borkman,* he reaches beyond the social dimension to the intense dramas of inner conflict. These plays have been called "dramas of conversion" in that they show a man wrestling with his whole past life, with what he has been and what it means to him now. And in these plays, if Ibsen is still scrupulously the realist, he is also a symbolist, building his drama around a few large, suggestive images of man's struggles, choices, successes, and defeats.

The Master Builder

CHARACTERS

HALVARD SOLNESS, *Master Builder.*
ALINE SOLNESS, *his wife.*
DOCTOR HERDAL, *physician.*
KNUT BROVIK, *formerly an architect, now in Solness's employment.*
RAGNAR BROVIK, *his son, draughtsman.*
KAIA FOSLI, *his niece, bookkeeper.*
MISS HILDA WANGEL.
SOME LADIES.
A CROWD IN THE STREET.

The action passes in and about Solness's house.

ACT I

A plainly furnished workroom in the house of HALVARD SOLNESS. *Folding doors on the left lead out to the hall. On the right is the door leading to the inner rooms of the house. At the back is an open door into the draughtsmen's office. In front, on the left, a desk with books, papers and writing materials. Further back than the folding door, a stove. In the right-hand corner, a sofa, a table, and one or two chairs. On the table a water bottle and glass. A smaller table, with a rocking chair and armchair, in front on the right. Lighted lamps, with shades, on the table in the draughtsmen's office, on the table in the corner, and on the desk.*

In the draughtsmen's office sit KNUT BROVIK *and his son* RAGNAR, *occupied with plans and calculations. At the desk in the outer office stands* KAIA FOSLI, *writing in the ledger.* KNUT BROVIK *is a spare old man with white hair and beard. He wears a rather threadbare but well-brushed black coat, spectacles, and a somewhat discolored white neckcloth.* RAGNAR BROVIK *is a well-dressed, light-haired man in his thirties, with a slight stoop.* KAIA FOSLI *is a slightly built girl, a little over twenty, carefully dressed, and delicate-looking. She has a green shade over her eyes.*

All three go on working for some time in silence.

KNUT BROVIK [*rises suddenly, as if in distress, from the table; breathes heavily and laboriously as he comes forward into the doorway*]. No, I can't bear it much longer!

KAIA [*going up to him*]. You are feeling very ill this evening, are you not, uncle?

BROVIK. Oh, I seem to get worse every day.

RAGNAR [*has risen and advances*]. You ought to go home, father. Try to get a little sleep—

BROVIK [*impatiently*]. Go to bed, I suppose? Would you have me stifled outright?

KAIA. Then take a little walk.

RAGNAR. Yes, do. I will come with you.

BROVIK [*with warmth*]. I will not go till he comes! I am determined to have it out this evening with—[*in a tone of suppressed bitterness*]—with him —with the chief.

KAIA [*anxiously*]. Oh no, uncle—do wait awhile before doing that.

RAGNAR. Yes, better wait, father!

BROVIK [*draws his breath laboriously*]. Ha—ha—! I haven't much time for waiting.

KAIA [*listening*]. Hush! I hear him on the stairs. [*All three go back to their work. A short silence.*]

[HALVARD SOLNESS *comes in through the hall door. He is a man no longer young, but healthy and vigorous, with close-cut curly hair, dark moustache, and dark thick eyebrows. He wears a grayish-green buttoned jacket with an upstanding collar and broad lapels. On his head he wears a soft gray felt hat, and he has one or two light portfolios under his arm.*]

SOLNESS [*near the door, points towards the draughtsmen's office, and asks in a whisper*]. Are they gone?

KAIA [*softly, shaking her head*]. No.

[*She takes the shade off her eyes.* SOLNESS *crosses the room, throws his hat on a chair, places the portfolios on the table by the sofa, and approaches the desk again.* KAIA *goes on writing without intermission, but seems nervous and uneasy.*]

SOLNESS [*aloud*]. What is that you are entering, Miss Fosli?

KAIA [*starts*]. Oh, it is only something that—

SOLNESS. Let me look at it, Miss Fosli. [*Bends over her, pretends to be looking into the ledger, and whispers.*] Kaia!

KAIA [*softly, still writing*]. Well?

SOLNESS. Why do you always take that shade off when I come?

KAIA [*as before*]. I look so ugly with it on.

SOLNESS [*smiling*]. Then you don't like to look ugly, Kaia?

KAIA [*half glancing up at him*]. Not for all the world. Not in your eyes.

SOLNESS [*stroking her hair gently*]. Poor, poor little Kaia—

KAIA [*bending her head*]. Hush—they can hear you.

[SOLNESS *strolls across the room to the right, turns and pauses at the door of the draughtsmen's office.*]

SOLNESS. Has any one been here for me?

RAGNAR [*rising*]. Yes, the young couple who want a villa built, out at Lövstrand.

SOLNESS [*growling*]. Oh, those two! They must wait. I am not quite clear about the plans yet.

RAGNAR [*advancing, with some hesitation*]. They were very anxious to have the drawings at once.

SOLNESS [*as before*]. Yes, of course—so they all are.

BROVIK [*looks up*]. They say they are longing so to get into a house of their own.

SOLNESS. Yes, yes—we know all that! And so they are content to take whatever is offered them. They get a—a roof over their heads—an address—but nothing to call a home. No thank you! In that case, let them apply to somebody else. Tell them that, the next time they call.

BROVIK [*pushes his glasses up on to his forehead and looks in astonishment at him*]. To somebody else? Are you prepared to give up the commission?

SOLNESS [*impatiently*]. Yes, yes, yes, devil take it! If that is to be the way of it—. Rather that, than build away at random. [*Vehemently.*] Besides, I know very little about these people as yet.

BROVIK. The people are safe enough. Ragnar knows them. He is a friend of the family. Perfectly safe people.

SOLNESS. Oh, safe—safe enough! That is not at all what I mean. Good Lord—don't you understand me either? [*Angrily.*] I won't have anything to do with these strangers. They may apply to whom they please, so far as I am concerned.

BROVIK [*rising*]. Do you really mean that?

SOLNESS [*sulkily*]. Yes I do,—For once in a way. [*He comes forward.*]

[BROVIK *exchanges a glance with* RAGNAR, *who makes a warning gesture. Then* BROVIK *comes into the front room.*]

BROVIK. May I have a few words with you?

SOLNESS. Certainly.

BROVIK [*to* KAIA]. Just go in there for a moment, Kaia.

KAIA [*uneasily*]. Oh, but uncle—

BROVIK. Do as I say, child. And shut the door after you.

[KAIA *goes reluctantly into the draughtsmen's office, glances anxiously and imploringly at* SOLNESS, *and shuts the door.*]

BROVIK [*lowering his voice a little*]. I don't want the poor children to know how ill I am.

SOLNESS. Yes, you have been looking very poorly of late.

BROVIK. It will soon be all over with me. My strength is ebbing—from day to day.

SOLNESS. Won't you sit down?

BROVIK. Thanks—may I?

SOLNESS [*placing the armchair more conveniently*]. Here—take this chair. —And now?

BROVIK [*has seated himself with difficulty*]. Well, you see, it's about Ragnar. That is what weighs most upon me. What is to become of him?

SOLNESS. Of course your son will stay with me as long as ever he likes.

BROVIK. But that is just what he does not like. He feels that he cannot stay here any longer.

SOLNESS. Why, I should say he was very well off here. But if he wants more money, I should not mind—

BROVIK. No, no! It is not that. [*Impatiently.*] But sooner or later he, too, must have a chance of doing something on his own account.

SOLNESS [*without looking at him*]. Do you think that Ragnar has quite talent enough to stand alone?

BROVIK. No, that is just the heartbreaking part of it—I have begun to have my doubts about the boy. For you have never said so much as—as one encouraging word about him. And yet I cannot but think there must be something in him—he can't be without talent.

SOLNESS. Well, but he has learnt nothing—nothing thoroughly, I mean. Except, of course, to draw.

BROVIK [*looks at him with covert hatred, and says hoarsely*]. You had learned little enough of the business when you were in my employment. But that did not prevent you from setting to work—[*breathing with difficulty*]—and pushing your way up, and taking the wind out of my sails—mine, and so many other people's.

SOLNESS. Yes, you see—circumstances favored me.

BROVIK. You are right there. Everything favored you. But then how can you have the heart to let me go to my grave—without having seen what Ragnar is fit for? And of course I am anxious to see them married, too—before I go.

SOLNESS [*sharply*]. Is it she who wishes it?

BROVIK. Not Kaia so much as Ragnar—he talks about it every day. [*Appealingly.*] You must—you must help him to get some independent work now! I must see something that the lad has done. Do you hear?

SOLNESS [*peevishly*]. Hang it, man, you can't expect me to drag commissions down from the moon for him!

BROVIK. He has the chance of a capital commission at this very moment. A big bit of work.

SOLNESS [*uneasily, startled*]. Has he?

BROVIK. If you would give your consent.

SOLNESS. What sort of work do you mean?

BROVIK [*with some hesitation*]. He can have the building of that villa out at Lövstrand.

SOLNESS. That! Why, I am going to build that myself.

BROVIK. Oh, you don't much care about doing it.

SOLNESS [*flaring up*]. Don't care! I? Who dares to say that?

BROVIK. You said so yourself just now.

SOLNESS. Oh, never mind what I say. Would they give Ragnar the building of that villa?

BROVIK. Yes. You see, he knows the family. And then—just for the fun of the thing—he has made drawings and estimates and so forth—

SOLNESS. Are they pleased with the drawings? The people who will have to live in the house?

BROVIK. Yes. If you would only look through them and approve of them.

SOLNESS. Then they would let Ragnar build their home for them?

BROVIK. They were immensely pleased with his idea. They thought it exceedingly original, they said.

SOLNESS. Oho! Original! Not the old-fashioned stuff that *I* am in the habit of turning out!

BROVIK. It seemed to them different.

SOLNESS [*with suppressed irritation*]. So it was to see Ragnar that they came here—whilst I was out!

BROVIK. They came to call upon you—and at the same time to ask whether you would mind retiring—

SOLNESS [*angrily*]. Retire? I?

BROVIK. In case you thought that Ragnar's drawings—

SOLNESS. I? Retire in favor of your son!

BROVIK. Retire from the agreement, they meant.

SOLNESS. Oh, it comes to the same thing. [*Laughs angrily.*] So that is it, is it? Halvard Solness is to see about retiring now! To make room for younger men! For the very youngest, perhaps! He must make room! Room! Room!

BROVIK. Why, good heavens! there is surely room for more than one single man—

SOLNESS. Oh, there's not so very much room to spare either. But, be that as it may—I will never retire! I will never give way to anybody! Never of my own free will. Never in this world will I do that!

BROVIK [*rises with difficulty*]. Then I am to pass out of life without any certainty? Without a gleam of happiness? Without any faith or trust in Ragnar? Without having seen a single piece of work of his doing? Is that to be the way of it?

SOLNESS [*turns half aside, and mutters*]. H'm—don't ask more just now.

BROVIK. I must have an answer to this one question. Am I to pass out of life in such utter poverty?

SOLNESS [*seems to struggle with himself; finally he says, in a low but firm voice*] You must pass out of life as best you can.

BROVIK. Then be it so. [*He goes up the room.*]

SOLNESS [*following him, half in desperation*]. Don't you understand that I cannot help it? I am what I am, and I cannot change my nature!

BROVIK. No, no; I suppose you can't. [*Reels and supports himself against the sofa table.*] May I have a glass of water?

SOLNESS. By all means. [*Fills a glass and hands it to him.*]

BROVIK. Thanks. [*Drinks and puts the glass down again.*]

[SOLNESS *goes up and opens the door of the draughtsmen's office.*]

SOLNESS. Ragnar—you must come and take your father home. [RAGNAR *rises quickly. He and* KAIA *come into the workroom.*]

RAGNAR. What is the matter, father?

BROVIK. Give me your arm. Now let us go.

RAGNAR. Very well. You had better put your things on, too, Kaia.

SOLNESS. Miss Fosli must stay—just for a moment. There is a letter I want written.

BROVIK [*looks at* SOLNESS]. Good night. Sleep well—if you can.

SOLNESS. Good night.

[BROVIK *and* RAGNAR *go out by the hall door.* KAIA *goes to the desk.* SOLNESS *stands with bent head, to the right, by the armchair.*]

KAIA [*dubiously*]. Is there any letter—?

SOLNESS [*curtly*]. No, of course not. [*Looks sternly at her.*] Kaia!

KAIA [*anxiously, in a low voice*]. Yes!

SOLNESS [*points imperatively to a spot on the floor*]. Come here! At once!

KAIA [*hesitatingly*]. Yes.

SOLNESS [*as before*]. Nearer!

KAIA [*obeying*]. What do you want with me?

SOLNESS [*looks at her for a while*]. Is it you I have to thank for all this?

KAIA. No, no, don't think that!

SOLNESS. But confess now—you want to get married!

KAIA [*softly*]. Ragnar and I have been engaged for four or five years, and so—

SOLNESS. And so you think it time there were an end to it. Is not that so?

KAIA. Ragnar and Uncle say I must. So I suppose I shall have to give in.

SOLNESS [*more gently*]. Kaia, don't you really care a little bit for Ragnar, too?

KAIA. I cared very much for Ragnar once—before I came here to you.

SOLNESS. But you don't now? Not in the least?

KAIA [*passionately, clasping her hands and holding them out towards him*]. Oh, you know very well there is only one person I care for now! One, and one only, in all the world! I shall never care for any one else.

SOLNESS. Yes, you say that. And yet you go away from me—leave me alone here with everything on my hands.

KAIA. But could I not stay with you, even if Ragnar—?

SOLNESS [*repudiating the idea*]. No, no, that is quite impossible. If Ragnar leaves me and starts work on his own account, then of course he will need you himself.

KAIA [*wringing her hands*]. Oh, I feel as if I could not be separated from you! It's quite, quite impossible!

SOLNESS. Then be sure you get those foolish notions out of Ragnar's head. Marry him as much as you please—[*alters his tone*]—I mean—don't let him throw up his good situation with me. For then I can keep you too, my dear Kaia.

KAIA. Oh yes, how lovely that would be, if it could only be managed!

SOLNESS [*clasps her head with his two hands and whispers*]. For I cannot get on without you, you see. I must have you with me every single day.

KAIA [*in nervous exaltation*]. My God! My God!

SOLNESS [*kisses her hair*]. Kaia—Kaia!

KAIA [*sinks down before him*]. Oh, how good you are to me! How unspeakably good you are!

SOLNESS [*vehemently*]. Get up! For goodness' sake get up! I think I hear some one! [*He helps her to rise. She staggers over to the desk.*]

[MRS. SOLNESS *enters by the door on the right. She looks thin and wasted with grief, but shows traces of bygone beauty. Blonde ringlets. Dressed with good taste, wholly in black. Speaks somewhat slowly and in a plaintive voice.*]

MRS. SOLNESS [*in the doorway*]. Halvard!

SOLNESS [*turns*]. Oh, are you there, my dear—?

MRS. SOLNESS [*with a glance at* KAIA]. I am afraid I am disturbing you.

SOLNESS. Not in the least. Miss Fosli has only a short letter to write.

MRS. SOLNESS. Yes, so I see.

SOLNESS. What do you want with me, Aline?

MRS. SOLNESS. I merely wanted to tell you that Dr. Herdal is in the drawing room. Won't you come and see him, Halvard?

SOLNESS [*looks suspiciously at her*]. H'm—is the doctor so very anxious to talk to me?

MRS. SOLNESS. Well, not exactly anxious. He really came to see me; but he would like to say how-do-you-do to you at the same time.

SOLNESS [*laughs to himself*]. Yes, I daresay. Well, you must ask him to wait a little.

MRS. SOLNESS. Then you will come in presently?

SOLNESS. Perhaps I will. Presently, presently, dear. In a little while.

MRS. SOLNESS [*glancing again at* KAIA]. Well, now, don't forget, Halvard. [*Withdraws and closes the door behind her.*]

KAIA [*softly*]. Oh dear, oh dear—I am sure Mrs. Solness thinks ill of me in some way!

SOLNESS. Oh, not in the least. Not more than usual at any rate. But all the same, you had better go now, Kaia.

KAIA. Yes, yes, now I must go.

SOLNESS [*severely*]. And mind you get that matter settled for me. Do you hear?

KAIA. Oh, if it only depended on me—

SOLNESS. I will have it settled, I say! And tomorrow too—not a day later!

KAIA [*terrified*]. If there's nothing else for it, I am quite willing to break off the engagement.

SOLNESS [*angrily*]. Break it off. Are you mad? Would you think of breaking it off?

KAIA [*distracted*]. Yes, if necessary. For I must—I must stay here with you! I can't leave you! That is utterly—utterly impossible!

SOLNESS [*with a sudden outburst*]. But deuce take it—how about Ragnar then! It's Ragnar that I—

KAIA [*looks at him with terrified eyes*]. It is chiefly on Ragnar's account, that—that you—

SOLNESS [*collecting himself*]. No, no, of course not! You don't understand me either. [*Gently and softly.*] Of course it is you I want to keep—you above everything, Kaia. But for that very reason, you must prevent Ragnar, too, from throwing up his situation. There, there, now go home.

KAIA. Yes, yes—good night, then.

SOLNESS. Good night. [*As she is going.*] Oh, stop a moment! Are Ragnar's drawings in there?

KAIA. I did not see him take them with him.

SOLNESS. Then just go and find them for me. I might perhaps glance over them, after all.

KAIA [*happy*]. Oh yes, please do!

SOLNESS. For your sake, Kaia dear. Now, let me have them at once, please. [KAIA *hurries into the draughtsmen's office, searches anxiously in the table drawer, finds a portfolio and brings it with her.*]

KAIA. Here are all the drawings.

SOLNESS. Good. Put them down there on the table.

KAIA [*putting down the portfolio*]. Good night, then. [*Beseechingly.*] And please, please think kindly of me.

SOLNESS. Oh, that I always do. Good night, my dear little Kaia. [*Glances to the right.*] Go, go now!

[MRS. SOLNESS *and* DR. HERDAL *enter by the door on the right. He is a stoutish, elderly man, with a round, good-humored face; clean-shaven, with thin, light hair, and gold spectacles.*]

MRS. SOLNESS [*still in the doorway*]. Halvard, I cannot keep the doctor any longer.

SOLNESS. Well then, come in here.

MRS. SOLNESS [*to* KAIA, *who is turning down the desk lamp*]. Have you finished the letter already, Miss Fosli?

KAIA [*in confusion*]. The letter—?

SOLNESS. Yes, it was quite a short one.

MRS. SOLNESS. It must have been very short.

SOLNESS. You may go now, Miss Fosli. And please come in good time tomorrow morning.

KAIA. I will be sure to. Good night, Mrs. Solness. [*She goes out by the hall door.*]

MRS. SOLNESS. She must be quite an acquisition to you, Halvard, this Miss Fosli.

SOLNESS. Yes, indeed. She is useful in all sorts of ways.

MRS. SOLNESS. So it seems.

DR. HERDAL. Is she good at bookkeeping too?

SOLNESS. Well—of course she has had a good deal of practice during these two years. And then she is so nice and willing to do whatever one asks of her.

MRS. SOLNESS. Yes, that must be very delightful—

SOLNESS. It is. Especially when one is not too much accustomed to that sort of thing.

MRS. SOLNESS [*in a tone of gentle remonstrance*]. Can you say that, Halvard?

SOLNESS. Oh, no, no, my dear Aline; I beg your pardon.

MRS. SOLNESS. There's no occasion. Well then, doctor, you will come back later on, and have a cup of tea with us?

DR. HERDAL. I have only that one patient to see, and then I'll come back.

MRS. SOLNESS. Thank you. [*She goes out by the door on the right.*]

SOLNESS. Are you in a hurry, doctor?

DR. HERDAL. No, not at all.

SOLNESS. May I have a little chat with you?

DR. HERDAL. With the greatest of pleasure.

SOLNESS. Then let us sit down. [*He motions the doctor to take the rocking chair, and sits down himself in the armchair. Looks searchingly at him.*] Tell me—did you notice anything odd about Aline?

DR. HERDAL. Do you mean just now, when she was here?

SOLNESS. Yes, in her manner to me. Did you notice anything?

DR. HERDAL [*smiling*]. Well, I admit—one couldn't well avoid noticing that your wife—h'm—

SOLNESS. Well?

DR. HERDAL. —that your wife is not particularly fond of this Miss Fosli.

SOLNESS. Is that all? I have noticed that myself.

DR. HERDAL. And I must say I am scarcely surprised at it.

SOLNESS. At what?

DR. HERDAL. That she should not exactly approve of your seeing so much of another woman, all day and every day.

SOLNESS. No, no, I suppose you are right there—and Aline too. But it's impossible to make any change.

DR. HERDAL. Could you not engage a clerk?

SOLNESS. The first man that came to hand? No, thank you—that would never do for me.

DR. HERDAL. But now, if your wife—? Suppose, with her delicate health, all this tries her too much?

SOLNESS. Even then—I might almost say—it can make no difference. I must keep Kaia Fosli. No one else could fill her place.

DR. HERDAL. No one else?

SOLNESS [*curtly*]. No, no one.

DR. HERDAL [*drawing his chair closer*]. Now listen to me, my dear Mr. Solness. May I ask you a question, quite between ourselves?

SOLNESS. By all means.

DR. HERDAL. Women, you see—in certain matters, they have a deucedly keen intuition—

SOLNESS. They have, indeed. There is not the least doubt of that. But—?

DR. HERDAL. Well, tell me now—if your wife can't endure this Kaia Fosli—?

SOLNESS. Well, what then?

DR. HERDAL. —may she not have just—just the least bit of reason for this instinctive dislike?

SOLNESS [*looks at him and rises*]. Oho!

DR. HERDAL. Now don't be offended—but hasn't she?

SOLNESS [*with curt decision*]. No.

DR. HERDAL. No reason of any sort?

SOLNESS. No other reason than her own suspicious nature.

DR. HERDAL. I know you have known a good many women in your time.

SOLNESS. Yes, I have.

DR. HERDAL. And have been a good deal taken with some of them, too.

SOLNESS. Oh yes, I don't deny it.

DR. HERDAL. But as regards Miss Fosli, then? There is nothing of that sort in the case?

SOLNESS. No; nothing at all—on my side.

DR. HERDAL. But on her side?

SOLNESS. I don't think you have any right to ask that question, doctor.

DR. HERDAL. Well, you know, we were discussing your wife's intuition.

SOLNESS. So we were. And for that matter—[*lowers his voice*]—Aline's intuition, as you call it—in a certain sense, it has not been so far astray.

DR. HERDAL. Aha! there we have it!

SOLNESS [*sits down*]. Dr. Herdal—I am going to tell you a strange story —if you care to listen to it.

DR. HERDAL. I like listening to strange stories.

SOLNESS. Very well then. I daresay you recollect that I took Knut Brovik and his son into my employment—after the old man's business had gone to the dogs.

DR. HERDAL. Yes, so I have understood.

SOLNESS. You see, they really are clever fellows, these two. Each of them has talent in his own way. But then the son took it into his head to get engaged; and the next thing, of course, was that he wanted to get married—and begin to build on his own account. That is the way with all these young people.

DR. HERDAL [*laughing*]. Yes, they have a bad habit of wanting to marry.

SOLNESS. Just so. But of course that did not suit my plans; for I needed Ragnar myself—and the old man too. He is exceedingly good at calculating bearing strains and cubic contents—and all that sort of devilry, you know.

DR. HERDAL. Oh yes, no doubt that's indispensable.

SOLNESS. Yes, it is. But Ragnar was absolutely bent on setting to work for himself. He would hear of nothing else.

DR. HERDAL. But he has stayed with you all the same.

SOLNESS. Yes, I'll tell you how that came about. One day this girl, Kaia Fosli, came to see them on some errand or other. She had never been here before. And when I saw how utterly infatuated they were with each other, the thought occurred to me: if I could only get her into the office here, then perhaps Ragnar too would stay where he is.

DR. HERDAL. That was not at all a bad idea.

SOLNESS. Yes, but at the time I did not breathe a word of what was in my mind. I merely stood and looked at her—and kept on wishing intently that I could have her here. Then I talked to her a little, in a friendly way—about one thing and another. And then she went away.

DR. HERDAL. Well?

SOLNESS. Well, then, next day, pretty late in the evening, when old Brovik and Ragnar had gone home, she came here again, and behaved as if I had made an arrangement with her.

DR. HERDAL. An arrangement? What about?

SOLNESS. About the very thing my mind had been fixed on. But I hadn't said one single word about it.

DR. HERDAL. That was most extraordinary.

SOLNESS. Yes, was it not? And now she wanted to know what she was to do here—whether she could begin the very next morning, and so forth.

DR. HERDAL. Don't you think she did it in order to be with her sweetheart?

SOLNESS. That was what occurred to me at first. But no, that was not it. She seemed to drift quite away from him—when once she had come here to me.

DR. HERDAL. She drifted over to you, then?

SOLNESS. Yes, entirely. If I happen to look at her when her back is turned, I can tell that she feels it. She quivers and trembles the moment I come near her. What do you think of that?

DR. HERDAL. H'm—that's not very hard to explain.

SOLNESS. Well, but what about the other thing? That she believed I had said to her what I had only wished and willed—silently—inwardly—to myself? What do you say to that? Can you explain that, Dr. Herdal?

DR. HERDAL. No, I won't undertake to do that.

SOLNESS. I felt sure you would not; and so I have never cared to talk about it till now. But it's a cursed nuisance to me in the long run, you understand. Here I have to go on day after day pretending—. And it's a shame to treat her so, too, poor girl. [*Vehemently.*] But I cannot do anything else. For if she runs away from me—then Ragnar will be off too.

DR. HERDAL. And you have not told your wife the rights of the story?

SOLNESS. No.

DR. HERDAL. Then why on earth don't you?

SOLNESS [*looks fixedly at him, and says in a low voice*]. Because I seem to find a sort of—of salutary self-torture in allowing Aline to do me an injustice.

DR. HERDAL [*shakes his head*]. I don't in the least understand what you mean.

SOLNESS. Well, you see—it is like paying off a little bit of a huge, immeasurable debt—

DR. HERDAL. To your wife?

SOLNESS. Yes; and that always helps to relieve one's mind a little. One can breathe more freely for a while, you understand.

DR. HERDAL. No, goodness knows, I don't understand at all—

SOLNESS [*breaking off, rises again*]. Well, well, well—then we won't talk any more about it. [*He saunters across the room, returns, and stops beside the table. Looks at the doctor with a sly smile.*] I suppose you think you have drawn me out nicely now, doctor?

DR. HERDAL [*with some irritation*]. Drawn you out? Again I have not the faintest notion what you mean, Mr. Solness.

SOLNESS. Oh come, out with it; I have seen it quite clearly, you know.

DR. HERDAL. What have you seen?

SOLNESS [*in a low voice, slowly*]. That you have been quietly keeping an eye upon me.

DR. HERDAL. That *I* have! And why in all the world should I do that?

SOLNESS. Because you think that I—[*Passionately.*] Well, devil take it—you think the same of me as Aline does.

DR. HERDAL. And what does she think about you?

SOLNESS [*having recovered his self-control*]. She has begun to think that I am —that I am—ill.

DR. HERDAL. Ill! You! She has never hinted such a thing to me. Why, what can she think is the matter with you?

SOLNESS [*leans over the back of the chair and whispers*]. Aline has made up her mind that I am mad. That is what she thinks.

DR. HERDAL [*rising*]. Why, my dear good fellow—!

SOLNESS. Yes, on my soul she does! I tell you it is so. And she has got you to think the same! Oh, I can assure you, doctor, I see it in your face as clearly as possible. You don't take me in so easily, I can tell you.

DR. HERDAL [*looks at him in amazement*]. Never, Mr. Solness—never has such a thought entered my mind.

SOLNESS [*with an incredulous smile*]. Really? Has it not?

DR. HERDAL. No, never! Nor your wife's mind either, I am convinced. I could almost swear to that.

SOLNESS. Well, I wouldn't advise you to. For, in a certain sense, you see, perhaps—perhaps she is not so far wrong in thinking something of the kind.

DR. HERDAL. Come now, I really must say—

SOLNESS [*interrupting, with a sweep of his hand*]. Well, well, my dear doctor—don't let us discuss this any further. We had better agree to differ. [*Changes to a tone of quiet amusement.*] But look here now, doctor—h'm—

DR. HERDAL. Well?

SOLNESS. Since you don't believe that I am—ill—and crazy, and mad, and so forth—

DR. HERDAL. What then?

SOLNESS. Then I daresay you fancy that I am an extremely happy man.

DR. HERDAL. Is that mere fancy?

SOLNESS [*laughs*]. No, no—of course not! Heaven forbid! Only think—to be Solness the master builder! Halvard Solness! What could be more delightful?

DR. HERDAL. Yes, I must say it seems to me you have had the luck on your side to an astounding degree.

SOLNESS [*suppresses a gloomy smile*]. So I have, I can't complain on that score.

DR. HERDAL. First of all that grim old robbers' castle was burnt down for you. And that was certainly a great piece of luck.

SOLNESS [*seriously*]. It was the home of Aline's family. Remember that.

DR. HERDAL. Yes, it must have been a great grief to her.

SOLNESS. She has not got over it to this day—not in all these twelve or thirteen years.

DR. HERDAL. Ah, but what followed must have been the worst blow for her.

SOLNESS. The one thing with the other.

DR. HERDAL. But you—yourself—you rose upon the ruins. You began as a poor boy from a country village—and now you are at the head of your profession. Ah, yes, Mr. Solness, you have undoubtedly had the luck on your side.

SOLNESS [*looking at him with embarrassment*]. Yes, but that is just what makes me so horribly afraid.

DR. HERDAL. Afraid? Because you have the luck on your side!

SOLNESS. It terrifies me—terrifies me every hour of the day. For sooner or later the luck must turn, you see.

DR. HERDAL. Oh nonsense! What should make the luck turn?

SOLNESS [*with firm assurance*]. The younger generation.

DR. HERDAL. Pooh! The younger generation! You are not laid on the shelf yet, I should hope. Oh, no—your position here is probably firmer now than it has ever been.

SOLNESS. The luck will turn. I know it—I feel the day approaching. Some one or other will take it into his head to say: Give me a chance! And then all the rest will come clamoring after him, and shake their fists at me and shout: Make room—make room—make room! Yes, just you see, doctor—presently the younger generation will come knocking at my door—

DR. HERDAL [*laughing*]. Well, and what if they do?

SOLNESS. What if they do? Then there's an end of Halvard Solness.

[*There is a knock at the door on the left.*]

SOLNESS [*starts*]. What's that? Did you not hear something?

DR. HERDAL. Some one is knocking at the door.

SOLNESS [*loudly*]. Come in.

[HILDA WANGEL *enters by the hall door. She is of middle height, supple, and delicately built. Somewhat sunburnt. Dressed in a tourist costume, with skirt caught up for walking, a sailor's collar open at the throat, and a small sailor hat on her head. Knapsack on back, plaid in strap, and alpenstock.*]

HILDA [*goes straight up to* SOLNESS, *her eyes sparkling with happiness*]. Good evening!

SOLNESS [*looks doubtfully at her*]. Good evening—

HILDA [*laughs*]. I almost believe you don't recognize me!

SOLNESS. No—I must admit that—just for the moment—

DR. HERDAL [*approaching*]. But I recognize you, my dear young lady—

HILDA [*pleased*]. Oh, is it you that—

DR. HERDAL. Of course it is. [*To* SOLNESS.] We met at one of the mountain stations this summer. [*To* HILDA.] What became of the other ladies?

HILDA. Oh, they went westward.

DR. HERDAL. They didn't much like all the fun we used to have in the evenings.

HILDA. No, I believe they didn't.

DR. HERDAL [*holds up his finger at her*]. And I am afraid it can't be denied that you flirted a little with us.

HILDA. Well that was better fun than to sit there knitting stockings with all those old women.

DR. HERDAL [*laughs*]. There I entirely agree with you.

SOLNESS. Have you come to town this evening?

HILDA. Yes, I have just arrived.

DR. HERDAL. Quite alone, Miss Wangel?

HILDA. Oh yes!

SOLNESS. Wangel? Is your name Wangel?

HILDA [*looks in amused surprise at him*]. Yes, of course it is.

SOLNESS. Then you must be a daughter of the district doctor up at Lysanger?

HILDA [*as before*]. Yes, who else's daughter should I be?

SOLNESS. Oh, then I suppose we met up there, that summer when I was building a tower on the old church.

HILDA [*more seriously*]. Yes, of course it was then we met.

SOLNESS. Well, that is a long time ago.

HILDA [*looks hard at him*]. It is exactly the ten years.

SOLNESS. You must have been a mere child then, I should think.

HILDA [*carelessly*]. Well, I was twelve or thirteen.

DR. HERDAL. Is this the first time you have ever been up to town, Miss Wangel?

HILDA. Yes, it is indeed.

SOLNESS. And don't you know any one here?

HILDA. Nobody but you. And of course, your wife.

SOLNESS. So you know her, too?

HILDA. Only a little. We spent a few days together at the sanatorium.

SOLNESS. Ah, up there?

HILDA. She said I might come and pay her a visit if ever I came up to town. [*Smiles.*] Not that that was necessary.

SOLNESS. Odd that she should never have mentioned it.

[HILDA *puts her stick down by the stove, takes off the knapsack and lays it and the plaid on the sofa.* DR. HERDAL *offers to help her.* SOLNESS *stands and gazes at her.*]

HILDA [*going towards him*]. Well, now I must ask you to let me stay the night here.

SOLNESS. I am sure there will be no difficulty about that.

HILDA. For I have no other clothes than those I stand in, except a change of linen in my knapsack. And that has to go to the wash, for it's very dirty.

SOLNESS. Oh yes, that can be managed. Now I'll just let my wife know—

DR. HERDAL. Meanwhile I will go and see my patient.

SOLNESS. Yes, do; and come again later on.

DR. HERDAL [*playfully, with a glance at* HILDA]. Oh, that I will, you may be very certain! [*Laughs.*] So your prediction has come true, Mr. Solness!

SOLNESS. How so?

DR. HERDAL. The younger generation did come knocking at your door.

SOLNESS [*cheerfully*]. Yes, but in a very different way from what I meant.

DR. HERDAL. Very different, yes. That's undeniable.

[*He goes out by the hall door.* SOLNESS *opens the door on the right and speaks into the side room.*]

SOLNESS. Aline! Will you come in here, please. Here is a friend of yours—Miss Wangel.

MRS. SOLNESS [*appears in the doorway*]. Who do you say it is? [*Sees* HILDA.] Oh, is it you, Miss Wangel? [*Goes up to her and offers her hand.*] So you have come to town after all.

SOLNESS. Miss Wangel has this moment arrived; and she would like to stay the night here.

MRS. SOLNESS. Here with us? Oh yes, certainly.

SOLNESS. Till she can get her things a little in order, you know.

MRS. SOLNESS. I will do the best I can for you. It's no more than my duty. I suppose your trunk is coming on later?

HILDA. I have no trunk.

MRS. SOLNESS. Well, it will be all right, I daresay. In the meantime, you must excuse my leaving you here with my husband, until I can get a room made a little comfortable for you.

SOLNESS. Can we not give her one of the nurseries? They are all ready as it is.

MRS. SOLNESS. Oh yes. There we have room and to spare. [*To* HILDA.] Sit down now, and rest a little. [*She goes out to the right.*]

[HILDA, *with her hands behind her back, strolls about the room and looks at various objects.* SOLNESS *stands in front, beside the table, also with his hands behind his back, and follows her with his eyes.*]

HILDA [*stops and looks at him*]. Have you several nurseries?

SOLNESS. There are three nurseries in the house.

HILDA. That's a lot. Then I suppose you have a great many children?

SOLNESS. No. We have no child. But now you can be the child here, for the time being.

HILDA. For tonight, yes. I shall not cry. I mean to sleep as sound as a stone.

SOLNESS. Yes, you must be very tired, I should think.

HILDA. Oh no! But all the same— It's so delicious to lie and dream.

SOLNESS. Do you dream much of nights?

HILDA. Oh yes! Almost always.

SOLNESS. What do you dream about most?

HILDA. I shan't tell you tonight. Another time, perhaps. [*She again strolls about her room, stops at the desk and turns over the books and papers a little.*]

SOLNESS [*approaching*]. Are you searching for anything?

HILDA. No, I am merely looking at all these things. [*Turns.*] Perhaps I mustn't?

SOLNESS. Oh, by all means.

HILDA. Is it you that write in this great ledger?

SOLNESS. No, it's my bookkeeper.

HILDA. Is it a woman?

SOLNESS [*smiles*]. Yes.

HILDA. One you employ here, in your office?

SOLNESS. Yes.

HILDA. Is she married?

SOLNESS. No, she is single.

HILDA. Oh, indeed!

SOLNESS. But I believe she is soon going to be married.

HILDA. That's a good thing for her.

SOLNESS. But not such a good thing for me. For then I shall have nobody to help me.

HILDA. Can't you get hold of some one else who will do just as well?

SOLNESS. Perhaps you would stay here and write in the ledger?

HILDA [*measures him with a glance*]. Yes, I daresay! No, thank you—nothing of that sort for me.

[*She again strolls across the room, and sits down in the rocking chair.* SOLNESS *too goes to the table.*]

HILDA [*continuing*]. For there must surely be plenty of other things to be done here. [*Looks smiling at him.*] Don't you think so, too?

SOLNESS. Of course. First of all, I suppose, you want to make a round of the shops, and get yourself up in the height of fashion.

HILDA [*amused*]. No, I think I shall let that alone!

SOLNESS. Indeed.

HILDA. For you must know I have run through all my money.

SOLNESS [*laughs*]. Neither trunk nor money, then.

HILDA. Neither one nor the other. But never mind—it doesn't matter now.

SOLNESS. Come now, I like you for that.

HILDA. Only for that?

SOLNESS. For that among other things. [*Sits in the armchair.*] Is your father alive still?

HILDA. Yes, father's alive.

SOLNESS. Perhaps you are thinking of studying here?

HILDA. No, that hadn't occurred to me.

SOLNESS. But I suppose you will be staying for some time?

HILDA. That must depend upon circumstances. [*She sits awhile rocking herself and looking at him, half-seriously, half with a suppressed smile. Then she takes off her hat and puts it on the table in front of her.*] Mr. Solness!

SOLNESS. Well?

HILDA. Have you a very bad memory?

SOLNESS. A bad memory? No, not that I am aware of.

HILDA. Then have you nothing to say to me about what happened up there?

SOLNESS [*in momentary surprise*]. Up at Lysanger? [*Indifferently.*] Why, it was nothing much to talk about, it seems to me.

HILDA [*looks reproachfully at him*]. How can you sit there and say such things?

SOLNESS. Well, then, you talk to me about it.

HILDA. When the tower was finished, we had grand doings in the town.

SOLNESS. Yes, I shall not easily forget that day.

HILDA [*smiles*]. Will you not? That comes well from you.

SOLNESS. Comes well?

HILDA. There was music in the churchyard—and many, many hundreds of people. We school girls were dressed in white; and we all carried flags.

SOLNESS. Ah yes, those flags—I can tell you I remember them!

HILDA. Then you climbed right up the scaffolding, straight to the very top; and you had a great wreath with you; and you hung that wreath right away up on the weathervane.

SOLNESS [*curtly interrupting*]. I always did that in those days. It was an old custom.

HILDA. It was so wonderfully thrilling to stand below, and look up at you. Fancy, if he should fall over! He—the master builder himself!

SOLNESS [*as if to divert her from the subject*]. Yes, yes, yes, that might very well have happened, too. For one of those white-frocked little devils, she went on in such a way, and screamed up at me so—

HILDA [*sparkling with pleasure*]. "Hurrah for Master Builder Solness!" Yes!

SOLNESS. —and waved and flourished with her flag, so that I—so that it almost made me giddy to look at it.

HILDA [*in a lower voice, seriously*]. That little devil—that was *I*.

SOLNESS [*fixes his eyes steadily upon her*]. I am sure of that now. It must have been you.

HILDA [*lively again*]. Oh, it was so gloriously thrilling! I could not have believed there was a builder in the whole world that could build such a tremendously high tower. And then, that you yourself should stand at the very top of it, as large as life! And that you should not be the least bit dizzy! It was that above everything that made one—made one dizzy to think of.

SOLNESS. How could you be so certain that I was not—?

HILDA [*scouting the idea*]. No indeed! Oh no! I knew that instinctively. For if you had been, you could never have stood up there and sung.

SOLNESS [*looks at her in astonishment*]. Sung? Did *I* sing?

HILDA. Yes, I should think you did.

SOLNESS [*shakes his head*]. I have never sung a note in my life.

HILDA. Yes indeed, you sang then. It sounded like harps in the air.

SOLNESS [*thoughtfully*]. This is very strange—all this.

HILDA [*is silent awhile, looks at him and says in a low voice*] But then,—it was after that—and the real thing happened.

SOLNESS. The real thing?

HILDA [*sparkling with vivacity*]. Yes, I surely don't need to remind you of that?

SOLNESS. Oh yes, do remind me a little of that, too.

HILDA. Don't you remember that a great dinner was given in your honor at the Club?

SOLNESS. Yes, to be sure. It must have been the same afternoon, for I left the place next morning.

HILDA. And from the Club you were invited to come round to our house to supper.

SOLNESS. Quite right, Miss Wangel. It is wonderful how all these trifles have impressed themselves on your mind.

HILDA. Trifles! I like that! Perhaps it was a trifle, too, that I was alone in the room when you came in?

SOLNESS. Were you alone?

HILDA [*without answering him*]. You didn't call me a little devil then?

SOLNESS. No, I suppose I did not.

HILDA. You said I was lovely in my white dress, and that I looked like a little princess.

SOLNESS. I have no doubt you did, Miss Wangel. And besides—I was feeling so buoyant and free that day—

HILDA. And then you said that when I grew up I should be your princess.

SOLNESS [*laughing a little*]. Dear, dear—did I say that too?

HILDA. Yes, you did. And when I asked how long I should have to wait, you said that you would come again in ten years—like a troll and carry me off—to Spain or some such place. And you promised you would buy me a kingdom there.

SOLNESS [*as before*]. Yes, after a good dinner one doesn't haggle about the halfpence. But did I really say all that?

HILDA [*laughs to herself*]. Yes. And you told me, too, what the kingdom was to be called.

SOLNESS. Well, what was it?

HILDA. It was to be called the kingdom of Orangia,[1] you said.

[1] In the original "Appelsinia," "appelsin" meaning "orange."

SOLNESS. Well, that was an appetizing name.

HILDA. No, I didn't like it a bit; for it seemed as though you wanted to make game of me.

SOLNESS. I am sure that cannot have been my intention.

HILDA. No, I should hope not—considering what you did next—

SOLNESS. What in the world did I do next?

HILDA. Well, that's the finishing touch, if you have forgotten that too. I should have thought no one could help remembering such a thing as that.

SOLNESS. Yes, yes, just give me a hint, and then perhaps—Well—

HILDA [*looks fixedly at him*]. You came and kissed me, Mr. Solness.

SOLNESS [*open mouthed, rising from his chair*]. *I* did!

HILDA. Yes, indeed you did. You took me in both your arms, and bent my head back, and kissed me—many times.

SOLNESS. Now really, my dear Miss Wangel—!

HILDA [*rises*]. You surely cannot mean to deny it?

SOLNESS. Yes, I do. I deny it altogether!

HILDA [*looks scornfully at him*]. Oh, indeed! [*She turns and goes slowly close up to the stove, where she remains standing motionless, her face averted from him, her hands behind her back. Short pause.*]

SOLNESS [*goes cautiously up behind her*]. Miss Wangel—!

[HILDA *is silent and does not move.*]

SOLNESS. Don't stand there like a statue. You must have dreamt all this. [*Lays his hand on her arm.*] Now just listen—

[HILDA *makes an impatient movement with her arm.*]

SOLNESS [*as a thought flashes upon him*]. Or—! Wait a moment! There is something under all this, you may depend!

[HILDA *does not move.*]

SOLNESS [*in a low voice, but with emphasis*]. I must have thought all that. I must have wished it—have willed it—have longed to do it. And then—. May not that be the explanation?

[HILDA *is still silent.*]

SOLNESS [*impatiently*]. Oh very well, deuce take it all—then I did it, I suppose.

HILDA [*turns her head a little, but without looking at him*]. Then you admit it now?

SOLNESS. Yes—whatever you like.

HILDA. You came and put your arms around me?

SOLNESS. Oh yes!

HILDA. And bent my head back?

SOLNESS. Very far back.

HILDA. And kissed me?

SOLNESS. Yes, I did.

HILDA. Many times?

SOLNESS. As many as ever you like.

HILDA [*turns quickly towards him and has once more the sparkling expression of gladness in her eyes*]. Well, you see, I got it out of you at last!

SOLNESS [*with a slight smile*]. Yes—just think of my forgetting such a thing as that.

HILDA [*again a little sulky, retreats from him*]. Oh, you have kissed so many people in your time, I suppose.

SOLNESS. No, you mustn't think that of me. [HILDA *seats herself in the armchair.* SOLNESS *stands and leans against the rocking chair. Looks observantly at her.*] Miss Wangel!

HILDA. Yes!

SOLNESS. How was it now? What came of all this—between us two?

HILDA. Why, nothing more came of it. You know that quite well. For then the other guests came in, and then—bah!

SOLNESS. Quite so! The others came in. To think of my forgetting that too!

HILDA. Oh, you haven't really forgotten anything: you are only a little ashamed of it all. I am sure one doesn't forget things of that kind.

SOLNESS. No, one would suppose not.

HILDA [*lively again, looks at him*]. Perhaps you have even forgotten what day it was?

SOLNESS. What day—?

HILDA. Yes, on what day did you hang the wreath on the tower? Well? Tell me at once!

SOLNESS. Him—I confess I have forgotten the particular day. I only know it was ten years ago. Some time in the autumn.

HILDA [*nods her head slowly several times*]. It was ten years ago—on the 19th of September.

SOLNESS. Yes, it must have been about that time. Fancy your remembering that too! [*Stops.*] But wait a moment—! Yes—it's the 19th of September today.

HILDA. Yes, it is; and the ten years are gone. And you didn't come—as you promised me.

SOLNESS. Promised you? Threatened, I suppose you mean?

HILDA. I don't think there was any sort of threat in that.

SOLNESS. Well then, a little bit of fun.

HILDA. Was that all you wanted? To make fun of me?

SOLNESS. Well, or to have a little joke with you. Upon my soul, I don't recollect. But it must have been something of that kind; for you were a mere child then.

HILDA. Oh, perhaps I wasn't quite such a child either. Not such a mere chit as you imagine.

SOLNESS [*looks searchingly at her*]. Did you really and seriously expect me to come again?

HILDA [*conceals a half-teasing smile*]. Yes, indeed; I did expect that of you.

SOLNESS. That I should come back to your home, and take you away with me?

HILDA. Just like a troll—yes.

SOLNESS. And make a princess of you?

HILDA. That's what you promised.

SOLNESS. And give you a kingdom as well?

HILDA [*looks up at the ceiling*]. Why not? Of course it need not have been an actual, everyday sort of a kingdom.

SOLNESS. But something else just as good?

HILDA. Yes, at least as good. [*Looks at him a moment.*] I thought, if you could build the highest church towers in the world, you could surely manage to raise a kingdom of one sort or another as well.

SOLNESS [*shakes his head*]. I can't quite make you out, Miss Wangel.

HILDA. Can you not? To me it seems all so simple.

SOLNESS. No, I can't make up my mind whether you mean all you say, or are simply having a joke with me.

HILDA [*smiles*]. Making fun of you, perhaps? I, too?

SOLNESS. Yes, exactly. Making fun—of both of us. [*Looks at her.*] Is it long since you found out that I was married?

HILDA. I have known it all along. Why do you ask me that?

SOLNESS [*lightly*]. Oh, well, it just occurred to me. [*Looks earnestly at her, and says in a low voice*] What have you come for?

HILDA. I want my kingdom. The time is up.

SOLNESS [*laughs involuntarily*]. What a girl you are!

HILDA [*gaily*]. Out with my kingdom, Mr. Solness! [*Raps with her fingers.*] The kingdom on the table!

SOLNESS [*pushing the rocking chair nearer and sitting down*]. Now, seriously speaking—what have you come for? What do you really want to do here?

HILDA. Oh, first of all, I want to go around and look at all the things that you have built.

SOLNESS. That will give you plenty of exercise.

HILDA. Yes, I know you have built a tremendous lot.

SOLNESS. I have indeed—especially of late years.

HILDA. Many church towers among the rest? Immensely high ones?

SOLNESS. No. I build no more church towers now. Nor churches either.

HILDA. What do you build then?

SOLNESS. Homes for human beings.

HILDA [*reflectively*]. Couldn't you build a little—a little bit of a church tower over these homes as well?

SOLNESS [*starting*]. What do you mean by that?

HILDA. I mean—something that points—points up into the free air. With the vane at a dizzy height.

SOLNESS [*pondering a little*]. Strange that you should say that—for that is just what I am most anxious to do.

HILDA [*impatiently*]. Why don't you do it, then?

SOLNESS [*shakes his head*]. No, the people will not have it.

HILDA. Fancy their not wanting it!

SOLNESS [*more lightly*]. But now I am building a new home for myself—just opposite here.

HILDA. For yourself?

SOLNESS. Yes. It is almost finished. And on that there is a tower.

HILDA. A high tower?

SOLNESS. Yes.

HILDA. Very high?

SOLNESS. No doubt people will say it is too high—too high for a dwelling house.

HILDA. I'll go out and look at that tower the first thing tomorrow morning.

SOLNESS [*sits resting his cheek on his hand, and gazes at her*]. Tell me, Miss Wangel—what is your name? Your Christian name, I mean?

HILDA. Why, Hilda, of course.

SOLNESS [*as before*]. Hilda? Indeed?

HILDA. Don't you remember that? You called me Hilda yourself—that day when you misbehaved.

SOLNESS. Did I really?

HILDA. But then you said "little Hilda"; and I didn't like that.

SOLNESS. Oh, you didn't like that, Miss Hilda?

HILDA. No, not at such a time as that. But—"Princess Hilda"—that will sound very well, I think.

SOLNESS. Very well indeed. Princess Hilda of—of—what was to be the name of the kingdom?

HILDA. Pooh! I won't have anything to do with that stupid kingdom. I have set my heart upon quite a different one!

SOLNESS [*has leaned back in the chair, still gazing at her*]. Isn't it strange—? The more I think of it now, the more it seems to me as though I had gone about all these years torturing myself with—h'm—

HILDA. With what?

SOLNESS. With the effort to recover something—some experience, which I seemed to have forgotten. But I never had the leasting inkling of what it could be.

HILDA. You should have tied a knot in your pockethandkerchief, Mr. Solness.

SOLNESS. In that case, I should simply have had to go racking my brains to discover what the knot could mean.

HILDA. Oh, yes, I suppose there are trolls of that kind in the world, too.

SOLNESS [*rises slowly*]. What a good thing it is that you have come to me now.

HILDA [*looks deeply into his eyes*]. Is it a good thing?

SOLNESS. For I have been so lonely here. I have been gazing so helplessly at it all. [*In a lower voice.*] I must tell you—I have begun to be so afraid—so terribly afraid of the younger generation.

HILDA [*with a little snort of contempt*]. Pooh—is the younger generation a thing to be afraid of?

SOLNESS. It is indeed. And that is why I have locked and barred myself in. [*Mysteriously*] I tell you the younger generation will one day come and thunder at my door! They will break in upon me!

HILDA. Then I should say you ought to go out and open the door to the younger generation.

SOLNESS. Open the door?

HILDA. Yes. Let them come in to you on friendly terms, as it were.

SOLNESS. No, no, no! The younger generation—it means retribution, you see. It comes, as if under a new banner, heralding the turn of fortune.

HILDA [*rises, looks at him, and says with a quivering twitch of her lips*]. Can I be of any use to you, Mr. Solness?

SOLNESS. Yes, you can indeed! For you, too, come—under a new banner, it seems to me. Youth marshalled against youth—!

[DR. HERDAL *comes in by the hall door.*]

DR. HERDAL. What—you and Miss Wangel here still?

SOLNESS. Yes. We have had no end of things to talk about.

HILDA. Both old and new.

DR. HERDAL. Have you really?

HILDA. Oh, it has been the greatest fun. For Mr. Solness—he has such a miraculous memory. All the least little details he remembers instantly.

[MRS. SOLNESS *enters by the door on the right.*]

MRS. SOLNESS. Well, Miss Wangel, your room is quite ready for you now.

HILDA. Oh, how kind you are to me!

SOLNESS [*to* MRS. SOLNESS]. The nursery?

MRS. SOLNESS. Yes, the middle one. But first let us go in to supper.

SOLNESS [*nods to* HILDA]. Hilda shall sleep in the nursery, she shall.

MRS. SOLNESS [*looks at him*]. Hilda?

SOLNESS. Yes, Miss Wangel's name is Hilda. I knew her when she was a child.

MRS. SOLNESS. Did you really, Halvard? Well, shall we go? Supper is on the table.

[*She takes* DR. HERDAL'*s arm and goes out with him to the right.* HILDA *has meanwhile been collecting her traveling things.*]

HILDA [*softly and rapidly to* SOLNESS]. Is it true, what you said? Can I be of use to you?

SOLNESS [*takes the things from her*]. You are the very being I have needed most.

HILDA [*looks at him with happy, wondering eyes and clasps her hands*]. But then, great heavens—!

SOLNESS [*eagerly*]. What—?

HILDA. Then I have my kingdom!

SOLNESS [*involuntarily*]. Hilda—!

HILDA [*again with the quivering twitch of her lips*]. Almost—I was going to say.

[*She goes out to right,* SOLNESS *follows her.*]

ACT II

A prettily furnished small drawing room in SOLNESS' *house. In the back, a glass door leading out to the verandah and garden. The right-hand corner is cut off transversely by a large bay window, in which are flower stands. The left-hand corner is similarly cut off by a transverse wall, in which is a small door papered like the wall. On each side, an ordinary door. In front, on the right, a console table with a large mirror over it. Well-filled stands of plants and flowers. In front, on the left, a sofa with a table and chairs. Further back, a bookcase. Well forward in the room, before the bay window, a small table and some chairs. It is early in the day.*

SOLNESS *sits by the little table with* RAGNAR BROVIK'S *portfolio open in front of him. He is turning the drawings over and closely examining some of them.* MRS. SOLNESS *moves about noiselessly with a small watering pot, attending to her flowers. She is dressed in black as before. Her hat, cloak and parasol lie on a chair near the mirror. Unobserved by her,* SOLNESS *now and again follows her with his eyes. Neither of them speaks.*

KAIA FOSLI *enters quietly by the door on the left.*

SOLNESS [*turns his head, and says in an offhand tone of indifference*]. Well, is that you?

KAIA. I merely wished to let you know that I have come.

SOLNESS. Yes, yes, that's all right. Hasn't Ragnar come too?

KAIA. No, not yet. He had to wait a little while to see the doctor. But he is coming presently to hear—

SOLNESS. How is the old man today?

KAIA. Not well. He begs you to excuse him; he is obliged to keep his bed today.

SOLNESS. Why, of course; by all means let him rest. But now, get to work.

KAIA. Yes. [*Pauses at the door.*] Do you wish to speak to Ragnar when he comes?

SOLNESS. No—I don't know that I have anything particular to say to him.

[KAIA *goes out again to the left.* SOLNESS *remains seated, turning over the drawings.*]

MRS. SOLNESS [*over beside the plants*]. I wonder if he isn't going to die now, as well?

SOLNESS [*looks up to her*]. As well as who?

MRS. SOLNESS [*without answering*]. Yes, yes—depend upon it, Halvard, old Brovik is going to die too. You'll see that he will.

SOLNESS. My dear Aline, ought you not to go out for a little walk?

MRS. SOLNESS. Yes, I suppose I ought to. [*She continues to attend to the flowers.*]

SOLNESS [*bending over the drawings*]. Is she still asleep?

MRS. SOLNESS [*looking at him*]. Is it Miss Wangel you are sitting there thinking about?

SOLNESS [*indifferently*]. I just happened to recollect her.

MRS. SOLNESS. Miss Wangel was up long ago.

SOLNESS. Oh, was she?

MRS. SOLNESS. When I went in to see her, she was busy putting her things in order. [*She goes in front of the mirror and slowly begins to put on her hat.*]

SOLNESS [*after a short pause*]. So we have found a use for one of our nurseries after all, Aline.

MRS. SOLNESS. Yes, we have.

SOLNESS. That seems to me better than to have them all standing empty.

MRS. SOLNESS. That emptiness is dreadful; you are right there.

SOLNESS [*closes the portfolio, rises and approaches her*]. You will find that we shall get on far better after this, Aline. Things will be more comfortable. Life will be easier—especially for you.

MRS. SOLNESS [*looks at him*]. After this?

SOLNESS. Yes, believe me, Aline—

MRS. SOLNESS. Do you mean—because she has come here?

SOLNESS [*checking himself*]. I mean, of course—when once we have moved into the new house.

MRS. SOLNESS [*takes her cloak*]. Ah, do you think so, Halvard? Will it be better then?

SOLNESS. I can't think otherwise. And surely you think so too?

MRS. SOLNESS. I think nothing at all about the new house.

SOLNESS [*cast down*]. It's hard for me to hear you say that; for you know it is mainly for your sake that I have built it. [*He offers to help her on with her cloak.*]

MRS. SOLNESS [*evades him*]. The fact is, you do far too much for my sake.

SOLNESS [*with a certain vehemence*]. No, no, you really mustn't say that, Aline! I cannot bear to hear you say such things!

MRS. SOLNESS. Very well, then I won't say it, Halvard.

SOLNESS. But I stick to what *I* said. You'll see that things will be easier for you in the new place.

MRS. SOLNESS. O heavens—easier for me—!

SOLNESS [*eagerly*]. Yes, indeed they will! You may be quite sure of that! For you see—there will be so very, very much there that will remind you of your own home—

MRS. SOLNESS. The home that used to be father's and mother's—and that was burnt to the ground—

SOLNESS [*in a low voice*]. Yes, yes, my poor Aline. That was a terrible blow for you.

MRS. SOLNESS [*breaking out in lamentation*]. You may build as much as ever you like, Halvard—you can never build up again a real home for me!

SOLNESS [*crosses the room*]. Well, in heaven's name, let us talk no more about it then.

MRS. SOLNESS. Oh yes, Halvard, I understand you very well. You are so anxious to spare me—and to find excuses for me too—as much as ever you can.

SOLNESS [*with astonishment in his eyes*]. You! Is it you—yourself, that you are talking about, Aline?

MRS. SOLNESS. Yes, who else should it be but myself?

SOLNESS [*involuntarily to himself*]. That too!

MRS. SOLNESS. As for the old house, I wouldn't mind so much about that. When once misfortune was in the air—why—

SOLNESS. Ah, you are right there. Misfortune will have its way—as the saying goes.

MRS. SOLNESS. But it's what came of the fire—the dreadful thing that followed—! That is the thing! That, that, that!

SOLNESS [*vehemently*]. Don't think about that, Aline!

MRS. SOLNESS. Ah, that is exactly what I cannot help thinking about. And now, at last, I must speak about it, too; for I don't seem able to bear it any longer. And then never to be able to forgive myself—

SOLNESS [*exclaiming*]. Yourself—!

MRS. SOLNESS. Yes, for I had duties on both sides—both towards you and towards the little ones. I ought to have hardened myself—not to have let the horror take such hold upon me—nor the grief for the burning of my old home. [*Wrings her hands.*] Oh, Halvard, if I had only had the strength!

SOLNESS [*softly, much moved, comes closer*]. Aline—you must promise me never to think these thoughts any more. Promise me that, dear!

MRS. SOLNESS. Oh, promise, promise! One can promise anything.

SOLNESS [*clenches his hands and crosses the room*]. Oh, but this is hopeless, hopeless! Never a ray of sunlight! Not so much as a gleam of brightness to light up our home!

MRS. SOLNESS. This is no home, Halvard.

SOLNESS. Oh no, you may well say that. [*Gloomily.*] And God knows whether you are not right in saying that it will be no better for us in the new house, either.

MRS. SOLNESS. It will never be any better. Just as empty—just as desolate—there as here.

SOLNESS [*vehemently*]. Why in all the world have we built it then? Can you tell me that?

MRS. SOLNESS. No; you must answer that question for yourself.

SOLNESS [*glances suspiciously at her*]. What do you mean by that, Aline?

MRS. SOLNESS. What do I mean?

SOLNESS. Yes, in the devil's name! You said it so strangely—as if you had hidden some meaning in it.

MRS. SOLNESS. No, indeed, I assure you—

SOLNESS [*comes closer*]. Oh, come now—I know what I know. I have both my eyes and my ears about me, Aline—you may depend upon that!

MRS. SOLNESS. Why what are you talking about? What is it?

SOLNESS [*places himself in front of her*]. Do you mean to say you don't find a kind of lurking, hidden meaning in the most innocent word I happen to say?

MRS. SOLNESS. *I*, do you say? *I* do that?

SOLNESS [*laughs*]. Ho-ho-ho! It's natural enough, Aline! When you have a sick man on your hands—

MRS. SOLNESS [*anxiously*]. Sick? Are you ill, Halvard?

SOLNESS [*violently*]. A half-mad man then! A crazy man! Call me what you will.

MRS. SOLNESS [*feels blindly for a chair and sits down*]. Halvard—for God's sake—

SOLNESS. But you are wrong, both you and the doctor. I am not in the state you imagine.

[*He walks up and down the room.* MRS. SOLNESS *follows him anxiously with her eyes. Finally he goes up to her.*]

SOLNESS [*calmly*]. In reality there is nothing whatever the matter with me.

MRS. SOLNESS. No, there isn't, is there? But then what is it that troubles you so?

SOLNESS. Why this, that I often feel ready to sink under this terrible burden of debt—

MRS. SOLNESS. Debt, do you say? But you owe no one anything, Halvard!

SOLNESS [*softly, with emotion*]. I owe a boundless debt to you—to you—to you, Aline.

MRS. SOLNESS [*rises slowly*]. What is behind all this? You may just as well tell me at once.

SOLNESS. But there is nothing behind it; I have never done you any wrong—not wittingly and willfully, at any rate. And yet—and yet it seems as though a crushing debt rested upon me and weighed me down.

MRS. SOLNESS. A debt to me?

SOLNESS. Chiefly to you.

MRS. SOLNESS. Then you are—ill after all, Halvard.

SOLNESS [*gloomily*]. I suppose I must be—or not far from it. [*Looks towards the door to the right, which is opened at this moment.*] Ah! now it grows lighter.

[HILDA WANGEL *comes in. She has made some alteration in her dress, and let down her skirt.*]

HILDA. Good morning, Mr. Solness!

SOLNESS [*nods*]. Slept well?

HILDA. Quite deliciously! Like a child in a cradle. Oh—I lay and stretched myself like—like a princess!

SOLNESS [*smiles a little*]. You were thoroughly comfortable then?

HILDA. I should think so.

SOLNESS. And no doubt you dreamed, too.

HILDA. Yes, I did. But that was horrid.

SOLNESS. Was it?

HILDA. Yes, for I dreamed I was falling over a frightfully high, sheer precipice. Do you never have that kind of dream?

SOLNESS. Oh yes—now and then—

HILDA. It's tremendously thrilling—when you fall and fall—

SOLNESS. It seems to make one's blood run cold.

HILDA. Do you draw your legs up under you while you are falling?

SOLNESS. Yes, as high as ever I can.

HILDA. So do I.

MRS. SOLNESS [*takes her parasol*]. I must go into town now, Halvard. [*To* HILDA.] And I'll try to get one or two things that you may require.

HILDA [*making a motion to throw her arms round her neck*]. Oh, you dear, sweet Mrs. Solness! You are really much too kind to me! Frightfully kind—

MRS. SOLNESS [*deprecatingly, freeing herself*]. Oh, not at all. It's only my duty, so I am very glad to do it.

HILDA [*offended, pouts*]. But really, I think I am quite fit to be seen in the streets—now that I've put my dress to rights. Or do you think I am not?

MRS. SOLNESS. To tell you the truth, I think people would stare at you a little.

HILDA [*contemptuously*]. Pooh! Is that all? That only amuses me.

SOLNESS [*with suppressed ill-humor*]. Yes, but people might take it into their heads that you were mad too, you see.

HILDA. Mad? Are there so many mad people here in town, then?

SOLNESS [*points to his own forehead*]. Here you see one at all events.

HILDA. You—Mr. Solness!

MRS. SOLNESS. Oh, don't talk like that, my dear Halvard!

SOLNESS. Have you not noticed that yet?

HILDA. No, I certainly have not. [*Reflects and laughs a little.*] And yet—perhaps in one single thing.

SOLNESS. Ah, do you hear that, Aline?

MRS. SOLNESS. What is that one single thing, Miss Wangel?

HILDA. No, I won't say.

SOLNESS. Oh yes, do!

HILDA. No thank you—I am not so mad as that.

MRS. SOLNESS. When you and Miss Wangel are alone, I daresay she will tell you, Halvard.

SOLNESS. Ah—you think she will?

MRS. SOLNESS. Oh yes, certainly. For you have known her so well in the past. Ever since she was a child—you tell me. [*She goes out by the door on the left.*]

HILDA [*after a little while*]. Does you wife dislike me very much?

SOLNESS. Did you think you noticed anything of the kind?

HILDA. Did you not notice it yourself?

SOLNESS [*evasively*]. Aline has become exceedingly shy with strangers of late years.

HILDA. Has she really?

SOLNESS. But if only you could get to know her thoroughly—! Ah! she is so good—so kind—so excellent a creature—

HILDA [*impatiently*]. But if she is all that—what made her say that about her duty?

SOLNESS. Her duty?

HILDA. She said that she would go out and buy something for me, because it was her duty. Oh I can't bear that ugly, horrid word!

SOLNESS. Why not?

HILDA. It sounds so cold, and sharp, and stinging. Duty—duty—duty. Don't you think so, too? Doesn't it seem to sting you?

SOLNESS. H'm—haven't thought much about it.

HILDA. Yes, it does. And if she is so good—as you say she is—why should she talk in that way?

SOLNESS. But, good Lord, what would you have had her say, then?

HILDA. She might have said she would do it because she had taken a tremendous fancy to me. She might have said something like that—something really warm and cordial, you understand.

SOLNESS [*looks at her*]. Is that how you would like to have it?

HILDA. Yes, precisely. [*She wanders about the room, stops at the bookcase and looks at the books.*] What a lot of books you have.

SOLNESS. Yes, I have got together a good many.

HILDA. Do you read them all, too?

SOLNESS. I used to try to. Do you read much?

HILDA. No, never! I have given it up. For it all seems so irrelevant.

SOLNESS. That is just my feeling.

[HILDA *wanders about a little, stops at the small table, opens the portfolio and turns over the contents.*]

HILDA. Are all these drawings yours?

SOLNESS. No, they are drawn by a young man whom I employ to help me.

HILDA. Someone you have taught?

SOLNESS. Oh yes, no doubt he has learnt something from me, too.

HILDA [*sits down*]. Then I suppose he is very clever. [*Looks at a drawing.*] Isn't he?

SOLNESS. Oh, he might be worse. For my purpose—

HILDA. Oh yes—I'm sure he is frightfully clever.

SOLNESS. Do you think you can see that in the drawings?

HILDA. Pooh—these scrawlings! But if he has been learning from you—

SOLNESS. Oh, so far as that goes—there are plenty of people that have learnt from me, and have come to little enough for all that.

HILDA [*looks at him and shakes her head*]. No, I can't for the life of me understand how you can be so stupid.

SOLNESS. Stupid? Do you think I am so very stupid?

HILDA. Yes, I do indeed. If you are content to go about here teaching all these people—

SOLNESS [*with a slight start*]. Well, and why not?

HILDA [*rises, half serious, half laughing*]. No indeed, Mr. Solness! What can be the good of that? No one but you should be allowed to build. You should stand quite alone—do it all yourself. Now you know it.

SOLNESS [*involuntarily*]. Hilda—!

HILDA. Well!

SOLNESS. How in the world did that come into your head?

HILDA. Do you think I am so very far wrong then?

SOLNESS. No, that's not what I mean. But now I'll tell you something.

HILDA. Well?

SOLNESS. I keep on—incessantly—in silence and alone—brooding on that very thought.

HILDA. Yes, that seems to me perfectly natural.

SOLNESS [*looks somewhat searchingly at her*]. Perhaps you have noticed it already?

HILDA. No, indeed I haven't.

SOLNESS. But just now—when you said you thought I was—off my balance? In one thing, you said—

HILDA. Oh, I was thinking of something quite different.

SOLNESS. What was it?

HILDA. I am not going to tell you.

SOLNESS [*crosses the room*]. Well, well—as you please. [*Stops at the bow-window.*] Come here, and I will show you something.

HILDA [*approaching*]. What is it?

SOLNESS. Do you see—over there in the garden—?

HILDA. Yes?

SOLNESS [*points*]. Right above the great quarry—?

HILDA. That new house, you mean?

SOLNESS. The one that is being built, yes. Almost finished.

HILDA. It seems to have a very high tower.

SOLNESS. The scaffolding is still up.

HILDA. Is that your new house?

SOLNESS. Yes.

HILDA. The house you are soon going to move into?

SOLNESS. Yes.

HILDA [*looks at him*]. Are there nurseries in that house, too?

SOLNESS. Three, as there are here.

HILDA. And no child.

SOLNESS. And there never will be one.

HILDA [*with a half-smile*]. Well, isn't it just as I said—?

SOLNESS. That—?

HILDA. That you are a little—a little mad after all.

SOLNESS. Was that what you were thinking of?

HILDA. Yes, of all the empty nurseries I slept in.

SOLNESS [*lowers his voice*]. We have had children—Aline and I.

HILDA [*looks eagerly at him*]. Have you—?

SOLNESS. Two little boys. They were of the same age.

HILDA. Twins, then.

SOLNESS. Yes, twins. It's eleven or twelve years ago now.

HILDA [*cautiously*]. And so both of them—? You have lost both the twins, then?

SOLNESS [*with quiet emotion*]. We kept them only about three weeks. Or scarcely so much. [*Bursts forth.*] Oh, Hilda, I can't tell you what a good thing it is for me that you have come! For now at last I have some one I can talk to!

HILDA. Can you not talk to—her, too?

SOLNESS. Not about this. Not as I want to talk and must talk. [*Gloomily.*] And not about so many other things, either.

HILDA [*in a subdued voice*]. Was that all you meant when you said you needed me?

SOLNESS. That was mainly what I meant—at all events, yesterday. For today I am not so sure— [*breaking off*] Come here and let us sit down, Hilda. Sit there on the sofa—so that you can look into the garden. [HILDA *seats herself in the corner of the sofa.* SOLNESS *brings a chair closer.*] Should you like to hear about it?

HILDA. Yes, I shall love to sit and listen to you.

SOLNESS [*sits down*]. Then I will tell you all about it.

HILDA. Now I can see both the garden and you, Mr. Solness. So now, tell away! Begin!

SOLNESS [*points towards the bow-window*]. Out there on the rising ground—where you see the new house—

HILDA. Yes?

SOLNESS. Aline and I lived there in the first years of our married life. There was an old house up there that had belonged to her mother; and we inherited it, and the whole of the great garden with it.

HILDA. Was there a tower on that house, too?

SOLNESS. No, nothing of the kind. From the outside it looked like a great, dark, ugly wooden box; but all the same, it was snug and comfortable enough inside.

HILDA. Then did you pull down the ramshackle old place?

SOLNESS. No, it burnt down.

HILDA. The whole of it?

SOLNESS. Yes.

HILDA. Was that a great misfortune for you?

SOLNESS. That depends on how you look at it. As a builder, the fire was the making of me—

HILDA. Well, but—?

SOLNESS. It was just after the birth of the two little boys—

HILDA. The poor little twins, yes.

SOLNESS. They came healthy and bonny into the world. And they were growing too—you could see the difference from day to day.

HILDA. Little children do grow quickly at first.

SOLNESS. It was the prettiest sight in the world to see Aline lying with the two of them in her arms. But then came the night of the fire—

HILDA [*excitedly*]. What happened? Do tell me! Was any one burnt?

SOLNESS. No, not that. Every one got safe and sound out of the house—

HILDA. Well, and what then—?

SOLNESS. The fright had shaken Aline terribly. The alarm—the escape—the breakneck hurry—and then the ice-cold night air—for they had to be carried out just as they lay—both she and the little ones.

HILDA. Was it too much for them?

SOLNESS. Oh no, they stood it well enough. But Aline fell into a fever, and it affected her milk. She would insist on nursing them herself; because it was her duty, she said. And both our little boys, they—[*clenching his hands*]—they—oh!

HILDA. They did not get over that?

SOLNESS. No, that they did not get over. That was how we lost them.

HILDA. It must have been terribly hard for you.

SOLNESS. Hard enough for me; but ten times harder for Aline. [*Clenching his hands in suppressed fury.*] Oh, that such things should be allowed to happen here in the world! [*Shortly and firmly.*] From the day I lost them, I had no heart for building churches.

HILDA. Did you not like the church tower in our town?

SOLNESS. I didn't like it. I know how free and happy I felt when that tower was finished.

HILDA. *I* know that, too.

SOLNESS. And now I shall never—never build anything of that sort again! Neither churches nor church towers.

HILDA [*nods slowly*]. Nothing but houses for people to live in.

SOLNESS. Homes for human beings, Hilda.

HILDA. But homes with high towers and pinnacles upon them.

SOLNESS. If possible. [*Adopts a lighter tone.*] But, as I said before, that fire was the making of me—as a builder, I mean.

HILDA. Why don't you call yourself an architect, like the others?

SOLNESS. I have not been systematically enough taught for that. Most of what I know I have found out for myself.

HILDA. But you succeeded all the same.

SOLNESS. Yes, thanks to the fire. I laid out almost the whole of the garden in villa lots; and there I was able to build after my own heart. So I came to the front with a rush.

HILDA [*looks keenly at him*]. You must surely be a very happy man, as matters stand with you.

SOLNESS [*gloomily*]. Happy? Do you say that, too—like all the rest of them?

HILDA. Yes, I should say you must be. If you could only cease thinking about the two little children—

SOLNESS [*slowly*]. The two little children—they are not so easy to forget, Hilda.

HILDA [*somewhat uncertainly*]. Do you still feel their loss so much—after all these years?

SOLNESS [*looks fixedly at her, without replying*]. A happy man you said—

HILDA. Well, now, are you not happy—in other respects?

SOLNESS [*continues to look at her*]. When I told you all this about the fire—h'm—

HILDA. Well?

SOLNESS. Was there not one special thought that you—that you seized upon?

HILDA [*reflects in vain*]. No. What thought should that be?

SOLNESS [*with subdued emphasis*]. It was simply and solely by that fire that I was enabled to build homes for human beings. Cozy, comfortable, bright homes, where father and mother and the whole troop of children can live in safety and gladness, feeling what a happy thing it is to be alive in the world—and most of all to belong to each other—in great things and in small.

HILDA [*ardently*]. Well, and is it not a great happiness for you to be able to build such beautiful homes?

SOLNESS. The price, Hilda! The terrible price I had to pay for the opportunity!

HILDA. But can you never get over that?

SOLNESS. No. That I might build homes for others, I had to forego—to forego for all time—the home that might have been my own. I mean a home for a troop of children—and for father and mother, too.

HILDA [*cautiously*]. But need you have done that? For all time, you say?

SOLNESS [*nods slowly*]. That was the price of this happiness that people talk about. [*Breathes heavily.*] This happiness—h'm—this happiness was not to be bought any cheaper, Hilda.

HILDA [*as before*]. But may it not come right even yet?

SOLNESS. Never in this world—never. That is another consequence of the fire—and of Aline's illness afterwards.

HILDA [*looks at him with an indefinable expression*]. And yet you build all these nurseries?

SOLNESS [*seriously*]. Have you never noticed, Hilda, how the impossible—how it seems to beckon and cry aloud to one?

HILDA [*reflecting*]. The impossible? [*With animation.*] Yes, indeed! Is that how you feel too?

SOLNESS. Yes, I do.

HILDA. There must be—a little of the troll in you too.

SOLNESS. Why of the troll?

HILDA. What would you call it, then?

SOLNESS [*rises*]. Well, well, perhaps you are right. [*Vehemently.*] But how can I help turning into a troll, when this is how it always goes with me in everything—in everything!

HILDA. How do you mean?

SOLNESS [*speaking low, with inward emotion*]. Mark what I say to you, Hilda. All that I have succeeded in doing, building, creating—all the beauty, security, cheerful comfort—ay, and magnificence too—[*Clenches his hands.*] Oh, is it not terrible even to think of—!

HILDA. What is so terrible?

SOLNESS. That all this I have to make up for, to pay for—not in money, but in human happiness. And not with my own happiness only, but with other people's too. Yes, yes, do you see that, Hilda? That is the price which my position as an artist has cost me—and others. And every single day I have to look on while the price is paid for me anew. Over again, and over again—and over again for ever!

HILDA [*rises and looks steadily at him*]. Now I can see that you are thinking of—of her.

SOLNESS. Yes, mainly of Aline. For Aline—she, too, had her vocation in life, just as much as I had mine. [*His voice quivers.*] But her vocation has had to be stunted, and crushed, and shattered—in order that mine might force its way to—to a sort of great victory. For you must know that Aline—she, too, had a talent for building.

HILDA. She! For building?

SOLNESS [*shakes his head*]. Not houses and towers, and spires—not such things as I work away at—

HILDA. Well, but what then?

SOLNESS [*softly, with emotion*]. For building up the souls of little children, Hilda. For building up children's souls in perfect balance, and in noble and beautiful forms. For enabling them to soar up into erect and full-grown human souls. That was Aline's talent. And there it all lies now—unused and unusable for ever—of no earthly service to anyone—just like the ruins left by a fire.

HILDA. Yes, but even if this were so—?

SOLNESS. It is so! It is so! I know it!

HILDA. Well, but in any case it is not your fault.

SOLNESS [*fixes his eyes on her, and nods slowly*]. Ah, that is the great, terrible question. That is the doubt that is gnawing me—night and day.

HILDA. That?

SOLNESS. Yes. Suppose the fault was mine—in a certain sense.

HILDA. Your fault! The fire!

SOLNESS. All of it; the whole thing. And yet, perhaps—I may not have had anything to do with it.

HILDA [*looks at him with a troubled expression*]. Oh, Mr. Solness—if you can talk like that, I am afraid you must be—ill, after all.

SOLNESS. H'm—I don't think I shall ever be of quite sound mind on that point.

[RAGNAR BROVIK *cautiously opens the little door in the left-hand corner.* HILDA *comes forward.*]

RAGNAR [*when he sees* HILDA]. Oh. I beg pardon, Mr. Solness— [*He makes a movement to withdraw.*]

SOLNESS. No, no, don't go. Let us get it over.

RAGNAR. Oh, yes—if only we could.

SOLNESS. I hear your father is no better?

RAGNAR. Father is fast growing weaker—and therefore I beg and implore you to write a few kind words for me on one of the plans! Something for father to read before he—

SOLNESS [*vehemently*]. I won't hear anything more about those drawings of yours!

RAGNAR. Have you looked at them?

SOLNESS. Yes—I have.

RAGNAR. And they are good for nothing? And *I* am good for nothing, too?

SOLNESS [*evasively*]. Stay here with me, Ragnar. You shall have everything your own way. And then you can marry Kaia, and live at your ease—and happily too, who knows? Only don't think of building on your own account.

RAGNAR. Well, well, then I must go home and tell father what you say—I promised I would. Is this what I am to tell father—before he dies?

SOLNESS [*with a groan*]. Oh tell him—tell him what you will, for me. Best to say nothing at all to him! [*With a sudden outburst.*] I cannot do anything else, Ragnar!

RAGNAR. May I have the drawings to take with me?

SOLNESS. Yes, take them—take them by all means! They are lying there on the table.

RAGNAR [*goes to the table*]. Thanks.

HILDA [*puts her hand on the portfolio*]. No, no; leave them here.

SOLNESS. Why?

HILDA. Because I want to look at them, too.

SOLNESS. But you have been— [*To* RAGNAR.] Well, leave them here, then.

RAGNAR. Very well.

SOLNESS. And go home at once to your father.

RAGNAR. Yes. I suppose I must.

SOLNESS [*as if in desperation*]. Ragnar—you must not ask me to do what is beyond my power! Do you hear, Ragnar? You must not!

RAGNAR. No, no. I beg your pardon—

[*He bows, and goes out by the corner door.* HILDA *goes over and sits down on a chair near the mirror.*]

HILDA [*looks angrily at* SOLNESS]. That was a very ugly thing to do.

SOLNESS. Do you think so, too?

HILDA. Yes, it was horribly ugly—and hard and bad and cruel as well.

SOLNESS. Oh, you don't understand my position.

HILDA. No matter—. I say you ought not to be like that.

SOLNESS. You said yourself, only just now, that no one but *I* ought to be allowed to build.

HILDA. *I* may say such things—but you must not.

SOLNESS. I most of all, surely, who have paid so dear for my position.

HILDA. Oh yes—with what you call domestic comfort—and that sort of thing.

SOLNESS. And with my peace of soul into the bargain.

HILDA [*rising*]. Peace of soul! [*With feeling.*] Yes, yes, you are right in that! Poor Mr. Solness—you fancy that—

SOLNESS [*with a quiet, chuckling laugh*]. Just sit down again, Hilda, and I'll tell you something funny.

HILDA [*sits down; with intent interest*]. Well?

SOLNESS. It sounds such a ludicrous little thing; for, you see, the whole story turns upon nothing but a crack in a chimney.

HILDA. No more than that?

SOLNESS. No, not to begin with. [*He moves a chair nearer to* HILDA *and sits down.*]

HILDA [*impatiently, taps on her knee*]. Well, now for the crack in the chimney!

SOLNESS. I had noticed the split in the flue long, long before the fire. Every time I went up into the attic, I looked to see if it was still there.

HILDA. And it was?

SOLNESS. Yes; for no one else knew about it.

HILDA. And you said nothing?

SOLNESS. Nothing.

HILDA. And did not think of repairing the flue either?

SOLNESS. Oh yes, I thought about it—but never got any further. Every time I intended to set to work, it seemed just as if a hand held me back. Not today, I thought—tomorrow; and nothing ever came of it.

HILDA. But why did you keep putting it off like that?

SOLNESS. Because I was revolving something in my mind. [*Slowly, and in a low voice.*] Through that little black crack in the chimney, I might, perhaps, force my way upwards—as a builder.

HILDA [*looking straight in front of her*]. That must have been thrilling.

SOLNESS. Almost irresistible—quite irresistible. For at that time it appeared to me a perfectly simple and straightforward matter. I would have had it happen in the wintertime—a little before midday. I was to be out driving Aline in the sleigh. The servants at home would have made huge fires in the stoves.

HILDA. For, of course, it was to be bitterly cold that day?

SOLNESS. Rather biting, yes—and they would want Aline to find it thoroughly snug and warm when she came home.

HILDA. I suppose she is very chilly by nature?

SOLNESS. She is. And as we drove home, we were to see the smoke.

HILDA. Only the smoke?

SOLNESS. The smoke first. But when we came up to the garden gate, the whole of the old timber box was to be a rolling mass of flames. That is how I wanted it to be, you see.

HILDA. Oh why, why could it not have happened so!

SOLNESS. You may well say that, Hilda.

HILDA. Well, but now listen, Mr. Solness. Are you perfectly certain that the fire was caused by that little crack in the chimney?

SOLNESS. No, on the contrary—I am perfectly certain that the crack in the chimney had nothing whatever to do with the fire.

HILDA. What?

SOLNESS. It has been clearly ascertained that the fire broke out in a clothes cupboard—in a totally different part of the house.

HILDA. Then what is all this nonsense you are talking about the crack in the chimney?

SOLNESS. May I go on talking to you a little, Hilda?

HILDA. Yes, if you'll only talk sensibly—

SOLNESS. I will try. [*He moves his chair nearer.*]

HILDA. Out with it, then, Mr. Solness.

SOLNESS [*confidentially*]. Don't you agree with me, Hilda, that there exist special, chosen people who have been endowed with the power and faculty of desiring a thing, craving for a thing, willing a thing—so persistently and so—so inexorably—that at last it has to happen? Don't you believe that?

HILDA [*with an indefinable expression in her eyes*]. If that is so, we shall see, one of these days, whether *I* am one of the chosen.

SOLNESS. It is not one's self alone that can do such great things. Oh, no—the helpers and the servers—they must do their part too, if it is to be of any good. But they never come of themselves. One has to call upon them very persistently—inwardly, you understand.

HILDA. What are these helpers and servers?

SOLNESS. Oh, we can talk about that some other time. For the present, let us keep to this business of the fire.

HILDA. Don't you think that fire would have happened all the same—even without your wishing for it?

SOLNESS. If the house had been old Knut Brovik's, it would never have burnt down so conveniently for him. I am sure of that; for he does not know how to call for the helpers—no, nor for the servers, either. [*Rises in unrest.*] So you see, Hilda—it is my fault, after all, that the lives of the two little boys had to be sacrificed. And do you think it is not my fault, too, that Aline has never been the woman she should and might have been—and that she most longed to be?

HILDA. Yes, but if it is all the work of those helpers and servers—?

SOLNESS. Who called for the helpers and servers? It was I! And they came and obeyed my will. [*In increasing excitement.*] That is what people call having the luck on your side; but I must tell you what this sort of luck feels like! It feels like a great raw place here on my breast. And the helpers and servers keep on flaying pieces of skin off other people in order to close my sore! But still the sore is not healed—never, never! Oh, if you knew how it can sometimes gnaw and burn.

HILDA [*looks attentively at him*]. You are ill, Mr. Solness. Very ill, I almost think.

SOLNESS. Say mad; for that is what you mean.

HILDA. No, I don't think there is much amiss with your intellect.

SOLNESS. With what then? Out with it!

HILDA. I wonder whether you were not sent into the world with a sickly conscience.

SOLNESS. A sickly conscience? What devilry is that?

HILDA. I mean that your conscience is feeble—too delicately built, as it were —hasn't strength to take a grip of things—to lift and bear what is heavy.

SOLNESS [*growls*]. H'm! May I ask, then, what sort of a conscience one ought to have?

HILDA. I should like your conscience to be—to be thoroughly robust.

SOLNESS. Indeed? Robust, eh? Is your own conscience robust, may I ask?

HILDA. Yes, I think it is. I have never noticed that it wasn't.

SOLNESS. It has not been put very severely to the test, I should think.

HILDA [*with a quivering of the lips*]. Oh, it was no such simple matter to leave father—I am so awfully fond of him.

SOLNESS. Dear me! for a month or two—

HILDA. I think I shall never go home again.

SOLNESS. Never? Then why did you leave him?

HILDA [*half seriously, half banteringly*]. Have you forgotten that the ten years are up?

SOLNESS. Oh nonsense. Was anything wrong at home? Eh?

HILDA [*quite seriously*]. It was this impulse within me that urged and goaded me to come—and lured and drew me on, as well.

SOLNESS [*eagerly*]. There we have it! There we have it, Hilda! There is a troll in you too, as in me. For it's the troll in one, you see—it is that that calls to the powers outside us. And then you must give in—whether you will or no.

HILDA. I almost think you are right, Mr. Solness.

SOLNESS [*walks about the room*]. Oh, there are devils innumerable abroad in the world, Hilda, that one never sees!

HILDA. Devils, too?

SOLNESS [*stops*]. Good devils and bad devils; light-haired devils and black-haired devils. If only you could always tell whether it is the light or dark ones that have got hold of you! [*Paces about.*] Ho-ho! Then it would be simple enough.

HILDA [*follows him with her eyes*]. Or if one had a really vigorous, radiantly healthy conscience—so that one dared to do what one would.

SOLNESS [*stops beside the console table*]. I believe, now, that most people are just as puny creatures as I am in that respect.

HILDA. I shouldn't wonder.

SOLNESS [*leaning against the table*]. In the sagas— Have you read any of the old sagas?

HILDA. Oh yes! When I used to read books, I—

SOLNESS. In the sagas you read about vikings, who sailed to foreign lands, and plundered and burned and killed men—

HILDA. And carried off women—

SOLNESS. —and kept them in captivity—

HILDA. —took them home in their ships—

SOLNESS. —and behaved to them like—like the very worst of trolls.

HILDA [*looks straight before her, with a half-veiled look*]. I think that must have been thrilling.

SOLNESS [*with a short, deep laugh*]. To carry off women.

HILDA. To be carried off.

SOLNESS [*looks at her a moment*]. Oh, indeed.

HILDA [*as if breaking the thread of the conversation*]. But what made you speak of these vikings, Mr. Solness?

SOLNESS. Why, those fellows must have had robust consciences, if you like! When they got home again, they could eat and drink, and be as happy as children. And the women, too! They often would not leave them on any account. Can you understand that, Hilda?

HILDA. Those women I can understand exceedingly well.

SOLNESS. Oho! Perhaps you could do the same yourself?

HILDA. Why not?

SOLNESS. Live—of your own free will—with a ruffian like that?

HILDA. If it was a ruffian I had come to love—

SOLNESS. Could you come to love a man like that?

HILDA. Good heavens, you know very well one can't choose whom one is going to love.

SOLNESS [*looks meditatively at her*]. Oh no, I suppose it is the troll within one that's responsible for that.

HILDA [*half laughing*]. And all those blessed devils, that you know so well—both the light-haired and the dark-haired ones.

SOLNESS [*quietly and warmly*]. Then I hope with all my heart that the devils will choose carefully for you, Hilda.

HILDA. For me they have chosen already—once and for all.

SOLNESS [*looks earnestly at her*]. Hilda—you are like a wild bird of the woods.

HILDA. Far from it. I don't hide myself away under the bushes.

SOLNESS. No, no. There is rather something of the bird of prey in you.

HILDA. That is nearer it—perhaps. [*Very earnestly.*] And why not a bird of prey? Why should not *I* go a-hunting—I, as well as the rest. Carry off the prey I want—if only I can get my claws into it, and do with it as I will.

SOLNESS. Hilda—do you know what you are?

HILDA. Yes, I suppose I am a strange sort of bird.

SOLNESS. No. You are like a dawning day. When I look at you—I seem to be looking towards the sunrise.

HILDA. Tell me, Mr. Solness—are you certain that you have never called me to you? Inwardly, you know?

SOLNESS [*softly and slowly*]. I almost think I must have.

HILDA. What did you want with me?

SOLNESS. You are the younger generation, Hilda.

HILDA [*smiles*]. That younger generation that you are so afraid of?

SOLNESS [*nods slowly*]. And which, in my heart, I yearn towards so deeply.

[HILDA *rises, goes to the little table, and fetches* RAGNAR BROVIK'S *portfolio.*]

HILDA [*holds out the portfolio to him*]. We were talking of these drawings—

SOLNESS [*shortly, waving them away*]. Put those things away! I have seen enough of them.

HILDA. Yes, but you have to write your approval on them.

SOLNESS. Write my approval on them? Never!

HILDA. But the poor old man is lying at death's door! Can't you give him and his son this pleasure before they are parted? And perhaps he might get the commission to carry them out, too.

SOLNESS. Yes, that is just what he would get. He has made sure of that—has my fine gentleman!

HILDA. Then, good heavens—if that is so—can't you tell the least little bit of a lie for once in a way?

SOLNESS. A lie? [*Raging.*] Hilda—take those devil's drawings out of my sight!

HILDA [*draws the portfolio a little nearer to herself*]. Well, well, well—don't bite me. You talk of trolls—but I think you go on like a troll yourself. [*Looks around.*] Where do you keep your pen and ink?

SOLNESS. There is nothing of the sort in here.

HILDA [*goes towards the door*]. But in the office where that young lady is—

SOLNESS. Stay where you are, Hilda! I ought to tell a lie, you say. Oh yes, for the sake of his old father I might well do that—for in my time I have crushed him, trodden him under foot—

HILDA. Him, too?

SOLNESS. I needed room for myself. But this Ragnar—he must on no account be allowed to come to the front.

HILDA. Poor fellow, there is surely no fear of that. If he has nothing in him—

SOLNESS [*comes closer, looks at her, and whispers*]. If Ragnar Brovik gets his chance, he will strike me to the earth. Crush me—as I crushed his father.

HILDA. Crush you? Has he the ability for that?

SOLNESS. Yes, you may depend upon it he has the ability! He is the younger generation that stands ready to knock at my door—to make an end of Halvard Solness.

HILDA [*looks at him with quiet reproach*]. And yet you would bar him out. Fie, Mr. Solness!

SOLNESS. The fight I have been fighting has cost heart's blood enough. And I am afraid, too, that the helpers and servers will not obey me any longer.

HILDA. Then you must go ahead without them. There is nothing else for it.

SOLNESS. It is hopeless, Hilda. The luck is bound to turn. A little sooner or a little later. Retribution is inexorable.

HILDA [*in distress, putting her hands over her ears*]. Don't talk like that! Do you want to kill me? To take from me what is more than my life?

SOLNESS. And what is that?

HILDA. The longing to see you great. To see you, with a wreath in your hand, high, high up upon a church tower. [*Calm again.*] Come, out with your pencil now. You must have a pencil about you?

SOLNESS [*takes out his pocketbook*]. I have one here.

HILDA [*lays the portfolio on the sofa table*]. Very well. Now let us two sit down here, Mr. Solness. [SOLNESS *seats himself at the table.* HILDA *stands behind him, leaning over the back of the chair.*] And now we will write on the drawings. We must write very, very nicely and cordially—for this horrid Ruar—or whatever his name is.

SOLNESS [*writes a few words, turns his head and looks at her*]. Tell me one thing, Hilda.

HILDA. Yes!

SOLNESS. If you have been waiting for me all these ten years—

HILDA. What then?

SOLNESS. Why have you never written to me? Then I could have answered you.

HILDA [*hastily*]. No, no, no! That was just what I did not want.

SOLNESS. Why not?

HILDA. I was afraid the whole thing might fall to pieces. But we were going to write on the drawings, Mr. Solness.

SOLNESS. So we were.

HILDA [*bends forward and looks over his shoulder while he writes*]. Mind now, kindly and cordially! Oh how I hate—how I hate this Ruald—

SOLNESS [*writing*]. Have you never really cared for anyone, Hilda?

HILDA [*harshly*]. What do you say?

SOLNESS. Have you never cared for anyone?

HILDA. For anyone else, I suppose you mean?

SOLNESS [*looks up at her*]. For anyone else, yes. Have you never? In all these ten years? Never?

HILDA. Oh yes, now and then. When I was perfectly furious with you for not coming.

SOLNESS. Then you did take an interest in other people, too?

HILDA. A little bit—for a week or so. Good heavens, Mr. Solness, you surely know how such things come about.

SOLNESS. Hilda—what is it you have come for?

HILDA. Don't waste time talking. The poor old man might go and die in the meantime.

SOLNESS. Answer me, Hilda. What do you want of me?

HILDA. I want my kingdom.

SOLNESS. H'm—

[*He gives a rapid glance towards the door on the left, and then goes on writing on the drawings. At the same moment* MRS. SOLNESS *enters; she has some packages in her hand.*]

MRS. SOLNESS. Here are a few things I have got for you, Miss Wangel. The large parcels will be sent later on.

HILDA. Oh, how very, very kind of you!

MRS. SOLNESS. Only my simple duty. Nothing more than that.

SOLNESS [*reading over what he has written*]. Aline!

MRS. SOLNESS. Yes?

SOLNESS. Did you notice whether the—the bookkeeper was out there?

MRS. SOLNESS. Yes, of course, she was out there.

SOLNESS [*puts the drawings in the portfolio*]. H'm—

MRS. SOLNESS. She was standing at the desk, as she always is—when *I* go through the room.

SOLNESS [*rises*]. Then I'll give this to her, and tell her that—

HILDA [*takes the portfolio from him*]. Oh, no, let me have the pleasure of doing that! [*Goes to the door, but turns.*] What is her name?

SOLNESS. Her name is Miss Fosli.

HILDA. Pooh, that sounds too cold! Her Christian name, I mean?

SOLNESS. Kaia—I believe.

HILDA [*opens the door and calls out*]. Kaia, come in here! Make haste! Mr. Solness wants to speak to you.

[KAIA FOSLI *appears at the door.*]

KAIA [*looking at him in alarm*]. Here I am—?

HILDA [*handing her the portfolio*]. See here, Kaia! You can take this home; Mr. Solness has written on them now.

KAIA. Oh, at last!

SOLNESS. Give them to the old man as soon as you can.

KAIA. I will go straight home with them.

SOLNESS. Yes, do. Now Ragnar will have a chance of building for himself.

KAIA. Oh, may he come and thank you for all—?

SOLNESS [*harshly*]. I won't have any thanks! Tell him that from me.

KAIA. Yes, I will—

SOLNESS. And tell him at the same time that henceforward I do not require his services—nor yours either.

KAIA [*softly and quiveringly*]. Not mine either?

SOLNESS. You will have other things to think of now, and to attend to; and that is a very good thing for you. Well, go home with the drawings now, Miss Fosli. At once! Do you hear?

KAIA [*as before*]. Yes, Mr. Solness. [*She goes out.*]

MRS. SOLNESS. Heavens! what deceitful eyes she has.

SOLNESS. She? That poor little creature?

MRS. SOLNESS. Oh—I can see what I can see, Halvard. Are you really dismissing them?

SOLNESS. Yes.

MRS. SOLNESS. Her as well?

SOLNESS. Was not that what you wished?

MRS. SOLNESS. But how can you get on without her—? Oh, well, no doubt you have someone else in reserve, Halvard.

HILDA [*playfully*]. Well, I for one am not the person to stand at that desk.

SOLNESS. Never mind, never mind—it will be all right, Aline. Now all you have to do is to think about moving into our new home—as quickly as you can. This evening we will hang up the wreath—[*turns to* HILDA] —right on the very pinnacle of the tower. What do you say to that, Miss Hilda?

HILDA [*looks at him with sparkling eyes*]. It will be splendid to see you so high up once more.

SOLNESS. Me!

MRS. SOLNESS. For heaven's sake, Miss Wangel, don't imagine such a thing! My husband!—when he always gets so dizzy!

HILDA. He get dizzy! No, I know quite well he does not!

MRS. SOLNESS. Oh yes, indeed he does.

HILDA. But I have seen him with my own eyes right up at the top of a high church tower!

MRS. SOLNESS. Yes, I hear people talk of that; but it is utterly impossible—

SOLNESS [*vehemently*]. Impossible—impossible, yes! But there I stood all the same!

MRS. SOLNESS. Oh, how can you say so, Halvard? Why, you can't even bear to go out on the second-story balcony here. You have always been like that.

SOLNESS. You may perhaps see something different this evening.

MRS. SOLNESS [*in alarm*]. No, no, no! Please God I shall never see that. I will write at once to the doctor—and I am sure he won't let you do it.

SOLNESS. Why, Aline—!

MRS. SOLNESS. Oh, you know you're ill, Halvard. This proves it! Oh God—Oh God! [*She goes hastily out to the right.*]

HILDA [*looks intently at him*]. Is it so, or is it not?

SOLNESS. That I turn dizzy?

HILDA. That my master builder dares not—cannot—climb as high as he builds?

SOLNESS. Is that the way you look at it?

HILDA. Yes.

SOLNESS. I believe there is scarcely a corner in me that is safe from you.

HILDA [*looks towards the bow-window*]. Up there, then. Right up there—

SOLNESS [*approaches her*]. You might have the topmost room in the tower, Hilda—there you might live like a princess.

HILDA [*indefinably, between earnest and jest*]. Yes, that is what you promised me.

SOLNESS. Did I really?

HILDA. Fie, Mr. Solness! You said I should be a princess, and that you would give me a kingdom. And then you went and—Well!

SOLNESS [*cautiously*]. Are you quite certain that this is not a dream—a fancy, that has fixed itself in your mind?

HILDA [*sharply*]. Do you mean that you did not do it?

SOLNESS. I scarcely know myself. [*More softly.*] But now I know so much for certain, that I—

HILDA. That you—? Say it at once!

SOLNESS. —that I ought to have done it.

HILDA [*exclaims with animation*]. Don't tell me you can ever be dizzy!

SOLNESS. This evening, then, we will hang up the wreath—Princess Hilda.

HILDA [*with a bitter curve of the lips*]. Over your new home, yes.

SOLNESS. Over the new house, which will never be a home for me. [*He goes out through the garden door.*]

HILDA [*looks straight in front of her with a faraway expression, and whispers to herself. The only words audible are*]—frightfully thrilling—

ACT III

The large, broad verandah of SOLNESS'S *dwelling house. Part of the house, with outer door leading to the verandah, is seen to the left. A railing along the verandah to the right. At the back, from the end of the verandah, a flight of steps leads down to the garden below. Tall old trees in the garden spread their branches over the verandah and towards the house. Far to the right, in among the trees, a glimpse is caught of the lower part of the new villa, with scaffolding round so much as is seen of the tower. In the background the garden is bounded by an old wooden fence. Outside the fence, a street with low, tumble-down cottages.*

Evening sky with sunlit clouds.

On the verandah, a garden bench stands along the wall of the house, and in front of the bench a long table. On the other side of the table, an armchair and some stools. All the furniture is of wicker-work.

MRS. SOLNESS, *wrapped in a large white crepe shawl, sits resting in the armchair and gazes over to the right. Shortly after,* HILDA WANGEL *comes up the flight of steps from the garden. She is dressed as in the last act, and wears her hat. She has in her bodice a little nosegay of small common flowers.*

MRS. SOLNESS [*turning her head a little*]. Have you been round the garden, Miss Wangel?

HILDA. Yes, I have been taking a look at it.

MRS. SOLNESS. And found some flowers too, I see.

HILDA. Yes, indeed! There are such heaps of them in among the bushes.

MRS. SOLNESS. Are there really? Still? You see I scarcely ever go there.

HILDA [*closer*]. What! Don't you take a run down into the garden every day, then?

MRS. SOLNESS. [*with a faint smile*]. I don't "run" anywhere, nowadays.

HILDA. Well, but do you not go down now and then to look at all the lovely things there?

MRS. SOLNESS. It has all become so strange to me. I am almost afraid to see it again.

HILDA. Your own garden!

MRS. SOLNESS. I don't feel that it is mine any longer.

HILDA. What do you mean—?

MRS. SOLNESS. No, no, it is not—not as it was in my mother's and father's time. They have taken away so much—so much of the garden, Miss Wangel. Fancy—they have parceled it out—and built houses for strangers—people that I don't know. And they can sit and look in upon me from their windows.

HILDA [*with a bright expression*]. Mrs. Solness!

MRS. SOLNESS. Yes!

HILDA. May I stay here with you a little?

MRS. SOLNESS. Yes, by all means, if you care to.

[HILDA *moves a stool close to the armchair and sits down.*]

HILDA. Ah—here one can sit and sun oneself like a cat.

MRS. SOLNESS [*lays her hand softly on* HILDA'S *neck*]. It is nice of you to be willing to sit with me. I thought you wanted to go in to my husband.

HILDA. What should I want with him?

MRS. SOLNESS. To help him, I thought.

HILDA. No, thank you. And besides, he is not in. He is over there with the workmen. But he looked so fierce that I did not care to talk to him.

MRS. SOLNESS. He is so kind and gentle in reality.

HILDA. He!

MRS. SOLNESS. You do not really know him yet, Miss Wangel.

HILDA [*looks affectionately at her*]. Are you pleased at the thought of moving over to the new house?

MRS. SOLNESS. I ought to be pleased; for it is what Halvard wants—

HILDA. Oh, not just on that account, surely.

MRS. SOLNESS. Yes, yes, Miss Wangel; for it is only my duty to submit myself to him. But very often it is dreadfully difficult to force one's mind to obedience.

HILDA. Yes, that must be difficult indeed.

MRS. SOLNESS. I can tell you it is—when one has so many faults as I have—

HILDA. When one has gone through so much trouble as you have—

MRS. SOLNESS. How do you know about that?

HILDA. Your husband told me.

MRS. SOLNESS. To me he very seldom mentions these things. Yes, I can tell you I have gone through more than enough trouble in my life, Miss Wangel.

HILDA [*looks sympathetically at her and nods slowly*]. Poor Mrs. Solness. First of all there was the fire—

MRS. SOLNESS [*with a sigh*]. Yes, everything that was mine was burnt.

HILDA. And then came what was worse.

MRS. SOLNESS [*looking inquiringly at her*]. Worse?

HILDA. The worst of all.

MRS. SOLNESS. What do you mean?

HILDA [*softly*]. You lost the two little boys.

MRS. SOLNESS. Oh yes, the boys. But, you see, that was a thing apart. That was a dispensation of Providence; and in such things one can only bow in submission—yes, and be thankful, too.

HILDA. Then you are so?

MRS. SOLNESS. Not always, I am sorry to say. I know well enough that it is my duty—but all the same I cannot.

HILDA. No, no, I think that is only natural.

MRS. SOLNESS. And often and often I have to remind myself that it was a righteous punishment for me—

HILDA. Why?

MRS. SOLNESS. Because I had not fortitude enough in misfortune.

HILDA. But I don't see that—

MRS. SOLNESS. Oh, no, no, Miss Wangel—do not talk to me any more about the two little boys. We ought to feel nothing but joy in thinking of them; for they are so happy—so happy now. No, it is the small losses in life that cut one to the heart—the loss of all that other people look upon as almost nothing.

HILDA [*lays her arms on* MRS. SOLNESS'S *knees, and looks up at her affectionately*]. Dear Mrs. Solness—tell me what things you mean!

MRS. SOLNESS. As I say, only little things. All the old portraits were burnt on the walls. And all the old silk dresses were burnt, that had belonged to the family for generations and generations. And all mother's and grandmother's lace—that was burnt, too. And only think—the jewels too! [*Sadly.*] And then all the dolls.

HILDA. The dolls?

MRS. SOLNESS [*choking with tears*]. I had nine lovely dolls.

HILDA. And they were burnt, too?

MRS. SOLNESS. All of them. Oh, it was hard—so hard for me.

HILDA. Had you put by all these dolls, then? Ever since you were little?

MRS. SOLNESS. I had not put them by. The dolls and I had gone on living together.

HILDA. After you were grown up?

MRS. SOLNESS. Yes, long after that.

HILDA. After you were married, too?

MRS. SOLNESS. Oh yes, indeed. So long as he did not see it—. But they were all burnt up, poor things. No one thought of saving them. Oh, it is so miserable to think of. You mustn't laugh at me, Miss Wangel.

HILDA. I am not laughing in the least.

MRS. SOLNESS. For you see, in a certain sense, there was life in them, too. I carried them under my heart—like little unborn children.

[DR. HERDAL, *with his hat in his hand, comes out through the door, and observes* MRS. SOLNESS *and* HILDA.]

DR. HERDAL. Well, Mrs. Solness, so you are sitting out here catching cold?

MRS. SOLNESS. I find it so pleasant and warm here today.

DR. HERDAL. Yes, yes. But is there anything going on here? I got a note from you.

MRS. SOLNESS [*rises*]. Yes, there is something I must talk to you about.

DR. HERDAL. Very well; then perhaps we had better go in. [*To* HILDA.] Still in your mountaineering dress, Miss Wangel?

HILDA [*gaily, rising*]. Yes—in full uniform! But today I am not going climbing and breaking my neck. We two will stop quietly below and look on, doctor.

DR. HERDAL. What are we to look on at?

MRS. SOLNESS [*softly, in alarm, to* HILDA]. Hush, hush—for God's sake! He is coming. Try to get that idea out of his head. And let us be friends, Miss Wangel. Don't you think we can?

HILDA [*throws her arms impetuously round* MRS. SOLNESS' *neck*]. Oh, if we only could!

MRS. SOLNESS [*gently disengages herself*]. There, there, there! There he comes, doctor. Let me have a word with you.

DR. HERDAL. Is it about him?

MRS. SOLNESS. Yes, to be sure it's about him. Do come in.

[*She and the doctor enter the house. Next moment* SOLNESS *comes up from the garden by the flight of steps. A serious look comes over* HILDA'S *face.*]

SOLNESS [*glances at the house door, which is closed cautiously from within*]. Have you noticed, Hilda, that as soon as I come, she goes?

HILDA. I have noticed that as soon as you come, you make her go.

SOLNESS. Perhaps so. But I cannot help it. [*Looks observantly at her.*] Are you cold, Hilda? I think you look cold.

HILDA. I have just come up out of a tomb.

SOLNESS. What do you mean by that?

HILDA. That I have got chilled through and through, Mr. Solness.

SOLNESS [*slowly*]. I believe I understand—

HILDA. What brings you up here just now?

SOLNESS. I caught sight of you from over there.

HILDA. But then you must have seen her too?

SOLNESS. I knew she would go at once if I came.

HILDA. Is it very painful for you that she should avoid you in this way?

SOLNESS. In one sense, it's a relief as well.

HILDA. Not to have her before your eyes?

SOLNESS. Yes.

HILDA. Not to be always seeing how heavily the loss of the little boys weighs upon her?

SOLNESS. Yes. Chiefly that.

[HILDA *drifts across the verandah with her hands behind her back, stops at the railing and looks out over the garden.*]

SOLNESS [*after a short pause*]. Did you have a long talk with her?

[HILDA *stands motionless and does not answer.*]

SOLNESS. Had you a long talk, I asked?

[HILDA *is silent as before.*]

SOLNESS. What was she talking about, Hilda?

[HILDA *continues silent.*]

SOLNESS. Poor Aline! I suppose it was about the little boys.

[*A nervous shudder runs through* HILDA; *then she nods hurriedly once or twice.*]

SOLNESS. She will never get over it—never in this world. [*Approaches her.*] Now you are standing there again like a statue; just as you stood last night.

HILDA [*turns and looks at him, with great serious eyes*]. I am going away.

SOLNESS [*sharply*]. Going away!

HILDA. Yes.

SOLNESS. But I won't allow you to!

HILDA. What am I to do here now?

SOLNESS. Simply to be here, Hilda!

HILDA [*measures him with a look*]. Oh, thank you. You know it wouldn't end there.

SOLNESS [*heedlessly*]. So much the better!

HILDA [*vehemently*]. I cannot do any harm to one whom I know! I can't take away anything that belongs to her.

SOLNESS. Who wants you to do that?

HILDA [*continuing*]. A stranger, yes! for that is quite a different thing! A person I have never set eyes on. But one that I have come into close contact with—! Oh no! Oh no! Ugh!

SOLNESS. Yes, but I never proposed you should.

HILDA. Oh, Mr. Solness, you know quite well what the end of it would be. And that is why I am going away.

SOLNESS. And what is to become of me when you are gone? What shall I have to live for then? After that?

HILDA [*with the indefinable look in her eyes*]. It is surely not so hard for you. You have your duties to her. Live for those duties.

SOLNESS. Too late. These powers—these—these—

HILDA. —devils—

SOLNESS. Yes, these devils! And the troll within me as well—they have drawn all the lifeblood out of her. [*Laughs in desperation.*] They did it for my happiness! Yes, yes! [*Sadly.*] And now she is dead—for my sake. And I am chained alive to a dead woman. [*In wild anguish.*] *I—I* who cannot live without joy in life!

[HILDA *moves round the table and seats herself on the bench, with her elbows on the table, and her head supported by her hands.*]

HILDA [*sits and looks at him awhile*]. What will you build next?

SOLNESS [*shakes his head*]. I don't believe I shall build much more.

HILDA. Not those cozy, happy homes for mother and father, and for the troop of children?

SOLNESS. I wonder whether there will be any use for such homes in the coming time.

HILDA. Poor Mr. Solness! And you have gone all these ten years—and staked your whole life—on that alone.

SOLNESS. Yes, you may well say so, Hilda.

HILDA [*with an outburst*]. Oh, it all seems to me so foolish—so foolish!

SOLNESS. All what?

HILDA. Not to be able to grasp at your own happiness—at your own life! Merely because someone you know happens to stand in the way!

SOLNESS. One whom you have no right to set aside.

HILDA. I wonder whether one really has not the right! And yet, and yet—. Oh, if one could only sleep the whole thing away! [*She lays her arms flat on the table, rests the left side of her head on her hands, and shuts her eyes.*]

SOLNESS [*turns the armchair and sits down at the table*]. Had you a cozy happy home—up there with your father, Hilda?

HILDA [*without stirring, answers as if half asleep*]. I had only a cage.

SOLNESS. And you are determined not to go back to it?

HILDA [*as before*]. The wild bird never wants to go into the cage.

SOLNESS. Rather range through the free air—

HILDA [*still as before*]. The bird of prey loves to range—

SOLNESS [*lets his eyes rest on her*]. If only one had the viking spirit in life—

HILDA [*in her usual voice; opens her eyes but does not move*]. And the other thing? Say what that was!

SOLNESS. A robust conscience.

[HILDA *sits erect on the bench, with animation. Her eyes have once more the sparkling expression of gladness.*]

HILDA [*nods to him*]. I know what you are going to build next!

SOLNESS. Then you know more than I do, Hilda.

HILDA. Yes, builders are such stupid people.

SOLNESS. What is it to be then?

HILDA [*nods again*]. The castle.

SOLNESS. What castle?

HILDA. My castle, of course.

SOLNESS. Do you want a castle now?

HILDA. Don't you owe me a kingdom, I should like to know?

SOLNESS. You say I do.

HILDA. Well—you admit you owe me this kingdom. And you can't have a kingdom without a royal castle, I should think!

SOLNESS [*more and more animated*]. Yes, they usually go together.

HILDA. Good! Then build it for me! This moment!

SOLNESS [*laughing*]. Must you have that on the instant too?

HILDA. Yes, to be sure! For the ten years are up now, and I am not going to wait any longer. So—out with the castle, Mr. Solness!

SOLNESS. It's no light matter to owe you anything, Hilda.

HILDA. You should have thought of that before. It is too late now. So—[*tapping the table*]—the castle on the table! It is my castle! I will have it at once!

SOLNESS [*more seriously, leans over towards her, with his arms on the table*]. What sort of castle have you imagined, Hilda?

[*Her expression becomes more and more veiled. She seems gazing inwards at herself.*]

HILDA [*slowly*]. My castle shall stand on a height—on a very great height—with a clear outlook on all sides, so that I can see far—far around.

SOLNESS. And no doubt it is to have a high tower!

HILDA. A tremendously high tower. And at the very top of the tower there shall be a balcony. And I will stand out upon it—

SOLNESS [*involuntarily clutches at his forehead*]. How can you like to stand at such a dizzy height—?

HILDA. Yes, I will, right up there will I stand and look down on the other people—on those that are building churches, and homes for mother and father and the troop of children. And you may come up and look on at it, too.

SOLNESS [*in a low tone*]. Is the builder to be allowed to come up beside the princess?

HILDA. If the builder will.

SOLNESS [*more softly*]. Then I think the builder will come.

HILDA [*nods*]. The builder—he will come.

SOLNESS. But he will never be able to build any more. Poor builder!

HILDA [*animated*]. Oh yes, he will! We two will set to work together. And then we will build the loveliest—the very loveliest—thing in all the world.

SOLNESS [*intently*]. Hilda—tell me what that is!

HILDA [*looks smilingly at him, shakes her head a little, pouts, and speaks as if to a child*]. Builders—they are such very—very stupid people.

SOLNESS. Yes, no doubt they are stupid. But now tell me what it is—the loveliest thing in the world—that we two are to build together?

HILDA [*is silent a little while, then says with an indefinable expression in her eyes*]. Castles in the air.

SOLNESS. Castles in the air?

HILDA [*nods*]. Castles in the air, yes! Do you know what sort of thing a castle in the air is?

SOLNESS. It is the loveliest thing in the world, you say.

HILDA [*rises with vehemence, and makes a gesture of repulsion with her hand*]. Yes, to be sure it is! Castles in the air—they are so easy to take refuge in. And so easy to build, too—[*looks scornfully at him*]—especially for the builders who have a—a dizzy conscience.

SOLNESS [*rises*]. After this day we two will build together, Hilda.

HILDA [*with a half-dubious smile*]. A real castle in the air?

SOLNESS. Yes. One with a firm foundation under it.

[RAGNAR BROVIK *comes out from the house. He is carrying a large, green wreath with flowers and silk ribbons.*]

HILDA [*with an outburst of pleasure*]. The wreath! Oh, that will be glorious!

SOLNESS [*in surprise*]. Have you brought the wreath, Ragnar?

RAGNAR. I promised the foreman I would.

SOLNESS [*relieved*]. Ah, then I suppose your father is better?

RAGNAR. No.

SOLNESS. Was he not cheered by what I wrote?

RAGNAR. It came too late.

SOLNESS. Too late!

RAGNAR. When she came with it he was unconscious. He had had a stroke.

SOLNESS. Why, then, you must go home to him! You must attend to your father!

RAGNAR. He does not need me any more.

SOLNESS. But surely you ought to be with him.

RAGNAR. She is sitting by his bed.

SOLNESS [*rather uncertainly*]. Kaia?

RAGNAR [*looking darkly at him*]. Yes—Kaia.

SOLNESS. Go home, Ragnar—both to him and to her. Give me the wreath.

RAGNAR [*suppresses a mocking smile*]. You don't meant that you yourself—?

SOLNESS. I will take it down to them myself. [*Takes the wreath from him.*] And now you go home; we don't require you today.

RAGNAR. I know you do not require me any more; but today I shall remain.

SOLNESS. Well, remain then, since you are bent upon it.

HILDA [*at the railing*]. Mr. Solness, I will stand here and look on at you.

SOLNESS. At me!

HILDA. It will be fearfully thrilling.

SOLNESS [*in a low tone*]. We will talk about that presently, Hilda. [*He goes down the flight of steps with the wreath, and away through the garden.*]

HILDA [*looks after him, then turns to* RAGNAR]. I think you might at least have thanked him.

RAGNAR. Thanked him? Ought I to have thanked him?

HILDA. Yes, of course you ought!

RAGNAR. I think it is rather you I ought to thank.

HILDA. How can you say such a thing?

RAGNAR [*without answering her*]. But I advise you to take care, Miss Wangel! For you don't know him rightly yet.

HILDA [*ardently*]. Oh, no one knows him as I do!

RAGNAR [*laughs in exasperation*]. Thank him, when he has held me down year after year! When he made father disbelieve in me—made me disbelieve in myself! And all merely that he might—!

HILDA [*as if divining something*]. That he might—? Tell me at once!

RAGNAR. That he might keep her with him.

HILDA [*with a start towards him*]. The girl at the desk.

RAGNAR. Yes.

HILDA [*threateningly, clenching her hands*]. That is not true! You are telling falsehoods about him!

RAGNAR. I would not believe it either until today—when she said so herself.

HILDA [*as if beside herself*]. What did she say? I will know! At once! at once!

RAGNAR. She said that he had taken possession of her mind—her whole mind—centered all her thoughts upon himself alone. She says that she can never leave him—that she will remain here, where he is—

HILDA [*with flashing eyes*]. She will not be allowed to!

RAGNAR [*as if feeling his way*]. Who will not allow her?

HILDA [*rapidly*]. He will not either!

RAGNAR. Oh no—I understand the whole thing now. After this, she would merely be—in the way.

HILDA. You understand nothing—since you can talk like that! No, *I* will tell you why he kept hold of her.

RAGNAR. Well then, why?

HILDA. In order to keep hold of you.

RAGNAR. Has he told you so?

HILDA. No, but it is so. It must be so! [*Wildly.*] I will—I will have it so!

RAGNAR. And at the very moment when you came—he let her go.

HILDA. It was you—you that he let go; what do you suppose he cares about strange women like her?

RAGNAR [*reflects*]. Is it possible that all this time he has been afraid of me?

HILDA. He afraid! I would not be so conceited if I were you.

RAGNAR. Oh, he must have seen long ago that I had something in me, too. Besides—cowardly—that is just what he is, you see.

HILDA. He! Oh yes, I am likely to believe that!

RAGNAR. In a certain sense he is cowardly—he, the great master builder. He is not afraid of robbing others of their life's happiness—as he has done both for my father and for me. But when it comes to climbing up a paltry bit of scaffolding—he will do anything rather than that.

HILDA. Oh, you should just have seen him high, high up—at the dizzy height where I once saw him.

RAGNAR. Did you see that?

HILDA. Yes, indeed I did. How free and great he looked as he stood and fastened the wreath to the church vane!

RAGNAR. I know that he ventured that, once in his life—one solitary time. It is a legend among us younger men. But no power on earth would induce him to do it again.

HILDA. Today he will do it again!

RAGNAR [*scornfully*]. Yes, I daresay!

HILDA. We shall see it!

RAGNAR. That neither you nor I will see.

HILDA [*with uncontrollable vehemence*]. I will see it! I will and must see it!

RAGNAR. But he will not do it. He simply dare not do it. For you see he cannot get over this infirmity—master builder though he be.

[MRS. SOLNESS *comes from the house on to the verandah.*]

MRS. SOLNESS [*looks around*]. Is he not here? Where has he gone to?

RAGNAR. Mr. Solness is down with the men.

HILDA. He took the wreath with him.

MRS. SOLNESS [*terrified*]. Took the wreath with him! Oh, God! oh God! Brovik—you must go down to him! Get him to come back here!

RAGNAR. Shall I say you want to speak to him, Mrs. Solness?

MRS. SOLNESS. Oh yes, do! No, no—don't say that *I* want anything! You can say that somebody is here, and that he must come at once.

RAGNAR. Good. I will do so, Mrs. Solness. [*He goes down the flight of steps and away through the garden.*]

MRS. SOLNESS. Oh, Miss Wangel, you can't think how anxious I feel about him.

HILDA. Is there anything in this to be so terribly frightened about?

MRS. SOLNESS. Oh yes; surely you can understand. Just think, if he were really to do it! If he should take it into his head to climb up the scaffolding!

HILDA [*eagerly*]. Do you think he will?

MRS. SOLNESS. Oh, one can never tell what he might take into his head. I am afraid there is nothing he mightn't think of doing.

HILDA. Aha! Perhaps you too think that he is—well—?

MRS. SOLNESS. Oh, I don't know what to think about him now. The doctor has been telling me all sorts of things; and putting it all together with several things I have heard him say—

[DR. HERDAL *looks out, at the door.*]

DR. HERDAL. Is he not coming soon?

MRS. SOLNESS. Yes, I think so. I have sent for him at any rate.

DR. HERDAL [*advancing*]. I am afraid you will have to go in, my dear lady—

MRS. SOLNESS. Oh no! Oh no! I shall stay out here and wait for Halvard.

DR. HERDAL. But some ladies have just come to call on you—

MRS. SOLNESS. Good heavens, that too! And just at this moment!

DR. HERDAL. They say they positively must see the ceremony.

MRS. SOLNESS. Well, well, I suppose I must go to them after all. It is my duty.

HILDA. Can't you ask the ladies to go away?

MRS. SOLNESS. No, that would never do. Now that they are here, it is my duty to see them. But do you stay out here in the meantime—and receive him when he comes.

DR. HERDAL. And try to occupy his attention as long as possible—

MRS. SOLNESS. Yes, do, dear Miss Wangel. Keep a firm hold of him as ever you can.

HILDA. Would it not be best for you to do that?

MRS. SOLNESS. Yes; God knows that is my duty. But when one has duties in so many directions—

DR. HERDAL [*looks towards the garden*]. There he is coming.

MRS. SOLNESS. And I have to go in!

DR. HERDAL [*to* HILDA]. Don't say anything about my being here.

HILDA. Oh no! I daresay I shall find something else to talk to Mr. Solness about.

MRS. SOLNESS. And be sure you keep firm hold of him. I believe you can do it best.

[MRS. SOLNESS *and* DR. HERDAL *go into the house.* HILDA *remains standing on the verandah.* SOLNESS *comes from the garden, up the flight of steps.*]

SOLNESS. Somebody wants me, I hear.

HILDA. Yes; it is I, Mr. Solness.

SOLNESS. Oh, is it you, Hilda? I was afraid it might be Aline or the doctor.

HILDA. You are very easily frightened, it seems!

SOLNESS. Do you think so?

HILDA. Yes; people say that you are afraid to climb about—on the scaffoldings, you know.

SOLNESS. Well, that is quite a special thing.

HILDA. Then it is true that you are afraid to do it?

SOLNESS. Yes, I am.

HILDA. Afraid of falling down and killing yourself?

SOLNESS. No, not of that.

HILDA. Of what, then?

SOLNESS. I am afraid of retribution, Hilda.

HILDA. Of retribution? [*Shakes her head.*] I don't understand that.

SOLNESS. Sit down and I will tell you something.

HILDA. Yes, do! At once! [*She sits on a stool by the railing, and looks expectantly at him.*]

SOLNESS [*throws his hat on the table*]. You know that I began by building churches.

HILDA [*nods*]. I know that well.

SOLNESS. For, you see, I came as a boy from a pious home in the country; and so it seemed to me that this church-building was the noblest task I could set myself.

HILDA. Yes, yes.

SOLNESS. And I venture to say that I built those poor little churches with such honest and warm and heartfelt devotion that—that—

HILDA. That—? Well?

SOLNESS. Well, that I think that he ought to have been pleased with me.

HILDA. He? What he?

SOLNESS. He who was to have the churches, of course! He to whose honor and glory they were dedicated.

HILDA. Oh, indeed! But are you certain, then, that—that he was not—pleased with you?

SOLNESS [*scornfully*]. He pleased with me! How can you talk so, Hilda? He who gave the troll in me leave to lord it just as it pleased. He who bade them be at hand to serve me, both day and night—all these—all these—

HILDA. Devils—

SOLNESS. Yes, of both kinds. Oh no, he made me feel clearly enough that he was not pleased with me. [*Mysteriously.*] You see, that was really the reason why he made the old house burn down.

HILDA. Was that why?

SOLNESS. Yes, don't you understand? He wanted to give me the chance of becoming an accomplished master in my own sphere—so that I might build all the more glorious churches for him. At first I did not understand what he was driving at; but all of a sudden it flashed upon me.

HILDA. When was that?

SOLNESS. It was when I was building the church tower up at Lysanger.

HILDA. I thought so.

SOLNESS. For you see, Hilda—up there, amidst those new surroundings, I used to go about musing and pondering within myself. Then I saw plainly why he had taken my little children from me. It was that I should have nothing else to attach myself to. No such thing as love and happiness, you understand. I was to be only a master builder—nothing else. And all my life long I was to go on building for him. [*Laughs.*] But I can tell you nothing came of that!

HILDA. What did you do, then?

SOLNESS. First of all, I searched and tried my own heart—

HILDA. And then?

SOLNESS. Then I did the impossible—I no less than he.

HILDA. The impossible?

SOLNESS. I had never before been able to climb up to a great, free height. But that day I did it.

HILDA [*leaping up*]. Yes, yes, you did!

SOLNESS. And when I stood there, high over everything, and was hanging the wreath over the vane, I said to him: Hear me now, thou Mighty One! From this day forward I will be a free builder—I, too, in my sphere—just as thou in thine. I will never more build churches for thee—only homes for human beings.

HILDA [*with great sparkling eyes*]. That was the song that I heard through the air!

SOLNESS. But afterwards his turn came.

HILDA. What do you mean by that?

SOLNESS [*looks despondently at her*]. Building homes for human beings—is not worth a rap, Hilda.

HILDA. Do you say that now?

SOLNESS. Yes, for now I see it. Men have no use for these homes of theirs—to be happy in. And I should not have had any use for such a home, if I had had one. [*With a quiet, bitter laugh.*] See, that is the upshot of the whole affair, however far back I look. Nothing really built; nor anything sacrificed for the chance of building. Nothing, nothing! the whole is nothing.

HILDA. Then you will never build anything more?

SOLNESS [*with animation*]. On the contrary, I am just going to begin!

HILDA. What, then? What will you build? Tell me at once!

SOLNESS. I believe there is only one possible dwelling place for human happiness—and that is what I am going to build now.

HILDA [*looks fixedly at him*]. Mr. Solness—you mean our castle?

SOLNESS. The castles in the air—yes.

HILDA. I am afraid you would turn dizzy before we got halfway up.

SOLNESS. Not if I can mount hand in hand with you, Hilda.

HILDA [*with an expression of suppressed resentment*]. Only with me? Will there be no others of the party?

SOLNESS. Who else should there be?

HILDA. Oh—that girl—that Kaia at the desk. Poor thing—don't you want to take her with you too?

SOLNESS. Oho! Was it about her that Aline was talking to you?

HILDA. Is it so—or is it not?

SOLNESS. [*vehemently*]. I will not answer such a question. You must believe in me, wholly and entirely!

HILDA. All these ten years I have believed in you so utterly—so utterly.

SOLNESS. You must go on believing in me!

HILDA. Then let me see you stand free and high up!

SOLNESS [*sadly*]. Oh Hilda—it is not everyday that I can do that.

HILDA [*passionately*]. I will have you do it! I will have it! [*Imploringly.*] Just once more, Mr. Solness! Do the impossible once again!

SOLNESS [*stands and looks deep into her eyes*]. If I try it, Hilda, I will stand up there and talk to him as I did that time before.

HILDA [*in rising excitement*]. What will you say to him?

SOLNESS. I will say to him: Hear me, Mighty Lord—thou may'st judge me as seems best to thee. But hereafter I will build nothing but the loveliest thing in the world—

HILDA [*carried away*]. Yes—yes—yes!

SOLNESS. —build it together with a princess, whom I love—

HILDA. Yes, tell him that! Tell him that!

SOLNESS. Yes. And then I will say to him: Now I shall go down and throw my arms round her and kiss her—

HILDA. —many times! Say that!

SOLNESS. —many, many times, I will say.

HILDA. And then—?

SOLNESS. Then I will wave my hat—and come down to the earth—and do as I said to him.

HILDA [*with outstretched arms*]. Now I see you again as I did when there was song in the air.

SOLNESS [*looks at her with his head bowed*]. How have you become what you are, Hilda?

HILDA. How have you made me what I am?

SOLNESS [*shortly and firmly*]. The princess shall have her castle.

HILDA [*jubilant, clapping her hands*]. Oh, Mr. Solness—! My lovely, lovely castle. Our castle in the air!

SOLNESS. On a firm foundation.

[*In the street a crowd of people has assembled, vaguely seen through the trees. Music of wind instruments is heard far away behind the new house.*]

[MRS. SOLNESS, *with a fur collar round her neck,* DR. HERDAL *with her white shawl on his arm, and some ladies, come out on the verandah.* RAGNAR BROVIK *comes at the same time up from the garden.*]

MRS. SOLNESS [*to* RAGNAR]. Are we to have music, too?

RAGNAR. Yes. It's the band of the Mason's Union. [*To* SOLNESS.] The foreman asked me to tell you that he is ready now to go up with the wreath.

SOLNESS [*takes his hat*]. Good. I will go down to him myself.

MRS. SOLNESS [*anxiously*]. What have you to do down there, Halvard?

SOLNESS [*curtly*]. I must be down below with the men.

MRS. SOLNESS. Yes, down below—only down below.

SOLNESS. That is where I always stand—on everyday occasions. [*He goes down the flight of steps and away through the garden.*]

MRS. SOLNESS [*calls after him over the railing*]. But do beg the man to be careful when he goes up? Promise me that, Halvard!

DR. HERDAL [*to* MRS. SOLNESS]. Don't you see that I was right? He has given up all thought of that folly.

MRS. SOLNESS. Oh, what a relief! Twice workmen have fallen, and each time they were killed on the spot. [*Turns to* HILDA.] Thank you, Miss Wangel, for having kept such a firm hold upon him. I should never have been able to manage him.

DR. HERDAL [*playfully*]. Yes, yes, Miss Wangel, you know how to keep firm hold on a man, when you give your mind to it.

[MRS. SOLNESS *and* DR. HERDAL *go up to the ladies, who are standing nearer to the steps and looking over the garden.* HILDA *remains standing beside the railing in the foreground.* RAGNAR *goes up to her.*]

RAGNAR [*with suppressed laughter, half whispering*]. Miss Wangel—do you see all those young fellows down in the street?

HILDA. Yes.

RAGNAR. They are my fellow students, come to look at the master.

HILDA. What do they want to look at him for?

RAGNAR. They want to see how he daren't climb to the top of his own house.

HILDA. Oh, that is what those boys want, is it?

RAGNAR [*spitefully and scornfully*]. He has kept us down so long—now we are going to see him keep quietly down below himself.

HILDA. You will not see that—not this time.

RAGNAR [*smiles*]. Indeed! Then where shall we see him?

HILDA. High—high up by the vane! That is where you will see him!

RAGNAR [*laughs*]. Him! Oh yes, I daresay!

HILDA. His will is to reach the top—so at the top you shall see him.

RAGNAR. His will, yes; that I can easily believe. But he simply cannot do it. His head would swim round, long, long before he got halfway. He would have to crawl down again on his hands and knees.

DR. HERDAL [*points across*]. Look! There goes the foreman up the ladders.

MRS. SOLNESS. And of course he has the wreath to carry, too. Oh, I do hope he will be careful!

RAGNAR [*stares incredulously and shouts*]. Why, but it's—

HILDA [*breaking out in jubilation*]. It is the master builder himself!

MRS. SOLNESS [*screams with terror*]. Yes, it is Halvard! Oh, my great God—! Halvard! Halvard!

DR. HERDAL. Hush! Don't shout to him!

MRS. SOLNESS [*half beside herself*]. I must go to him! I must get him to come down again!

DR. HERDAL [*holds her*]. Don't move, any of you! Not a sound!

HILDA [*immovable, follows* SOLNESS *with her eyes*]. He climbs and climbs. Higher and higher! Higher and higher! Look! Just look!

RAGNAR [*breathless*]. He must turn now. He can't possibly help it.

HILDA. He climbs and climbs. He will soon be at the top now.

MRS. SOLNESS. Oh, I shall die of terror. I cannot bear to see it.

DR. HERDAL. Then don't look up at him.

HILDA. There he is standing on the topmost planks. Right at the top!

DR. HERDAL. Nobody must move! Do you hear?

HILDA [*exulting, with quiet intensity*]. At last! At last! Now I see him great and free again!

RAGNAR [*almost voiceless*]. But this is im—

HILDA. So I have seen him all through these ten years. How secure he stands! Frightfully thrilling all the same. Look at him! Now he is hanging the wreath round the vane.

RAGNAR. I feel as if I were looking at something utterly impossible.

HILDA. Yes, it is the impossible that he is doing now! [*With the indefinable expression in her eyes.*] Can you see anyone else up there with him?

RAGNAR. There is no one else.

HILDA. Yes, there is one he is striving with.

RAGNAR. You are mistaken.

HILDA. Then do you hear no song in the air, either?

RAGNAR. It must be the wind in the treetops.

HILDA. *I* hear a song—a mighty song! [*Shouts in wild jubilation and glee.*] Look, look! Now he is waving his hat! He is waving it to us down here! Oh, wave, wave back to him. For now it is finished! [*Snatches the white shawl from the doctor, waves it, and shouts up to* SOLNESS.] Hurrah for Master Builder Solness!

DR. HERDAL. Stop! Stop! For God's sake—!

[*The ladies on the verandah wave their pockethandkerchiefs, and the shouts of "Hurrah" are taken up in the street below. Then they are suddenly silenced, and the crowd bursts out into a shriek of horror. A human body, with planks and fragments of wood, is vaguely perceived crashing down behind the trees.*]

MRS. SOLNESS AND THE LADIES [*at the same time*]. He is falling! He is falling!

[MRS. SOLNESS *totters, falls backwards, swooning, and is caught, amid cries and confusion, by the ladies. The crowd in the street breaks down the fence and storms into the garden. At the same time* DR. HERDAL, *too, rushes down thither. A short pause.*]

HILDA [*stares fixedly upwards and says, as if petrified*]. My Master Builder.

RAGNAR [*supports himself, trembling, against the railing*]. He must be dashed to pieces—killed on the spot.

ONE OF THE LADIES [*while* MRS. SOLNESS *is carried into the house*]. Run down for the doctor—

RAGNAR. I can't stir a foot—

ANOTHER LADY. Then call to someone!

RAGNAR [*tries to call out*]. How is it? Is he alive?

A VOICE [*below in the garden*]. Mr. Solness is dead!

OTHER VOICES [*nearer*]. The head is all crushed. He fell right into the quarry.

HILDA [*turns to* RAGNAR, *and says quietly*]. I can't see him up there now

RAGNAR. This is terrible. So, after all, he could not do it.

HILDA [*as if in quiet spellbound triumph*]. But he mounted right to the top. And I heard harps in the air. [*Waves her shawl in the air, and shrieks with wild intensity.*] My—my Master Builder!

Giovanni Verga

Malaria

TRANSLATED BY D. H. LAWRENCE

Giovanni Verga (1840–1922)

GIOVANNI VERGA WAS BORN IN CATANIA, SICILY, INTO A WEALTHY and proud upper middle-class family. He was educated by a tutor who was himself a poet in the Romantic tradition, which pervades Verga's early writings. Verga left Sicily to study in Florence, the literary capital of Italy, then moved to Milan, where he was associated with a group of easy-living, elegant, Bohemian young writers. In both Florence and Milan he came into contact with the works of such French novelists as Gustave Flaubert, Émile Zola, and Guy de Maupassant and absorbed the doctrines of Realism and Naturalism, especially the belief that the artist should be impersonal, a precise and detached observer who lets the details of reality speak for themselves and remains invisible behind his creation. He became the best representative of *verismo,* the Italian form of Naturalism which found its most convincing expression in writers attached to the soil—the customs, the language, the outlook—of a single region.

The important turning point in Verga's career was his rediscovery of his native Sicily as the frame and subject of his fiction. The work of his Florentine and Milanese periods had generally been elegant and somewhat artificial novels about love, the rich, and society. In 1874, in a tale called *Nedda,* he first discovered the possibilities that could be found in a Sicilian setting. A few years later, with the collection of tales called *Life in the Fields,* he found his true subject and style in the lives of Sicilian peasants. In 1881 he published *The House by the Meddlar Tree,* the first in what was planned as a series of five novels under the general title of *The Defeated.* In fact, only one more novel was completed—*Mastro-Don Gesualdo,* —but the two, along with his numerous short stories, were sufficient to secure Verga's fame as an acute and profoundly sensitive observer of the injustices of society and the harshness of nature, pessimistic about man's ability to control his destiny.

Verga made the decision to break with the literary language accepted as correct in Florence and filled his stories with the speech rhythms and dialect of Sicily, to convey the impression of the peasants' own perspective on a world seemingly ruled by a dimly understood but brutally rigid fatality. *Malaria* uses what could be called a "choral technique," also evident in *The House by the Meddlar Tree.* There is no central character and no fixed story line; rather, the collective consciousness of the peasants, their collective travail, and the way they view it are the true subjects of the story.

The translation is by D. H. Lawrence, an admirer of Verga who was instrumental in making him known to English readers.

*Malaria**

And you feel you could touch it with your hand—as if it smoked up from the fat earth, there, everywhere, round about the mountains that shut it in, from Agnone to Mount Etna capped with snow—stagnating in the plain like the sultry heat of June. There the red-hot sun rises and sets, and the livid moon, and the *Puddara* which seems to float through a sea of exhalations, and the birds and the white marguerites of spring, and the burnt-up summer; and there the wild duck in long black files fly through the autumn clouds, and the river gleams as if it were of metal, between the wide, lonely banks, that are broken here and there, scattered with pebbles, and in the background the Lake of Lentini, like a mere, with its flat shores, and not a boat, not a tree on its sides, smooth and motionless. By the lake bed the oxen pasture at will, forlorn, muddied up to the breast, hairy. When the sheep bell resounds in the great silence, the wagtails fly away, noiselessly, and the shepherd himself, yellow with fever, and white as well with dust, lifts his swollen lids for a moment, raising his head in the shadow of the dry reeds.

And truly the malaria gets into you with the bread you eat, or if you open your mouth to speak as you walk, suffocating in the dust and sun of the roads, and you feel your knees give way beneath you, or you sink discouraged on the saddle as your mule ambles along, with its head down. In vain the villages of Lentini and Francoforte and Paternò try to clamber up like strayed sheep onto the first hills that rise from the plain, and surround themselves with orange groves, and vineyards, and evergreen gardens and orchards; the malaria seizes the inhabitants in the depopulated streets, and nails them in front of the doors of their houses whose plaster is all falling with the sun, and there they tremble with fever under their brown cloaks, with all the bed blankets over their shoulders.

Down below, on the plain, the houses are rare and sad-looking, beside the roads wasted by the sun, standing between two heaps of smoking dung, propped up by dilapidated sheds, where the change horses wait with extinguished eyes, tied to the empty manger. Or by the shore of the lake, with the decrepit bough of the inn sign hung over the doorway, the great

* Literally, "bad air," believed to be the cause of the disease.

bare rooms, and the host dozing squatted on the doorstep, with his head tied up in a kerchief, spying round the deserted country every time he wakes up, to see if a thirsty traveler is coming. Or else what looks like little huts of white wood, plumed with four meager, gray eucalyptus trees, along the railway that cuts the plain in two like a hatchet cleft, where the locomotive flies whistling as the autumn wind, and where at night are coruscations of fiery sparks. Or finally here and there, at the boundaries of the farmlands marked by a little stone pillar very roughly squared, the farmplaces with their roofs shoved up from outside, with their doorframes collapsing, in front of the cracked threshing-floors, in the shade of the tall ricks of straw where the hens sleep with their heads under their wing, and the donkey lets his head hang, with his mouth still full of straw, and the dog rises suspiciously, and barks hoarsely at the stone which falls out from the plaster, at the firefly which flickers past, at the leaf which stirs in the inert countryside.

At evening, as soon as the sun sinks, sun-burnt men appear in the doorways, wearing big straw hats and wide canvas drawers, yawning and stretching their arms; and half-naked women, with blackened shoulders, suckling babies that are already pale and limp, so that you can't imagine that they'll ever get big and swarthy and romp on the grass when winter comes again, and the yard-floor will be green once more, and the sky blue, and the country all round laughing in the sun. And you can't imagine where all the people live who go to mass on Sundays, or why they live there, all those who come to the little church surrounded by cactus hedges, from ten miles around, from as far as ever the clanging of the little cracked bell can be heard over the endless plain.

However, wherever there is malaria there is earth blessed by God. In June the ears of wheat hang weighted down, and the furrows smoke as if they had blood in their veins the moment the ploughshare enters them in November. And then those who reap and those who sow must fall like ripe ears as well, for the Lord has said, "In the sweat of thy brow shalt thou eat bread." And when the sweats of fever leave some one of them stiff upon the mattress of maize-sheathes, and there's no need any more of sulphate or of decoction of eucalyptus, they put him on the haycart, or across an ass' pack-saddle, or on a ladder, or any way they can, with a sack over his face, and they take him to bury him by the lonely little church, under the thorny cactuses whose fruit no one for that reason eats. The women weep in a cluster, and the men stand looking on, smoking.

So they had carried away the estate-keeper of Valsavoia, who was called Farmer Croce, after he'd been swallowing sulphate and eucalyptus decoction for thirty years. In spring he was better, but at autumn, when the wild ducks passed again, he put his kerchief on his head and showed himself not oftener than every other day in the doorway; till he was reduced to skin and bone, and had a big belly like a drum, so that they called him the Toad, partly because of his rude, savage manner, and partly because his eyes had become livid and stuck out of his head. He kept on saying before he died, "Don't you bother, the master will see after my children!" And with his wondering eyes he looked them one after another in the face, all those who stood round the bed, the last evening, when they put the candle under his nose. Uncle Menico the goatherd, who understood those things, said that his liver must be as hard as a stone, and weighed five pounds. But somebody added:

"Well, now he needn't worry about it! He's got fat and rich at his master's expense, and his children don't stand in need of anybody! Do you think he took all that sulphate and put up with all that malaria for thirty years, just to please his master?"

Neighbor Carmine, the host by the lake, had lost all his five children one after the other in the same way, three boys and two girls! Never mind about the girls! But the boys died just when they were getting old enough to earn their bread. So now he was used to it; and as the fever got the last boy under, after having harassed him for two or three years, he didn't spend another farthing, neither for sulphate nor for decoctions, but drew off some good wine and set himself to make all the good fish stews he could think of, to provoke the appetite of the sick youth. He went fishing specially in the mornings, and came back laden with mullet and eels as thick as your arm, and when it was ready he stood before the bed with tears in his eyes and said to his son, "There you are, eat that!" And the rest of the fish Nanni the carter took to town to sell.

"The lake gives, and the lake takes away," said Nanni, seeing Neighbor Carmine weeping in secret. "What's the good, brother?"

The lake had given him good wages. And at Christmas, when eels fetch a good price, they used to have merry suppers before the fire, in the house by the lake, macaroni, sausages, everything you could think of, while the wind howled outside like a wolf that is cold and hungry. And in that way those that were left behind consoled themselves for the ones that were dead. But little by little they were wasting away, so that the mother grew bent like a hook with heartbrokenness, and the father, who was big and fat, was always on the doorstep, so that he needn't see those empty rooms, where his boys used to sing and work. The last one absolutely didn't want to die, and cried and grew desperate when the fever seized him, and even went and threw himself into the lake out of fear of death. But his father could swim, and fished him out again, and shouted at him that that cold bath would bring back the fever worse than ever.

"Ah," sobbed the youth, clutching his hair with his hands, "there's no hope for me, there's no hope for me!" "Just like his sister Agatha, who didn't want to die because she was a bride," observed Neighbor Carmine in private to his wife, sitting on the side of the bed; and she, who for some time now had left off weeping, nodded assent, bent as she was like a hook.

But she, though she was so reduced, and her big fat husband, they both had tough skins, and lived on alone to mind the house. The malaria doesn't finish everybody. Sometimes there's one who will live to be a hundred, like Cirino the simpleton, who had neither king nor kingdom, nor wit nor wish, nor father nor mother, nor house to sleep in, nor bread to eat, and everybody knew him for forty miles around, since he went from farm to farm, helping to tend the oxen, to carry the manure, to skin the dead cattle, and do all the dirty jobs; and got kicks and a bit of bread; he slept in the ditches, on the edges of the fields, under the hedges, or under the sheds for the standing cattle; and lived by charity, straying round like a dog without a master, with two ends of old drawers held together with bits of string on his thin black legs; and he went singing at the top of his voice under the sun which beat down on his bare head, yellow as saffron. He neither took sulphate any more, nor medicines, nor did he catch the fever. A hundred times they had found him stretched out across the road, as if he was dead, and picked him up; but at last the malaria had left him, because it could do no more with him. After it had eaten up his brain and the calves of his legs, and had got into his belly till it was swollen like a waterbag, it had left him as happy as an Easter Day, singing in the sun better than a cricket. The simpleton liked best to stand in front of the stables at Valsavoia, because people passed by, and he ran after them for miles, crying, "Uuh! uuh!" until they threw him a few cents. The host took the cents from him and kept him to sleep under the shed, on the horses' bedding, and when the horses gave him a kick Cirino ran to wake up the master crying, "Uuh!" and then in the morning he currycombed them and groomed them.

Later he had been attracted by the railway which they were building in the neighborhood. The coach drivers and wayfarers had become rarer on the road, and the idiot didn't know what to think, watching the swallows in the air for hours, and blinking his eyelids at the sun to make it out. Then the first time he saw all those people stuffed into the big cars that were leaving the station, he seemed to understand. And after that every day he waited for the train, never a minute wrong in his time, as if he had a clock in his head; and while it fled before him, hurling its noise and smoke in his face, he began to run after it, throwing his arms in the air and howling in a tone of anger and menace, "uuh! uuh!" . . .

The host too, whenever he saw the train passing in the distance puffing through the malaria, said nothing, but spat after it all he felt, shaking his head before the deserted sheds and the empty jugs. Formerly affairs had gone so well with him that he had had four wives, so that they called him

"Killwife," and they said he'd got case-hardened to it, and that he was for taking the fifth, if the daughter of Farmer Turi Oricchiazza hadn't given him answer: "God preserve us! not if he was made of gold, that Christian there! He eats up his fellow man like a crocodile!"

But it wasn't true that he'd got case-hardened to it, because when Goodwife Santa had died, his third, he had never taken a mouthful of food till midday, nor a drop of water, and he really cried behind the counter of the inn. "This time I want to take one who is used to the malaria," he had said after that event. "I don't want to suffer like this any more."

The malaria killed off his wives, one after the other, but they left him just the same, old and wrinkled, so that it was really hard to imagine that such a man had his own brave homicide on his conscience, intending for all that to take a fourth wife. However, each new time he wanted his wife young and appetizing, for the inn could never prosper without a wife, and for this reason customers had become scarce. Now there was nobody left but Neighbor Mommu, the signalman from the railway just near, a man who never spoke a word, and came to drink his glass between train and train, sitting himself down on the bench by the door with his shoes in his hand, to rest his legs.

"The malaria doesn't get those lot!" thought Killwife, also never opening his mouth, because if the malaria had made them fall like flies there'd have been nobody to keep that railway going. The poor wretch, since the only man who had poisoned his existence had been removed from his sight, had now only two enemies in the world: the railway which took away his customers, and the malaria which carried off his wives. All the other people on the plain, as far as the eye could reach, had their moments of blessedness, even if they had someone in bed sinking bit by bit, or if the fever was beating them down on the doorstep, with their handkerchiefs on their heads and their cloaks over their shoulders. They took pleasure looking round on the young wheat that was rising prosperous and green as velvet, or the wheat-ears waxing like a sea, and they listened to the long singing of the reapers, stretched out in a line like soldiers, and in every little road the bagpipes were heard, behind which swarms of peasants were just arriving from Calabria for the harvest, dusty people bent under their heavy saddle-sacks, the men in front and the women trailing behind, limping and looking with burnt, tired faces at the road which stretched before them. And on the brink of every ditch, behind every clump of aloes, at the hour when evening drops down like a gray veil, the pipes of the watchmen fluted among the ripe ears of grain, which fell silent, motionless, as the wind sank, invaded by the same silence of night.

"There you are!" thought Killwife. "If all that lot of folks can only manage not to leave their bones behind them, and get back home, they'll get back with money in their pockets, they will."

As for him, no! He waited neither for harvest nor anything, and he hadn't the spirit to sing. The evening fell sadly enough, through the empty stables and the dark inn. At that hour the train passed whistling in the distance, and Neighbor Mommu stood beside his signalbox with his flag in his hand; but away up there, when the train had vanished in the shadows, they heard Cirino the simpleton running after it shouting, "Uuh!" And Killwife, in the doorway of the dark, deserted inn, thought to himself that there was no malaria for that lot.

At last, when he could no longer pay the rent for the inn and the stabling, the landlord turned him out after he'd lived there fifty-seven years, and Killwife was reduced to looking for a job on the railway himself, and holding the little flag in his hand when the train passed.

And then, tired with running all day up and down the track, worn out with years and misfortunes, he saw twice a day the long line of carriages crowded with people pass by; the jolly companies of shooters spreading over the plain; sometimes a peasant lad playing the accordion with his head bent, bunched up on the seat of a third-class compartment; the beautiful ladies who looked out of the windows with their heads swathed in a veil; the silver and the tarnished steel of the bags and valises which shone under the polished lamps; the high stuffed seat-backs with their crochet-work covers. Ah, how lovely it must be traveling in there, snatching a wink of sleep! It was as if a piece of a city were sliding past, with the lit-up streets and the glittering shops. Then the train lost itself in the vast mist of the evening, and the poor fellow, taking off his shoes for a moment, and sitting on the bench, muttered, "Ah! for that lot there isn't any malaria."

Thomas Mann

Tristan

TRANSLATED BY H. T. LOWE-PORTER

Thomas Mann (1875–1955)

THOMAS MANN WAS BORN IN THE GERMAN CITY OF LÜBECK, INTO a solid, established merchant family. Upon his father's death, his family moved to Munich, where Mann went to the university (without ever taking a degree), worked in an insurance company, and wrote for *Simplicissimus,* a literary-satirical weekly. When he was about twenty-three, he began his first novel, *Buddenbrooks,* the story of the decline of a solid middle-class burgher family that loses its grip on life as the younger generations turn from the practical to art, spiritual values, introspection, and sickly weakness. This theme of the incompatibility of the artist's sensitive—and morbid—spirituality with the normal practical life of the dominant middle classes was pursued in much of Mann's earlier work, notably in the long short stories "Tristan," "Tonio Kröger," and "Death in Venice."

During World War I, Mann was an ardent patriot and defender of German culture, authoritarian and antidemocratic in his stance—a position he would later repudiate. He indeed became a boldly outspoken opponent of emergent fascism in Germany, and in 1933, when Hitler and the Nazis came to power, he went into exile, first in Switzerland, then, with the coming of the World War II, in the United States. Much of Mann's reflection on the evolution of European civilization, its warring forces and its sicknesses, is expressed in his novel *The Magic Mountain* (1924), a book that both sums up and offers a critique of a period of history, as it underwent a crisis in its traditional values. He moved on, in the thirties and forties, to a four-volume retelling of the Joseph story from the Old Testament, *Joseph and His Brethren,* then explored further the uses of mythic material in *Doctor Faustus.* His last novel was *Confessions of Felix Krull, Confidence Man.*

Mann is a slow, patient, and erudite author who prepares his ground and establishes his themes with deliberation, weaving a complex texture of meaning and implication. "Tristan," which prefigures *The Magic Mountain* by its setting—a sanatorium in which the weak and dying, those who cannot face "real life," gather to be treated—develops its exploration of the artistic sensibility in part through reference to the overpoweringly romantic music of Richard Wagner's opera, *Tristan and Isolde.* In both the opera and the story, the *sehnsuchtsmotiv,* the motif or theme of passionate longing of the lovers Tristan and Isolde for one another, returns to express an impossible, doomed love. In Wagner's opera—as in the old Celtic legend that is its source—Isolde's husband, King Mark, kills Tristan, and Isolde dies on her lover's body.

Tristan

Einfried, the sanatorium. A long, white, rectilinear building with a side wing, set in a spacious garden pleasingly equipped with grottoes, bowers, and little bark pavilions. Behind its slate roofs the mountains tower heavenwards, evergreen, massy, cleft with wooded ravines.

Now as then Dr. Leander directs the establishment. He wears a two-pronged black beard as curly and wiry as horse-hair stuffing; his spectacle-lenses are thick, and glitter; he has the look of a man whom science has cooled and hardened and filled with silent, forbearing pessimism. And with this beard, these lenses, this look, and in his short, reserved, preoccupied way, he holds his patients in his spell: holds those sufferers who, too weak to be laws unto themselves, put themselves into his hands that his severity may be a shield unto them.

As for Fräulein von Osterloh, hers it is to preside with unwearying zeal over the housekeeping. Ah, what activity! How she plies, now here, now there, now upstairs, now down, from one end of the building to the other! She is queen in kitchen and storerooms, she mounts the shelves of the linen-presses, she marshals the domestic staff; she ordains the bill of fare, to the end that the table shall be economical, hygienic, attractive, appetizing, and all these in the highest degree; she keeps house diligently, furiously; and her exceeding capacity conceals a constant reproach to the world of men, to no one of whom has it yet occurred to lead her to the altar. But ever on her cheeks there glows, in two round, carmine spots, the unquenchable hope of one day becoming Frau Dr. Leander.

Ozone, and stirless, stirless air! Einfried, whatever Dr. Leander's rivals and detractors may choose to say about it, can be most warmly recommended for lung patients. And not only these, but patients of all sorts, gentlemen, ladies, even children, come to stop here. Dr. Leander's skill is challenged in many different fields. Sufferers from gastric disorders come, like Frau Magistrate Spatz—she has ear trouble into the bargain—people with defective hearts, paralytics, rheumatics, nervous sufferers of all kinds and degrees. A diabetic general here consumes his daily bread amid continual grumblings. There are several gentlemen with gaunt, fleshless faces who fling their legs about in that uncontrollable way that bodes no good. There is an elderly lady, a Frau Pastor Höhlenrauch, who has brought fourteen children into the world and is now incapable of a single thought, yet has not thereby attained to any peace of mind, but must go roving specter-like all day long up and down through the house, on the arm of her private attendant, as she has been doing this year past.

Sometimes a death takes place among the "severe cases," those who lie in their chambers, never appearing at meals or in the reception rooms. When this happens no one knows of it, not even the person sleeping next door. In the silence of the night the waxen guest is put away and life at Einfried goes tranquilly on, with its massage, its electric treatment, douches, baths; with its exercises, its steaming and inhaling, in rooms especially equipped with all the triumphs of modern therapeutic.

Yes, a deal happens hereabouts—the institution is in a flourishing way. When new guests arrive, at the entrance to the side wing, the porter sounds the great gong; when there are departures, Dr. Leander, together with Fräulein von Osterloh, conducts the traveler in due form to the waiting carriage. All sorts and kinds of people have received hospitality at Einfried. Even an author is here stealing time from God Almighty—a queer sort of man, with a name like some kind of mineral or precious stone.

Lastly there is, besides Dr. Leander, another physician, who takes care of the slight cases and the hopeless ones. But he bears the name of Müller and is not worth mentioning.

At the beginning of January a business man named Klöterjahn—of the firm of A. C. Klöterjahn & Co.—brought his wife to Einfried. The porter rang the gong, and Fräulein von Osterloh received the guests from a distance in the drawing room on the ground floor, which, like nearly all the fine old mansion, was furnished in wonderfully pure Empire style. Dr. Leander appeared straightway. He made his best bow, and a preliminary conversation ensued, for the better information of both sides.

Beyond the windows lay the wintry garden, the flower beds covered with straw, the grottoes snowed under, the little temples forlorn. Two porters were dragging in the guests' trunks from the carriage drawn up before the wrought iron gate—for there was no drive up to the house.

"Be careful, Gabriele, *doucement, doucement,*[1] my angel, keep your mouth closed," Herr Klöterjahn had said as he led his wife through the garden; and nobody could look at her without tenderheartedly echoing the caution—though, to be sure, Herr Klöterjahn might quite as well have uttered it all in his own language.

The coachman who had driven the pair from the station to the sanatorium was an uncouth man, and insensitive; yet he sat with his tongue between his teeth as the husband lifted down his wife. The very horses, steaming in

[1] "Gently, gently."

the frosty air, seemed to follow the procedure with their eyeballs rolled back in their heads out of sheer concern for so much tenderness and fragile charm.

The young wife's trouble was her trachea; it was expressly so set down in the letter Herr Klöterjahn had sent from the shores of the Baltic to announce their impending arrival to the director of Einfried—the trachea, and not the lungs, thank God! But it is a question whether, if it had been the lungs, the new patient could have looked any more pure and ethereal, any remoter from the concerns of this world, than she did now as she leaned back pale and weary in her chaste white-enameled armchair, beside her robust husband, and listened to the conversation.

Her beautiful white hands, bare save for the simple wedding ring, rested in her lap, among the folds of a dark, heavy cloth skirt; she wore a close-fitting waist of silver-gray with a stiff collar—it had an allover pattern of arabesques in high-pile velvet. But these warm, heavy materials only served to bring out the unspeakable delicacy, sweetness, and langor of the little head, to make it look more than ever touching, exquisite, and unearthly. Her light-brown hair was drawn smoothly back and gathered in a knot low on her neck, but near the right temple a single lock fell loose and curling, not far from the place where an odd little vein branched across one well-marked eyebrow, pale blue and sickly amid all that pure, well-nigh transparent spotlessness. That little blue vein above the eye dominated quite painfully the whole fine oval of the face. When she spoke, it stood out still more; yes, even when she smiled—and lent her expression a touch of strain, if not actually of distress, that stirred vague fear in the beholder. And yet she spoke, and she smiled: spoke frankly and pleasantly in her rather husky voice, with a smile in her eyes—though they again were sometimes a little difficult and showed a tendency to avoid a direct gaze. And the corners of her eyes, both sides the base of the slender little nose, were deeply shadowed. She smiled with her mouth too, her beautiful wide mouth, whose lips were so pale and yet seemed to flash—perhaps because their contours were so exceedingly pure and well-cut. Sometimes she cleared her throat, then carried her handkerchief to her mouth and afterwards looked at it.

"Don't clear your throat like that, Gabriele," said Herr Klöterjahn. "You know, darling, Dr. Hinzpeter expressly forbade it, and what we have to do is to exercise self-control, my angel. As I said, it is the trachea," he repeated. "Honestly, when it began, I thought it was the lungs, and it gave me a scare, I do assure you. But it isn't the lungs—we don't mean to let ourselves in for that, do we, Gabriele, my love, eh? Ha ha!"

"Surely not," said Dr. Leander, and glittered at her with his eyeglasses.

Whereupon Herr Klöterjahn ordered coffee, coffee and rolls; and the speaking way he had of sounding the *c* far back in his throat and exploding the *b* in "butter" must have made any soul alive hungry to hear it.

His order was filled; and rooms were assigned to him and his wife, and they took possession with their things.

And Dr. Leander took over the case himself, without calling in Dr. Müller.

The population of Einfried took unusual interest in the fair new patient; Herr Klöterjahn, used as he was to see homage paid her, received it all with great satisfaction. The diabetic general, when he first saw her, stopped grumbling a minute; the gentlemen with the fleshless faces smiled and did their best to keep their legs in order; as for Frau Magistrate Spatz, she made her her oldest friend on the spot. Yes, she made an impression, this woman who bore Herr Klöterjahn's name! A writer who had been sojourning a few weeks in Einfried, a queer sort, he was, with a name like some precious stone or other, positively colored up when she passed him in the corridor, stopped stock-still and stood there as though rooted to the ground, long after she had disappeared.

Before two days were out, the whole little population knew her history. She came originally from Bremen, as one could tell by certain pleasant small twists in her pronunciation; and it had been in Bremen that, two years gone by, she had bestowed her hand upon Herr Klöterjahn, a successful business man, and become his life-partner. She had followed him to his native town on the Baltic coast, where she had presented him, some ten months before the time of which we write, and under circumstances of the greatest difficulty and danger, with a child, a particularly well-formed and vigorous son and heir. But since that terrible hour she had never fully recovered her strength—granting, that is, that she had ever had any. She had not been long up, still extremely weak, with extremely impoverished vitality, when one day after coughing she brought up a little blood—oh, not much, an insignificant quantity in fact; but it would have been much better to be none at all; and the suspicious thing was, that the same trifling but disquieting incident recurred after another short while. Well, of course, there were things to be done, and Dr. Hinzpeter, the family physician, did them. Complete rest was ordered, little pieces of ice swallowed; morphine administered to check the cough, and other medicines to regulate the heart action. But recovery failed to set in; and while the child, Anton Klöterjahn, junior, a magnificent specimen of a baby, seized on his place in life and held it with prodigious energy and ruthlessness, a low, unobservable fever seemed to waste the young mother daily. It was, as we have heard, an affection of the trachea—a word that in Dr. Hinzpeter's mouth sounded so soothing, so consoling, so reassuring, that it raised their spirits to a surprising degree. But even though it was not the lungs, the doctor presently found that a milder climate and a stay in a sanatorium were imperative if the cure was to be hastened. The reputation enjoyed by Einfried and its director had done the rest.

Such was the state of affairs; Herr Klöterjahn himself related it to all and sundry. He talked with a slovenly pronunciation, in a loud, good-humored voice, like a man whose digestion is in as capital order as his pocketbook; shoveling out the words pell-mell, in the broad accents of the northern coast-dweller; hurtling some of them forth so that each sound was a little explosion, at which he laughed as at a successful joke.

He was of medium height, broad, stout, and short-legged; his face full and red, with watery blue eyes shaded by very fair lashes; with wide nostrils and humid lips. He wore English sidewhiskers and English clothes, and it enchanted him to discover at Einfried an entire English family, father, mother, and three pretty children with their nurse, who were stopping here for the simple and sufficient reason that they knew not where else to go. With this family he partook of a good English breakfast every morning. He set great store by good eating and drinking and proved to be a connoisseur both of food and wines, entertaining the other guests with the most exciting accounts of dinners given in his circle of acquaintance back home, with full descriptions of the choicer and rarer dishes; in the telling his eyes would narrow benignly, and his pronunciation take on certain palatal and nasal sounds, accompanied by smacking noises at the back of his throat. That he was not fundamentally averse to earthly joys of another sort was evinced upon an evening when a guest of the cure, an author by calling, saw him in the corridor trifling in not quite permissible fashion with a chambermaid—a humorous little passage at which the author in question made a laughably disgusted face.

As for Herr Klöterjahn's wife, it was plain to see that she was devotedly attached to her husband. She followed his words and movements with a smile: not the rather arrogant toleration the ailing sometimes bestow upon the well and sound, but the sympathetic participation of a well-disposed invalid in the manifestations of people who rejoice in the blessing of abounding health.

Herr Klöterjahn did not stop long in Einfried. He had brought his wife hither, but when a week had gone by and he knew she was in good hands and well looked after, he did not linger. Duties equally weighty—his flourishing child, his no less flourishing business—took him away; they compelled him to go, leaving her rejoicing in the best of care.

Spinell was the name of that author who had been stopping some weeks in Einfried—Detlev Spinell was his name, and his looks were quite out of the common. Imagine a dark man at the beginning of the thirties, impressively tall, with hair already distinctly gray at the temples, and a round, white, slightly bloated face, without a vestige of beard. Not that it was shaven—that you could have told; it was soft, smooth, boyish, with at most a downy hair here and there. And the effect was singular. His bright, doelike brown eyes had a gentle expression, the nose was thick and rather too fleshy. Also, Herr Spinell had an upper lip like an ancient Roman's, swelling and full of pores; large, carious teeth, and feet of uncommon size. One of the gentlemen with the rebellious legs, a cynic and ribald wit, had christened him "the dissipated baby;" but the epithet was malicious, and not very apt. Herr Spinell dressed well, in a long black coat and a waistcoat with colored spots.

He was unsocial and sought no man's company. Only once in a while he might be overtaken by an affable, blithe, expansive mood; and this always happened when he was carried away by an aesthetic fit at the sight of beauty, the harmony of two colors, a vase nobly formed, or the range of mountains lighted by the setting sun. "How beautiful!" he would say, with his head on one side, his shoulders raised, his hands spread out, his lips and nostrils curled and distended. "My God! look, how beautiful!" And in such moments of ardor he was quite capable of flinging his arms blindly round the neck of anybody, high or low, male or female, that happened to be near.

On his table, for anybody to see who entered his room, there always lay the book he had written. It was a novel of medium length, with a perfectly bewildering drawing on the jacket, printed on a sort of filter paper. Each letter of the type looked like a Gothic cathedral. Fräulein von Osterloh had read it once, in a spare quarter-hour, and found it "very cultured"—which was her circumlocution for inhumanly boresome. Its scenes were laid in fashionable salons, in luxurious boudoirs full of choice *objets d'art,* old furniture, gobelins, rare porcelains, priceless stuffs, and art treasures of all sorts and kinds. On the description of these things was expended the most loving care; as you read you constantly saw Herr Spinell, with distended nostrils, saying: "How beautiful! My God! look, how beautiful!" After all, it was strange he had not written more than this one book; he so obviously adored writing. He spent the greater part of the day doing it, in his room, and sent an extraordinary number of letters to the post, two or three nearly every day—and that made it more striking, even almost funny, that he very seldom received one in return.

Herr Spinell sat opposite Herr Klöterjahn's wife. At the first meal of which the new guests partook, he came rather late into the dining room, on the ground floor of the side wing, bade good day to the company generally in a soft voice, and betook himself to his own place, whereupon Dr. Leander perfunctorily presented him to the newcomers. He bowed, and self-consciously began to eat, using his knife and fork rather affectedly with the large, finely shaped white hands that came out from his very narrow coat-sleeves. After a little he grew more at ease and looked tranquilly first at Herr Klöterjahn and then at his wife, by turns. And in the course of the meal Herr Klöterjahn addressed to him sundry queries touching the general situation and climate of Einfried; his wife, in her charming way, added a word or two, and Herr Spinell gave courteous answers. His voice was mild, and really agreeable; but he had a halting way of speaking that almost amounted to an impediment—as though his teeth got in the way of his tongue.

After luncheon, when they had gone into the salon, Dr. Leander came up to the new arrivals to wish them *Mahlzeit*,[2] and Herr Klöterjahn's wife took occasion to ask about their *vis-à-vis*.

"What was the gentleman's name?" she asked. "I did not quite catch it. Spinelli?"

"Spinell, not Spinelli, madame. No, he is not an Italian; he only comes from Lemberg, I believe."

"And what was it you said? He is an author, or something of the sort?" asked Herr Klöterjahn. He had his hands in the pockets of his very easy-fitting English trousers, cocked his head towards the doctor, and opened his mouth, as some people do, to listen the better.

"Yes . . . I really don't know," answered Dr. Leander. "He writes. . . . I believe he has written a book, some sort of novel. I really don't know what."

By which Dr. Leander conveyed that he had no great opinion of the author and declined all responsibility on the score of him.

"But I find that most interesting," said Herr Klöterjahn's wife. Never before had she met an author face to face.

"Oh, yes," said Dr. Leander obligingly. "I understand he has a certain amount of reputation," which closed the conversation.

But a little later, when the new guests had retired and Dr. Leander himself was about to go, Herr Spinell detained him in talk to put a few questions for his own part.

"What was their name?" he asked. "I did not understand a syllable, of course."

"Klöterjahn," answered Dr. Leander, turning away.

"What's that?" asked Herr Spinell.

"*Klöterjahn* is their name," said Dr. Leander, and went his way. He set no great store by the author.

. . .

Have we got as far on as where Herr Klöterjahn went home? Yes, he was back on the shore of the Baltic once more, with his business and his babe, that ruthless and vigorous little being who had cost his mother great suffering and a slight weakness of the trachea; while she herself, the young wife, remained in Einfried and became the intimate friend of Frau Spatz. Which did not prevent Herr Klöterjahn's wife from being on friendly terms with the rest of the guests—for instance with Herr Spinell, who, to the astonish-

[2] That is, *gesegnete Mahlzeit*, "May your meal be blessed." A greeting used at the finish of a meal.

ment of everybody, for he had up to now held communion with not a single soul, displayed from the very first an extraordinary devotion and courtesy, and with whom she enjoyed talking, whenever she had any time left over from the stern service of the cure.

He approached her with immense circumspection and reverence, and never spoke save with his voice so carefully subdued that Frau Spatz, with her bad hearing, seldom or never caught anything he said. He tiptoed on his great feet up to the armchair in which Herr Klöterjahn's wife leaned, fragilely smiling; stopped two paces off, with his body bent forward and one leg poised behind him, and talked in his halting way, as though he had an impediment in his speech; with ardor, yet prepared to retire at any moment and vanish at the first sign of fatigue or satiety. But he did not tire her; she begged him to sit down with her and the Rätin;[3] she asked him questions and listened with curious smiles, for he had a way of talking sometimes that was so odd and amusing, different from anything she had ever heard before.

"Why are you in Einfried, really?" she asked. "What cure are you taking, Herr Spinell?"

"Cure? Oh, I'm having myself electrified a bit. Nothing worth mentioning. I will tell you the real reason why I am here, madame. It is a feeling for style."

"Ah?" said Herr Klöterjahn's wife; supported her chin on her hand and turned to him with exaggerated eagerness, as one does to a child who wants to tell a story.

"Yes, madame. Einfried is perfect Empire. It was once a castle, a summer residence, I am told. This side wing is a later addition, but the main building is old and genuine. There are times when I cannot endure Empire, and then times when I simply must have it in order to attain any sense of well-being. Obviously, people feel one way among furniture that is soft and comfortable and voluptuous, and quite another among the straight lines of these tables, chairs, and draperies. This brightness and hardness, this cold, austere simplicity and reserved strength, madame—it has upon me the ultimate effect of an inward purification and rebirth. Beyond a doubt, it is morally elevating."

"Yes, that is remarkable," she said. "And when I try I can understand what you mean."

Whereto he responded that it was not worth her taking any sort of trouble, and they laughed together. Frau Spatz laughed too and found it remarkable in her turn, though she did not say she understood it.

The reception room was spacious and beautiful. The high, white folding doors that led to the billiard room were wide open, and the gentlemen with the rebellious legs were disporting themselves within, others as well. On the

[3] Magistrate's wife.

opposite side of the room a glass door gave on the broad veranda and the garden. Near the door stood a piano. At a green-covered folding table the diabetic general was playing whist with some other gentlemen. Ladies sat reading or embroidering. The rooms were heated by an iron stove, but the chimney-piece, in the purest style, had coals pasted over with red paper to simulate a fire, and chairs were drawn up invitingly.

"You are an early riser, Herr Spinell," said Herr Klöterjahn' wife. "Two or three times already I have chanced to see you leaving the house at half past seven in the morning."

"An early riser? Ah, with a difference, madame, with a vast difference. The truth is, I rise early because I am such a late sleeper."

"You really must explain yourself, Herr Spinell." Frau Spatz too said she demanded an explanation.

"Well, if one is an early riser, one does not need to get up so early. Or so it seems to me. The conscience, madame, is a bad business. I, and other people like me, work hard all our lives to swindle our consciences into feeling pleased and satisfied. We are feckless creatures, and aside from a few good hours we go around weighted down, sick and sore with the knowledge of our own futility. We hate the useful; we know it is vulgar and unlovely, and we defend this position, as a man defends something that is absolutely necessary to his existence. Yet all the while conscience is gnawing at us, to such an extent that we are simply one wound. Added to that, our whole inner life, our view of the world, our way of working, is of a kind—its effect is frightfully unhealthy, undermining, irritating, and this only aggravates the situation. Well, then, there are certain little counterirritants, without which we would most certainly not hold out. A kind of decorum, a hygienic regimen, for instance, becomes a necessity for some of us. To get up early, to get up ghastly early, take a cold bath, and go out walking in a snowstorm—that may give us a sense of self-satisfaction that lasts as much as an hour. If I were to act out my true character, I should be lying in bed late into the afternoon. My getting up early is all hypocrisy, believe me."

"Why do you say that, Herr Spinell? On the contrary, I call it self-abnegation." Frau Spatz, too, called it self-abnegation.

"Hypocrisy or self-abnegation—call it what you like, madame. I have such a hideously downright nature—"

"Yes, that's it. Surely you torment yourself far too much."

"Yes, madame, I torment myself a great deal."

The fine weather continued. Rigid and spotless white the region lay, the mountains, house and garden, in a windless air that was blinding clear and cast bluish shadows; and above it arched the spotless pale-blue sky, where myriads of bright particles of glittering crystals seemed to dance. Herr Klöterjahn's wife felt tolerably well these days: free of fever, with scarce any cough, and able to eat without too great distaste. Many days she sat taking her cure for hours on end in the sunny cold on the terrace. She sat in the snow, bundled in wraps and furs, and hopefully breathed in the pure icy air to do her trachea good. Sometimes she saw Herr Spinell, dressed like herself, and in fur boots that made his feet a fantastic size, taking an airing in the garden. He walked with tentative tread through the snow, holding his arms in a certain careful pose that was stiff yet not without grace; coming up to the terrace he would bow very respectfully and mount the first step or so to exchange a few words with her.

"Today on my morning walk I saw a beautiful woman—good Lord! how beautiful she was!" he said; laid his head on one side and spread out his hands.

"Really, Herr Spinell. Do describe her to me."

"That I cannot do. Or, rather, it would not be a fair picture. I only saw the lady as I glanced at her in passing, I did not actually see her at all. But that fleeting glimpse was enough to rouse my fancy and make me carry away a picture so beautiful that—good Lord! how beautiful it is!"

She laughed. "Is that the way you always look at beautiful women, Herr Spinell? Just a fleeting glance?"

"Yes, madame; it is a better way than if I were avid of actuality, stared them plump in the face, and carried away with me only a consciousness of the blemishes they in fact possess."

" 'Avid of actuality'—what a strange phrase, a regular literary phrase, Herr Spinell; no one but an author could have said that. It impresses me very much, I must say. There is a lot in it that I dimly understand; there is something free about it, and independent, that even seems to be looking down on reality though it is so very respectable—is respectability itself, as you might say. And it makes me comprehend, too, that there is something else besides the tangible, something more subtle—"

"I know only one face," he said suddenly, with a strange lift in his voice, carrying his closed hands to his shoulders as he spoke and showing his carious teeth in an almost hysterical smile, "I know only one face of such lofty nobility that the mere thought of enhancing it through my imagination would be blasphemous; at which I could wish to look, on which I could wish to dwell, not minutes and not hours, but my whole life long; losing myself utterly therein, forgotten to every earthly thought. . . ."

"Yes, indeed, Herr Spinell. And yet don't you find Fräulein von Osterloh has rather prominent ears?"

He replied only by a profound bow; then, standing erect, let his eyes rest with a look of embarrassment and pain on the strange little vein that branched pale blue and sickly across her pure translucent brow.

An odd sort, a very odd sort. Herr Klöterjahn's wife thought about him sometimes; for she had much leisure for thought. Whether it was that the change of air began to lose its effect or some positively detrimental influence was at work, she began to go backward, the condition of her trachea left much to be desired, she had fever not infrequently, felt tired and exhausted, and could not eat. Dr. Leander most emphatically recommended rest, quiet, caution, care. So she sat, when indeed she was not forced to lie, quite motionless, in the society of Frau Spatz, holding some sort of sewing which she did not sew, and following one or another train of thought.

Yes, he gave her food for thought, this very odd Herr Spinell; and the strange thing was she thought not so much about him as about herself, for he had managed to rouse in her a quite novel interest in her own personality. One day he had said, in the course of conversation:

"No, they are positively the most enigmatic facts in nature—women, I mean. That is a truism, and yet one never ceases to marvel at it afresh. Take some wonderful creature, a sylph, an airy wraith, a fairy dream of a thing, and what does she do? Goes and gives herself to a brawny Hercules at a country fair, or maybe to a butcher's apprentice. Walks about on his arm, even leans her head on his shoulder and looks round with an impish smile as if to say: 'Look on this, if you like, and break your heads over it.' And we break them."

With this speech Herr Klöterjahn's wife had occupied her leisure again and again.

Another day, to the wonderment of Frau Spatz, the following conversation took place:

"May I ask, madame—though you may very likely think me prying—what your name really is?"

"Why, Herr Spinell, you know my name is Klöterjahn!"

"H'm. Yes, I know that—or, rather, I deny it. I mean your own name, your maiden name, of course. You will in justice, madame, admit that anybody who calls you Klöterjahn ought to be thrashed."

She laughed so hard that the little blue vein stood out alarmingly on her brow and gave the pale sweet face a strained expression most disquieting to see.

"Oh, no! Not at all, Herr Spinell! Thrashed, indeed! Is the name Klöterjahn so horrible to you?"

"Yes, madame. I hate the name from the bottom of my heart. I hated it the first time I heard it. It is the abandonment of ugliness; it is grotesque to make you comply with the custom so far as to fasten your husband's name upon you; is barbarous and vile."

"Well, and how about Eckhof? Is that any better? Eckhof is my father's name."

"Ah, you see! Eckhof is quite another thing. There was a great actor named Eckhof. Eckhof will do nicely. You spoke of your father— Then is your mother—?"

"Yes, my mother died when I was little."

"Ah! Tell me a little more of yourself, pray. But not if it tires you. When it tires you, stop, and I will go on talking about Paris, as I did the other day. But you could speak very softly, or even whisper—that would be more beautiful still. You were born in Bremen?" He breathed, rather than uttered, the question with an expression so awed, so heavy with import, as to suggest that Bremen was a city like no other on earth, full of hidden beauties and nameless adventures, and ennobling in some mysterious way those born within its walls.

"Yes, imagine," said she involuntarily. "I was born in Bremen."

"I was there once," he thoughtfully remarked.

"Goodness me, you have been there, too? Why, Herr Spinell, it seems to me you must have been everywhere there is between Spitzbergen and Tunis!"

"Yes, I was there once," he repeated. "A few hours, one evening. I recall a narrow old street, with a strange, warped-looking moon above the gabled roofs. Then I was in a cellar that smelled of wine and mold. It is a poignant memory."

"Really? Where could that have been, I wonder? Yes, in just such a gray old gabled house I was born, one of the old merchant houses, with echoing wooden floor and white-painted gallery."

"Then your father is a business man?" he asked hesitatingly.

"Yes, but he is also, and in the first place, an artist."

"Ah! In what way?"

"He plays the violin. But just saying that does not mean much. It is *how* he plays, Herr Spinell—it is that that matters! Sometimes I cannot listen to some of the notes without the tears coming into my eyes and making them burn. Nothing else in the world makes me feel like that. You won't believe it—"

"But I do. Oh, very much I believe it! Tell me, madame, your family is old, is it not? Your family has been living for generations in the old gabled house—living and working and closing their eyes on time?"

"Yes. Tell me why you ask."

"Because it not infrequently happens that a race with sober, practical bourgeois traditions will towards the end of its days flare up in some form of art."

"Is that a fact?"

"Yes."

"It is true, my father is surely more of an artist than some that call themselves so and get the glory of it. I only play the piano a little. They have forbidden me now, but at home, in the old days, I still played. Father and I played together. Yes, I have precious memories of all those years; and especially of the garden, our garden, back of the house. It was dreadfully wild and overgrown, and shut in by crumbling mossy walls. But it was just that gave it such charm. In the middle was a mountain with a wide border of sword-lilies. In the summer I spent long hours there with my friends. We all sat round the fountain on little camp-stools—"

"How beautiful!" said Herr Spinell, and flung up his shoulders. "You sat there and sang?"

"No, we mostly crocheted."

"But still—"

"Yes, we crocheted and chattered, my six friends and I—"

"How beautiful! Good Lord! think of it, *how beautiful!*" cried Herr Spinell again, his face quite distorted with emotion.

"Now, what is it you find so particularly beautiful about that, Herr Spinell?"

"Oh, there being six of them besides you, and your being not one of the six, but a queen among them . . . set apart from your six friends. A little gold crown showed in your hair—quite a modest, unostentatious little crown, still it was there—"

"Nonsense, there was nothing of the sort."

"Yes, there was; it shone unseen. But if I had been there, standing among the shrubbery, one of those times, I should have seen it."

"God knows what you would have seen. But you were not there. Instead of that, it was my husband who came out of the shrubbery one day, with my father. I was afraid they had been listening to our prattle—"

"So it was there, then, madame, that you first met your husband?"

"Yes, there it was I saw him first," she said, in quite a glad, strong voice; she smiled, and as she did so the little blue vein came out and gave her face a constrained and anxious expression. "He was calling on my father on business, you see. Next day he came to dinner, and three days later he proposed for my hand."

"Really? It all happened as fast as that?"

"Yes. Or, rather, it went a little slower after that. For my father was not very much inclined to it, you see, and consented on condition that we wait a long time first. He would rather I had stopped with him, and he had doubts in other ways too. But—"

"But?"

"But I had set my heart on it," she said, smiling; and once more the little vein dominated her whole face with its look of constraint and anxiety.

"Ah, so you set your heart on it."

"Yes, and I displayed great strength of purpose, as you see—"

"As I see. Yes."

"So that my father had to give way in the end."

"And so you forsook him and his fiddle and the old house with the overgrown garden, and the fountain and your six friends, and clave unto Herr Klöterjahn—"

" 'And clave unto'—you have such a strange way of saying things, Herr Spinell. Positively biblical. Yes, I forsook all that; nature has arranged things that way."

"Yes, I suppose that is it."

"And it was a question of my happiness—"

"Of course. And happiness came to you?"

"It came Herr Spinell, in the moment when they brought little Anton to me, our little Anton, and he screamed so lustily with his strong little lungs—he is very, very strong and healthy, you know—"

"This is not the first time, madame, that I have heard you speak of your little Anton's good health and great strength. He must be quite uncommonly healthy?"

"That he is. And looks so absurdly like my husband!"

"Ah! . . . So that was the way of it. And now you are no longer called by the name of Eckhof, but a different one, and you have your healthy little Anton, and are troubled with your trachea."

"Yes. And you are a perfectly enigmatic man, Herr Spinell, I do assure you."

"Yes. God knows you certainly are," said Frau Spatz, who was present on this occasion.

And that conversation, too, gave Herr Klöterjahn's wife food for reflection. Idle as it was, it contained much to nourish those secret thoughts of hers about herself. Was this the baleful influence which was at work? Her weakness increased and fever often supervened, a quiet glow in which she rested with a feeling of mild elevation, to which she yielded in a pensive mood that was a little affected, self-satisfied, even rather self-righteous. When she had not to keep her bed, Herr Spinell would approach her with immense caution, tiptoeing on his great feet; he would pause two paces off, with his body inclined and one leg behind him, and speak in a voice that was hushed with awe, as though he would lift her higher and higher on the tide of his devotion until she rested on billowy cushions of cloud where no shrill sound nor any earthly touch might reach her. And when he did this she would think of the way Herr Klöterjahn said: "Take care, my angel, keep your mouth closed, Gabriele," a way that made her feel as though he had struck her roughly though well-meaningly on the shoulder. Then as fast as she could she would put the memory away and rest in her weakness and elevation of spirit upon the clouds which Herr Spinell spread out for her.

One day she abruptly returned to the talk they had had about her early life. "Is it really true, Herr Spinell," she asked, "that you would have seen the little gold crown?"

Two weeks had passed since that conversation, yet he knew at once what she meant, and his voice shook as he assured her that he would have seen the little crown as she sat among her friends by the fountain—would have caught its fugitive gleam among her locks.

A few days later one of the guests chanced to make a polite inquiry after the health of little Anton. Herr Klöterjahn's wife gave a quick glance at Herr Spinell, who was standing near, and answered in a perfunctory voice:

"Thanks, how should he be? He and my husband are quite well, of course."

There came a day at the end of February, colder, purer, more brilliant than any that had come before it, and high spirits held sway at Einfried. The "heart cases" consulted in groups, flushed of cheek, the diabetic general caroled like a boy out of school, and the gentlemen of the rebellious legs cast aside all restraint. And the reason for all these things was that a sleighing party was in prospect, an excursion in sledges into the mountains, with cracking whips and sleigh bells jingling. Dr. Leander had arranged this diversion for his patients.

The serious cases, of course, had to stop at home. Poor things! The other guests arranged to keep it from them; it did them good to practice this much sympathy and consideration. But a few of those remained at home who might very well have gone. Fräulein von Osterloh was of course excused, she had too much on her mind to permit her even to think of going. She was needed at home, and at home she remained. But the disappointment was general when Herr Klöterjahn's wife announced her intention of stopping away. Dr. Leander exhorted her to come and get the benefit of the fresh air —but in vain. She said she was not up to it, she had a headache, she felt too weak—they had to resign themselves. The cynical gentleman took occasion to say:

"You will see, the dissipated baby will stop at home too."

And he proved to be right, for Herr Spinell gave out that he intended to "work" that afternoon—he was prone thus to characterize his dubious activities. Anyhow, not a soul regretted his absence; nor did they take more to heart the news that Frau Magistrate Spatz had decided to keep her young friend company at home—sleighing made her feel seasick.

Luncheon on the great day was eaten as early as twelve o'clock, and immediately thereafter the sledges drew up in front of Einfried. The guests came through the garden in little groups, warmly wrapped, excited, full of eager anticipation. Herr Klöterjahn's wife stood with Frau Spatz at the glass door which gave on the terrace, while Herr Spinell watched the setting forth from above, at the window of his room. They saw the little struggles that took place for the best seats, amid joking and laughter; and Fräulein von Osterloh, with a fur boa round her neck, running from one sleigh to the other and shoving baskets of provisions under the seats: they saw Dr. Leander, with his fur cap pulled low on his brow, marshaling the whole scene with his spectacle-lenses glittering, to make sure everything was ready. At last he took his own seat and gave the signal to drive off. The horses started up, a few of the ladies shrieked and collapsed, the bells jingled, the short-shafted whips cracked and their long lashes trailed across the snow; Fräulein von Osterloh stood at the gate waving her handkerchief until the train rounded a curve and disappeared; slowly the merry tinkling died away. Then she turned and hastened back through the garden in pursuit of her duties; the two ladies left the glass door, and almost at the same time Herr Spinell abandoned his post of observation above.

Quiet reigned at Einfried. The party would not return before evening. The serious cases lay in their rooms and suffered. Herr Klöterjahn's wife took a short turn with her friend, then they went to their respective chambers. Herr Spinell kept to his, occupied in his own way. Towards four o'clock the ladies were served with half a liter of milk apiece, and Herr Spinell with a light tea. Soon after, Herr Klöterjahn's wife tapped on the wall between her room and Frau Spatz's and called:

"Shan't we go down to the salon, Frau Spatz? I have nothing to do up here."

"In just a minute, my dear," answered she. "I'll just put on my shoes—if you will wait a minute. I have been lying down."

The salon, naturally, was empty. The ladies took seats by the fireplace. The Frau Magistrate embroidered flowers on a strip of canvas; Herr Klöterjahn's wife took a few stitches too, but soon let her work fall in her lap and, leaning on the arm of her chair, fell to dreaming. At length she made some remark, hardly worth the trouble of opening her lips for; the Frau Magistrate asked what she said, and she had to make the effort of saying it all over again, which quite wore her out. But just then steps were heard outside, the door opened, and Herr Spinell came in.

"Shall I be disturbing you?" he asked mildly from the threshold, addressing Herr Klöterjahn's wife and her alone; bending over her, as it were, from a distance, in the tender, hovering way he had.

The young wife answered:

"Why should you? The room is free to everybody—and besides, why would it be disturbing us? On the contrary, I am convinced that I am boring Frau Spatz."

He had no ready answer, merely smiled and showed his carious teeth, then went hesitatingly up to the glass door, the ladies watching him, and stood with his back to them looking out. Presently he half turned round, still gazing into the garden, and said:

"The sun has gone in. The sky clouded over without our seeing it. The dark is coming on already."

"Yes, it is all overcast," replied Herr Klöterjahn's wife. "It looks as though our sleighing party would have some snow after all. Yesterday at this hour it was still broad daylight, now it is already getting dark."

"Well," he said, "after all these brilliant weeks a little dullness is good for the eyes. The sun shines with the same penetrating clearness upon the lovely and the commonplace, and I for one am positively grateful to it for finally going under a cloud."

"Don't you like the sun, Herr Spinell?"

"Well, I am no painter . . . when there is no sun one becomes more profound. . . . It is a thick layer of grayish-white cloud. Perhaps it means thawing weather for tomorrow. But, madame, let me advise you not to sit there at the back of the room looking at your embroidery."

"Don't be alarmed; I am not looking at it. But what else is there to do?"

He had sat down on the piano stool, resting one arm on the lid of the instrument.

"Music," he said. "If we could only have a little music here. The English children sing darky songs, and that is all."

"And yesterday afternoon Fräulein von Osterloh rendered 'Cloister Bells' at top speed," remarked Herr Klöterjahn's wife.

"But you play, madame!" said he, in an imploring tone. He stood up. "Once you used to play every day with your father."

"Yes, Herr Spinell, in those days I did. In the time of the fountain, you know."

"Play to us today," he begged. "Just a few notes—this once. If you knew how I long for some music—"

"But our family physician, as well as Dr. Leander, expressly forbade it, Herr Spinell."

"But they aren't here—either of them. We are free agents. Just a few bars—"

"No, Herr Spinell, it would be no use. Goodness knows what marvels you expect of me—and I have forgotten everything I knew. Truly. I know scarcely anything by heart."

"Well, then, play that scarcely anything. But there are notes here too. On top of the piano. No, that is nothing. But here is some Chopin." [4]

"Chopin?"

"Yes, the Nocturnes. All we have to do is to light the candles—"

"Pray don't ask me to play, Herr Spinell. I must not. Suppose it were to be bad for me—"

He was silent; standing there in the light of the two candles, with his great feet, in his long black tailcoat, with his beardless face and graying hair. His hands hung down at his sides.

[4] Frédéric Chopin (1810–1849), Polish composer, especially known for his piano music.

"Then, madame, I will ask no more," he said at length, in a low voice. "If you are afraid it will do you harm, then we shall leave the beauty dead and dumb that might have come alive beneath your fingers. You were not always so sensible; at least not when it was the opposite question from what it is today, and you had to decide to take leave of beauty. Then you did not care about your bodily welfare; you showed a firm and unhesitating resolution when you left the fountain and laid aside the little gold crown. Listen," he said, after a pause, and his voice dropped still lower; "if you sit down and play as you used to play when your father stood behind you and brought tears to your eyes with the tones of his violin—who knows but the little gold crown might glimmer once more in your hair. . . ."

"Really," said she, with a smile. Her voice happened to break on the word, it sounded husky and barely audible. She cleared her throat and went on:

"Are those really Chopin's Nocturnes you have there?"

"Yes, here they are open at the place; everything is ready."

"Well, then, in God's name, I will play one," said she. "But only one—do you hear? In any case, one will do you, I am sure."

With which she got up, laid aside her work, and went to the piano. She seated herself on the music stool, on a few bound volumes, arranged the lights, and turned over the notes. Herr Spinell had drawn up a chair and sat beside her, like a music-master.

She played the Nocturne in E-flat major, opus 9, number 2. If her playing had really lost very much then she must originally have been a consummate artist. The piano was mediocre, but after the first few notes she learned to control it. She displayed a nervous feeling for modulations of timbre and a joy in mobility of rhythm that amounted to the fantastic. Her attack was at once firm and soft. Under her hands the very last drop of sweetness was wrung from the melody; the embellishments seemed to cling with slow grace about her limbs.

She wore the same frock as on the day of her arrival, the dark, heavy bodice with the velvet arabesques in high relief, that gave her head and hands such an unearthly fragile look. Her face did not change as she played, but her lips seemed to become more clear-cut, the shadows deepened at the corners of her eyes. When she finished she laid her hands in her lap and went on looking at the notes. Herr Spinell sat motionless.

She played another Nocturne, and then a third. Then she stood up but only to look on the top of the piano for more music.

It occurred to Herr Spinell to look at the black-bound volumes on the piano stool. All at once he uttered an incoherent exclamation, his large white hands clutching at one of the books.

"Impossible! No,it cannot be," he said. "But yes, it is. Guess what this is—what was lying here! Guess what I have in my hands."

"What?" she asked.

Mutely he showed her the title page. He was quite pale; he let the book sink and looked at her, his lips trembling.

"Really? How did that get here? Give it me," was all she said; set the notes on the piano and after a moment's silence began to play.

He sat beside her, bent forward, his hands between his knees, his head bowed. She played the beginning with exaggerated and tormenting slowness, with painfully long pauses between the single figures. The *Sehnsuchts-motiv,*[5] roving lost and forlorn like a voice in the night, lifted its trembling question. Then silence, a waiting. And lo, an answer: the same timorous, lonely note, only clearer, only tenderer. Silence again. And then, with that marvelous muted *sforzando,*[6] like mounting passion, the love-motif came in; reared and soared and yearned ecstatically upward to its consummation, sank back, was resolved; the cellos taking up the melody to carry it on with their deep, heavy notes of rapture and despair.

Not unsuccessfully did the player seek to suggest the orchestral effects upon the poor instrument at her command. The violin runs of the great climax rang out with brilliant precision. She played with a fastidious reverence, lingering on each figure, bringing out each detail, with the self-forgotten concentration of the priest who lifts the Host above his head. Here two forces, two beings, strove towards each other, in transports of joy and pain; here they embraced and became one in delirious yearning after eternity and the absolute. . . . The prelude flamed up and died away. She stopped at the point where the curtains part, and sat speechless, staring at the keys.

But the boredom of Frau Spatz had now reached that pitch where it distorts the countenance of man, makes the eyes protrude from the head, and lends the features a corpselike and terrifying aspect. More than that, this music acted on the nerves that controlled her digestion, producing in her dyspeptic organism such *malaise* that she was really afraid she would have an attack.

"I shall have to go up to my room," she said weakly. Good-bye; I will come back soon."

She went out. Twilight was far advanced. Outside the snow fell thick and soundlessly upon the terrace. The two tapers cast a flickering, circumscribed light.

"The Second Act," he whispered, and she turned the pages and began.

What was it dying away in the distance—the ring of a horn? The rustle of leaves? The rippling of a brook? Silence and night crept up over grove and house; the power of longing had full sway, no prayers or warnings could avail against it. The holy mystery was consummated. The light was

[5] The "longing motif" from Richard Wagner's opera, *Tristan and Isolde.* [6] Literally, forcing. A musical notation meaning to render with special emphasis.

quenched; with a strange clouding of the timbre the death-motif sank down: white-veiled desire, by passion driven, fluttered towards love as through the dark it groped to meet her.

Ah, boundless, unquenchable exultation of union in the eternal beyond! Freed from torturing error, escaped from fettering space and time, the Thou and the I, the Thine and the Mine at one forever in a sublimity of bliss! The day might part them with deluding show; but when night fell, then by the power of the potion they would see clear. To him who has looked upon the night of death and known its secret sweets, to him day never can be aught but vain, nor can he know a longing save for night, eternal, real, in which he is made one with love.

O night of love, sink downwards and enfold them, grant them the oblivion they crave, release them from this world of partings and betrayals. Lo, the last night is quenched. Fancy and thought alike are lost, merged in the mystic shade that spread its wings of healing above their madness and despair. "Now, when deceitful daylight pales, when my raptured eye grows dim, then all that from which the light of day would shut my sight, seeking to blind me with false show, to the stanchless torments of my longing soul—then, ah, then, O wonder of fulfillment, even then I am the world!" Followed Brangäna's dark notes of warning, and then those soaring violins so higher than all reason.

"I cannot understand it all, Herr Spinell. Much of it I only divine. What does it mean, this 'even then I am the world'?"

He explained, in a few low-toned words.

"Yes, yes. It means that. How is it you can understand it all so well yet cannot play it?"

Strangely enough, he was not proof against this simple question. He colored, twisted his hands together, shrank into his chair.

"The two things seldom happen together," he wrung from his lips at last. "No, I cannot play. But go on."

And on they went, into the intoxicated music of the love-mystery. Did love ever die? Tristan's love? The love of thy Isolde, and of mine? Ah, no, death cannot touch that which can never die—and what of him could die, save what distracts and tortures love and severs united lovers? Love joined the two in sweet conjunction, death was powerless to sever such a bond, save only when death was given to one with the very life of the other. Their voices rose in mystic unison, rapt in the wordless hope of that death-in-love, of endless oneness in the wonder-kingdom of the night. Sweet night! Eternal night of love! And all-encompassing land of rapture! Once envisaged or divined, what eye could bear to open again on desolate dawn? Forfend such fears, most gentle death! Release these lovers quite from need of waking. Oh, tumultuous storm of rhythms! Oh, glad chromatic upward surge of metaphysical perception! How find, how bind this bliss so far remote from parting's torturing pangs? Ah, gentle glow of longing, soothing and kind, ah, yielding sweet-sublime, ah, raptured sinking into the twilight of eternity! Thou Isolde, Tristan I, yet no more Tristan, no more Isolde. . . .

All at once something startling happened. The musician broke off and peered into the darkness with her hand above her eyes. Herr Spinnell turned round quickly in his chair. The corridor door had opened, a sinister form appeared, leant on the arm of a second form. It was a guest of Einfried, one of those who, like themselves, had been in no state to undertake the sleigh-ride, but had passed this twilight hour in one of her pathetic, instinctive rounds of the house. It was that patient who had borne fourteen children and was no longer capable of a single thought; it was Frau Pastor Höhlenrauch, on the arm of her nurse. She did not look up; with groping step she paced the dim background of the room and vanished by the opposite door, rigid and still, like a lost and wandering soul. Stillness reigned once more.

"That was Frau Pastor Höhlenrauch," he said.

"Yes, that was poor Frau Höhlenrauch," she answered. Then she turned over some leaves and played the finale, played Isolde's song of love and death.

How colorless and clear were her lips, how deep the shadows lay beneath her eyes! The little pale-blue vein in her transparent brow showed fearfully plain and prominent. Beneath her flying fingers the music mounted to its unbelievable climax and was resolved in that ruthless, sudden *pianissimo* which is like having the ground glide from beneath one's feet, yet like a sinking too into the very deeps of desire. Followed the immeasurable plenitude of that vast redemption and fulfillment; it was repeated, swelled into a deafening, unquenchable tumult of immense appeasement that wove and welled and seemed about to die away, only to swell again and weave the *Sehnsuchtsmotiv* into its harmony; at length to breathe an outward breath and die, faint on the air, and soar away. Profound stillness.

They both listened, their heads on one side.

"Those are bells," she said.

"It is the sleighs," he said. "I will go now."

He rose and walked across the room. At the door he halted, then turned and shifted uneasily from one foot to the other. And then, some fifteen or twenty paces from her, it came to pass that he fell upon his knees, both knees, without a sound. His long black coat spread out on the floor. He held his hands clasped over his mouth, and his shoulders heaved.

She sat there with hands in her lap, leaning forward, turned away from the piano, and looked at him. Her face wore a distressed, uncertain smile, while her eyes searched the dimness at the back of the room, searched so painfully, so dreamily, she seemed hardly able to focus her gaze.

The jingling of sleigh bells came nearer and nearer, there was the crack of whips, a babel of voices.

The sleighing party had taken place on the twenty-sixth of February, and was talked of for long afterwards. The next day, February twenty-seventh, a day of thaw, that set everything to melting and dripping, splashing and running, Herr Klöterjahn's wife was in capital health and spirits. On the twenty-eighth she brought up a little blood—not much, still it was blood, and accompanied by a far greater loss of strength than ever before. She went to bed.

Dr. Leander examined her, stony-faced. He prescribed according to the dictates of science—morphia, little pieces of ice, absolute quiet. Next day, on account of pressure of work, he turned her case over to Dr. Müller, who took it on in humility and meekness of spirit and according to the letter of his contract—a quiet, pallid, insignificant little man, whose unadvertised activities were consecrated to the care of the slight cases and the hopeless ones.

Dr. Müller presently expressed the view that the separation between Frau Klöterjahn and her spouse had lasted overlong. It would be well if Herr Klöterjahn, in case his flourishing business permitted, were to make another visit to Einfried. One might write him—or even wire. And surely it would benefit the young mother's health and spirits if he were to bring young Anton with him—quite aside from the pleasure it would give the physicians to behold with their own eyes this so healthy little Anton.

And Herr Klöterjahn came. He got Dr. Müller's little wire and arrived from the Baltic coast. He got out of the carriage, ordered coffee and rolls, and looked considerably aggrieved.

"My dear sir," he asked, "what is the matter? Why have I been summoned?"

"Because it is desirable that you should be near your wife," Dr. Müller replied.

"Desirable! Desirable! But is it *necessary?* It is a question of expense with me—times are poor and railway journeys cost money. Was it imperative I should take this whole day's journey? If it were the lungs that are attacked, I should say nothing. But as it is only the trachea, thank God—"

"Herr Klöterjahn," said Dr. Müller mildly, "in the first place the trachea is an important organ. . . ." He ought not to have said "in the first place," because he did not go on to the second.

But there also arrived at Einfried, in Herr Klöterjahn's company, a full-figured personage arrayed all in red and gold and plaid, and she it was who carried on her arm Anton Klöterjahn, junior, that healthy little Anton. Yes, there he was, and nobody could deny that he was healthy even to excess. Pink and white and plump and fragrant, in fresh and immaculate attire, he rested heavily upon the bare red arm of his bebraided body-servant, consumed huge quantities of milk and chopped beef, shouted and screamed, and in every way surrendered himself to his instincts.

Our author from the window of his chamber had seen him arrive. With a peculiar gaze, both veiled and piercing, he fixed young Anton with his eye as he was carried from the carriage into the house. He stood there a long time with the same expression on his face.

Herr Spinell was sitting in his room "at work."

His room was like all the others at Einfried—old-fashioned, simple, and distinguished. The massive chest of drawers was mounted with brass lions' heads; the tall mirror on the wall was not a single surface, but made up of many little panes set in lead. There was no carpet on the polished blue paved floor, the stiff legs of the furniture prolonged themselves on it in clear-cut shadows. A spacious writing table stood at the window, across whose panes the author had drawn the folds of a yellow curtain, in all probability that he might feel more retired.

In the yellow twilight he bent over the table and wrote—wrote one of those numerous letters which he sent weekly to the post and to which, quaintly enough, he seldom or never received an answer. A large, thick quire of paper lay before him, in whose upper left-hand corner was a curious involved drawing of a landscape and the name Detlev Spinell in the very latest thing in lettering. He was covering the page with a small, painfully neat, and punctiliously traced script.

"Sir:" he wrote, "I address the following lines to you because I cannot help it; because what I have to say so fills and shakes and tortures me, the words come in such a rush, that I should choke if I did not take this means to relieve myself."

If the truth were told, this about the rush of words was quite simply wide of the fact. And God knows what sort of vanity it was made Herr Spinell put it down. For his words did not come in a rush; they came with such pathetic slowness, considering the man was a writer by trade, you would have drawn the conclusion, watching him, that a writer is one to whom writing comes harder than to anybody else.

He held between two fingertips one of those curious downy hairs he had on his cheek, and twirled it round and round, whole quarter-hours at a time, gazing into space and not coming forwards by a single line; then wrote a few words, daintily, and stuck again. Yet so much was true: that what had managed to get written sounded fluent and vigorous, though the matter was odd enough, even almost equivocal, and at times impossible to follow.

"I feel," the letter went on, "an imperative necessity to make you see what I see; to show you through my eyes, illuminated by the same power of language that clothes them for me, all the things which have stood before my inner eye for weeks, like an indelible vision. It is my habit to yield to the impulse which urges me to put my own experiences into flamingly right and unforgettable words and to give them to the world. And therefore hear me.

"I will do no more than relate what has been and what is: I will merely tell a story, a brief, unspeakable touching story, without comment, blame, or passing of judgment; simply in my own words. It is the story of Gabriele Eckhof, of the woman whom you, sir, call your wife—and mark you this: it is your story, it happened to you, yet it will be I who will for the first time lift it for you to the level of an experience.

"Do you remember the garden, the old, overgrown garden behind the gray patrician house? The moss was green in the crannies of its weather-beaten wall, and behind the wall dreams and neglect held sway. Do you remember the fountain in the center? The pale mauve lilies leaned over its crumbling rim, the little stream prattled softly as it fell upon the riven paving. The summer day was drawing to its close.

"Seven maidens sat circlewise round the fountain; but the seventh, or rather the first and only one, was not like the others, for the sinking sun seemed to be weaving a queenly coronal among her locks. Her eyes were like troubled dreams, and yet her pure lips wore a smile.

"They were singing. They lifted their little faces to the leaping streamlet and watched its charming curve droop earthward—their music hovered round it as it leaped and danced. Perhaps their slim hands were folded in their laps the while they sang.

"Can you, sir, recall the scene? Or did you ever see it? No, you saw it not. Your eyes were not formed to see it nor your ears to catch the chaste music of their song. You saw it not, or else you would have forbade your lungs to breathe, your heart to beat. You must have turned aside and gone back to your own life, taking with you what you had seen to preserve it in the depth of your soul to the end of your earthly life, a sacred and inviolable relic. But what did you do?

"That scene, sir, was an end and culmination. Why did you come to spoil it, to give it a sequel, to turn it into the channels of ugly and commonplace life? It was a peaceful apotheosis and a moving, bathed in a sunset beauty of decadence, decay, and death. An ancient stock, too exhausted and refined for life and action, stood there at the end of its days; its latest manifestations were those of art: violin notes, full of that melancholy understanding which is ripeness for death. . . . Did you look into her eyes—those eyes where tears so often stood, lured by the dying sweetness of the violin? Her six friends may have had souls that belonged to life; but hers, the queen's and sister's, death and beauty had claimed for their own.

"You saw it, that deathly beauty; saw, and coveted. The sight of that touching purity moved you with no awe or trepidation. And it was not enough for you to see, you must possess, you must use, you must desecrate. . . . It was the refinement of a choice you made—you are a gourmand, sir, a plebeian gourmand, a peasant with taste.

"Once more let me say that I have no wish to offend you. What I have just said is not an affront; it is a statement, a simple, psychological statement of your simple personality—a personality which for literary purposes is entirely uninteresting. I make the statement solely because I feel an impulse to clarify for you your own thoughts and actions; because it is my inevitable task on this earth to call things by their right names, to make them speak, to illuminate the unconscious. The world is full of what I call the unconscious type, and I cannot endure it; I cannot endure all these unconscious types! I cannot bear all this dull, uncomprehending, unperceiving living and behaving, this world of maddening naiveté about me! It tortures me until I am driven irresistibly to set it all in relief, in the round, to explain, express, and make self-conscious everything in the world—so far as my powers will reach—quite unhampered by the result, whether it be for good or evil, whether it brings consolation and healing or piles grief on grief.

"You, sir, as I said, are a plebeian gourmand, a peasant with taste. You stand upon an extremely low evolutionary level; your own constitution is coarse-fibered. But wealth and a sedentary habit of life have brought about in you a corruption of the nervous system, as sudden as it is unhistoric; and this corruption has been accompanied by a lascivious refinement in your choice of gratifications. It is altogether possible that the muscles of your gullet began to contract, as at the sight of some particularly rare dish, when you conceived the idea of making Gabriele Eckhof your own.

"In short, you lead her idle will astray, you beguile her out of that moss-grown garden into the ugliness of life, you give her your own vulgar name and make of her a married woman, a housewife, a mother. You take that deathly beauty—spent, aloof, flowering in lofty unconcern of the uses of this world—and debase it to the service of common things, you sacrifice it to that stupid, contemptible, clumsy graven image we call 'nature'—and not the faintest suspicion of the vileness of your conduct visits your peasant soul.

"Again. What is the result? This being, whose eyes are like troubled dreams, she bears you a child; and so doing she endows the new life, a gross continuation of its author's own, with all the blood, all the physical energy she possesses—and she dies. She dies, sir! And if she does not go hence with your vulgarity upon her head; if at the very last she has lifted herself out of the depths of degradation, and passes in an ecstasy, with the deathly kiss of beauty on her brow—well, it is I, sir, who have seen to that! You, meanwhile, were probably spending your time with chambermaids in dark corners.

"But your son, Gabriele Eckhof's son, is alive; he is living and flourishing. Perhaps he will continue in the way of his father, become a well-fed, trading, tax-paying citizen; a capable, philistine pillar of society; in any case, a tone-deaf, normally functioning individual, responsible, sturdy, and stupid, troubled by not a doubt.

"Kindly permit me to tell you, sir, that I hate you. I hate you and your child, as I hate the life of which you are the representative: cheap, ridiculous, but yet triumphant life, the everlasting antipodes and deadly enemy of beauty. I cannot say I despise you—for I am honest. You are stronger than I. I have no armor for the struggle between us, I have only the Word, avenging weapon of the weak. Today I have availed myself of this weapon. This letter is nothing but an act of revenge—you see how honorable I am —and if any word of mine is sharp and bright and beautiful enough to strike home, to make you feel the presence of a power you do not know, to shake even a minute your robust equilibrium, I shall rejoice indeed.—DETLEV SPINELL."

And Herr Spinell put this screed into an envelope, applied a stamp and a many-flourished address, and committed it to the post.

Herr Klöterjahn knocked on Herr Spinell's door. He carried a sheet of paper in his hand covered with neat script, and he looked like a man bent on energetic action. The post office had done its duty, the letter had taken its appointed way: it had traveled from Einfried to Einfried and reached the hand for which it was meant. It was now four o'clock in the afternoon.

Herr Klöterjahn's entry found Herr Spinell sitting on the sofa reading his own novel with the appalling cover design. He rose and gave his caller a surprised and inquiring look, though at the same time he distinctly flushed.

"Good afternoon," said Herr Klöterjahn. "Pardon the interruption. But may I ask if you wrote this?" He held up in his left hand the sheet inscribed with fine clear characters and struck it with the back of his right and made it crackle. Then he stuffed that hand into the pocket of his easy-fitting trousers, put his head on one side, and opened his mouth, in a way some people have, to listen.

Herr Spinell, curiously enough, smiled; he smiled engagingly, with a rather confused, apologetic air. He put his hand to his head as though trying to recollect himself, and said:

"Ah!—yes, quite right, I took the liberty—"

The fact was, he had given in to his natural man today and slept nearly up to midday, with the result that he was suffering from a bad conscience and a heavy head, was nervous and incapable of putting up a fight. And the spring air made him limp and good-for-nothing. So much we must say in extenuation of the utterly silly figure he cut in the interview which followed.

"Ah? Indeed! Very good!" said Herr Klöterjahn. He dug his chin into his chest, elevated his brows, stretched his arms, and indulged in various other antics by way of getting down to business after his introductory question.

But unfortunately he so much enjoyed the figure he cut that he rather overshot the mark, and the rest of the scene hardly lived up to this preliminary pantomime. However, Herr Spinell went rather pale.

"Very good!" repeated Herr Klöterjahn. "Then permit me to give you an answer in person; it strikes me as idiotic to write pages of letter to a person when you can speak to him any hour of the day."

"Well, idiotic . . ." Herr Spinell said, with his apologetic smile. He sounded almost meek.

"Idiotic!" repeated Herr Klöterjahn, nodding violently in token of the soundness of his position. "And I should not demean myself to answer this scrawl; to tell the truth, I should have thrown it away at once if I had not found in it the explanation of certain changes—however, that is no affair of yours, and has nothing to do with the thing anyhow. I am a man of action, I have other things to do than to think about your unspeakable visions."

"I wrote *'indelible vision,'* " said Herr Spinell, drawing himself up. This was the only moment at which he displayed a little self-respect.

"Indelible, unspeakable," responded Herr Klöterjahn, referring to the text. "You write a villainous hand, sir; you would not get a position in my office, let me tell you. It looks clear enough at first, but when you come to study it, it is full of shakes and quavers. But that is your affair, it's no business of mine. What I have come to say to you is that you are a tomfool—which you probably know already. Furthermore, you are a cowardly sneak; I don't suppose I have to give the evidence for that either. My wife wrote me once that when you meet a woman you don't look her square in the face, but just give her a side squint, so as to carry away a good impression, because you are afraid of the reality. I should probably have heard more of the same sort of stories about you, only unfortunately she stopped mentioning you. But this is the kind of thing you are: you talk so much about 'beauty'; you are all chicken-livered hypocrisy and cant—which is probably at the bottom of your impudent allusion to out-of-the-way corners too. That ought to crush me, of course, but it just makes me laugh—it doesn't do a thing but make me laugh! Understand? Have I clarified your thoughts and actions for you, you pitiable object, you? Though of course it is not my invariable calling—"

" *'Inevitable'* was the word I used," Herr Spinell said; but he did not insist on the point. He stood there, crestfallen, like a big, unhappy, chidden, gray-haired schoolboy.

"Invariable or inevitable, whichever you like—anyhow you are a contemptible cur, and that I tell you. You see me every day at table, you bow and smirk and say good morning—and one fine day you send me a scrawl full of idiotic abuse. Yes, you've a lot of courage—on paper! And it's not only this ridiculous letter—you have been intriguing behind my back. I can see that now. Though you need not flatter yourself it did any good. If you imagine you put any ideas into my wife's head you never were more mistaken in your life. And if you think she behaved any different when we came from what she always does, then you just put the cap onto your own foolishness. She did not kiss the little chap, that's true, but it was only a precaution, because they have the idea now that the trouble is with her lungs, and in such cases you can't tell whether—though that still remains to be proved, no matter what you say with your 'She dies, sir,' you silly ass!"

Here Herr Klöterjahn paused for breath. He was in a furious passion; he kept stabbing the air with his right forefinger and crumpling the sheet of paper in his other hand. His face, between the blond English muttonchops, was frightfully red and his dark brow was rent with swollen veins like lightnings of scorn.

"You hate me," he went on, "and you would despise me if I were not stronger than you. Yes, you're right there! I've got my heart in the right place, by God, and you've got yours mostly in the seat of your trousers. I would most certainly hack you into bits if it weren't against the law, you and your gabble about the 'Word,' you skulking fool! But I have no intention of putting up with your insults; and when I show this part about the vulgar name to my lawyer at home, you will very likely get a little surprise. My name, sir, is a first-rate name, and I have made it so by my own efforts. You know better than I do whether anybody would ever lend you a penny piece on yours, you lazy lout! The law defends people against the kind you are! You are a common danger, you are enough to drive a body crazy! But you're left this time, my master! I don't let individuals like you get the best of me so fast! I've got my heart in the right place—"

Herr Klöterjahn's excitement had really reached a pitch. He shrieked, he bellowed, over and over again, that his heart was in the right place.

" 'They were singing.' Exactly. Well, they weren't. They were knitting. And if I heard what they said, it was about a recipe for potato pancakes; and when I show my father-in-law that about the old decayed family you'll probably have a libel suit on your hands. 'Did you see the picture?' Yes, of course I saw it; only I don't see why that should make me hold my breath and run away. I don't leer at women out of the corner of my eye; I look at them square, and if I like their looks I go for them. I have my heart in the right place—"

Somebody knocked. Knocked eight or ten times, quite fast, one after the other—a sudden, alarming little commotion that made Herr Klöterjahn pause; and an unsteady voice that kept tripping over itself in its haste and distress said:

"Herr Klöterjahn, Herr Klöterjahn—oh, is Herr Klöterjahn there?"

"Stop outside," said Herr Klöterjahn, in a growl. . . . "What's the matter? I'm busy talking."

"Oh, Herr Klöterjahn," said the quaking, breaking voice, "you must come! The doctors are there too—oh, it is all so dreadfully sad—"

He took one step to the door and tore it open. Frau Magistrate Spatz was standing there. She had her handkerchief before her mouth, and great egg-shaped tears rolled into it, two by two.

"Herr Klöterjahn," she got out. "It is so frightfully sad. . . . She has brought up so much blood, such a horrible lot of blood. . . . She was sitting up quite quietly in bed and humming a little snatch of music . . . and there it came . . . my God, such a quantity you never saw. . . ."

"Is she dead?" yelled Herr Klöterjahn. As he spoke he clutched the Rätin by the arm and pulled her to and fro on the sill. "Not quite? Not dead; she can see me, can't she? Brought up a little blood again, from the lung, eh? Yes, I give in, it may be from the lung. Gabriele!" he suddenly cried out, and his eyes filled with tears; you could see what a burst of good, warm, honest human feeling came over him. "Yes, I'm coming," he said, and dragged the Rätin after him as he went with long strides down the corridor. You could still hear his voice, from quite a distance, sounding fainter and fainter. "Not quite, eh? From the lung?"

Herr Spinell stood still on the spot where he had stood during the whole of Herr Klöterjahn's rudely interrupted call and looked out the open door. At length he took a couple of steps and listened down the corridor. But all was quiet, so he closed the door and came back into the room.

He looked at himself awhile in the glass, then he went up to the writing table, took a little flask and a glass out of a drawer, and drank a cognac—for which nobody can blame him. Then he stretched himself out on the sofa and closed his eyes.

The upper half of the window was down. Outside in the garden birds were twittering; those dainty, saucy little notes held all the spring, finely and penetratingly expressed. Herr Spinell spoke once: *"Invariable calling,"* he said, and moved his head and drew in the air through his teeth as though his nerves pained him violently.

Impossible to recover any poise or tranquillity. Crude experiences like this were too much—he was not made for them. By a sequence of emotions, the analysis of which would lead us too far afield, Herr Spinell arrived at the decision that it would be well for him to have a little out-of-doors exercise. He took his hat and went downstairs.

As he left the house and issued into the mild, fragrant air, he turned his head and lifted his eyes, slowly, scanning the house until he reached one of the windows, a curtained window, on which his gaze rested awhile, fixed and somber. Then he laid his hands on his back and moved away across the gravel path. He moved in deep thought.

The beds were still straw-covered, the trees and bushes bare; but the snow was gone, the path was only damp in spots. The large garden with its grottoes, bowers and little pavilions lay in the splendid colorful afternoon light, strong shadow and rich, golden sun, and the dark network of branches stood out sharp and articulate against the bright sky.

It was about that hour of the afternoon when the sun takes shape, and from being a formless volume of light turns to a visibly sinking disk, whose milder, more saturated glow the eye can tolerate. Herr Spinell did not see the sun, the direction the path took hid it from his view. He walked with bent head and hummed a strain of music, a short phrase, a figure that mounted wailingly and complainingly upward—the *Sehnsuchtsmotiv*. . . . But suddenly, with a start, a quick, jerky intake of breath, he stopped, as though rooted to the path, and gazed straight ahead of him, with brows fiercely gathered, staring eyes, and an expression of horrified repulsion.

The path had curved just here, he was facing the setting sun. It stood large and slantwise in the sky, crossed by two narrow strips of gold-rimmed cloud; it set the tree tops aglow and poured its red-gold radiance across the garden. And there, erect in the path, in the midst of the glory, with the sun's mighty aureola above her head, there confronted him an exuberant figure, all arrayed in red and gold and plaid. She had one hand on her swelling hip, with the other she moved to and fro the graceful little perambulator. And in this perambulator sat the child—sat Anton Klöterjahn, junior, Gabriele Eckhof's fat son.

There he sat among his cushions, in a woolly white jacket and large white hat, plump-cheeked, well cared for, and magnificent; and his blithe unerring gaze encountered Herr Spinell's. The novelist pulled himself together. Was he not a man, had he not the power to pass this unexpected, sun-kindled apparition there in the path and continue on his walk? But Anton Klöterjahn began to laugh and shout—most horrible to see. He squealed, he crowed with inconceivable delight—it was positively uncanny to hear him.

God knows what had taken him; perhaps the sight of Herr Spinell's long, black figure set him off; perhaps an attack of sheer animal spirits gave rise to his wild outburst of merriment. He had a bone teething ring in one hand and a tin rattle in the other; and these two objects he flung aloft with shoutings, shook them to and fro, and clashed them together in the air, as though purposely to frighten Herr Spinell. His eyes were almost shut, his mouth gaped open till all the rosy gums were displayed; and as he shouted he rolled his head about in excess of mirth.

Herr Spinell turned round and went thence. Pursued by the youthful Klöterjahn's joyous screams, he went away across the gravel, walking stiffly, yet not without grace; his gait was the hesitating gait of one who would disguise the fact that, inwardly, he is running away.

Selected Poems

of

William Butler Yeats

William Butler Yeats (1865–1939)

WILLIAM BUTLER YEATS WAS BORN IN DUBLIN, BUT IT WAS Sligo, in the west of Ireland—a land of Celtic myth and mystery—that was Yeats's true homeland, and it was there that he eventually settled. As a young man he pursued a literary career in London, where he joined the circle of poets known as the Rhymers' Club, came under the influence of French Symbolism (especially Mallarmé), and also became interested in the Irish nationalist movement and the Irish cultural "renaissance." In 1900, back in Dublin, he helped to found the famous Abbey Theatre, where much of the revival of Irish culture found expression. He also fell in love with the beautiful Maud Gonne, but she became involved in the Irish nationalist movement and gave her life to revolutionary politics. Yeats became an immensely respected poet in Ireland, was elected a senator in the new Irish Free State, and was awarded the Nobel Prize in 1923.

Yeats's poetic career shows an extraordinary record of self-renewal, of growth, of constant movement toward new achievements. Beginning as a poet within the late Romantic tradition (his first master was Tennyson), identified with the writers of the "Celtic Twilight" school, employing a mystical and incantatory style, he then moved toward a more direct and dramatic poetry, influenced by his experience writing for the Abbey Theatre. In the poems of *The Tower,* he seemed to have reached the height of his powers with intense and difficult lyrics that return again and again to central questions of art and its relation to life. But Yeats did not stop there; in the last years of his life, he moved to a new style of spare, almost awkward, lyricism, to ballad forms, popular speech, and wrote a poetry of "madness," that celebrates the body and its desires, confronts age and decay, and proclaims the necessity of constant self-renewal.

Yeats stands with Shakespeare, Milton, and Wordsworth as one of the greatest English poets. The six poems given here represent a range from his middle period of dramatic lyrics ("No Second Troy") through the complex philosophical lyrics of *The Tower* ("Sailing to Byzantium," "Leda and the Swan," "Among School Children"), in which he asks questions about the artistic life removed from the world's flux (a life symbolized by the "holy city of Byzantium") and about the relation of the art produced by such a life to human history. The last two poems ("Crazy Jane Talks with the Bishop" and "An Acre of Grass") are from Yeats' poetry of "mad old age."

Selected Poems

No Second Troy

Why should I blame her that she filled my days
With misery, or that she would of late
Have taught to ignorant men most violent ways,
Or hurled the little streets upon the great,
Had they but courage equal to desire?
What could have made her peaceful with a mind
That nobleness made simple as a fire,
With beauty like a tightened bow, a kind
That is not natural in an age like this,
Being high and solitary and most stern?
Why, what could she have done, being what she is?
Was there another Troy for her to burn? °

*Sailing to Byzantium**

I

That is no country for old men. The young
In one another's arms, birds in the trees
—Those dying generations—at their song,
The salmon-falls, the mackerel-crowded seas,
Fish, flesh, or fowl, commend all summer long
Whatever is begotten, born, and dies.
Caught in that sensual music all neglect
Monuments of unageing intellect.

12. her: reference to Yeats's love, Maud Gonne, who became active in the Irish revolutionary movement. She is implicitly compared to Helen, whose abduction by Paris caused the Trojan War. * *Byzantium:* capital of the Eastern Roman Empire and holy city of the Greek Orthodox Church, noted for its stylized art and high intellectual traditions.

II

An aged man is but a paltry thing,
A tattered coat upon a stick, unless
Soul clap its hands and sing, and louder sing
For every tatter in its mortal dress,
Nor is there singing school but studying
Monuments of its own magnificence;
And therefore I have sailed the seas and come
To the holy city of Byzantium.

III

O sages standing in God's holy fire
As in the gold mosaic of a wall,
Come from the holy fire, perne in a gyre,°
And be the singing-masters of my soul.
Consume my heart away; sick with desire
And fastened to a dying animal
It knows not what it is; and gather me
Into the artifice of eternity.

IV

Once out of nature I shall never take
My bodily form from any natural thing,
But such a form° as Grecian goldsmiths make
Of hammered gold and gold enamelling
To keep a drowsy Emperor awake;
Or set upon a golden bough to sing
To lords and ladies of Byzantium
Of what is past, or passing, or to come.

Leda and the Swan*

A sudden blow: the great wings beating still
Above the staggering girl, her thighs caressed

19. perne in a gyre: spin in a spiral motion, like a spool. *27. form:* "I have read somewhere that in the Emperor's palace at Byzantium was a tree made of gold and silver, and artificial birds that sang" (Yeats). * *Leda:* raped by Zeus (Jupiter), who had taken the form of a swan to disguise himself. From this union was born the world's most beautiful woman, Helen, whose abduction from her husband, Menelaus, by the Trojan Paris caused the Trojan war. (See "No Second Troy" and, in Volume I, *The Iliad.*)

By the dark webs, her nape caught in his bill
He holds her helpless breast upon his breast.

How can those terrified vague fingers push
The feathered glory from her loosening thighs?
And how can body, laid in that white rush,
But feel the strange heart beating where it lies?

A shudder in the loins engenders there
The broken wall, the burning roof and tower°
And Agamemnon° dead.
                    Being so caught up,
So mastered by the brute blood of the air,
Did she put on his knowledge with his power
Before the indifferent beak could let her drop?

Among School Children

I

I walk through the long schoolroom questioning;
A kind old nun in a white hood replies;
The children learn to cipher and to sing
To study reading-books and history,
To cut and sew, be neat in everything
In the best modern way—the children's eyes
In momentary wonder stare upon
A sixty-year-old smiling public man.

II

I dream of a Ledaean° body, bent
Above a sinking fire, a tale that she
Told of a harsh reproof, or trivial event
That changed some childish day to tragedy—
Told, and it seemed that our two natures blent
Into a sphere from youthful sympathy,
Or else, to alter Plato's parable,°
Into the yolk and white of the one shell.

10. broken wall . . . to war: References to the destruction of Troy by the Greeks. *11. Agamemnon:* brother of Menelaus and leader of the Greek army. He met death at the hands of his unfaithful wife, Clytemnestra, upon his return from the Trojan War. (See Aeschylus, *Agamemnon,* in Volume I.) *9. Ledean:* like Leda and her daughter, Helen of Troy. *15: Plato's parable:* parable in which human beings were originally spherical, then divided in half; one half continued to long to rejoin the other.

III

And thinking of that fit of grief or rage
I look upon one child or t'other there
And wonder if she stood so at that age—
For even daughters of the swan can share
Something of every paddler's heritage—
And had that colour upon cheek or hair,
And thereupon my heart is driven wild:
She stands before me as a living child.

IV

Her present image floats into the mind—
Did Quattrocento finger° fashion it
Hollow of cheek as though it drank the wind
And took a mess of shadows for its meat?
And I though never of Ledaean kind
Had pretty plumage once—enough of that,
Better to smile on all that smile, and show
There is a comfortable kind of old scarecrow.

V

What youthful mother, a shape upon her lap
Honey of generation° had betrayed,
And that must sleep, shriek, struggle to escape
As recollection or the drug decide,
Would think her son, did she but see that shape
With sixty or more winters on its head,
A compensation for the pang of his birth,
Or the uncertainty of his setting forth?

VI

Plato° thought nature but a spume that plays
Upon a ghostly paradigm of things;
Solider Aristotle° played the taws°
Upon the bottom of a king of kings;

26. *Quattrocento finger:* artists of the fifteenth century in Italy, such as Botticelli (1444?–1510), who painted thin women with hollowed cheeks. 34. *Honey of generation:* this may mean sexual desire or the pleasure the soul feels in first being born. 41. *Plato:* nature to Plato is an appearance or shadow; the true reality lies in the spiritual form. 43. *Aristotle:* called "solider" because he located reality in matter as well. *played the taws:* Aristotle was tutor to Alexander the Great, whom he is here imagined as having whipped with a leather strap (the taws).

World-famous golden-thighed Pythagoras°
Fingered upon a fiddle-stick or strings
What a star sang and careless Muses heard:
Old clothes upon old sticks to scare a bird.

VII

Both nuns and mothers worship images,
But those the candles light are not as those
That animate a mother's reveries,
But keep a marble or a bronze repose.
And yet they too break hearts—O Presences
That passion, piety or affection knows,
And that all heavenly glory symbolize—
O self-born mockers of man's enterprise;

VIII

Labour is blossoming or dancing where
The body is not bruised to pleasure soul,
Nor beauty born out of its own despair,
Nor blear-eyed wisdom out of midnight oil.
O chestnut-tree, great-rooted blossomer,
Are you the leaf, the blossom or the bole?
O body swayed to music, O brightening glance,
How can we know the dancer from the dance?

Crazy Jane Talks with the Bishop

I met the Bishop on the road
And much said he and I.
"Those breasts are flat and fallen now,
Those veins must soon be dry;
Live in a heavenly mansion,
Not in some foul sty."

"Fair and foul are near of kin,
And fair needs foul," I cried.
"My friends are gone, but that's a truth
Nor grave nor bed denied,

45. *Pythagoras:* early Greek philosopher regarded by his disciples as a god with a golden thigh. He formulated the doctrine of the "harmony of the spheres."

Learned in bodily lowliness
And in the heart's pride.

"A woman can be proud and stiff
When on love intent;
But Love has pitched his mansions in
The place of excrement;
For nothing can be sole or whole
That has not been rent."

An Acre of Grass

Picture and book remain,
An acre of green grass
For air and exercise,
Now strength of body goes;
Midnight, an old house
Where nothing stirs but a mouse.

My temptation is quiet.
Here at life's end
Neither loose imagination,
Nor the mill of the mind
Consuming its rag and bone,
Can make the truth known.

Grant me an old man's frenzy,
Myself must I remake
Till I am Timon and Lear°
Or that William Blake°
Who beat upon the wall
Till Truth obeyed his call;

A mind Michael Angelo° knew
That can pierce the clouds.
Or inspired by frenzy
Shake the dead in their shrouds;
Forgotten else by mankind,
An old man's eagle mind.

15. Timon and Lear: two of Shakespeare's "mad old men" who come to their own visions of truth. *16. Blake:* poet and mystic who perceived visions of divine Truth. (See "Mock on, Mock on," p. 121.) *19. Michael Angelo:* Italian painter and sculptor (1475–1564), who painted the Sistine Ceiling and the Last Judgment.

Symbolist and Modernist Poetry

Symbolism as a poetic movement develops from Romanticism. It continues and intensifies the Romantic emphasis on inner experience and the high role given to the poetic imagination as the chief force for ordering the world's phenomena. But in relation to Romanticism, Symbolism marks a turning-away from direct confrontation with the world toward a confrontation with art itself. The Symbolist poem typically is about the act of artistic creation itself, the mind's attempt to bring order out of chaos, and the poet's difficult relation to the world and to his art. The language of Symbolist poetry tends to be less direct than it was in the emotional outpourings of Romanticism, and more elusive in its relation to reality. The poetic image takes on a new value and autonomy that gives it the status of an all-pervasive "symbol." Symbolism may indeed be regarded as man's concerted effort, in a world where religious belief no longer holds sway, to devise a secular religion of art.

Symbolism was initially a French movement that later penetrated other European countries. Charles Baudelaire was the key figure in the transition from Romanticism to Symbolism because he summed up all the Romantic themes and first developed the expressive techniques of the Symbolists. Stéphane Mallarmé was the most typical figure; his dedication to an art of almost impossible perfection and difficulty made him an artistic hero to young writers from many countries, among them James Joyce, W. B. Yeats, Rainer Maria Rilke, and Wallace Stevens, who were all directly or indirectly influenced by his example.

Modernist is a vaguer term than Symbolist. It may be taken to encompass all the attempts by English and American poets around the turn of the century to renew poetic forms and language and to infuse into poetry a sense of modern life and its issues. It represents a reaction against Romanticism, especially the late-Romantic style of the Victorians—a desire to "make it new" (in the words of Ezra Pound, a chief spokesman and influence), to forge a more direct and muscular style, and to give new vividness to the poetic image as a unique marriage of the abstract and the concrete.

Movements and labels are finally less important than the fact that the poets represented in the following pages are all among the major shapers of twentieth-century poetry, the modern masters in terms of whom younger generations of poets still must define themselves.

Symbolist and Modernist Poetry

Charles Baudelaire (1821–1867)

With his volume *Les Fleurs du mal* (in which "Spleen" is a central poem), Baudelaire brought to French poetry a revolution in style and theme comparable to that worked by Wordsworth in England. In his esthetic theories and his poetic art, he is a prime source of the modern temper in literature.

Spleen

I am like the king of a rainy country,
rich but powerless, senile and yet still young,
who scorning his councillors' flattery, tires
of his dogs and of other animals too—
neither hunt nor hawking can entertain him,
nor his subjects dying outside the palace.
His favorite fool's songs no longer brighten
the eyes in this cruel invalid's face.
The royal bed is becoming a royal tomb,
and the court ladies, who find all princes fair
game, can no longer invent gowns daring enough
to draw a smile from this callow skeleton.
His alchemist turns lead to gold, yet never
could distill the corruption out of his soul,
and even bloodbaths in the true Roman style
(the kind grand old men still reminisce about)
fail to warm this besotted corpse in whose veins,
rather than blood, green Lethe's absinthe° runs.

—TR. RICHARD HOWARD

18. absinthe: a drugging drink, made from wormwood.

Arthur Rimbaud (1854–1891)

Rimbaud shot like a meteor across the firmament of French poetry; he wrought increasingly bold experiments in what he called "the alchemy of the word." Then, at the age of nineteen, he abandoned poetry forever, and set out for a life of money-grubbing and adventure in Africa.

Dawn

I have embraced the summer dawn.

On the brow of the palaces, nothing stirred. The water was dead. Nor did the encampments of shadow retreat from the forest road. I walked, waking the warm living breath of things, and the luminous stones watched, and the wings rose soundlessly.

The first adventure, on the path already glowing with cool pale light, was a flower that told me its name.

I laughed at the blond *wasserfall* [1] running dishevelled through the pines: on the silver hilltop, I recognized the goddess.

Then I lifted her veils, one by one: in the lane, waving my arms; across the field, where I betrayed her to the cock; in the city, she fled among the steeples and domes, and staggering like a beggar across the marble wharves, I ran after.

Above the road, near a laurel grove, I wrapped her in her own gathered veils, and I could feel her tremendous body—could I smell it as well? Dawn and the child fell together below the woods.

Waking, it was noon.

—TR. RICHARD HOWARD

1. *Wasserfall:* German for waterfall.

Stéphane Mallarmé (1842–1898)

Mallarmé was to a generation of European writers and artists "the Master"—the poet who best incarnated the striving after perfection of form and mastery of art's difficulties. Some of the most important poets and artists of the modern period came to his "soirées" on Tuesday evenings: the roster of great names includes Edgar Degas, André Gide, Paul Claudel, J. A. M. Whistler, and Paul Valéry.

Le Cygne

The virgin, the blind, the beautiful today,
dares it break the mirror of this lake,
hard, neglectful, hoarding under ice
a great glacier of flights that never fly?
The swan worsens, remembers it is he,
the magnificence that gives itself no hope,
the fortitude that finds no *raison d'être*—
the great boredoms blaze in the sterile winter.
The whole neck shakes in this white agony
inflicted by the space the swan denies;
he cannot deny the ice that ties his feet.
His pure brilliance led him to this grand asylum,
governed by staccato cries of grandeur,
pride that clothes the swan in useless exile.

—TR. ROBERT LOWELL

Emily Dickinson (1830–1886)

Emily Dickinson lived a quiet, secluded life in Massachusetts. She saw only a few people and wrote to a few others. After her death, a large number of poems were found among her papers. They were short, delicate lyrics for the most part, written with unconventional syntax and startling imagery.

After Great Pain, a Formal Feeling Comes

After great pain, a formal feeling comes—
The Nerves sit ceremonious, like Tombs—
The stiff Heart questions was it He, that bore,
And Yesterday, or Centuries before?

The Feet, mechanical, go round—
Of Ground, or Air, or Ought—
A Wooden way
Regardless grown,
A Quartz contentment, like a stone—

This is the Hour of Lead—
Remembered, if outlived,
As Freezing persons, recollect the Snow—
First—Chill—then Stupor, then the letting go—

Ezra Pound (1885–   )

Born in Idaho, Ezra Pound spent the major part of his life abroad, chiefly in England and Italy. During his youth he acted as a polemicist for avant-garde poetry, although his own interests ranged throughout the whole past of literature. His own poetic practice has had immense influence on the writings of younger poets.

*Portrait d'une Femme**

Your mind and you are our Sargasso Sea,°
London has swept about you this score years
And bright ships left you this or that in fee:

* *Portrait d'une Femme:* portrait of a lady. 1. *Sargasso Sea:* a part of the Atlantic Ocean clogged with seaweed.

Ideas, old gossip, oddments of all things,
Strange spars of knowledge and dimmed wares of price.
Great minds have sought you—lacking someone else.
You have been second always. Tragical?
No. You preferred it to the usual thing:
One dull man, dulling and uxorious,°
One average mind—with one thought less, each year.
Oh, you are patient, I have seen you sit
Hours, where something might have floated up.
And now you pay one. Yes, you richly pay.
You are a person of some interest, one comes to you
And takes strange gain away:
Trophies fished up; some curious suggestion;
Fact that leads nowhere; and a tale or two,
Pregnant with mandrakes,° or with something else
That might prove useful and yet never proves,
That never fits a corner or shows use,
Or finds its hour upon the loom of days:
The tarnished, gaudy, wonderful old work;
Idols and ambergris° and rare inlays,
These are your riches, your great store; and yet
For all this sea-hoard of deciduous° things,
Strange woods half sodden, and new brighter stuff:
In the slow float of different light and deep,
No! there is nothing! In the whole and all,
Nothing that's quite your own.
Yet this is you.

T. S. Eliot (1888–1965)

Although Eliot was born in the United States, he became a British citizen and spent the major part of his life in England. His critical writings, as well as his poems, revolutionized contemporary poetry in both England and America.

9. *uxorious:* doting on his wife. 18. *mandrakes:* plants with forked roots traditionally thought to promote fertility. 23. *ambergris:* secreted by the sperm whale, used in making perfume. 25. *deciduous:* as of trees that lose their leaves in the autumn.

The Love Song of J. Alfred Prufrock

S'io credesse che mia risposta fosse
A persona che mai tornasse al mondo,
Questa fiamma staria senza piu scosse.
Ma perciocche giammai di questo fondo
Non torno vivo alcum, s'i' odo il vero,
*Senza terna d'infamia ti rispondo.**

Let us go then, you and I,
When the evening is spread out against the sky
Like a patient etherized upon a table;
Let us go, through certain half-deserted streets,
The muttering retreats
Of restless nights in one-night cheap hotels
And sawdust restaurants with oyster-shells:
Streets that follow like a tedious argument
Of insidious intent
To lead you to an overwhelming question. . . .
Oh, do not ask, "What is it?"
Let us go and make our visit.

In the room the women come and go
Talking of Michelangelo.

The yellow fog that rubs its back upon the window-panes,
The yellow smoke that rubs its muzzle on the window-panes
Licked its tongue into the corners of the evening,
Lingered upon the pools that stand in drains,
Let fall upon its back the soot that falls from chimneys,
Slipped by the terrace, made a sudden leap,
And seeing that it was a soft October night,
Curled once about the house, and fell asleep.
And indeed there will be time
For the yellow smoke that slides along the street,
Rubbing its back upon the window-panes;
There will be time, there will be time
To prepare a face to meet the faces that you meet;

* *S'io credesse* . . . : "If I thought that my reply were to one who would ever return to the world, this flame would stand without further movement. But since no one has ever returned alive from this depth, if what I hear is true, I answer you without fear of infamy." Dante, *Inferno,* xxvii, 61–66. Guido da Montefeltro, caught in the flames that surround the false counselors, is confessing his crimes to Dante.

There will be time to murder and create,
And time for all the works and days of hands
That lift and drop a question on your plate;
Time for you and time for me,
And time yet for a hundred indecisions,
And for a hundred visions and revisions,
Before the taking of a toast and tea.
In the room the women come and go
Talking of Michelangelo.

And indeed there will be time
To wonder, "Do I dare?" and, "Do I dare?"
Time to turn back and descend the stair,
With a bald spot in the middle of my hair—
(They will say: "How his hair is growing thin!")
My morning coat, my collar mounting firmly to the chin,
My necktie rich and modest, but asserted by a simple pin—
(They will say: "But how his arms and legs are thin!")
Do I dare
Disturb the universe?
In a minute there is time
For decisions and revisions which a minute will reverse.

For I have known them all already, known them all:
Have known the evenings, mornings, afternoons,
I have measured out my life with coffee spoons;
I know the voices dying with a dying fall
Beneath the music from a farther room.
  So how should I presume?

And I have known the eyes already, known them all—
The eyes that fix you in a formulated phrase,
And when I am formulated, sprawling on a pin,
When I am pinned and wriggling on the wall,
Then how should I begin
To spit out all the butt-ends of my days and ways?
  And how should I presume?

And I have known the arms already, known them all—
Arms that are braceleted and white and bare
(But in the lamplight, downed with light brown hair!)
Is it perfume from a dress
That makes me so digress?
Arms that lie along a table, or wrap about a shawl,
  And should I then presume?

And how should I begin?

Shall I say, I have gone at dusk through narrow streets
And watched the smoke that rises from the pipes
Of lonely men in shirt-sleeves, leaning out of windows? . . .

I should have been a pair of ragged claws
Scuttling across the floors of silent seas.
And the afternoon, the evening, sleeps so peacefully!
Smoothed by long fingers,
Asleep . . . tired . . . or it malingers,
Stretched on the floor, here beside you and me.
Should I, after tea and cakes and ices,
Have the strength to force the moment to its crisis?
But though I have wept and fasted, wept and prayed,
Though I have seen my head (grow slightly bald) brought in
upon a platter,°
I am no prophet—and here's no great matter;
I have seen the moment of my greatness flicker,
And I have seen the eternal Footman hold my coat, and snicker,
And in short, I was afraid.

And would it have been worth it, after all,
After the cups, the marmalade, the tea,
Among the porcelain, among some talk of you and me,
Would it have been worth while,
To have bitten off the matter with a smile,
To have squeezed the universe into a ball
To roll it toward some overwhelming question,
To say: "I am Lazarus,° come from the dead,
Come back to tell you all, I shall tell you all"—
If one, settling a pillow by her head,
Should say: "That is not what I meant at all;
That is not it, at all."

And would it have been worth it, after all,
Would it have been worth while,
After the sunsets and the dooryards and the sprinkled streets,
After the novels, after the teacups, after the skirts that trail along
the floor—
And this, and so much more?—

82. *platter:* like the prophet John the Baptist. 94. *Lazarus:* raised from the dead by Christ, John 12:1–18; also, the beggar carried to Abraham's bosom, Luke 16:19–31.

It is impossible to say just what I mean!
But as if a magic lantern threw the nerves in patterns on a screen:
Would it have been worth while
If one, settling a pillow or throwing off a shawl,
And turning toward the window, should say:
  "That is not it at all,
  That is not what I meant, at all."
No! I am not Prince Hamlet, nor was meant to be;
Am an attendant lord, one that will do
To swell a progress,° start a scene or two,
Advise the prince; no doubt, an easy tool,
Deferential, glad to be of use,
Politic, cautious, and meticulous;
Full of high sentence,° but a bit obtuse;
At times, indeed, almost ridiculous—
Almost, at times, the Fool.

I grow old. . . . I grow old. . . .
I shall wear the bottoms of my trousers rolled.
Shall I part my hair behind? Do I dare to eat a peach?
I shall wear white flannel trousers, and walk upon the beach.
I have heard the mermaids singing, each to each.

I do not think that they will sing to me.

I have seen them riding seaward on the waves
Combing the white hair of the waves blown back
When the wind blows the water white and black.

We have lingered in the chambers of the sea
By sea-girls wreathed with seaweed red and brown
Till human voices wake us, and we drown.

113. swell a progress: add to a royal procession. *117. sentence:* judgments, pronouncements.

Rainer Maria Rilke (1875–1926)

Rilke, Germany's most notable poet of the early years of this century, was considerably influenced by the Symbolist movement. Much of the Symbolists' use of unusual imagery and striking metaphor is visible in Lowell's translation of Rilke's "Self-Portrait."

Self-Portrait

The bone-build of the eyebrows has a mule's
or Pole's noble and narrow steadfastness.
A scared blue child is peering through the eyes,
and there's a kind of weakness, not a fool's,
yet womanish—the gaze of one who serves.
The mouth is just a mouth . . . untidy curves,
quite unpersuasive, yet it says its *yes,*
when forced to act. The forehead cannot frown
and likes the shade of dumbly looking down.

A still life, *nature morte*°—hardly a whole!
It has done nothing worked through or alive,
in spite of pain, in spite of comforting . . .
Out of this distant and disordered thing
something in earnest labors to unroll.

—TR. ROBERT LOWELL

Alexander Blok (1880–1921)

As Rilke was a German Symbolist, Blok was a Russian one. His long poem "The Twelve" is a passionate, fragmented, imaginative, picture of Russia in the throes of revolution.

From *The Twelve*

5

Our sons have gone
to serve the Reds
to serve the Reds

10. *nature morte:* the French term for "still life"; literally, "dead nature."

to risk their heads!

O bitter, bitter pain,
sweet living!
a torn overcoat!
an Austrian gun!

—To get the bourgeois
We'll start a fire
a worldwide fire, and drench it in blood—
the good Lord bless us!

8

—O you bitter bitterness,
boring boredom,
deadly boredom.
This is how I will
spend my time.

This is how I will
scratch my head,

munch on seeds,
some sunflower seeds,

play with my knife
play with my knife.

You bourgeois, fly as a sparrow!
I'll drink your blood,

your warm blood, for love,
for dark-eyed love.

God, let this soul, your servant, rest in peace

Such boredom!

11

Thus they march ever ready,
all twelve, on and on.
They are without pity,
without icon.

Their steel rifles are seeking
the invisible foe,

in the dark side streets,
in the deepest snow.

A red flag is flapping
against their eyes.
Their rhythmic steps
march on and on.

The fierce enemy
will soon be found.
The snow is blinding them.
they are marching on,

day and night.

"Power to the People!"

12

The Twelve step steadfastly.
"Who's there? Come on out!"
It's the wind which is playing
with a red flag.

The snowdrifts are icy.
"Come out from the drift!"
But they are followed only
by a hungry dog.

"Get away, else we'll tickle you
with our bayonets!"
The Old World is no better
than a mangy old dog.

Hungry wolf,
he will follow
baring his teeth.
"Who goes there?"

"Who is that in the distance
waving a flag?
In the darkness rushing
by the shadow of walls?

Never mind, we'll get you!
Better give yourself up alive!
Comrade, we'll kill you.
Come out or we'll shoot!"

Only an echo,
from beyond the walls.
Only the laughing
of the huge snowstorm.

And they march steadfastly,
a dog trailing behind—
while ahead—
with a bloody red flag,
unseen in the snow,
immune to their bullets,
in a scattering of pearls,
in a crown of white roses,
our Lord is walking with a tender step.

January 1918

—TR. OLGA CARLISLE

Federico García Lorca (1899–1936)

One of the many tragic occurrences of the Spanish Civil War was the murder of García Lorca by the Falangists. With his death, Spain lost one of its most outstanding poets and playwrights. Lorca has often been linked with the Surrealists because of his unusual combination of images, which frequently suggest the workings of the subconscious mind. However, he was never properly part of any artistic movement and always followed an independent path.

Casida* of Flight

I want to sleep the sleep of the apples,
to get away from the tumult of the cemeteries,
I want to sleep the sleep of that child
who wanted to cut his heart on the high seas.

I don't want him to repeat to me that the dead do not lose their
blood,
that the putrid mouth goes on asking for water;
I don't want to inform myself of the tortures of the grass
nor of the moon with a serpent's mouth,
which works before dawn.

* *Casida:* originally a short Arabic or Persian poem, usually on an amorous theme.

I want to sleep for a while,
a while, a minute, a century,
but all must know that I have not died,
that there is a stable of gold in my lips,
that I am the small friend of the West wind,
that I am the immense shadow of my tears.

Cover me at dawn with a veil
because dawn will throw me fists full of ants,
and wets with hard water my shoes,
so that the pincers of the scorpion slides.

Because I want to sleep the sleep of the apples,
to learn a lament which purifies the earth.

Because I want to live with that obscure child
who wanted to cut his heart on the high seas.

—TR. STEPHEN SPENDER AND J. L. GILI

Eugenio Montale (1896–)

Montale is often regarded as one of Italy's finest poets. He also wrote many excellent critical studies of literature and served a while as an editor in a publishing house and as a librarian in Florence.

The Sunflower

Bring me the sunflower to plant in my garden here
Where the salt of the flung spray has parched a space,
And all day long to the blue and mirroring air
Let it turn the ardor of its yellow face.

These dark things to the source of brightness turn,
In a flow of colors into music flowing, spend
Themselves forever. Thus to burn
Is consummation, of all ends the end.

Bring me within your hands that flower which yearns
Up to the ultimate transparent white
Where all of life into its essence burns:
Bring me that flower impassioned of the light.

—TR. MAURICE ENGLISH

Wallace Stevens (1879–1955)

Stevens was an insurance executive in Connecticut and, unlike most other poets in this volume, did not begin writing until quite late in life. Influenced by the French Symbolists, he wrote poetry of a rare intellectual concentration and brilliance.

Final Soliloquy of the Interior Paramour

Light the first light of evening, as in a room
In which we rest and, for small reason, think
The world imagined is the ultimate good.

This is, therefore, the intensest rendezvous.
It is in that thought that we collect ourselves,
Out of all the indifferences, into one thing:

Within a single thing, a single shawl
Wrapped tightly round us, since we are poor, a warmth,
A light, a power, the miraculous influence.

Here, now, we forget each other and ourselves.
We feel the obscurity of an order, a whole,
A knowledge, that which arranged the rendezvous.

Within its vital boundary, in the mind.
We say God and the imagination are one . . .
How high that highest candle lights the dark.

Out of this same light, out of the central mind,
We make a dwelling in the evening air,
In which being there together is enough.

James Joyce

Araby

James Joyce (1882–1941)

JAMES JOYCE WAS BORN IN DUBLIN—THE CITY WHOSE SIGHTS, smells, sounds, and citizens pervade all his writing—into a large family which would, as the years went on, be increasingly beset by financial difficulties. He was educated at Jesuit schools, and at one point thought of becoming a priest, but then decisively rejected the Church for the secular religion of art. After taking his B.A. at University College Dublin, he also rejected Ireland and set off for Paris to study and to write, to live—in the words of Stephen Daedalus, the hero of *Portrait of the Artist as a Young Man*—in "silence, exile, and cunning." Most of the rest of his life would be spent on the Continent, in Trieste, Zurich, and Paris, teaching English and elaborating his fiction, facing the difficulties of publication and encroaching blindness. He lived in poverty until a series of gifts made him financially independent for the last twenty years of his life.

From *Dubliners,* through *Portrait of the Artist as a Young Man,* to *Ulysses* (published in Paris in 1922, and for many years banned in England and America), and finally to *Finnegans Wake,* Joyce never ceased to experiment audaciously, pushing literary form and language to their utmost limits. Beginning within a Symbolist esthetic and a realist manner—both Flaubert and Ibsen were important masters—he created with *Ulysses* a work that is at once one of the most detailed realistic renderings of life ever composed and a vastly complex symbolic patterning of reality. The book appeared to many later novelists as a final use of the novel form, one that nearly exhausted the form's possibilities. In *Finnegans Wake,* he carried experimentation with language—especially multilayered punning—to a point close to the invention of a new language. The demands he made on his readers were enormous; he said that he expected them to spend their whole lives attempting to understand his books.

The stories in *Dubliners* realize, perhaps better than anything else Joyce wrote, the artistic intent announced by Stephen Daedalus: "to forge in the smithy of my soul the uncreated conscience of my race." These stories lay bare in a series of special moments of revelation and illumination—moments Joyce liked to refer to as "epiphanies"—central truths about characters' lives and about life. If they do not show the bold experimentation of his later work, they are among the highest artistic accomplishments in the form; each is perfectly "realistic" in its presentation yet suggestive of a full symbolic resonance of meaning.

Araby

North Richmond Street, being blind,[1] was a quiet street except at the hour when the Christian Brothers' School set the boys free. An uninhabited house of two stories stood at the blind end, detached from its neighbors in a square ground. The other houses of the street, conscious of decent lives within them, gazed at one another with brown imperturbable faces.

The former tenant of our house, a priest, had died in the back drawing room. Air, musty from having been long enclosed, hung in all the rooms, and the waste room behind the kitchen was littered with old useless papers. Among these I found a few paper-covered books, the pages of which were curled and damp: *The Abbot*, by Walter Scott, *The Devout Communicant* and *The Memoirs of Vidocq*.[2] I liked the last best because its leaves were yellow. The wild garden behind the house contained a central apple tree and a few straggling bushes under one of which I found the late tenant's rusty bicycle pump. He had been a very charitable priest; in his will he had left all his money to institutions and the furniture of his house to his sister.

When the short days of winter came dusk fell before we had well eaten our dinners. When we met in the street the houses had grown somber. The space of sky above us was the color of ever changing violet and towards it the lamps of the street lifted their feeble lanterns. The cold air stung us and we played till our bodies glowed. Our shouts echoed in the silent street. The career of our play brought us through the dark muddy lanes behind the houses where we ran the gauntlet of the rough tribes from the cottages, to the back doors of the dark dripping gardens where odors arose from the ashpits, to the dark odorous stables where a coachman smoothed and combed the horse or shook music from the buckled harness. When we returned to the street light from the kitchen windows had filled the areas. If my uncle was seen turning the corner we hid in the shadow until we had seen him safely housed. Or if Mangan's sister came out on the doorstep to call her brother in to his tea we watched her from our shadow peer up and down the street. We waited to see whether she would remain

[1] A dead end street. [2] Respectively, an historical novel by Walter Scott (1771–1832); a devotional book; and the celebrated memoirs of Vidocq (1775–1857), a French criminal who became chief of the police.

or go in and, if she remained, we left our shadow and walked up to Mangan's steps resignedly. She was waiting for us, her figure defined by the light from the half-opened door. Her brother always teased her before he obeyed and I stood by the railings looking at her. Her dress swung as she moved her body and the soft rope of her hair tossed from side to side.

Every morning I lay on the floor in the front parlor watching her door. The blind was pulled down to within an inch of the sash so that I could not be seen. When she came out on the doorstep my heart leaped. I ran to the hall, seized my books and followed her. I kept her brown figure always in my eye and, when we came near the point at which our ways diverged, I quickened my pace and passed her. This happened morning after morning. I had never spoken to her, except for a few casual words, and yet her name was like a summons to all my foolish blood.

Her image accompanied me even in places the most hostile to romance. On Saturday evenings when my aunt went marketing I had to go to carry some of the parcels. We walked through the flaring streets, jostled by drunken men and bargaining women, amid the curses of laborers, the shrill litanies of shopboys who stood on guard by the barrels of pigs' cheeks, the nasal chanting of street-singers, who sang a *come-all-you* about O'Donovan Rossa, or a ballad about the troubles in our native land. These noises converged in a single sensation of life for me: I imagined that I bore my chalice safely through a throng of foes. Her name sprang to my lips at moments in strange prayers and praises which I myself did not understand. My eyes were often full of tears (I could not tell why) and at times a flood from my heart seemed to pour itself out into my bosom. I thought little of the future. I did not know whether I would ever speak to her or not or, if I spoke to her, how I could tell her of my confused adoration. But my body was like a harp and her words and gestures were like fingers running upon the wires.

One evening I went into the back drawing room in which the priest had died. It was a dark rainy evening and there was no sound in the house. Through one of the broken panes I heard the rain impinge upon the earth, the fine incessant needles of water playing in the sodden beds. Some distant lamp or lighted window gleamed below me. I was thankful that I could see so little. All my senses seemed to desire to veil themselves and, feeling that I was about to slip from them, I pressed the palms of my hands together until they trembled, murmuring: *"O love! O love!"* many times.

At last she spoke to me. When she addressed the first words to me I was so confused that I did not know what to answer. She asked me was I going to *Araby*. I forgot whether I answered yes or no. It would be a splendid bazaar, she said she would love to go.

"And why can't you?" I asked.

While she spoke she turned a silver bracelet round and round her wrist.

She could not go, she said, because there would be a retreat that week in her convent. Her brother and two other boys were fighting for their caps and I was alone at the railings. She held one of the spikes, bowing her head towards me. The light from the lamp opposite our door caught the white curve of her neck, lit up her hair that rested there and, falling, lit up the hand upon the railing. It fell over one side of her dress and caught the white border of a petticoat, just visible as she stood at ease.

"It's well for you," she said.

"If I go," I said, "I will bring you something."

What innumerable follies laid waste my waking and sleeping thoughts after that evening! I wished to annihilate the tedious intervening days. I chafed against the work of school. At night in my bedroom and by day in the classroom her image came between me and the page I strove to read. The syllables of the word *Araby* were called to me through the silence in which my soul luxuriated and cast an Eastern enchantment over me. I asked for leave to go to the bazaar on Saturday night. My aunt was surprised and hoped it was not some Freemason affair. I answered few questions in class. I watched my master's face pass from amiability to sternness; he hoped I was not beginning to idle. I could not call my wandering thoughts together. I had hardly any patience with the serious work of life which, now that it stood between me and my desire, seemed to me child's play, ugly monotonous child's play.

On Saturday morning I reminded my uncle that I wished to go to the bazaar in the evening. He was fussing at the hallstand, looking for the hat brush, and answered me curtly:

"Yes, boy, I know."

As he was in the hall I could not go into the front parlor and lie at the window. I left the house in bad humor and walked slowly towards the school. The air was pitilessly raw and already my heart misgave me.

When I came home to dinner my uncle had not yet been home. Still it was early. I sat staring at the clock for some time and, when its ticking began to irritate me, I left the room. I mounted the staircase and gained the upper part of the house. The high cold empty gloomy rooms liberated me and I went from room to room singing. From the front window I saw my companions playing below in the street. Their cries reached me weakened and indistinct and, leaning my forehead against the cool glass, I looked over at the dark house where she lived. I may have stood there for an hour, seeing nothing but the brown-clad figure cast by my imagination, touched discreetly by the lamplight at the curved neck, at the hand upon the railings and at the border below the dress.

When I came downstairs again I found Mrs. Mercer sitting at the fire. She was an old garrulous woman, a pawnbroker's widow, who collected used stamps for some pious purpose. I had to endure the gossip of the tea table. The meal was prolonged beyond an hour and still my uncle did not come. Mrs. Mercer stood up to go: she was sorry she couldn't wait any longer, but it was after eight o'clock and she did not like to be out late, as the night air was bad for her. When she had gone I began to walk up and down the room, clenching my fists. My aunt said:

"I'm afraid you may put off your bazaar for this night of Our Lord."

At nine o'clock I heard my uncle's latchkey in the hall door. I heard him talking to himself and heard the hallstand rocking when it had received the weight of his overcoat. I could interpret these signs. When he was midway through his dinner I asked him to give me the money to go to the bazaar. He had forgotten.

"The people are in bed and after their first sleep now," he said.

I did not smile. My aunt said to him energetically:

"Can't you give him the money and let him go? You've kept him late enough as it is."

My uncle said he was very sorry he had forgotten. He said he believed in the old saying: "All work and no play makes Jack a dull boy." He asked me where I was going and, when I had told him a second time he asked me did I know *The Arab's Farewell to His Steed.* When I left the kitchen he was about to recite the opening lines of the piece to my aunt.

I held a florin tightly in my hand as I strode down Buckingham Street towards the station. The sight of the streets thronged with buyers and glaring with gas recalled to me the purpose of my journey. I took my seat in a third-class carriage of a deserted train. After an intolerable delay the train moved out of the station slowly. It crept onward among ruinous houses and over the twinkling river. At Westland Row Station a crowd of people pressed to the carriage doors; but the porters moved them back, saying that it was a special train for the bazaar. I remained alone in the bare carriage. In a few minutes the train drew up beside an improvised wooden platform. I passed out on to the road and saw by the lighted dial of a clock that it was ten minutes to ten. In front of me was a large building which displayed the magical name.

I could not find any sixpenny entrance and, fearing that the bazaar would be closed, I passed in quickly through a turnstile, handing a shilling to a weary-looking man. I found myself in a big hall girdled at half its height by a gallery. Nearly all the stalls were closed and the greater part of the hall was in darkness. I recognized a silence like that which pervades a churce after a service. I walked into the center of the bazaar timidly. A few people were gathered about the stalls which were still open. Before a curtain, over which the words *Café Chantant* were written in colored lamps, two men were counting money on a salver. I listened to the fall of the coins.

Remembering with difficulty why I had come I went over to one of the stalls and examined porcelain vases and flowered tea sets. At the door of the stall a young lady was talking and laughing with two young gentlemen. I remarked their English accents and listened vaguely to their conversation.

"O, I never said such a thing!"

"O, but you did!"

"O, but I didn't!"

"Didn't she say that?"

"Yes. I heard her."

"O, there's a . . . fib!"

Observing me the young lady came over and asked me did I wish to buy anything. The tone of her voice was not encouraging; she seemed to have spoken to me out of a sense of duty. I looked humbly at the great jars that stood like eastern guards at either side of the dark entrance to the stall and murmured:

"No, thank you."

The young lady changed the position of one of the vases and went back to the two young men. They began to talk of the same subject. Once or twice the young lady glanced at me over her shoulder.

I lingered before her stall, though I knew my stay was useless, to make my interest in her wares seem the more real. Then I turned away slowly and walked down the middle of the bazaar. I allowed the two pennies to fall against the sixpence in my pocket. I heard a voice call from one end of the gallery that the light was out. The upper part of the hall was now completely dark.

Gazing up into the darkness I saw myself as a creature driven and derided by vanity; and my eyes burned with anguish and anger.

D. H. Lawrence

Tickets, Please

D. H. Lawrence (1885–1930)

DAVID HERBERT LAWRENCE WAS BORN NEAR NOTTINGHAM, IN the Midlands region of England. His father was a coal miner, his mother a possessive and ambitious woman who had visions of a more refined life for her children. Lawrence went to secondary school on a scholarship. Ill health prevented his becoming a miner; he went to the university in Nottingham and for a time was a school teacher. Then he met Frieda von Richthofen, a German aristocrat married to an English professor, and left with her for Germany in 1912. They were married in England in 1914, and their passionate, quarrelsome, self-torturing relationship was a central fact in Lawrence's life and in his fiction. Lawrence's first major novel, *Sons and Lovers,* was published in 1913, followed by a volume of short stories, *The Prussian Officer and Other Stories,* and the novel *The Rainbow,* which was the first of Lawrence's works to be banned as obscene. *Women in Love* had to be privately printed and it, too, was denounced in the press as perverse, degrading, and obscene. Meanwhile, the Lawrences, depressed by wartime England, had left for the Continent, then made their way to Ceylon, Australia, and Taos, New Mexico, where Lawrence hoped to establish a utopian community. He later settled in Italy, completing *Lady Chatterly's Lover* there. He died in the south of France.

Working-class in origins, sensitive to issues of social class, both rejecting his background and reveling in a kind of primitive coarseness, a man who both repelled and fascinated some of his most sympathetic contemporaries, the preacher and prophet on a range of subjects, Lawrence was one of the most unconventional and powerful figures in modern literature. If he was not really an innovator in terms of literary form, his subjects and his way of talking about them made him a revolutionary writer. Notably, he brought a new form of consciousness and a new mode of apprehension to relations between men and women and to man's relation to his subconscious knowledge. He sought to bring about new relationships freed from the cant, hypocrisy, and slavery of convention. Although didactic and irrational at times, he is brilliantly illuminating about man's degradation in modern civilization and his need to locate once again the sources of wholeness and power.

In addition to his novels, Lawrence published some striking poetry and essays and wrote letters of rare vitality and force. He also wrote over a hundred short stories, which are often more easily approachable than his novels and contain in small compass the essential Lawrentian conflicts. Such a story is "Tickets, Please", published in *England, My England.*

Tickets, Please

There is in the Midlands a single-line tramway system which boldly leaves the county town and plunges off into the black, industrial countryside, up hill and down dale, through the long ugly villages of workmen's houses, over canals and railways, past churches perched high and nobly over the smoke and shadows, through stark, grimy cold little marketplaces, tilting away in a rush past cinemas and shops down to the hollow where the collieries are, then up again, past a little rural church, under the ash trees, on in a rush to the terminus, the last little ugly place of industry, the cold little town that shivers on the edge of the wild, gloomy country beyond. There the green and creamy colored tram-car seems to pause and purr with curious satisfaction. But in a few minutes—the clock on the turret of the Cooperative Wholesale Society's shops gives the time—away it starts once more on the adventure. Again there are the reckless swoops downhill, bouncing the loops: again the chilly wait in the hilltop marketplace: again the breathless slithering round the precipitous drop under the church: again the patient halts at the loops, waiting for the outcoming car: so on and on, for two long hours, till at last the city looms beyond the fat gasworks, the narrow factories draw near, we are in the sordid streets of the great town, once more we sidle to a standstill at our terminus, abashed by the great crimson and cream-colored city cars, but still perky, jaunty, somewhat dare-devil, green as a jaunty sprig of parsley out of a black colliery garden.

To ride on these cars is always an adventure. Since we are in wartime, the drivers are men unfit for active service: cripples and hunchbacks. So they have the spirit of the devil in them. The ride becomes a steeplechase. Hurray! we have leapt in a clear jump over the canal bridges—now for the four-lane corner. With a shriek and a trail of sparks we are clear again. To be sure, a tram often leaps the rails—but what matter! It sits in a ditch till other trams come to haul it out. It is quite common for a car, packed with one solid mass of living people, to come to a dead halt in the midst of unbroken blackness, the heart of nowhere on a dark night, and for the driver and the girl conductor to call, "All get off—car's on fire!" Instead, however, of rushing out in a panic, the passengers stolidly reply: "Get on

—get on! We're not coming out. We're stopping where we are. Push on, George." So till flames actually appear.

The reason for this reluctance to dismount is that the nights are howlingly cold, black, and windswept, and a car is a haven of refuge. From village to village the miners travel, for a change of cinema, of girl, of pub. The trams are desperately packed. Who is going to risk himself in the black gulf outside, to wait perhaps an hour for another tram, then to see the forlorn notice "Depot Only," because there is something wrong! Or to greet a unit of three bright cars all so tight with people that they sail past with a howl of derision. Trams that pass in the night.

This, the most dangerous tram service in England, as the authorities themselves declare, with pride, is entirely conducted by girls, and driven by rash young men, a little crippled, or by delicate young men, who creep forward in terror. The girls are fearless young hussies. In their ugly blue uniform, skirts up to their knees, shapeless old peaked caps on their heads, they have all the sang-froid of an old noncommissioned officer. With a tram packed with howling colliers, roaring hymns downstairs and a sort of antiphony of obscenities upstairs, the lasses are perfectly at their ease. They pounce on the youths who try to evade their ticket machine. They push off the men at the end of their distance. They are not going to be done in the eye—not they. They fear nobody—and everybody fears them.

"Hello, Annie!"

"Hello, Ted!"

"Oh, mind my corn, Miss Stone. It's my belief you've got a heart of stone, for you've trod on it again."

"You should keep it in your pocket," replies Miss Stone, and she goes sturdily upstairs in her high boots.

"Tickets, please."

She is peremptory, suspicious, and ready to hit first. She can hold her own against ten thousand. The step of that tram-car is her Thermopylae.[1]

Therefore, there is a certain wild romance aboard these cars—and in the sturdy bosom of Annie herself. The time for soft romance is in the morning, between ten o'clock and one, when things are rather slack: that is, except market day and Saturday. Thus Annie has time to look about her. Then she often hops off her car and into a shop where she has spied something, while the driver chats in the main road. There is very good feeling between the girls and the drivers. Are they not companions in peril, shipments aboard this careering vessel of a tram-car, for ever rocking on the waves of a stormy land.

Then, also, during the easy hours, the inspectors are most in evidence.

[1] Site of a famous battle in 480 B.C., in which three hundred Spartans fought to the last man to hold the pass against the Persian army.

For some reason, everybody employed in this tram service is young: there are no gray heads. It would not do. Therefore the inspectors are of the right age, and one, the chief, is also good-looking. See him stand on a wet, gloomy morning, in his long oilskin, his peaked cap well down over his eyes, waiting to board a car. His face is ruddy, his small brown mustache is weathered, he has a faint impudent smile. Fairly tall and agile, even in his waterproof, he springs aboard a car and greets Annie.

"Hello, Annie! Keeping the wet out?"

"Trying to."

There are only two people in the car. Inspecting is soon over. Then for a long and impudent chat on the foot board, a good, easy, twelve-mile chat.

The inspector's name is John Thomas Raynor—always called John Thomas, except sometimes, in malice, Coddy. His face sets in fury when he is addressed, from a distance, with this abbreviation. There is considerable scandal about John Thomas in half a dozen villages. He flirts with the girl conductors in the morning, and walks out with them in the dark night, when they leave their tram-car at the depot. Of course, the girls quit the service frequently. Then he flirts and walks out with the newcomer: always providing she is sufficiently attractive, and that she will consent to walk. It is remarkable, however, that most of the girls are quite comely, they are all young, and this roving life aboard the car gives them a sailor's dash and recklessness. What matter how they behave when the ship is in port? Tomorrow they will be aboard again.

Annie, however, was something of a Tartar, and her sharp tongue had kept John Thomas at arm's length for many months. Perhaps, therefore, she liked him all the more: for he always came up smiling, with impudence. She watched him vanquish one girl, then another. She could tell by the movement of his mouth and eyes, when he flirted with her in the morning, that he had been walking out with this lass, or the other, the night before. A fine cock-of-the-walk he was. She could sum him up pretty well.

In this subtle antagonism they knew each other like old friends, they were as shrewd with one another almost as man and wife. But Annie had always kept him sufficiently at arm's length. Besides, she had a boy of her own.

The Statutes fair, however, came in November, at Bestwood. It happened that Annie had the Monday night off. It was a drizzling ugly night, yet she dressed herself up and went to the fair ground. She was alone, but she expected soon to find a pal of some sort.

The roundabouts were veering round and grinding out their music, the side shows were making as much commotion as possible. In the coconut shies there were no coconuts, but artificial wartime substitutes, which the lads declared were fastened into the irons. There was a sad decline in brilliance and luxury. Nonetheless, the ground was muddy as ever, there was the same crush, the press of faces lighted up by the flares and the electric lights, the same smell of naphtha and a few fried potatoes, and of electricity.

Who should be the first to greet Miss Annie on the show ground but John Thomas. He had a black overcoat buttoned up to his chin, and a tweed cap pulled down over his brows, his face between was ruddy and smiling and handy as ever. She knew so well the way his mouth moved.

She was very glad to have a "boy." To be at the Statutes without a fellow was no fun. Instantly, like the gallant he was, he took her on the Dragons, grim-toothed, roundabout switchbacks. It was not nearly so exciting as a tram-car actually. But, then, to be seated in a shaking, green dragon, uplifted above the sea of bubble faces, careering in a rickety fashion in the lower heavens, while John Thomas leaned over her, his cigarette in his mouth, was after all the right style. She was a plump, quick, alive little creature. So she was quite excited and happy.

John Thomas made her stay on for the next round. And therefore she could hardly for shame repulse him when he put his arm round her and drew her a little nearer to him, in a very warm and cuddly manner. Besides, he was fairly discreet, he kept his movement as hidden as possible. She looked down, and saw that his red, clean hand was out of sight of the crowd. And they knew each other so well. So they warmed up to the fair.

After the dragons they went on the horses. John Thomas paid each time, so she could but be complaisant. He, of course, sat astride on the outer horse—named "Black Bess"—and she sat sideways, towards him, on the inner horse—named "Wildfire." But of course John Thomas was not going to sit discreetly on "Black Bess," holding the brass bar. Round they spun and heaved, in the light. And round he swung on his wooden steed, flinging one leg across her mount, and perilously tipping up and down, across the space, half lying back, laughing at her. He was perfectly happy; she was afraid her hat was on one side, but she was excited.

He threw quoits on a table, and won for her two large, pale blue hatpins. And then, hearing the noise of the cinemas, announcing another performance, they climbed the boards and went in.

Of course, during these performances pitch darkness falls from time to time, when the machine goes wrong. Then there is a wild whooping, and a loud smacking of simulated kisses. In these moments John Thomas drew Annie towards him. After all, he had a wonderfully warm, cozy way of holding a girl with his arm, he seemed to make such a nice fit. And, after all, it was pleasant to be so held: so very comforting and cozy and nice. He leaned over her and she felt his breath on her hair; she knew he wanted to kiss her on the lips. And, after all, he was so warm and she fitted in to him so softly. After all, she wanted him to touch her lips.

But the light sprang up; she also started electrically, and put her hat straight. He left his arm lying nonchalantly behind her. Well, it was fun, it was exciting to be at the Statutes with John Thomas.

When the cinema was over they went for a walk across the dark, damp fields. He had all the arts of lovemaking. He was especially good at holding a girl, when he sat with her on a stile in the black, drizzling darkness. He seemed to be holding her in space, against his own warmth and gratification. And his kisses were soft and slow and searching.

So Annie walked out with John Thomas, though she kept her own boy dangling in the distance. Some of the tram-girls chose to be huffy. But there, you must take things as you find them, in this life.

There was no mistake about it, Annie liked John Thomas a good deal. She felt so rich and warm in herself whenever he was near. And John Thomas really liked Annie, more than usual. The soft, melting way in which she could flow into a fellow, as if she melted into his very bones, was something rare and good. He fully appreciated this.

But with a developing acquaintance there began a developing intimacy. Annie wanted to consider him a person, a man: she wanted to take an intelligent interest in him, and to have an intelligent response. She did not want a mere nocturnal presence, which was what he was so far. And she prided herself that he could not leave her.

Here she made a mistake. John Thomas intended to remain a nocturnal presence; he had no idea of becoming an all-round individual to her. When she started to take an intelligent interest in him and his life and his character, he sheered off. He hated intelligent interest. And he knew that the only way to stop it was to avoid it. The possessive female was aroused in Annie. So he left her.

It is no use saying she was not surprised. She was at first startled, thrown out of her count. For she had been so *very* sure of holding him. For a while she was staggered, and everything became uncertain to her. Then she wept with fury, indignation, desolation, and misery. Then she had a spasm of despair. And then, when he came, still impudently, on to her car, still familiar, but letting her see by the movement of his head that he had gone away to somebody else for the time being, and was enjoying pastures new, then she determined to have her own back.

She had a very shrewd idea what girls John Thomas had taken out. She went to Nora Purdy. Nora was a tall, rather pale, but well-built girl, with beautiful yellow hair. She was rather secretive.

"Hey!" said Annie, accosting her; then softly, "Who's John Thomas on with now?"

"I don't know," said Nora.

"Why, tha does," said Annie, ironically lapsing into dialect. "Tha knows as well as I do."

"Well, I do, then," said Nora. "It isn't me, so don't bother."

"It's Cissy Meakin, isn't it?"

"It is, for all I know."

"Hasn't he got a face on him!" said Annie. "I don't half like his cheek. I could knock him off the footboard when he comes round at me."

"He'll get dropped on one of these days," said Nora.

"Ay, he will, when somebody makes up their mind to drop it on him. I should like to see him taken down a peg or two, shouldn't you?"

"I shouldn't mind," said Nora.

"You've got quite as much cause to as I have," said Annie. "But we'll drop on him one of these days, my girl. What? Don't you want to?"

"I don't mind," said Nora.

But as a matter of fact, Nora was much more vindictive than Annie.

One by one Annie went the round of the old flames. It so happened that Cissy Meakin left the tramway service in quite a short time. Her mother made her leave. Then John Thomas was on the *qui vive*. He cast his eyes over his old flock. And his eyes lighted on Annie. He thought she would be safe now. Besides, he liked her.

She arranged to walk home with him on Sunday night. It so happened that her car would be in the depot at half-past nine: the last car would come in at ten fifteen. So John Thomas was to wait for her there.

At the depot the girls had a little waiting room of their own. It was quite rough, but cozy, with a fire and an oven and a mirror, and table and wooden chairs. The half-dozen girls who knew John Thomas only too well had arranged to take service this Sunday afternoon. So, as the cars began to come in, early, the girls dropped into the waiting room. And instead of hurrying off home, they sat around the fire and had a cup of tea. Outside was the darkness and lawlessness of wartime.

John Thomas came on the car after Annie, at about a quarter to ten. He poked his head easily into the girls' waiting room.

"Prayer meeting?" he asked.

"Ay," said Laura Sharp. "Ladies only."

"That's me!" said John Thomas. It was one of his favorite exclamations.

"Shut the door, boy," said Muriel Baggaley.

"On which side of me?" said John Thomas.

"Which tha likes," said Polly Birkin.

He had come in and closed the door behind him. The girls moved in their circle, to make a place for him near the fire. He took off his greatcoat and pushed back his hat.

"Who handles the teapot?" he said.

Nora Purdy silently poured him out a cup of tea.

"Want a bit o' my bread and drippin'?" said Muriel Baggaley to him.

"Ay, give us a bit."

And he began to eat his piece of bread.

"There's no place like home, girls," he said.

They all looked at him as he uttered this piece of impudence. He seemed to be sunning himself in the presence of so many damsels.

"Especially if you're not afraid to go home in the dark," said Laura Sharp.

"Me! By myself I am."

They sat till they heard the last tram come in. In a few minutes Emma Houselay entered.

"Come on, my old duck!" cried Polly Birkin.

"It *is* perishing," said Emma, holding her fingers to the fire.

"But—I'm afraid to, go home in, the dark," sang Laura Sharp, the tune having got into her mind.

"Who're you going with tonight, John Thomas?" asked Muriel Baggaley, coolly.

"Tonight?" said John Thomas. "Oh, I'm going home by myself tonight—all on my lonely-o."

"That's me!" said Nora Purdy, using his own ejaculation.

The girls laughed shrilly.

"Me as well, Nora," said John Thomas.

"Don't know what you mean," said Laura.

"Yes, I'm toddling," said he, rising and reaching for his overcoat.

"Nay," said Polly. "We're all here waiting for you."

"We've got to be up in good time in the morning," he said, in the benevolent official manner.

They all laughed.

"Nay," said Muriel. "Don't leave us all lonely, John Thomas. Take one!"

"I'll take the lot, if you like," he responded gallantly.

"That you won't, either," said Muriel. "Two's company; seven's too much of a good thing."

"Nay—take one," said Laura. "Fair and square, all above board and say which."

"Ay," cried Annie, speaking for the first time. "Pick, John Thomas; let's hear thee."

"Nay," he said. "I'm going home quiet tonight. Feeling good, for once."

"Whereabouts?" said Annie. "Take a good 'un, then. But tha's got to take one of us!"

"Nay, how can I take one," he said, laughing uneasily. "I don't want to make enemies."

"You'd only make *one*," said Annie.

"The chosen *one*," added Laura.

"Oh, my! Who said girls!" exclaimed John Thomas, again turning, as if to escape. "Well—good night."

"Nay, you've got to make your pick," said Muriel. "Turn your face to the wall, and say which one touches you. Go on—we shall only just touch your back—one of us. Go on—turn your face to the wall, and don't look, and say which one touches you."

He was uneasy, mistrusting them. Yet he had not the courage to break away. They pushed him to a wall and stood him there with his face to it. Behind his back they all grimaced, tittering. He looked so comical. He looked around uneasily.

"Go on!" he cried.

"You're looking—you're looking!" they shouted.

He turned his head away. And suddenly, with a movement like a swift cat, Annie went forward and fetched him a box on the side of the head that sent his cap flying and himself staggering. He started round.

But at Annie's signal they all flew at him, slapping him, pinching him, pulling his hair, though more in fun than in spite or anger. He, however, saw red. His blue eyes flamed with strange fear as well as fury, and he butted through the girls to the door. It was locked. He wrenched at it. Roused, alert, the girls stood round and looked at him. He faced them, at bay. At that moment they were rather horrifying to him, as they stood in their short uniforms. He was distinctly afraid.

"Come on, John Thomas! Come on! Choose!" said Annie.

"What are you after? Open the door," he said.

"We shan't—not till you've chosen!" said Muriel.

"Chosen what?" he said.

"Chosen the one you're going to marry," she replied.

He hesitated a moment.

"Open the blasted door," he said, "and get back to your senses." He spoke with official authority.

"You've got to choose!" cried the girls.

"Come on!" cried Annie, looking him in the eye. "Come on! Come on!"

He went forward, rather vaguely. She had taken off her belt, and swinging it, she fetched him a sharp blow over the head with the buckle end. He sprang and seized her. But immediately the other girls rushed upon him, pulling and tearing and beating him. Their blood was now thoroughly up. He was their sport now. They were going to have their own back, out of him. Strange, wild creatures, they hung on him and rushed at him to bear him down. His tunic was torn right up the back, Nora had hold at the back of his collar, and was actually strangling him. Luckily the button burst. He struggled in a wild frenzy of fury and terror, almost mad terror. His tunic was simply torn off his back, his shirt sleeves were torn away, his arms were naked. The girls rushed at him, clenched their hands on him and pulled at him: or they rushed at him and pushed him, butted him with all their might: or they struck him wild blows. He ducked and cringed and struck sideways. They became more intense.

At last he was down. They rushed on him, kneeling on him. He had neither breath nor strength to move. His face was bleeding with a long scratch, his brow was bruised.

Annie knelt on him, the other girls knelt and hung on to him. Their faces were flushed, their hair wild, their eyes were all glittering strangely. He lay at last quite still, with face averted, as an animal lies when it is defeated and at the mercy of the captor. Sometimes his eye glanced back at the wild faces of the girls. His breast rose heavily, his wrists were torn.

"Now, then, my fellow!" gasped Annie at length. "Now then—now—"

At the sound of her terrifying, cold triumph, he suddenly started to struggle as an animal might, but the girls threw themselves upon him with unnatural strength and power, forcing him down.

"Yes—now, then!" gasped Annie at length.

And there was a dead silence, in which the thud of heart-beating was to be heard. It was a suspense of pure silence in every soul.

"Now you know where you are," said Annie.

The sight of his white, bare arm maddened the girls. He lay in a kind of trance of fear and antagonism. They felt themselves filled with super natural strength.

Suddenly Polly started to laugh—to giggle wildly—helplessly—and Emma and Muriel joined in. But Annie and Nora and Laura remained the same, tense, watchful, with gleaming eyes. He winced away from these eyes.

"Yes," said Annie, in a curious low tone, secret and deadly. "Yes! You've got it now. You know what you've done, don't you? You know what you've done."

He made no sound nor sign, but lay with bright, averted eyes, and averted, bleeding face.

"You ought to be *killed,* that's what you ought," said Annie, tensely. "You ought to be *killed.*" And there was a terrifying lust in her voice.

Polly was ceasing to laugh, and giving long-drawn Oh-h-hs and sighs as she came to herself.

"He's got to choose," she said vaguely.

"Oh, yes, he has," said Laura, with vindictive decision.

"Do you hear—do you hear?" said Annie. And with a sharp movement, that made him wince, she turned his face to her.

"Do you hear?" she repeated, shaking him.

But he was quite dumb. She fetched him a sharp slap on the face. He started, and his eyes widened. Then his face darkened with defiance, after all.

"Do you hear?" she repeated.

He only looked at her with hostile eyes.

"Speak!" she said, putting her face devilishly near his.

"What?" he said, almost overcome.

"You've got to *choose!*" she cried, as if it were some terrible menace, and as if it hurt her that she could not exact more.

"What?" he said, in fear.

"Choose your girl, Coddy. You've got to choose her now. And you'll get your neck broken if you play any more of your tricks, my boy. You're settled now."

There was a pause. Again he averted his face. He was cunning in his overthrow. He did not give in to them really—no, not if they tore him to bits.

"All right, then," he said, "I choose Annie." His voice was strange and full of malice. Annie let go of him as if he had been a hot coal.

"He's chosen Annie!" said the girls in chorus.

"Me!" cried Annie. She was still kneeling, but away from him. He was still lying prostrate, with averted face. The girls grouped uneasily around.

"Me!" repeated Annie, with a terrible bitter accent.

Then she got up, drawing away from him with strange disgust and bitterness.

"I wouldn't touch him," she said.

But her face quivered with a kind of agony, she seemed as if she would fall. The other girls turned aside. He remained lying on the floor, with his torn clothes and bleeding, averted face.

"Oh, if he's chosen—" said Polly.

"I don't want him—he can choose again," said Annie, with the same rather bitter hopelessness.

"Get up," said Polly, lifting his shoulder. "Get up."

He rose slowly, a strange, ragged, dazed creature. The girls eyed him from a distance, curiously, furtively, dangerously.

"Who wants him?" cried Laura, roughly.

"Nobody," they answered, with contempt. Yet each one of them waited for him to look at her, hoped he would look at her. All except Annie, and something was broken in her.

He, however, kept his face closed and averted from them all. There was a silence of the end. He picked up the torn pieces of his tunic, without knowing what to do with them. The girls stood about uneasily, flushed, panting, tidying their hair and their dress unconsciously, and watching him. He looked at none of them. He espied his cap in a corner, and went and picked it up. He put it on his head, and one of the girls burst into a shrill, hysteric laugh at the sight he presented. He, however, took no heed, but went straight to where his overcoat hung on a peg. The girls moved away from contact with him as if he had been an electric wire. He put on his coat and buttoned it down. Then he rolled his tunic-rags into a bundle, and stood before the locked door, dumbly.

"Open the door, somebody," said Laura.

"Annie's got the key," said one.

Annie silently offered the key to the girls. Nora unlocked the door.

"Tit for tat, old man," she said. "Show yourself a man, and don't bear a grudge."

But without a word or sign he had opened the door and gone, his face closed, his head dropped.

"That'll learn him," said Laura.

"Coddy!" said Nora.

"Shut up, for God's sake!" cried Annie fiercely, as if in torture.

"Well, I'm about ready to go, Polly. Look sharp!" said Muriel.

The girls were all anxious to be off. They were tidying themselves hurriedly, with mute, stupefied faces.

Luigi Pirandello

Six Characters in Search of an Author

TRANSLATED BY EDWARD STORER

Luigi Pirandello (1867–1936)

LUIGI PIRANDELLO WAS BORN IN AGRIGENTO, IN SICILY, AND WAS directed by his father toward a business career. But a love of study took him instead to a series of universities: in Palermo, in Rome, and in Bonn, where he wrote a dissertation in philology. His father arranged for his son to marry a rich Sicilian girl so that he would be free to write without financial worries. But a landslide in a Sicilian sulphur mine brought an end to his wife's fortune and also the start of her mental disorders. Teaching and writing to subsist, Pirandello lived with material difficulties and psychological problems for many years, but in time became an international success and a nationally honored figure.

Pirandello's early literary efforts—mostly short stories—were very much under the influence of Giovanni Verga and the Sicilian brand of *verismo*. Yet even in his early work there was evidence of his love of paradox and of probing questions about the nature of illusion and reality, which became the essence of his work in the theater. Pirandello had made an unsuccessful attempt at theater as early as 1898, but it was not until 1917 with *It* Is *So (If You Think So)* that he found his principal theme and entered into the period of his major plays. *Six Characters in Search of an Author* and *Henry IV*, probably his two best plays, were presented in 1921 and 1922, and international fame arrived with the Parisian production of *Six Characters* in 1923.

With *Six Characters* and the plays that followed it, Pirandello made explicit a theme implicit in almost all great drama (it is important in Shakespeare, for example): the "theatricality" of the drama—the play's consciousness of itself as a play, as an artificial, but possibly truer, version of reality. Pirandello's favored structure is the play within the play, by which the drama reflects on its own mode of existence through the creation of a facsimile of itself. Pirandello described *Six Characters,* along with *Each in His Own Way* and *Tonight We Improvise,* as "theater in the theater," dramas showing the birth of drama and of theater. For Pirandello, this structure is a means to explore different layers of appearance and to question their degree of reality or unreality for different observers and actors. He probes the ways in which people use roles and masks in their lives and the ways in which life and theater are inextricably intertwined. Pirandello's extreme self-consciousness about the theater has influenced almost all subsequent dramatists of any importance; in part because of him, they have not been able to approach their work naively and "innocently."

Six Characters in Search of an Author

A COMEDY IN THE MAKING

CHARACTERS OF THE COMEDY IN THE MAKING

THE FATHER	THE BOY
THE MOTHER	THE CHILD
THE STEP-DAUGHTER	*(The last two do not speak)*
THE SON	MADAME PACE

ACTORS OF THE COMPANY

THE MANAGER	OTHERS ACTORS AND ACTRESSES
LEADING LADY	PROPERTY MAN
LEADING MAN	PROMPTER
SECOND LADY	MACHINIST
LEAD	MANAGER'S SECRETARY
L'INGÉNUE	DOOR-KEEPER
JUVENILE LEAD	SCENE-SHIFTERS

Daytime. The Stage of a Theater

N. B. The Comedy is without acts or scenes. The performance is interrupted once, without the curtain being lowered, when the manager and the chief characters withdraw to arrange the scenario. A second interruption of the action takes place when, by mistake, the stage hands let the curtain down.

ACT I

The spectators will find the curtain raised and the stage as it usually is during the daytime. It will be half dark, and empty, so that from the beginning the public may have the impression of an impromptu performance.

Prompter's box and a small table and chair for the manager.

Two other small tables and several chairs scattered about as during rehearsals.

The ACTORS *and* ACTRESSES *of the company enter from the back of the stage:*

first one, then another, then two together; nine or ten in all. They are about to rehearse a Pirandello play: Mixing It Up.[1] *Some of the company move off towards their dressing rooms. The* PROMPTER *who has the "book" under his arm, is waiting for the* MANAGER *in order to begin the rehearsal.*

The ACTORS *and* ACTRESSES, *some standing, some sitting, chat and smoke. One perhaps reads a paper; another cons his part.*

Finally, the MANAGER *enters and goes to the table prepared for him. His* SECRETARY *brings him his mail, through which he glances. The* PROMPTER *takes his seat, turns on a light, and opens the "book."*

THE MANAGER [*throwing a letter down on the table*]. I can't see. [*To* PROPERTY MAN.] Let's have a little light, please!

PROPERTY MAN. Yes sir, yes, at once. [*A light comes down on to the stage.*]

THE MANAGER [*clapping his hands*]. Come along! Come along! Second act of "Mixing It Up." [*Sits down.*]

[*The* ACTORS *and* ACTRESSES *go from the front of the stage to the wings, all except the three who are to begin the rehearsal.*]

PROMPTER [*reading the "book"*]. "Leo Gala's house. A curious room serving as dining-room and study."

THE MANAGER [*to* PROPERTY MAN]. Fix up the old red room.

PROPERTY MAN [*noting it down*]. Red set. All right!

PROMPTER [*continuing to read from the "book"*]. "Table already laid

[1] That is, *Il giuoco delle parti.*

and writing desk with books and papers. Book-shelves. Exit rear to Leo's bedroom. Exit left to kitchen. Principal exit to right."

THE MANAGER [*energetically*]. Well, you understand: The principal exit over there; here, the kitchen. [*Turning to actor who is to play the part of* SOCRATES.] You make your entrances and exits here. [*To* PROPERTY MAN.] The baize doors at the rear, and curtains.

PROPERTY MAN [*noting it down*]. Right!

PROMPTER [*reading as before*]. "When the curtain rises, Leo Gala, dressed in cook's cap and apron is busy beating an egg in a cup. Philip, also dressed as a cook, is beating another egg. Guido Venanzi is seated and listening."

LEADING MAN [*to* MANAGER]. Excuse me, but must I absolutely wear a cook's cap?

THE MANAGER [*annoyed*]. I imagine so. It says so there anyway. [*Pointing to the "book."*]

LEADING MAN. But it's ridiculous!

THE MANAGER [*jumping up in a rage*]. Ridiculous? Ridiculous? Is it my fault if France won't send us any more good comedies, and we are reduced to putting on Pirandello's works, where nobody understands anything, and where the author plays the fool with us all? [*The* ACTORS *grin. The* MANAGER *goes to* LEADING MAN *and shouts.*] Yes sir, you put on the cook's cap and beat eggs. Do you suppose that with all this egg-beating business you are on an ordinary stage? Get that out of your head. You represent the shell of the eggs you are beating! [*Laughter and comments among the* ACTORS.] Silence! and listen to my explanations, please! [*To* LEADING MAN.] "The empty form of reason without the fullness of instinct, which is blind."—You stand for reason, your wife is instinct. It's a mixing up of the parts, according to which you who act your own part become the puppet of yourself. Do you understand?

LEADING MAN. I'm hanged if I do.

THE MANAGER. Neither do I. But let's get on with it. It's sure to be a glorious failure anyway. [*Confidentially.*] But I say, please face three-quarters. Otherwise, what with the abstruseness of the dialogue, and the public that won't be able to hear you, the whole thing will go to hell. Come on! come on!

PROMPTER. Pardon sir, may I get into my box? There's a bit of a draught.

THE MANAGER. Yes, yes, of course!

At this point, the DOOR-KEEPER *has entered from the stage door and advances towards the* MANAGER'S *table, taking off his braided cap. During this manoeuvre, the*

SIX CHARACTERS *enter, and stop by the door at back of stage, so that when the* DOOR-KEEPER *is about to announce their coming to the* MANAGER, *they are already on the stage. A tenuous light surrounds them, almost as if irradiated by them—the faint breath of their fantastic reality.*

This light will disappear when they come forward towards the actors. They preserve, however, something of the dream lightness in which they seem almost suspended; but this does not detract from the essential reality of their forms and expressions.

He who is known as the FATHER *is a man of about 50: hair, reddish in color, thin at the temples; he is not bald, however; thick moustaches, falling over his still fresh mouth, which often opens in an empty and uncertain smile. He is fattish, pale; with an especially wide forehead. He has blue, oval-shaped eyes, very clear and piercing. Wears light trousers and a dark jacket. He is alternatively mellifluous and violent in his manner.*

The MOTHER *seems crushed and terrified as if by an intolerable weight of shame and abasement. She is dressed in modest black and wears a thick widow's veil of crêpe. When she lifts this, she reveals a waxlike face. She always keeps her eyes downcast.*

The STEP-DAUGHTER, *is dashing, almost impudent, beautiful. She wears mourning too, but with great elegance. She shows contempt for the timid half-frightened manner of the wretched* BOY *(14 years old, and also dressed in black); on the other hand, she displays a lively tenderness for her little sister, the* CHILD *(about four), who is dressed in white, with a black silk sash at the waist.*

The SON *(22) tall, severe in his attitude of contempt for the* FATHER, *supercilious and indifferent to the* MOTHER. *He looks as if he had come on the stage against his will.*

DOOR-KEEPER [*cap in hand*]. Excuse me, sir . . .

THE MANAGER [*rudely*]. Eh? What is it?

DOOR-KEEPER [*timidly*]. These people are asking for you, sir.

THE MANAGER [*furious*]. I am rehearsing, and you know perfectly well no one's allowed to come in during rehearsals! [*Turning to the* CHARACTERS.] Who are you, please. What do you want?

THE FATHER [*coming forward a little, followed by the others who seem embarrassed*]. As a matter of fact . . . we have come here in search of an author . . .

THE MANAGER [*half angry, half amazed*]. An author? What author?

THE FATHER. Any author, sir.

THE MANAGER. But there's no author here. We are not rehearsing a new piece.

THE STEP-DAUGHTER [*vivaciously*]. So much the better, so much the better! We can be your new piece.

AN ACTOR [*coming forward from the others*]. Oh, do you hear that?

THE FATHER [*to* STEP-DAUGHTER]. Yes, but if the author isn't here . . . [*to* MANAGER] unless you would be willing . . .

THE MANAGER. You are trying to be funny.

THE FATHER. No, for Heaven's sake, what are you saying? We bring you a drama, sir.

THE STEP-DAUGHTER. We may be your fortune.

THE MANAGER. Will you oblige me by going away? We haven't time to waste with mad people.

THE FATHER [*mellifluously*]. Oh sir, you know well that life is full of infinite absurdities, which, strangely enough, do not even need to appear plausible, since they are true.

THE FATHER. I say that to reverse the ordinary process may well be considered a madness: that is, to create credible situations, in order that they may appear true. But permit me to observe that if this be madness, it is the sole *raison d'être* of your profession, gentlemen. [*The* ACTORS *look hurt and perplexed.*]

THE MANAGER [*getting up and looking at him*]. So our profession seems to you one worthy of madmen then?

THE FATHER. Well, to make seem true that which isn't true . . . without any need . . . for a joke as it were. . . . Isn't that your mission, gentlemen: to give life to fantastic characters on the stage?

THE MANAGER [*interpreting the rising anger of the* COMPANY]. But I would beg you to believe, my dear sir, that the profession of the comedian is a noble one. If today, as things go, the playwrights give us stupid comedies to play and puppets to represent instead of men, remember we are proud to have given life to immortal works here on these very boards! [*The* ACTORS, *satisfied, applaud their* MANAGER.]

THE FATHER [*interrupting furiously*]. Exactly, perfectly, to living beings more alive than those who breathe and wear clothes: beings less real perhaps, but truer! I agree with you entirely. [*The* ACTORS *look at one another in amazement.*]

THE MANAGER. But what do you mean? Before, you said . . .

THE FATHER. No, excuse me, I meant it for you, sir, who were crying out that you had no time to lose with madmen, while no one better than yourself knows that nature uses the instrument of human fantasy in order to pursue her high creative purpose.

THE MANAGER. Very well—but where does all this take us?

THE FATHER. Nowhere! It is merely to show you that one is born to life in many forms, in many shapes, as tree, or as stone, as water, as butterfly, or as woman. So one may also be born a character in a play.

THE MANAGER [*with feigned comic dismay*]. So you and these other friends of yours have been born characters?

THE FATHER. Exactly, and alive as you see! [MANAGER *and* ACTORS *burst out laughing.*]

THE FATHER [*hurt*]. I am sorry you laugh, because we carry in us a drama, as you can guess from this woman here veiled in black.

THE MANAGER [*losing patience at last and almost indignant*]. Oh, chuck it! Get away please! Clear out of here! [*To* PROPERTY MAN.] For Heaven's sake, turn them out!

THE FATHER [*resisting*]. No, no, look here, we . . .

THE MANAGER [*roaring*]. We come here to work, you know.

LEADING ACTOR. One cannot let oneself be made such a fool of.

THE FATHER [*determined, coming forward*]. I marvel at your incredulity, gentlemen. Are you not accustomed to see the characters created by an author spring to life in yourselves and face each other? Just because there is no "book" [*pointing to the* PROMPTER'S *box*] which contains us, you refuse to believe . . .

THE STEP-DAUGHTER [*advances towards* MANAGER, *smiling and coquettish*]. Believe me, we are really six most interesting characters, sir; side-tracked however.

THE FATHER. Yes, that is the word! [*To* MANAGER *all at once.*] In the sense, that is, that the author who created us alive no longer wished, or was no longer able, materially to put us into a work of art. And this was a real crime, sir; because he who has had the luck to be born a character can laugh even at death. He cannot die. The man, the writer, the instrument of the creation will die, but his creation does not die. And to live for ever, it does not need to have extraordinary gifts or to be able to work wonders. Who was Sancho Panza? Who was Don Abbondio? Yet they live eternally because—live germs as they were—they had the fortune to find a fecundating matrix, a fantasy which could raise and nourish them: make them live for ever!

THE MANAGER. That is quite all right. But what do you want here, all of you?

THE FATHER. We want to live.

THE MANAGER [*ironically*]. For Eternity?

THE FATHER. No, sir, only for a moment . . . in you.

AN ACTOR. Just listen to him!

LEADING LADY. They want to live, in us . . . !

JUVENILE LEAD [*pointing to the* STEP-DAUGHTER]. I've no objection, as far as that one is concerned!

THE FATHER. Look here! look here! The comedy has to be made. [*To the* MANAGER.] But if you and your actors are willing, we can soon concert it among ourselves.

THE MANAGER [*annoyed*]. But what do you want to concert? We don't go in for concerts here. Here we play dramas and comedies!

THE FATHER. Exactly! That is just why we have come to you.

THE MANAGER. And where is the "book"?

THE FATHER. It is in us! [*The* ACTORS *laugh.*] The drama is in us, and we are the drama. We are impatient to play it. Our inner passion drives us on to this.

THE STEP-DAUGHTER [*disdainful, alluring, treacherous, full of impudence*]. My passion, sir! Ah, if you only knew! My passion for him! [*Points to the* FATHER *and makes a pretense of embracing him. Then she breaks out into a loud laugh.*]

THE FATHER [*angrily*]. Behave yourself! And please don't laugh in that fashion.

THE STEP-DAUGHTER. With your permission, gentlemen, I, who am a two months' orphan, will show you how I can dance and sing. [*Sings and then dances* Prenez garde à Tchou-Tchin-Tchou.]

> Les chinois sont un peuple malin,
> De Shangaî à Pekin,
> Ils ont mis des écriteaux partout:
> Prenez garde à Tchou-Tchin-Tchou.[2]

ACTORS AND ACTRESSES. Bravo! Well done! Tip-top!

THE MANAGER. Silence! This isn't a cafe concert, you know! [*Turning to the* FATHER *in consternation.*] Is she mad?

THE FATHER. Mad? No, she's worse than mad.

THE STEP-DAUGHTER [*to* MANAGER]. Worse? Worse? Listen! Stage this drama for us at once! Then you will see that at a certain moment I . . . when this little darling here . . . [*Takes the* CHILD *by the hand and leads her to the* MANAGER.] Isn't she a dear? [*Takes her up and kisses her.*] Darling! Darling! [*Puts her down again and adds feelingly.*] Well, when God suddenly takes this dear little child away from that poor mother there; and this imbecile here [*seizing hold of the* BOY *roughly and pushing him forward*] does the stupidest things,

[2] "The Chinese are a clever people, / From Shanghai to Peking / They have put signs everywhere: / Watch out for Chou-Ching-Chou."

like the fool he is, you will see me run away. Yes, gentlemen, I shall be off. But the moment hasn't arrived yet. After what has taken place between him and me [*indicates the* FATHER *with a horrible wink*] I can't remain any longer in this society, to have to witness the anguish of this mother here for that fool . . . [*Indicates the* SON.] Look at him! Look at him! See how indifferent, how frigid he is, because he is the legitimate son. He despises me, despises him [*pointing to the* BOY], despises this baby here; because . . . we are bastards. [*Goes to the* MOTHER *and embraces her.*] And he doesn't want to recognize her as his mother—she who is the common mother of us all. He looks down upon her as if she were only the mother of us three bastards. Wretch! [*She says all this very rapidly, excitedly. At the word "bastards" she raises her voice, and almost spits out the final "Wretch!"*]

THE MOTHER [*to the* MANAGER, *in anguish*]. In the name of these two little children, I beg you . . . [*She grows faint and is about to fall.*] Oh God!

THE FATHER [*coming forward to support her as do some of the* ACTORS]. Quick, a chair, a chair for this poor widow!

THE ACTORS. Is it true? Has she really fainted?

THE MANAGER. Quick, a chair! Here!

[*One of the* ACTORS *brings a chair, the* OTHERS *proffer assistance. The* MOTHER *tries to prevent the* FATHER *from lifting the veil which covers her face.*]

THE FATHER. Look at her! Look at her!

THE MOTHER. No, no; stop it please!

THE FATHER [*raising her veil*]. Let them see you!

THE MOTHER [*rising and covering her face with her hands, in desperation*]. I beg you, sir, to prevent this man from carrying out his plan which is loathsome to me.

THE MANAGER [*dumbfounded*]. I don't understand at all. What is the situation? Is this lady your wife? [*To the* FATHER.]

THE FATHER. Yes, gentlemen: my wife!

THE MANAGER. But how can she be a widow if you are alive? [*The* ACTORS *find relief for their astonishment in a loud laugh.*]

THE FATHER. Don't laugh! Don't laugh like that, for Heaven's sake. Her drama lies just here in this: she has had a lover, a man who ought to be here.

THE MOTHER [*with a cry*]. No! No!

THE STEP-DAUGHTER. Fortunately for her, he is dead. Two months ago as I said. We are in mourning, as you see.

THE FATHER. He isn't here you see, not because he is dead. He isn't here —look at her a moment and you will understand—because her drama isn't a drama of the love of two men for whom she was incapable of feeling anything except possibly a little gratitude—gratitude not for me but for the other. She isn't a woman, she is a mother, and her drama—powerful sir, I assure you—lies, as a matter of fact, all in these four children she has had by two men.

THE MOTHER. I had them? Have you got the courage to say that I wanted them? [*To the* COMPANY.] It was his doing. It was he who gave me that other man, who forced me to go away with him.

THE STEP-DAUGHTER. It isn't true.

THE MOTHER [*startled*]. Not true, isn't it?

THE STEP-DAUGHTER. No, it isn't true, it just isn't true.

THE MOTHER. And what can you know about it?

THE STEP-DAUGHTER. It isn't true. Don't believe it. [*To* MANAGER.] Do you know why she says so? For that fellow there. [*Indicates the* SON.] She tortures herself, destroys herself on account of the neglect of that son there; and she wants him to believe that if she abandoned him when he was only two years old, it was because he [*indicates the* FATHER] made her do so.

THE MOTHER [*vigorously*]. He forced me to it, and I call God to witness it. [*To the* MANAGER.] Ask him [*indicates* HUSBAND] if it isn't true. Let him speak. You [*to* STEP-DAUGHTER] are not in a position to know anything about it.

THE STEP-DAUGHTER. I know you lived in peace and happiness with my father while he lived. Can you deny it?

THE MOTHER. No, I don't deny it . . .

THE STEP-DAUGHTER. He was always full of affection and kindness for you. [*To the* BOY, *angrily*.] It's true, isn't it? Tell them! Why don't you speak, you little fool?

THE MOTHER. Leave the poor boy alone. Why do you want to make me appear ungrateful, daughter? I don't want to offend your father. I have answered him that I didn't abandon my house and my son through any fault of mine, nor from any willful passion.

THE FATHER. It is true. It was my doing.

LEADING MAN [*to the* COMPANY]. What a spectacle!

LEADING LADY. We are the audience this time.

JUVENILE LEAD. For once, in a way.

THE MANAGER [*beginning to get really interested*]. Let's hear them out. Listen!

THE SON. Oh yes, you're going to hear a fine bit now. He will talk to you of the Demon of Experiment.

THE FATHER. You are a cynical imbecile. I've told you so already a hundred times. [*To the* MANAGER.] He tries to make fun of me on account of this expression which I have found to excuse myself with.

THE SON [*with disgust*]. Yes, phrases! phrases!

THE FATHER. Phrases! Isn't everyone consoled when faced with a trouble or fact he doesn't understand, by a word, some simple word, which tells us nothing and yet calms us?

THE STEP-DAUGHTER. Even in the case of remorse. In fact, especially then.

THE FATHER. Remorse? No, that isn't true. I've done more than use words to quieten the remorse in me.

THE STEP-DAUGHTER. Yes, there was a bit of money too. Yes, yes, a bit of money. There were the hundred lire he was about to offer me in payment, gentlemen. . . . [*Sensation of horror among the* ACTORS.]

THE SON [*to the* STEP-DAUGHTER]. This is vile.

THE STEP-DAUGHTER. Vile? There they were in a pale blue envelope on a little mahogany table in the back of Madame Pace's shop. You know Madame Pace—one of those ladies who attract poor girls of good family into their ateliers, under the pretext of their selling *robes et manteaux.*

THE SON. And he thinks he has bought the right to tyrannize over us all with those hundred lire he was going to pay; but which, fortunately —note this, gentlemen—he had no chance of paying.

THE STEP-DAUGHTER. It was a near thing, though, you know! [*Laughs ironically.*]

THE MOTHER [*protesting*]. Shame, my daughter, shame!

THE STEP-DAUGHTER. Shame indeed! This is my revenge! I am dying to live that scene. . . . The room . . . I see it. . . . Here is the window with the mantles exposed, there the divan, the looking-glass, a screen, there in front of the window the little mahogany table with the blue envelope containing one hundred lire. I see it. I see it. I could take hold of it. . . . But you, gentlemen, you ought to turn your backs now: I am almost nude, you know. But I don't blush: I leave that to him [*indicating* FATHER].

THE MANAGER. I don't understand this at all.

THE FATHER. Naturally enough. I would ask you, sir, to exercise your authority a little here, and let me speak before you believe all she is trying to blame me with. Let me explain.

THE STEP-DAUGHTER. Ah yes, explain it in your own way.

THE FATHER. But don't you see that the whole trouble lies here. In words, words. Each one of us has within him a whole world of things, each man of us his own special world. And how can we ever come to an understanding if I put in the words I utter the sense and value of things as I see them; while you who listen to me must inevitably translate them according to the conception of things each one of you has within himself. We think we understand each other, but we never really do. Look here! This woman [*indicating the* MOTHER] takes all my pity for her as a specially ferocious form of cruelty.

THE MOTHER. But you drove me away.

THE FATHER. Do you hear her? I drove her away! She believes I really sent her away.

THE MOTHER. You know how to talk, and I don't; but, believe me, sir [*to* MANAGER], after he had married me . . . who knows why? . . . I was a poor insignificant woman. . . .

THE FATHER. But, good Heavens! it was just for your humility that I married you. I loved this simplicity in you. [*He stops when he sees she makes signs to contradict him, opens his arms wide in sign of desperation, seeing how hopeless it is to make himself understood.*] You see she denies it. Her mental deafness, believe me, is phenomenal, the limit: [*touches his forehead*] deaf, deaf, mentally deaf! She has plenty of feeling. Oh yes, a good heart for the children; but the brain —deaf, to the point of desperation—!

THE STEP-DAUGHTER. Yes, but ask him how his intelligence has helped us.

THE FATHER. If we could see all the evil that may spring from good, what should we do? [*At this point the* LEADING LADY *who is biting her lips with rage at seeing the* LEADING MAN *flirting with the* STEP-DAUGHTER, *comes forward and says to the* MANAGER.]

LEADING LADY. Excuse me, but are we going to rehearse today?

THE MANAGER. Of course, of course; but let's hear them out.

JUVENILE LEAD. This is something quite new.

L'INGÉNUE. Most interesting!

LEADING LADY. Yes, for the people who like that kind of thing. [*Casts a glance at* LEADING MAN.]

THE MANAGER [*to* FATHER]. You must please explain yourself quite clearly. [*Sits down.*]

THE FATHER. Very well then: listen! I had in my service a poor man, a clerk, a secretary of mine, full of devotion, who became friends with her. [*Indicating the* MOTHER.] They understood one another, were kindred souls in fact, without, however, the least suspicion of any evil existing. They were incapable even of thinking of it.

THE STEP-DAUGHTER. So he thought of it—for them!

THE FATHER. That's not true. I meant to do good to them—and to myself, I confess, at the same time. Things had come to the point that I could not say a word to either of them without their making a mute appeal, one to the other, with their eyes. I could see them silently asking each other how I was to be kept in countenance, how I was to be kept quiet. And this, believe me, was just about enough of itself to keep me in a constant rage, to exasperate me beyond measure.

THE MANAGER. And why didn't you send him away then—this secretary of yours?

THE FATHER. Precisely what I did, sir. And then I had to watch this poor woman drifting forlornly about the house like an animal without a master, like an animal one has taken in out of pity.

THE MOTHER. Ah yes . . . !

THE FATHER [*suddenly turning to the* MOTHER]. It's true about the son anyway, isn't it?

THE MOTHER. He took my son away from me first of all.

THE FATHER. But not from cruelty. I did it so that he should grow up healthy and strong by living in the country.

THE STEP-DAUGHTER [*pointing to him ironically*]. As one can see.

THE FATHER [*quickly*]. Is it my fault if he has grown up like this? I sent him to a wet nurse in the country, a peasant, as *she* did not seem to me strong enough, though she is of humble origin. That was, anyway, the reason I married her. Unpleasant all this may be, but how can it be helped? My mistake possibly, but there we are! All my life I have had these confounded aspirations towards a certain moral sanity. [*At this point the* STEP-DAUGHTER *bursts into a noisy laugh.*] Oh, stop it! Stop it! I can't stand it.

THE MANAGER. Yes, please stop it, for Heaven's sake.

THE STEP-DAUGHTER. But imagine moral sanity from him, if you please—the client of certain ateliers like that of Madame Pace!

THE FATHER. Fool! That is the proof that I am a man! This seeming contradiction, gentlemen, is the strongest proof that I stand here a live man before you. Why, it is just for this very incongruity in my nature that I have had to suffer what I have. I could not live by the side of that woman [*indicating the* MOTHER] any longer; but not so much for the boredom she inspired me with as for the pity I felt for her.

THE MOTHER. And so he turned me out—.

THE FATHER. —well provided for! Yes, I sent her to that man, gentlemen . . . to let her go free of me.

THE MOTHER. And to free himself.

THE FATHER. Yes, I admit it. It was also a liberation for me. But great evil has come of it. I meant well when I did it; and I did it more for her sake than mine. I swear it. [*Crosses his arms on his chest; then turns suddenly to the* MOTHER.] Did I ever lose sight of you until that other man carried you off to another town, like the angry fool he was? And on account of my pure interest in you . . . my pure interest, I repeat, that had no base motive in it. . . . I watched with the tenderest concern the new family that grew up around her. She can bear witness to this. [*Points to the* STEP-DAUGHTER.]

THE STEP-DAUGHTER. Oh yes, that's true enough. When I was a kiddie, so so high, you know, with plaits over my shoulders and knickers longer than my skirts, I used to see him waiting outside the school for me to come out. He came to see how I was growing up.

THE FATHER. This is infamous, shameful!

THE STEP-DAUGHTER. No. Why?

THE FATHER. Infamous! infamous! [*Then excitedly to* MANAGER, *explaining.*] After she [*indicating* MOTHER] went away, my house seemed suddenly empty. She was my incubus, but she filled my house. I was like a dazed fly alone in the empty rooms. This boy here [*indicating the* SON] was educated away from home, and when he came back, he seemed to me to be no more mine. With no mother to stand between him and me, he grew up entirely for himself, on his own, apart, with no tie of intellect or affection binding him to me. And then—strange but true—I was driven, by curiosity at first and then by some tender sentiment, towards her family, which had come into being through my will. The thought of her began gradually to fill up the emptiness I felt all around me. I wanted to know if she were happy in living out the simple daily duties of life. I wanted to think of her as fortunate and happy because far away from the complicated torments of my spirit. And so, to have proof of this, I used to watch that child coming out of school.

THE STEP-DAUGHTER. Yes, yes. True. He used to follow me in the street and smiled at me, waved his hand, like this. I would look at him with interest, wondering who he might be. I told my mother, who guessed at once. [*The* MOTHER *agrees with a nod.*] Then she didn't want to send me to school for some days; and when I finally went back, there he was again—looking so ridiculous—with a paper parcel in his hands. He came close to me, caressed me, and drew out a fine straw hat from the parcel, with a bouquet of flowers—all for me!

THE MANAGER. A bit discursive this, you know!

THE SON [*contemptuously*]. Literature! Literature!

THE FATHER. Literature indeed! This is life, this is passion!

THE MANAGER. It may be, but it won't act.

THE FATHER. I agree. This is only the part leading up. I don't suggest this should be staged. She [*pointing to the* STEP-DAUGHTER], as you see, is no longer the flapper with plaits down her back—

THE STEP-DAUGHTER. —and the knickers showing below the skirt!

THE FATHER. The drama is coming now, sir; something new, complex, most interesting.

THE STEP-DAUGHTER. As soon as my father died . . .

THE FATHER. —there was absolute misery for them. They came back here, unknown to me. Through her stupidity! [*Pointing to the* MOTHER.] It is true she can barely write her own name; but she could anyhow have got her daughter to write to me that they were in need. . . .

THE MOTHER. And how was I to divine all this sentiment in him?

THE FATHER. That is exactly your mistake, never to have guessed any of my sentiments.

THE MOTHER. After so many years apart, and all that had happened . . .

THE FATHER. Was it my fault if that fellow carried you away? It happened quite suddenly; for after he had obtained some job or other, I could find no trace of them; and so, not unnaturally, my interest in them dwindled. But the drama culminated unforeseen and violent on their return, when I was impelled by my miserable flesh that still lives. . . . Ah! what misery, what wretchedness is that of the man who is alone and disdains debasing *liaisons!* Not old enough to do without women, and not young enough to go and look for one without shame. Misery? It's worse than misery; it's a horror; for no woman can any longer give him love; and when a man feels this . . . One ought to do without, you say? Yes, yes, I know. Each of us when he appears before his fellows is clothed in a certain dignity. But every man knows what unconfessable things pass within the secrecy of his own heart. One gives way to the temptation, only to rise from it again, afterwards, with a great eagerness to reestablish one's dignity, as if it were a tombstone to place on the grave of one's shame, and a monument to hide and sign the memory of our weaknesses. Everybody's in the same case. Some folks haven't the courage to say certain things, that's all!

THE STEP-DAUGHTER. All appear to have the courage to do them though.

THE FATHER. Yes, but in secret. Therefore, you want more courage to say these things. Let a man but speak these things out, and folks at once label him a cynic. But it isn't true. He is like all the others, better indeed, because he isn't afraid to reveal with the light of the intelligence the red shame of human bestiality on which most men close their eyes so as not to see it.

Woman—for example, look at her case! She turns tantalizing inviting glances on you. You seize her. No sooner does she feel herself in your grasp than she closes her eyes. It is the sign of her mission, the sign by which she says to man: "Blind yourself, for I am blind."

THE STEP-DAUGHTER. Sometimes she can close them no more: when she no longer feels the need of hiding her shame to herself, but dry-eyed and dispassionately, sees only that of the man who has blinded himself without love. Oh, all these intellectual complications make me sick, disgust me—all this philosophy that uncovers the beast in man, and then seeks to save him, excuse him. . . . I can't stand it, sir. When a man seeks to "simplify" life bestially, throwing aside every relic of humanity, every chaste aspiration, every pure feeling, all sense of ideality, duty, modesty, shame . . . then nothing is more revolting and nauseous than a certain kind of remorse—crocodiles' tears, that's what it is.

THE MANAGER. Let's come to the point. This is only discussion.

THE FATHER. Very good, sir! But a fact is like a sack which won't stand up when it is empty. In order that it may stand up, one has to put into it the reason and sentiment which have caused it to exist. I couldn't possibly know that after the death of that man, they had decided to return here, that they were in misery, and that she [*pointing to the* MOTHER] had gone to work as a modiste, and at a shop of the type of that of Madame Pace.

THE STEP-DAUGHTER. A real high-class modiste, you must know, gentlemen. In appearance, she works for the leaders of the best society; but she arranges matters so that these elegant ladies serve her purpose . . . without prejudice to other ladies who are . . . well . . . only so so.

THE MOTHER. You will believe me, gentlemen, that it never entered my mind that the old hag offered me work because she had her eye on my daughter.

THE STEP-DAUGHTER. Poor mamma! Do you know, sir, what that woman did when I brought her back the work my mother had finished? She would point out to me that I had torn one of my frocks, and she would give it back to my mother to mend. It was I who paid for it, always I; while this poor creature here believed she was sacrificing herself for me and these two children here, sitting up at night sewing Madame Pace's robes.

THE MANAGER. And one day you met there . . .

THE STEP-DAUGHTER. Him, him. Yes sir, an old client. There's a scene for you to play! Superb!

THE FATHER. She, the Mother arrived just then. . . .

THE STEP-DAUGHTER [*treacherously*]. Almost in time!

THE FATHER [*crying out*]. No, in time! in time! Fortunately I recognized her . . . in time. And I took them back home with me to my house. You can imagine now her position and mine; she, as you see her; and I who cannot look her in the face.

THE STEP-DAUGHTER. Absurd! How can I possibly be expected—after that —to be a modest young miss, a fit person to go with his confounded aspirations for "a solid moral sanity"?

THE FATHER. For the drama lies all in this—in the conscience that I have, that each one of us has. We believe this conscience to be a single thing, but it is many-sided. There is one for this person, and another for that. Diverse consciences. So we have this illusion of being one person for all, of having a personality that is unique in all our acts. But it isn't true. We perceive this when, tragically perhaps, in something we do, we are as it were, suspended, caught up in the air on a kind of hook. Then we perceive that all of us was not in that act, and that it would be an atrocious injustice to judge us by that action alone, as if all our existence were summed up in that one deed. Now do you understand the perfidy of this girl? She surprised me in a place, where she ought not to have known me, just as I could not exist for her; and she now seeks to attach to me a reality such as I could never suppose I should have to assume for her in a shameful and fleeting moment of my life. I feel this above all else. And the drama, you will see, acquires a tremendous value from this point. Then there is the position of the others . . . his . . . [*indicating the* SON].

THE SON [*shrugging his shoulders scornfully*]. Leave me alone! I don't come into this.

THE FATHER. What? You don't come into this?

THE SON. I've got nothing to do with it, and don't want to have; because you know well enough I wasn't made to be mixed up in all this with the rest of you.

THE STEP-DAUGHTER. We are only vulgar folk! He is the fine gentleman. You may have noticed, Mr. Manager, that I fix him now and again with a look of scorn while he lowers his eyes—for he knows the evil he has done me.

THE SON [*scarcely looking at her*]. I?

THE STEP-DAUGHTER. You! you! I owe my life on the streets to you. Did you or did you not deny us, with your behavior, I won't say the intimacy of home, but even that mere hospitality which makes guests feel at their ease? We were intruders who had come to disturb the kingdom of your legitimacy. I should like to have you witness, Mr. Manager, certain scenes between him and me. He says I have tyrannized over everyone. But it was just his behavior which made me insist on the reason for which I had come into the house—this reason he calls "vile"—into his house, with my mother who is his mother too. And I came as mistress of the house.

THE SON. It's easy for them to put me always in the wrong. But imagine, gentlemen, the position of a son, whose fate it is to see arrive one day at his home a young woman of impudent bearing, a young woman who inquires for his father, with whom who knows what business she has. This young man has then to witness her return bolder than ever, accompanied by that child there. He is obliged to watch her treat his father in an equivocal and confidential manner. She asks money of him in a way that lets one suppose he must give it her, *must,* do you understand, because he has every obligation to do so.

THE FATHER. But I have, as a matter of fact, this obligation. I owe it to your mother.

THE SON. How should I know? When had I ever seen or heard of her? One day there arrive with her [*indicating* STEP-DAUGHTER] that lad and this baby here. I am told: "This is *your* mother too, you know." I divine from her manner [*indicating* STEP-DAUGHTER *again*] why it is they have come home. I had rather not say what I feel and think about it. I shouldn't even care to confess to myself. No action can therefore be hoped for from me in this affair. Believe me, Mr. Manager, I am an "unrealized" character, dramatically speaking; and I find myself not at all at ease in their company. Leave me out of it, I beg you.

THE FATHER. What? It is just because you are so that . . .

THE SON. How do you know what I am like? When did you ever bother your head about me?

THE FATHER. I admit it. I admit it. But isn't that a situation in itself? This aloofness of yours which is so cruel to me and to your mother, who returns home and sees you almost for the first time grown up, who doesn't recognize you but knows you are her son . . . [*pointing out the* MOTHER *to the* MANAGER]. See, she's crying!

THE STEP-DAUGHTER [*angrily, stamping her foot*]. Like a fool!

THE FATHER [*indicating* STEP-DAUGHTER]. She can't stand him you know. [*Then referring again to the* SON.] He says he doesn't come into the affair, whereas he is really the hinge of the whole action. Look at that lad who is always clinging to his mother, frightened and humiliated. It is on account of this fellow here. Possibly his situation is the most painful of all. He feels himself a stranger more than the others. The poor little chap feels mortified, humiliated at being brought into a home out of charity as it were. [*In confidence.*] He is the image of his father. Hardly talks at all. Humble and quiet.

THE MANAGER. Oh, we'll cut him out. You've no notion what a nuisance boys are on the stage. . . .

THE FATHER. He disappears soon, you know. And the baby too. She is the first to vanish from the scene. The drama consists finally in this: when that mother reenters my house, her family born outside of it, and shall we say superimposed on the original, ends with the death of the little girl, the tragedy of the boy and the flight of the elder daughter. It cannot go on, because it is foreign to its surroundings. So after much torment, we three remain: I, the mother, that son. Then, owing to the disappearance of that extraneous family, we too find ourselves strange to one another. We find we are living in an atmosphere of mortal desolation which is the revenge, as he [*indicating* SON] scornfully said of the Demon of Experiment, that unfortunately hides in me. Thus, sir, you see when faith is lacking, it becomes impossible to create certain states of happiness, for we lack the necessary humility. Vaingloriously, we try to substitute ourselves for this faith, creating thus for the rest of the world a reality which we believe after their fashion, while, actually, it doesn't exist. For each one of us has his own reality to be respected before God, even when it is harmful to one's very self.

THE MANAGER. There is something in what you say. I assure you all this interests me very much. I begin to think there's the stuff for a drama in all this, and not a bad drama either.

THE STEP-DAUGHTER [*coming forward*]. When you've got a character like me.

THE FATHER [*shutting her up, all excited to learn the decision of the* MANAGER]. You be quiet!

THE MANAGER [*reflecting, heedless of interruption*]. It's new . . . hem . . . yes. . . .

THE FATHER. Absolutely new!

THE MANAGER. You've got a nerve though, I must say, to come here and fling it at me like this. . . .

THE FATHER. You will understand, sir, born as we are for the stage . . .

THE MANAGER. Are you amateur actors then?

THE FATHER. No. I say born for the stage, because . . .

THE MANAGER. Oh, nonsense. You're an old hand, you know.

THE FATHER. No sir, no. We act that role for which we have been cast, that role which we are given in life. And in my own case, passion itself, as usually happens, becomes a trifle theatrical when it is exalted.

THE MANAGER. Well, well, that will do. But you see, without an author . . . I could give you the address of an author if you like. . . .

THE FATHER. No, no. Look here! You must be the author.

THE MANAGER. I? What are you talking about?

THE FATHER. Yes, you, you! Why not?

THE MANAGER. Because I have never been an author: that's why.

THE FATHER. Then why not turn author now? Everybody does it. You don't want any special qualities. Your task is made much easier by the fact that we are all here alive before you. . . .

THE MANAGER. It won't do.

THE FATHER. What? When you see us live our drama . . .

THE MANAGER. Yes, that's all right. But you want someone to write it.

THE FATHER. No, no. Someone to take it down, possibly, while we play it, scene by scene! It will be enough to sketch it out at first, and then try it over.

THE MANAGER. Well . . . I am almost tempted. It's a bit of an idea. One might have a shot at it.

THE FATHER. Of course. You'll see what scenes will come out of it. I can give you one, at once . . .

THE MANAGER. By Jove, it tempts me. I'd like to have a go at it. Let's try it out. Come with me to my office. [*Turning to the* ACTORS.] You are at liberty for a bit, but don't step out of the theatre for long. In a quarter of an hour, twenty minutes, all back here again! [*To the* FATHER.] We'll see what can be done. Who knows if we don't get something really extraordinary out of it?

THE FATHER. There's no doubt about it. They [*indicating the* CHARACTERS] had better come with us too, hadn't they?

THE MANAGER. Yes, yes. Come on! come on! [*Moves away and then turning to the* ACTORS.] Be punctual, please! [MANAGER *and the* SIX CHARACTERS *cross the stage and go off. The other* ACTORS *remain, looking at one another in astonishment.*]

LEADING MAN. Is he serious? What the devil does he want to do?

JUVENILE LEAD. This is rank madness.

THIRD ACTOR. Does he expect to knock up a drama in five minutes?

JUVENILE LEAD. Like the improvisers!

LEADING LADY. If he thinks I'm going to take part in a joke like this . . .

JUVENILE LEAD. I'm out of it anyway.

FOURTH ACTOR. I should like to know who they are. [*Alludes to* CHARACTERS.]

THIRD ACTOR. What do you suppose? Madmen or rascals?

JUVENILE LEAD. And he takes them seriously!

L'INGÉNUE. Vanity! He fancies himself as an author now.

LEADING MAN. It's absolutely unheard of. If the stage has come to this . . . well I'm . . .

FIFTH ACTOR. It's rather a joke.

THIRD ACTOR. Well, we'll see what's going to happen next.

[*Thus talking, the* ACTORS *leave the stage; some going out by the little door at the back; others retiring to their dressing-rooms.*

The curtain remains up.

The action of the play is suspended for twenty minutes.]

ACT II

The stage call-bells ring to warn the company that the play is about to begin again.

The STEP-DAUGHTER *comes out of the* MANAGER'S *office along with the* CHILD *and the* BOY. *As she comes out of the office, she cries:—*

Nonsense! nonsense! Do it yourselves! I'm not going to mix myself up in this mess. [*Turning to the* CHILD *and coming quickly with her on to the stage.*] Come on, Rosetta, let's run!

[*The* BOY *follows them slowly, remaining a little behind and seeming perplexed.*]

THE STEP-DAUGHTER [*stops, bends over the* CHILD *and takes the latter's face between her hands*]. My little darling! You're frightened, aren't you? You don't know where we are, do you? [*Pretending to reply to a question of the* CHILD.] What is the stage? It's a place, baby, you know, where people play at being serious, a place where they act comedies. We've got to act a comedy now, dead serious, you know; and you're in it also, little one. [*Embraces her, pressing the little head to her breast, and rocking the* CHILD *for a moment.*] Oh darling, darling, what a horrid comedy you've got to play! What a wretched part they've found for you! A garden . . . a fountain . . . look . . . just suppose, kiddie, it's here. Where, you say? Why, right here in the middle. It's all pretense you know. That's the trouble, my pet: it's all make-believe here. It's better to imagine it though, because if they fix it up for you, it'll only be painted cardboard, painted cardboard for the rockery, the water, the plants. . . . Ah, but I think a baby like this one would sooner have a make-believe fountain than a real one, so she could play with it. What a joke it'll be for the others! But for you, alas! not quite such a joke: you who are real, baby dear, and really play by a real fountain that is big and green and beautiful, with ever so many bamboos around it that are reflected in the water, and a whole lot of little ducks swimming about. . . . No, Rosetta, no, your mother doesn't bother about you on account of that wretch of a son there. I'm in the devil of a temper, and as for that lad . . . [*Seizes* BOY *by the arm to force him to take one of his hands out of his pockets.*] What have you got there? What are you hiding? [*Pulls his hand out of his pocket, looks into it and catches the glint of a revolver.*] Ah! where did you get this? [*The* BOY, *very pale in the face, looks at her, but does not answer.*] Idiot! If I'd been in your place, instead of killing myself, I'd have shot one of those two, or both of them: father and son.

[*The* FATHER *enters from the office, all excited from his work. The* MANAGER *follows him.*]

THE FATHER. Come on, come on dear! Come here for a minute! We've arranged everything. It's all fixed up.

THE MANAGER [*also excited*]. If you please, young lady, there are one or two points to settle still. Will you come along?

THE STEP-DAUGHTER [*following him towards the office*]. Ouff! what's the good, if you've arranged everything.

[*The* FATHER, MANAGER *and* STEP-DAUGHTER *go back into the office again (off) for a moment. At the same time, the* SON *followed by the* MOTHER, *comes out.*]

THE SON [*looking at the three entering office*]. Oh this is fine, fine! And to think I can't even get away!

[*The* MOTHER *attempts to look at him, but lowers her eyes immediately when he turns away from her. She then sits down. The* BOY *and the* CHILD *approach her. She casts a glance again at the* SON, *and speaks with humble tones, trying to draw him into conversation.*]

THE MOTHER. And isn't my punishment the worst of all? [*Then seeing from the* SON'S *manner that he will not bother himself about her.*] My God! Why are you so cruel? Isn't it enough for one person to support all this torment? Must you then insist on others seeing it also?

THE SON [*half to himself, meaning the* MOTHER *to hear, however*]. And they want to put it on the stage! If there was at least a reason for it! He thinks he has got at the meaning of it all. Just as if each one of us in every circumstance of life couldn't find his own explanation of it! [*Pauses.*] He complains he was discovered in a place where he ought not to have been seen, in a moment of his life which ought to have remained hidden and kept out of the reach of that convention which he has to maintain for other people. And what about my case? Haven't I had to reveal what no son ought ever to reveal: how father and mother live and are man and wife for themselves quite apart from that idea of father and mother which we give them? When this idea is revealed, our life is then linked at one point only to that man and that woman; and as such it should shame them, shouldn't it?

[*The* MOTHER *hides her face in her hands. From the dressing-rooms and the little door at the back of the stage the* ACTORS *and* STAGE MANAGER *return, followed by the* PROPERTY MAN, *and the* PROMPTER. *At the same moment, the* MANAGER *comes out of his office, accompanied by the* FATHER *and the* STEP-DAUGHTER.]

THE MANAGER. Come on, come on, ladies and gentlemen! Heh! you there, machinist!

MACHINIST. Yes sir?

THE MANAGER. Fix up the white parlor with the floral decorations. Two wings and a drop with a door will do. Hurry up!

[*The* MACHINIST *runs off at once to prepare the scene, and arranges it while the* MANAGER *talks with the* STAGE MANAGER, *the* PROPERTY MAN, *and the* PROMPTER *on matters of detail.*]

THE MANAGER [*to* PROPERTY MAN]. Just have a look, and see if there isn't a sofa or divan in the wardrobe. . . .

PROPERTY MAN. There's the green one.

THE STEP-DAUGHTER. No no! Green won't do. It was yellow, ornamented with flowers—very large! and most comfortable!

PROPERTY MAN. There isn't one like that.

THE MANAGER. It doesn't matter. Use the one we've got.

THE STEP-DAUGHTER. Doesn't matter? It's most important!

THE MANAGER. We're only trying it now. Please don't interfere. [*To* PROPERTY MAN.] See if we've got a shop window—long and narrowish.

THE STEP-DAUGHTER. And the little table! The little mahogany table for the pale blue envelope!

PROPERTY MAN [*to* MANAGER]. There's that little gilt one.

THE MANAGER. That'll do fine.

THE FATHER. A mirror.

THE STEP-DAUGHTER. And the screen! We must have a screen. Otherwise how can I manage?

PROPERTY MAN. That's all right, Miss. We've got any amount of them.

THE MANAGER [*to the* STEP-DAUGHTER]. We want some clothes pegs too, don't we?

THE STEP-DAUGHTER. Yes, several, several!

THE MANAGER. See how many we've got and bring them all.

PROPERTY MAN. All right!

[*The* PROPERTY MAN *hurries off to obey his orders. While he is putting the things in their places, the* MANAGER *talks to the* PROMPTER *and then with the* CHARACTERS *and the* ACTORS.]

THE MANAGER [*to* PROMPTER]. Take your seat. Look here: this is the outline of the scenes, act by act. [*Hands him some sheets of paper.*] And now I'm going to ask you to do something out of the ordinary.

PROMPTER. Take it down in shorthand?

THE MANAGER [*pleasantly surprised*]. Exactly! Can you do shorthand?

PROMPTER. Yes, a little.

THE MANAGER. Good! [*Turning to a* STAGE HAND.] Go and get some paper from my office, plenty, as much as you can find.

[*The* STAGE HAND *goes off, and soon returns with a handful of paper which he gives to the* PROMPTER.]

THE MANAGER [*to* PROMPTER]. You follow the scenes as we play them, and try and get the points down, at any rate the most important ones. [*Then addressing the* ACTORS.] Clear the stage, ladies and gentlemen! Come over here [*pointing to the left*] and listen attentively.

LEADING LADY. But excuse me, we . . .

THE MANAGER [*guessing her thought*]. Don't worry! You won't have to improvise.

LEADING MAN. What have we to do then?

THE MANAGER. Nothing. For the moment you just watch and listen. Everybody will get his part written out afterwards. At present we're going to try the thing as best we can. They're going to act now.

THE FATHER [*as if fallen from the clouds into the confusion of the stage*]. We? What do you mean, if you please, by a rehearsal?

THE MANAGER. A rehearsal for them. [*Points to the* ACTORS.]

THE FATHER. But since we are the characters . . .

THE MANAGER. All right: "characters" then, if you insist on calling yourselves such. But here, my dear sir, the characters don't act. Here the actors do the acting. The characters are there, in the "book" [*pointing towards* PROMPTER'S *box*]—when there is a "book"!

THE FATHER. I won't contradict you; but excuse me, the actors aren't the characters. They want to be, they pretend to be, don't they? Now if these gentlemen here are fortunate enough to have us alive before them . . .

THE MANAGER. Oh this is grand! You want to come before the public yourselves then?

THE FATHER. As we are . . .

THE MANAGER. I can assure you it would be a magnificent spectacle!

LEADING MAN. What's the use of us here anyway then?

THE MANAGER. You're not going to pretend that you can act? It makes me laugh! [*The* ACTORS *laugh.*] There, you see, they are laughing at the notion. But, by the way, I must cast the parts. That won't be difficult. They cast themselves. [*To the* SECOND LADY LEAD.] You play the Mother. [*To the* FATHER.] We must find her a name.

THE FATHER. Amalia, sir.

THE MANAGER. But that is the real name of your wife. We don't want to call her by her real name.

THE FATHER. Why ever not, if it is her name? . . . Still, perhaps, if that lady must . . . [*makes a slight motion of the hand to indicate the* SECOND LADY LEAD]. I see this woman here [*means the* MOTHER] as Amalia. But do as you like. [*Gets more and more confused.*] I don't know what to say to you. Already, I begin to hear my own words ring false, as if they had another sound. . . .

THE MANAGER. Don't you worry about it. It'll be our job to find the right tones. And as for her name, if you want her Amalia, Amalia it shall be; and if you don't like it, we'll find another! For the moment though, we'll call the characters in this way: [*to* JUVENILE LEAD] You are the Son. [*To the* LEADING LADY.] You naturally are the Step-Daughter. . . .

THE STEP-DAUGHTER [*excitedly*]. What? what? I, that woman there? [*Bursts out laughing.*]

THE MANAGER [*angry*]. What is there to laugh at?

LEADING LADY [*indignant*]. Nobody has ever dared to laugh at me. I insist on being treated with respect; otherwise I go away.

THE STEP-DAUGHTER. No, no, excuse me . . . I am not laughing at you. . . .

THE MANAGER [*to* STEP-DAUGHTER]. You ought to feel honored to be played by . . .

LEADING LADY [*at once, contemptuously*]. "That woman there" . . .

THE STEP-DAUGHTER. But I wasn't speaking of you, you know. I was speaking of myself—whom I can't see at all in you! That is all. I don't know . . . but . . . you . . . aren't in the least like me. . . .

THE FATHER. True. Here's the point. Look here, sir, our temperaments, our souls . . .

THE MANAGER. Temperament, soul, be hanged! Do you suppose the spirit of the piece is in you? Nothing of the kind!

THE FATHER. What, haven't we our own temperaments, our own souls?

THE MANAGER. Not at all. Your soul or whatever you like to call it takes shape here. The actors give body and form to it, voice and gesture. And my actors—I may tell you—have given expression to much more lofty material than this little drama of yours, which may or may not hold up on the stage. But if it does, the merit of it, believe me, will be due to my actors.

THE FATHER. I don't dare contradict you, sir; but, believe me, it is a terrible suffering for us who are as we are, with these bodies of ours, these features to see . . .

THE MANAGER [*cutting him short and out of patience*]. Good heavens! The make-up will remedy all that, man, the make-up . . .

THE FATHER. Maybe. But the voice, the gestures . . .

THE MANAGER. Now, look here! On the stage, you as yourself, cannot exist. The actor here acts you, and that's an end to it!

THE FATHER. I understand. And now I think I see why our author who conceived us as we are, all alive, didn't want to put us on the stage after all. I haven't the least desire to offend your actors. Far from it! But when I think that I am to be acted by . . . I don't know by whom . . .

LEADING MAN [*on his dignity*]. By me, if you've no objection!

THE FATHER [*humbly, mellifluously*]. Honored, I assure you, sir. [*Bows.*] Still, I must say that try as this gentleman may, with all his good will and wonderful art, to absorb me into himself . . .

LEADING MAN. Oh chuck it! "Wonderful art!" Withdraw that, please!

THE FATHER. The performance he will give, even doing his best with make-up to look like me . . .

LEADING MAN. It will be a bit difficult! [*The* ACTORS *laugh.*]

THE FATHER. Exactly! It will be difficult to act me as I really am. The effect will be rather—apart from the make-up—according as to how he supposes I am, as he senses me—if he does sense me—and not as I inside of myself feel myself to be. It seems to me then that account should be taken of this by everyone whose duty it may become to criticize us. . . .

THE MANAGER. Heavens! The man's starting to think about the critics now! Let them say what they like. It's up to us to put on the play if we can. [*Looking around.*] Come on! come on! Is the stage set? [*To the* ACTORS *and* CHARACTERS.] Stand back—stand back! Let me see, and don't let's lose any more time! [*To the* STEP-DAUGHTER.] Is it all right as it is now?

THE STEP-DAUGHTER. Well, to tell the truth, I don't recognize the scene.

THE MANAGER. My dear lady, you can't possibly suppose that we can construct that shop of Madame Pace piece by piece here? [*To the* FATHER.] You said a white room with flowered wallpaper, didn't you?

THE FATHER. Yes.

THE MANAGER. Well then. We've got the furniture right more or less. Bring that little table a bit further forward. [*The* STAGE HANDS *obey the order. To* PROPERTY MAN.] You go and find an envelope, if possible, a pale blue one; and give it to that gentleman. [*Indicates* FATHER.]

PROPERTY MAN. An ordinary envelope?

MANAGER AND FATHER. Yes, yes, an ordinary envelope.

PROPERTY MAN. At once, sir. [*Exit.*]

THE MANAGER. Ready, everyone! First scene—the Young Lady. [*The* LEADING LADY *comes forward.*] No, no, you must wait. I meant her [*indicating the* STEP-DAUGHTER]. You just watch—

THE STEP-DAUGHTER [*adding at once*]. How I shall play it, how I shall live it! . . .

LEADING LADY [*offended*]. I shall live it also, you may be sure, as soon as I begin!

THE MANAGER [*with his hands to his head*]. Ladies and gentlemen, if you please! No more useless discussions! Scene I: the Young Lady with Madame Pace: Oh! [*Looks around as if lost.*] And this Madame Pace, where is she?

THE FATHER. She isn't with us, sir.

THE MANAGER. Then what the devil's to be done?

THE FATHER. But she is alive too.

THE MANAGER. Yes, but where is she?

THE FATHER. One minute. Let me speak! [*Turning to the* ACTRESSES.] If these ladies would be so good as to give me their hats for a moment . . .

THE ACTRESSES [*half surprised, half laughing, in chorus*]. What?
Why?
Our hats?
What does he say?

THE MANAGER. What are you going to do with the ladies' hats? [*The* ACTORS *laugh.*]

THE FATHER. Oh nothing. I just want to put them on these pegs for a moment. And one of the ladies will be so kind as to take off her mantle . . .

THE ACTORS. Oh, what d'you think of that?
Only the mantle?
He must be mad.

SOME ACTRESSES. But why?
Mantles as well?

THE FATHER. To hang them up here for a moment. Please be so kind, will you?

THE ACTRESSES [*taking off their hats, one or two also their cloaks, and going to hang them on the racks*]. After all, why not?
There you are!
This is really funny.
We've got to put them on show.

THE FATHER. Exactly; just like that, on show.

THE MANAGER. May we know why?

THE FATHER. I'll tell you. Who knows if, by arranging the stage for her, she does not come here herself, attracted by the very articles of her trade? [*Inviting the* ACTORS *to look towards the exit at back of stage.*] Look! Look!

[*The door at the back of stage opens and* MADAME PACE *enters and takes a few steps forward. She is a fat, oldish woman with puffy oxygenated hair. She is rouged and powdered, dressed with a comical elegance in black silk. Round her waist is a long silver chain from which hangs a pair of scissors. The* STEP-DAUGHTER *runs over to her at once amid the stupor of the* ACTORS.]

THE STEP-DAUGHTER [*turning towards her*]. There she is! There she is!

THE FATHER [*radiant*]. It's she! I said so, didn't I? There she is!

THE MANAGER [*conquering his surprise, and then becoming indignant*]. What sort of a trick is this?

LEADING MAN [*almost at the same time*]. What's going to happen next?

JUVENILE LEAD. Where does *she* come from?

L'INGÉNUE. They've been holding her in reserve, I guess.

LEADING LADY. A vulgar trick!

THE FATHER [*dominating the protests*]. Excuse me, all of you! Why are you so anxious to destroy in the name of a vulgar, commonplace sense of truth, this reality which comes to birth attracted and formed by the magic of the stage itself, which has indeed more right to live here than you, since it is much truer than you—if you don't mind my saying so? Which is the actress among you who is to play Madame Pace? Well, here is Madame Pace herself. And you will allow, I fancy, that the actress who acts her will be less true than this woman here, who is herself in person. You see my daughter recognized her and went over to her at once. Now you're going to witness the scene!

[*But the scene between the* STEP-DAUGHTER *and* MADAME PACE *has already begun despite the protest of the* ACTORS *and the reply of the* FATHER. *It has begun quietly, naturally, in a manner impossible for the stage. So when the* ACTORS, *called to attention by the* FATHER, *turn round the see* MADAME PACE, *who has placed one hand under the* STEP DAUGHTER'S *chin to raise her head, they observe her at first with great attention, but hearing her speak in an unintelligible manner their interest begins to wane.*]

THE MANAGER. Well? well?

LEADING MAN. What does she say?

LEADING LADY. One can't hear a word.

JUVENILE LEAD. Louder! Louder please!

THE STEP-DAUGHTER [*leaving* MADAME PACE, *who smiles a Sphinx-like smile, and advancing towards the* ACTORS]. Louder? Louder? What are you talking about? These aren't matters which can be shouted at the top of one's voice. If I have spoken them out loud, it was to shame him and have my revenge. [*Indicates* FATHER.] But for Madame it's quite a different matter.

THE MANAGER. Indeed? indeed? But here, you know, people have got to make themselves heard, my dear. Even we who are on the stage can't hear you. What will it be when the public's in the theatre? And anyway, you can very well speak up now among yourselves, since we shan't be present to listen to you as we are now. You've got to pretend to be alone in a room at the back of a shop where no one can hear you.

[*The* STEP-DAUGHTER *coquettishly and with a touch of malice makes a sign of disagreement two or three times with her finger.*]

THE MANAGER. What do you mean by no?

THE STEP-DAUGHTER [*sotto voce, mysteriously*]. There's someone who will hear us if she [*indicating* MADAME PACE] speaks out loud.

THE MANAGER [*in consternation*]. What? Have you got someone else to spring on us now? [*The* ACTORS *burst out laughing.*]

THE FATHER. No, no sir. She is alluding to me. I've got to be here—there behind that door, in waiting; and Madame Pace knows it. In fact, if you will allow me, I'll go there at once, so I can be quite ready. [*Moves away.*]

THE MANAGER [*stopping him*]. No! Wait! wait! We must observe the conventions of the theatre. Before you are ready . . .

THE STEP-DAUGHTER [*interrupting him*]. No, get on with it at once! I'm just dying, I tell you, to act this scene. If he's ready, I'm more than ready.

THE MANAGER [*shouting*]. But, my dear young lady, first of all, we must have the scene between you and this lady . . . [*indicates* MADAME PACE]. Do you understand? . . .

THE STEP-DAUGHTER. Good Heavens! She's been telling me what you know already: that mamma's work is badly done again, that the material's ruined; and that if I want her to continue to help us in our misery I must be patient. . . .

MADAME PACE [*coming forward with an air of great importance*]. Yes indeed, sir, I no wanta take advantage of her, I no wanta be hard . . .

[*Note:* MADAME PACE *is supposed to talk in a jargon half Italian, half English.*]

THE MANAGER [*alarmed*]. What? What? She talks like that? [*The* ACTORS *burst out laughing again.*]

THE STEP-DAUGHTER [*also laughing*]. Yes yes, that's the way she talks, half English, half Italian! Most comical it is!

MADAME PACE. Itta seem not verra polite gentlemen laugha atta me eef I trya best speaka English.

THE MANAGER. *Diamine!* Of course! Of course! Let her talk like that! Just what we want. Talk just like that, Madame, if you please! The effect will be certain. Exactly what was wanted to put a little comic relief into the crudity of the situation. Of course she talks like that! Magnificent!

THE STEP-DAUGHTER. Magnificent? Certainly! When certain suggestions are made to one in language of that kind, the effect is certain, since it seems almost a joke. One feels inclined to laugh when one hears her talk about an "old signore" "who wanta talka nicely with you." Nice old signore, eh, Madame?

MADAME PACE. Not so old my dear, not so old! And even if you no lika him, he won't make any scandal!

THE MOTHER [*jumping up amid the amazement and consternation of the actors who had not been noticing her. They move to restrain her.*] You old devil! You murderess!

THE STEP-DAUGHTER [*running over to calm her* MOTHER]. Calm yourself, Mother, calm yourself! Please don't . . .

THE FATHER [*going to her also at the same time*]. Calm yourself! Don't get excited! Sit down now!

THE MOTHER. Well then, take that woman away out of my sight!

THE STEP-DAUGHTER [*to* MANAGER]. It is impossible for my mother to remain here.

THE FATHER [*to* MANAGER]. They can't be here together. And for this reason, you see: that woman there was not with us when we came. . . . If they are on together, the whole thing is given away inevitably, as you see.

THE MANAGER. It doesn't matter. This is only a first rough sketch—just to get an idea of the various points of the scene, even confusedly. . . . [*Turning to the* MOTHER *and leading her to her chair.*] Come along, my dear lady, sit down now, and let's get on with the scene. . . .

[*Meanwhile, the* STEP-DAUGHTER, *coming forward again, turns to* MADAME PACE.]

THE STEP-DAUGHTER. Come on, Madame, come on!

MADAME PACE [*offended*]. No, no, *grazie*. I not do anything witha your mother present.

THE STEP-DAUGHTER. Nonsense! Introduce this "old signore" who wants to talk nicely to me. [*Addressing the* COMPANY *imperiously.*] We've got to do this scene one way or another, haven't we? Come on! [*To* MADAME PACE.] You can go!

MADAME PACE. Ah yes! I go 'way! I go 'way! Certainly! [*Exits furious.*]

THE STEP-DAUGHTER [*to the* FATHER]. Now you make your entry. No, you needn't go over here. Come here. Let's suppose you've already come in. Like that, yes! I'm here with bowed head, modest like. Come on! Out with your voice! Say "Good morning, Miss" in that peculiar tone, that special tone . . .

THE MANAGER. Excuse me, but are you the Manager, or am I? [*To the* FATHER, *who looks undecided and perplexed.*] Get on with it, man! Go down there to the back of the stage. You needn't go off. Then come right forward here.

[*The* FATHER *does as he is told, looking troubled and perplexed at first. But as soon as he begins to move, the reality of the action affects him, and he begins to smile and to be more natural. The* ACTORS *watch intently.*]

THE MANAGER [*sotto voce, quickly to the* PROMPTER *in his box*]. Ready! ready? Get ready to write now.

THE FATHER [*coming forward and speaking in a different tone*]. Good afternoon, Miss!

THE STEP-DAUGHTER [*head bowed down slightly, with restrained disgust*]. Good afternoon!

THE FATHER [*looks under her hat which partly covers her face. Perceiving she is very young, he makes an exclamation, partly of surprise, partly of fear lest he compromise himself in a risky adventure*]. Ah . . . but . . . ah . . . I say . . . this is not the first time that you have come here, is it?

THE STEP-DAUGHTER [*modestly*]. No sir.

THE FATHER. You've been here before, eh? [*Then seeing her nod agreement.*] More than once? [*Waits for her to answer, looks under her hat, smiles, and then says.*] Well then, there's no need to be so shy, is there? May I take off your hat?

THE STEP-DAUGHTER [*anticipating him and with veiled disgust*]. No sir . . . I'll do it myself. [*Takes it off quickly.*]

[*The* MOTHER, *who watches the progress of the scene with the* SON *and the other two children who cling to her, is on thorns; and follows with varying expressions of sorrow, indignation, anxiety, and horror the words and actions of the other two. From time to time she hides her face in her hands and sobs.*]

THE MOTHER. Oh, my God, my God!

THE FATHER [*playing his part with a touch of gallantry*]. Give it to me! I'll put it down. [*Takes hat from her hands.*] But a dear little head like yours ought to have a smarter hat. Come and help me choose one from the stock, won't you?

L'INGÉNUE [*interrupting*]. I say . . . those are our hats you know.

THE MANAGER [*furious*]. Silence! silence! Don't try and be funny, if you please. . . . We're playing the scene now I'd have you notice. [*To the* STEP-DAUGHTER.] Begin again, please!

THE STEP-DAUGHTER [*continuing*]. No thank you, sir.

THE FATHER. Oh, come now. Don't talk like that. You must take it. I shall be upset if you don't. There are some lovely little hats here; and then— Madame will be pleased. She expects it, anyway, you know.

THE STEP-DAUGHTER. No, no! I couldn't wear it!

THE FATHER. Oh, you're thinking about what they'd say at home if they saw you come in with a new hat? My dear girl, there's always a way round these little matters, you know.

THE STEP-DAUGHTER [*all keyed up*]. No, it's not that I couldn't wear it because I am . . . as you see . . . you might have noticed. . . . [*Showing her black dress.*]

THE FATHER. . . . in mourning! Of course: I beg your pardon: I'm frightfully sorry. . . .

THE STEP-DAUGHTER [*forcing herself to conquer her indignation and nau-

sea]. Stop! Stop! It's I who must thank you. There's no need for you to feel mortified or specially sorry. Don't think any more of what I've said. [*Tries to smile.*] I must forget that I am dressed so . . .

THE MANAGER [*interrupting and turning to the* PROMPTER]. Stop a minute! Stop! Don't write that down. Cut out that last bit. [*Then to the* FATHER *and* STEP-DAUGHTER.] Fine! it's going fine! [*To the* FATHER *only.*] And now you can go on as we arranged. [*To the* ACTORS.] Pretty good that scene, where he offers her the hat, eh?

THE STEP-DAUGHTER. The best's coming now. Why can't we go on?

THE MANAGER. Have a little patience! [*To the* ACTORS.] Of course, it must be treated rather lightly.

LEADING MAN. Still, with a bit of go in it!

LEADING LADY. Of course! It's easy enough! [*To* LEADING MAN.] Shall you and I try it now?

LEADING MAN. Why, yes! I'll prepare my entrance. [*Exit in order to make his entrance.*]

THE MANAGER [*to* LEADING LADY]. See here! The scene between you and Madame Pace is finished. I'll have it written out properly after. You remain here . . . oh, where are you going?

LEADING LADY. One minute. I want to put my hat on again. [*Goes over to hat-rack and puts her hat on her head.*]

THE MANAGER. Good! You stay here with your head bowed down a bit.

THE STEP-DAUGHTER. But she isn't dressed in black.

LEADING LADY. But I shall be, and much more effectively than you.

THE MANAGER [*to* STEP-DAUGHTER]. Be quiet please, and watch! You'll be able to learn something. [*Clapping his hands.*] Come on! come on! Entrance, please!

[*The door at rear of stage opens, and the* LEADING MAN *enters with the lively manner of an old gallant. The rendering of the scene by the* ACTORS *from the very first words is seen to be quite a different thing, though it has not in any way the air of a parody. Naturally, the* STEP-DAUGHTER *and the* FATHER, *not being able to recognize themselves in the* LEADING LADY *and the* LEADING MAN, *who deliver their words in different tones and with a different psychology, express, sometimes with smiles, sometimes with gestures, the impression they receive.*]

LEADING MAN. Good afternoon, Miss . . . .

THE FATHER [*at once unable to contain himself*]. No! no!

[*The* STEP-DAUGHTER *noticing the way the* LEADING MAN *enters, bursts out laughing.*]

THE MANAGER [*furious*]. Silence! And you please just stop that laughing. If we go on like this, we shall never finish.

THE STEP-DAUGHTER. Forgive me, sir, but it's natural enough. This lady [*indicating* LEADING LADY] stands there still; but if she is supposed to be me, I can assure you that if I heard anyone say "Good afternoon" in that manner and in that tone, I should burst out laughing as I did.

THE FATHER. Yes, yes, the manner, the tone . . .

THE MANAGER. Nonsense! Rubbish! Stand aside and let me see the action.

LEADING MAN. If I've got to represent an old fellow who's coming into a house of an equivocal character . . .

THE MANAGER. Don't listen to them, for Heaven's sake! Do it again! It goes fine. [*Waiting for the* ACTORS *to begin again.*] Well?

LEADING MAN. Good afternoon, Miss.

LEADING LADY. Good afternoon.

LEADING MAN [*imitating the gesture of the* FATHER *when he looked under the hat, and then expressing quite clearly first satisfaction and then fear*]. Ah, but . . . I say . . . this is not the first time you have come here, is it?

THE MANAGER. Good, but not quite so heavily. Like this. [*Acts himself.*] "This isn't the first time that you have come here" . . . [*To* LEADING LADY.] And you say: "No, sir."

LEADING LADY. No, sir.

LEADING MAN. You've been here before, more than once.

THE MANAGER. No, no, stop! Let her nod "yes" first. "You've been here before, eh?" [*The* LEADING LADY *lifts up her head slightly and closes her eyes as though in disgust. Then she inclines her head twice.*]

THE STEP-DAUGHTER [*unable to contain herself*]. Oh my God! [*Puts a hand to her mouth to prevent herself from laughing.*]

THE MANAGER [*turning round*]. What's the matter?

THE STEP-DAUGHTER. Nothing, nothing!

THE MANAGER [*to* LEADING MAN]. Go on!

LEADING MAN. You've been here before, eh? Well then, there's no need to be so shy, is there? May I take off your hat?

[*The* LEADING MAN *says this last speech in such a tone and with such gestures that the* STEP-DAUGHTER, *though she has her hand to her mouth, cannot keep from laughing.*]

LEADING LADY [*indignant*]. I'm not going to stop here to be made a fool of by that woman there.

LEADING MAN. Neither am I! I'm through with it!

THE MANAGER [*shouting to* STEP-DAUGHTER]. Silence! for once and all, I tell you!

THE STEP-DAUGHTER. Forgive me! forgive me!

THE MANAGER. You haven't any manners: that's what it is! You go too far.

THE FATHER [*endeavoring to intervene*]. Yes, it's true, but excuse her . . .

THE MANAGER. Excuse what? It's absolutely disgusting.

THE FATHER. Yes, sir, but believe me, it has such a strange effect when . . .

THE MANAGER. Strange? Why strange? Where is it strange?

THE FATHER. No, sir; I admire your actors—this gentleman here, this lady; but they are certainly not us!

THE MANAGER. I should hope not. Evidently they cannot be you, if they are actors.

THE FATHER. Just so: actors! Both of them act our parts exceedingly well. But, believe me, it produces quite a different effect on us. They want to be us, but they aren't, all the same.

THE MANAGER. What is it then anyway?

THE FATHER. Something that is . . . that is theirs—and no longer ours. . . .

THE MANAGER. But naturally, inevitably. I've told you so already.

THE FATHER. Yes, I understand . . . I understand . . .

THE MANAGER. Well then, let's have no more of it! [*Turning to the* ACTORS.] We'll have the rehearsals by ourselves, afterwards, in the ordinary way. I never could stand rehearsing with the author present. He's never satisfied! [*Turning to* FATHER *and* STEP DAUGHTER.] Come on! Let's get on with it again; and try and see if you can't keep from laughing.

THE STEP-DAUGHTER. Oh, I shan't laugh any more. There's a nice little bit coming for me now: you'll see.

THE MANAGER. Well then: when she says "Don't think any more of what I've said. I must forget, etc.," you [*addressing the* FATHER] come in sharp with "I understand, I understand"; and then you ask her . . .

THE STEP-DAUGHTER [*interrupting*]. What?

THE MANAGER. Why she is in mourning.

THE STEP-DAUGHTER. Not at all! See here: when I told him that it was useless for me to be thinking about my wearing mourning, do you know how he answered me? "Ah well," he said, "then let's take off this little frock."

THE MANAGER. Great! Just what we want, to make a riot in the theatre!

THE STEP-DAUGHTER. But it's the truth!

THE MANAGER. What does that matter? Acting is our business here. Truth up to a certain point, but no further.

THE STEP-DAUGHTER. What do you want to do then?

THE MANAGER. You'll see, you'll see! Leave it to me.

THE STEP-DAUGHTER. No sir! What you want to do is to piece together a little romantic sentimental scene out of my disgust, out of all the reasons, each more cruel and viler than the other, why I am what I am. He is to ask me why I'm in mourning; and I'm to answer with tears in my eyes, that it is just two months since papa died. No sir, no! He's got to say to me; as he did say: "Well, let's take off this little dress at once." And I; with my two months' mourning in my heart, went there behind that screen, and with these fingers tingling with shame. . . .

THE MANAGER [*running his hands through his hair*]. For Heaven's sake! What are you saying?

THE STEP-DAUGHTER [*crying out excitedly*]. The truth! The truth!

THE MANAGER. It may be. I don't deny it, and I can understand all your horror; but you must surely see that you can't have this kind of thing on the stage. It won't go.

THE STEP-DAUGHTER. Not possible, eh? Very well! I'm much obliged to you —but I'm off!

THE MANAGER. Now be reasonable! Don't lose your temper!

THE STEP-DAUGHTER. I won't stop here! I won't! I can see you've fixed it all up with him in your office. All this talk about what is possible for the stage . . . I understand! He wants to get at his complicated "cerebral drama," to have his famous remorses and torments acted; but I want to act my part, *my part!*

THE MANAGER [*annoyed, shaking his shoulders*]. Ah! Just *your* part! But, if you will pardon me, there are other parts than yours: His [*indicating the* FATHER] and hers! [*Indicating the* MOTHER.] On the stage you can't have a character becoming too prominent and overshadowing all the others. The thing is to pack them all into a neat little framework and then act what is actable. I am aware of the fact that everyone has his own interior life which he wants very much to put forward. But the difficulty lies in this fact: to set out just so much as is necessary for the stage, taking the other characters into consideration, and at the same time hint at the unrevealed interior life of each. I am willing to admit, my dear young lady, that from your point of view it would be a fine idea if each character could tell the public all his troubles in a nice monologue or a regular one hour lecture. [*Good humoredly.*] You must restrain yourself, my dear, and in your own interest, too; because this fury of yours, this exaggerated disgust you show, may make a bad impression, you know. After you have confessed to me that there were others before him at Madame Pace's and more than once . . .

THE STEP-DAUGHTER [*bowing her head, impressed*]. It's true. But remember those others mean him for me all the same.

THE MANAGER [*not understanding*]. What? The others? What do you mean?

THE STEP-DAUGHTER. For one who has gone wrong, sir, he who was responsible for the first fault is responsible for all that follow. He is responsible for my faults, was, even before I was born. Look at him, and see if it isn't true!

THE MANAGER. Well, well! And does the weight of so much responsibility seem nothing to you? Give him a chance to act it, to get it over!

THE STEP-DAUGHTER. How? How can he act all his "noble remorses," all his "moral torments," if you want to spare him the horror of being discovered one day—after he had asked her what he did ask her—in the arms of her, that already fallen woman, that child, sir, that child he used to watch come out of school? [*She is moved.*]

[*The* MOTHER *at this point is overcome with emotion, and breaks out into a fit of crying. All are touched. A long pause.*]

THE STEP-DAUGHTER [*as soon as the* MOTHER *becomes a little quieter, adds resolutely and gravely*]. At present, we are unknown to the public. Tomorrow, you will act us as you wish, treating us in your own manner. But do you really want to see drama, do you want to see it flash out as it really did?

THE MANAGER. Of course! That's just what I do want, so I can use as much of it as is possible.

THE STEP-DAUGHTER. Well then, ask that Mother there to leave us.

THE MOTHER [*changing her low plaint into a sharp cry*]. No! No! Don't permit it, sir, don't permit it!

THE MANAGER. But it's only to try it.

THE MOTHER. I can't bear it. I can't.

THE MANAGER. But since it has happened already . . . I don't understand!

THE MOTHER. It's taking place now. It happens all the time. My torment isn't a pretended one. I live and feel every minute of my torture. Those two children there—have you heard them speak? They can't speak any more. They cling to me to keep up my torment actual and vivid for me. But for themselves, they do not exist, they aren't any more. And she [*indicating the* STEP-DAUGHTER] has run away, she has left me, and is lost. If I now see her here before me, it is only to renew for me the tortures I have suffered for her too.

THE FATHER. The eternal moment! She [*indicating the* STEP-DAUGHTER] is here to catch me, fix me, and hold me eternally in the stocks for that one fleeting and shameful moment of my life. She can't give it up! And you sir, cannot either fairly spare me it.

THE MANAGER. I never said I didn't want to act it. It will form, as a matter of fact, the nucleus of the whole first act right up to her surprise. [*Indicates the* MOTHER.]

THE FATHER. Just so! This is my punishment: the passion in all of us that must culminate in her final cry.

THE STEP-DAUGHTER. I can hear it still in my ears. It's driven me mad, that cry!—You can put me on as you like; it doesn't matter. Fully dressed, if you like—provided I have at least the arm bare; because, standing like this [*She goes close to the* FATHER *and leans her head on his breast.*] with my head so, and my arms round his neck, I saw a vein pulsing in my arm here; and then, as if that live vein had awakened disgust in me,

I closed my eyes like this, and let my head sink on his breast. [*Turning to the* MOTHER.] Cry out mother! Cry out! [*Buries head in* FATHER'S *breast, and with her shoulders raised as if to prevent her hearing the cry, adds in tones of intense emotion.*] Cry out as you did then!

THE MOTHER [*coming forward to separate them*]. No! My daughter, my daughter! [*And after having pulled her away from him.*] You brute! you brute! She is my daughter! Don't you see she's my daughter?

THE MANAGER [*walking backwards towards footlights*]. Fine! fine! Damned good! And then, of course—curtain!

THE FATHER [*going towards him excitedly*]. Yes, of course, because that's the way it really happened.

THE MANAGER [*convinced and pleased*]. Oh, yes, no doubt about it. Curtain here, curtain!

[*At the reiterated cry of the* MANAGER, *the* MACHINIST *lets the curtain down, leaving the* MANAGER *and the* FATHER *in front of it before the footlights.*]

THE MANAGER. The darned idiot! I said "curtain" to show the act should end there, and he goes and lets it down in earnest. [*To the* FATHER, *while he pulls the curtain back to go on to the stage again.*] Yes, yes, it's all right. Effect certain! That's the right ending. I'll guarantee the first act at any rate.

ACT III

When the curtain goes up again, it is seen that the stage hands have shifted the bit of scenery used in the last part, and have rigged up instead at the back of the stage a drop, with some trees, and one or two wings. A portion of a fountain basin is visible. The MOTHER *is sitting on the right with the two children by her side. The* SON *is on the same side, but away from the others. He seems bored, angry, and full of shame. The* FATHER *and the* STEP-DAUGHTER *are also seated towards the right front. On the other side (left) are the* ACTORS, *much in the positions they occupied before the curtain was lowered. Only the* MANAGER *is standing up in the middle of the stage, with his hand closed over his mouth in the act of meditating.*

THE MANAGER [*shaking his shoulders after a brief pause*]. Ah yes: the second act! Leave it to me, leave it all to me as we arranged, and you'll see! It'll go fine!

THE STEP-DAUGHTER. Our entry into his house [*indicates* FATHER] in spite of him . . . [*indicates the* SON].

THE MANAGER [*out of patience*]. Leave it to me, I tell you!

THE STEP-DAUGHTER. Do let it be clear, at any rate, that it is in spite of my wishes.

THE MOTHER [*from her corner, shaking her head*]. For all the good that's come of it . . .

THE STEP-DAUGHTER [*turning towards her quickly*]. It doesn't matter. The more harm done us, the more remorse for him.

THE MANAGER [*impatiently*]. I understand! Good Heavens! I understand! I'm taking it into account.

THE MOTHER [*supplicatingly*]. I beg you, sir, to let it appear quite plain that for conscience' sake I did try in every way . . .

THE STEP-DAUGHTER [*interrupting indignantly and continuing for the* MOTHER] . . . to pacify me, to dissuade me from spiting him. [*To* MANAGER.] Do as she wants: satisfy her, because it is true! I enjoy it immensely. Anyhow, as you can see, the meeker she is, the more she tries to get at his heart, the more distant and aloof does he become.

THE MANAGER. Are we going to begin this second act or not?

THE STEP-DAUGHTER. I'm not going to talk any more now. But I must tell you this: you can't have the whole action take place in the garden, as you suggest. It isn't possible!

THE MANAGER. Why not?

THE STEP-DAUGHTER. Because he [*indicates the* SON *again*] is always shut up alone in his room. And then there's all the part of that poor dazed-looking boy there which takes place indoors.

THE MANAGER. Maybe! On the other hand, you will understand—we can't change scenes three or four times in one act.

THE LEADING MAN. They used to once.

THE MANAGER. Yes, when the public was up to the level of that child there.

THE LEADING LADY. It makes the illusion easier.

THE FATHER [*irritated*]. The illusion! For Heaven's sake, don't say illusion. Please don't use that word, which is particularly painful for us.

THE MANAGER [*astounded*]. And why, if you please?

THE FATHER. It's painful, cruel, really cruel; and you ought to understand that.

THE MANAGER. But why? What ought we to say then? The illusion, I tell you, sir, which we've got to create for the audience . . .

THE LEADING MAN. With our acting.

THE MANAGER. The illusion of a reality.

THE FATHER. I understand; but you, perhaps, do not understand us. Forgive me! You see . . . here for you and your actors, the thing is only—and rightly so . . . a kind of game . . .

THE LEADING LADY [*interrupting indignantly*]. A game! We're not children here, if you please! We are serious actors.

THE FATHER. I don't deny it. What I mean is the game, or play, of your art, which has to give, as the gentleman says, a perfect illusion of reality.

THE MANAGER. Precisely—!

THE FATHER. Now, if you consider the fact that we [*indicates himself and the other five* CHARACTERS], as we are, have no other reality outside of this illusion . . .

THE MANAGER [*astonished, looking at his* ACTORS, *who are also amazed*]. And what does that mean?

THE FATHER [*after watching them for a moment with a wan smile*]. As I say, sir, that which is a game of art for you is our sole reality. [*Brief pause. He goes a step or two nearer the* MANAGER *and adds.*] But not only for us, you know, by the way. Just you think it over well. [*Looks him in the eyes.*] Can you tell me who you are?

THE MANAGER [*perplexed, half smiling*]. What? Who am I? I am myself.

THE FATHER. And if I were to tell you that that isn't true, because you and I . . . ?

THE MANAGER. I should say you were mad—! [*The* ACTORS *laugh.*]

THE FATHER. You're quite right to laugh: because we are all making believe here. [*To* MANAGER.] And you can therefore object that it's only for a joke that that gentleman there [*indicates the* LEADING MAN], who naturally is himself, has to be me, who am on the contrary myself—this thing you see here. You see I've caught you in a trap! [*The* ACTORS *laugh.*]

THE MANAGER [*annoyed*]. But we've had all this over once before. Do you want to begin again?

THE FATHER. No, no! That wasn't my meaning! In fact, I should like to request you to abandon this game of art [*looking at the* LEADING LADY *as if anticipating her*] which you are accustomed to play here with your actors, and to ask you seriously once again: who are you?

THE MANAGER [*astonished and irritated, turning to his* ACTORS]. If this fellow here hasn't got a nerve! A man who calls himself a character comes and asks me who I am!

THE FATHER [*with dignity, but not offended*]. A character, sir, may always ask a man who he is. Because a character has really a life of his own, marked with his especial characteristics; for which reason he is always "somebody." But a man—I'm not speaking of you now—may very well be "nobody."

THE MANAGER. Yes, but you are asking these questions of me, the boss, the manager! Do you understand?

THE FATHER. But only in order to know if you, as you really are now, see yourself as you once were with all the illusions that were yours then, with all the things both inside and outside of you as they seemed to you—as they were then indeed for you. Well, sir, if you think of all those illusions that mean nothing to you now, of all those things which don't even *seem* to you to exist any more, while once they *were* for you, don't you feel that—I won't say these boards—but the very earth under your feet is sinking away from you when you reflect that in the same way this *you* as you feel it today—all this present reality of yours—is fated to seem a mere illusion to you tomorrow?

THE MANAGER [*without having understood much, but astonished by the specious argument*]. Well, well! And where does all this take us anyway?

THE FATHER. Oh, nowhere! It's only to show you that if we [*indicating the* CHARACTERS] have no other reality beyond the illusion, you too must not count overmuch on your reality as you feel it today, since, like that of yesterday, it may prove an illusion for you tomorrow.

THE MANAGER [*determining to make fun of him*]. Ah, excellent! Then you'll be saying next that you, with this comedy of yours that you brought here to act, are truer and more real than I am.

THE FATHER [*with the greatest seriousness*]. But of course; without doubt!

THE MANAGER. Ah, really?

THE FATHER. Why, I thought you'd understand that from the beginning.

THE MANAGER. More real than I?

THE FATHER. If your reality can change from one day to another . . .

THE MANAGER. But everyone knows it can change. It is always changing, the same as anyone else's.

THE FATHER [*with a cry*]. No, sir, not ours! Look here! That is the very difference! Our reality doesn't change: it can't change! It can't be other than what it is, because it is already fixed for ever. It's terrible. Ours is an immutable reality which should make you shudder when you approach us if you are really conscious of the fact that your reality is a mere transitory and fleeting illusion, taking this form today and that tomorrow, according to the conditions, according to your will, your sentiments, which in turn are controlled by an intellect that shows them to you today in one manner and tomorrow . . . who knows how? . . . Illusions of reality represented in this fatuous comedy of life that never ends, nor can ever end! Because if tomorrow it were to end . . . then why, all would be finished.

THE MANAGER. Oh for God's sake, will you *at least* finish with this philosophizing and let us try and shape this comedy which you yourself have brought me here? You argue and philosophize a bit too much, my dear sir. You know you seem to me almost, almost . . . [*Stops and looks him over from head to foot.*] Ah, by the way, I think you introduced yourself to me as a—what shall . . . we say—a "character," created by an author who did not afterward care to make a drama of his own creations.

THE FATHER. It is the simple truth, sir.

THE MANAGER. Nonsense! Cut that out, please! None of us believes it, because it isn't a thing, as you must recognize yourself, which one can believe seriously. If you want to know, it seems to me you are trying to imitate the manner of a certain author whom I heartily detest—I warn you—although I have unfortunately bound myself to put on one of his works. As a matter of fact, I was just starting to rehearse it, when you arrived. [*Turning to the* ACTORS.] And this is what we've gained—out of the frying-pan into the fire!

THE FATHER. I don't know to what author you may be alluding, but believe me I feel what I think; and I seem to be philosophizing only for those who do not think what they feel, because they blind themselves with their own sentiment. I know that for many people this self-blinding seems much more "human"; but the contrary is really true. For man never reasons so much and becomes so introspective as when he suffers; since he is anxious to get at the cause of his sufferings, to learn who has produced them, and whether it is just or unjust that he should have to bear them. On the other hand, when he is happy, he takes his happiness as it comes and doesn't analyze it, just as if happiness were his right. The animals suffer without reasoning about their sufferings. But take the case of a man who suffers and begins to reason about it. Oh no! it can't be allowed! Let him suffer like an animal, and then—ah yet, he is "human"!

THE MANAGER. Look here! Look here! You're off again, philosophizing worse than ever.

THE FATHER. Because I suffer, sir! I'm not philosophizing: I'm crying aloud the reason of my sufferings.

THE MANAGER [*makes brusque movement as he is taken with a new idea*]. I should like to know if anyone has ever heard of a character who gets right out of his part and perorates and speechifies as you do. Have you ever heard of a case? I haven't.

THE FATHER. You have never met such a case, sir, because authors, as a rule, hide the labor of their creations. When the characters are really alive before their author, the latter does nothing but follow them in their action, in their words, in the situations which they suggest to him; and he has to will them the way they will themselves—for there's trouble if he doesn't. When a character is born, he acquires at once such an independence, even of his own author, that he can be imagined by everybody even in many other situations where the author never dreamed of placing him; and so he acquires for himself a meaning which the author never thought of giving him.

THE MANAGER. Yes, yes, I know this.

THE FATHER. What is there then to marvel at in us? Imagine such a misfortune for characters as I have described to you: to be born of an author's fantasy, and be denied life by him; and then answer me if these characters left alive, and yet without life, weren't right in doing what they did do and are doing now, after they have attempted everything in their power to persuade him to give them their stage life. We've all tried him in turn, I, she [*indicating the* STEP-DAUGHTER] and she [*indicating the* MOTHER.]

THE STEP-DAUGHTER. It's true. I too have sought to tempt him, many, many times, when he has been sitting at his writing table, feeling a bit melancholy, at the twilight hour. He would sit in his armchair too lazy to switch on the light, and all the shadows that crept into his room were full of our presence coming to tempt him. [*As if she saw herself still there by the writing table, and was annoyed by the presence of the* ACTORS.] Oh, if you would only go away, go away and leave us alone—mother here with that son of hers—I with that Child—that Boy there always alone—and then I with him [*just hints at the* FATHER]—and then I alone, alone . . . in those shadows! [*Makes a sudden movement as if in the vision she has of herself illuminating those shadows she wanted to seize hold of herself.*] Ah! my life! my life! Oh, what scenes we proposed to him—and I tempted him more than any of the others!

THE FATHER. Maybe. But perhaps it was your fault that he refused to give us life: because you were too insistent, too troublesome.

THE STEP-DAUGHTER. Nonsense! Didn't he make me so himself? [*Goes close to the* MANAGER *to tell him as if in confidence.*] In my opinion he abandoned us in a fit of depression, of disgust for the ordinary theatre as the public knows it and likes it.

THE SON. Exactly what it was, sir; exactly that!

THE FATHER. Not at all! Don't believe it for a minute. Listen to me! You'll be doing quite right to modify, as you suggest, the excesses both of this girl here, who wants to do too much, and of this young man, who won't do anything at all.

THE SON. No, nothing!

THE MANAGER. You too get over the mark occasionally, my dear sir, if I may say so.

THE FATHER. I? When? Where?

THE MANAGER. Always! Continuously! Then there's this insistence of yours in trying to make us believe you are a character. And then too, you must really argue and philosophize less, you know, much less.

THE FATHER. Well, if you want to take away from me the possibility of representing the torment of my spirit which never gives me peace, you will be suppressing me: that's all. Every true man, sir, who is a little above the level of the beasts and plants does not live for the sake of living, without knowing how to live; but he lives so as to give a meaning and a value of his own to life. For me this is *everything*. I cannot give up this, just to represent a mere fact as she [*indicating the* STEP-DAUGHTER] wants. It's all very well for her, since her "vendetta" lies in the "fact." I'm not going to do it. It destroys my *raison d'être*.

THE MANAGER. Your *raison d'être!* Oh, we're going ahead fine! First she starts off, and then you jump in. At this rate, we'll never finish.

THE FATHER. Now, don't be offended! Have it your own way—provided, however, that within the limits of the parts you assign us each one's sacrifice isn't too great.

THE MANAGER. You've got to understand that you can't go on arguing at your own pleasure. Drama is action, sir, action and not confounded philosophy.

THE FATHER. All right. I'll do just as much arguing and philosophizing as everybody does when he is considering his own torments.

THE MANAGER. If the drama permits! But for Heaven's sake, man, let's get along and come to the scene.

THE STEP-DAUGHTER. It seems to me we've got too much action with our coming into his house. [*Indicating* FATHER.] You said, before, you couldn't change the scene every five minutes.

THE MANAGER. Of course not. What we've got to do is to combine and group up all the facts in one simultaneous, close-knit, action. We can't have it as you want, with your little brother wandering like a ghost from room to room, hiding behind doors and meditating a project which—what did you say it did to him?

THE STEP-DAUGHTER. Consumes him, sir, wastes him away!

THE MANAGER. Well, it may be. And then at the same time, you want the little girl there to be playing in the garden . . . one in the house, and the other in the garden: isn't that it?

THE STEP-DAUGHTER. Yes, in the sun, in the sun! That is my only pleasure: to see her happy and careless in the garden after the misery and squalor of the horrible room where we all four slept together. And I had to sleep with her—I, do you understand?—with my vile contaminated body next to hers; with her folding me fast in her loving little arms. In the garden, whenever she spied me, she would run to take me by the hand. She didn't care for the big flowers, only the little ones; and she loved to show me them and pet me.

THE MANAGER. Well then, we'll have it in the garden. Everything shall happen in the garden; and we'll group the other scenes there. [*Calls a* STAGE HAND.] Here, a backcloth with trees and something to do as a fountain basin. [*Turning round to look at the back of the stage.*] Ah, you've fixed it up. Good! [*To* STEP-DAUGHTER.] This is just to give an idea, of course. The boy, instead of hiding behind the doors, will wander about here in the garden, hiding behind the trees. But it's going to be rather difficult to find a child to do that scene with you where she shows you the flowers. [*Turning to the* BOY.] Come forward a little, will you please? Let's try it now! Come along! come along! [*Then seeing him come shyly forward, full of fear and looking lost.*] It's a nice business, this lad here. What's the matter with him? We'll have to give him a word or two to say. [*Goes close to him, puts a hand on his shoulders, and leads him behind one of the trees.*] Come on! come on! Let me see you a little! Hide here . . . yes, like that. Try and show your head just a little as if you were looking for someone . . . [*Goes back to observe the effect, when the* BOY *at once goes through the action.*] *Excellent! fine!* [*Turning to* STEP-DAUGHTER.] Suppose the little girl there were to surprise him as he looks round, and run over to him, so we could give him a word or two to say?

THE STEP-DAUGHTER. It's useless to hope he will speak, as long as that fellow there is here . . . [*indicates the* SON]. You must send him away first.

THE SON [*jumping up*]. Delighted! Delighted! I don't ask for anything better. [*Begins to move away.*]

THE MANAGER [*at once stopping him*]. No! No! Where are you going? Wait a bit!

> [*The* MOTHER *gets up alarmed and terrified at the thought that he is really about to go away. Instinctively she lifts her arms to prevent him, without, however, leaving her seat.*]

THE SON [*to* MANAGER *who stops him*]. I've got nothing to do with this affair. Let me go please! Let me go!

THE MANAGER. What do you mean by saying you've got nothing to do with this?

THE STEP-DAUGHTER [*calmly, with irony*]. Don't bother to stop him: he won't go away.

THE FATHER. He has to act the terrible scene in the garden with his mother.

THE SON [*suddenly resolute and with dignity*]. I shall act nothing at all. I've said so from the very beginning. [*To the* MANAGER.] Let me go!

THE STEP-DAUGHTER [*going over to the* MANAGER]. Allow me? [*Puts down the* MANAGER'S *arm which is restraining the* SON.] Well, go away then, if you want to! [*The* SON *looks at her with contempt and hatred. She laughs and says.*] You see, he can't, he can't go away! He is obliged to stay here, indissolubly bound to the chain. If I, who fly off when that happens which has to happen, because I can't bear him—if I am still here and support that face and expression of his, you can well imagine that he is unable to move. He has to remain here, has to stop with that nice father of his, and that mother whose only son he is. [*Turning to the* MOTHER.] Come on, mother, come along! [*Turning to* MANAGER *to indicate her.*] You see, she was getting up to keep him back. [*To the* MOTHER, *beckoning her with her hand.*] Come on! come on! [*Then to* MANAGER.] You can imagine how little she wants to show these actors of yours what she really feels; but so eager is she to get near him that . . . There, you see? She is willing to act her part. [*And in fact, the* MOTHER *approaches him; and as soon as the* STEP-DAUGHTER *has finished speaking, opens her arms to signify that she consents.*]

THE SON [*suddenly*]. No! no! If I can't go away, then I'll stop here; but I repeat: I act nothing!

THE FATHER [*to* MANAGER *excitedly*]. You can force him, sir.

THE SON. Nobody can force me.

THE FATHER. I can.

THE STEP-DAUGHTER. Wait a minute, wait . . . First of all, the baby has to go to the fountain . . . [*Runs to take the* CHILD *and leads her to the fountain.*]

THE MANAGER. Yes, yes of course; that's it. Both at the same time.

[*The second* LADY LEAD *and the* JUVENILE LEAD *at this point separate themselves from the group of* ACTORS. *One watches the* MOTHER *attentively; the other moves about studying the movements and manner of the* SON *whom he will have to act.*]

THE SON [*to* MANAGER]. What do you mean by both at the same time? It isn't right. There was no scene between me and her. [*Indicates the* MOTHER.] Ask her how it was!

THE MOTHER. Yes, it's true. I had come into his room . . .

THE SON. Into my room, do you understand? Nothing to do with the garden.

THE MANAGER. It doesn't matter. Haven't I told you we've got to group the action?

THE SON [*observing the* JUVENILE LEAD *studying him*]. What do you want?

JUVENILE LEAD. Nothing! I was just looking at you.

THE SON [*turning towards the second* LADY LEAD]. Ah! she's at it too: to re-act her part! [*Indicating the* MOTHER.]

THE MANAGER. Exactly! And it seems to me that you ought to be grateful to them for their interest.

THE SON. Yes, but haven't you yet perceived that it isn't possible to live in front of a mirror which not only freezes us with the image of ourselves, but throws our likeness back at us with a horrible grimace?

THE FATHER. That is true, absolutely true. You must see that.

THE MANAGER [*to second* LADY LEAD *and* JUVENILE LEAD]. He's right! Move away from them!

THE SON. Do as you like. I'm out of this!

THE MANAGER. Be quiet, you, will you? And let me hear your mother! [*To* MOTHER.] You were saying you had entered . . .

THE MOTHER. Yes, into his room, because I couldn't stand it any longer. I went to empty my heart to him of all the anguish that tortures me. . . . But as soon as he saw me come in . . .

THE SON. Nothing happened! There was no scene. I went away, that's all! I don't care for scenes!

THE MOTHER. It's true, true. That's how it was.

THE MANAGER. Well now, we've got to do this bit between you and him. It's indispensable.

THE MOTHER. I'm ready . . . when you are ready. If you could only find a chance for me to tell him what I feel here in my heart.

THE FATHER [*going to* SON *in a great rage*]. You'll do this for your mother, for your mother, do you understand?

THE SON [*quite determined*]. I do nothing!

THE FATHER [*taking hold of him and shaking him*]. For God's sake, do as I tell you! Don't you hear your mother asking you for a favor? Haven't you even got the guts to be a son?

THE SON [*taking hold of the* FATHER]. No! No! And for God's sake stop it, or else . . . [*General agitation. The* MOTHER, *frightened, tries to separate them.*]

THE MOTHER [*pleading*]. Please! please!

THE FATHER [*not leaving hold of the* SON]. You've got to obey, do you hear?

THE SON [*almost crying from rage*]. What does it mean, this madness you've got? [*They separate.*] Have you no decency, that you insist on showing everyone our shame? I won't do it! I won't! And I stand for the will of our author in this. He didn't want to put us on the stage, after all!

THE MANAGER. Man alive! You came here . . .

THE SON [*indicating* FATHER]. *He* did! I didn't!

THE MANAGER. Aren't you here now?

THE SON. It was his wish, and he dragged us along with him. He's told you not only the things that did happen, but also things that have never happened at all.

THE MANAGER. Well, tell me then what did happen. You went out of your room without saying a word?

THE SON. Without a word, so as to avoid a scene!

THE MANAGER. And then what did you do?

THE SON. Nothing . . . walking in the garden . . . [*Hesitates for a moment with expression of gloom.*]

THE MANAGER [*coming closer to him, interested by his extraordinary reserve*]. Well, well . . . walking in the garden . . .

THE SON [*exasperated*]. Why on earth do you insist? It's horrible! [*The* MOTHER *trembles, sobs, and looks towards the fountain.*]

THE MANAGER [*slowly observing the glance and turning towards the* SON *with increasing apprehension*]. The baby?

THE SON. There in the fountain . . .

THE FATHER [*pointing with tender pity to the* MOTHER]. She was following him at the moment . . .

THE MANAGER [*to the* SON *anxiously*]. And then you . . .

THE SON. I ran over to her; I was jumping in to drag her out when I saw something that froze my blood . . . the boy standing stock still, with eyes like a madman's, watching his little drowned sister, in the fountain! [*The* STEP-DAUGHTER *bends over the fountain to hide the* CHILD. *She sobs.*] Then . . . [*A revolver shot rings out behind the trees where the* BOY *is hidden.*]

THE MOTHER [*with a cry of terror runs over in that direction together with several of the* ACTORS *amid general confusion*]. My son! My son! [*Then amid the cries and exclamations one hears her voice.*] Help! Help!

THE MANAGER [*pushing the* ACTORS *aside while they lift up the* BOY *and carry him off.*] Is he really wounded?

SOME ACTORS. He's dead! dead!

OTHER ACTORS. No, no, it's only make believe, it's only pretense!

THE FATHER [*with a terrible cry*]. Pretense? Reality, sir, reality!

THE MANAGER. Pretense? Reality? To hell with it all! Never in my life has such a thing happened to me. I've lost a whole day over these people, a whole day!

Curtain.

André Gide

The Return of the Prodigal Son

TRANSLATED BY WALLACE FOWLIE

André Gide (1869–1951)

ANDRÉ GIDE WAS BORN IN PARIS INTO A WELL-TO-DO FAMILY. He liked to see in his dual inheritance—his father was a Protestant, his mother, converted to Protestantism, was born a Catholic—a source of the unending debate within himself about ethical systems and styles of life. His childhood was austere; as a young man, he frequented the Symbolist writers, especially the group gathered around Stéphane Mallarmé.

A major revolution in his life came with a trip to North Africa in 1893: he discovered his homosexual leanings, the rich sensuality of the Mediterranean landscape, and the possibilities of a life unfettered by convention—a life that he would celebrate in *Fruits of the Earth*. "Families, I hate you," he wrote in that book. He did in fact marry eventually and established himself in Paris and on a country estate in Normandy, but he sought always to avoid becoming structured into a bourgeois existence. He remained a traveler and avid seeker for new knowledge and experience. He was one of the founders of *La Nouvelle Revue Française,* a periodical that for years published the best and most advanced writing in France and from abroad. He became a Communist during the thirties but was totally disillusioned during a trip to Soviet Russia.

To generations of young Frenchmen, Gide was a liberating influence; to their elders, he was a "corrupter of youth." He questioned unceasingly all dogmas and conventions and believed that man should remain "available" to any new passion or idea that came his way and should be ready to embrace life fully in all its forms. "It is good to follow your inclination, so long as it leads you upwards," says one of Gide's characters, and this desire to be in harmony with life and nature and yet to attain ever higher self-realization is typical of Gide.

Much of Gide's writing is confessional in nature: in books like *Corydon, If It Die,* and his *Journal,* Gide wrestled with his own desires and shortcomings and tried to lay himself utterly bare under an introspective gaze of great intensity. He was also a master of the middle-length, first-person narrative that the French call a *récit,* of which *The Immoralist* is the most brilliant example.

The Return of the Prodigal Son is typically Gidean in its use of a mythical story as a vehicle for a very personal discussion of values, in its use of dialogue, debate, and contest to reach elusive truths, and in its searching examination of the demands of freedom and individual commitment, of social rules and individual conscience. The Parable of the Prodigal Son, on which Gide has based his story, is told in Luke 15:11–32.

The Return of the Prodigal Son

As was done in old triptychs,[1] I have painted here, for my secret pleasure, the parable told to us by Our Lord Jesus Christ. Leaving scattered and indistinct the double inspiration which moves me, I have not tried to prove the victory of any god over me—or my victory. And yet, if the reader demands of me some expression of piety, he will not perhaps look for it in vain in my painting, where, like a donor in the corner of the picture, I am kneeling, a pendant to the prodigal son, smiling like him and also like him, my face soaked with tears.

The Prodigal Son

When, after a long absence, tired of his fancies and as if fallen out of love with himself, the prodigal son, from the depths of that destitution he sought, thinks of his father's face; of that not too small room where his mother used to bend over his bed; of that garden, watered with a running stream, but enclosed and from which he had always wanted to escape; of his thrifty older brother whom he never loved, but who still holds, in the expectation of his return, that part of his fortune which, as a prodigal, he was not able to squander—the boy confesses to himself that he did not find happiness, nor even succeed in prolonging very much that disorderly excitement which he sought in place of happiness. "Ah!" he thinks, "if my father, after first being angry with me, believed me dead, perhaps, in spite of my sins, he would rejoice at seeing me again. Ah, if I go back to him very humbly, my head bowed and covered with ashes, and if, bending down before him and saying to him: 'Father, I have sinned against heaven, and before you,' what shall I do if, raising me with his hand, he says, 'Come into the house, my son'?" And already the boy is piously on his way.

When from the top of the hill he sees at last the smoking roofs of the house, it is evening. But he waits for the shadows of night in order to veil somewhat his poverty. In the distance he hears his father's voice. His

[1] Altarpiece paintings that have three panels to them.

knees give way. He falls and covers his face with his hands because he is ashamed of his shame, and yet he knows that he is the lawful son. He is hungry. In a fold of his tattered cloak he has only one handful of those sweet acorns which were his food, as they were the food of the swine he herded. He sees the preparations for supper. He makes out his mother coming on to the doorstep. . . . He can hold back no longer. He runs down the hill and comes into the courtyard where his dog, failing to recognize him, barks. He tries to speak to the servants. But they are suspicious and move away in order to warn the master. Here he is!

Doubtless he was expecting his prodigal son, because he recognizes him immediately. He opens his arms. The boy then kneels before him, and hiding his forehead with one arm, he raises his right hand for pardon:

"Father! Father! I have gravely sinned against heaven and against you. I am not worthy to be called. But at least, like one of your servants, the humblest, let me live in a corner of our house."

The father raises him and embraces him.

"My son, blessed is this day when you come back to me!" And his joy weeps as it overflows his heart. He raises his head from his son's brow which he was kissing, and turns toward his servants:

"Bring forth the best robe. Put shoes on his feet, and a precious ring on his finger. Look in our stables for the fattest calf and kill it. Prepare a joyful feast, for my son whom I thought dead is alive."

And as the news spreads rapidly, he hastens. He does not want another to say:

"Mother, the son we wept for has returned to us."

Everyone's joy mounting up like a hymn troubles the older son. He sits down at the common table because his father invites him and urges him forcibly. Alone, among all the guests, for even the humblest servant is invited, he shows an angry expression. To the repentant sinner why is there more honor than to himself, who has never sinned? He esteems order more than love. If he consents to appear at the feast, it is because by giving credit to his brother, he can lend him joy for one evening. It is also because his father and mother have promised him to rebuke the prodigal tomorrow, and because he himself is preparing to admonish him seriously.

The torches send up their smoke toward heaven. The meal is over. The servants have cleared the tables. Now, in the night, when not a breath is stirring, soul after soul, in the weary house, goes to sleep. And yet, in the room next to the prodigal's, I know a boy, his younger brother, who throughout the night until dawn will try in vain to sleep.

The Father's Reprimand

Lord, like a child I kneel before You today, my face soaked with tears. If I remember and transcribe here your compelling parable, it is because I know who your prodigal child was. I see myself in him. At times I hear in myself and repeat in secret those words which, from the depth of his great distress, You have him cry:

"How many hirelings of my father have bread enough and to spare, and I perish with hunger!"

I imagine the father's embrace, and in the warmth of such love my heart melts. I imagine an earlier distress, and even—ah! I imagine all kinds of things. This I believe: I am the very one whose heart beats when, from the top of the hill, he sees again the blue roofs of the house he left. What keeps me then from running toward my home and going in?—I am expected. I can see the fatted calf they are preparing. . . . Stop! Do not set up the feast too quickly!—Prodigal son, I am thinking of you. Tell me first what your Father said to you the next day, after the feast of welcome. Ah! even if the elder son prompts you, Father, let me hear your voice sometimes through his words!

"My son, why did you leave me?"

"Did I really leave you? Father, are you not everywhere? Never did I cease loving you."

"Let us not split hairs. I had a house which kept you in. It was built for you. Generations worked so that in it your soul could find shelter, luxury worthy of it, comfort and occupation. Why did you, the heir, the son, escape from the House?"

"Because the House shut me in. The House is not You, Father."

"It is I who built it, and for you."

"Ah! you did not say that, my brother did. You built the whole world, the House and what is not the House. The House was built by others. In your name, I know, but by others."

"Man needs a roof under which he can lay his head. Proud boy! Do you think you can sleep in the open?"

"Do you need pride to do that? Some poorer than I have done so."

"They are the poor. You are not poor. No one can give up his wealth. I had made you rich above all men."

"Father, you know that when I left, I took with me all the riches I could. What do I care about goods that cannot be carried away?"

"All that fortune you took away, you have spent recklessly."

"I changed your gold into pleasures, your precepts into fantasy, my chastity into poetry, and my austerity into desires."

"Was it for that your thrifty parents strove to instill into you so much virtue?"

"So that I should burn with a brighter flame perhaps, being kindled by a new fervor."

"Think of that pure flame Moses saw on the sacred bush. It shone, but without consuming."

"I have known love which consumes."

"The love which I want to teach you, refreshes. After a short time, what did you have left, prodigal son?"

"The memory of those pleasures."

"And the destitution which comes after them."

"In that destitution, I felt close to you, Father."

"Was poverty needed to drive you back to me?"

"I do not know. I do not know. It was in the dryness of the desert that I loved my thirst more."

"Your poverty made you feel more deeply the value of riches."

"No, not that! Can't you understand me, Father? My heart, emptied of everything, became filled with love. At the cost of all my goods, I bought fervor."

"Were you happy, then, far from me?"

"I did not feel far from you."

"Then, what made you come back? Tell me."

"I don't know. Laziness perhaps."

"Laziness, my son? What! Wasn't it love?"

"Father, I have told you. I never loved you better than in the desert. But each morning I was tired of looking for my subsistence. In the House, at least there is food to eat."

"Yes, servants look after that. So, what brought you back was hunger."

"Cowardice also perhaps, and sickness. . . . In the end, that food I was never sure of finding weakened me. Because I fed on wild fruit and locusts and honey. I grew less and less able to stand the discomfort which at first quickened my fervor. At night, when I was cold, I thought of my tucked-in bed in my father's house. When I fasted, I thought of my father's home where the abundance of food served always exceeded my hunger. I weakened; I didn't feel enough courage, enough strength to struggle much longer and yet . . ."

"So yesterday's fatted calf seemed good to you?"

The prodigal son throws himself down sobbing, with his face against the ground.

"Father! Father! The wild taste of sweet acorns is still in my mouth, in spite of everything. Nothing could blot out their savor."

"Poor child!" says the father as he raises him up. "I spoke to you perhaps too harshly. Your brother wanted me to. Here it is he who makes the law.

It is he who charged me to say to you: 'Outside of the House, there is no salvation for you.' But listen. It was I who made you. I know what is in you. I know what sent you out on your wanderings. I was waiting for you at the end of the road. If you had called me . . . I was there."

"Father! might I then have found you without coming back?"

"If you felt weak, you did well to come back. Go now. Go back to the room I had prepared for you. Enough for today. Rest. Tomorrow you will speak with your brother."

The Elder Brother's Reprimand

The prodigal son first tries to bluster.

"Big brother," he begins, "we aren't very much alike. Brother, we aren't alike at all."

The elder brother says:

"It's your fault."

"Why mine?"

"Because I live by order. Whatever differs from it is the fruit or the seed of pride."

"Am I different only in my faults?"

"Only call quality what brings you back to order, and curtail all the rest."

"It is that mutilation I fear. What you plan to suppress comes also from the Father."

"Not suppress—curtail, I said."

"I understand. All the same, that is how I curtailed my virtues."

"And that is also why now I still see them in you. You must exaggerate them. Understand me. It is not a diminution of yourself, but an exaltation I propose, in which the most diverse, the most unruly elements of your flesh and your spirit must join together harmoniously, in which the worst in you must nourish the best, in which the best must submit to . . ."

"It was exaltation which I also sought and found in the desert—and perhaps not very different from the one you propose to me."

"To tell the truth, I wanted to impose it on you."

"Our Father did not speak so harshly."

"I know what the Father said to you. It was vague. He no longer expresses himself very clearly, so that he can be made to say what one wants. But I understand his thought very well. With the servants, I am the one interpreter, and who wants to understand the Father must listen to me."

"I understand him quite easily without you."

"You thought you did. But you understood incorrectly. There are not several ways of understanding the Father. There are not several ways of listening to him. There are not several ways of loving him, so that we may be united in his love."

"In his House."

"This love brings one back here. You see this, for you have come back. Tell me now, what impelled you to leave?"

"I felt too clearly that the House is not the entire universe. I myself am not completely in the boy you wanted me to be. I could not help imagining other cultures, other lands, and roads by which to reach them, roads not yet traced. I imagined in myself the new being which I felt rushing down those roads. I ran away."

"Think what could have happened if, like you, I had deserted our Father's House. Servants and thieves would have pillaged all our goods."

"That would not have mattered to me, since I was catching sight of other goods . . ."

"Which your pride exaggerated. My brother, indiscipline is over. You will learn, if you don't yet know it, out of what chaos man has emerged. He has just barely emerged. With all of his artless weight, he falls back into it as soon as the Spirit no longer supports him above it. Do not learn this at your own expense. The well-ordered elements which make up your being wait only for an acquiescence, a weakening on your part in order to return to anarchy . . . But what you will never know is the length of time it was needed for man to elaborate man. Now that we have the model, let us keep it. 'Hold that fast which thou hast,' says the Spirit to the Angel of the Church, and He adds, 'that no man take thy crown.' *The which thou hast* is your crown, that royalty over others and over yourself. The usurper lies in wait for your crown. He is everywhere. He prowls around you and in you. *Hold fast,* my brother! Hold fast."

"Too long ago I let go my hold. And now I cannot close my hand over my own wealth."

"Yes, you can. I will help you. I have watched over your wealth during your absence."

"And moreover, I know those words of the Spirit. You did not quote them all."

"You are right. It goes on: 'Him that overcometh will I make a pillar in the temple of my God, and he shall go no more out.' "

" 'And he shall go no more out.' That is precisely what terrifies me."

"If it is for his happiness."

"Oh! I understand. But I had been in that temple . . ."

"You found you were wrong to have left, since you wanted to return."

"I know, I know. I am back now. I agree."

"What good can you look for elsewhere, which here you do not find in abundance? Or better—here alone your wealth is to be found."

"I know that you kept my riches for me."

"The part of your fortune which you did not squander, namely that part which is common to all of us: the property."

"Then do I personally own nothing else?"

"Yes. That special allotment of gifts which perhaps our Father will still consent to grant you."

"That is all I want. I agree to own only that."

"How proud you are! You will not be consulted. Between you and me, that portion is risky. I would advise your giving it up. It was that allotment of personal gifts which already brought on your downfall. That was the wealth you squandered immediately."

"The other kind I couldn't take with me."

"Therefore you will find it intact. Enough for today. Find rest now in the House."

"That suits me well, for I am tired."

"Then blessed be your fatigue! Now go and sleep. Tomorrow your mother will speak to you."

The Mother

Prodigal son, whose mind still rebels against the words of your brother, let your heart now speak. How sweet it is, as you lie at the feet of your mother, with your head hidden on her lap, to feel her caressing hand bow your stubborn neck!

"Why did you leave me for so long a time?"

And since you answer only with tears:

"Why weep now, my son? You have been given back to me. In waiting for you, I have shed all my tears."

"Were you still waiting for me?"

"Never did I give up hoping for you. Before going to sleep, every evening I would think: if he returns tonight, will he be able to open the door? And it took me a long time to fall asleep. Every morning, before I was totally awake, I would think: isn't it today he will come back? Then I prayed. I prayed so hard that it was not possible for you not to come back."

"Your prayers forced me to come back."

"Don't smile because of me, my child."

"Oh mother, I have come back to you very humble. See how I place my forehead lower than your heart! There is not one of my thoughts of yesterday which does not become empty today. When close to you, I can hardly understand why I left the house."

"You will not leave it again?"

"I cannot leave it again."

"What then attracted you outside?"

"I don't want to think of it any more. Nothing . . . Myself . . ."

"Did you think then that you would be happy away from us?"

"I was not looking for happiness."

"What were you looking for?"

"I was looking for . . . who I was."

"Oh! son of your parents, and brother among your brothers."

"I was not like my brothers. Let's not talk any more about it. I have come back now."

"Yes, let's talk of it further. Do not believe that your brothers are so unlike you."

"Henceforth my one care is to be like all of you."

"You say that as if with resignation."

"Nothing is more fatiguing than to realize one's difference. Finally my wandering tired me out."

"You have aged, that is true."

"I have suffered."

"My poor child! Doubtless your bed was not made every evening, nor the table set for all your meals?"

"I ate what I found and often it was green or spoiled fruit which my hunger made into food."

"At least did you suffer only from hunger?"

"The sun at mid-day, the cold wind in the heart of the night, the shifting sand of the desert, the thorns which made my feet bloody, nothing of all that stopped me, but—I didn't tell this to my brother—I had to serve . . ."

"Why did you conceal it?"

"Bad masters who harmed me bodily, exasperated my pride, and gave me barely enough to eat. That is when I thought: 'Serving for the sake of serving! . . .' In dreams I saw my house, and I came home."

The prodigal son again lowers his head and his mother caresses it tenderly.

"What are you going to do now?"

"I have told you. Try to become like my big brother, look after our property, like him choose a wife . . ."

"You have doubtless someone in mind, as you say that."

"Oh, anyone at all will be my first preference, as soon as you have chosen her. Do as you did for my brother."

"I should have preferred someone you love."

"What does that matter? My heart had made a choice. I renounce the pride which took me far away from you. Help me in my choice. I submit, I tell you. And I will have my children submit also. In that way, my adventure will not seem pointless to me."

"Listen to me. There is at this moment a child you could take on already as a charge."

"What do you mean and of whom are you speaking?"

"Of your younger brother who was not ten when you left, whom you hardly recognized, but who . . ."

"Go on, mother! What are you worried about now?"

"In whom you might well have recognized yourself because he is like what you were when you left."

"Like me?"

"Like what you were, I said, not yet, alas, what you have become."

"What he will become."

"What you must make him become immediately. Speak to him. He will listen to you, doubtless, you the prodigal. Tell him what disappointment you met on your way. Spare him . . ."

"But what causes you such alarm about my brother? Perhaps simply a resemblance of features . . ."

"No, no! the resemblance between you two is deeper. I worry now for him about what first did not worry me enough for you. He reads too much, and doesn't always prefer good books."

"Is that all it is?"

"He is often perched on the highest part of the garden, from where, as you know, you can see the countryside over the walls."

"I remember. Is that all?"

"He spends less time with us than in the farm."

"Ah! what does he do there?"

"Nothing wrong. But it is not the farmers he stays with, it is the farm hands who are as different from us as possible and those who are not from this country. There is one in particular, who comes from some distance, and who tells him stories."

"Ah! the swineherd."

"Yes. Did you know him? . . . Your brother each evening in order to listen to him, follows him into the pigsties. He comes back only for dinner, but with no appetite, and his clothes reeking. Remonstrances have no effect. He stiffens under constaint. On certain mornings, at dawn, before any of us are up, he runs off to accompany that swineherd to the gate when he is leading off his herd to graze."

"He knows he must not leave."

"You knew also! One day he will escape from me, I am sure. One day he will leave . . ."

"No, I will speak to him, mother. Don't be alarmed."

"I know he will listen to a great deal from you. Did you see how he watched you that first evening, with what prestige your rags were covered, and the purple robe your father put on you! I was afraid that in his mind he will confuse one with the other, and that he is attracted first by the rags. But now this idea seems ridiculous to me. For if you, my child, had been able to foresee such unhappiness, you would not have left us, would you?"

"I don't know now how I was able to leave you, you who are my mother."

"Well, tell him all that."

"I will tell him that tomorrow evening. Now kiss me on my forehead as you used to when I was small and you watched me fall asleep. I am sleepy."

"Go to bed. I am going to pray for all of you."

Dialogue with the Younger Brother

Beside the prodigal's, there is a room not too small, with bare walls. The prodigal, a lamp in his hand, comes close to the bed where his younger brother is lying, his face toward the wall. He begins in a low voice, so as not to disturb him if the boy is sleeping.

"I would like to talk to you, brother."

"What is stopping you?"

"I thought you were sleeping."

"I don't have to sleep in order to dream."

"You were dreaming? Of what?"

"What do you care? If I can't understand my dreams, I don't think you will be able to explain them to me."

"Are they that subtle, then? If you told them to me, I would try."

"Do you choose your dreams? Mine are what they want to be, and are freer than I . . . What have you come here for? Why are you disturbing me in my sleep?"

"You aren't sleeping, and I'm here to speak gently to you."

"What have you to say to me?"

"Nothing, if that is the tone you take."

"Then goodbye."

The prodigal goes toward the door, but puts the lamp on the floor so that the room is barely lighted. Then, coming back, he sits on the edge of the bed and in the dark strokes for a long time the boy's forehead which is kept turned away.

"You answer me more gruffly than I ever did your brother. Yet I too rebelled against him."

The stubborn boy suddenly sat up.

"Tell me, is it my brother that sent you?"

"No, not him, but our mother."

"So, you wouldn't have come of your own accord."

"But I came as a friend."

Half sitting up on his bed, the boy looks straight at the prodigal.

"How could one of my family be my friend?"

"You are mistaken about our brother . . ."

"Don't speak to me about him! I hate him. My whole heart cries out against him. He's the reason for my answering you gruffly."

"Explain why."

"You wouldn't understand."

"Tell me just the same."

The prodigal rocks his brother in his arms and already the boy begins to yield.

"The evening you returned, I couldn't sleep. All night I kept thinking: I had another brother, and I didn't know it . . . That is why my heart beat so hard when, in the courtyard of our house, I saw you come covered with glory."

"Alas, I was covered then with rags."

"Yes, I saw you. You were already glorious. And I saw what our father did. He put a ring on your finger, a ring the like of which our brother does not have. I did not want to question anyone about you. All that I knew was that you had come from very far away, and that your eyes, at table . . ."

"Were you at the feast?"

"Oh! I know you did not see me. During the whole meal you looked far off without seeing anything. And it was all right when on the second evening you spoke with our father, but on the third . . ."

"Go on."

"Ah! you could have said to me at least one word of love!"

"You were expecting me then?"

"Impatiently! Do you think I would hate our brother so much if you had not gone to talk with him that evening and for so long? What did you find to say to each other? You certainly know, if you are like me, that you can have nothing in common with him."

"I had behaved very wrong toward him."

"Is that possible?"

"At any rate toward our father and mother. You know that I ran away from home."

"Yes, I know. A long time ago, wasn't it?"

"When I was about your age."

"Ah! And that's what you call behaving wrong?"

"Yes, it was wrong, it was my sin."

"When you left, did you feel you were doing wrong?"

"No, I felt duty-bound to leave."

"What has happened since then to change your first truth into an error?"

"I suffered."

"And is that what makes you say: I did wrong?"

"No, not exactly. That is what made me reflect."

"Then, before, you didn't reflect?"

"Yes, but my weak reason let itself be conquered by my desires."

"As later by your suffering. So that today you have come back . . . conquered."

"No, not exactly,—resigned."

"At any rate, you have given up being what you wanted to be."

"What my pride persuaded me to be."

The boy remains silent a moment, then suddenly cries with a sob:

"Brother! I am the boy you were when you left. Tell me. Did you find nothing but disappointments on your wanderings? Is all that I imagine outside and different from here, only an illusion? All the newness I feel in me, is that madness? Tell me, what did you meet on your way that seemed so tragic? Oh! what made you come back?"

"The freedom I was looking for, I lost. When captive, I had to serve."

"I am captive here."

"Yes, but I mean serving bad masters. Here you are serving your parents."

"Ah! serving for the sake of serving! At least don't we have the freedom of choosing our bondage?"

"I had hoped for that. As far as my feet carried me, I walked, like Saul in search of his she-asses, in search of my desire. But there where a kingdom was waiting for him, I found wretchedness. And yet . . ."

"Didn't you mistake the road?"

"I walked straight ahead."

"Are you sure? And yet there are still other kingdoms, and lands without kings, to discover."

"Who told you?"

"I know it, I feel it. I have already the impression of being the lord over them."

"Proud boy!"

"Ah! ah! that's something our brother said to you. Why do you repeat it to me now? Why didn't you keep that pride? You would not have come back."

"Then I would never have known you."

"Yes, yes, out there where I would have joined you, you would have recognized me as your brother. It seems to me even that I am leaving in order to find you."

"That you are leaving?"

"Haven't you understood? Aren't you yourself encouraging me to leave?"

"I wanted to spare your returning, but by sparing your departure."

"No, no, don't tell me that. No, you don't mean that. You yourself left like a conqueror, didn't you?"

"And that is what made my bondage seem harder to me."

"Then, why did you give in to it? Were you already so tired?"

"No, not then. But I had doubts."

"What do you mean?"

"Doubts about everything, about myself. I wanted to stop and settle down somewhere. The comfort which this master promised me was a temptation . . . Yes, I feel it clearly now. I failed."

The prodigal bows his head and hides his face in his hands.

"But at first?"

"I had walked for a long time through large tracts of wild country."

"The desert?"

"It wasn't always the desert."

"What were you looking for there?"

"I myself do not understand now."

"Get up from my bed. Look, on the table beside it, there, near that torn book."

"I see a pomegranate split open."

"The swineherd brought it to me the other evening, after he had not been back for three days."

"Yes, it is a wild pomegranate."

"I know. It is almost unbearably bitter. And yet I feel, if I were sufficiently thirsty, I would bite into it."

"Ah! now I can tell you. That is the thirst I was looking for in the desert."

"A thirst which that sour fruit alone can quench . . ."

"No, but it makes you love that thirst."

"Do you know where it can be picked?"

"In a small deserted orchard you reach before evening. No longer does any wall separate it from the desert. A stream flowed through it. Some half-ripe fruit hung from the branches."

"What fruit?"

"The same which grows in our garden, but wild. It had been very hot all day."

"Listen. Do you know why I was expecting you this evening? I am leaving before the end of the night. Tonight, this night, as soon as it grows pale . . . I have girded my loins. Tonight I have kept on my sandals."

"So, what I was not able to do, you will do?"

"You opened the way for me, and it will help me to think of you."

"It is for me to admire you, and for you to forget me, on the contrary. What are you taking with you?"

"You know that as the youngest, I have no share in the inheritance. I am taking nothing."

"That is better."

"What are you looking at through the window?"

"The garden where our dead forefathers are sleeping."

"Brother . . ." (and the boy who has gotten out of bed, puts, around the prodigal's neck, his arm which has become as tender as his voice)—"Come with me."

"Leave me! leave me! I am staying to console our mother. Without me you will be braver. It is time now. The sky turns pale. Go without making any noise. Come! kiss me, my young brother, you are taking with you all my hopes. Be strong. Forget us. Forget me. May you never come back . . . Go down quietly. I am holding the lamp . . ."

"Ah! give me your hand as far as the door."

"Be careful of the steps as you go down."

Franz Kafka

A Hunger Artist

TRANSLATED BY WILLA AND EDWIN MUIR

Franz Kafka (1883–1924)

FRANZ KAFKA WAS BORN IN PRAGUE, AT THAT TIME PART OF the Austro-Hungarian Empire, into a middle-class Jewish family. His father was a practical, competent, and domineering man next to whom Kafka felt insignificant and inadequate, and whom he regarded with mixed feelings of love, hate, and guilt. Kafka studied law at the German University of Prague. Soon after taking his doctorate, he went to work for a workmen's insurance company, a semiofficial bureau. His private life was marked by anxiety, indecision, and frustration. He was twice engaged to the same woman, but could not bring himself to the point of marriage. He felt caught between loyalties to the Jewish intellectual community of Prague and the more official German society to which his family belonged. He was also suffering from tuberculosis. In 1923, he met a gifted and cultivated actress and left Prague to live with her in Berlin, a brief idyll that ended a year later when he died of tuberculosis in a sanatorium near Vienna.

During his lifetime, Kafka published mainly short stories and novellas. Doubting the value of his work, he ordered Max Brod, his closest friend, to burn all the manuscripts left at his death. This Brod did not do, and Kafka's three major novels—*The Trial, The Castle,* and *Amerika*—were published after his death. They were followed in 1931 by a volume of shorter pieces, *The Great Wall of China.* Kafka's reputation gained international dimensions, and his influence on younger writers became immense.

Kafka's fiction takes us into a world that has the precision and horror of nightmare. He can be described as a Surrealist because his reality is dislocated, distorted, and neurotic, but he rarely abandons a precise and analytical style in his descriptions of this reality. The disjunction between style and the hallucinated material it conveys expresses a vision of a world in which intention and action are divorced from one another and the mind is no longer adequate to what is happening. Many of Kafka's stories are fablelike in their texture, developing ambiguous, riddling images of man's situation in a world that is both absurd and menacing. A favorite theme is that of total devotion to a task, an institution, or a role, with the ambiguities of motive and value that such devotion entails. *A Hunger Artist* gives a compelling version of this theme.

A Hunger Artist

During these last decades the interest in professional fasting has markedly diminished. It used to pay very well to stage such great performances under one's own management, but today that is quite impossible. We live in a different world now. At one time the whole town took a lively interest in the hunger artist; from day to day of his fast the excitement mounted; everybody wanted to see him at least once a day; there were people who bought season tickets for the last few days and sat from morning till night in front of his small barred cage; even in the nighttime there were visiting hours, when the whole effect was heightened by torch flares; on fine days the cage was set out in the open air, and then it was the children's special treat to see the hunger artist; for their elders he was often just a joke that happened to be in fashion, but the children stood open-mouthed, holding each other's hands for greater security, marveling at him as he sat there pallid in black tights, with his ribs sticking out so prominently, not even on a seat but down among straw on the ground, sometimes giving a courteous nod, answering questions with a constrained smile, or perhaps stretching an arm through the bars so that one might feel how thin it was, and then again withdrawing deep into himself, paying no attention to anyone or anything, not even to the all-important striking of the clock that was the only piece of furniture in his cage, but merely staring into vacancy with half-shut eyes, now and then taking a sip from a tiny glass of water to moisten his lips.

Besides casual onlookers there were also relays of permanent watchers selected by the public, usually butchers, strangely enough, and it was their task to watch the hunger artist day and night, three of them at a time, in case he should have some secret recourse to nourishment. This was nothing but a formality, instituted to reassure the masses, for the initiates knew well enough that during his fast the artist would never in any circumstances, not even under forcible compulsion, swallow the smallest morsel of food; the honor of his profession forbade it. Not every watcher, of course, was capable of understanding this, there were often groups of night watchers who were very lax in carrying out their duties and deliberately huddled together in a retired corner to play cards with great absorption, obviously intending to give the hunger artist the chance of a little refreshment, which they supposed he could draw from some private hoard. Nothing annoyed the artist more than such watchers; they made him miserable; they made his fast seem unendurable; sometimes he mastered his feebleness sufficiently to sing during their watch for as long as he could keep going, to show them how unjust their suspicions were. But that was of little use; they only wondered at his cleverness in being able to fill his mouth even while singing. Much more to his taste were the watchers who sat close up to the bars, who were not content with the dim night lighting of the hall but focused him in the full glare of the electric pocket torch given them by the impresario. The harsh light did not trouble him at all, in any case he could never sleep properly, and he could always drowse a little, whatever the light, at any hour, even when the hall was thronged with noisy onlookers. He was quite happy at the prospect of spending a sleepless night with such watchers; he was ready to exchange jokes with them, to tell them stories out of his nomadic life, anything at all to keep them awake and demonstrate to them again that he had no eatables in his cage and that he was fasting as not one of them could fast. But his happiest moment was when the morning came and an enormous breakfast was brought them, at his expense, on which they flung themselves with the keen appetite of healthy men after a weary night of wakefulness. Of course there were people who argued that this breakfast was an unfair attempt to bribe the watchers, but that was going rather too far, and when they were invited to take on a night's vigil without a breakfast, merely for the sake of the cause, they made themselves scarce, although they stuck stubbornly to their suspicions.

Such suspicions, anyhow, were a necessary accompaniment to the profession of fasting. No one could possibly watch the hunger artist continuously, day and night, and so no one could produce first-hand evidence that the fast had really been rigorous and continuous; only the artist himself could know that, he was therefore bound to be the sole completely satisfied spectator of his own fast. Yet for other reasons he was never satisfied; it was not perhaps mere fasting that had brought him to such skeleton thinness that many people had regretfully to keep away from his exhibitions, because the sight of him was too much for them, perhaps it was dissatisfaction with himself that had worn him down. For he alone knew, what no other initiate knew, how easy it was to fast. It was the easiest thing in the world. He made no secret of this, yet people did not believe him, at the best they set him down as modest, most of them, however, thought he was out for publicity or else was some kind of cheat who found it easy to fast because he had discovered a way of making it easy, and then had the impudence to admit the fact, more or less. He had to put up with all that, and in the course of time had got used to it, but his inner dissatisfaction always rankled, and never yet, after any term of fasting—this must be granted to his credit—had he left the cage of his own free will. The longest period of fasting was fixed by his impresario at forty days, beyond that term he was not allowed to go, not even in great cities, and there was good reason for it, too. Experience had proved that for about forty days the interest of the public could be stimulated by a steadily increasing pressure of advertisement, but after that the town began to lose interest, sympathetic support began notably to fall off; there were of course local variations as between one town and another or one country and another, but as a general rule forty days marked the limit. So on the fortieth day the flower-bedecked cage was opened, enthusiastic spectators filled the hall, a military band played, two doctors entered the cage to measure the results of the fast, which were announced through a megaphone, and finally two young ladies appeared, blissful at having been selected for the honor, to help the hunger artist down the few steps leading to a small table on which was spread a carefully chosen invalid repast. And at this very moment the artist always turned stubborn. True, he would entrust his bony arms to the outstretched helping hands of the ladies bending over him, but stand up he would not. Why stop fasting at this particular moment, after forty days of it? He had held out for a long time, an illimitably long time; why stop now, when he was in his best fasting form, or rather, not yet quite in his best fasting form? Why should he be cheated of the fame he would get for fasting longer, for being not only the record hunger artist of all time, which presumably he was already, but for beating his own record by a performance beyond human imagination, since he felt that there were no limits to his capacity for fasting? His public pretended to admire him so much, why should it have so little patience with him; if he could endure fasting longer, why shouldn't the public endure it? Besides, he was tired, he was comfortable sitting in the straw, and now he was supposed to lift himself to his full height and go down to a meal the very thought of which gave him a nausea that only the presence of the ladies kept him from betraying, and even that with an effort. And he looked up into the eyes of the ladies who were apparently so friendly and in reality so cruel, and shook his head, which felt too heavy on its strengthless neck. But then there happened yet again what always happened. The impresario came forward, without a word —for the band made speech impossible—lifted his arms in the air above the artist, as if inviting Heaven to look down upon its creature here in the straw, this suffering martyr, which indeed he was, although in quite another sense; grasped him round the emaciated waist, with exaggerated caution, so that the frail condition he was in might be appreciated; and committed him to the care of the blenching ladies, not without secretly giving him a shaking so that his legs and body tottered and swayed. The artist now submitted completely; his head lolled on his breast as if it had landed there by chance; his body was hollowed out; his legs in a spasm of self-preservation clung close to each other at the knees, yet scraped on the ground as if it were not really solid ground, as if they were only trying to find solid ground; and the whole weight of his body, a featherweight after all, relapsed onto one of the ladies, who, looking round for help and panting a little—this post of honor was not at all what she had expected it to be—first stretched her neck as far as she could to keep her face at least free from contact with the artist, then finding this impossible, and her more fortunate companion not coming to her aid but merely holding extended on her own trembling hand the little bunch of knucklebones that was the artist's, to the great delight of the spectators burst into tears and had to be replaced by an attendant who had long been stationed in readiness. Then came the food, a little of which the impresario managed to get between the artist's lips, while he sat in a kind of half-fainting trance, to the accompaniment of cheerful patter designed to distract the public's attention from the artist's condition; after that, a toast was drunk to the public, supposedly prompted by a whisper from the artist in the impresario's ear; the band confirmed it with a mighty flourish, the spectators melted away, and no one had any cause to be dissatisfied with the proceedings, no one except the hunger artist himself, he only, as always.

So he lived for many years, with small regular intervals of recuperation, in visible glory, honored by the world, yet in spite of that troubled in spirit, and all the more troubled because no one would take his trouble seriously. What comfort could he possibly need? What more could he possibly wish for? And if some good-natured person, feeling sorry for him, tried to console him by pointing out that his melancholy was probably caused by fasting, it could happen, especially when he had been fasting for some time, that he reacted with an outburst of fury and to the general alarm began to shake the bars of his cage like a wild animal. Yet the impresario had a way of punishing these outbreaks which he rather enjoyed putting into operation. He would apologize publicly for the artist's behavior, which was only to be excused, he admitted, because of the irritability caused by fasting; a condition hardly to be understood by well-fed people; then by natural transition he went on to mention the artist's equally incomprehensible boast that he could fast for much longer than he was doing; he praised the high ambition, the good will, the great self-denial undoubtedly implicit in such a statement; and then quite simply countered it by bringing out photographs, which were also on sale to the public, showing the artist on the fortieth day of a fast lying in bed almost dead from exhaustion. This perversion of the truth, familiar to the artist though it was, always unnerved him afresh and proved too much for him. What was a consequence of the premature ending of his fast was here presented as the cause of it! To fight against this lack of understanding, against a whole world of nonunderstanding, was impossible. Time and again in good faith he stood by the bars listening to the impresario, but as soon as the photographs appeared he always let go and sank with a groan back on to his straw, and the reassured public could once more come close and gaze at him.

A few years later when the witnesses of such scenes called them to mind, they often failed to understand themselves at all. For meanwhile the aforementioned change in public interest had set in; it seemed to happen almost overnight; there may have been profound causes for it, but who was going to bother about that; at any rate the pampered hunger artist suddenly found himself deserted one fine day by the amusement seekers, who went streaming past him to other more favored attractions. For the last time the impresario hurried him over half Europe to discover whether the old interest might still survive here and there; all in vain; everywhere, as if by secret agreement, a positive revulsion from professional fasting was in evidence. Of course it could not really have sprung up so suddenly as all that, and many premonitory symptoms which had not been sufficiently remarked or suppressed during the rush and glitter of success now came retrospectively to mind, but it was now too late to take any countermeasures. Fasting would surely come into fashion again at some future date, yet that was no comfort for those living in the present. What, then, was the hunger artist to do? He had been applauded by thousands in his time and could hardly come down to showing himself in a street booth at village fairs, and as for adopting another profession, he was not only too old for that but too fanatically devoted to fasting. So he took leave of the impresario, his partner in an unparalleled career, and hired himself to a large circus; in order to spare his own feelings he avoided reading the conditions of his contract.

A large circus with its enormous traffic in replacing and recruiting men, animals and apparatus can always find a use for people at any time, even for a hunger artist, provided of course that he does not ask too much, and in this particular case anyhow it was not only the artist who was taken on but his famous and long-known name as well, indeed considering the peculiar nature of his performance, which was not impaired by advancing age, it could not be objected that here was an artist past his prime, no longer at the height of his professional skill, seeking a refuge in some quiet corner of a circus, on the contrary, the hunger artist averred that he could fast as well as ever, which was entirely credible, he even alleged that if he were allowed to fast as he liked, and this was at once promised him without more ado, he could astound the world by establishing a record never yet achieved, a statement which certainly provoked a smile among the other professionals, since it left out of account the change in public opinion, which the hunger artist in his zeal conveniently forgot.

He had not, however, actually lost his sense of the real situation and took it as a matter of course that he and his cage should be stationed, not in the middle of the ring as a main attraction, but outside, near the animal cages, on a site that was after all easily accessible. Large and gaily painted placards made a frame for the cage and announced what was to be seen inside it. When the public came thronging out in the intervals to see the animals, they could hardly avoid passing the hunger artist's cage and stopping there for a moment, perhaps they might even have stayed longer had not those pressing behind them in the narrow gangway, who did not understand why they should be held up on their way towards the excitements of the menagerie, made it impossible for anyone to stand gazing quietly for any length of time. And that was the reason why the hunger artist, who had of course been looking forward to these visiting hours as the main achievement of his life, began instead to shrink from them. At first he could hardly wait for the intervals; it was exhilarating to watch the crowds come streaming his way, until only too soon—not even the most obstinate self-deception, clung to almost consciously, could hold out against the fact—the conviction was borne in upon him that these people, most of them, to judge from their actions, again and again, without exception, were all on their way to the menagerie. And the first sight of them from the distance remained the best. For when they reached his cage he was at once deafened by the storm of shouting and abuse that arose from the two contending factions, which renewed themselves continuously, of those who wanted to stop and stare at him—he soon began to dislike them more than the others—not out of real interest but only out of obstinate self-assertiveness, and those who wanted to go straight on to the animals. When the first great rush was past, the stragglers came along, and these, whom nothing could have prevented from stopping to look at him as long as they had breath, raced past with long strides, hardly even glancing at him, in their haste to get to the menagerie in time. And all too rarely did it happen that he had a stroke of luck, when some father of a family fetched up before him with his children, pointed a finger at the hunger artist and explained at length what the phenomenon meant, telling stories of earlier years when he himself had watched similar but much more thrilling performances, and the children, still rather uncomprehending, since neither inside nor outside school had they been sufficiently prepared for this lesson—what did they care about fasting?—yet showed by the brightness of their intent eyes that new and better times might be coming. Perhaps, said the hunger artist to himself many a time, things would be a little better if his cage were set not quite so near the menagerie. That made it too easy for people to make their choice, to say nothing of what he suffered from the stench of the menagerie, the animals' restlessness by night, the carrying past of raw lumps of flesh for the beasts of prey, the roaring at feeding times, which depressed him continually. But he did not dare to lodge a complaint with the management; after all, he had the animals to thank for the troops of people who passed his cage, among whom there might always be one here and there to take an interest in him, and who could tell where they might seclude him if he called attention to his existence and thereby to the fact that, strictly speaking, he was only an impediment on the way to the menagerie.

A small impediment, to be sure, one that grew steadily less. People grew familiar with the strange idea that they could be expected, in times like these, to take an interest in a hunger artist, and with this familiarity the verdict went out against him. He might fast as much as he could, and he did so; but nothing could save him now, people passed him by. Just try to explain to anyone the art of fasting! Anyone who has no feeling for it cannot be made to understand it. The fine placards grew dirty and illegible, they were torn down; the little notice board telling the number of fast days achieved, which at first was changed carefully every day, had long stayed at the same figure, for after the first few weeks even this small task seemed pointless to the staff; and so the artist simply fasted on and on, as he had once dreamed of doing, and it was no trouble to him, just as he had always foretold, but no one counted the days, no one, not even the artist himself, knew what records he was already breaking, and his heart grew heavy. And when once in a time some leisurely passer-by stopped, made merry over the old figure on the board and spoke of swindling, that was in its way the stupidest lie ever invented by indifference and inborn malice, since it was not the hunger artist who was cheating, he was working honestly, but the world was cheating him of his reward.

Many more days went by, however, and that too came to an end. An overseer's eye fell on the cage one day and he asked the attendants why this perfectly good stage should be left standing there unused with dirty straw inside it; nobody knew, until one man, helped out by the notice board, remembered about the hunger artist. They poked into the straw with sticks and found him in it. "Are you still fasting?" asked the overseer, "when on earth do you mean to stop?" "Forgive me, everybody," whispered the hunger artist; only the overseer, who had his ear to the bars, understood him. "Of course," said the overseer, and tapped his forehead with a finger to let the attendants know what state the man was in, "we forgive you." "I always wanted you to admire my fasting," said the hunger artist. "We do admire it," said the overseer, affably. "But you shouldn't admire it," said the hunger artist. "Well then we don't admire it," said the overseer, "but why shouldn't we admire it?" "Because I have to fast, I can't help it," said the hunger artist. "What a fellow you are," said the overseer, "and why can't you help it?" "Because," said the hunger artist, lifting his head a little and speaking, with his lips pursed, as if for a kiss, right into the overseer's ear, so that no syllable might be lost, "because I couldn't find the food I liked. If I had found it, believe me, I should have made no fuss and stuffed myself like you or anyone else." These were his last words, but in his dimming eyes remained the firm though no longer proud persuasion that he was still continuing to fast.

"Well, clear this out now!" said the overseer, and they buried the hunger artist, straw and all. Into the cage they put a young panther. Even the most insensitive felt it refreshing to see this wild creature leaping around the cage that had so long been dreary. The panther was all right. The food he liked was brought him without hesitation by the attendants; he seemed not even to miss his freedom; his noble body, furnished almost to the bursting point with all that it needed, seemed to carry freedom around with it too; somewhere in his jaws it seemed to lurk; and the joy of life streamed with such ardent passion from his throat that for the onlookers it was not easy to stand the shock of it. But they braced themselves, crowded round the cage, and did not want ever to move away.

Ernest Hemingway

A Clean, Well-Lighted Place

Ernest Hemingway (1899–1961)

Ernest Hemingway's life was a continual adventure and search for adventure, a refusal to accept the patterns of modern American middle-class existence. Born in Oak Park, Illinois, educated in the public schools, he did not go to college, but instead became a cub reporter for the *Kansas City Star* and served his literary apprenticeship in journalism. During World War I, he went to Italy as an ambulance driver, and was severely wounded in 1918.

Back in the United States, in Chicago and Michigan, Hemingway could not adapt to America's postwar complacency, and in 1921 returned to France as a reporter for the *Toronto Star*. Here he discovered the "lost generation" of American expatriates, partook of the "moveable feast" that was Paris, and sampled life in many European countries. Later he explored Africa and, when the Spanish Civil War broke out in 1936, went to Spain as a war correspondent. Following World War II he lived mostly in Cuba. He died in Ketchum, Idaho, of a self-inflicted gunshot wound.

Hemingway's first important publication was *In Our Time* (short stories), followed by *The Sun Also Rises,* a novel about the lost generation, postwar Europe, the frantic search for pleasure, and the frustrated search for love. In *A Farewell to Arms,* he recalled his wartime experiences in Italy, and in *For Whom the Bell Tolls* he evoked the betrayal and the tragedy of the Spanish Civil War. A later novel, *Across the River and into the Trees,* is generally considered a falling-off in his talent, a failure redeemed by *The Old Man and the Sea,* a short novel that won him the Nobel Prize.

Hemingway began with short stories and published them throughout his career. And it may be in his short stories that he has left his most characteristic and enduring work. The form is perfectly suited to Hemingway's style: the terse, spare, understated, supple prose, suspicious of rhetoric and always alive to the sensations of life, the feel of the earth and the body, which came as a revelation to Hemingway's contemporaries and has influenced writers ever since. Writing, Hemingway once remarked, should be architecture, not interior decoration; and each of his great stories has the strength, necessity, and economy of architecture.

A Clean, Well-Lighted Place

It was late and every one had left the café except an old man who sat in the shadow the leaves of the tree made against the electric light. In the day time the street was dusty, but at night the dew settled the dust and the old man liked to sit late because he was deaf and now at night it was quiet and he felt the difference. The two waiters inside the café knew that the old man was a little drunk, and while he was a good client they knew that if he became too drunk he would leave without paying, so they kept watch on him.

"Last week he tried to commit suicide," one waiter said.

"Why?"

"He was in despair."

"What about?"

"Nothing."

"How do you know it was nothing?"

"He has plenty of money."

They sat together at a table that was close against the wall near the door of the café and looked at the terrace where the tables were all empty except where the old man sat in the shadow of the leaves of the tree that moved slightly in the wind. A girl and a soldier went by in the street. The street light shone on the brass number on his collar. The girl wore no head covering and hurried beside him.

"The guard will pick him up," one waiter said.

"What does it matter if he gets what he's after?"

"He had better get off the street now. The guard will get him. They went by five minutes ago."

The old man sitting in the shadow rapped on his saucer with his glass. The younger waiter went over to him.

"What do you want?"

The old man looked at him. "Another brandy," he said.

"You'll be drunk," the waiter said. The old man looked at him. The waiter went away.

"He'll stay all night," he said to his colleague. "I'm sleepy now. I never get into bed before three o'clock. He should have killed himself last week."

The waiter took the brandy bottle and another saucer from the counter inside the café and marched out to the old man's table. He put down the saucer and poured the glass full of brandy.

"You should have killed yourself last week," he said to the deaf man. The old man motioned with his finger. "A little more," he said. The waiter poured on into the glass so that the brandy slopped over and ran down the stem into the top saucer of the pile. "Thank you," the old man said. The waiter took the bottle back inside the café. He sat down at the table with his colleague again.

"He's drunk now," he said.

"He's drunk every night."

"What did he want to kill himself for?"

"How should I know."

"How did he do it?"

"He hung himself with a rope."

"Who cut him down?"

"His niece."

"Why did they do it?"

"Fear for his soul."

"How much money has he got?"

"He's got plenty."

"He must be eighty years old."

"Anyway I should say he was eighty."

"I wish he would go home. I never get to bed before three o'clock. What kind of hour is that to go to bed?"

"He stays up because he likes it."

"He's lonely. I'm not lonely. I have a wife waiting in bed for me."

"He had a wife once too."

"A wife would be no good to him now."

"You can't tell. He might be better with a wife."

"His niece looks after him. You said she cut him down."

"I know."

"I wouldn't want to be that old. An old man is a nasty thing."

"Not always. This old man is clean. He drinks without spilling. Even now, drunk. Look at him."

"I don't want to look at him. I wish he would go home. He has no regard for those who must work."

The old man looked from his glass across the square, then over at the waiters.

"Another brandy," he said, pointing to his glass. The waiter who was in a hurry came over.

"Finished," he said, speaking with that omission of syntax stupid people employ when talking to drunken people or foreigners. "No more tonight. Close now."

"Another," said the old man.

"No. Finished." The waiter wiped the edge of the table with a towel and shook his head.

The old man stood up, slowly counted the saucers, took a leather coin purse from his pocket and paid for the drinks, leaving half a peseta tip.

The waiter watched him go down the street, a very old man walking unsteadily but with dignity.

"Why didn't you let him stay and drink?" the unhurried waiter asked. They were putting up the shutters. "It is not half-past two."

"I want to go home to bed."

"What is an hour?"

"More to me than to him."

"An hour is the same."

"You talk like an old man yourself. He can buy a bottle and drink at home."

"It's not the same."

"No, it is not," agreed the waiter with a wife. He did not wish to be unjust. He was only in a hurry.

"And you? You have no fear of going home before your usual hour?"

"Are you trying to insult me?"

"No, hombre, only to make a joke."

"No," the waiter who was in a hurry said, rising from pulling down the metal shutters. "I have confidence. I am all confidence."

"You have youth, confidence, and a job," the older waiter said. "You have everything."

"And what do you lack?"

"Everything but work."

"You have everything I have."

"No. I have never had confidence and I am not young."

"Come on. Stop talking nonsense and lock up."

"I am of those who like to stay late at the café," the older waiter said. "With all those who do not want to go to bed. With all those who need a light for the night."

"I want to go home and into bed."

"We are of two different kinds," the older waiter said. He was now dressed to go home. "It is not only a question of youth and confidence although those things are very beautiful. Each night I am reluctant to close up because there may be some one who needs the café."

"Hombre, there are bodegas[1] open all night long."

"You do not understand. This is a clean and pleasant café. It is well lighted. The light is very good and also, now, there are shadows of the leaves."

[1] General stores with bars.

"Good night," said the younger waiter.

"Good night," the other said. Turning off the electric light he continued the conversation with himself. It is the light of course but it is necessary that the place be clean and pleasant. You do not want music. Certainly you do not want music. Nor can you stand before a bar with dignity although that is all that is provided for these hours. What did he fear? It was not fear or dread. It was a nothing that he knew too well. It was all a nothing and a man was nothing too. It was only that and light was all it needed and a certain cleanness and order. Some lived in it and never felt it but he knew it all was nada y pues nada y nada y pues nada.[2] Our nada who art in nada, nada be thy name thy kingdom nada thy will be nada in nada as it is in nada. Give us this nada our daily nada and nada us our nada as we nada our nadas and nada us not into nada but deliver us from nada; pues nada. Hail nothing full of nothing, nothing is with thee. He smiled and stood before a bar with a shining steam pressure coffee machine.

"What's yours?" asked the barman.

"Nada."

"Otro loco mas," [3] said the barman and turned away.

"A little cup," said the waiter.

The barman poured it for him.

"The light is very bright and pleasant but the bar is unpolished," the waiter said.

The barman looked at him but did not answer. It was too late at night for conversation.

"You want another copita?" [4] the barman asked.

"No, thank you," said the waiter and went out. He disliked bars and bodegas. A clean, well-lighted café was a very different thing. Now, without thinking further, he would go home to his room. He would lie in the bed and finally, with daylight, he would go to sleep. After all, he said to himself, it is probably only insomnia. Many must have it.

[2] "Nothing and again nothing." [3] "Another crazy one." [4] Glass.

Albert Camus

The Guest

TRANSLATED BY JUSTIN O'BRIEN

Albert Camus (1913–1960)

ALBERT CAMUS' DEATH IN AN AUTOMOBILE ACCIDENT AT THE age of forty-six silenced the voice that in many ways expressed the conscience of an age. In his novels, plays, philosophical essays, and journalistic writings, Camus confronted the problems of a European generation stunned by total war and the concentration camp with a stark lucidity and a moral commitment which were to earn him the title of *le Juste,* "the just man."

Camus was born in Algeria and grew up in the working-class districts of Algiers. He obtained a scholarship to go to high school, then studied philosophy at the University of Algiers until tuberculosis made him abandon the idea of a scholarly career. He soon turned to the theater, organized a troupe, and directed plays. He also became active in journalism, which in 1938 brought him to Paris. After the start of the war and the German occupation of France, he joined the resistance to work for the liberation of France.

Camus' fame dates from the publication of *The Stranger* and *The Myth of Sisyphus* in 1942, a short novel and a volume of philosophical reflections in which he sought to explore man's place in an absurd universe—absurd because of the discrepancy between man's rational consciousness and the irrationality of nature. His next novel, *The Plague,* depicts the human condition in the plague-visited Algerian city of Oran, where heroism is simply the struggle, pursued without religious faith or any transcendant hope, to conquer some small portion of the world's destructive forces. "I cry out that I believe in nothing and that everything is absurd, but I cannot doubt my cry . . . *I revolt, therefore we are,*" writes Camus in his major philosophical work, *The Rebel.* It is man's consciousness of his refusal to accept the universe as it is that provides the very basis of his free existence, and his solidarity with other men.

Camus' last novel, *The Fall,* has as its protagonist a man both vile and compelling, a "penitent" whose endlessly repeated confession allows him to assume the position of judge and to implicate the reader—and all mankind—in a system of universal guilt. *The Fall* may reflect Camus' own tortured problems of conscience brought on by the outbreak of the Algerian war of independence, a rebellion in which he, as both Algerian and Frenchman, found it impossible to take sides. "We must be neither victims nor torturers," he wrote in one of the essays published posthumously in *Resistance, Rebellion and Death. The Fall* demonstrates the enormous difficulties of attaining this state of being. In *The Guest,* one of the short stories in *Exile and the Kingdom,* the situation of Daru, a school teacher in an Algeria of divided loyalties, has a similar resonance.

The Guest

The schoolmaster was watching the two men climb toward him. One was on horseback, the other on foot. They had not yet tackled the abrupt rise leading to the schoolhouse built on the hillside. They were toiling onward, making slow progress in the snow, among the stones, on the vast expanse of the high, deserted plateau. From time to time the horse stumbled. Without hearing anything yet, he could see the breath issuing from the horse's nostrils. One of the men, at least, knew the region. They were following the trail although it had disappeared days ago under a layer of dirty white snow. The schoolmaster calculated that it would take them half an hour to get onto the hill. It was cold; he went back into the school to get a sweater.

He crossed the empty, frigid classroom. On the blackboard the four rivers of France, drawn with four different colored chalks, had been flowing toward their estuaries for the past three days. Snow had suddenly fallen in mid-October after eight months of drought without the transition of rain, and the twenty pupils, more or less, who lived in the villages scattered over the plateau had stopped coming. With fair weather they would return. Daru now heated only the single room that was his lodging, adjoining the classroom and giving also onto the plateau to the east. Like the class windows, his window looked to the south too. On that side the school was a few kilometers from the point where the plateau began to slope toward the south. In clear weather could be seen the purple mass of the mountain range where the gap opened onto the desert.

Somewhat warmed, Daru returned to the window from which he had first seen the two men. They were no longer visible. Hence they must have tackled the rise. The sky was not so dark, for the snow had stopped falling during the night. The morning had opened with a dirty light which had scarcely become brighter as the ceiling of clouds lifted. At two in the afternoon it seemed as if the day were merely beginning. But still this was better than those three days when the thick snow was falling amidst unbroken darkness with little gusts of wind that rattled the double door of the classroom. Then Daru had spent long hours in his room, leaving it only to go to the shed and feed the chickens or get some coal. Fortunately the delivery truck from Tadjid, the nearest village to the north, had brought his supplies two days before the blizzard. It would return in forty-eight hours.

Besides, he had enough to resist a siege, for the little room was cluttered with bags of wheat that the administration left as a stock to distribute to those of his pupils whose families had suffered from the drought. Actually they had all been victims because they were all poor. Every day Daru would distribute a ration to the children. They had missed it, he knew, during these bad days. Possibly one of the fathers or big brothers would come this afternoon and he could supply them with grain. It was just a matter of carrying them over to the next harvest. Now shiploads of wheat were arriving from France and the worst was over. But it would be hard to forget that poverty, that army of ragged ghosts wandering in the sunlight, the plateaus burned to a cinder month after month, the earth shriveled up little by little, literally scorched, every stone bursting into dust under one's foot. The sheep had died then by thousands and even a few men, here and there, sometimes without anyone's knowing.

In contrast with such poverty, he who lived almost like a monk in his remote schoolhouse, nonetheless satisfied with the little he had and with the rough life, had felt like a lord with his white-washed walls, his narrow couch, his unpainted shelves, his well, and his weekly provision of water and food. And suddenly this snow, without warning, without the foretaste of rain. This is the way the region was, cruel to live in, even without men—who didn't help matters either. But Daru had been born here. Everywhere else, he felt exiled.

He stepped out onto the terrace in front of the schoolhouse. The two men were now halfway up the slope. He recognized the horseman as Balducci, the old gendarme he had known for a long time. Balducci was holding on the end of a rope an Arab who was walking behind him with hands bound and head lowered. The gendarme waved a greeting to which Daru did not reply, lost as he was in contemplation of the Arab dressed in a faded blue jellaba, his feet in sandals but covered with socks of heavy raw wool, his head surmounted by a narrow, short *chèche*.[1] They were approaching. Balducci was holding back his horse in order not to hurt the Arab, and the group was advancing slowly.

Within earshot, Balducci shouted: "One hour to do the three kilometers from El Ameur!" Daru did not answer. Short and square in his thick sweater, he watched them climb. Not once had the Arab raised his head. "Hello," said Daru when they got up onto the terrace. "Come in and warm up." Balducci painfully got down from his horse without letting go the rope. From under his bristling mustache he smiled at the schoolmaster.

[1] A long scarf worn as a turban.

His little dark eyes, deep-set under a tanned forehead, and his mouth surrounded with wrinkles made him look attentive and studious. Daru took the bridle, led the horse to the shed, and came back to the two men, who were now waiting for him in the school. He led them into his room. "I am going to heat up the classroom," he said. "We'll be more comfortable there." When he entered the room again, Balducci was on the couch. He had undone the rope tying him to the Arab, who had squatted near the stove. His hands still bound, the *chèche* pushed back on his head, he was looking toward the window. At first Daru noticed only his huge lips, fat, smooth, almost Negroid; yet his nose was straight, his eyes were dark and full of fever. The *chèche* revealed an obstinate forehead and, under the weathered skin now rather discolored by the cold, the whole face had a restless and rebellious look that struck Daru when the Arab, turning his face toward him, looked him straight in the eyes. "Go into the other room," said the schoolmaster, "and I'll make you some mint tea." "Thanks," Balducci said. "What a chore! How I long for retirement." And addressing his prisoner in Arabic: "Come on, you." The Arab got up and, slowly, holding his bound wrists in front of him, went into the classroom.

With the tea, Daru brought a chair. But Balducci was already enthroned on the nearest pupil's desk and the Arab had squatted against the teacher's platform facing the stove, which stood between the desk and the window. When he held out the glass of tea to the prisoner, Daru hesitated at the sight of his bound hands. "He might perhaps be untied." "Sure," said Balducci. "That was for the trip." He started to get to his feet. But Daru, setting the glass on the floor, had knelt beside the Arab. Without saying anything, the Arab watched him with his feverish eyes. Once his hands were free, he rubbed his swollen wrists against each other, took the glass of tea, and sucked up the burning liquid in swift little sips.

"Good," said Daru. "And where are you headed?"

Balducci withdrew his mustache from the tea. "Here, son."

"Odd pupils! And you're spending the night?"

"No. I'm going back to El Ameur. And you will deliver this fellow to Tinguit. He is expected at police headquarters."

Balducci was looking at Daru with a friendly little smile.

"What's this story?" asked the schoolmaster. "Are you pulling my leg?"

"No, son. Those are the orders."

"The orders? I'm not . . ." Daru hesitated, not wanting to hurt the old Corsican. "I mean, that's not my job."

"What! What's the meaning of that? In wartime people do all kinds of jobs."

"Then I'll wait for the declaration of war!"

Balducci nodded.

"O.K. But the orders exist and they concern you too. Things are brewing, it appears. There is talk of a forthcoming revolt. We are mobilized, in a way."

Daru still had his obstinate look.

"Listen, son," Balducci said. "I like you and you must understand. There's only a dozen of us at El Ameur to patrol throughout the whole territory of a small department and I must get back in a hurry. I was told to hand this guy over to you and return without delay. He couldn't be kept there. His village was beginning to stir; they wanted to take him back. You must take him to Tinguit tomorrow before the day is over. Twenty kilometers shouldn't faze a husky fellow like you. After that, all will be over. You'll come back to your pupils and your comfortable life."

Behind the wall the horse could be heard snorting and pawing the earth. Daru was looking out the window. Decidedly, the weather was clearing and the light was increasing over the snowy plateau. When all the snow was melted, the sun would take over again and once more would burn the fields of stone. For days, still, the unchanging sky would shed its dry light on the solitary expanse where nothing had any connection with man.

"After all," he said, turning around toward Balducci, "what did he do?" And, before the gendarme had opened his mouth, he asked: "Does he speak French?"

"No, not a word. We had been looking for him for a month, but they were hiding him. He killed his cousin."

"Is he against us?"

"I don't think so. But you can never be sure."

"Why did he kill?"

"A family squabble, I think. One owed the other grain, it seems. It's not at all clear. In short, he killed his cousin with a billhook. You know, like a sheep, *kreezk!*"

Balducci made the gesture of drawing a blade across his throat and the Arab, his attention attracted, watched him with a sort of anxiety. Daru felt a sudden wrath against the man, against all men with their rotten spite, their tireless hates, their blood lust.

But the kettle was singing on the stove. He served Balducci more tea, hesitated, then served the Arab again, who, a second time, drank avidly. His raised arms made the jellaba fall open and the schoolmaster saw his thin, muscular chest.

"Thanks, kid," Balducci said. "And now, I'm off."

He got up and went toward the Arab, taking a small rope from his pocket.

"What are you doing?" Daru asked dryly.

Balducci, disconcerted, showed him the rope.

"Don't bother."

The old gendarme hesitated. "It's up to you. Of course, you are armed?"

"I have my shotgun."

"Where?"

"In the trunk."

"You ought to have it near your bed."

"Why? I have nothing to fear."

"You're crazy, son. If there's an uprising, no one is safe, we're all in the same boat."

"I'll defend myself. I'll have time to see them coming."

Balducci began to laugh, then suddenly the mustache covered the white teeth.

"You'll have time? O.K. That's just what I was saying. You have always been a little cracked. That's why I like you, my son was like that."

At the same time he took out his revolver and put it on the desk.

"Keep it; I don't need two weapons from here to El Ameur."

The revolver shone against the black paint of the table. When the gendarme turned toward him, the schoolmaster caught the smell of leather and horseflesh.

"Listen, Balducci," Daru said suddenly, "every bit of this disgusts me, and first of all your fellow here. But I won't hand him over. Fight, yes, if I have to. But not that."

The old gendarme stood in front of him and looked at him severely.

"You're being a fool," he said slowly. "I don't like it either. You don't get used to putting a rope on a man even after years of it, and you're even ashamed—yes, ashamed. But you can't let them have their way."

"I won't hand him over," Daru said again.

"It's an order, son, and I repeat it."

"That's right. Repeat to them what I've said to you: I won't hand him over."

Balducci made a visible effort to reflect. He looked at the Arab and at Daru. At last he decided.

"No, I won't tell them anything. If you want to drop us, go ahead; I'll not denounce you. I have an order to deliver the prisoner and I'm doing so. And now you'll just sign this paper for me."

"There's no need. I'll not deny that you left him with me."

"Don't be mean with me. I know you'll tell the truth. You're from hereabouts and you are a man. But you must sign, that's the rule."

Daru opened his drawer, took out a little square bottle of purple ink, the red wooden penholder with the "sergeant-major" pen he used for making models of penmanship, and signed. The gendarme carefully folded the paper and put it into his wallet. Then he moved toward the door.

"I'll see you off," Daru said.

"No," said Balducci. "There's no use being polite. You insulted me."

He looked at the Arab, motionless in the same spot, sniffed peevishly, and turned away toward the door. "Good-by, son," he said. The door shut behind him. Balducci appeared suddenly outside the window and then disappeared. His footsteps were muffled by the snow. The horse stirred on the other side of the wall and several chickens fluttered in fright. A moment later Balducci reappeared outside the window leading the horse by the bridle. He walked toward the little rise without turning around and disappeared from sight with the horse following him. A big stone could be heard bouncing down. Daru walked back toward the prisoner, who, without stirring, never took his eyes off him. "Wait," the schoolmaster said in Arabic and went toward the bedroom. As he was going through the door, he had a second thought, went to the desk, took the revolver, and stuck it in his pocket. Then, without looking back, he went into his room.

For some time he lay on his couch watching the sky gradually close over, listening to the silence. It was this silence that had seemed painful to him during the first days here, after the war. He had requested a post in the little town at the base of the foothills separating the upper plateaus from the desert. There, rocky walls, green and black to the north, pink and lavender to the south, marked the frontier of eternal summer. He had been named to a post farther north, on the plateau itself. In the beginning, the solitude and the silence had been hard for him on these wastelands peopled only by stones. Occasionally, furrows suggested cultivation, but they had been dug to uncover a certain kind of stone good for building. The only plowing here was to harvest rocks. Elsewhere a thin layer of soil accumulated in the hollows would be scraped out to enrich paltry village gardens. This is the way it was: bare rock covered three quarters of the region. Towns sprang up, flourished, then disappeared; men came by, loved one another or fought bitterly, then died. No one in this desert, neither he nor his guest, mattered. And yet, outside this desert neither of them, Daru knew, could have really lived.

When he got up, no noise came from the classroom. He was amazed at the unmixed joy he derived from the mere thought that the Arab might have fled and that he would be alone with no decision to make. But the prisoner was there. He had merely stretched out between the stove and the desk. With eyes open, he was staring at the ceiling. In that position, his thick lips were particularly noticeable, giving him a pouting look. "Come," said Daru. The Arab got up and followed him. In the bedroom, the schoolmaster pointed to a chair near the table under the window. The Arab sat down without taking his eyes off Daru.

"Are you hungry?"

"Yes," the prisoner said.

Daru set the table for two. He took flour and oil, shaped a cake in a frying pan, and lighted the little stove that functioned on bottled gas. While the cake was cooking, he went out to the shed to get cheese, eggs, dates, and condensed milk. When the cake was done he set it on the window sill to cool, heated some condensed milk diluted with water, and beat up the eggs into an omelette. In one of his motions he knocked against the revolver stuck in his right pocket. He set the bowl down, went into the classroom, and put the revolver in his desk drawer. When he came back to the room, night was falling. He put on the light and served the Arab. "Eat," he said. The Arab took a piece of the cake, lifted it eagerly to his mouth, and stopped short.

"And you?" he asked.

"After you. I'll eat too."

The thick lips opened slightly. The Arab hesitated, then bit into the cake determinedly.

The meal over, the Arab looked at the schoolmaster. "Are you the judge?"

"No, I'm simply keeping you until tomorrow."

"Why do you eat with me?"

"I'm hungry."

The Arab fell silent. Daru got up and went out. He brought back a folding bed from the shed, set it up between the table and the stove, perpendicular to his own bed. From a large suitcase which, upright in a corner, served as a shelf for papers, he took two blankets and arranged them on the camp bed. Then he stopped, felt useless, and sat down on his bed. There was nothing more to do or to get ready. He had to look at this man. He looked at him, therefore, trying to imagine his face bursting with rage. He couldn't do so. He could see nothing but the dark yet shining eyes and the animal mouth.

"Why did you kill him?" he asked in a voice whose hostile tone surprised him.

The Arab looked away.

"He ran away. I ran after him."

He raised his eyes to Daru again and they were full of a sort of woeful interrogation. "Now what will they do to me?"

"Are you afraid?"

He stiffened, turning his eyes away.

"Are you sorry?"

The Arab stared at him openmouthed. Obviously he did not understand. Daru's annoyance was growing. At the same time he felt awkward and self-conscious with his big body wedged between the two beds.

"Lie down there," he said impatiently. "That's your bed."

The Arab didn't move. He called to Daru:

"Tell me!"

The schoolmaster looked at him.

"Is the gendarme coming back tomorrow?"

"I don't know."

"Are you coming with us?"

"I don't know. Why?"

The prisoner got up and stretched out on top of the blankets, his feet toward the window. The light from the electric bulb shone straight into his eyes and he closed them at once.

"Why?" Daru repeated, standing beside the bed.

The Arab opened his eyes under the blinding light and looked at him, trying not to blink.

"Come with us," he said.

In the middle of the night, Daru was still not asleep. He had gone to bed after undressing completely; he generally slept naked. But when he suddenly realized that he had nothing on, he hesitated. He felt vulnerable and the temptation came to him to put his clothes back on. Then he shrugged his shoulders; after all, he wasn't a child and, if need be, he could break his adversary in two. From his bed he could observe him, lying on his back, still motionless with his eyes closed under the harsh light. When Daru turned out the light, the darkness seemed to coagulate all of a sudden. Little by little, the night came back to life in the window where the starless sky was stirring gently. The schoolmaster soon made out the body lying at his feet. The Arab still did not move, but his eyes seemed open. A faint wind was prowling around the schoolhouse. Perhaps it would drive away the clouds and the sun would reappear.

During the night the wind increased. The hens fluttered a little and then were silent. The Arab turned over on his side with his back to Daru, who thought he heard him moan. Then he listened for his guest's breathing, become heavier and more regular. He listened to that breath so close to him and mused without being able to go to sleep. In this room where he had been sleeping alone for a year, this presence bothered him. But it bothered him also by imposing on him a sort of brotherhood he knew well but refused to accept in the present circumstances. Men who share the same rooms, soldiers or prisoners, develop a strange alliance as if, having cast off their armor with their clothing, they fraternized every evening, over and above their differences, in the ancient community of dream and fatigue. But Daru shook himself; he didn't like such musings, and it was essential to sleep.

A little later, however, when the Arab stirred slightly, the schoolmaster was still not asleep. When the prisoner made a second move, he stiffened, on the alert. The Arab was lifting himself slowly on his arms with almost the motion of sleepwalker. Seated upright in bed, he waited motionless without turning his head toward Daru, as if he were listening attentively.

Daru did not stir; it had just occurred to him that the revolver was still in the drawer of his desk. It was better to act at once. Yet he continued to observe the prisoner, who, with the same slithery motion, put his feet on the ground, waited again, then began to stand up slowly. Daru was about to call out to him when the Arab began to walk, in a quite natural but extraordinarily silent way. He was heading toward the door at the end of the room that opened into the shed. He lifted the latch with precaution and went out, pushing the door behind him but without shutting it. Daru had not stirred. "He is running away," he merely thought. "Good riddance!" Yet he listened attentively. The hens were not fluttering; the guest must be on the plateau. A faint sound of water reached him, and he didn't know what it was until the Arab again stood framed in the doorway, closed the door carefully, and came back to bed without a sound. Then Daru turned his back on him and fell asleep. Still later he seemed, from the depths of his sleep, to hear furtive steps around the schoolhouse. "I'm dreaming! I'm dreaming!" he repeated to himself. And he went on sleeping.

When he awoke, the sky was clear; the loose window let in a cold, pure air. The Arab was asleep, hunched up under the blankets now, his mouth open, utterly relaxed. But when Daru shook him, he started dreadfully, staring at Daru with wild eyes as if he had never seen him and such a frightened expression that the schoolmaster stepped back. "Don't be afraid. It's me. You must eat." The Arab nodded his head and said yes. Calm had returned to his face, but his expression was vacant and listless.

The coffee was ready. They drank it seated together on the folding bed as they munched their pieces of the cake. Then Daru led the Arab under the shed and showed him the faucet where he washed. He went back into the room, folded the blankets and the bed, made his own bed and put the room in order. Then he went through the classroom and out onto the terrace. The sun was already rising in the blue sky; a soft, bright light was bathing the deserted plateau. On the ridge the snow was melting in spots. The stones were about to reappear. Crouched on the edge of the plateau, the schoolmaster looked at the deserted expanse. He thought of Balducci. He had hurt him, for he had sent him off in a way as if he didn't want to be associated with him. He could still hear the gendarme's farewell and, without knowing why, he felt strangely empty and vulnerable. At that moment, from the other side of the schoolhouse, the prisoner coughed. Daru listened to him almost despite himself and then, furious, threw a pebble that whistled through the air before sinking into the snow. That man's stupid crime revolted him, but to hand him over was contrary to honor. Merely thinking of it made him smart with humiliation. And he cursed at one and the same time his own people who had sent him this Arab and the Arab too who had dared to kill and not managed to get away. Daru got up, walked in a circle on the terrace, waited motionless, and then went back into the schoolhouse.

The Arab, leaning over the cement floor of the shed, was washing his teeth with two fingers. Daru looked at him and said: "Come." He went back into the room ahead of the prisoner. He slipped a hunting-jacket on over his sweater and put on walking-shoes. Standing, he waited until the Arab had put on his *chèche* and sandals. They went into the classroom and the schoolmaster pointed to the exit, saying: "Go ahead." The fellow didn't budge. "I'm coming," said Daru. The Arab went out. Daru went back into the room and made a package of pieces of rusk, dates, and sugar. In the classroom, before going out, he hesitated a second in front of his desk, then crossed the threshold and locked the door. "That's the way," he said. He started toward the east, followed by the prisoner. But, a short distance from the schoolhouse, he thought he heard a slight sound behind them. He retraced his steps and examined the surroundings of the house; there was no one there. The Arab watched him without seeming to understand. "Come on," said Daru.

They walked for an hour and rested beside a sharp peak of limestone. The snow was melting faster and faster and the sun was drinking up the puddles at once, rapidly cleaning the plateau, which gradually dried and vibrated like the air itself. When they resumed walking, the ground rang under their feet. From time to time a bird rent the space in front of them with a joyful cry. Daru breathed in deeply the fresh morning light. He felt a sort of rapture before the vast familiar expanse, now almost entirely yellow under its dome of blue sky. They walked an hour more, descending toward the south. They reached a level height made up of crumbly rocks. From there on, the plateau sloped down, eastward, toward a low plain where there were a few spindly trees and, to the south, toward outcroppings of rock that gave the landscape a chaotic look.

Daru surveyed the two directions. There was nothing but the sky on the horizon. Not a man could be seen. He turned toward the Arab, who was looking at him blankly. Daru held out the package to him. "Take it," he said. "There are dates, bread, and sugar. You can hold out for two days. Here are a thousand francs too." The Arab took the package and the money but kept his full hands at chest level as if he didn't know what to do with what was being given him. "Now look," the schoolmaster said as he pointed in the direction of the cast, "there's the way to Tinguit. You have a two-hour walk. At Tinguit you'll find the administration and the police. They are expecting you." The Arab looked toward the east, still holding the package and the money against his chest. Daru took his elbow and turned him rather roughly toward the south. At the foot of the height on which they stood could be seen a faint path. "That's the trail across the plateau. In a day's walk from here you'll find pasturelands and the first nomads. They'll take you in and shelter you according to their law." The Arab had now turned toward Daru and a sort of panic was visible in his expression. "Listen," he said. Daru shook his head: "No, be quiet. Now I'm leaving you." He turned his back on him, took two long steps in the direction of the school, looked hesitantly at the motionless Arab, and started off again. For a few minutes he heard nothing but his own step resounding on the cold ground and did not turn his head. A moment later, however, he turned around. The Arab was still there on the edge of the hill, his arms hanging now, and he was looking at the schoolmaster. Daru felt something rise in his throat. But he swore with impatience, waved vaguely, and started off again. He had already gone some distance when he again stopped and looked. There was no longer anyone on the hill.

Daru hesitated. The sun was now rather high in the sky and was beginning to beat down on his head. The schoolmaster retraced his steps, at first somewhat uncertainly, then with decision. When he reached the little hill, he was bathed in sweat. He climbed it as fast as he could and stopped, out of breath, at the top. The rock fields to the south stood out sharply against the blue sky, but on the plain to the east a steamy heat was already rising. And in that slight haze, Daru, with heavy heart, made out the Arab walking slowly on the road to prison.

A little later, standing before the window of the classroom, the schoolmaster was watching the clear light bathing the whole surface of the plateau, but he hardly saw it. Behind him on the blackboard, among the winding French rivers, sprawled the clumsily chalked-up words he had just read: "You handed over our brother. You will pay for this." Daru looked at the sky, the plateau, and, beyond, the invisible lands stretching all the way to the sea. In this vast landscape he had loved so much, he was alone.

Jorge Luis Borges

The Babylon Lottery

TRANSLATED BY ANTHONY KERRIGAN

Jorge Luis Borges (1899–)

THE AWARD TO JORGE LUIS BORGES OF THE INTERNATIONAL Publishers' Prize in 1961 finally brought wide public attention to a writer who had long been recognized by some connoisseurs as one of the masters of contemporary literature. Borges was born in Buenos Aires, Argentina. His father imparted to him a taste for reading, especially English literature; by the age of nine, Borges had read all of Dickens, Kipling, Mark Twain, Poe, and H. G. Wells. His secondary education was completed in Geneva, Switzerland. He then lived for a time in Spain and returned to Buenos Aires in 1921, where he became a leader in *ultraismo,* a poetic movement that had affinities with Surrealism. In the 1930s he began publishing stories and essays, mostly in *Sur,* a new and influential literary review. He later became professor of English Literature at the University of Buenos Aires and director of the Argentine National Library, and has also taught at universities in the United States. He continues to live in Buenos Aires.

At present Borges is almost completely blind, a condition which he maintains is no handicap to a creator of imaginary worlds. And the imaginary worlds of Borges are extraordinarily rich and complex, labyrinths in which the mind restlessly explores its capacities and possibilities. Borges is a man of prodigious erudition, matched only by his inventiveness, and he loves to create imaginary encyclopedias, bestiaries, libraries, and maps, which bring together other men's commentaries on the world and permit Borges' own commentary on the commentaries. His stories are fables, in which he invents mythologies and works out highly ambiguous morals. They are—in the title he has given one of his volumes of stories—"fictions," fabulations in the purest state. The translator of William Faulkner, André Gide, James Joyce, Franz Kafka, and many others, Borges commands modern (as well as ancient) literature, and his stories are among the best commentaries on the tendencies of modern literature, especially its self-reflexiveness and its central concern with the processes of its own creation.

The Babylon Lottery

Like all men in Babylon I have been a proconsul; like all, a slave; I have also known omnipotence, opprobrium, jail. Look: the index finger of my right hand is missing. Look again: through this rent in my cape you can see a ruddy tatoo on my belly. It is the second symbol, Beth. This letter, on nights of full moon, gives me power over men whose mark is Ghimel; but it also subordinates me to those marked Aleph, who on moonless nights owe obedience to those marked Ghimel. In a cellar at dawn, I have severed the jugular vein of sacred bulls against a black rock. During one lunar year, I have been declared invisible: I shrieked and was not heard, I stole my bread and was not decapitated. I have known what the Greeks did not: uncertainty. In a bronze chamber, faced with the silent handkerchief of a strangler, hope has been faithful to me; in the river of delights, panic has not failed me. Heraclitus of Pontica admiringly relates that Pythagoras recalled having been Pyrrho, and before that Euphorbus, and before that some other mortal. In order to recall analogous vicissitudes I do not need to have recourse to death, nor even to imposture.

I owe this almost atrocious variety to an institution which other republics know nothing about, or which operates among them imperfectly and in secret: the lottery. I have not delved into its history; I do know that the wizards have been unable to come to any agreement; of its powerful designs I know what a man not versed in astrology might know of the moon. I come from a vertiginous country where the lottery forms a principal part of reality: until this very day I have thought about all this as little as I have about the behavior of the indecipherable gods or about the beating of my own heart. Now, far from Babylon and its beloved customs, I think of the lottery with some astonishment and ponder the blasphemous conjectures murmured by men in the shadows at twilight.

My father related that anciently—a matter of centuries; of years?—the lottery in Babylon was a game of plebeian character. He said (I do not know with what degree of truth) that barbers gave rectangular bits of bone or decorated parchment in exchange for copper coins. A drawing of the lottery was held in the middle of the day: the winners received, without further corroboration from chance, silver-minted coins. The procedure, as you see, was elemental.

Naturally, these "lotteries" failed. Their mortal virtue was nil. They did not appeal to all the faculties of men: only to their hope. In the face of public indifference, the merchants who established these venal lotteries began to lose money. Someone attempted to introduce a slight reform: the interpolation of a certain small number of adverse outcomes among the favored numbers. By means of this reform, the purchasers of numbered rectangles stood the double chance of winning a sum or of paying a fine often considerable in size. This slight danger—for each thirty favored numbers there would be one adverse number—awoke, as was only natural, the public's interest. The Babylonians gave themselves up to the game. Anyone who did not acquire lots was looked upon as pusillanimous, mean-spirited. In time, this disdain multiplied. The person who did not play was despised, but the losers who paid the fine were also scorned. The Company (thus it began to be known at that time) was forced to take measures to protect the winners, who could not collect their prizes unless nearly the entire amount of the fines was already collected. The Company brought suit against the losers: the judge condemned them to pay the original fine plus costs or to spend a number of days in jail. Every loser chose jail, so as to defraud the Company. It was from this initial bravado of a few men that the all-powerful position of the Company—its ecclesiastical, metaphysical strength—was derived.

A short while later, the reports on the drawings omitted any enumeration of fines and limited themselves to publishing the jail sentences corresponding to each adverse number. This laconism, almost unnoticed at the time, became of capital importance. *It constituted the first appearance in the lottery of nonpecuniary elements.* Its success was great. Pushed to such a measure by the players, the Company found itself forced to increase its adverse numbers.

No one can deny that the people of Babylonia are highly devoted to logic, even to symmetry. It struck them as incoherent that the fortunate numbers should be computed in round figures of money while the unfortunate should be figured in terms of days and nights in jail. Some moralists argued that the possession of money does not determine happiness and that other forms of fortune are perhaps more immediate.

There was another source of restlessness in the lower depths. The members of the sacerdotal college multiplied the stakes and plumbed the vicissitudes of terror and hope; the poor, with reasonable or inevitable envy, saw themselves excluded from this notoriously delicious exhilaration. The just anxiety of all, poor and rich alike, to participate equally in the lottery, inspired an indignant agitation, the memory of which the years have not erased. Certain obstinate souls did not comprehend, or pretended not to comprehend, that a new order had come, a necessary historical stage. . . . A slave stole a crimson ticket, a ticket which earned him the right to have his tongue burned in the next drawing. The criminal code fixed the same penalty for the theft of a ticket. A number of Babylonians argued that he deserved a red-hot poker by virtue of the theft; others, more magnanimous, held that the public executioner should apply the penalty of the lottery, since chance had so determined. . . .

Disturbances broke out, there was a lamentable shedding of blood; but the people of Babylon imposed their will at last, over the opposition of the rich. That is: the people fully achieved their magnanimous ends. In the first place, it made the Company accept complete public power. (This unification was necessary, given the vastness and complexity of the new operations.) In the second place, it forced the lottery to be secret, free, and general. The sale of tickets for money was abolished. Once initiated into the mysteries of Bel, every free man automatically participated in the sacred drawings of lots, which were carried out in the labyrinths of the gods every seventy nights and which determined every man's fate until the next exercise. The consequences were incalculable. A happy drawing might motivate his elevation to the council of wizards or his condemnation to the custody of an enemy (notorious or intimate), or to find, in the peaceful shadows of a room, the woman who had begun to disquiet him or whom he had never expected to see again. An adverse drawing might mean mutilation, a varied infamy, death. Sometimes a single event—the tavern killing of C, the mysterious glorification of B—might be the brilliant result of thirty or forty drawings. But it must be recalled that the individuals of the Company were (and are) all-powerful and astute as well. In many cases, the knowledge that certain joys were the simple doing of chance might have detracted from their excellence; to avoid this inconvenience the Company's agents made use of suggestion and magic. Their moves, their management, were secret. In the investigation of people's intimate hopes and intimate terrors, they made use of astrologers and spies. There were certain stone lions, there was a sacred privy called Qaphqa, there were fissures in a dusty aqueduct which, according to general opinion, *lead to the Company;* malign or benevolent people deposited accusations in these cracks. These denunciations were incorporated into an alphabetical archive of variable veracity.

Incredibly enough, there were still complaints. The Company, with its habitual discretion, did not reply directly. It preferred to scribble a brief argument—which now figures among sacred scriptures—in the debris of a mask factory. That doctrinal piece of literature observed that the lottery is an interpolation of chance into the order of the world and that to accept errors is not to contradict fate but merely to corroborate it. It also observed that those lions and that sacred recipient, though not unauthorized by the Company (which did not renounce the right to consult them), functioned without official guaranty.

This declaration pacified the public unease. It also produced other effects, not foreseen by the author. It deeply modified the spirit and operations of the Company. (I have little time left to tell what I know; we have been warned that the ship is ready to sail; but I will attempt to explain it.)

Improbable as it may be, no one had until then attempted to set up a general theory of games. A Babylonian is not highly speculative. He reveres the judgments of fate, he hands his life over to them, he places his hopes, his panic terror in them, but it never occurs to him to investigate their labyrinthian laws nor the giratory spheres which disclose them. Nevertheless, the unofficial declaration which I have mentioned inspired many discussions of a juridico-mathematical nature. From one of these discussions was born the following conjecture: if the lottery is an intensification of chance, a periodic infusion of chaos into the cosmos, would it not be desirable for chance to intervene at all stages of the lottery and not merely in the drawing? Is it not ridiculous for chance to dictate the death of someone, while the circumstances of his death—its silent reserve or publicity, the time limit of one hour or one century—should remain immune to hazard? These eminently just scruples finally provoked a considerable reform, whose complexities (intensified by the practice of centuries) are not understood except by a handful of specialists, but which I will attempt to summarize, even if only in a symbolic manner.

Let us imagine a first drawing, which eventuates in a sentence of death against some individual. To carry out the sentence, another drawing is set up, and this drawing proposes (let us say) nine possible executioners. Of these executioners, four can initiate a third drawing which will reveal the name of the actual executioner, two others can replace the adverse order with a fortunate order (the finding of a treasure, let us say), another may exacerbate the death sentence (that is: make it infamous or enrich it with torture), still others may refuse to carry it out. . . .

Such is the symbolic scheme. In reality, *the number of drawings is infinite*. No decision is final, all diverge into others. The ignorant suppose that an infinite number of drawings require an infinite amount of time; in reality, it is quite enough that time be infinitely subdivisible, as is the case in the famous parable of the Tortoise and the Hare. This infinitude harmonizes in an admirable manner with the sinuous numbers of Chance and of the Celestial Archetype of the Lottery adored by the Platonists. . . .

A certain distorted echo of our ritual seems to have resounded along the Tiber: Aelius Lampridius, in his *Life of Antoninus Heliogabalus,* tells of how this emperor wrote down the lot of his guests on seashells, so that one would receive ten pounds of gold and another ten flies, ten dormice, ten bears. It is only right to remark that Heliogabalus was educated in Asia Minor, among the priests of the eponymous god.

There are also impersonal drawings, of undefined purpose: one drawing will decree that a sapphire from Taprobane be thrown into the waters of the Euphrates; another, that a bird be released from a tower roof; another, that a grain of sand be withdrawn (or added) to the innumerable grains on a beach. The consequences, sometimes, are terrifying.

Under the beneficent influence of the Company, our customs have become thoroughly impregnated with chance. The buyer of a dozen amphoras of Damascus wine will not be surprised if one of them contains a talisman or a viper. The scribe who draws up a contract scarcely ever fails to introduce some erroneous datum; I myself, in making this hasty declaration, have falsified or invented some grandeur, some atrocity; perhaps, too, a certain mysterious monotony. . . .

Our historians, the most discerning in the world, have invented a method for correcting chance. It is well known that the operations of this method are (in general) trustworthy; although, naturally, they are not divulged without a measure of deceit. In any case, there is nothing so contaminated with fiction as the history of the Company. . . .

A paleographic document, unearthed in a temple, may well be the work of yesterday's drawing or that of one lasting a century. No book is ever published without some variant in each copy. Scribes take a secret oath to omit, interpolate, vary.

The Company, with divine modesty, eludes all publicity. Its agents, as is only natural, are secret. The orders which it is continually sending out do not differ from those lavishly issued by imposters. Besides, who can ever boast of being a mere imposter? The inebriate who improvises an absurd mandate, the dreamer who suddenly awakes to choke the woman who lies at his side to death, do they not both, perhaps, carry out a secret decision by the Company? This silent functioning, comparable to that of God, gives rise to all manner of conjectures. One of them, for instance, abominably insinuates that the Company is eternal and that it will last until the last night of the world, when the last god annihilates the cosmos. Still another conjecture declares that the Company is omnipotent, but that it exerts its influence only in the most minute matters: in a bird's cry, in the shades of rust and the hues of dust, in the cat naps of dawn. There is one conjecture, spoken from the mouths of masked heresiarchs, to the effect that *the Company has never existed and never will.* A conjecture no less vile argues that it is indifferently inconsequential to affirm or deny the reality of the shadowy corporation, because Babylon is nothing but an infinite game of chance.

Robert Lowell

Old Glory: Benito Cereno

Robert Lowell (1917–   )

ROBERT LOWELL IS CONSIDERED ONE OF AMERICA'S MOST IMPORTANT contemporary poets and the most influential poet since the generation of Pound, Eliot, and Stevens. Lowell was born in Boston, the descendant of many distinguished New England ancestors, and educated at Harvard University and Kenyon College, from which he was graduated in 1940. He became a convert to Catholicism in 1940, but later left the Church. During World War II he was a conscientious objector, for which he went to prison. He has also been an outspoken opponent of the American involvement in Vietnam. He lives in New York and teaches poetry at Harvard.

Lowell began writing poetry in the thirties under the influence of the southern poets Allen Tate and John Crowe Ransom, from whom he learned the discipline of form and meter. He wrote as an inheritor of Pound and Eliot, but with more allegiance to the traditional forms and meters of English verse. His poetry has evolved toward a style of greater flexibility and freedom, although always with a strong sense of form.

His trilogy *The Old Glory* (1964) marks Lowell's first venture into the theater. Two of the plays, *Endecott and the Red Cross* and *My Kinsman, Major Molyneux,* are based on stories by Nathaniel Hawthorne; the third, *Benito Cereno,* on a novella by Herman Melville. The last two plays were first performed in 1964 in New York City. They marked a new departure in American drama—an experiment in poetic diction for the theater and a stately, operatic, antinaturalistic style. The plays are united, as the title of the trilogy suggests, by a concern with the symbolism of the American character and destiny. We feel, perhaps especially in *Benito Cereno,* the most powerful of the three, the reflection of a sensitive and concerned contemporary American consciousness on the work of one of his spiritual ancestors, who sought, over a century earlier, to understand the peculiar American admixture of virtue and blindness and to face the American relationship to "blackness." The result is a strong drama, both faithful to the spirit of Melville's tale and remarkably original and pertinent.

Benito Cereno

CHARACTERS

CAPTAIN AMASA DELANO
JOHN PERKINS
DON BENITO CERENO
BABU
ATUFAL
FRANCESCO
AMERICAN SAILORS
SPANISH SAILORS
NEGRO SLAVES

THE SCENE

About the year 1800, an American sealing vessel, the President Adams, *at anchor in an island harbor off the coast of Trinidad. The stage is part of the ship's deck. Everything is unnaturally clean, bare and shipshape. To one side, a polished, coal-black cannon. The American captain,* AMASA DELANO *from Duxbury, Massachusetts, sits in a cane chair. He is a strong, comfortable-looking man in his early thirties who wears a spotless blue coat and white trousers. Incongruously, he has on a straw hat and smokes a corncob pipe. Beside him stands* JOHN PERKINS, *his bosun, a very stiff, green young man, a relative of* DELANO'S. THREE SAILORS, *one carrying an American flag, enter.* EVERYONE *stands at attention and salutes with machinelike exactitude. Then the* THREE SAILORS *march off stage.* DELANO *and* PERKINS *are alone.*

DELANO. There goes the most beautiful woman in South America.
PERKINS. We never see any women, Sir;
just this smothering, overcast Equator,
a seal or two,
the flat dull sea,
and a sky like a gray wasp's nest.
DELANO. I wasn't talking about women,
I was calling your attention to the American flag.
PERKINS. Yes, Sir! I wish we were home in Duxbury.
DELANO. We are home. America is wherever her flag flies.
My own deck is the only place in the world
where I feel at home.
PERKINS. That's too much for me, Captain Delano.
I mean I wish I were at home with my wife;
these world cruises are only for bachelors.
DELANO. Your wife will keep. You should smoke, Perkins.
Smoking turns men into philosophers
and swabs away their worries.
I can see my wife and children or not see them
in each puff of blue smoke.
PERKINS. You are always tempting me, Sir!
I try to keep fit,
I want to return to my wife as fit as I left her.

DELANO. You're much too nervous, Perkins.
Travel will shake you up. You should let
a little foreign dirt rub off on you.
I've taught myself to speak Spanish like a Spaniard.
At each South American port, they mistake me for a
Castilian Don.
PERKINS. Aren't you lowering yourself a little, Captain?
Excuse me, Sir, I have been wanting to ask you a question.
Don't you think our President, Mr. Jefferson, is lowering himself
by being so close to the French?
I'd feel a lot safer in this unprotected place
if we'd elected Mr. Adams instead of Mr. Jefferson.
DELANO. The better man ran second!
Come to think of it, he rather let us down
by losing the election just after we had named this ship,
the *President Adams*. Adams is a nervous dry fellow.
When you've traveled as much as I have,
you'll learn that that sort doesn't export, Perkins.
Adams didn't get a vote outside New England!
PERKINS. He carried every New England state;
that was better than winning the election.
I'm afraid I'm a dry fellow, too, Sir.
DELANO. Not when I've educated you!
When I am through with you, Perkins,
you'll be as worldly as the Prince Regent of England,
only you'll be a first class American officer.
I'm all for Jefferson, he has the popular touch.
Of course he's read too many books,
but I've always said an idea or two won't sink our Republic.
I'll tell you this, Perkins,
Mr. Jefferson is a gentleman and an American.
PERKINS. They say he has two illegitimate negro children.
DELANO. The more the better! That's the quickest way
to raise the blacks to our level.
I'm surprised you swallow such Federalist bilge, Perkins!
I told you Mr. Jefferson is a gentleman and an American;
when a man's in office, Sir, we all pull behind him!
PERKINS. Thank God our Revolution ended where the French one
began.
DELANO. Oh the French! They're like the rest of the Latins,
they're hardly white people,
they start with a paper republic
and end with a toy soldier, like Bonaparte.

PERKINS. Yes, Sir. I see a strange sail making for the harbor.
They don't know how to sail her.
DELANO. Hand me my telescope.
PERKINS. Aye, aye, Sir!
DELANO [*with telescope*]. I see an ocean undulating in long scoops of swells;
it's set like the beheaded French Queen's high wig;
the sleek surface is like waved lead,
cooled and pressed in the smelter's mold.
I see flights of hurried gray fowl,
patches of fluffy fog.
They skim low and fitfully above the decks,
like swallows sabering flies before a storm.
This gray boat foreshadows something wrong.
PERKINS. It does, Sir!
They don't know how to sail her!
DELANO. I see a sulphurous haze above her cabin,
the new sun hangs like a silver dollar to her stern;
low creeping clouds blow on from them to us.
PERKINS. What else, Sir?
DELANO. The yards are woolly.
the ship is furred with fog.
On the cracked and rotten head-boards,
the tarnished, gilded letters say, the *San Domingo*.
A rat's-nest messing up the deck,
black faces in white sheets are fussing with the ropes.
I think it's a cargo of Dominican monks.
PERKINS. Dominican monks, Sir! God help us,
I thought they were outlawed in the new world.
DELANO. No, it's nothing. I see they're only slaves.
The boat's transporting slaves.
PERKINS. Do you believe in slavery, Captain Delano?
DELANO. In a civilized country, Perkins,
everyone disbelieves in slavery,
everyone disbelieves in slavery and wants slaves.
We have the perfect uneasy answer;
in the North, we don't have them and want them;
Mr. Jefferson has them and fears them.
PERKINS. Is that how you answer, Sir,
when a little foreign dirt has rubbed off on you?
DELANO. Don't ask me such intense questions.
You should take up smoking, Perkins.
There was a beautiful, dumb English actress—

I saw her myself once in London.
They wanted her to look profound,
so she read Plato and the Bible and Benjamin Franklin,
and thought about them every minute.
She still looked like a moron.
Then they told her to think about nothing.
She thought about nothing, and looked like Socrates.
That's smoking, Perkins, you think about nothing and look deep.

PERKINS. I don't believe in slavery, Sir.

DELANO. You don't believe in slavery or Spaniards
or smoking or long cruises or monks or Mr. Jefferson!
You are a Puritan, all faith and fire.

PERKINS. Yes, Sir.

DELANO. God save America from Americans! [*Takes up the telescope.*]
I see octagonal network bagging out
from her heavy top like decayed beehives.
The battered forecastle looks like a raped Versailles.
On the stern-piece, I see the fading arms of Spain.
There's a masked satyr, or something
with its foot on a big white goddess.
She has quite a figure.

PERKINS. They oughtn't to be allowed on the ocean!

DELANO. Who oughtn't? Goddesses?

PERKINS. I mean Spaniards, who cannot handle a ship,
and mess up its hull with immoral statues.

DELANO. You're out of step. You're much too dry.
Bring me my three-cornered hat.
Order some men to clear a whaleboat.
I am going to bring water and fresh fish to the *San Domingo*.
These people have had some misfortune, Perkins!

PERKINS. Aye, aye, Sir.

DELANO. Spaniards? The name gets you down,
you think their sultry faces and language
make them Zulus.
You take the name *Delano*—
I've always thought it had some saving
Italian or Spanish virtue in it.

PERKINS. Yes, Sir.

DELANO. A Spaniard isn't a negro under the skin,
particularly a Spaniard from Spain—
these South American ones mix too much with the Indians.
Once you get inside a Spaniard,
he talks about as well as your wife in Duxbury.

PERKINS [*shouting*]. A boat for the captain! A whaleboat for Captain Delano!

[*A bosun's whistle is heard, the lights dim. When they come up, we are on the deck of the* San Domingo, *the same set, identical except for litter and disorder.* THREE AMERICAN SAILORS *climb on board. They are followed by* PERKINS *and* DELANO, *now wearing a three-cornered hat. Once on board, the* AMERICAN SAILORS *salute* DELANO *and stand stiffly at attention like toys.* NEGROES *from the* San Domingo *drift silently and furtively forward.*]

DELANO. I see a wen of barnacles hanging to the waterline of this ship.
It sticks out like the belly of a pregnant woman.
Have a look at our dory Bosun.

PERKINS. Aye, aye, Sir!

[*By now, about twenty blacks and two Spanish sailors have drifted in. They look like some gaudy, shabby, unnautical charade, and pay no attention to the Americans, until an unseen figure in the rigging calls out a single sharp warning in an unknown tongue. Then they all rush forward, shouting, waving their arms and making inarticulate cries like birds. Three shrill warnings come from the rigging. Dead silence. The men from the* San Domingo *press back in a dense semicircle. One by one, individuals come forward, make showy bows to* DELANO, *and speak.*]

FIRST NEGRO. Scurvy, Master Yankee!

SECOND NEGRO. Yellow fever, Master Yankee!

THIRD NEGRO. Two men knocked overboard rounding Cape Horn, Master Yankee!

FOURTH NEGRO. Nothing to eat, Master Yankee!

NEGRO WOMAN. Nothing to drink, Master Yankee!

SECOND NEGRO WOMAN. Our mouths are dead wood, Master Yankee!

DELANO. You see, Perkins,
these people have had some misfortune.

[*General hubbub, muttering, shouts, gestures, ritual and dumbshow of distress. The rigging, hitherto dark, lightens, as the sun comes out of a cloud, and shows* THREE OLD NEGROES, *identical down to their shabby patches. They perch on cat's-heads; their heads are grizzled like dying willow tops; each is picking bits of unstranded rope for oakum. It is they who have been giving the warnings that control the people below. Everyone,* DELANO *along with the rest, looks up.* DELANO *turns aside and speaks to* PERKINS.]

It is like a Turkish bazaar.

PERKINS. They are like gypsies showing themselves for money at a county fair, Sir.

DELANO. This is enchanting after the blank gray roll of the ocean!
Go tell the Spanish captain I am waiting for him.

[PERKINS *goes off. Sharp warnings from the* OAKUM-PICKERS. *A big black spread of canvas is pulled creakingly and ceremoniously aside.* SIX FIGURES *stand huddled on a platform about four feet from the deck. They look like weak old invalids in bathrobes and nightcaps until they strip to the waist and turn out to be huge, shining young negroes. Saying nothing, they set to work cleaning piles of rusted hatchets. From time to time, they turn and clash their hatchets together with a rhythmic shout.* PERKINS *returns.*]

PERKINS. Their captain's name is Don Benito Cereno,
he sends you his compliments, Sir.
He looks more like a Mexican planter than a seaman.
He's put his fortune on his back:
he doesn't look as if he had washed since they left port.

DELANO. Did you tell him I was waiting for him?
A captain should be welcomed by his fellow-captain.
I can't understand this discourtesy.

PERKINS. He's coming, but there's something wrong with him.

[BENITO CERENO, *led by his negro servant,* BABU, *enters.* BENITO, *looking sick and dazed, is wearing a sombrero and is dressed with a singular but shabby richness. Head bent to one side, he leans in a stately coma against the rail, and stares unseeingly at* DELANO. BABU, *all in scarlet, and small and quick, keeps whispering, pointing and pulling at* BENITO*'s sleeve.* DELANO *walks over to them.*]

DELANO. Your hand, Sir. I am Amasa Delano,
captain of the *President Adams,*
a sealing ship from the United States.
This is your lucky day,
the sun is out of hiding for the first time in two weeks,
and here I am aboard your ship
like the Good Samaritan with fresh food and water.

BENITO. The Good Samaritan? Yes, yes,
we mustn't use the Scriptures lightly.

Welcome, Captain. It is the end of the day.
DELANO. The end? It's only morning.
I loaded and lowered a whaleboat
as soon as I saw how awkwardly your ship was making for the harbor.
BENITO. Your whaleboat's welcome, Captain.
I am afraid I am still stunned by the storm.
DELANO. Buck up. Each day is a new beginning.
Assign some sailors to help me dole out my provisions.
BENITO. I have no sailors.
BABU [*in a quick sing-song*]. Scurvy, yellow fever,
ten men knocked off on the Horn,
doldrums, nothing to eat, nothing to drink!
By feeding us, you are feeding the King of Spain.
DELANO. Sir, your slave has a pretty way of talking.
What do you need?

[DELANO *waits for* BENITO *to speak. When nothing more is said, he shifts awkwardly from foot to foot, then turns to his* SAILORS.]

Stand to, men!

[*The* AMERICAN SAILORS, *who have been lounging and gaping, stand in a row, as if a button had been pressed.*]

Lay our fish and water by the cabin!

[*The* SAILORS *arrange the watercans and baskets of fish by the cabin. A sharp whistle comes from the* OAKUM-PICKERS. *Almost instantly, the provisions disappear.*]

Captain Cereno, you are surely going to taste my water!
BENITO. A captain is a servant, almost a slave, Sir.
DELANO. No, a captain's a captain.
I am sending for more provisions.
Stand to!

[*The* AMERICAN SAILORS *stand to.*]

Row back to the ship. When you get there,
take on five hogsheads of fresh water,
and fifty pounds of soft bread.

[FIRST SAILOR *salutes and goes down the ladder.*]

Bring all our remaining pumpkins!

[SECOND *and* THIRD SAILORS *salute and go down the ladder.*]

My bosun and I will stay on board,
until our boat returns.
I imagine you can use us.
BENITO. Are you going to stay here alone?

Won't your ship be lost without you?
Won't you be lost without your ship?

BABU. Listen to Master!
He is the incarnation of courtesy, Yankee Captain.
Your ship doesn't need you as much as we do.

DELANO. Oh, I've trained my crew.
I can sail my ship in my sleep. [*Leaning over the railing and calling.*]
Men, bring me a box of lump sugar,
and six bottles of my best cider. [*Turning to* BENITO.]
Cider isn't my favorite drink, Don Benito,
but it's a New England specialty;
I'm ordering six bottles for your table.

[BABU *whispers and gestures to* DON BENITO, *who is exhausted and silent.*]

BABU. *Une bouteille du vin* [*to* NEGROES].
My master wishes to give you a bottle
of the oldest wine in Seville.

[*He whistles. A negro woman rushes into the cabin and returns with a dusty beribboned bottle, which she holds like a baby.* BABU *ties a rope around the bottle.*]

BABU. I am sending this bottle of wine to your cabin.
When you drink it, you will remember us.
Do you see these ribbons? The crown of Spain is tied to one.
Forgive me for tying a rope around the King of Spain's neck.
[*Lowers the wine on the rope to the whaleboat.*]

DELANO [*shouting to his* SAILORS]. Pick up your oars!

SAILORS. Aye, aye, Sir!

DELANO. We're New England Federalists;
we can drink the King of Spain's health.

[BENITO *stumbles off stage on* BABU's *arm.*]

PERKINS. Captain Cereno hasn't traveled as much as you have;
I don't think he knew what you meant by the New England Federalists.

DELANO [*leaning comfortably on the rail; half to himself and half to* PERKINS].
The wind is dead. We drift away.
We will be left alone all day,
here in this absentee empire.
Thank God, I know my Spanish!

PERKINS. You'll have to watch them, Sir.
Brown men in charge of black men—
it doesn't add up to much!

This Babu, I don't trust him!
Why doesn't he talk with a Southern accent,
Like Mr. Jefferson? They're out of hand, Sir!
DELANO. Nothing relaxes order more than misery.
They need severe superior officers.
They haven't one.
Now, if this Benito were a man of energy . . .
a Yankee . . .
PERKINS. How can a Spaniard sail?
DELANO. Some can. There was Vasco da Gama and Columbus . . .
No, I guess they were Italians. Some can,
but this captain is tubercular.
PERKINS. Spaniards and negroes have no business on a ship.
DELANO. Why is this captain so indifferent to me?
If only I could stomach his foreign reserve!
This absolute dictator of his ship
only gives orders through his slaves!
He is like some Jesuit-haunted Hapsburg king
about to leave the world and hope the world will end.
PERKINS. He said he was lost in the storm.
DELANO. Perhaps it's only policy,
a captain's icy dignity
obliterating all democracy—
PERKINS. He's like someone walking in his sleep.
DELANO. Ah, slumbering dominion!
He is so self-conscious in his imbecility . . .
No, he's sick. He sees his men no more than me.
This ship is like a crowded immigration boat;
it needs severe superior officers,
the friendly arm of a strong mate.
Perhaps, I ought to take it over by force.
No, they're sick, they've been through the plague.
I'll go and speak and comfort my fellow captain.
I think you can help me, Captain. I'm feeling useless.
My own thoughts oppress me, there's so much to do.
I wonder if you would tell me the whole sad story of your voyage.
Talk to me as captain to captain.
We have sailed the same waters.
Please tell me your story.
BENITO. A story? A story! That's out of place.
When I was a child, I used to beg for stories back in Lima.
Now my tongue's tied and my heart is bleeding.

[*Stops talking, as if his breath were gone. He stares for a few moments, then looks up at the rigging, as if he were counting the ropes one by one.* DELANO *turns abruptly to* PERKINS.]

DELANO. Go through the ship, Perkins,
and see if you can find me a Spaniard who can talk.
BENITO. You must be patient, Captain Delano;
if we only see with our eyes,
sometimes we cannot see at all.
DELANO. I stand corrected, Captain;
tell me about your voyage.
BENITO. It's now a hundred and ninety days . . .
This ship, well manned, well officered, with several cabin passengers,
carrying a cargo of Paraguay tea and Spanish cutlery.
That parcel of negro slaves, less than four score now,
was once three hundred souls.
Ten sailors and three officers fell from the mainyard off the Horn;
part of our rigging fell overboard with them,
as they were beating down the icy sail.
We threw away all our cargo,
Broke our waterpipes,
Lashed them on deck
this was the chief cause of our suffering.
DELANO. I must interrupt you, Captain.
How did you happen to have three officers on the mainyard?
I never heard of such a disposal,
it goes against all seamanship.
BABU. Our officers never spared themselves;
if there was any danger, they rushed in
to save us without thinking.
DELANO. I can't understand such an oversight.
BABU. There was no oversight. My master had a hundred eyes.
He had an eye for everything.
Sometimes the world falls on a man.
The sea wouldn't let Master act like a master,
yet he saved himself and many lives.
He is still a rich man, and he saved the ship.
BENITO. Oh my God, I wish the world had fallen on me,
and the terrible cold sea had drowned me;
that would have been better than living through what I've
lived through!
BABU. He is a good man, but his mind is off;

he's thinking about the fever when the wind stopped—
poor, poor Master!
Be patient, Yankee Captain, these fits are short,
Master will be the master once again.
BENITO. The scurvy was raging through us.
We were on the Pacific. We were invalids
and couldn't man our mangled spars.
A hurricane blew us northeast through the fog.
Then the wind died.
We lay in irons fourteen days in unknown waters,
our black tongues stuck through our mouths,
but we couldn't mend our broken waterpipes.
BABU. Always those waterpipes,
he dreams about them like a pile of snakes!
BENITO. Yellow fever followed the scurvy,
the long heat thickened in the calm,
my Spaniards turned black and died like slaves,
The blacks died too. I am my only officer left.
BABU. Poor, poor Master! He had a hundred eyes,
he lived our lives for us.
He is still a rich man.
BENITO. In the smart winds beating us northward,
our torn sails dropped like sinkers in the sea;
each day we dropped more bodies.
Almost without a crew, canvas, water, or a wind,
we were bounced about by the opposing waves
through cross-currents and the weedy calms,
and dropped our dead.
Often we doubled and redoubled on our track
like children lost in jungle. The thick fog
hid the Continent and our only port from us.
BABU. We were poor kidnapped jungle creatures.
We only lived on what he could give us.
He had a hundred eyes, he was the master.
BENITO. These negroes saved me, Captain.
Through the long calamity,
they were as gentle as their owner, Don Aranda, promised.
Don Aranda took away their chains before he died.
BABU. Don Aranda saved our lives, but we couldn't save his.
Even in Africa I was a slave.
He took away my chains.
BENITO. I gave them the freedom of my ship.
I did not think they were crates or cargo or cannibals.

But it was Babu—under God, I swear I owe my life to Babu!
He calmed his ignorant, wild brothers,
never left me, saved the *San Domingo*.

BABU. Poor, poor Master. He is still a rich man.
Don't speak of Babu. Babu is the dirt under your feet.
He did his best.

DELANO. You are a good fellow, Babu.
You are the salt of the earth. I envy you, Don Benito;
he is no slave, Sir, but your friend.

BENITO. Yes, he is salt in my wounds.
I can never repay him, I mean.
Excuse me, Captain, my strength is gone.
I have done too much talking. I want to rest.

[BABU *leads* BENITO *to a shabby straw chair at the side.* BENITO *sits.* BABU *fans him with his sombrero.*]

PERKINS. He's a fine gentleman, but no seaman.
A cabin boy would have known better
than to send his three officers on the mainyard.

DELANO [*paying no attention*]. A terrible story. I would have been unhinged myself.

[*Looking over toward* BABU *and* BENITO.]

There's a true servant. They do things better
in the South and in South America—
trust in return for trust!
The beauty of that relationship is unknown
in New England. We're too much alone
in Massachusetts, Perkins.
How do our captains and our merchants live,
each a republic to himself.
Even Sam Adams had no friends and only loved the mob.

PERKINS. Sir, you are forgetting that
New England seamanship brought them their slaves.

DELANO. Oh, just our Southern slaves;
we had nothing to do with these fellows.

PERKINS. The ocean would be a different place
if every Spaniard served an apprenticeship on an American ship
before he got his captain's papers.

DELANO. This captain's a gentleman, not a sailor.
His little yellow hands
got their command before they held a rope—
in by the cabin-window, not the hawse-hole!
Do you want to know why
they drifted hog-tied in those easy calms—

inexperience, sickness, impotence and aristocracy!
PERKINS. Here comes Robinson Crusoe and his good man Friday.
DELANO. We don't beat a man when he's down.
[BENITO *advances uncertainly on* BABU'S *arm.*]
I am glad to see you on your feet again,
That's the only place for a Captain, sir!
I have the cure for you, I have decided
to bring you medicine and a sufficient supply of water.
A first class deck officer, a man from Salem,
shall be stationed on your quarter deck,
a temporary present from my owners.
We shall refit your ship and clear this mess.
BENITO. You will have to clear away the dead.
BABU. This excitement is bad for him, Yankee Master.
He's lived with death. He lives on death still;
this sudden joy will kill him. You've heard
how thirsty men die from overdrinking!
His heart is with his friend, our owner, Don Aranda.
BENITO. I am the only owner. [*He looks confused and shaken.*]
[BABU *scurries off and brings up the straw chair.* BENITO *sits.*]
DELANO. Your friend is dead? He died of fever?
BENITO. He died very slowly and in torture.
He was the finest man in Lima.
We were brought up together,
I am lost here.
DELANO. Pardon me, Sir. You are young at sea.
My experience tells me what your trouble is:
this is the first body you have buried in the ocean.
I had a friend like yours, a warm honest fellow,
who would look you in the eye—
we had to throw him to the sharks.
Since then I've brought embalming gear on board.
Each man of mine shall have a Christian grave on land.
You wouldn't shake so, if Don Aranda were on board,
I mean, if you'd preserved the body.
BENITO. If he were on board this ship?
If I had preserved his body?
BABU. Be patient, Master!
We still have the figurehead.
DELANO. You have the figurehead?
BABU. You see that thing wrapped up in black cloth?
It's a figurehead Don Aranda bought us in Spain.

It was hurt in the storm. It's very precious.
Master takes comfort in it,
he is going to give it to Don Aranda's widow.
It's time for the pardon ceremony, Master.

[*Sound of clashing hatchets.*]

DELANO. I am all for these hatchet-cleaners.
They are saving cargo. They make
an awful lot of pomp and racket though
about a few old, rusty knives.

BENITO. They think steel is worth its weight in gold.

[*A slow solemn march is sounded on the gongs and other instruments. A gigantic coal-black* NEGRO *comes up the steps. He wears a spiked iron collar to which a chain is attached that goes twice around his arms and ends padlocked to a broad band of iron. The* NEGRO *comes clanking forward and stands dumbly and like a dignitary in front of* BENITO. *Two small* BLACK BOYS *bring* BENITO *a frail rattan cane and a silver ball, which they support on a velvet cushion.* BENITO *springs up, holds the ball, and raises the cane rigidly above the head of the negro in chains. For a moment, he shows no trace of sickness. The assembled blacks sing, "Evviva, Benito!" three times.*]

BABU [*at one side with the Americans, but keeping an eye on* BENITO].
You are watching the humiliation of King Atufal,
once a ruler in Africa. He ruled as much land there as your President.
Poor Babu was a slave even in Africa,
a black man's slave, and now a white man's.

BENITO [*in a loud, firm voice*]. Former King Atufal, I call on you to kneel!
Say, "My sins are black as night,
I ask the King of Spain's pardon
through his servant, Don Benito."

[*Pause.* ATUFAL *doesn't move.*]

NEGROES. Your sins are black as night, King Atufal!
Your sins are black as night, King Atufal!

DELANO. What has King Atufal done?

BABU. I will tell you later, Yankee Captain.

BENITO. Ask pardon, former King Atufal.
If you will kneel,
I will strike away your chains.

[ATUFAL *slowly raises his chained arms and lets them drop.*]

Ask pardon!

WOMAN SLAVE. Ask pardon King Atufal.

BENITO. Go!

[*Sound of instruments. The* BLACK BOYS *take* BENITO*'s ball and cane. The straw chair is brought up.* BENITO *sits.* FRANCESCO *then leads him off stage.*]

BABU. Francesco!
I will be with you in a moment, Master.
You mustn't be afraid,
Francesco will serve you like a second Babu.

BENITO. Everyone serves me alike here,
but no one can serve me as you have.

BABU. I will be with you in a moment.
The Yankee master is at sea on our ship.
He wants me to explain our customs.

[BENITO *is carried off stage.*]

You would think Master's afraid of dying,
if Babu leaves him!

DELANO. I can imagine your tenderness during his sickness.
You were part of him,
you were almost a wife.

BABU. You say such beautiful things,
the United States must be a paradise for people like Babu.

DELANO. I don't know.
We have our faults. We have many states,
some of them could stand improvement.

BABU. The United States must be heaven.

DELANO. I suppose we have fewer faults than other countries.
What did King Atufal do?

BABU. He used the Spanish flag for toilet paper.

DELANO. That's treason.
Did Atufal know what he was doing?
Perhaps the flag was left somewhere it shouldn't have been.
Things aren't very strict here.

BABU. I never thought of that.
I will go and tell Master.

DELANO. Oh, no, you mustn't do that!
I never interfere with another man's ship.
Don Benito is your lord and dictator.
How long has this business with King Atufal been going on?

BABU. Ever since the yellow fever,
and twice a day.

DELANO. He did a terrible thing, but he looks like a royal fellow.

You shouldn't call him a king, though,
it puts ideas into his head.

BABU. Atufal had gold wedges in his ears in Africa;
now he wears a padlock and Master bears the key.

DELANO. I see you have a feeling for symbols of power.
You had better be going now,
Don Benito will be nervous about you.

[BABU *goes off.*]

That was a terrible thing to do with a flag;
everything is untidy and unraveled here—
this sort of thing would never happen on the *President Adams.*

PERKINS. Your ship is as shipshape as our country, Sir.

DELANO. I wish people wouldn't take me as representative of our country:
America's one thing, I am another;
we shouldn't have to bear one another's burdens.

PERKINS. You are a true American for all your talk, Sir;
I can't believe you were mistaken for a Castilian Don.

DELANO. No one would take me for Don Benito.

PERKINS. I wonder if he isn't an imposter, some traveling actor from a circus?

DELANO. No, Cereno is a great name in Peru, like Winthrop or Adams with us.
I recognize the family features in our captain.

[*An* OLD SPANISH SAILOR, *grizzled and dirty, is seen crawling on all fours with an armful of knots toward the Americans. He points to where* BENITO *and* BABU *have disappeared and whistles. He holds up the knots as though he were in chains, then throws them out loosely on the deck in front of him. A* GROUP OF NEGROES *forms a circle around him, holding hands and singing childishly. Then, laughing, they carry the* SPANIARD *off stage on their shoulders.*]

These blacks are too familiar!
We are never alone!

[*Sound of gongs. Full minute's pause, as if time were passing.* DELANO *leans on the railing. The sun grows brighter.*]

This ship is strange.
These people are too spontaneous—all noise and show, no character!
Real life is a simple monotonous thing.
I wonder about that story about the calms;

it doesn't stick.
Don Benito hesitated himself in telling it.
No one could run a ship so stupidly,
and place three officers on one yard.
[BENITO *and* BABU *return.*]
A captain has unpleasant duties;
I am sorry for you, Don Benito.
BENITO. You find my ship unenviable, Sir?
DELANO. I was talking about punishing Atufal;
he acted like an animal!
BENITO. Oh, yes, I was forgetting . . .
He was a King,
How long have you lain in at this island, Sir?
DELANO. Oh, a week today.
BENITO. What was your last port, Sir?
DELANO. Canton.
BENITO. You traded seal-skins and American muskets
for Chinese tea and silks, perhaps?
DELANO. We took in some silks.
BENITO. A little gold and silver too?
DELANO. Just a little silver. We are only merchants.
We take in a dollar here and there. We have no Peru,
or a Pizarro who can sweat gold out of the natives.
BENITO. You'll find things have changed
a little in Peru since Pizarro, Captain.
[*Starts to move away.* BABU *whispers to him, and he comes back abruptly, as if he had forgotten something important.*]
How many men have you on board, Sir?
DELANO. Some twenty-five, Sir. Each man is at his post.
BENITO. They're all on board, Sir, now?
DELANO. They're all on board. Each man is working.
BENITO. They'll be on board tonight, Sir?
DELANO. Tonight? Why do you ask, Don Benito?
BENITO. Will they all be on board tonight, Captain?
DELANO. They'll be on board for all I know.
[PERKINS *makes a sign to* DELANO.]
Well, no, to tell the truth, today's our Independence Day.
A gang is going ashore to see the village.
A little diversion improves their efficiency,
a little regulated corruption.
BENITO. You North Americans take no chances. Generally, I suppose,
even your merchant ships go more or less armed?

DELANO. A rack of muskets, sealing spears and cutlasses.
Oh, and a six-pounder or two; we are a sealing ship,
but with us each merchant is a privateer—
only in case of oppression, of course.
You've heard about how we shoot pirates.

BABU. Boom, boom, come Master.

[BENITO *walks away on* BABU'*s arm and sits down, almost off stage in his straw chair. They whisper. Meanwhile, a* SPANISH SAILOR *climbs the rigging furtively, spread-eagles his arms and shows a lace shirt under his shabby jacket. He points to* BENITO *and* BABU *and winks. At a cry from one of the* OAKUM-PICKERS, THREE NEGROES *help the* SPANIARD *down with servile, ceremonious attentions.*]

PERKINS. Did you see that sailor's lace shirt, Sir?
He must have robbed one of the cabin passengers.
I hear that people strip the dead
in these religious countries.

DELANO. No, you don't understand the Spaniards.
In these old Latin countries,
each man's a beggar or a noble, often both;
they have no middle class. With them it's customary
to sew a mess of gold and pearls on rags—
that's how an aristocracy that's going to the dogs
keeps up its nerve.
It's odd though,
that Spanish sailor seemed to want to tell me something.
He ought to dress himself properly and speak his mind.
That's what we do. That's why we're strong:
everybody trusts us. Nothing gets done
when every man's a noble. I wonder why
the captain asked me all those questions?

PERKINS. He was passing the time of day, Sir;
It's a Latin idleness.

DELANO. It's strange. Did you notice how Benito stopped rambling?
He was conventional . . . consecutive for the first time since we met him.
Something's wrong. Perhaps, they've men below the decks,
a sleeping volcano of Spanish infantry. The Malays do it,
play sick and cut your throat.
A drifting boat, a dozen doped beggars on deck,
two hundred sweating murderers packed below like sardines—
that's rot! Anyone can see these people are really sick,

sicker than usual. Our countries are at peace.
I wonder why he asked me all those questions?

PERKINS. Just idle curiosity. I hear
the gentlemen of Lima sit at coffee tables from sun to sun
and gossip. They don't even have women to look at;
they're all locked up with their aunts.

DELANO. Their sun is going down. These old empires go.
They are much too familiar with their blacks.
I envy them though, they have no character,
they feel no need to stand alone.
We stand alone too much,
that's why no one can touch us for sailing a ship;
When a country loses heart, it's easier to live.
Ah, Babu! I suppose Don Benito's indisposed again!
Tell him I want to talk to his people;
there's nothing like a well man to help the sick.

BABU. Master is taking his siesta, Yankee Master.
His siesta is sacred, I am afraid to disturb it.
Instead, let me show you our little entertainment.

DELANO. Let's have your entertainment;
if you know a man's pleasure
you know his measure.

BABU. We are a childish people. Our pleasures are childish.
No one helped us, we know nothing
about your important amusements,
such as killing seals and pirates.

DELANO. I'm game. Let's have your entertainment.

[BABU *signals. The gong sounds ten times and the canvas is pulled from the circular structure. Enclosed in a triangular compartment, an* OLD SPANISH SAILOR *is dipping naked white dolls in a tar-pot.*]

BABU. This little amusement keeps him alive, Yankee Master.
He is especially fond of cleaning the dolls
after he has dirtied them.

[*The* OLD SPANISH SAILOR *laughs hysterically, and then smears his whole face with tar.*]

OLD SPANISH SAILOR. My soul is white!

BABU. The yellow fever destroyed his mind.

DELANO. Let's move on. This man's brain,
as well as his face, is defiled with pitch!

BABU. He says his soul is white.

[*The structure is pushed around and another triangular compartment appears. A* NEGRO BOY *is playing chess against a splendid Spanish doll with a crown on its head. He stops and holds two empty wine bottles to his ears.*]

This boy is deaf.
The yellow fever destroyed his mind.

DELANO. Why is he holding those bottles to his ears?

BABU. He is trying to be a rabbit,
or listening to the ocean, his mother—
who knows?

DELANO. If he's deaf, how can he hear the ocean?
Anyway, he can't hear me.
I pass, let's move on.

[*The structure is pushed around to a third compartment. A* SPANISH SAILOR *is holding a big armful of rope.*]

What are you knotting there, my man?

SPANISH SAILOR. The knot.

DELANO. So I see, but what's it for?

SPANISH SAILOR. For someone to untie. Catch! [*Throws the knot to* DELANO.]

BABU [*snatching the knot from* DELANO]. It's dirty, it will dirty your uniform.

DELANO. Let's move on. Your entertainment
is rather lacking in invention, Babu.

BABU. We have to do what we can
We are just beginners at acting.
This next one will be better.

[*The structure is pushed around and shows a beautiful* NEGRO WOMAN. *She is dressed and posed as the Virgin Mary. A Christmas crèche is arranged around her. A* VERY WHITE SPANIARD *dressed as Saint Joseph stands behind her. She holds a Christchild, the same crowned doll, only black, the* NEGRO BOY *was playing chess against.*]

She is the Virgin Mary. That man is not the father.

DELANO. I see. I suppose her son is the King of Spain.

BABU. The Spaniards taught us everything,
there's nothing we can learn from you, Yankee Master.
When they took away our country, they gave us a better world.
Things do not happen in that world as they do here.

DELANO. That's a very beautiful,
though unusual Virgin Mary.

BABU. Yes, the Bible says, "I am black not white."
When Don Aranda was dying,
we wanted to give him the Queen of Heaven

because he took away our chains.
PERKINS. The Spaniards must have taught them everything;
they're all mixed up, they don't even know their religion.
DELANO. No, no! The Catholic Church doesn't just teach,
it knows how to take from its converts.
BABU. Do you want to shake hands with the Queen of Heaven, Yankee Master?
DELANO. No, I'm not used to royalty.
Tell her I believe in freedom of religion,
if people don't take liberties.
Let's move on.
BABU [*kneeling to the Virgin Mary*]. I present something Your Majesty has never seen,
a white man who doesn't believe in taking liberties,
Your Majesty.
[*The structure is pushed around and shows* ATUFAL *in chains but with a crown on his head.*]
This is the life we believe in.
THE NEGROES ALL TOGETHER. Ask pardon, King Atufal!
Kiss the Spanish flag!
DELANO. Please don't ask me to shake hands with King Atufal!
[*The canvas is put back on the structure.*]
BABU. You look tired and serious, Yankee Master.
We have to have what fun we can.
We never would have lived through the deadly calms
without a little amusement. [*Bows and goes off.*]
[*The* NEGROES *gradually drift away.* DELANO *sighs with relief.*]
DELANO. Well, that wasn't much!
I suppose Shakespeare started that way.
PERKINS. Who cares?
I see a speck on the blue sea, Sir,
our whaleboat is coming.
DELANO. A speck? My eyes are speckled.
I seem to have been dreaming. What's solid? [*Touches the ornate railing; a piece falls onto the deck.*]
This ship is nothing, Perkins!
I dreamed someone was trying to kill me!
How could he? Jack-of-the-beach,
they used to call me on the Duxbury shore.
Carrying a duck-satchel in my hand, I used to paddle
along the waterfront from a hulk to school.
I didn't learn much there. I was always shooting duck

or gathering huckleberries along the marsh with Cousin Nat!
I like nothing better than breaking myself on the surf.
I used to track the seagulls down the five-mile stretch of beach for eggs.
How can I be killed now at the ends of the earth
by this insane Spaniard?
Who could want to murder Amasa Delano?
My conscience is clean. God is good.
What am I doing on board this nigger-pirate ship?

PERKINS. You're not talking like a skipper, Sir.
Our boat's a larger spot now.

DELANO. I am childish.
I am doddering and drooling into my second childhood.
God help me, nothing's solid!

PERKINS. Don Benito, Sir. Touch him,
he's as solid as his ship.

DELANO. Don Benito? He's a walking ghost!

[BENITO *comes up to* DELANO. BABU *is a few steps behind him.*]

BENITO. I am the ghost of myself, Captain.
Excuse me, I heard you talking about dreams and childhood.
I was a child, too, once, I have dreams about it.

DELANO [*starting*]. I'm sorry.
This jumping's just a nervous habit.
I thought you were part of my dreams.

BENITO. I was taking my siesta,
I dreamed I was a boy back in Lima.
I was with my brothers and sisters,
and we were dressed for the festival of Corpus Christi
like people at our Bourbon court.
We were simple children, but something went wrong;
little black men came on us with beetle backs.
They had caterpillar heads and munched away on our fine clothes.
They made us lick their horned and varnished insect legs.
Our faces turned brown from their spit,
we looked like bugs, but nothing could save our lives!

DELANO. Ha, ha, Captain. We are like two dreams meeting head-on.
My whaleboat's coming,
we'll both feel better over a bottle of cider.

[BABU *blows a bosun's whistle. The gongs are sounded with descending notes. The* NEGROES *assemble in ranks.*]

BABU. It's twelve noon, Master Yankee.

Master wants his midday shave.

ALL THE NEGROES. Master wants his shave! Master wants his shave!

BENITO. Ah, yes, the razor! I have been talking too much.
You can see how badly I need a razor.
I must leave you, Captain.

BABU. No, Don Amasa wants to talk.
Come to the cabin, Don Amasa.
Don Amasa will talk, Master will listen.
Babu will lather and strop.

DELANO. I want to talk to you about navigation.
I am new to these waters.

BENITO. Doubtless, doubtless, Captain Delano.

PERKINS. I think I'll take my siesta, Sir. [*He walks off.*]

[BENITO, BABU, *and* DELANO *walk toward the back of the stage. A scrim curtain lifts, showing a light deck cabin that forms a sort of attic. The floor is matted, partitions that still leave splintered traces have been knocked out. To one side, a small table screwed to the floor; on it, a dirty missal; above it, a small crucifix, rusty crossed muskets on one side, rusty crossed cutlasses on the other.* BENITO *sits down in a broken thronelike and gilded chair.* BABU *begins to lather. A magnificent array of razors, bottles and other shaving equipment lies on a table beside him. Behind him, a hammock with a pole in it and a dirty pillow.*]

DELANO. So this is where you took your siesta.

BENITO. Yes, Captain, I rest here when my fate will let me.

DELANO. This seems like a sort of dormitory, sitting-room,
sail-loft, chapel, armory, and private bedroom all together.

BENITO. Yes, Captain: events have not been favorable
to much order in my personal arrangements.

[BABU *moves back and opens a locker. A lot of flags, torn shirts and socks tumble out. He takes one of the flags, shakes it with a flourish, and ties it around* BENITO'S *neck.*]

BABU. Master needs more protection.
I do everything I can to save his clothes.

DELANO. The Castle and the Lion of Spain.
Why, Don Benito, this is the flag of Spain you're using!
It's well it's only I and not the King of Spain who sees this!
All's one, though, I guess, in this carnival world.
I see you like gay colors as much as Babu.

BABU [*giggling*]. The bright colors draw the yellow fever
from Master's mind. [*Raises the razor.* BENITO *begins to shake.*]

Now, Master, now, Master!
BENITO. You are talking while you hold the razor.
BABU. You mustn't shake so, Master.
Look, Don Amasa, Master always shakes when I shave him,
though he is braver than a lion and stronger than a castle.
Master knows Babu has never yet drawn blood.
I may, though, sometime, if he shakes so much.
Now, Master!
Come, Don Amasa, talk to Master about the gales and calms,
he'll answer and forget to shake.
DELANO. Those calms, the more I think of them the more I wonder.
You say you were two months sailing here;
I made that stretch in less than a week.
We never met with any calms.
If I'd not heard your story from your lips,
and seen your ruined ship,
I would have said something was missing,
I would have said this was a mystery ship.
BENITO. For some men the whole world is a mystery;
they cannot believe their senses. [BENITO *shakes, the razor gets out of hand and cuts his cheek.*]
Santa Maria!
BABU. Poor, poor Master, see, you shook so;
this is Babu's first blood.
Please answer Don Amasa, while I wipe
this ugly blood from the razor and strop it again.
BENITO. The sea was like the final calm of the world
On, on it went. It sat on us and drank our strength,
crosscurrents eased us out to sea,
the yellow fever changed our blood to poison.
BABU. You stood by us. Some of us stood by you!
BENITO. Yes, my Spanish crew was weak and surly, but the blacks,
the blacks were angels. Babu has kept me in this world.
I wonder what he is keeping me for?
You belong to me. I belong to you forever.
BABU. Ah, Master, spare yourself.
Forever is a very long time;
nothing's forever.

[*With great expertness, delicacy and gentleness,* BABU *massages* BENITO*'s cheeks, shakes out the flag, pours lotion from five bottles on* BENITO*'s hair, cleans the shaving materials, and stands off admiring his work.*]

Master looks just like a statue.

He's like a figurehead, Don Amasa!

[DELANO *looks, then starts to walk out leaving* BENITO *and* BABU. *The curtain drops upon them.* DELANO *rejoins* PERKINS, *lounging at the rail.*]

PERKINS. Our boat is coming.

DELANO [*gaily*]. I know!
I don't know how I'll explain this pomp
and squalor to my own comfortable family of a crew.
Even shaving here is like a High Mass.
There's something in a negro, something
that makes him fit to have around your person.
His comb and brush are castanets.
What tact Babu had!
What noiseless, gliding briskness!

PERKONS. Our boat's about alongside, Sir.

DELANO. What's more, the negro has a sense of humor.
I don't mean their boorish giggling and teeth-showing,
I mean his easy cheerfulness in every glance and gesture.
You should have see Babu toss that Spanish flag like
a juggler,
and change it to a shaving napkin!

PERKINS. The boat's here, Sir.

DELANO. We need inferiors, Perkins,
more manners, more docility, no one has an inferior mind
in America.

PERKINS. Here is your crew, Sir.

[BABU *runs out from the cabin. His cheek is bleeding.*]

DELANO. Why, Babu, what has happened?

BABU. Master will never get better from his sickness.
His bad nerves and evil fever made him use me so.
I gave him one small scratch by accident,
the only time I've nicked him, Don Amasa.
He cut me with his razor. Do you think I will die?
I'd rather die than bleed to death!

DELANO. It's just a pinprick, Babu. You'll live.

BABU. I must attend my master. [*Runs back into cabin.*]

DELANO. Just a pinprick, but I wouldn't have thought
Don Benito had the stuff to swing a razor.
Up north we use our fists instead of knives.
I hope Benito's not dodging around some old grindstone
in the hold, and sharpening a knife for me.
Here, Perkins, help our men up the ladder.

[*Two immaculate* AMERICAN SAILORS *appear carrying*

great casks of water. Two more follow carrying net baskets of wilted pumpkins. The NEGROES *begin to crowd forward, shouting, "We want Yankee food, we want Yankee drink!"* DELANO *grandiosely holds up a pumpkin; an* OLD NEGRO *rushes forward, snatches at the pumpkin, and knocks* DELANO *off balance into* PERKIN'S *arms.* DELANO *gets up and knocks the* NEGRO *down with his fist. All is tense and quiet. The* SIX HATCHET-CLEANERS *lift their hatchets above their heads.*]

DELANO [*furious*]. Americans, stand by me! Stand by your captain!

[*Like lightning, the* AMERICANS *unsling their muskets, fix bayonets, and kneel with their guns pointing at the* NEGROES.]

Don Benito, Sir, call your men to order!

BABU. We're starving, Yankee Master. We mean no harm;
we've never been so scared.

DELANO. You try my patience, Babu.
I am talking to Captain Cereno;
call your men to order, Sir.

BENITO. Make them laugh, Babu. The Americans aren't going to shoot.

[BABU *airily waves a hand. The* NEGROES *smile.* DELANO *turns to* BENITO.]

You mustn't blame them too much; they're sick and hungry.
We have kept them cooped up for ages.

DELANO [*as the* NEGROES *relax*]. Form them in lines, Perkins!
Each man shall have his share.
That's how we run things in the States—
to each man equally, no matter what his claims.

NEGROES [*standing back, bleating like sheep*]. Feed me, Master Yankee! Feed me, Master Yankee!

DELANO. You are much too close.
Here, Perkins, take the provisions aft.
You'll save lives by giving each as little as you can,
Be sure to keep a tally.

[FRANCESCO, *a majestic, yellow-colored mulatto, comes up to* DELANO.]

FRANCESCO. My master requests your presence at dinner, Don Amasa.

DELANO. Tell him I have indigestion.
Tell him to keep better order on his ship.
It's always the man of good will that gets hurt;
my fist still aches from hitting that old darky.

FRANCESCO. My master has his own methods of discipline

that are suitable for our unfortunate circumstances.
Will you come to dinner, Don Amasa?

DELANO. I'll come. When in Rome, do as the Romans.
Excuse my quick temper, Sir.
It's better to blow up than to smolder.

[*The scrim curtain is raised. In the cabin, a long table loaded with silver has been laid out. The locker has been closed and the Spanish flag hangs on the wall.* DON BENITO *is seated,* BABU *stands behind him. As soon as* DELANO *sits down,* FRANCESCO *begins serving with great dignity and agility.*]

FRANCESCO. A finger bowl, Don Amasa. [*After each statement, he moves about the table.*]
A napkin, Don Amasa.
A glass of American water, Don Amasa.
A slice of American pumpkin, Don Amasa.
A goblet of American cider, Don Amasa.

[DELANO *drinks a great deal of cider,* BENITO *hardly touches his.*]

DELANO. This is very courtly for a sick ship, Don Benito.
The Spanish Empire will never go down, if she keeps her chin up.

BENITO. I'm afraid I shan't live long enough to enjoy your prophecy.

DELANO. I propose a toast to the Spanish Empire
on which the sun never sets;
may you find her still standing, when you land, Sir!

BENITO. Our Empire has lasted three hundred years,
I suppose she will last another month.
I wish I could say the same for myself. My sun is setting,
I hear the voices of the dead in this calm.

DELANO. You hear the wind lifting;
it's bringing our two vessels together.
We are going to take you into port, Don Benito.

BENITO. You are either too late or too early with your good works.
Our yellow fever may break out again.
You aren't going to put your men in danger, Don Amasa?

DELANO. My boys are all healthy, Sir.

BENITO. Health isn't God, I wouldn't trust it.

FRANCESCO. May I fill your glass, Don Amasa?

BABU. New wine in new bottles,
that's the American spirit, Yankee Master.
They say all men are created equal in North America.

DELANO. We prefer merit to birth, boy.

[BABU *motions imperiously for* FRANCESCO *to leave. As he goes, bowing to the* CAPTAINS, FOUR NEGROES *play the* Marseillaise.]

Why are they playing the *Marseillaise*?

BABU. His uncle is supposed to have been in the French Convention,
and voted for the death of the French King.

DELANO. This polite and royal fellow is no anarchist!

BABU. Francesco is very *ancien régime,*
he is even frightened of the Americans.
He doesn't like the way you treated King George.
Babu is more liberal.

DELANO. A royal fellow,
this usher of yours, Don Benito!
He is as yellow as a goldenrod.
He is a king, a king of kind hearts.
What a pleasant voice he has!

BENITO [*glumly*]. Francesco is a good man.

DELANO. As long as you've known him,
he's been a worthy fellow, hasn't he?
Tell me, I am particularly curious to know.

BENITO. Francesco is a good man.

DELANO. I'm glad to hear it, I am glad to hear it!
You refute the saying of a planter friend of mine.
He said, "When a mulatto has a regular European face,
look out for him, he is a devil."

BENITO. I've heard your planter's remark applied
to intermixtures of Spaniards and Indians;
I know nothing about mulattoes.

DELANO. No, no, my friend's refuted;
if we're so proud of our white blood,
surely a little added to the blacks improves their breed.
I congratulate you on your servants, Sir.

BABU. We've heard that Jefferson, the King of your Republic,
would like to free his slaves.

DELANO. Jefferson has read too many books, boy,
but you can trust him. He's a gentleman and an American!
He's not lifting a finger to free his slaves.

BABU. We hear you have a new capital modelled on Paris,
and that your President is going to set up
a guillotine on the Capitol steps.

DELANO. Oh, Paris! I told you you could trust Mr. Jefferson, boy,
he stands for law and order like your mulatto.
Have you been to Paris, Don Benito?

BENITO. I'm afraid I'm just a provincial Spaniard, Captain.
DELANO. Let me tell you about Paris.
You know what French women are like—
nine parts sex and one part logic.
Well, one of them in Paris heard
that my ship was the *President Adams*. She said,
"You are descended from Adam, Captain,
you must know everything,
tell me how Adam and Eve learned to sleep together."
Do you know what I said?
BENITO. No, Captain.
DELANO. I said, "I guess Eve was a Frenchwoman,
the first Frenchwoman."
Do you know what she answered?
BENITO. No, Captain Delano.
DELANO. She said, "I was trying to provoke a philosophical discussion, Sir."
A philosophical discussion, ha, ha!
You look serious, Sir. You know, something troubles me.
BENITO. Something troubles you, Captain Delano?
DELANO. I still can't understand those calms,
but let that go. The scurvy,
why did it kill off three Spaniards in every four,
and only half the blacks?
Negroes are human, but surely you couldn't have favored them
before your own flesh and blood!
BENITO. This is like the Inquisition, Captain Delano.
I have done the best I could.

[BABU *dabs* BENITO'*s forehead with cider.*]

BABU. Poor, poor Master; since Don Aranda died,
he trusts no one except Babu.
DELANO. Your Babu is an uncommonly intelligent fellow;
you are right to trust him, Sir.
Sometimes I think we overdo our talk of freedom.
If you looked into our hearts, we all want slaves.
BENITO. Disease is a mysterious thing;
it takes one man, and leaves his friend.
Only the unfortunate can understand misfortune.
DELANO. I must return to my bosun;
he's pretty green to be left alone here.
Before I go I want to propose a last toast to you!
A good master deserves good servants!

[He gets up. As he walks back to PERKINS, *the scrim curtain falls, concealing* BENITO *and* BABU.]

That captain must have jaundice,
I wish he kept better order.
I don't like hitting menials.

PERKINS. I've done some looking around, Sir. I've used my eyes.

DELANO. That's what they're for, I guess. You have to watch your step,
this hulk, this rotten piece of finery,
will fall part. This old world needs new blood
and Yankee gunnery to hold it up.
You shouldn't mess around, though, it's their ship;
you're breaking all the laws of the sea.

PERKINS. Do you see that man-shaped thing in canvas?

DELANO. I see it.

PERKINS. Behind the cloth, there's a real skeleton,
a man dressed up like Don Benito.

DELANO. They're Catholics, and worship bones.

PERKINS. There's writing on its coat. It says,
"I am Don Aranda," and, "Follow your leader."

DELANO. Follow your leader?

PERKINS. I saw two blacks unfurling a flag,
a black skull and crossbones on white silk.

DELANO. That's piracy. We've been ordered
to sink any ship that flies that flag.
Perhaps they were playing.

PERKINS. I saw King Atufal throw away his chains,
He called for food, the Spaniards served him two pieces of pumpkin,
and a whole bottle of your cider.

DELANO. Don Benito has the only key to Atufal's padlock.
My cider was for the captain's table.

PERKINS. Atufal pointed to the cabin where you were dining,
and drew a finger across his throat.

DELANO. Who could want to kill Amasa Delano?

PERKINS. I warned our men to be ready for an emergency.

DELANO. You're a mind reader,
I couldn't have said better myself;
but we're at peace with Spain.

PERKINS. I told them to return with loaded muskets
and fixed bayonets.

DELANO. Here comes Benito. Watch how I'll humor him
and sound him out.

[BABU *brings out* BENITO's *chair.* BENITO *sits in it.*]
It's good to have you back on deck, Captain.
Feel the breeze! It holds and will increase.
My ship is moving nearer. Soon we will be together.
We have seen you through your troubles.
BENITO. Remember, I warned you about the yellow fever.
I am surprised you haven't felt afraid.
DELANO. Oh, that will blow away.
Everything is going to go better and better;
the wind's increasing, soon you'll have no cares.
After the long voyage, the anchor drops into the harbor.
It's a great weight lifted from the captain's heart.
We are getting to be friends, Don Benito.
My ship's in sight, the *President Adams*!
How the wind braces a man up!
I have a small invitation to issue to you.
BENITO. An invitation?
DELANO. I want you to take a cup of coffee
with me on my quarter deck tonight.
The Sultan of Turkey never tasted such coffee
as my old steward makes. What do you say, Don Benito?
BENITO. I cannot leave my ship.
DELANO. Come, come, you need a change of climate.
The sky is suddenly blue, Sir,
my coffee will make a man of you.
BENITO. I cannot leave my ship.
Even now, I don't think you understand my position here.
DELANO. I want to speak to you alone.
BENITO. I am alone, as much as I ever am.
DELANO. In America, we don't talk about money
in front of servants and children.
BENITO. Babu is not my servant.
You spoke of money—since the yellow fever,
he has had a better head for figures than I have.
DELANO. You embarrass me, Captain,
but since circumstances are rather special here,
I will proceed.
BENITO. Babu takes an interest in all our expenses.
DELANO. Yes, I am going to talk to you about your expenses.
I am responsible to my owners for all
the sails, ropes, food and carpentry I give you.
You will need a complete rerigging, almost a new ship, in fact,
You shall have our services at cost.

BENITO. I know, you are a merchant.
I suppose I ought to pay you for our lives.
DELANO. I envy you, Captain. You are the only owner
of the *San Domingo,* since Don Aranda died.
I am just an employee. Our owners would sack me,
if I followed my better instincts.
BENITO. You can give your figures to Babu, Captain.
DELANO. You are very offhand about money, Sir;
I don't think you realize the damage that has been done to your ship.
Ah, you smile. I'm glad you're loosening up.
Look, the water gurgles merrily, the wind is high,
a mild light is shining. I sometimes think
such a tropical light as this must have shone
on the tents of Abraham and Isaac.
It seems as if Providence were watching over us.
PERKINS. There are things that need explaining here, Sir.
DELANO. Yes, Captain, Perkins saw some of your men
unfurling an unlawful flag,
a black skull and crossbones.
BENITO. You know my only flag is the Lion and Castle of Spain.
DELANO. No, Perkins says he saw a skull and crossbones.
That's piracy. I trust Perkins.
You've heard about how my government blew
the bowels out of the pirates at Tripoli?
BENITO. Perhaps my Negroes . . .
DELANO. My government doesn't intend to
let you play at piracy!
BENITO. Perhaps my Negroes were playing.
When you take away their chains . . .
DELANO. I'll see that you are all put back in chains,
if you start playing pirates!
PERKINS. There's something else he can explain, Sir.
DELANO. Yes, Perkins saw Atufal throw off his chains
and order dinner.
BABU. Master has the key, Yankee Master.
BENITO. I have the key.
You can't imagine how my position exhausts me, Captain.
DELANO. I can imagine. Atufal's chains are fakes.
You and he are in cahoots, Sir!
PERKINS. They don't intend to pay for our sails and service.
They think America is Santa Claus.
DELANO. The United States are death on pirates and debtors.

PERKINS. There's one more thing for him to explain, Sir.
DELANO. Do you see that man-shaped thing covered with black cloth, Don Benito?
BENITO. I always see it.
DELANO. Take away the cloth. I order you to take away the cloth!
BENITO. I cannot. Oh, Santa Maria, have mercy!
DELANO. Of course, you can't. It's no Virgin Mary.
You have done something terrible to your friend, Don Aranda.
Take away the cloth, Perkins!

[*As* PERKINS *moves forward,* ATUFAL *suddenly stands chainless and with folded arms, blocking his way.*]

BABU [*dancing up and down beside himself*].
Let them see it! Let them see it!
I can't stand any more of their insolence;
the Americans treat us like their slaves!

[BABU *and* PERKINS *meet at the man-shaped object and start pulling away the cloth.* BENITO *rushes between them, and throws them back and sprawling on the deck.* BABU *and* PERKINS *rise and stand hunched like wrestlers, about to close in on* BENITO, *who draws his sword with a great gesture. It is only a hilt. He runs at* BABU *and knocks him down.* ATUFAL *throws off his chains and signals to the* HATCHET-CLEANERS. *They stand behind* BENITO *with raised hatchets. The* NEGROES *shout ironically,* "Evviva Benito!"]

You too, Yankee Captain!
If you shoot, we'll kill you.
DELANO. If a single American life is lost,
I will send this ship to the bottom,
and all Peru after it.
Do you hear me, Don Benito?
BENITO. Don't you understand? I am as powerless as you are!
BABU. He is as powerless as you are.
BENITO. Don't you understand? He has been holding a knife at my back.
I have been talking all day to save your life.
BABU [*holding a whip*].
Do you see this whip? When Don Aranda was out of temper,
he used to snap pieces of flesh off us with it.
Now I hold the whip.
When I snap it, Don Benito jumps!

[*Snaps the whip.* DON BENITO *flinches.*]

DELANO [*beginning to understand*].
It's easy to terrorize the defenseless.
BABU. That's what we thought when Don Aranda held the whip.
DELANO. You'll find I am made of tougher stuff than your Spaniards.
ATUFAL. We want to kill you.
NEGROES. We want to kill you, Yankee Captain.
DELANO. Who could want to kill Amasa Delano?
BABU. Of course. We want to keep you alive.
We want you to sail us back to Africa.
Has anyone told you how much you are worth, Captain?
DELANO. I have another course in mind.
BABU. Yes, there's another course if you don't like Africa, there's another course.
King Atufal, show the Yankee captain
the crew that took the other course!
[*Three dead* SPANISH SAILORS *are brought on stage.*]
ATUFAL. Look at Don Aranda?
BABU. Yes, you are hot-tempered and discourteous, Captain.
I am going to introduce you to Don Aranda.
You have a new command, Captain. You must meet your new owner.
[*The black cloth is taken from the man-shaped object and shows a chalk-white skeleton dressed like* DON BENITO.]
Don Amasa, Don Aranda!
You can see that Don Aranda was a white man like you,
because his bones are white.
NEGROES. He is a white because his bones are white!
He is a white because his bones are white!
ATUFAL [*pointing to the ribbon on the skeleton's chest*].
Do you see that ribbon?
It says, "Follow the leader."
We wrote it in his blood.
BABU. He was a white man
even though his blood was red as ours.
NEGROES. He is white because his bones are white!
BABU. Don Aranda is our figurehead,
we are going to chain him to the bow of our ship
to scare off devils.
ATUFAL. This is the day of Jubilee,
I am raising the flag of freedom!
NEGROES. Freedom! Freedom! Freedom!
[*The black skull and crossbones is raised on two poles.*

The NEGROES *form two lines, leading up to the flag, and leave an aisle. Each man is armed with some sort of weapon.*]

BABU. Spread out the Spanish flag!

[*The Lion and Castle of Spain is spread out on the deck in front of the skull and crossbones.*]

The Spanish flag is the road to freedom.
Don Benito mustn't hurt his white feet on the splinters.

[*Kneeling in front of* BENITO.]

Your foot, Master!

[BENITO *holds out his foot.* BABU *takes off* BENITO'S *shoes.*]

Give Don Benito back his sword!

[*The sword-hilt is fastened back in* BENITO'S *scabbard.*]

Load him with chains!

[*Two heavy chains are draped on* BENITO'S *neck. The cane and ball are handed to him.*]

Former Captain Benito Cereno, kneel!
Ask pardon of man!

BENITO [*kneeling*]. I ask pardon for having been born a Spaniard.
I ask pardon for having enslaved my fellow man.

BABU. Strike off the oppressor's chain!

[*One of* BENITO'S *chains is knocked off, then handed to* ATUFAL, *who dashes it to the deck.*]

Former Captain Benito Cereno,
you must kiss the flag of freedom. [*Points to* DON ARANDA.]
Kiss the mouth of the skull!

[BENITO *walks barefoot over the Spanish flag and kisses the mouth of* DON ARANDA.]

NEGROES. *Evviva Benito! Evviva Benito!*

[*Sounds are heard from* PERKINS, *whose head has been covered with the sack.*]

ATUFAL. The bosun wants to kiss the mouth of freedom.

BABU. March over the Spanish flag, Bosun.

[PERKINS *starts forward.*]

DELANO. You are dishonoring your nation, Perkins!
Don't you stand for anything?

PERKINS. I only have one life, Sir.

[*Walks over the Spanish flag and kisses the mouth of the skull.*]

NEGROES. *Evviva* Bosun! *Evviva* Bosun!

DELANO. You are no longer an American, Perkins!

BABU. He was free to choose freedom, Captain.

ATUFAL. Captain Delano wants to kiss the mouth of freedom.
BABU. He is jealous of the bosun.
ATUFAL. In the United States, all men are created equal.
BABU. Don't you want to kiss the mouth of freedom, Captain?
DELANO [*lifting his pocket and pointing the pistol*].
Do you see what I have in my hand?
BABU. A pistol.
DELANO. I am unable to miss at this distance.
BABU. You must take your time, Yankee Master.
You must take your time.
DELANO. I am unable to miss.
BABU. You can stand there like a block of wood
as long as you want to, Yankee Master.
You will drop asleep, then we will tie you up,
and make you sail us back to Africa.

[*General laughter. Suddenly, there's a roar of gunfire. Several* NEGROES, *mostly women, fall.* AMERICAN SEAMEN *in spotless blue and white throw themselves in a lying position on deck. More kneel above them, then more stand above these. All have muskets and fixed bayonets. The First Row fires. More* NEGROES *fall. They start to retreat. The Second Row fires. More* NEGROES *fall. They retreat further. The Third Row fires. The Three* AMERICAN LINES *march forward, but all the* NEGROES *are either dead or in retreat.* DON BENITO *has been wounded. He staggers over to* DELANO *and shakes his hand.*]

BENITO. You have saved my life.
I thank you for my life.
DELANO. A man can only do what he can,
We have saved American lives.
PERKINS [*pointing to* ATUFAL'*s body*]. We have killed King Atufal,
we have killed their ringleader.

[BABU *jumps up. He is unwounded.*]

BABU. I was the King. Babu, not Atufal
was the king, who planned, dared and carried out
the seizure of this ship, the *San Domingo*.
Untouched by blood myself, I had all
the most dangerous and useless Spaniards killed.
I freed my people from their Egyptian bondage.
The heartless Spaniards slaved for me like slaves.

[BABU *steps back, and quickly picks up a crown from the litter.*]

This is my crown.

[*Puts crown on his head. He snatches* BENITO's *rattan cane.*]

This is my rod.

[*Picks up silver ball.*]

This is the earth.

[*Holds the ball out with one hand and raises the cane.*]

This is the arm of the angry God.

[*Smashes the ball.*]

PERKINS. Let him surrender. Let him surrender.
We want to save someone.

BENITO. My God how little these people understand!

BABU [*holding a white handkerchief and raising both his hands*].
Yankee Master understand me. The future is with us.

DELANO [*raising his pistol*]. This is your future.

[BABU *falls and lies still.* DELANO *pauses, then slowly empties the five remaining barrels of his pistol into the body. Lights dim.*]

Curtain